Mr. Cheap's Seattle

Mark Waldstein

Associate Editor
Kim Camlet

Assistant Editor
Tami Monahan

Editorial Assistant
Jerald Tenenbaum

ADAMS PUBLISHING
Holbrook, Massachusetts

Also in the Mr. Cheap's® Series:

Mr. Cheap's® Atlanta
Mr. Cheap's® Boston
Mr. Cheap's® Chicago
Mr. Cheap's® New York
Mr. Cheap's® San Francisco

More cities are still being added—check the travel
section of your favorite bookstore!

ACKNOWLEDGMENTS

A book of this magnitude takes a ton of help from all corners, especially when its author and assistants divided their time between two corners of the country. Mr. C is *never* stingy when it comes to extending his gratitude. First of all, a heartfelt thank you to dear pal Stan Gill, for his friendship and warm hospitality. Thanks also to Sara Anderson and Rob Falk, who were dispatched upon many local errands and always came through with flying colors. And, for further suggestions and/or inspiration, thanks to Paul Kanter and Sue Meyer, Phil Emerson, and Mark Maravalli.

From Kim: Thanks to the friendly bus driver, Diane, "who made sure I got to my hotel safely." And back home, special thanks to Karen and Mike Camlet, Helen and Rex Hammock, and Kris Glover for their support and encouragement.

Tami wishes to thank Alan Goldwasser at Ticket/Ticket for providing invaluable arts and entertainment information. Thanks also to Glenn McGibbon for helping out whenever and wherever necessary. A big "thank you" goes to Susan Beale for production wizardry and an endless supply of patience and good humor.

Published by Adams Media Corporation
260 Center Street, Holbrook, MA 02343

Mr. Cheap's® is a registered trademark of Adams Media Corporation

ISBN: 1-55850-445-1

Printed in the United States of America

A B C D E F G H I J

Library of Congress Cataloging-in-Publication Data
Waldstein, Mark.
    Mr. Cheap's Seattle / Mark Waldstein ; contributing editors, Tami Monahan, Kim Camlet ;
editorial assistant Jerald Tenenbaum.
    p.   cm.
    Includes index.
    ISBN: 1-55850-445-1
    1. Seattle (Wash.)—Guidebooks. 2. Shopping—Washington (State)—Seattle—Guidebooks.
3. Restaurants—Washington (State)—Seattle—Guidebooks. 4. Bed and breakfast accomoda-
tions—Washington (State)—Seattle—Guidebooks. 5. Hotels—Washington (State)—Seattle—Guidebooks. 6. Outlet Stores—Washington (State)—Seattle—Guidebooks. I. Title.
    F899.S43W35   1995
    917.97'7720443—dc20   94-32651
                                                                                       CIP

This publication is designed to provide accurate and authoritative information with regard to the subject matter covered. It is sold with the understanding that the publisher is not engaged in rendering
legal, accounting, or other professional advice. If legal advice or other expert assistance is required,
the services of a qualified professional person should be sought.
            — From a *Declaration of Principles* jointly adopted by a Committee of the
            American Bar Association and a Committee of Publishers and Associations.

This book is available at quantity discounts for bulk purchases.
For information, call 1-800-872-5627.

CONTENTS

A FEW (CAREFULLY CHOSEN) WORDS FROM MR. CHEAP

About this "cheap" business. I'll admit, there are more elegant ways to put the idea. Lots of folks want to save money, especially in these tough times. When it comes to low *prices*, few people know as many good places as I do. But, strictly speaking, that doesn't make these stores and restaurants "cheap." Nor does it make anyone who uses this book a "cheapskate." I think *thrifty* would be a better word. Or perhaps *frugal*.

In my mind, a cheap person is someone who has plenty of money to burn, and refuses to touch it; whereas a thrifty person would probably spend the cash if he or she had it—especially for something of good value. Most of us fall into the latter category, don't we?

Anyway, everyone loves a bargain, and it's my pleasure to pass these tips along. This whole idea grew out of my own personal experience, from years of living on the financial edge as a "starving artist." My background is in theater and writing; and, as most people know, actors don't make any money—even with steady work! I learned to live "cheaply" out of necessity, and developed my first book, *Mr. Cheap's Boston*, as a way to put this knowledge to good use, helping out folks in similar straits. That book wound up on the *Boston Globe* bestseller list; *Mr. Cheap's New York* and others soon followed. Suddenly, I discovered myself on a mission!

There is, by now, a research technique behind these books, but "cheaping" is hardly an exact science. Prices change all the time. Stores come and go. Restaurants change their menus. Now, you won't find the exact same items on the shelves tomorrow that I found during my travels; but the descriptions in this book are sure to help you track down just about anything you may be looking for, at the lowest possible price.

A few words of caution: "You gets what you pays for." It's been said many times, and it's generally true. With new merchandise in particular, prices are always discounted for a reason. It may be that the item is simply a leftover from last year, yet still perfectly good; in other cases, if the price is low, the quality may not be far behind. I have tried to point out, wherever I could, items that are cheap because they are less well made, or because they are irregular or damaged. Even these "IR" goods may be useful to the reader who only needs them to last for a short time—students furnishing a dorm room, for example—or, to shoppers who happen to be handy with a hammer, or a needle and thread. Sometimes, the "truly cheap" is all you need.

A few last notes: As of 1995, the Seattle region has a second area code. In this book, all phone numbers are the familiar ol' (206), unless stated otherwise. Also, in the "Shopping" and "Entertainment" sections, places with multiple locations show the Seattle addresses first, followed by suburban branches in alphabetical order. And finally, though I've attempted to give store hours, these can change at any time; it's always a good idea to call ahead.

I fully expect to hear from readers who insist I've left out their favorite diner, or some resale boutique they love. To these fellow bargain hunters, I say, Mr. C can't be *everywhere*; but I encourage you to please pass along the information, and I'll be happy to scout your suggestions out for our next edition. The address is:

Mr. Cheap
c/o Adams Media Corporation
260 Center St.
Holbrook, MA 02343

So, get ready to use the book—but be careful how you use the name! As you see, "cheap" can mean many things. And when you tell your friends that you paid only $45 for your designer outfit, nobody will be laughing. They'll just want to know how you did it.

On to the goodies!

Mark Waldstein
a.k.a. Mr. Cheap

SHOPPING

All area codes (206) unless otherwise noted

The hundreds of stores in this section are all places which will save you money in some way. They actually cover a broad spectrum of discount shopping, from the latest designer clothing to thrift shops, new furniture and used, major brands and second-rate imitations. Mr. Cheap wants to cover it all, giving his fellow Cheapsters as many options as possible for saving cash.

Whenever possible, Mr. C points out *why* an item is marked down—whether it's discontinued, second-quality (imperfect), or just plain cheap stuff. Thus informed, it is up to you to decide which stores and merchandise are for you.

The prices quoted, again, are based upon items Mr. C found at the time of his research. You shouldn't expect to find the same items, at the same prices, when you shop; these prices are just examples which are similar to what you may find. Even as prices go up overall, you should still find the book completely useful in comparing one place against another.

Many stores which sell several kinds of merchandise have been cross-referenced for you, appearing in each appropriate chapter; but remember to consult "Discount Department Stores" and "Flea Markets and Emporia" for many of the same items which have their own chapters. Similarly, the "General Markets" portion of the "Food Shops" chapter gives you more places to look for individual kinds of foods.

Okay, enough talking—*Go to it!*

PREFACE:
GOING TO THE OUTLETS

Many of the cities Mr. Cheap has written about have one or more "outlet malls" at least an hour's drive from downtown. Seattle is fortunate enough to have one of these even closer than that, surrounded by an area that's equally worth a day trip in itself. **The Great Northwest Factory Stores**, located in the Snoqualmie Valley town of North Bend, is actually part of a national chain of outlet malls. Here, some forty stores—with more being built at the time of this writing—tout 30% to 70% savings on famous name clothing and shoes, housewares, toys, gifts, luggage, and more.

Shopping at such outlet malls can save you money, but it does not always guarantee incredible deals that you would not be able to find anywhere else. Here are some important things to keep in mind:

- You won't clothe your entire family for $9.99.
- Not every item in these stores is sold at discount; many stores offer a mix of clearance *and* regular merchandise.
- Some outlet stores sell goods made specifically for them— close, but not identical, to goods in full-price stores.
- Go in knowing what you want, and how much it costs elsewhere, so you'll know a bargain when you see it.

Having gotten that off his chest, Mr. C certainly recommends that you check the mall out. Careful shoppers will indeed come away with some good deals, especially those who are willing to wait until late in the retail season. This makes perfect sense; only retailers want you to think about winter coats in the height of summer.

Among the many name-brand stores found at Great Northwest, some of which are described elsewhere in the book, are:

American Tourister—luggage
Bass Shoes
B.U.M. Equipment—sportswear
Champion/Hanes—sweats, underwear
Corning/Revere—dishware
Famous Footwear—name brand shoes
Fieldcrest Cannon—linens
Izod—sportswear
L'eggs/Hanes/Bali—lingerie, underwear
OshKosh B'Gosh—children's wear
Perfumania—designer fragrances
Toy Liquidators
Van Heusen—sportswear

The mall is located just off Exit 31 from Route I-90, north of the highway. It's open daily from 10 A.M. to 8 P.M., except Sundays from 10 A.M. to 6 P.M.; winter hours may vary. For more information, call 888-4505.

Meanwhile, make a day of it and drive through the Snoqualmie Valley area itself. North Bend sits at the western edge of Mt. Baker-Snoqualmie National Forest; great for drives, picnics, and hikes. You can get booklet of self-guided tours from the **USDA Forest Service District Office**, located at 42404 SE North Bend Way; telephone 888-1421.

What else can you do here? Take a train ride on the lovingly restored **Puget Sound and Snoqualmie Valley Railroad**, a turn-of-the-century steam train that runs between Snoqualmie and North Bend; information, 746-4025. Visit the **Snoqualmie Valley Historical Museum**, to see what the area was like in the days *before* shopping malls; telephone 888-3200. Catch an evening movie at the **North Bend Cinema**, at 125 North Bend Blvd. N, where tickets cost no more than $3.50; telephone 888-1232. And of course, don't miss the nearby **Snoqualmie Falls** , higher than Niagara, with its dramatic viewing post which juts out over the river. Just follow the signs from either Exit 27 or Exit 31 off Route I-90.

Further away, the **Centralia Factory Outlet Center** is another mall devoted to outlets. Located at 1324 Lum Road in Centralia, it's about an hour-and-a-half drive from Seattle. The telephone number is (360) 736-3327.

APPLIANCES

Apollo Spas

- 29225 Pacific Hwy. S, Federal Way; 839-7847
- 13123 NE 124th St., Kirkland; 820-4141
- 4510 168th Ave. SW, Lynnwood; 787-0248
- 5831 Tacoma Mall Blvd., Tacoma; 471-0321

Apollo Spas furnishes a small chain of showrooms right from its factory in Spokane—meaning *you* can furnish your home with one of these whirlpools o' pleasure for $1,000 to $2,000 less than they'd cost at retail home centers. They save on shipping and middleman costs; you save on those physical therapist bills.

Of course, a hot tub is a complex creature, and you don't want a cheap price to mean cheap construction. Well, Apollo's parent company has been in the boating business for over three decades—so they do these spas right. They use space-age materials, they molly bolt all the corners, and everything is double- and triple-layered. Thus, they can warranty the tub for thirty years, and add a one-year parts and labor warranty.

Even so, a basic 6' x 8' model, big enough for four people, starts around $1,595. Adding a cover and wooden outer cabinet brings the price tag up to $2,495—still less than the same item would cost elsewhere. They've got a two-person spa around $2,000 complete, good for decks and patios. And smaller jetted bathtubs start around $500.

There are several styles to choose from, in an array of sizes, designs and fancy colors. The spas look downright futuristic, molded to let your body rest in a variety of sitting and reclining positions. Store hours vary, but most are open seven days a week.

Black & Decker Service Center

- 421 S Michigan St., Seattle; 763-1948
- 2602 S 38th St., Tacoma; 473-6040

Official Black & Decker service shops are also good places to look for bargain prices on factory-reconditioned appliances and power tools. It's hardly the grimy workshop you may expect; these pleasant stores have a separate sales area, and several aisles are filled with a full selection of current B & D machines from blenders to drills to lawn mowers. They're sold at 10% to 20% below retail prices, and they all carry the full 1-2 year manufacturer's warranty.

Among the items Mr. C found on these shelves were a coffee bean grinder for $15.99; Dustbusters for $17.99; and a five-speed mixer, with built-in timer, for $90. A ten-inch band saw had $15 knocked off the price just because it came in a "blemished carton." And a 19-inch, rear-bag electric lawn mower was marked down from $250 to $189. The Seattle store, in the industrial Georgetown area, is open from 8 A.M. to 5 P.M. on weekdays, and from 9-2 on Saturdays; the Tacoma branch is open weekdays only.

Dave's Appliance Rebuild

- 1601 15th Ave. E, Seattle; 324-3270

The name says it all. In a corner of this Shop Rite parking lot in First Hill, Dave's is a small store packed with reconditioned appliances of all kinds. Before you scoff at this notion, consider the fact that every single unit on display during Mr. C's visit bore a "Sold" tag. Consider also that these included items like a Hotpoint washing machine for $189, and a GE electric stove for $209. It's possible to come out with a washer/dryer set for a clean $300. Refrigerators start as low as $100 for a single door unit, heading up to $400 or so for a frost-free side-by-side. Furthermore, prices are openly referred to as "nego-tiable"; this store does a high-volume business, and wants to get its machines out the door.

Many of these look just like new (and some don't); some are still under the original manufacturer's warranty. Dave backs up his friendly crew's own work with a 90-day store warranty on parts and labor. And, if you don't see what you need, come back soon—these guys are offered more than 200 items *each week*, most of which are too worn out for resale. But even these contribute to Dave's used parts collection; so, if a belt breaks on your own washing machine, chances are that you can get a replacement here for half the price of a new one.

These guys know what they're doing; they've been at it for over twenty years. Dave's Rebuild is open weekdays from 9 A.M. to 5:30 P.M., and Saturdays from 9 to 3.

Dick 'n Dale's Appliance and TV
- 4538 California Ave. SW, Seattle; 938-0445

Along with good prices on first-quality new appliances and televisions, this West Seattle shop specializes in what retailers call "freight-damaged" goods. These too are brand-new units, but because they've been jostled a bit on some truck—usually leading to a torn box, and maybe a scratch or two—they can no longer be sold in department stores at full-price.

That's where Dick Egge and Dale Schindler come in. They snap up as many of these babies as they can get their hands on, thanks to their connections in the industry. They are, for example, one of only four dealers in western Washington getting freight-damaged deals directly from General Electric and Hotpoint.

How much can this save you? How about $200 on a vertical washer/dryer set. Many items are sold even below dealer cost. Mr. C was also shown a GE refrigera-

tor/freezer with an in-door ice and water dispenser, and a white vinyl finish (the current fashion); it would cost over $1,000 at full-price, but was selling for only $750. All of these carry the full manufacturers' warranties, in every area but cosmetics—but if you don't mind a scuff mark here or there, you can make out like a bandit.

Of course, another drawback is the limited selection. But Dick 'n Dale do get a fair number of these, in a good variety of models and name brands. If you're in the market, stop in and see what's available. If they don't have what you need, leave your name and number—they'll keep an eye out for your request. Open from 9 A.M. to 6 P.M., Mondays through Saturdays.

Fremont Appliance
- 6200 15th Ave. NW, Seattle; 789-7348

A husband and wife team has been running this appliance store for the past thirty years. Located not in Fremont but in Ballard, rebuilt appliances sold here include refrigerators, washers, dryers, and ranges (electric only); all carry a six-month store warranty, very commendable indeed.

Among the appliances Mr. C noticed were a Whirlpool large-capacity washer and dryer set for $399. Refrigerators and ranges started at $199. Delivery in Seattle is free, but you're on your own when it comes to hooking up the ice-maker on your fridge. Open from 10 A.M. to 6 P.M., Tuesdays through Saturdays.

Guaranteed Appliance Repair

• 7705 15th Ave. NW, Seattle; 789-2397

Another Ballard shop, this small but flourishing business is very up-front and honest about its used appliances. Nothing here is sold broken—everything leaves the store clean, working, and with a sturdy six-month guarantee.

Now, not everything in the showroom fits that criteria when you see it—since Guaranteed Appliance is such a small operation, they can't afford to fix every item as soon as it comes in. You're likely to see worn-out appliances sitting alongside units that are ready to go, but marked "CIO" ("Check It Out"); this indicates that work has not yet been done on that particular appliance. If it's the one you want, the staff will recondition it ASAP, bring it up to the established standards, and call you when it's ready.

Mr. C noticed names like Amana, Hotpoint, Kenmore, and General Electric. Dishwashers are priced between $125 and $175, refrigerators start at $250, and stoves (Guaranteed Appliance doesn't deal with gas ranges) begin at $150.

There is a fee for delivery. GAR is open Mondays through Fridays from 10 A.M. to 6 P.M., and Saturdays from 10 A.M. to 5 P.M.

Jack Roberts Appliance

• 10416 Aurora Ave. N, Seattle; 527-2775
• 17900 Highway 99, Lynnwood; 743-2777
• 325 Sunset Blvd. N, Renton; 255-8484

Like Dick 'n Dale (see above), Jack Roberts offers some freight-damaged appliances at greatly reduced prices.

Mr. C found a Westinghouse 24-cubic foot refrigerator/freezer, in a soft white vinyl finish, reduced from a list price of $1,299 to $899. These deals also extend to their audio and video department, like a recently-seen Pioneer stereo receiver marked down from $650 to $489. You'll find the largest selection of these specials at their main branch in Lynnwood.

But JRA also works to keep its prices low on everything in the store; they employ two shoppers to track major competitors in the area, and adjust their prices to within $20 of the best deals they find elsewhere. They even admit to some room for negotiation on new models. Mr. C found new refrigerators as low as $400 here—very cool indeed. They carry most major brands, and are open seven days a week.

Monarch Appliance

• 18400 Aurora Ave. N, Seattle; 546-3420

Up the road apiece from Jack Roberts (see above), Monarch Appliance is another place to check into on your pricing tour. They carry all the big brands, and do a high-volume business with contractors in free-standing and built-in refrigerators, deep freezers, dishwashers, ranges, compactors, washers and dryers, and more.

Furthermore, Mr. C was told—quite clearly—that they offer the same prices to the general public that licensed contractors get. So, a KitchenAid washer and dryer set which lists for $1,100 can sell for $900 here. A Hotpoint electric range was marked down from $630 to $500, and so on. Give 'em a look. Open weekdays from 9 A.M. to 6 P.M., and Saturdays from 9 to 5.

Seattle Vacuum

• 14022 Aurora Ave. N, Seattle; 632-6277

Looking to clean up on a vacuum deal? Consider a second-hand unit—after all, *good* machines are made to last for years. Along with retailing new models, this small shop near the northern border of the city excels in the repair and restoration of all kinds of vacs, and usually has a good selection on hand—which can start as low as $35. Some are sold "as is"; but fully reconditioned models get all-new bearings, belts, brushes, and even trim. A very fancy commercial-grade machine which might have sold for $1,800 new (!) can be gotten for $250 here.

In between, you may find a Hoover upright for $55, or a three-amp motor Kirby for $99. Other brands recently seen here included Electrolux and Eureka. You can even trade in your old model toward the price of another new or used machine. Reconditioned vacuums carry an unheard-of *two year* store warranty; hey, these guys can really keep 'em going. They had one baby on sale here that had to be fifty years old if it was a day.

SV also carries a full line of replacement parts, accessories, bags, shampoos, and attachments, too. Open 9 A.M. to 6 P.M. on weekdays, and on Saturdays from 10 A.M. to 3 P.M.

Another nearby store offering similar deals, but a much smaller selection, is the **Hoover Factory Service Center** at 13250 Aurora Avenue N, Seattle (telephone 367-4425). Here, Mr. C found a spiffy new-looking "refurb" with an original price of $210 selling for only $142. Others were priced under $100, but again, there aren't always that many to see. These units do carry store warranties, natch, since the store is a service center. It's tucked away in the K-Mart Plaza, and is open from 8 A.M. to 6 P.M. on weekdays, and 9-5 on Saturdays.

T-Dee Appliance
● 13339 Lake City Way NE, Seattle; 361-7368

This all-purpose budget shop combines used appliances with freight-damaged models, giving you a variety of options and conditions. Some of these units are downright scary-looking, but most are in fine shape; come to think of it, the store itself could use a bit of reconditioning.

All appliances carry a one-year parts and labor warranty, truly rare in the used *anything* business. Mr. C found refrigerators for as little as $150 here, as well as a washer and dryer set for $295. The store also does repairs, and rents out appliances of various kinds, including microwave ovens, televisions, VCRs, and CD players. Open Mondays through Thursdays from 9 A.M. to 6 P.M., Fridays and Saturdays until 5.

Weiskind Appliance
● 10316 Aurora Ave. N, Seattle; 522-9391

An authorized Maytag dealer, that's mostly what you'll find at this north end store. In a smaller room at the back, they sell extensively reconditioned appliances—with an equally earnest store guarantee of six months, up there with the best Mr. C has ever found (any non-Maytag used items get a standard 30-day pledge).

Many of these babies look as good as new, and some are not far from it. Among the deals seen on a recent visit was a shiny white, recent washer-dryer set going for $550. You could pay almost that much for a new washer alone. Color models tend to go for even less, since white is where it's at these days. If you can live with avocado (maybe you have a dark basement), so much the better for you!

There were a few fridges (priced from $200-$400) on hand, as well as gas and electric ranges ($275 or so). And if you're not in a hurry to get your laundry done, go out to the "graveyard" behind the store and pick out a handyman's special—then you can *really* get clean for dirt cheap. Weiskind is open weekdays from 8 A.M. to 5:30 P.M., closing up at 5 P.M. on Saturdays.

BOOKS

As with appliances, used books can save you lots of money, especially if you are a voracious reader. Seattle is blessed with enough second-hand bookshops to give the hungriest bookworm indigestion; several are mixed into the listings below. Save even more by bringing in books that you no longer want. Most stores will give you a choice of cash or in-store credit; you'll usually get a higher figure by choosing the credit. It's a good, cheap way to check out new authors—and to keep your library lean.

A/K/A Fine Used Books

- 4142 Brooklyn Ave. NE, Seattle; 632-5870

This place is just what you think of when you picture a typical college-area bookshop. Two floors, joined by a winding staircase, are absolutely packed with books of every kind. So is the staircase. The broad selection ranges from *Silent Spring* to *Serpico*, with everything in between. After all, most stores have a "Humor" shelf. But, how many divide this up into things like a "Circus, Hobos, Tramps, and Related" section?

You'll also find subjects like art, women's studies, world politics, labor (in the "Radical Room"), and literature well-represented. And it's not all esoteric: Recent discoveries included John Grisham's *The Client* (just as the movie was coming out), reduced from $23.95 to $11, and a new copy of Mickey Mantle's *All My Octobers* at half-price—most likely a reviewer's copy. Plus plenty of science fiction, mysteries, and other novels.

A/K/A runs monthly sales by subject: All books on the Far East and Africa, for example, may be reduced a further 20% for a month. The store offers a free book search service, too. And don't miss the $1 and $2 bargain shelves, just as jammed as all the others. They're all ready for the browsing from 10 A.M. to 9 P.M., Mondays through Saturdays, and from 12-6 P.M. on Sundays. They are closed on some Sundays, though; call ahead if you're going then.

Arkadian Bookshop

- 5232 University Way NE, Seattle; 522-6575

It's Mr. C's continuing mission to seek out strange, great deals, to boldly go where no bargain hunter has gone before...Yes, the Arkadian Bookshop specializes in science fiction/fantasy stuff. Lots of it, new and used. While visiting, Mr. C scanned paperback copies of *Time Trap*, *Vulcan Glory*, and *Final Nexus*—each one was $2.50. All books are very reasonable here, some starting at just $1.25; comics also start that low, but are marked at list price. Videos can be rented, or purchased at prices starting at $14.95. Arkadian is open from 11 A.M. to 7 P.M., and noon to 6 P.M. on Sundays.

B. Dalton Bookseller

- 823 First Ave., Seattle; 246-4373
- Northgate Mall, Seattle; 364-6330
- 14725 NE 20th St., Bellevue; 641-3004
- Factoria Square Mall, Bellevue; 746-2924
- Bellevue Square Mall, Bellevue; 455-9115
- 6830 Bothell Way, Bothell; 486-4372
- Southcenter Shopping Center, Tukwila; 246-4373

One of the biggies in the bookselling wars, B. Dalton wins the race in its computer section, which encompasses more subjects than many competitors do. Dalton's also discounts current hardcover *New York Times* bestsellers by 25%.

Here's another Mr. C moneysaving tip: If you join B. Dalton's "Booksavers Club," you'll get an automatic 10% off every book every day, even if they're already discounted. The club costs $10 per year to join, but for true bookworms, it soon pays for itself. Store hours vary; open seven days a week.

Barnes & Noble Booksellers
- 626 106th Ave. NE, Bellevue; 451-8463
- Crossroads Shopping Center, Bellevue; 644-1650
- 300 Andover Park W, Tukwila; 575-3965

Barnes & Noble is right up there with the other bookstore biggies offering everyday discount prices. This includes reductions of 30% on current *New York Times* bestsellers. B & N's spiffy, refined shops are part of the new wave of book superstores. It's big, but comfortable. Classical music wafts softly in the background. There's a cafe at one end of the store, too; browsing and hanging out are definitely encouraged.

Every hardcover book in the store sells for at least 10% off the jacket price; "staff recommendations" are reduced by 30%. For more bargains, a large selection of remainders and overstocks are sold at up to 80% off their original prices. Special-ordering is a breeze here, and B & N's own publishing house reprints literary classics at super savings. Hours vary with each location, but all are open seven days a week, including evenings. In fact, B & N sponsors special events, including author signings and readings; see the listing under "Entertainment—Readings and Literary Events."

Beatty Books
- 1925 Third Ave., Seattle; 728-2665

Beatty offers a large selection of used books, covering literature, modern fiction, and history, to name a few topics. Some of the books are rare, and their uniqueness affects their price. However, most paperbacks are about $1, some going as high as $7 or $8. Mr. C was especially impressed by a $15 Ansel Adams book of photographs, half its original cover price. Beatty is fine for a quick browse, but it's definitely a place where you could comfortably curl up for a few hours with a new find. The shop is open from 11 A.M. to 5:30 P.M., Mondays through Saturdays.

Beauty and the Books
- 4213 University Way NE, Seattle; 632-8510

Love the name. Come in here to browse and stay a while; there are comfy couches and stools throughout the shop. Beauty and the Books offers quite a range of children's books, including classics you may have grown up with. A perfect-looking, big, colorful copy of *The Velveteen Rabbit* was seen for $12.50, down from $16.95, and shelved next to a $6.95 copy of the illustrated classic, *Treasure Island*.

The grown-up selection is also very broad; larger subject headings roam from standard fiction, to poetry, to biographies, to sci-fi, to medical. A hodgepodge of worn paperbacks is available in the center of the store (and just outside it) for 50 cents apiece. Beauty is open from 10 A.M. to 10 P.M. daily.

Beyond the Closet Bookstore
- 1501 Belmont Ave. E, Seattle; 322-4609

This bright, comfortable shop is "Seattle's exclusively lesbian & gay bookstore," as their card proclaims. Most of their new books are sold at full-price, but you'll find more than that here: There's a large selection of magazines, pins, cards and bargain books, too. Some of these are used, but in such excellent condition that they blend right in with the new books discounted by the wholesaler.

A hardcover copy of Quentin Crisp's *Book of Quotations*, originally $18.95, was seen for $7.98, while a complete multi-volume set of

Armistead Maupin's *Tales of the City*—as seen on TV!—could go for $40. The staff is very friendly and knowledgeable, ready to help you find whatever you're looking for. The Closet is open from 10 A.M. to 10 P.M. daily, 'til 11 P.M. Fridays and Saturdays.

Borders Books and Music

● 1505 Fourth Ave., Seattle; 622-4599

Borders crossed into downtown Seattle in the spring of '94. What does this mean for devoted Cheapsters? It means 30% off *New York Times* bestsellers in hardcover, and 30% off staff-recommended titles; 10% discounts are offered on many other hardcovers. There are also plenty of brand-new remainders at super-bargain prices. For information on music discounts, see the listing under "CDs, Records, Tapes, and Video."

Live music, mostly classical, usually rings forth from the upstairs cafe on Sunday afternoons to accompany their "Sunday Tea at the Borders" events. Pick up their monthly brochure to keep track of upcoming events, like author signings, discussion groups, and story times, all free to the public. For more information about special events, see the listing under "Entertainment—Readings and Literary Events." Borders is open Mondays through Thursdays, from 8 A.M. to 10 P.M., Fridays and Saturdays 'til 11 P.M., and Sundays from 11 A.M. to 8 P.M.

Brentano's Bookstore

● Westlake Center, 400 Pine St., Seattle; 467-9626

Like so many other large chain stores, Brentano's can keep its prices down while offering a wide selection of books. Discounts include 25% off remainders and overstocks—many tables are covered with these bargain books—and 10% off Brentano's top ten best sellers. For the serious book buyer, a Brentano's book card is a wise investment. A fee of $10 a year gets you 10% off each purchase—and you can use this card in Waldenbooks, too. After you spend a total of $100, a $5 gift certificate is mailed to you. Drop by and check out the

schedule for author signings. Brentano's is open daily.

Chameleon

● 514 15th Ave. E., Seattle; 323-0154

True to its name, this used book store seems to shift between dealing in used books, and exhibiting and selling African artwork. The bookshelves are predominantly filled with second-hand hardcovers, all in excellent condition. Henry Miller's *Moloch, or This Gentle World*, was recently seen for $9, half its original price.

Meanwhile, the walls, most table tops, and sides of bookcases are covered with African jewelry and masks. Not all pieces on display were for sale—ask for assistance—but you can find some cool bead necklaces for $7.50. Chameleon is open from 11 A.M. to 9 P.M. Mondays through Fridays, 'til 6 P.M. on the weekends.

Cinema Books

● 4753 Roosevelt Way NE, Seattle; 547-7667

Lights! Camera! Books! This U-District shop only carries books, magazines, calendars and postcards that have to do with the silver screen—or the smaller, home version, TV. The store sells most of its merchandise at list price; however, a table in back is loaded with discounted books. Among the deals found were a pictorial history of the Beatles on sale for $14.98—half its original cover price. Along the same line, Mr. C noted a large, behind-the-scenes study of *Gone with the Wind* marked down from $38 to $18.95. Most of the books are new remainders, and all are in excellent condition. Cinema Books is open from 10 A.M. to 7 P.M. Mondays through Saturdays.

The Couth Buzzard

● 7221 Greenwood Ave. N, Seattle; 789-8965

Why the name? Good question. Could be because you can circle these shelves for hours before swooping down upon that one perfect find. The place is just enormous. To help you find your way around, there are fairly accurate (and highly specialized) subject directories throughout the store. So, if you want to find "Neo-Pagan" books, you would look in section 27 to find hardcovers, and section 10 for paperbacks.

Not only does the Buzzard have such esoteric topics, but every section has an over-abundance of titles. Tickle your funny bone with a hardcover copy of Erma Bombeck's *The Family Ties that Bind...and Gag!* ($4.50, originally $15.95). Or, if you'd like to bend your funny bone into a pretzel, take a look at the yoga section. A book called *American Yoga Association Beginners Manual* was seen for $8. Then, to see color pictures of bones and other educational stuff, pick up a few copies of *National Geographic*, ranging between $1 and $3—some issues date back to the 1940s.

Used paperbacks are 60% off the cover price, while hardcover discounts vary. Further bargains can be found in the front of the store; books in the "Garbage to current fiction" boxes are on sale for 25¢ each, or five for a dollar. When Mr. C visited, Leon Uris's novel *Trinity* happened to be tucked in one of these cartons—not garbage at all. Also, each month offers a sale on some specific genre, like spy novels or true crime. And look for their annual sale when everything in the store is sold at 50% off.

Couth Buzzard is open Mondays through Thursdays, from noon to 8 P.M.; Fridays through Sundays, from 10 A.M. to 6 P.M. There's a complimentary cup of coffee waiting for you, too.

Crown Books
- 216 Broadway E, Seattle; 328-2665
- 4522 University Way NE, Seattle; 545-7117
- 11023 Eighth Ave. NE, Seattle; 365-5143
- 2212 NW Market St., Seattle; 782-5472
- 17370 Southcenter Pkwy., Tukwila; 575-0051

This national chain store offers big discounts on new releases. *New York Times* bestsellers are sold at 35% off in hardcover, 25% off in paperback. Large-sized art, reference, and cook-

books are 20% to 50% off, with lots of remainders available for under $5. The selection is as good as the prices, especially in their humor, auto, and computer sections.

To give you an idea of what all these percentages mean, you can buy a copy of *Men are from Mars, Women are from Venus* for $13.80—as opposed to $23 elsewhere. And an older, oversized, full-color, bound edition of Picasso artwork was recently seen for $5.99. Store hours vary; open seven days a week.

Half Price Books
- 4709 Roosevelt Way NE, Seattle; 547-7859
- Crossroads Shopping Center, Bellevue; 747-6616
- 23632 Highway 99, Edmonds; 670-6199
- 6409 Sixth Ave., Tacoma; 566-1238
- 16828 Southcenter Pkwy., Tukwila; 575-3173

Half Price Books is a chain with close to fifty stores in eight Western states. They have a huge selection of new and used books, most of which are marked at half off the cover prices—and some even less. They also pay cash for books, CDs, LPs, magazines, and other printed or recorded material.

As Mr. C browsed the shelves, he came across such hardcover bargains as *The Client* by John Grisham; originally $23.50, a new copy was available here for just $7.98. The large-sized *Grateful Dead Family Album*, originally $29.95, was just $9.98. Used hardcovers included Amy Tan's *The Joy Luck Club* for $6.98. Most paperbacks are, again, half of the cover price—except for the 50¢ racks of used pulp novels, romance, and science fiction.

Half Price Books is a big advocate for getting young people to read, and so they have a great collection of kids' books. They also have a "Frequent Reader" program for children under 15, and a 10% discount for all you teachers and librarians out there.

Upstairs at the U-District branch, along with tons of computer manuals, there is a goodly selection of computer software. Some of these are used, while others are unused but outdated versions of popular programs. This can be a clever way to save money: Often, buying last year's version of, say, "Word for Windows"—*plus* an upgrade disk—still costs less than buying the current version outright.

Used records are priced at $2 to $5 each, and used cassette tapes from $3 to $5. Mr. C didn't run across too much in the way of CDs. Books are the main attraction here, anyway. Half Price Books is open from 10 A.M. to 10 P.M. daily.

Horizon Books
● 425 15th Ave. E, Seattle; 329-3586
This little Capitol Hill shop is just bursting at the seams with books. Every shelf, from the dusty floorboards to the ceiling, is lined with books, with stacks of books in front of those, and piles of books on the floor in front of them. It's bookworm-bargain-hunter nirvana, but be prepared to spend some time searching if you've got a specific title in mind. Most paperbacks are only a dollar or two, and the vast fiction section ranged from classics, to science fiction, to gay/lesbian, to beatnik. There's also a good children's section, containing such favorites as Laura Ingalls Wilder's *Little House on the Prairie* series, each book marked $1 or $2.

Perhaps to keep you from being completely overwhelmed by the written word, a third of the back room is taken up by records and sheet music. There is an extensive jazz and classical collection on vinyl, with prices starting at $2.50. Horizon is open from 10 A.M. to 10 P.M. during the week, and 'til 9 P.M. on the weekends.

Left Bank Books
● 92 Pike St., Seattle; 622-0195
Left Bank is the right place to go if you're looking for beat, radical, or all-out anarchistic writing (and by the way, Pike Place Market, not First Hill, is the place to go if you're looking for Left Bank). Their books are

new and used, and grouped into such categories as labor economics, environmental, and Western philosophy. The prices are just as varied. A copy of *In Search of the Working Class* was marked down to $8, while Nietzsche's *Twilight of the Idols/The Anti-Christ* was seen for $2.50.

For more savings, there is a special monthly sale. One or two subjects—say, poetry, or Middle Eastern history—may be marked down 20%. Stop by Mondays through Saturdays, from 10 A.M. to 9 P.M.; or Sundays, from 9 A.M. to 6 P.M.

Leisure Books
● 4461 California Ave. SW, Seattle; 935-7325
The name of this West Seattle shop says it all. Once you've made out your vacation reading list (or anytime, really), check out the selection here—big on fiction of all kinds. Tons of bestsellers, science fiction, romance, Westerns, and mystery titles are packed into this long, narrow storefront. Not to mention history, nature, gardening, and other hobby-related books.

Most of the stock is used, but not all of it. The store buys and sells books, and acquires some library and reviewers' copies. Most paperback fiction goes for 50¢ to $2.50, and up; a new hardcover edition of Tom Clancy's *Clear and Present Danger* was reduced from $21.95 to $15. Open seven days a week.

Page One Book Exchange
● 14220 NE 20th St., Bellevue; 474-6165
Here's a storefront shop, tucked into an Eastside strip mall, which caters to the avid fiction reader. The store is almost entirely filled with paperback novels, generally selling at half of the cover price. In fact, there is such a good selection of bestsellers, alphabetized by author, that you can frequently find multiple copies of hot titles by Grisham, Ludlum, Clancy, Steele, *et. al.* It's like going to the video store.

And, like videos, you can almost "rent" these books; the store takes trade-ins for cash or credit. So, you may buy a $6.99 paperback for $3.50, read it, and return it for a trade-in value of 20% of the cover. Net cost: $2.10. Go ahead; they're quite open about this policy, and many of the customers are regulars here.

There are some non-fiction books as well, plus a bargain shelf of books at 25¢ each, or six for a buck. Store hours are from 11 A.M. to 5 P.M. on weekdays, and from 10-5 on Saturdays. Closed Sundays.

The Penny Box
• 10052 NE 137th St., Kirkland; 820-0226

You may have to search a bit for this bookshop, tucked away in one of the gazillion shopping centers just north of Juanita. But, once you do, you're certain to find something among its 15,000 titles to reward your efforts. This charming and immaculate little emporium buys and sells used books only, specializing in the science fiction and fantasy genres. They also deal in vintage collectibles, as well as carrying a large variety of children's books. Most paperbacks are sold for half the cover price, with hardcovers going for about one-third of the cover. Open seven days a week, including Tuesdays through Saturdays until 9 P.M.

Pioneer Square Books
• 213 First Ave. S, Seattle; 343-BOOK (2665)

This is a good, run-of-the-mill used bookstore, with shelves full of hardcover and paperbacks. Prices and discounts vary, but however you read into this, you'll find some big savings. A hardcover biography of Jackie Kennedy Onassis, *A Woman Named Jackie*, was list-priced at $21.95. PSB had it for $6.95. Many titles are available in multiple copies, and the store also deals in rare and out-of-print books. Open from 10 A.M. to 6 P.M. Mondays through Saturdays, and from noon to 6 P.M. Sundays.

Pistil
• 1013 E Pike St., Seattle; 325-5401

Don't judge these books by their covers; Pistil mixes new and used copies

MR. CHEAP'S PICKS
Books

✔ **A/K/A Fine Used Books—** Also known as one of the U-District's best.

✔ **The Couth Buzzard—**This sprawling used bookstore has so much to see, you need a map—which they thoughtfully provide.

✔ **Shorey's—**Another vast used bookstore, specializing in the rare and unusual, which threatens to take over the Pike Place Market next door.

✔ **Twice Sold Tales—**Quirky charm, comfy seating, and big savings during their Friday all-nighter sales.

together on the shelves, and sometimes it's hard to tell which is which. However, if you look inside, you'll see that the used books are marked at half off the cover price, and therefore a much better buy. Betty Friedan's *The Feminine Mystique* was seen for $2.50, less than half of the original paperback's $5.40.

This First Hill shop is neatly arranged, with especially good children's and humor sections. Pick up a copy of *Raggedy Ann* for $3.50, or *Bloom County Babylon* for $6.50. Pistil is open from 10 A.M. to 10 P.M. Tuesdays through Sundays, and closed Mondays.

Rainy Day Books
• 8329 15th Ave. NW, Seattle; 783-3383

Nothing like curling up with a good book on a rainy day. Maybe that's why Seattleites buy more books than nearly everyone else in the country. Yes, Mr. C knows that soggy-weather thing is a ploy to keep away outsiders and Californians—just indulge this little contribution to the myth.

General fiction is the specialty at this Ballard bookseller: popular titles, favorite literature, and fairly recent bestsellers. Anne Rice's *Witching Hour*, plus several John Grisham novels, were all seen for $3.45. The store is filled mostly with paperbacks, and they're about half the cover price. Stop in Mondays through Saturdays, rain or shine, from 11 A.M. to 4 P.M. Rainy Day Books is, appropriately enough, closed on Sunday.

Red and Black Books Collective

● 432 15th Ave. E., Seattle; 322-READ (7323)

This bookstore is best-known for its multicultural and children's book sections. On the whole, R and B sells new books at retail prices. However, it does have a table of books marked down because of damage, overstock, or as other types of remainders. On this table, Mr. C found a copy of *Vanishing Arctic: Alaska's National Wildlife Refuge* for $12.95 (marked down from $25); *Jump and Other Stories*, by Nobel Prize winner Nadine Gordimer, for $4.98 (list price $20); and *Let Freedom Ring: A Ballad of Martin Luther King Jr.*, a children's pictorial, for $10 (originally $18.95).

For additional savings, take advantage of R and B's "Frequent Buyer" card. After you've bought twelve books at list price, they calculate the average and give you that much in store credit. In other words, it literally pays off to shop here.

R and B also has a fairly impressive calendar of literary events, all of which are free to the public. Alice Walker is among the artists and activists who've appeared here. See the listing under "Entertainment—Readings and Literary Events" for more information. Pick up a seasonal newsletter to find out about current events. Open from 10 A.M. to 8 P.M. Mondays through Thursdays, 'til 9 P.M. Fridays and Saturdays, and from 12-7 P.M. on Sundays.

Seattle Mystery Bookshop

● 117 Cherry St., Seattle; 587-5737

It *may* have been Colonel Mustard in the library with a candlestick. But it was definitely Mr. C in the Seattle Mystery Bookshop with a bargain. This cozy store near Pioneer Square specializes in mysteries, and lots of them are sold below list price. A mix of new and used books fills the store, with an impressive collection of writings from Northwest authors. Most used paperbacks are around $3. Hardcovers are a bit more: Mr. C spotted *The Disciples* by Joseph J. Andrew marked down from $20 to $11.98.

Seattle Mystery Bookshop also hosts a "Meet the Authors" series. While these names may not be recognized nationally, you will probably get a chance to chat with each writer, rather than just get a hastily scribbled signature. Call for details, or pick up a schedule at the store. Open Mondays through Saturdays, from 11 A.M. to 6 P.M., Sundays from 12-5.

Shakespeare & Company

● Pike Place Market, Seattle; 624-7151

Amid the hurly-burly of wandering minstrels and tourists at the Pike Place Market, this very well-stocked and reasonably priced used bookstore can be found. Located in the Main Arcade, Shakespeare & Company is owned by a mother-and-son team who are quite proud of the books therein. Tight but neatly arranged shelves reach from floor to ceiling, displaying far more than the Bard—contemporary and classical fiction, counter-culture/beat, nature, and architecture, to name but a few.

Pictures of deceased movie stars line the walls, under the caption "Too Young to Die." This is probably not a Morticia Addams decorating motif as much as an advertisement for the store's large collection of Hollywood movie books. A coffee table-sized photo biography of Marilyn Monroe was seen for $19.95; while Mr. C leafed through it, the folks offered it for $17.

Shakespeare's works, of course, are here in abundance—in paperbacks starting at $1.50, to hardcover editions for $24.95. If thou art not willing to readeth the real thingeth, the store also has Cliff's Notes in stock. Shakespeare & Company is open from 10 A.M. to 5:30 P.M. Wednesdays through Mondays, and closed Tuesdays.

Shorey's
• 1411 First Ave., Seattle; 624-0221
Literally attached to Pike Place Market, Shorey's is another fine place to browse. Gargantuan is one word that well describes this used book store, with more nooks and crannies than an English muffin. It's gotta be big to hold the one-million-plus books it claims to have in stock.

There's scarcely enough room here to mention every subject, but rest assured that Shorey's has them all covered (excuse the pun). Fiction and history, among others, have their own rooms. Other genres, like geology, mountaineering, and erotica, have designated bookcases throughout the store. And it's a good place to look for obscure, out-of-print poetry (isn't that redundant?).

Most paperbacks are a few dollars each, while hardcovers go around $10 and up. Rare and out of print books can be much more, but these are kept separately. The rare books in Room 2 can only be seen with permission! For more savings, check out the bargain shelves for 25¢ and 50¢ books. And look for a huge 50% off sale every year after Christmas. Shorey's also has favorite classic art prints for sale for around $4 apiece. Open Mondays through Saturdays, from 10 A.M. to 6 P.M.; Sundays, noon to 5 P.M.

Tower Books
• 20 Mercer St., Seattle; 283-6333
• 10635 NE Eighth St., Bellevue; 451-1110
• 2501 S 38th St., Tacoma; 473-3362
Not just for music anymore, Tower now sells brand-new books and magazines at considerable discounts. Current bestsellers are 30% off, as are a special selection of other new releases chosen by the staff. Various sales are also in progress everyday; when Mr. C stopped by, all audio books on tape were 30% off.

Crave the written word? Only have a buck or two? Browse the 50¢ rack just outside the front door. If you're completely broke but still want to hang with the *literati*, you can attend Tower's frequent book signings. One of these events, "Taste the Wine, Meet the Authors," held in honor of *Northwest Wines*, really encouraged the public to raise its glass to this subject. Tower is open daily from 9 A.M. to midnight. Check the store for upcoming events. For info about good deals on music, see the listing in "CDs, Records, Tapes, and Video."

And, for that really small used bookshop experience in Queen Anne, check out Titlewave Books nearby at 7 Mercer St.; telephone 282-7687.

Twice Sold Tales
• 905 E John St., Seattle; 324-2421
• 2210 N 45th St., Seattle; 545-4226
Warning: The Capitol Hill branch of these stores is guarded by five wandering/dozing cats by day, and a ferocious bubble machine at night. If you can handle these hazards, stop in on any Friday between midnight and 8 A.M.—yes, that's right—to take advantage of the 25% off everything sale. The night-owl catches the book worm, to mix an adage. These special hours and prices take place at the Capitol Hill branch only.

Otherwise, expect to pay $6 for Abbie Hoffman's *Soon to be a Major Motion Picture*, or $12 for *Dear Mili*, a Maurice Sendak children's story, color-illustrated in hardcover. Feeling glum about your own writing lately? Peruse the "Bad Poetry" shelf, where you can read such gems as Leonard Nimoy's *Warmed by Love*—marked down from the original $14.95 to $10 (Mr. C wonders if that's enough of a reduction). There's also a 50¢ rack out front if you're really strapped for cash. Twice Sold Tales in Capitol Hill is open from 10 A.M. to 2 A.M. Saturdays through Thursdays; and, as noted above, open all nights on Fridays; the Wallingford branch is open Sundays through Thursdays from 12-8 P.M., Fridays until 10 P.M., and Saturdays 10-10.

University Bookstore

- 4326 University Way NE, Seattle; 634-3400
- 990 102nd Ave. NE, Bellevue; 632-9500

Anyone who has stopped into the University Bookstore knows that they sell far more than textbooks or school materials. What may not be as well-known is that there are some "classy" deals on popular fiction, too.

Among the permanent discounts, University bestsellers are marked at 25% off the cover price. Better yet, the store has one of the city's best selections of remainder books, crammed onto several large bargain tables. You may find such books as a special edition of *The More Than Complete Hitchhiker's Guide* by Douglas Adams (a compilation of the entire series, including the hard-to-find *Young Zaphod Plays It Safe*), for $11.99, significantly less than combined the original price of $51.80. *Meditations for Men Who Do Too Much* was seen for $3.99, down from $9, perfect for any man (or woman) who doesn't want to *pay* too much. And a beautiful hardcover pictorial of the Pacific Northwest was spotted for $14.98.

UB is open Mondays through Saturdays from 9 A.M. to 6 P.M., Sundays noon to 5 P.M. Get on their mailing list for news about monthly author-signings, again, one of the best in the city. See the listing under "Entertainment—Readings and Literary Events" for more details.

Waldenbooks

- 1428 Fourth Ave., Seattle; 621-1143
- 701 Fifth Ave., Seattle; 442-9524
- Northgate Mall, Seattle; 365-2923
- Bellevue Square Mall, Bellevue; 455-9885
- Everett Mall, Everett; 347-1046
- Sea Tac Mall, Federal Way; 839-8448
- Alderwood Mall, Lynnwood; 771-7180
- Kitsap Mall, Silverdale; (360) 692-6901
- Lakewood Mall, Tacoma; 588-2888
- Tacoma Mall, Tacoma; 474-4402
- Southcenter Shopping Center, Tukwila; 248-0886
- *And other suburban locations*

In addition to discounting its own weekly in-store picks by 25%, Waldenbooks offers its customers a "Preferred Reader" discount card. Show it at the cash register wherever you buy something in any branch, nationwide. You'll get 10% off your purchase; and, for every $100 you spend during the course of a year, you'll get a $5 credit toward future purchases. This credit can likewise be redeemed at any Waldenbooks store, on anything except newspapers, magazines, and cards. Membership costs $10; sign up in any store. Waldenbooks also displays a good selection of publishers' overstocks and remainder books, at significant discounts. Hours vary with each location.

Westside Stories

- 12 Boston St., Seattle; 285-BOOK (2665)

*Could be....Who knows....*The inside of Westside Stories is just as cute as its name. The place is kinda small, but still has lots of open space between the wooden bookcases—sort of like a small-town library. There's no place to sit, unless you're a kid; only the children's/pre-teen section has chairs, and they're mini-sized.

Most of the books here are used, and some rare books are mixed in—so be sure to check the price carefully. While visiting, Mr. C spotted a hardcover copy of the *Dances with Wolves* novelization, originally $18.95, for $9.95. And Margaret Atwood's *Cat's Eye*, also in hardcover, was just $7.50. For many other books, $2 seems to be the average price. Open seven days a week.

CAMERAS

There are lots of places to save money on appliances and electronics in Seattle. Some, unfortunately, are as far below repute as they are below retail. With merchandise that is imported from foreign countries, there is a greater possibility of shady deals, or inferior quality. Mr. C says this not out of any kind of prejudice, but because he wants you to be careful. You should have no such worries with the stores listed here.

One of the best ways to protect yourself, if you have doubts as to *any* store's reliability, is to ask about their guarantee policy; make sure the item you want carries an American warranty. Since some stores deal directly with manufacturers in the Far East, their merchandise many carry a foreign warranty instead. Even for identical products, a foreign warranty can make repairs a hassle—unless you don't mind paying the postage to Japan! Remember, you are perfectly within your rights to inquire about this in the store.

Ballard Camera
- 1836 NW Market St., Seattle; 783-1121

This longtime cameras-only dealer also boasts one of the city's largest selections of used cameras for professionals and amateurs, saving you hundreds of dollars off the comparable cost of new models. Ballard Camera has been around for more than forty years, and many of its experienced staff have worked here for a decade or two themselves. They know their stuff.

On any given day, this comfortable shop will present you with dozens upon dozens of used cameras to choose from; Mr. C found about fifty SLR models alone, like a factory-overhauled Minolta 7XI reduced from its original $600 down to $349. A pro-grade Canon F-1 was selling for half of its $1,500 list price; Ballard is one of Seattle's busiest Canon dealers. And, for serious shutter-freaks, a Contax RTS-3—which currently lists for $2,500 new—was available here for $1,400. In fact, the store actually had *two* of these in their used department, even though it's one of that manufacturer's most recent styles.

All of which should give you some idea of how much business Ballard does in the second-hand area. Along with cameras, you can also find used deals on lenses (over 150 to choose from), filters, and other accessories. All used items are guaranteed to work, or the store will give you an exchange. They do, of course, sell new equipment as well, plus one-hour photo developing and next-day slide processing. Friendly service, too. Ballard Camera is open weekdays from 9:30 to 6 P.M., and on Saturdays until 5 P.M.

Cameras West
- 1908 Fourth Ave., Seattle; 622-0066
- Northgate Mall, Seattle; 365-0066
- 14309 NE 20th St., Bellevue; 641-6677

Along with a large selection of famous-name cameras and video camcorders at competitive prices, Cameras West is notable (in this volume) for its equally good choice of second-hand, like-new models. There's a good range of manual and fully-automatic models; each store has a few dozen cameras and bodies at any one time, as well as up to a hundred different lenses and filters. You're sure to see, as Mr. C has, such

25

MR. CHEAP'S PICKS
Cameras

✔ **Ballard Camera**—Perhaps Seattle's largest selection of used, last-a-lifetime cameras.

✔ **Ken's Camera**—Focusing on good deals on specific items, with a knowledgeable, helpful staff.

---

names as Minolta, Pentax, Olympus, and Nikon, depending on what's come in through trade-ins; a classic Canon AE-1, with a standard lens, was recently snapped up for $200. All used cameras carry a 90-day store warranty.

Cameras West also offers current equipment for rent—another way to save cash over buying at full-price, or trying something out before purchasing it. All branches are open seven days a week.

Ken's Camera
- 1327 Second Ave., Seattle; 223-5553
- 8907 Evergreen Way, Everett; 353-5553
- 4520 200th St. SW, Lynnwood; 771-3050

Ken's Camera "focuses" on high-quality equipment at reasonable costs. Not every item is the least expensive in town, but most of the prices are less than many other camera stores. Ken also offers a thirty-day price protection guarantee.

Mr. C did some price checking and found that basic point and shoot cameras start as low as $30. For the more advanced photographer, how's this for snappy savings: An Olympus IS3 35mm camera at Ken's was recently priced at $519, significantly better than the $600 seen elsewhere at the time. Stop by during the week between 9 A.M. and 5:30 P.M., and Saturdays from 10 A.M. to 5 P.M.

Lee's Video-Audio-Fax
- 15625 NE Eighth St., Bellevue; 643-5555

See the listing under "Electronics."

Tall's Camera
- 950 Third Ave., Seattle; 682-2233
- 1319 Fourth Ave., Seattle; 583-8111
- Bellevue Square Mall, Bellevue; 455-2233
- Alderwood Mall, Lynwood; 672-7177
- Tacoma Mall, Tacoma; 473-2233
- Southcenter Mall, Tukwila; 433-1111

Another major full-price retailer that takes trade-ins and sells them off at drastically reduced prices, Tall's tends to offer a dozen or so cameras at any given time in most of its stores. Some are sold "as is," but most carry a 30-day store warranty. Don't forget, of course, that such cameras are built to last decades. On his visit, Mr. C found a Minolta "Maxxum" 7000AF body for $95; and a Canon EOS 650 for $225. Plus plenty of assorted lenses, filters, and motor drives.

The Third Avenue store does not sell used cameras at all; check the Fourth Avenue branch a few blocks away. The downtown stores, however, are closed on Sundays.

CARPETING AND RUGS

Caravan Carpets
- 3500 Fremont Ave. N, Seattle; 547-6666

The carpets and kilims sold here are tribal or nomadic, showing a variety of ethnic styles. Most are hand-made with natural fibers, and colored with vegetable dyes. Surprisingly, these high-quality rugs are quite affordable—especially the large selection of good-condition used rugs found downstairs in the "bargain basement."

Some of the more impressive deals that Mr. C found were a handmade 5' x 8' Persian rug for $300, and a 5' x 7' kilim for $100. Hundreds of carpets are available, and the knowledgeable staff is patient and willing to help you find something nice within your price range.

Caravan is open from 11 A.M. to 7 P.M. Mondays through Saturdays, from noon to 5 P.M. Sundays.

Charles Roberts
• 410 First Ave. S, Seattle; 621-9580
One of the many rug dealers in Pioneer Square, Charles Roberts sells Orientals ranging in price from a few hundred dollars to many thousands—with just about as broad a range in age and style.

Even the most expensive rugs are still very reasonable. Mr. C was shown a 10' x 16' carpet dating from the 1920s, selling for $7,000. Elsewhere, this huge, antique rug could cost as much as $12,000. Okay, we can dream, right? That aside, there are plenty of choices that probably fit more in the Mr. C price range—a 9' x 12' carpet, used and slightly worn in parts ("the thin spots give it character," the saleswoman pointed out), was just $180. A 2' x 3' hand-made Pakistani rug with 200 knots per square inch—real quality here—was just $90. Charles Roberts also offers free delivery and shipping. Stop by between 10 A.M. and 4:30 P.M. Mondays through Saturdays.

Nearby, **Yam Oriental Rugs** at 78 S Washington Street (622-2439) is another good place to check out for serious deals on handmade rugs, with Persians starting as low as $169. Open seven days.

Consolidated Carpets
• 5935 Fourth Ave. S, Seattle; 762-6270
• 200 N 85th St., Seattle; 789-7737
• 11724 Lake City Way NE, Seattle; 440-8609
• 14150 NE 20th St., Bellevue; 641-4552

MR. CHEAP'S PICKS
Carpeting and Rugs

✔ **Caravan Carpets**—The "Bargain Basement" at this Eastern rug shop in Fremont is filled with a large and diverse collection.

✔ **4-Day Carpet Company**—From humble beginnings in a garage, they've moved up to...a larger garage. The deals on second-hand office carpeting, though, are amazing.

✔ **Seattle Carpet Center**—Also specializing in used commercial carpeting, along with good prices on new broadloom.

• 335 S Washington St., Kent; 852-7100
• 4601 200th Ave. SW, Lynnwood; 774-3303

From its large, main warehouse branch in the Georgetown industrial district, Consolidated Carpet furnishes half a dozen stores with closeouts and other deals which come in from manufacturers all over the country. They buy 'em by the truckload, ensuring low prices, from makers like Philadelphia, Shaw, and DuPont; plus similar deals in vinyl flooring from Armstrong and Congoleum.

The selection at the main store makes it worth the scouting trip. Brand-new remnants here sell for as little as $4 a yard, cash-and-carry. Many of these are huge, like a plush 12' x 16' piece seen for $99. Not that everything here is a remnant; there are full bolts of broadloom starting as low as $12.99 a yard. Installation can be arranged, at an extra cost; the rock-bottom prices on the tags are strictly no-frills. Open seven days a week.

4-Day Carpet Company
- 900 N Broad St., Seattle; 343-7628
- 1501 S Central Ave., Kent; 850-2144

What's in a name? Well, these guys are only open four days a week. Why make an effort to get there? Super-low prices on commercial carpeting. Most of it is second-hand—yes, that's right—or brand-new, second-quality (but you'd hardly know it).

Owner Bill Barks began as a contractor himself, ripping out yards and yards of still-good floor covering when offices chose to redecorate. Rather than toss it out, he began selling the used stuff on Saturdays out of a garage. He's in a bigger garage now (two, in fact); but the principle is the same, potentially saving you hundreds of dollars.

Some of this broadloom goes for a mere $2 or $3 per square yard (!). Styles which could once have cost up to $30 a yard may now be found here for no more than $13—with enough stock on hand to avoid using blemished areas, and enough variety to work within any color scheme. Bring in a drawing of your floor layout, and the experienced staff will work with you to find just what you need. You can even save more by going with used padding!

Among factory seconds (new), there are big "leftover" pieces taken from the ends of rolls; some whose rolls were damaged in warehouses, still perfectly good on the inside; and other remnants, some of which are bound into rugs. These can be selling here for half of their original prices.

It's strictly no-frills; you may have to dodge the occasional fork-lift. But the service is good, and the deals are first-rate. Open Wednesdays and Thursdays from 9 A.M. to 8 P.M., Fridays and Saturdays from 9 A.M. to 6 P.M.

JB Factory Carpets
- 13310 NE Bellevue-Redmond Rd., Bellevue; 746-7717
- 113 SW 153rd St., Burien; 242-6700
- 310 N Central Ave., Kent; 852-2797
- 4320 196th Ave. SW, Lynnwood; 776-4777
- 7002 Tacoma Mall Blvd., Tacoma; 472-1034

This major area chain applies high-volume pricing to lots of big-name flooring, including some brands, like Karastan, which few stores sell at discount. Other makers seen here are Mannington, Bigelow, and Congoleum vinyl. Frequent sales can swipe as much as 60% off retail prices; one recent sale offered Monsanto wear-dated nylon plush, reduced from JB's everyday $15.95 per yard (already good) to a paltry $8.95 a yard. In the large Kent store, Mr. C also found Karastan carpets marked down from $52 a yard to an amazing $20, as well as wool berbers from just $9.99 a yard. JB also pledges to beat any carpeting estimate by 5%.

Orientals and other rugs, imported from India, Belgium, and the like, carry a 20-year guarantee. A 6' x 9' Karastan wool rug, originally retailing for $1,629, was reduced all the way to $815. In all, there's quite a lot to see. Open seven days, including weeknights until 8 P.M.

Oriental Rug Warehouse
- Pavilion Mall, Tukwila; 575-0628

Upstairs in a mall known more for clothing than carpets, ORW offers good deals on a variety of woven rugs imported from India, Pakistan, China, Turkey, Belgium, and more. 90% of these are handmade. Whether you go for a Persian silk rug, reduced from a retail prices of $3,000 to $2,100, or a comparable wool version for $1,200 (or a machine-made one for $259), you're sure to find a design you like at a good price. Owner Selcuk Kaya has been at it for almost ten years, and does a surprisingly high-volume business for such a small store. Open seven days a week.

Remnant King Carpets
- 800 NW 65th St., Seattle; 789-7553
- 4117 Rucker St., Everett; 259-4922

A tiny Ballard shop is fed by a larger Everett branch in this mini-chain specializing in remnants only. A good variety starts around $4 per square yard for nylons, going up to $12 a yard for 100% wool styles. All of these are brand-new; shop in either store, or request something to be trucked from one to another within days. The in-town store is open every day; the Everett location is closed on Sundays.

Remnants To Go
- 2420 First Ave. S, Seattle; 382-1253
- 12505 Lake City Way NE, Seattle; 361-6260
- 15115 Highway 99, Lynnwood; 743-6930
- 145 SW 152nd St., Burien; 433-0556

Even with four branches, Remnants To Go is run as a local family business. They specialize in new carpeting from remnant pieces, with the motto, "You won't buy more than you need." They must mean it; during Mr. C's visit, they actually sold someone just enough carpeting to make a cat's scratching post. But don't be fooled—they do large-area projects just as well, including installation, if you wish.

You can find many major brands here, and the whole variety of weaves. Plush broadlooms start as low as $5.99 a square yard; and you may even find natural wool berbers at that price. Commercial loops start at $4.99 a yard. Oriental rugs were seen for $80, and bound 9' x 12' rugs from $100. RTG also does the same

kind of dealing in vinyl floor coverings, counter tops, and related home decor—and again, they can do the installation themselves. Open seven days a week.

Seattle Carpet Center
- 1416 Elliott Ave. W, Seattle; 285-7500

Two warehouses' worth of new and used carpeting stock this Queen Anne shop. The main showroom looks like any such store, with swatches of Shaw, Philadelphia, and other name brands. But these are sold at $4-$5 less per yard than at other comparable dealers, primarily due to the low overhead at this family-run business.

Step through to the garage, though, and you'll find the real deals—new and used remnants of commercial broadloom as low as $1 a square yard. Most used rems are more like $3.50, with unused remnants going from about $5 to $14 a yard. Many of the used pieces look like new. Mr. C was shown a handsome 7' x 10' aqua remnant with pink pin-dots, "only used a couple of days," selling for $89. Most of these are nylon commercial grades, Scotchguarded, and spot-cleaned.

SCC is closed Sundays and Mondays; otherwise, hours are from 9:30 A.M. to 6 P.M., except Thursdays until 8 and Saturdays until 5.

And you probably know about these major chains, weaving their way around the country:

Carpeteria
- 17720 Southcenter Pkwy., Tukwila; 575-1687

Carpet Exchange
- 1251 First Ave. S, Seattle; 624-7800
- 12802 Bellevue-Redmond Rd., Bellevue; 455-8332

- 30820 Pacific Hwy. S, Federal Way; 839-2142
- 5501 196th Ave. SW, Lynnwood; 771-1477
- 9021 S 180th St., Renton; 251-0200
- 3200 Randall Way, NW, Silverdale; (360) 692-7732
- 6818 Tacoma Mall Blvd., Tacoma; 474-9034

CDS, RECORDS, TAPES, AND VIDEO

You can save extra money on music by shopping second-hand. Like used bookshops, many of the stores below will allow you to trade in music you no longer want. Alas, they won't take just anything; used LPs, in particular, have become less marketable. Most stores will give you a choice of cash or in-store credit; you'll usually get a higher figure by choosing the credit. It's a good, cheap way to check out artists you might not take a chance on at full-price.

Be Dazzled Discs
• 101 Cherry St., Seattle; 382-6072
Mr. C be delighted with Be Dazzled. A third of the stock is used and discounted, while even some of the new discs are below list price, too. You'll always find various things on sale, making it worth a regular drop-in to see what the latest deals are. Used CDs, except for the rare or out-of-print ones, are generally priced between $4 and $8. Check out the good selection of alternative, garage, funk, and others, befitting a music shop in Pioneer Square. Be Dazzled is open from 11 A.M. to 7 P.M. Mondays through Saturdays, and from 12 noon to 6 P.M. Sundays.

Bop Street Records and CDs
• 5512 20th Ave. NW, Seattle; 783-3009
Collector Dave Voorhees found himself with so many record albums, he had to open a store to sell them off. Now, he buys, sells, and trades from a stock of over 10,000 records, discs, and cassettes—so many, in fact, that he can't even display them all in this long, narrow shoebox of a shop. This is progress?

There is an overwhelming selection of good ol' vinyl records here, from albums to 45s to 78s. Most are priced from $4.99 to $9.99. The entire history of rock is well-represented, from oldies to hip-hop, plus lots of jazz and classical music.

Compact discs are more like $9.99 to $11.99; Dave also specializes in live bootleg concert CDs, something of a rarity. Second-hand cassette tapes, meanwhile, are usually $3.99 to $5.99. The store is totally laid-back and friendly, and it's open Mondays through Saturdays from 12 noon to 6 P.M.

Borders Books and Music
• 1505 Fourth Ave., Seattle; 622-4599
Borders crossed into Seattle in the spring of '94. What does this mean for devoted Cheapsters? In the way of music, there are two important things to know. First, anything on Billboard's "Top 15" is reduced—that means CDs at the top of the charts are $12.99. Second, there is usually live music, mostly classical, played in the upstairs cafe on Sunday afternoons. It's part of the "Sunday Tea at the Borders" events.

The music selection itself is vast, as good as any other national chain. The classical department is particularly good, though rock and jazz are also well represented. Pick up their monthly brochure to keep track of upcoming music and literary events, all free to the public. For more information about special events, see the listing under "Entertainment—Readings and Literary Events." For information on book discounts see the listing under "Books." Borders is open Mondays through Thursdays, from 8 A.M. to 10 P.M., Fridays and Saturdays 'til 11 P.M., and Sundays from 11 A.M. to 8 P.M.

Bud's Jazz Records
- 102 S Jackson St., Seattle;
  628-0445

Jazz *aficionado* Bud Young has filled his walk-down shop in Pioneer Square with "jazz in all its forms." It's easily one of the deepest jazz collections Mr. C has come across in his many travels. Being rare or just hard to find, alas, many of these are sold at full-price; but there are some bargain bins any serious fan will want to check out. Used CDs go for $6.49 or so; cassettes around $3; and most LPs are $8 and up. Open daily from 11 A.M. to 7 P.M., Sundays from 12-6.

Cellophane Square
- 1315 NE 42nd St., Seattle;
  634-2280
- Bellevue Square Mall, Bellevue;
  454-5059

Cellophane Square sells new and used records, tapes, and compact discs—and has on display a fairly even amount of all three. In this era of all-CD-stores, that's something in itself. According to the sales guy, hundreds of new tunes come in each day, so you'll find different stuff every time you visit.

Pick up a used Stone Roses CD for $8.99, or a Breeders cassette tape for $6.99. If the condition of an album is questionable, they'll lower the price (don't be afraid to call them on it!). Anything priced at $2 or more comes with a one-week return guarantee; you don't have to worry about getting stuck with something you can't play. Cellophane Square is open seven days a week.

Easy Street CDs and Tapes
- 4559 California Ave. SW, Seattle;
  938-EASY (3279)
- Parkplace Center, Kirkland;
  827-8257

A latest-releases haven which also deals in used compact discs and cassette tapes, Easy Street makes it easy to keep the music flowing on the street where you live. Most new CDs go on sale for $12.99, not a bad price; used discs range from $4.99 to $8.99, however, including the likes of Rod Stewart and Billy Joel. Some recent hits

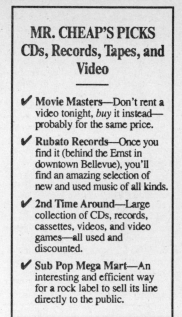

go up to $10.99, for hot bands like Pearl Jam and Nirvana. There's also a $2.99-$4.99 bin, and even this will turn up a few name artists.

This is mainly a rock 'n roll kinda place, but you can also find classical and jazz CDs among the used bins. Second-hand cassettes are mostly $2.49 and $3.49; Mr. C found the Rolling Stones' *Steel Wheels* and Bob Seger's *Like a Rock*. Jazz tapes included David Sanborn's *Voyeur* for $3.49. And don't pass up the 79¢ table, which yielded tapes by Lionel Richie and other stars. ES also sells rock posters, funky greeting cards, and other paraphernalia; during Mr. C's visit, they were having a poster clearance sale, with a table full of things like Aerosmith and the *Reality Bites* movie poster, all $2.50 each. Open seven days a week.

Movie Masters
- 213 SW 152nd Ave., Burien;
  431-5453

Entrepreneur Art Robbins believes he has the only store in the Seattle area which buys, sells, and trades movie videos to the public. In fact, though this may look like your corner video stop, Movie Masters does *not* rent any videotapes. Instead, Art gets trade-ins, as well as deals on overstocked new tapes, and sells them all at considerable savings off retail prices. He must be doing something right—from his start in 1989, he's now got some 1,500 new tapes (and hundreds more used) in the store at any one time.

New titles are priced at up to 35% below retail, even for fairly recent hits. *The Fugitive* was spotted here at a discount—*before* it turned up on cable. There are also lots of out-of-print titles. Second-hand tapes go for about half of retail, mostly $7.99 to $9.99. Often, Art can offer you a choice of new or used on a particular movie. And, don't miss his "$3 Each—Buy One, Get Two Free" bargain box. You can see how much turnover the man has, if he's literally giving clearance stock away. Own three videos for the price of renting one somewhere else!

Movie Masters also deals in video games, with all of the popular versions from Sega to 3DO. They've got as many as 150 Super Nintendo cartridges at any one time. Some cost as little as $5; Game Boy cartridges are mostly $12.99 to $14.99. Hotter games are more, but still discounted: "Virtual Racing," which at the time of this writing has not been seen under $79, could be had for $59 here. You'll find no prices on any of the boxes, however— Art uses up-to-the-minute price guides to keep his rates near their wholesale value (sometimes under it).

Another reason for the lack of price tags is that he likes to cut deals. Bring an armful up to the counter and make an offer. "A smile goes a long way in my store," says Art. "Just slap 'em on the counter and say, 'I got cash!'" Bring something in to trade for credit, too. The store is open Mondays through Fridays from 11 A.M. to 7 P.M., and Saturdays from 10-6.

Park Avenue Records
- 523 Queen Anne Ave. N, Seattle; 284-2390

As the name suggests, this store deals mainly in vinyl. About 80% of the stock is used, but you can still expect high quality sound here—because nothing with a scratch is ever put on the shelves. If you *should* get a record with a skip, you can return it within a week for store credit—no hassles. Not that paying $2.99 for the Police's *Synchronicity* or $8.99 for a Dylan CD is a huge investment in the first place, but it's nice to know you have the option.

Park Avenue also specializes in albums that are locally produced, as well as those imported from far and wide. You can also find plenty of jazz, R & B, and classical music. Store hours are from 11 A.M. to 9 P.M. Mondays through Saturdays, and from noon to 8 P.M. Sundays.

Rubato Records
- 136 105th St. NE, Bellevue; 455-9417

If there is an inexpensive one-stop shopping place for your home entertainment system, this small store fits the bill. Tucked into an alleyway between a strip mall and an Ernst hardware store, Rubato has been in business for almost twenty years. They've somehow crammed in over 15,000 new and used compact discs, in a price range from 49¢ to about $10; 10,000 record albums, starting as low as $3 apiece, plus 45rpm singles for $1 and up; and some 1,000 cassette tapes around $4-$5.

Mr. C found Hammer among the used CD bins (well, not the man himself, but one of his albums) for $4, and one by Pete Townshend for $6.50. Oh, and were you about to say, "But what about VHS and laser disc movies?" Sure, they've got 'em both—at prices that start under $10. Rubato is open daily from 11 A.M. to 9 P.M., Sundays from 12-5.

2nd Time Around
- 4209 University Way NE, Seattle; 632-1698

For good savings not only on music— but also stereo equipment, videos,

and video game cartridges—2nd
Time Around is practically 2nd to
none. The broad selection of CDs and
cassettes at this U-District shop will
take you a good while to browse
through, with a fair amount of LPs
available too. A special cassette sale
was going on when Mr. C stopped
by: 10% markdowns including such
gems as *This is Spinal Tap* for $9.99,
and $1.99 Devo tapes.

If you seek the other kind of
tape—the kind you can watch—videos are hardly priced much higher. A
copy of *Cocoon* was seen for $5.99,
while *sex, lies, and videotape* could
be yours for $9.99. Nintendo and
Sega Genesis cartridges are also available—prices start at $19.99 for
"Strike Gunner," and can go as high
as $44.99 for the ever-popular "Super
Mario All-Stars."

Don't forget to check out the used
stereo equipment behind the
counter—CD players start around
sixty bucks. 2nd Time Around is
open from 10 A.M. to 11 P.M. Mondays
through Thursdays, 'til midnight Fridays and Saturdays, and noon to 10
P.M. Sundays.

Sub Pop Mega Mart
- 1928 Second Ave., Seattle;
  443-0322

Sub Pop Mega Mart is an itty-bitty retail showroom for the Sub Pop recording label and its related divisions.
Check out the disk covers on the
wall, or in the laminated catalog, to
see what's available. The catalog also
gives you a band biography, track listing, and description of the album on
the back of each page. Very handy.
Once you know what you want, ask
for it at the counter. How about
prices? CDs are $11.98; records and
cassettes are $7.98. Band posters are
also available for just a few dollars,
and T-shirts are around $12.

Customers are encouraged to "try
before you buy" the music—Sub Pop
staff will play any disk you're interested in testing. No more bringing
your new music home with a mixture
of expectation and dread, hoping that
the songs you haven't heard yet are

as good as the one you bought the album for. Sub Pop is open daily until
6 P.M., 'til 5 P.M. on Sundays.

Tower Records & Video
- 500 Mercer St., Seattle; 283-4456
- 4321 University Way NE, Seattle;
  632-1187
- 2501 S 38th St., Tacoma; 475-9222
- 10635 NE Eighth St., Bellevue;
  451-2557

Open until midnight every single day
of the year, Tower discounts Billboard's top-selling CDs and tapes by
30% off list price; newer releases, rising up the charts, also tend to be
marked down—usually to about
$10.99 for CDs, $7.99 for cassettes.
And be sure to check the cut-out
bins, where overstock music is always drastically reduced. You can
usually find all varieties of music represented, from Patsy Cline to UB40.

The store also stocks a bowling-al-
ley-long aisle of magazines, from
Sassy to *Spin*. For information on
more substantial reading materials,
see the listing under "Books." And,
by the way, Tower opens at 9 A.M. for
you early risers.

The Wherehouse
- 206 Broadway E, Seattle; 324-2140
- 4501 Roosevelt Way NE, Seattle;
  633-4072
- 1100 Bellevue Way NE, Bellevue;
  454-2235
- 2301 148th Ave. NE, Bellevue;
  746-7022
- 31861 Gateway Center Blvd. S,
  Federal Way; 941-8221
- 3000 184th Ave. NW, Lynnwood;
  776-5099
- 19800 44th Ave. W, Lynnwood;
  670-2827
- 6409 Sixth Ave., Tacoma; 564-2336

Along with the latest releases, the
Wherehouse is a chain that carries a
wide selection of used CDs for $3.99
to $6.99 (most of them at the more
expensive end). Discs priced at $6.99
include *Best of Dark Horse* by
George Harrison, *Upfront* by jazzman
David Sanborn, Van Halen's *OU812*,
and many others. Discs by artists
from Robert Palmer to Dizzy
Gillespie were seen for $3.99. Where-

house is also a great place to sell or trade in your CDs; they'll give up to $6 credit for used CDs. They even have listening stations, so you can audition discs before you buy them; and they carry accessories like CD and tape holders, CD cleaners, and such.

There are used videos here, as well. Most are about $12.95, with titles like *Mr. Saturday Night*, *Sister Act*, and *Passenger 57*. Check out the section of videos under $10,

which on a recent visit included the Steve Martin/Lily Tomlin comedy *All of Me* and *Educating Rita* with Michael Caine. Some videos are very cheap indeed: *Necessary Roughness* and *Wayne's World* were seen for $4.95. That's almost the price of a rental! Speaking of which—they also rent videos, and sell new releases at reasonable prices. This is a total entertainment store. Hours vary for each store, but they're all open seven days.

CLOTHING—NEW

Know what you're buying! Clothes, like anything else, are sold at discount for many reasons. Let's quickly go over some basic terms.

With new merchandise, "First-quality" means perfect clothing—it has no flaws of any kind, just as you would find in any full-price store. Such items may be reduced in price as a sales promotion, because they're left over from a past season, or because too many were made. Some stores are able to discount first-quality clothing simply through high-volume selling and good connections with wholesalers. "Discontinued" styles are self-explanatory; again, these are usually new and still perfectly good.

"Second-quality," sometimes called "irregulars," "seconds," or "IRs," are new clothes which have some slight mistakes in their manufacture, or which have been damaged in shipping. Often, these blemishes are hard to find. Still, a reputable store will call your attention to the defects, either with a sign near the items, or a piece of masking tape directly on the problem area.

If you're not sure whether you're looking at a first or a second, go ahead and ask!

MEN'S AND WOMEN'S WEAR—GENERAL

Athletic Supply Company Outlet
- 224 Westlake Ave. N, Seattle; 623-8972

Downstairs at the Lake Union branch of this sporting goods colossus, check out the deals on sportswear basics and pro team-related clothing. Shelves of sweats separates by Russell, manufacturer to the big-leaguers, include irregular (but perfectly good-looking) tops, sweatpants, and more, in a full range of sizes and colors. Score a hooded sweatshirt for just $11.95. Kids' sizes, too.

On the major league level, ASC has ever-varying racks of IR's and closeouts. Starter NFL team jackets in lined nylon, originally $100, were seen for $70 here. Sonics sweatshirts, reduced from $40 to $14.88. Irregular (but authentic) Russell baseball jerseys, for a handful of pro teams, for an amazing $26.95. Plus a better selection of team hats that'll stay well under your salary cap at $9.88 each.

Toward the rear of the basement (which is as clean and bright as the main floor, by the way) are several bargain bins filled with mix 'n match separates: mesh jerseys ($4.88), nylon running shorts (88¢), and more. Sharing this level of the store is ASC's retail sneaker section; while these are mostly being sold at full-price, those prices are very competitive (no pun intended), and there are usually some good closeout deals mixed in with the regular stock. Athletic Supply is closed on Sundays.

Burlington Coat Factory
- 24111 Highway 99, Edmonds; 776-2221
- 10401 Gravelly Lake Dr. SW, Tacoma; 588-3595
- Pavilion Mall, Tukwila; 575-4269
See the listing under "Discount Department Stores."

Dress Barn
- Pavilion Mall, Tukwila; 575-1916
No, you won't look like a farm hand if you shop here; you'll just have more cash in hand, that's all. This national chain is a good place to stock up on basics like T-shirts and jeans. The store's full of name brands, too, like Gloria Vanderbilt (her jeans are half off at $20). A double-breasted rayon plaid suit by Sasson was recently seen here, reduced from $175 to $125.

A cotton cable-knit sweater by Sweater Exchange was marked down from $38 to $30, and casual cotton pants by Westport Ltd. were selling for the same price—about one-third of their original retail value. Stock up on basics here; cotton turtlenecks are two for $18, and crew socks are a bargain at $3 a pair. Open daily.

Fade-In Outlet
- 1233 Sixth Ave. S, Seattle; 447-1881
Plunge deep into the heart of the industrial district south of downtown Seattle, and you'll find this small but packed storefront where you can save on beachwear and athletic fashions. The manufacturer, Image Concepts, makes all-cotton separates that are sold in boutiques and department stores at much higher prices.

Their "U-Wear" line of dyed short pants can be found at Costco reduced from upwards of $20 down to $10.99; here at the factory, snap 'em up for $7.99. They also carry closeouts from other makers, like Jerzees sweatpants for $7.99. And check out the "Budget Balcony," a small mezzanine with boxes of T's, tank-tops, and shorts—or whatever they want to get rid of—for $1.99 each. Fade-In is open from 10 A.M. to 4:30 P.M., Mondays through Fridays only.

J. Thompson
- 205 Pine St., Seattle; 382-6661
The discount fashions seen at this downtown store are geared mainly toward working women. While designer names are not found in abundance here, the styles are classic and fresh, with looks for both the office and weekend getaways. There are even a few plus sizes available.

Most of the clothing is sold at 30% to 70% off the retail price, and there's always stuff on sale in the back—the day Mr. C visited, one rack of clothing was marked $9.90, any item. There are other bargains throughout the rest of the store, such as matching tee shirt and leggings sets for $14.50, while a kilt (!) was reduced from $28 to $10. Open from 9:15 A.M. to 5 P.M. Mondays through Fridays, closed weekends.

Jeans Direct
- 11822 NE Eighth St., Bellevue; 453-9517
- 6522 Bothell Way, Kenmore; 820-2207
- 326 W Meeker St., Kent; 854-4774
The name says it all. These stores mix famous maker closeouts and seconds with recycled denims and sportswear tops, all at fabulous discounts ("Some of them are shrink-to-fit jeans that just didn't shrink right," said the store manager). Mr. C was asked not to mention the brands, but

trust him, they're in. Most jeans go for $19.99, with lesser brands from $9.99 to $12.99. Women's relaxed-fit and stretch jeans were seen for $22.99, still a good price. Kids' sizes are here too, at $11.99.

You'll also find novelty print T-shirts and sportshirts around $10, and some at two for $10; in summer, bathing suits for $7.99; basic color lycra/cotton sport separates for $7-$8; and lots more. Fitting rooms are available. JD offers a 15-day refund policy with receipt, or an exchange without. Open seven days a week, including weekday evenings.

King's Sports Wear
- 202 Yesler Way, Seattle; 628-0815

Royal savings? You bet—well, at least, as regal as T-shirts can be. Disney, Looney Tunes, and professional sports teams are all represented at this Pioneer Square souvenir shop. Buy your little princess a Princess Jasmine T-shirt, or any other cartoon design, all at three for $10. A Chicago Bulls T-shirt will cost you more, but at $12, it's a still a winner. For the plain look, solid-color tees are two for $10, in a wide variety of colors. Heaps of cheap socks (five for $5) and used jeans ($13) for sale, too. King's is open from 10 A.M. to 5:30 P.M. Mondays through Saturdays.

LA Connection
- 2500 SW Barton St., Seattle; 935-5951
- 16805 Redmond Way, Redmond; 882-7955

Mr. C's fashion maven swears by these quiet strip-mall stores for deals on the latest womens' sportswear looks. LAC gets mid-grade brands direct from the factories; word-of-mouth advertising and other low-overhead practices result in bargain prices like cotton/ramie cable knit sweaters for $14.99 and college insignia sweatshirts for $9.99. $20 was the price seen on racks of floral cotton/lycra minidresses, as well as appliquéd cotton top-and-slacks ensembles.

Leggings and tees, all $4.99, are shelved by color; the store is also good for 99¢ "hair scrunchies" and earrings, as well as evening purses from $10-$20. Hours vary for each location; both open Mondays through Saturdays.

Loehmann's
- Loehmann's Plaza, Bellevue; 641-7596

Loehmann's means low prices on fancy women's clothing and shoes, plain and simple. These folks practically *invented* the designer close-out store years ago in New York; suave Manhattanites still shlep out to Brooklyn for their famous deals.

Mr. C found a rayon pantsuit by Karen Miller, which retails for $190, selling here for just $90; and a Gillian wool coatdress, list price $270, here just $150. Two-ply cashmere sweaters were just $100, but get to the store early if these are advertised, because they sell out *fast*.

Don't miss the better-name designer suits and eveningwear in the now-famous Back Room. Here, a Bill Blass silk plaid dress with pleated skirt was slashed from an original $390 to an amazing $60; and a Bob Mackie silk blouse was just $80, less than half-price. Calvin Klein fashions can usually be found here too, like a pure cashmere sweater listed at $750 but reduced to $400.

At the time of Mr. C's visit, Loehmann's was running a special sale, offering a selection of suits at a ridiculously low *two* for $199. These were originally valued at $225 to $300 each, made by designers like Kasper for A.S.L. and Oleg Cassini.

Note also that petites can do very well for themselves here—with plenty of suits, dresses, and pants to choose from. A petite dress by Depeche was seen for $299, almost $400 off the retail price. Loehmann's is the anchor store for the shopping plaza of the same name, across from Factoria Square. It's open from 10 A.M. to 9 P.M. on weekdays, 10-7 on Saturdays, and 12-6 on Sundays.

Mr. Rags Outlet Store

- 1415 Maple Ave. SW, Renton; 322-5000

Just off the Renton exit from I-405 are the home offices for this young men's sportswear chain of over thirty Northwest stores. Here too is the clearance center for all of the overstock from those stores—both their own label and those of other famous (can't be mentioned in print) makers, mostly at 50% to 75% off.

Mr. C found a quilted flannel jacket, just past season but still a hot style, marked down from a retail price of $120 to $60. Also half-price were canvas sneakers and nylon windbreakers. Oversized plaid shorts (yeah, you women love 'em too), usually $30-$40, were all $14.88. Baseball caps for seemingly everything famous *but* baseball teams were reduced from $25 to $10. And a selection of top-name jeans were cut from $58.95 to $29.88. Plus tons of brightly colored T-shirts, sweats, and underwear.

It's all first-quality stock, and all final sales; items may be returned for exchange only. Though you can see it from the freeway, getting to the store is tricky. Take the Rainier Avenue exit north; then a left on Grady, left on Lind, and left onto 16th. The store is open weekdays from 10 A.M. to 6 P.M., Saturdays 10-5.

"No Billy No" Outlet

- 1518 First Ave. S, Seattle; 623-5543

Taking its name from (presumably) the owner's dog, the minimalist motif of a barking canine forms the logo for this way-cool clothing manufacturer. NBN fashions are sold in boutiques all over town, but here at their factory just south of the Kingdome, you can buy seconds, samples, and overruns—and ideas that just plain didn't sell—at less than half of the retail prices.

Mr. C found 200-weight fleece pullovers, dyed in a variety of vivid colors, meant to sell for $70; here, they were being cleared out at $25. Oversize hip-hop-style drawstring shorts, once $28, were seen for $17.

MR. CHEAP'S PICKS
Men's and Women's
Wear—General

✔ **Loehmann's**—A New York discount classic, for classy women's fashions.

✔ **Mr. Rags Outlet**—You probably know this chain; now, get to know their Renton clearance center.

✔ **Nordstrom Rack**—Of course.

✔ **The Sample Shop**—As in salesman's samples, never-worn, from all the major lines in women's fashion.

✔ **Stars**—Everything for the kids in your life, all at discount.

✔ **Union Bay Outlet**—A Northwest original in casual looks for men, women, and kids; come to the Kent factory for incredible deals.

And racks of NBN logo T-shirts, with various renditions of that pooch, go for as little as $6 each. This small shop is filled with fashions that will land you squarely on the cutting edge, dude. All sales are final. Open Thursdays and Fridays from 11 A.M. to 6 P.M., and Saturdays from 11-5.

Nordstrom Rack

- 1601 Second Ave., Seattle; 448-8522
- 3115 Alderwood Mall Blvd., Lynnwood; 774-6569
- Pavilion Mall, Tukwila; 575-1058

Mr. C hardly needs to tell you about this local legend—but would a book like his be complete without it?

In olden times, "send him to the rack" was a kind of torture. When it comes to Nordstrom's clothing, going to this Rack is a delight—especially when it means relief from this otherwise-expensive store's prices. Each branch features multiple floors jampacked with great deals. Women will love dress slacks for $12.97, and junior dresses for $18.97. Gents can find double-breasted suits under $200. And for the kiddies, little girl's pajamas were seen for $9.97, and boy's T-shirts were seen for $5.97. Bring the whole family, synchronize your watches, then fan out to individual departments for a couple of hours.

Want designer names? There are tons of 'em here. A Donna Karan black dress, originally retailing for $650, was seen here for $189; a lined, all-weather Calvin Klein overcoat, reduced from $690 to $350; and a pair of 9 & Co. boots, once $55, here $35. Not to mention lots of workout gear, like Danskin leotards for $19.97 and Ryka aerobics sneakers, marked down from $75 to $36.90. Mr. C also found wool/cashmere blazers by Joseph Abboud reduced from $395 to $197; a Ralph Lauren "Polo" hand-knit wool sweater, once $325, now $160; Adolfo leather tassel loafers for $69; and denim shorts by Marithé and François Girbaud, marked down from $40 to $26.97.

All of this merchandise is marked down from 40% to 80% off the original store price—for the most current fashions, look for the "just arrived from Nordstrom's" signs. And, when the Rack advertises a clearance sale of its own—keep an eye on the newspapers and other media—look out. The crowds show up early and in full force, but it's worth it. Open seven days a week; hours vary with each location.

Outdoor & More
- 510 Westlake Ave. N, Seattle; 340-0677

Beginning with 10,000 square feet (not to mention thirty years of buying experience) and expanding from there, Steve Hess has created a no-frills paradise in the Lake Union area. He's filled his store with both sporting goods and the clothing to match,

mostly (but not all) closeouts. Mr. C found racks and racks of sweatshirts and bathing suits ($5 and up), waterproof fleece jackets for $40, and Rainskins slickers for $20. Plus leather and suede hiking boots from $30, cotton/lycra biking shorts for $5.99, and White Sierra walking shorts reduced from $30 to $9.99. Plenty of army/navy surplus here, too—"I've always got lots of clothing that's warm and cheap," says Steve.

There is also a full range of sporting gear (see the listing under "Sporting Goods"); and it all carries a 30-day refund (with receipt) or exchange policy. Open seven days.

The Sample Shop
- 613 Queen Anne Ave. N, Seattle; 282-8780

This small boutique does indeed have a sampling of many different styles, sizes, colors, and fabrics. Actually, these clothes are all manufacturer samples, used to show off their latest lines to major stores; they've never been worn. It's almost like getting brand-new designer clothing at used prices—as much as half off retail. On any given visit, you may find items by Jones New York, Marisa Nicoli, London Fog, and other names. And, while you'll only see one or two of each piece, the Sample Shop does have access to the entire lines these represent.

The garments appeal to the professional woman, but are not limited to clothes that would be worn at the office. There are many snazzy dresses for a night on the town, plus comfy, casual clothes for the weekend. As long as you wear a size between 4 and 20, they've got you covered. Alterations are available for an additional fee.

Accessorize your new duds from the *enormous* selection of costume jewelry available here. There's so much, in fact, that Mr. C has given the Sample Shop a separate entry under "Jewelry." Skip ahead for more details; and sample the fashions here Mondays through Saturdays from 10 A.M. to 6 P.M.

Take 2
- 430 15th Ave. E, Seattle; 324-2569
See the listing under "Clothing—Used."

Union Bay Sportswear Outlet
- 21216 72nd Ave. S, Kent; 872-2946
Talk about a success story. Every living being under the age of thirtysomething knows Union Bay, and it all originates right here in Kent. Come on down to the home office, where this large store sells the genuine articles at deep discounts.

The front room—smart-looking as any mall boutique, complete with dressing rooms—sells current lines for men and women at factory-direct prices of 35% off the suggested retail. Here, Mr. C found perfect denim shirts, not $36, but $23; plaid jam shorts discounted from $26 to $17; men's "Re-Union" sportcoats reduced from $122 to a handsome $81; and ribbed V-neck sweaters marked down from $72 to $47. Not to mention the ubiquitous UB jeans.

The back room, more warehousey, clears out past-season stock at prices near cost. All of these sales are final, but what deals: twill pants for $15, Mexican-style "blanket shirts" for $12, plus tons and tons of cool print shirts and shorts.

There are separate sections for juniors and kids as well; nearly everything here is first-quality. And, three special sales a year (like back-to-school time) knock an extra 25% off *everything* in the store. Gotta get on the mailing list for that one. As if you needed further incentive? The outlet is open weekdays from 10 A.M. to 5:30 P.M.; plus the second and fourth Saturdays of each month, same hours.

Valerie
- 4508 University Way NE, Seattle; 547-0918
This fashionable store caters primarily to young women of the high school and college-age crowd. These clothes are current, hip, and affordable, and also exceptionally wellmade. The deals are great because the garments are factory-direct closeouts—no defective merchandise here.

All the dresses range in price from $29 to $39; shirts are $7.99 and up, and most skirts are $19.99. And for the fabulous finale, all the earrings are just 99 cents! All of them, can you believe it? Valerie's is open from 10 A.M. to 6 P.M., Mondays through Saturdays.

Warshal's Sporting Goods
- 1000 First Ave., Seattle; 624-7304
Though they're equally well-known for things like fishing gear and cameras, this longtime Seattle landmark is in Mr. C's book for its 3,000-square foot clearance room on the second floor. It's filled with end-of-season closeouts and overstocks, mostly 25% to 50% off their original downstairs prices.

A Columbia ski parka, with a cloth exterior and "Thermaloft" filling, was recently reduced here from $135.99 to $89.99. Classic yellow rain slickers (gee, but *when* would you ever use one?) by Columbia were also seen, ten bucks off at $25.99. Cool-looking denim shirts by the rackful were marked from $44 down to $25, and all kinds of novelty print T-shirts and sweatshirts were half-price.

Warshal's is open Mondays through Saturdays from 9 A.M. to 5:30 P.M.; parking is darn near impossible here in the center of town, but the store hands out little maps directing you to nearby lots which offer an hour's free parking validation. 'Course, it's hard to get the maps until you've *parked*....

Winters Surplus
- 6169 Fourth Ave. S, Seattle; 763-2722
Camped out in the heart of industrial Georgetown, Winters has a little bit of everything for the budget-priced outdoorsman (or woman). The place is packed from floor to ceiling with new stuff, closeouts, and genuine army/navy surplus from various genuine armies and navies. Find good deals on raingear by Helly Hansen and Rainskins; Skor ski parkas, marked from $135 down to $60; and spiffy new Aerosport hiking shoes, reduced from $42.95 to $29.95. Of

course, if you prefer good ol' beat-up used GI boots, those are here too. There are also some more fashionable fashions, like a recent special on Brittania jeans for $12.95; and, out on the sidewalk, a rack of kids' Seahawks jerseys for $4.95 each.

Meanwhile, Winters is also another of those sporting-gear-army-navy-junk-havens, and a good one (see the listing under "Sporting Goods"). It's open weekdays from 9-6, and Saturdays from 9-5.

CHILDREN'S AND JUNIORS' WEAR

Burlington Coat Factory
- 24111 Highway 99, Edmonds; 776-2221
- 10401 Gravelly Lake Dr. SW, Tacoma; 588-3595
- Pavilion Mall, Tukwila; 575-4269

See the listing under "Discount Department Stores."

Cotton Caboodle Outlet Store
- 203 W Thomas St., Seattle; 282-2701

A tiny corner of this large Queen Anne factory is devoted to selling off Cotton Caboodle's flawed or discontinued merchandise. Normally sold in specialty stores, you can find lots of baby basics here at wholesale prices—and Mr. C defies you to find the flaws. Boys and girls separates range from infant (6 months) to sizes 14-16. These are 100% cotton basics in white and brightly dyed colors; racks of dresses are selling for $3 and $5 each, while bicycle shorts styles go for as little as $1.75. Plus boxes of thermals and sweats, socks, leggings, T-shirts, and the like.

Some discontinued items are sold below cost in this no-frills setting. No cash refunds are given, but clothing that's not on special sale can be exchanged. You'll certainly be able to snap up a ton of little ones' looks for short money! The store is open Tuesdays through Saturdays from 10 A.M. to 4 P.M. only.

Kids on 45th
- 1720 N 45th St., Seattle; 633-KIDS (5437)

See the listing under "Clothing—Used."

Stars
- 55 NE Gilman Blvd., Issaquah; 392-2900

Stars, new in late '93, calls itself "The Children's Wear Superstore." Indeed, they seem to have everything your kid will ever need, from layette through boys' size 20. Mr. C found Carter's infant sleepers at $5.99 and OshKosh overalls at $19.99, dresses by Jessica McClintock and Mousefeathers, and denim fashions by Lee and Levi's among the 500 or so labels at this vast store. There's quite a price range for everyone, from lower to better-grade brands. And it's all sold at discounts of 25% to 40% below retail.

But our young stars don't just want to be miniature fashion plates. There are *minds* to be developed. So, Stars also carries books, like the award-winning Caldicott & Newbury series at 25% off the cover, and Dr. Seuss favorites at $9.99. Tots to teeny-boppers will find just about every toy their peers are playing with. And, for a unique and classy gift, how about a four-piece setting of silver-plated Oneida baby dinnerware for $18?

Speaking of toys, Stars offers an (unsupervised) play area, which at least lets some parents get their shopping done more quickly. Entertainment is even provided in the store, three times a day on weekends: jugglers, magicians, and puppet shows help keep those kiddies smiling.

Stars is certainly off the beaten path, but with all this under one roof, it's well worth the trip. Open seven days a week, including weekday evenings; the exact schedule varies by season, so if this is a hike for you, do call ahead for current hours. Oh, and if you get put on hold, you'll hear every song ever written with the word "star" in the title. Cute!

Storks Nest
- Pike Place Market, Seattle; 382-9878

Literally the size of a stork's nest—or possibly just an egg—this cozy store hides some big savings on clothes for your little one. The store's regular-priced clothes are colorful, brightly patterned, and definitely not the typical designs you'd find in twenty other stores. They are a bit expensive, but these clothes are adorable and

unique; some are even hand-made, and worth a mention. Ah, but wait...

Just outside the store, Storks Nest has a good selection of clearance stork—er, stock. A pair of girl's floral overalls with a matching halter top was seen at $9 for the set; a pair of boys shorts and matching shirt, decorated in racing-flag style, was seen for $9.95; and a red and white sailor dress, size 9-12 months, was seen for $9. Check out these racks, and you'll walk out of the Storks Nest joyfully carrying a bundle of great buys. Drop in between 10:30 A.M. and 5:30 P.M., Mondays through Saturdays.

Not enough for ya? There are several national chains, on which Mr. C felt no need to waste precious ink—you *know* what they offer. Here are their addresses, though:

Clothestime
- Aurora Square, Seattle; 362-3571
- 325 Broadway E, Seattle; 325-7803
- 900 NE 45th St., Seattle; 632-0820
- Northgate Mall, Seattle; 362-9480
- 305 SE Everett Mall Way, Everett; 348-9566
- 3105 Alderwood Mall Blvd., Lynnwood; 774-7961
- 10406 Silverdale Way NW, Silverdale; (360) 698-1223
- 3304 S 23rd St., Tacoma; 305-0042
- 3815 S Steele St., Tacoma; 473-4279
- Pavilion Mall, Tukwila; 575-8110

Marshalls
- Aurora Square, Seattle; 367-85203205 Alderwood Mall Blvd., Lynnwood; 771-6045
- Overlake Fashion Plaza, Redmond; 644-2429
- Pavilion Mall, Tukwila; 575-0141

Ross Dress for Less
- 13201-B Aurora Ave. N, Seattle; 367-6030
- 10406 Silverdale Way NW, Silverdale; (360) 698-3180
- 2931 S 38th St., Tacoma; 474-3888
- 17672 Southcenter Pkwy., Tukwila; 575-0110

TJMaxx
- 11029 Roosevelt Way NE, Seattle; 363-9511

CLOTHING—USED

Second-hand clothing is another great way to save lots of money—and Seattleites seldom turn their noses up at the idea. In these recessionary times, people are taking this approach to nearly everything, and it makes a lot of sense. Used clothing offers every option, from trashy stuff to designer labels. Again, a few terms:

"Consignment" and "resale" shops are all the rage these days.

Most sell what they call "gently used" clothing—the original owner wore the article only a few times, then decided to resell it. Often, these are fancy outfits in which such people don't want to be seen in more than once. Fine! This is how you can get these high fashion clothes at super low prices. Since they still look new, your friends will never know the secret (unless, of course, you want to brag about your bargain-hunting prowess). You can also sell things from your own closets at these shops, if they are recent and in good shape; the store owners will split the cash with you.

"Vintage" clothing is usually older and more worn-looking, still hanging around from other decades. Sometimes it can cost more than you'd expect for used clothing, depending on which "retro" period is back in style at the moment.

Finally, "thrift shops" sell used clothing that has *definitely* seen better days. These items have generally been donated to the stores, most of which are run by charity organizations; in such places, you can often find great bargains, and help out a worthy cause at the same time.

CONSIGNMENT AND RESALE SHOPS

Alexandra's
• 415 Stewart St., Seattle; 623-1214
In the heart of Seattle's downtown, Alexandra's caters to women in the office world who want upscale looks but can't—or would prefer not to—pay upscale prices. Alexandra takes in about 200 "new" garments each week; there's always a big selection. A nice feature about the layout of this split-level boutique is that a large portion of the clothes are separated by designer. If, for example, you really like Oscar de la Renta, Christian Dior, or Calvin Klein, you can easily find a good-sized collection of your favorites.

Not all fashions are grouped in this manner, so do check out the other racks to find equally impressive prices on sophisticated styles. The day Mr. C visited, a Giorgio Armani jacket was seen for only $249—with matching slacks for $129. And a Donna Karan rayon jacket was on sale for $69. Items that have been in the store thirty days are reduced by a further 25%; over sixty days, they're 50% off; then, if they still haven't sold, they're marked 75% off. A short-sleeved Anne Klein II dress

was marked down twice—to $89, and then $49. Want more savings? Look through the store for the "A" sale items. The first week, these garments are reduced by 40%; the second week, 60%.

Alexandra's also has two huge yearly clearout sales, during the summer and winter. Call for the dates and times. The shop is open Mondays through Saturdays, 10 A.M. to 6 P.M., and Thursdays 'til 8. Closed Sundays.

Between Friends
• 818 Third Ave., Seattle; 624-2220
Between Friends resells women's clothing rather than consigning it, emphasizing career and casual wear. Among the great deals Mr. C found were a Liz Claiborne two-piece ensemble for $49.98, and a silk, long sleeve Calvin Klein mini-dress for $99.98. (The original $675.00 price tag was still on the garment.) Also, there are constant clearance markdowns, which start at 20% off the ticket price.

Some of the pieces are new, like the rack of silk tank tops for $13.98 each, and the $5.98 Ginnie Johansen earrings. Sizes are limited, but the savings make it worth a look.

Stop by Mondays through Fridays, from 10 A.M. to 6 P.M.

Cecil's
- 2224 Queen Anne Ave. N, Seattle; 283-3676

Mr. C was *quite* impressed with the selection, prices, better name brands, and overall feel of this store. Owner Kelly Morken has set up shop in one of those turn-of-the-century houses at the top of Queen Anne Hill; wander from room to room, upstairs and down, ladies, and you're sure to have a ball.

Shirts and jackets are arranged by color, skirts by size. A short-sleeve silk blouse from Nordstrom's was seen for $13.75, and a suede mini-skirt for $19. Upstairs, you'll find more casual looks—designer jeans range between $15 and $21. Most of the clothes, though, are dressier or professional attire, like a black-and-white-checked skirt suit by Jones New York for $68. Or, slip into a pair of $22 black patent leather heels.

A unique idea at Cecil's is called "Friends Night Out." Anyone can arrange to throw a little shopping party for herself and eight or more friends, any evening; the store provides hors d'oeuvres. Meanwhile, the "hostess" gets 15% off any purchases, and her friends get 10% off. Not a bad incentive, eh? Everyone makes out. Cecil's is open Mondays through Fridays from 10 A.M. to 7 P.M., Saturdays 'til 5 P.M., and Sundays from 12-5 P.M.

The Dark Horse Boutique
- 11810 NE Eighth St., Bellevue; 454-0990

Founded in 1962, the Dark Horse was one of the area's first consignment resale stores. Back then, selling used designer clothing from a strip-mall may well have been a long shot; but this horse has paid off royally. Not only is the store still here, it's in a larger space than the original—and more floor space means they can put out more stock, including menswear, which most resellers don't deal in at all. But Mr. C found a handsome all-wool suit from Ralph Lauren's "Chaps" line, selling here for $60.

On the female side of things, a

Kasper black and white linen blazer and print skirt ensemble was seen for $70. Plenty of good-quality casual clothes too (a LizSport sweater, $24), shoes (Joan & David pumps with bows on top, $18) and accessories, like handbags and scarves. Books, too, for something even more unusual in the mix. In all, a good selection, nice folks. Open every day but Sunday from 10:30 A.M. to 6 P.M.; Thursdays until 8, Saturdays 'til 5.

Far Fetched
- 2620 Bellevue Way NE, Bellevue; 827-3979

In business for more than a dozen years, owner Marlene Grosse has spent the last few at this rather far-flung location in a strip mall near Route 520. She has packed her large space not only with consignment clothing (which is mostly casual, mid-grade stuff), but also with house-wares, home furnishings, books, and more, making this look more like a thrift shop.

Much of the stock comes from estate sales and store closings; poke around and you may well find things like a Liz Claiborne blazer for $24 or a men's Hickey-Freeman suit for $70. There are tons of clothes for kids of all ages, plus a good selection of vintage clothing which can be rented out as costumes. Plenty of jewelry, too.

Other kinds of items Mr. C found here included a 53-piece set of Noritake china, selling for $150; a set of cocktail glasses for $12; small appliances, like a Black & Decker iron for $9 ("we guarantee satisfaction" with electrics), and the assorted gadgetry of a hundred emptied kitchen drawers. Open weekdays from 11 A.M. to 7 P.M. (6 P.M. in summer); Saturdays 11-5, and Sundays 12-4.

Gentlemen's Consignment
- 2809 E Madison St., Seattle; 328-8137

Here's a resale rarity—a consignment shop for men only. It's perfect if you've just entered the business world, and can't quite float the funds for a Wall Street wardrobe. The clothes, shoes, and accessories here are all in "like new" condition, contemporary in style, and feature many big names—Ralph Lauren, Giorgio Armani, and Hugo Boss, to name but a few.

Mr. C found a Polo all-wool checked blazer for $86, various dress shirts for $18, and a London Fog raincoat for $110. GC does have more casual attire, and a limited selection of shoes, hats, and accessories. There's also a separate front room for the *créme de la créme*; this includes Armani silk ties which the store gets regularly from a man who insists on wearing these twice only.

The store is just as handsome as its stock, elegant in an old-world fashion with a dark wood interior and ornate mirrors in which to see your "new" looks. Service is just as refined. Open Tuesdays through Saturdays from 10 A.M. to 6 P.M., Sundays from 11-4.

Mr. C's travels have revealed one other such specialty store, called **His: Consignment for Men** at 2226 Queen Anne Avenue N, Seattle (281-0265). Again, lots of classic tailored looks for professional types. Anything in the store longer than six weeks is reduced further, and there are always half-off racks in back. His: Consignment is open Tuesdays through Fridays from 10 A.M. to 6 P.M., and Saturdays 'til 5 P.M.

Gypsy Trader

● 1622 N 45th St., Seattle; 547-1430
In Wallingford, this fine recent addition to the resale scene trades mostly in consigned, contemporary women's clothes. You'll find some big names in this little store, like a Ralph Lauren skirt and a DKNY flannel pullover, each seen for $15. Other items are of good quality, if not fancy labels. Lots of the clothes are stylish fashions that can be worn either at the office, or at home after a long day. Gypsy Trader also has larger women's fashions at low prices, like a pair of size 18 wool dress pants for $10. For even more savings, check out the sale rack in front of the store—discounts of up to

50% off the store's prices can be found there.

There's also a good choice of consigned, contemporary jewelry available. Earrings are between $5 and $6, while necklaces are $5 or more. For additional accessorizing, try on some dress scarves, priced between $3 and $6. Gypsy Trader is open Tuesdays through Sundays, from 10 A.M. to 6 P.M.

Kathy's Kloset

● 4751 12th Ave., Seattle; 523-3019
This longtime U-District resale shop claims to be one of Seattle's very first; a favorite with both professionals and students, Kathy's does indeed boast a large and varied selection of everything from Oleg Cassini suits to good ol' worn-in jeans. One rack holds nothing but a bevy of black blazers: linen, lace, velvet, most $20-$25. Ascend the spiral staircase to the second floor, and you'll find more casual looks, like Esprit white cotton shorts for $11. Lots of shoes, dressy and non; a shiny pair of Ferragamo alligator pumps for $30, Bass canvas deck shoes for $8.99.

Near the front door are cosmetics and perfumes, not often found in resale stores, by the likes of Estee Lauder and Halston; plus lots of costume jewelry. Open daily from 10 A.M. to 6 P.M., Thursdays 'til 8, and Sundays 12-5.

Kathy used to operate a second branch in West Seattle, but this became a separate store a few years ago. It's now called **Funky Jane's**, at 4738 42nd Avenue SW; telephone 937-2637. The types of merchandise and prices are much the same, with hours from 10 A.M. to 8 P.M. on weekdays, 10-6 on Saturdays, and 12-5 on Sundays.

Labels

● 7212 Greenwood Ave. N, Seattle; 781-1194
Labels consigns women's and children's clothing and, yes, carries some pretty impressive name brands. Mr. C spotted a Liz Claiborne paisley rayon blouse ($17.50), and Eddie Bauer loafers ($13.95) while visiting. Of course, there are lots of good-quality

clothes there whose brand names you may not recognize, but these still offer fantastic savings—like $7 sweaters, $12 skirts, and $14 jeans. There are even some maternity clothes.

The children's section is large, though the boys' selection is rather limited. A girl's T-shirt with flowers hand-painted on it was seen for $3.75, and baby pajamas were $2.50. Toys, too. Further discounts include 20% and 30% markdowns on merchandise that has been in the store for a length of time. Labels is open every day but Monday.

L'Armoire
• 709 S Third St., Renton; 277-5705
Here's one for you south-enders. This area is really coming on for consignment shopping; L'Armoire has been around for a couple of years now, recently moved into a larger space filled with lots of goodies. Owner Madelaine Baum has put in a bit of everything—office fashions, fancy eveningwear, bridal gowns, casual looks, sleepwear and lingerie, new and used jewelry, gifts, and more. An Ann Taylor suit, originally $150, was reduced to $47; some new items are sold at a quarter of their retail prices.

Special sections cater to sizes from petite to plus, with plenty to choose from. There's also a selection of fine furs and leather coats. Lots of shoes, in very good shape. And, after 90 days on the selling floor, clothing gets sent to the rack—the 50% rack, that is. Nice dressing rooms, too.

Jewelry ranges from costume pieces to watches to estate stuff; one consignor recently brought in her entire collection of 18K gold-plated jewelry and hand-cut crystal. There's also a section of new and used gift items, like sachets, soaps, and collectibles. Open daily from 10 A.M. to 6 P.M.

In the near future, Ms. Baum intends to cover the suburbs with more branches of her successful store. In the meantime, she has already expanded the concept to include L'Armoire Children's Boutique at 807 S Third Street (telephone, 277-2444). This store features like-new clothing for

---

MR. CHEAP'S PICKS
Consignment and Resale Shops

✔ **Alexandra's**—Designer labels for women at decent prices, right downtown.

✔ **Cecil's**—Host a private "Friends Night Out" party here, and you'll all get even bigger savings off the already-low prices.

✔ **Gentlemen's Consignment and His: For Men**—Two classy shops, unique in the resale clothing biz: For men only.

✔ **Kathy's Kloset**—Longtime popular spot with the U-District crowd.

✔ **L'Armoire**—Chic consignment comes to Renton. Kids' stuff, too.

✔ **Ragamoffyn's**—Better wear your best jewels to shop for second-hand duds here.

---

boys and girls from infant to size 10; plus furniture, toys, car seats, and other accessories.

Elsewhere in Renton, **Fashion Quest** (123 Wells Street S; 271-2886) is another good place to check out for women's fashions—they're open Tuesdays through Saturdays from 11 A.M. to 6:30 P.M. Make a day of it!

The Last Tango
• 3033 78th Ave. NE, Mercer Island; 232-2205
As your humble author conducted his research in various consignment shops, he was often told, "Make sure you check out Last Tango." And sure enough, this is an Island paradise for women's finer fashions—and a busy

one. Interestingly, the store is organized entirely by color, not by size; the better to put ensembles together, with the help of the knowledgeable staff.

In a short period of time, LT has attracted a steady, upscale clientele, filling the store with such names as Escada, Ungaro, Chanel, Donna Karan, and the like. There is, Mr. C was assured, "no junk." In addition to those biggies, he was shown an all-cotton suit by Carlisle (*very* exclusive—sold privately in homes), selling here for $158; the skirt alone had originally retailed for $180, and the blazer $390.

Shoes are well represented, too: Via Spiga, Cole-Haan, and more, many priced around $40 and under. Plus jewelry in 14K gold, sterling silver, and semi-precious stones, at about half of department store rates. The Last Tango offers in-store alterations (at a fee) by a fashion expert who also conducts wardrobe seminars. It's all there for you to sigh over, Tuesdays through Saturdays from 10 A.M. to 5 P.M. (Thursdays until 7).

Pandora's Box
- 10867 NE Second Pl., Bellevue; 455-3883

Enter this tiny house just outside of downtown Bellevue, and you will indeed find a treasure trove of women's secondhand fashions. Like any treasure, it's hard to find (on a quiet side street), but worth it. In fact, a steady clientele has been finding its way here for twenty years.

Wander through the many small rooms, and you're likely to find such gems as an Armani silk blouse and skirt set, once $1,000, selling here for $140. Not everything is as high-powered, but Ellen Tracy, Jones New York, and Liz Claiborne are not uncommon labels here. Shoes are in great shape; a like-new pair of Joan & David pumps were seen for $35, while many others are priced at $10 and up. Plus belts, purses, and lots of good-quality costume jewelry (new $36 earrings for $8).

Each room features different types of clothes: professional, casual, evening wear. Clothing spends one month at "full" price, then is reduced by 20% each month thereafter until it sells. The store is open Mondays through Saturdays from 10 A.M. to 5 P.M.

Ragamoffyn's
- 127 and 132 Park Lane, Kirkland; 828-0396

It is widely agreed (not to put down any of the other stores in this chapter) that Ragamoffyn's is one of the standout resellers in the greater Seattle area. Owner Gisela Tipton certainly makes it distinctive, with a whitewashed interior and antique furniture making the shop look more like an art gallery.

High-class names on the racks add to the prestige factor. Mr. C found an Escada cotton sweater, like new, for $50; an Albert Nipon grey wool plaid suit for $62; and a selection of Chanel evening bags, originally $1,000, for $195. Lots of shoes here, too. The store even sells colognes, barely used (no doubt from consignors who didn't care for the scents); a bottle of White Diamonds, nearly full, was reduced from an original $80 to just $15.

Across the street, "Ragamoffyn's Rack" clears out slower-moving merchandise at *further* reductions of 50% and 75% off. A Christian Dior evening gown, black velvet with pink trim, was reduced from Ragamoffyn's own price of $125 to a mere $32. All sales here are final. Both stores are open weekdays from 10 A.M. to 5:30 P.M.; Saturdays, they close at 5.

A few doors down from this pair is another resale shop: Champagne Taste (147 Park Lane; telephone 828-4502). There is more stock here, in a wider range of tastes and styles. Labels like Scott McClintock, Karen Alexander, and Liz Claiborne were seen here; but so were lots of lesser-name brands. The store specializes in bridal gowns, with lots to see, from $300 up to $3,000; also, racks and racks of sparkly evening wear, all organized by color. The store has a very cozy feel, with couches, Oriental rugs, upholstered fitting rooms, and good service.

Open weekdays from 10 A.M. to 5:30 P.M., Saturdays 10-5, Sundays 12-5.

Razz M' Tazz

• 623 Queen Anne Ave. N, Seattle; 281-7900

This upscale consignment boutique is known for its exceptional women's fashions and personal service. The labels are designer, the garments are two years or younger, and every item is in "like new" condition.

The savings you'll find here are about 30% to 40% off department store prices, with ongoing sales of an additional 20% to 40% off the ticketed price on selected items. A few examples that Mr. C spotted were a $40 Karen Kane silk blouse, a $60 Anne Klein II silk jacket, and $65 Ellen Tracy wool/rayon slacks. Stop by Tuesdays through Saturdays, from 10 A.M. to 6 P.M.

ReRuns Consignment

• 413 15th Ave. E, Seattle; 329-0549

While this spacious First Hill consignment shop offers a wide variety of clothing, it also has many pieces of large furniture, kitchenware, and other items not always seen in consignment shops. In the back room, Mr. C found a large, round-back woven India chair for $18, a Japanese folding shoji screen for $89, and two golf bags, with clubs, for around $50 each. Nearby, a pair of children's oak chairs was selling for $49.

In the area of clothing, just about everything is in great shape. If there is a problem with a garment, a tag will either say "as is," or specifically spell out what's wrong. Still, you may get into a Christian Dior blazer for only $18—if you don't mind a tiny pale stain in front. Conveniently, there is a dry-cleaner nearby, and the ReRuns staff will let you take their clothing there for an expert assessment. Do be prepared to leave something behind with the staff to ensure your—and the piece's—prompt return. ReRun in

between 10:30 A.M. and 5 P.M. Mondays through Saturdays, noon to 4 P.M. Sundays.

Wonder-Full Size Consignment

• 8331 15th Ave. NW, Seattle; 783-8341

Generally speaking, most resale and consignment shops do not carry much in the way of larger sizes; they're limited to what their clients bring in. That makes this Ballard shop wonderful indeed for the larger woman—its clothes are stylish, inexpensive, and intended for the non-Kate Moss physique.

Wonder-Full carries high-quality professional and casualwear in the size 16 to 26 range. Dresses are priced at around $16; jeans, $12; and blouses, $7. Quite a few shoes were in stock when Mr. C stopped by, in sizes up to 11, including wide widths. Gently-worn, high quality heels, flats, and casual shoes in good shape can cost just $8-$10. The store is open Tuesdays through Saturdays, from 10 A.M. to 5 P.M.

Your Hidden Closet

• 1075 Bellevue Way NE, Bellevue; 453-5999

Located in the Belgate Plaza shopping center, this is to Mr. C's knowledge the only consumer/resale shop devoted to larger womens' sizes (14 and up) on the Eastside. They've been at it for almost ten years. Some of the clothing here is designer stuff, like a DKNY silk blouse, size 42, selling for $59. A size 18 black linen blazer by Jones New York was seen for the same price; lesser names on this rack were mostly $15-$30.

You'll also find jeans, sweaters, and shoes, along with handbags, scarves, and jewelry. And YHC has been doing more and more business in bridal fashions, including mother-of-the-bride; most bridal gowns seen here recently were around $200 to $400. Open Mondays through Thursdays from 10 A.M. to 6 P.M.; Fridays and Saturdays 'til 5.

CHILDREN'S RESALE SHOPS

Kids on 45th
- 1720 N 45th St., Seattle; 633-KIDS (5437)

The children's clothes in this cozy Wallingford store are a combination of new, used, and consigned. All are current fashions, in excellent condition.

The front of the store is filled with the new merchandise. Much of it is sold at list price, but because Kids has its own line of brightly colored activewear, these basics can save you plenty over department store prices. The store buys white cotton separates, and then dyes them in eye-catching colors. Leggings and long sleeve jerseys are $7.95 each, while other items, like sweatshirts and dresses, average about 30% below comparable retail prices. They also carry artsy clothing by local designers, an inexpensive way to find something unique, as well as a full range of infant needs.

Second-hand clothing is even more reasonable—and more plentiful. These range from baby fashions to pre-teens. During Mr. C's visit, he noted a $1 rack crammed with shirts, pants, and other items. A pair of girl's jeans was seen for $10, and a sweatshirt for $3. There was also an entire rack of shoes; rustle up a pair of size 4 cowboy boots for $6, or a pair of size 13 loafers for $3.95.

Carseats, swing-o-matics, books, toys, and accessories are all available here at good savings. Kids on 45th is open from 10 A.M. to 6 P.M. Mondays through Saturdays, from 11 A.M. to 5 P.M. Sundays.

Kym's Kiddy Corner
- 11721 15th Ave. NE, Seattle; 361-5974

Wow. If you've got kids, this place is well worth going out of your way for. Kym and Mike sell everything you could possibly need but babysitters. They pack a vast quantity of new and used goods into what seems from the outside like a small building—it even spills out into their tiny front parking lot, which is taken up with rocking horses, bikes, and car seats instead of cars.

In business for almost ten years, they've acquired a big list of consignors (although they also buy used items outright, a rarity) as well as the connections to get new stuff at or below list prices. A baby jogger—y'know, those aerodynamic "strollers" for the spandex crowd—can sell here for as much as $40 below specialty store prices, new. Car seats start from $50 new, $25 used.

In the clothing rooms, new (mid-grade brand) party dresses start around $25; while, among the used racks, a girl's size 2 ensemble of a black velvet jumper with a satiny white polka-dot blouse was seen for $9.95. Secondhand infants' sleepers go for $4.98. And there are tons of (new) baby accessories—from cribs, crib pads, and crib toys to pacifiers, socks, and bonnets.

Kym's also has a playroom, which can either serve as a testing laboratory for your kids to try out toys, or simply to keep them happily occupied while you shop. As noted above, Kym's will pay cash for used items, or take them in trade for credit toward new or used goods. Returns may be for credit only. The store is open daily from 10 A.M. to 5 P.M., Sundays from 12-5.

L'Armoire
- 709 S Third St., Renton; 277-5705

See the listing under "Consignment and Resale Shops" above.

Moms 'n Tots
- 137 106th Ave. NE, Bellevue; 451-4439

In a strip mall around the other side of the Bellevue Ernst, this is one of the Eastside's best choices for new and consignment clothing for the constituencies in the store's name. In other words, mothers, mothers-to-be, and children.

Good value new items recently seen here included infant sleepers by Peek-A-Boo for $15.95, and lovely floral print girls' dresses from Health-tex for $18.95. In the used department, Mr. C found lots more clothing, plus a Graco "Swyngomatic" high chair for $33.50. Also, maternity fashions like a Hayley Michaels dress (with far more European styling than one normally sees in such clothes) for $35. Plus lots of toys for the tots and other accessories. Open Mondays through Saturdays from 10 A.M. to 5 P.M.

Rainbow Boutique
- 9518 Roosevelt Way NE, Seattle; 522-1213

On the way up to Northgate, this storefront shop specializes in both aspects of baby bargain-hunting—in other words, children's clothing, shoes, and toys, plus women's and maternity apparel. On the maternity side, you can find jeans for $12, as well as dresses starting at $15.

Children's clothing is well organized, and arranged by size. A Nike "Air Jordan" T-shirt was seen for $10 on the boys' size 5 to 8 rack, while a girl's Osh Kosh top was seen for $4 on the newborn to 18 months rack. On the footwear scene, Sesame Street sneakers were selling for $6.50, while shiny patent leather shoes, complete with bows, were seen for $6.

At the rear of the store is another separate room, jam-packed with toys, games, and accessories. You may find a Graco "Swyngomatic" decorated with Disney characters for $20, a Kolcraft car seat for $32, or a Barbie Party Bake Oven set for $20. Clearance sales are held after the summer and winter seasons—check for specific dates. Open Mondays through Fridays between 10 A.M. and 5:30 P.M., and Saturdays 10 A.M. to 4 P.M.

MR. CHEAP'S PICKS
Children's Resale Shops

- ✔ **Kids on 45th**—A Wallingford bonanza of new and used bargains.

- ✔ **Kym's Kiddy Corner**—One of the largest selections Mr. C has ever seen in children's second-hand clothing and toys.

Sarah's Hope Chest, Ltd.
- 2123 Queen Anne Ave. N, Seattle; 281-5709

Sarah's Hope Chest is about as young as the people who wear her clothes. Open since February '94, Sarah's consigns new and used children's clothing, from newborn to size 14. Size 5 footed sleepers were seen for $3; girls' size 12 stretch pants were seen for $4, and boys' size 4 Levi's were $6. If an item has not been sold in sixty days, it goes over to the 50% off rack.

Accessories and toys are also sold here, though the selection varies. When Mr. C visited, a girl's bike was seen for $40, and a Perego stroller was going for $65. There was even a double stroller for $55. And, the maternity department was still growing (ooh—sorry); expect more of those fashions by the time you read this. Sarah's Hope Chest is open Mondays through Saturdays, from 10 A.M. to 6 P.M.

VINTAGE SHOPS

American Denim
- 401 NE 45th St., Seattle; 885-3317

This corner store, located in a nondescript stretch of 45th just west of Route 5, doesn't even have its name advertised outside. Only a standup sign on the sidewalk, with the Levi's logo, points the way to one of the best places in Seattle to find good, cheap, used jeans.

The storefront room is simply set out with about a dozen clothing racks. Most racks are marked $10, and there's usually a sale rack of jeans selling for $5. There are tons of styles and sizes to choose from, so it's likely you'll find a pair made for you. But there's more to life than jeans alone. When Mr. C visited, flannel shirts, normally only $12.99, were further reduced to $9.99. Remember, these versatile shirts are great for tying around your waist or cutting up—and the scraps make dandy dust rags! They even have some good deals on music—a used R.E.M. *Green* CD was seen for $8.95. And genuine flower-power stickers, left over from the sixties and perfect for covering your VW Bug, were just two bucks.

American Denim is open Mondays through Saturdays, 11 A.M. to 7 P.M., and Sundays from noon to 5 P.M. For a similar selection and savings, you should also check out the **Wild West Trading Company** at 7525 Aurora Avenue N (telephone 781-9781); they also have locations in Bremerton, Everett, and Lynnwood.

Clotheshorse Trading Co.
- 4241 University Way NE, Seattle; 632-7884

Be warned, fashion animals: Some of the clothing in here is brand new and pricey, while some of it is made by local artists, and yes, still pricey. However, much of the other goods are inexpensive, secondhand, and way cool. Fortunately, the truly budget-conscious won't confuse the new with the used—each is grouped into separate rooms, and some of the home-grown fashions are perched high atop the dressing rooms.

Among the used clothes, Mr. C found a velvet skirt for $7, a Wilson leather biker jacket for $65, and a lace-covered, 1920s style hat for $6. If you can resist the rest, Clotheshorse has some unique and inexpensive fashions that make it worth digging through the racks. Open from 11 A.M. to 7 P.M. daily, noon to 6 P.M. Sundays.

Cloud 9
- 6518 Roosevelt Way NE, Seattle; 525-4440

Housed in what was formerly a neighborhood movie theater—the marquee still rises over the door—Cloud 9 sells used clothing, furniture, and assorted items for the home. When Mr. C visited, a short-sleeve Nordstrom sweater ($21.60), a big straw hat ($4.50), a rocking chair ($80), and a pair of hiking boots ($24) all looked especially good. Lots of dishware and kitchen items were also for sale. Cloud 9 is open Mondays through Thursdays from 10 A.M. to 4 P.M., and Saturdays from noon to 4 P.M. Closed Fridays and Sundays.

The Daily Planet...Antiques
- 3416 Fremont Ave. N, Seattle; 633-0895

No Superman here, but super prices on super cool retro stuff is what you'll find at this Daily Planet. An eclectic mix fills this narrow Fremont store and covers every surface inside. In keeping with the ever-faster pace of modern society, "antique" here means as recent as the 1960s, and includes such period items as luggage starting at $4, lots of old cameras starting at $2 (do they work? Take a gamble!), and winter coats going for about $39.95. You can even pick up a working lava lamp for $65. Open from 10:30 A.M. to 6 P.M. everyday except Sundays, when the Planet stops the presses at 5 P.M.

Fritzi Ritz
- 3425 Fremont Pl. N, Seattle; 633-0929

Across the street from the Daily Planet (see above), this used clothing store seems to have a little bit of everything: some dressy stuff, some downright funky stuff, and some stuff to relax in. Going to a soirée that calls for something fancy? Gentlemen can choose from a number of unusual cummerbunds starting at $6.95, and top off their swanky look with a fedora for $16.95. Ladies have a variety of choices in the dress and skirt departments; most styles come from the '60s and '70s, and represent nearly every color known (plus a few you'd happily forgotten). Play Donna Reed and do your vacuuming in a pale green cotton housedress with an embroidered flower pattern, seen for $19.95. Apologies to the '90s feminist crowd.

The store also sells genuine high

school letters, only a dollar or two apiece; look for your school's colors, and then perplex your classmates at your next reunion. With probably the deepest clothing selection among Fremont's many vintage stores, Fritzi Ritz is open seven days a week.

Funk You
• 705-B E Pike St., Seattle; 329-7963
Somehow, the past two decades seem to have missed Funk You; everything in here, right down to the posters decorating the walls, date from the early '70s. Wild, bright, and very outrageous fashions fill the store, with plenty of accessories to complete the psychedelic look.

Make a fashion statement with your feet. Mr. C loved a pair of platform sandals ($12.95) with a lot of "sole"; so much, in fact, there was enough room to cut a big triangle clear through each heel. Equally eye-catching were the $9.95 bellbottoms and crocheted hats, $4.95 mood rings, and $16.95 "ultra suede" jackets (that ever-so-classy genuine fake stuff). Open from 12 noon to 8 P.M. Tuesdays through Saturdays, noon to 6 P.M. Sundays, and closed Mondays.

Grandma's Attic
• Pike Place Market, Seattle; 682-9281
For some reason, this attic is actually two levels *below* the street in the Main Arcade, but if you can brave the crowd scene, the genuine vintage clothing at Grandma's will make the quest worth it. While there are trinkets for the tourists, what Mr. C found truly impressive was the antique clothing itself. A pair of Victorian blouses dating back to the 1870s, for example, were selling for a reasonable $40 and $25! Many other equally impressive pieces are suspended from ceiling beams, though not all are for sale.

A 100% cashmere overcoat with a mink collar (who knew from "P.C." back then?) may sell for $50, while alligator bags range from $20 to $37. Guys have a whole rack of sportcoats to choose from; a particularly nice piece was a 100% wool Harris Tweed

jacket from the 1950s, marked at $37.50—the standard price here for men's coats. The women's clothing selection was quite diverse, broadly ranging in size and style. A black silk I. Magnin dress with full skirt, and a pre-1920s-style peach-colored Jantzen wool sweater, were both marked as $14.50.

Genuine antique glasses and costume jewelry round out the exceptional bargains, along with luggage. Venture, well, down to the Attic between 10 A.M. and 6 P.M. any day of the week.

Metropolis Vintage
• 423 15th Ave. E, Seattle; 322-2297
This First Hill store carries clothing, hats, shoes, and jewelry that is at least twenty or more years old. There are a few recent pieces, but even they have an old-fashioned look to them. In the mood to don a fedora and become as suave as Humphrey Bogart? This place has a fabulous selection of authentic men's hats from the '40s and '50s—with prices starting in the low 20s. And ladies can step out for the evening and paint the town red in a red linen Nordstrom dress for $18—adding some sparkle with a genuine art deco brooch for $28.

Got a question about the $1 silk ties? How about all the dresses around the store walls, grouped by color to save you time if you've got a certain shade in mind? The staff is friendly and well-armed with info about whatever piece interests you. More savings can be found even before you enter the store—a constantly changing sale rack on the sidewalk helps make room for new additions. Stop by any day of the week between 11:30 A.M. and 5:30 P.M.

The New Store
• 4542 University Way NE, Seattle; 633-5075
Strange, only about 10% of the stock in here is actually new, and among those items are jewelry such as piercing rings priced at $9 to $15 (they don't actually do the piercing). All the rest is used period stuff, some of which dates back as far as the 1920s.

Men's jackets start at $10, women's bathing suits start at $4, and Levi's jeans range in price from $16 to $24.

Some of the dresses are a bit more expensive, but still a bargain when you consider what you're buying. A black chantilly lace dress from the 1950s was seen at $68—there was also a $48 blue velvet dress from the 1940s that would make Isabella Rosselini jealous. If these are too pricey, there are still lots of lovely frocks available for under $35. The New Store is open from 11 A.M. to 8 P.M. Mondays through Saturdays, and from noon to 4 P.M. Sundays.

Ola Wyola
- 2211 First Ave., Seattle; 448-3325

Located below street level in Belltown, Ola Wyola sits at the bottom of a flight of pink stairs. Your reward for finding this nearly-hidden boutique is being able to take advantage of the reasonably priced and unusual clothing. Just about everything is either from the 1970s or earlier, and marked with equally unusual tags. On Mr. C's visit, "Someone's lovely wedding dress," as one particular tag read, was priced at $69.99, while a black "I Love Lucy dress" was seen for $29.99. There was also a silk "Beaded thing—36-inch waist" for sale.

Ola's is split into two parts; and the hallway connecting the two is lined with a bargain rack sporting 30% discounts. The second room also has a sale rack—10% is taken off these items. The day Mr. C visited, a 100% wool Pendleton suit was on this rack for $30. There was also a two-tone mod vinyl jacket from the '70s on sale for $20. Accessories and trinkets, some imported or antique, are also available. Or add a touch of class to your abode with a pair of candle sconces starting at $9.99. Hours are 12 P.M. to 6 P.M., seven days a week.

Old Duffers Stuff
- 1519 First Ave., Seattle; 621-1141

The things this Old Duffer has hung onto are quite remarkable. Most of the clothes were made from the 1940s through the 1970s, but several pieces of jewelry date back to Victorian times. In spite of their antiquity, there's plenty to choose from even at budget prices.

Both men's and women's clothes, shoes, and accessories are sold here. Victorian cuff links start at just $4.50 a pair and go as high as $45, while period tie pins start around $17.50. As for shoes, Mr. C spotted a classy pair of wingtips for $18, and cowboy boots for $45. Dresses started at $18, and jeans at $10. Lots of hats ($10.50 and up) and leather jackets ($30 and up) fill in the rest of the store. Old Duffers is set back in the 1519 First Avenue complex, so just wander in a ways until you find it—open 11 A.M. to 5 P.M. Mondays through Saturdays.

"Pin-Down Girl"
- 2224 Second Ave., Seattle; 441-1248

In case you're interested, "Pin-Down Girl" is named for an old B-movie about women wrestlers—which is about as far from Betty Grable as you can get. That said, here's what the "Pin-Down" store has to offer: jeans, jeans, and more jeans. Cut-offs are $10, vintage denims are $25, and plain-old regular second-hand Levi's are $18.

Of course, there's more to life than jeans. There's corduroys. Lot's of 'em, mostly $15 a pair. Flannel shirts range between $10 and $20, and nylon jackets start at $12. Leather jackets, sunglasses, and cowboy boots are available too, but you may want to try wrestling some of the prices down a bit on these. "Pin-Down Girl" is open from noon to 6 P.M. Mondays through Saturdays, closed Sundays.

Raghaus
- 1515 Broadway, Seattle; 726-1085

In the vicinity of Seattle Central Community College, this well-stocked used clothing store specializes in looks that are about twenty years old, with some newer and older items mixed in. Bigger sizes are plentiful, too, not common among vintage stores. Even more unusual, there are plenty of racks—arranged by type of clothing and color—and yet, plenty of room to move around.

Best buys include vests (ranging from $5.50 to $8), women's wool hats (starting at $8.95), and men's short sleeve button-down shirts (starting at $5). What Mr. C found especially interesting were a fluffy poodle sundress (!) for $14, a pair of funky curtains for $5—and the mannequin waiting for service in the shoe section. Perhaps it was contemplating the purchase of a cherished pair of clogs (they were only $16). Raghaus is open seven days a week.

Retro Viva
- 1151 First Ave., Seattle; 624-2529
- 215 Broadway E, Seattle; 328-7451
- 4515 University Way, Seattle; 632-8886

Three-quarters of Retro Viva is dedicated to new, funky fashions; the rest is very reasonably-priced used clothing. Take the $5 and $10 racks—both are loaded with trendy jerseys, miniskirts, and dresses—all just slightly worn, and from the current "retro" season. Other racks sport 25%, 40% and 50% reductions. And if these deals sound great, wait until February—when *everything* goes to 10%-70% off, including the new clothes. There are also huge savings in an annual November sale—stop by and see the deals for yourself. Retro Viva is open from 10:30 A.M. to 6 P.M. Mondays through Saturdays, noon to 5 P.M. Sundays.

Righteous Rags
- 506 E Pine St., Seattle; 329-7847

These clothes are divine, the prices, heavenly. Polyester, loud colors, and mod designs from the '60s and '70s leap out at you from every direction. To add to this visual smorgasbord, pierced mannequin body parts are aesthetically positioned throughout the store.

While visiting, Mr. C was nearly accosted by a $12 sparkling silver quilted mini-dress, a must in any woman's hip and happening wardrobe. T-shirts start at $5, really groovy corduroy pants start at $10, and quality imitation leather garments (or "pleather," if you will) start at $15. Righteous Rags is open from

---

MR. CHEAP'S PICKS
Vintage Shops

✔ **American Denim**—Largest selection and lowest prices on used jeans in town.

✔ **Fritzi Ritz**—Perhaps the best among Fremont's kitsch row.

✔ **Grandma's Attic**—In Pike Place Market, Grandma cleans house all the way back to the days of her youth.

✔ **Righteous Rags**—Digging for psychedelic duds is a gas in this uniquely decorated store, dude.

---

noon to 6 P.M. Mondays through Saturdays, and, sticking with the religious theme, closed Sundays.

For more good vintage fashions, head down the street to **Le Frock**, located at 317 E Pine Street (telephone 623-5339). Frock's bargain loft, although small, carries some big savings, like Levi's jeans starting from $10.

Rudy's Vintage Clothing
- 1424 First Ave., Seattle; 682-6586

Clearly geared more to the Pike Place Market crowd than your average vintage shop, Rudy's is cleaner and better organized than most; its stock is usually in better shape, too. There are lots of smart "classic" professional looks, for both genders, whether fairly recent stuff or styles from the *Father Knows Best* era. Naturally, with this downtown elegance comes a downtown rent, and prices here also tend to be higher than other retro shops—but give it a look. They're also open seven days a week, which is unusual in this line.

2nd Life
- 618 E Pine St., Seattle; 860-9974

This tiny shop makes up for its small size by offering huge savings on an eclectic mix of merchandise. Here's a sampling: A black tuxedo with matching pants for $50, a cocktail dress for $15, and a fringy suede jacket for $20; plus sunglasses ($3), wallets ($5), cowboy boots ($18), board games ($3), a toaster for $15 (all appliances are in working order), and metal lunch boxes ($12). How's that for a combination? There was even a $1,200 banjo selling for $600. If you need to get a life, 2nd Life will give you a good start. The store is open from noon to 7 P.M. Mondays through Saturdays, and 'til 6 P.M. Sundays.

Second Skins
● 112 Broadway E, Seattle; 329-8287
Second Skins deals mainly in new leather fetish items, many created by local artists; that's hardly unusual in the First Hill/Capitol Hill area. But, if you're not into the studded look, don't pass this by—there is also quite a bit of second-hand leather clothing of the more everyday variety, although sizes are somewhat limited. Between hats, vests, pants, and boots, you literally can dress from head to toe in a second skin of leather—assuming animal rights are not your priority.

A brown bomber jacket was seen here for $45, nicely broken in; a leather miniskirt was $35, and used combat boots were $20 for the pair. This may not be a place to bring little kids or gramma; but the, um, *interesting* art work, dance music, and super cool merchandise makes this place a lot of fun for the hip crowd. Second Skins is open from 11 A.M. to 6 P.M. Tuesdays through Fridays, from noon to 6 P.M. on Saturdays, and from noon to 5 P.M. Sundays. Closed Mondays.

Take 2
● 430 15th Ave. E, Seattle; 324-2569
Hike to the back of this trendy-looking store and you'll see big savings on their full-price clothes. Two sale racks—one offering 50% off, the other $5 per item—are both permanent fixtures holding a large selection of new shirts, shorts, and skirts. Then, there's the used clothing on nearby racks, like Gap and Eddie Bauer jeans for $16, and a $10 Karen Ellis polka dot blazer.

After perusing this section, don't make a beeline for the door just yet. Take 2 also sells current end-of-season new clothes—not last year's looks—which are discounted as well. Check out the tags and compare the "Our Price" of $39.95 with the "Reg. Price" of $59.95 on new floral rayon baby doll dresses. Accessorize your new outfit with something from the jewelry display—sterling silver rings start at just $5. Take 2's hours are from 10 A.M. to 7:30 P.M. Mondays through Fridays, from 10 A.M. to 7 P.M. Saturdays, and from noon to 6 P.M. Sundays.

Time Tunnel
● 1914 Second Ave., Seattle; 448-1030
Taking its cue from H. G. Wells, or perhaps that old '60s TV series, Time Tunnel tries to stock clothing from several different periods; however, there's a limited selection of each. The prices are quite good, speaking of yesteryear—jeans for just $12, denim overalls $25, and dresses starting at $19—but you may not find your size or the exact style you want. Still, if you've got the time to burrow through all the stuff, this place is worth a look. Open Mondays through Fridays between 11 A.M. and 6 P.M., and on the weekends, from noon to 5 P.M.

Vintage Voola
● 512 E Pike St., Seattle; 324-2808
Vintage Voola started as a small furniture store, yet has successfully held on to those roots as it expanded into clothing. An unusual combo—vintage clothes and furniture—but it works. Nicer used furniture is located in the front of the store, with the "scratch and dent" bargains found upstairs. Among the pieces up there, Mr. C spotted a small, slightly water-damaged table for $24, and set of three stacking stools for $45.

Vintage Voola's clothing is a small but varied collection of garments made between the 1940s and 1970s. Some of them are even personalized (Howard, where are you? Your bowling shirt is being sold here for $5). Dresses start at $12, cowboy boots at

$35, and men's button-down polyester shirts start at $7.50. Hoo-eeee. Vintage Voola is open from noon to 6 P.M. Mondays through Saturdays, and 'til 5 P.M. Sundays.

THRIFT SHOPS

Assistance League Thrift Shop

• 1419 N 45th St., Seattle; 547-4680
This small thrift store, in what was once a Wallingford house, is neatly arranged by clothing size—you can immediately find the styles that would fit you, and get through them quickly.

Most of the clothes seem to be for mature women and men—no nightclub duds here. A man's jacket was seen for $7.50, a complete suit for $25. A woman's seersucker suit was just $5, while a pair of casual pants with elastic waist were just $3. The clothes are in good condition, although they may not be the most current fashion or brand name. Kitchen items and costume jewelry are available, too—most items a dollar or two apiece. Proceeds benefit a number of programs, including Operation School Bell, which donates clothing to disadvantaged schoolchildren.

Bargain World

• 1600 Central Ave. S, Kent; 850-8884
• 729 Meridian Ave. E, Puyallup; 927-5629
• 18101 Pacific Ave. S, Spanaway; 846-8970
Big as any major national chain thrift, Bargain World has a ton of clothing for men, women, and kids; much of it is current or close to it, and the prices are microscopic. A Geoffrey Beene khaki shirt for $2.99, for example, or a pair of Kenneth Cole heels for $12.99. Plus a good selection of housewares and small appliances.

Oh, but that's not good enough for them. On top of that, BW offers a 30% discount to seniors (55 and over) all the time; a 30% discount for *everybody*, every Sunday; and, on some Sundays, certain color tags get 70% markdowns. Profits benefit the Family Renewal Shelter, for victims of domestic abuse. The stores are open seven days a week.

Chicken Soup Brigade

• 207 Harvard Ave. E, Seattle; 329-4563
• 2501 S Jackson St., Seattle; 322-7550
The Chicken Soup Brigade is an organization which enhances the quality of life for people with AIDS. You can find a wide variety of things at these shops, like sheets and pillow cases for $1, shorts for $5, dresses for $12, and books starting at 50 cents. You can also pick up cheap kitchen stuff, like a wire whisk (perfect for fluffy omelettes) for 39¢, wine glasses and coffee mugs for 50¢, and silverware for 25¢ apiece. You may even catch, as Mr. C did, a $95 futon sofa/bed and frame; but don't expect to find too much in the way of furniture at any given time.

Inexpensive as these all are, some items are even marked down an additional 25% to 75% until they sell. CSB stores are open seven days a week, from 10 A.M. to 7 P.M. Mondays through Saturdays, noon to 6 P.M. Sundays. Soup's on!

Deseret Industries

• 17935 Aurora Ave. N, Seattle; 542-9447
• 133 SW 157th St., Burien; 241-9447
These folks sure have made an industry of it, all right. Deseret is a large thrift shop stuffed with clothing, and a little bit of everything else, at very low prices. Blue jeans for $2.50, shoes for $3-$5, men's sportcoats in fairly nice condition for $8.25, women's fake fur coats for $13.25, and kids' clothes by the metric ton.

Meanwhile, you can also find major appliances from $50 to $150, vacuums for $15, color TVs for $50, bicycles from $35 to $50, and all kinds of housewares. Deseret also has a surprising selection of finer items, like china, antique clocks, musical instruments, and porcelain collectibles. These are displayed inside locked cabinets, and purchased by sealed bidding. Ask in the store for details. Open every day but Sunday.

Discovery Shop
- 2005 NW Market St., Seattle; 782-7763
- 6814 Roosevelt Way NE, Seattle; 524-3399
- 4535 California Ave. SW, Seattle; 937-7169
- 1001 W Broadway, Everett; 339-4141
- 225 First Ave. S, Kent; 852-9696
- 137 Park Lane, Kirkland; 827-3785
- *And other suburban locations*

All of the profits generated by these upscale thrift shops go to the American Cancer Society's research and service programs. In addition to selling clothing, different branches also specialize in various items, like books or appliances; so either call ahead if you need something specific, or just browse and see what you find. The Ballard shop, for example, mostly sells women's clothing. All of the gently-used styles are current, and range from fashions that could be worn to the office, to casualwear fit for a Sunday picnic. You can even find better-name labels if you're lucky. Pick up a short-sleeve Laura Ashley dress for $18, or a Gap blazer for $20. Jeans, starting at $7, and men's suits, starting at $20, are also great deals. For extra savings, watch for the half-price or $1 sale racks.

Children's clothing is usually available at each store, but the selection is limited. Most articles cost only a few dollars each, and are worth checking out. Because so much is regularly being donated, you can return in a couple of weeks and see lots of new items. These shops are open from 9:30 A.M. to 4 P.M., Mondays through Saturdays.

Goodwill Industries
- 1400 S Lane St., Seattle; 329-1000
- 1911 Auburn Way N, Auburn; 735-1051
- 3002 Hoyt Ave., Everett; 252-6163
- 19505 52nd Ave. W, Lynnwood; 774-6157
- 714 S 27th St., Tacoma; 272-5166
- 3121 S 38th St., Tacoma; 472-5160

If you're reading this book, you hardly need Mr. C to tell you about Goodwill. Their downtown branch (near the Dearborn/Rainier Ave. South split) is soooo big, they should've put the city inside the store instead of vice versa. You'll find the usual clothing bonanza of men's suits for $15, sweaters for $1, and the rest; unlike many other thrifts, Goodwill also gets deals on new clothing as well. Plus used furniture, electronics, books, jewelry, toys, and sporting goods. Special monthly sales put various categories at even further discounts. Store hours vary.

Hadassah Nearly New Shop
- 621 Broadway E, Seattle; 325-4974

Tucked away below street level, you may not expect to find like-new designer clothes in this far-from-glamorous thrift store—but believe it! Proceeds from the store go toward the Hadassah-Hebrew University Medical Center in Israel. Something is always on special sale; the day Mr. C visited, there was a group of blouses all priced at $2—including labels like Nordstrom and Christian Dior.

The regular racks, though close together, are packed with almost unbelievable bargains. You'll need to dig around a little, but here's a brief overview of the women's selection: Anne Klein linen slacks for $8, a Nordstrom 100% wool cardigan for $6, same price for a Lizwear ramie/cotton sweater, and women's Reeboks (worn a few times, but still sparkling white) for $7. Larger sizes are also available.

For men: $5 Levi's Dockers, $6 Dexter loafers, $1 silk ties, $18 jackets, $30 suits. There's not much in the way of children's clothing, but most of what you do find will cost a mere 50 cents. Sheets, pillow cases, vases, and kitchenware are also on display. Stop by during the week from 10 A.M. to 6 P.M., Saturdays 11 A.M. to 4 P.M., and Sundays noon to 4 P.M.

The Last White Elephant
• 902 NE 65th St., Seattle; 525-0170
This Roosevelt-area thrift benefits organizations working for animal rights and the protection of endangered species. While smaller than the big chains, there is a nicely eclectic selection (say *that* three times fast), as only the U-District could offer. You may find an Esprit cardigan for $5, a glazed earthen teapot for $8.50, and cruelty-free lipsticks for $1 each. A tape of birds in their natural environment chirps in the background. It's a fun place. Closed Mondays.

Meanwhile, to further benefit humane animal causes, you can also check out The PAWS Store at 8503 Greenwood Avenue N, Seattle; telephone 782-1700. Along with fundraising "PAWS" (Progressive Animal Welfare Society) merchandise for sale, they lend out educational books and videos on the subject. Open daily from 10 A.M. to 6 P.M., Sundays from 11-5.

Mercer Island Thrift Shop
• 7710 SE 34th St., Mercer Island; 236-3625
Does this sound like an oxymoron? Shame on you. Dedicated Cheapsters know that thrifts in upscale areas get more upscale donations. This attractive shop in a new, woodframe building, has two floors of good-quality clothing, housewares, furniture, books, sporting goods, tools, even older computers. It's all very clean and organized. Periodic special sales may offer deals like all T-shirts for a dime each. Proceeds benefit Mercer Island Youth and Family Services. Open Thursdays from 10 A.M. to 7 P.M., Fridays and Saturdays from 10-4.

Overlake Service League Thrift Shop
• Bellevue Square Mall, Bellevue; 454-6424
This Bellevue community service organization has scored a first in all of Mr. C's travels: It's in the middle of the ritziest shopping mall in town. That's because Kemper Freeman Sr., the developer of the mall, decreed it. Yes Virginia, you *can* find bargains in Bellevue Square—like an Evan-Pi-

---

MR. CHEAP'S PICKS
Thrift Shops

✔ **Hadassah Nearly New Shop**—It doesn't *look* chic from the outside, but nothing beats single-digit prices on like-new designer labels.

✔ **Overlake Service League**—A first in Mr. C's travels: A thrift shop in the ritziest mall in town (Bellevue, that is).

✔ **Shop 'n Save** and **Value Village**—Two chains of "commercial" thrifts, each with tons of clothing and housewares, all organized downright *fanatically*.

✔ **ThriftKo**—Not just tons of cheap clothing, but unused catalog closeouts as well.

---

cone linen blazer and skirt for $15, men's tuxedos for $35, and lots of costume jewelry for $5 and under (and real stuff, too). Being a small store, they only sell clothing, and only put out fashions appropriate to the season. There are special "New Today" and half-price sale racks, and it's all fine stuff. Open during mall hours, every day.

St. Vincent de Paul Retail Stores
• 17712 15th Ave. NE, Seattle; 364-1492
• 9835 16th Ave. SW, Seattle; 763-2130
• 13445 First Ave. S, Burien; 243-6370
• 2825 NE Sunset Blvd., Renton; 226-9426
Not only do these large stores sell the standard mix of clothing and housewares, at the standard incredibly low prices, but St. Vincent also distinguishes itself by selling new (and

used) mattresses at wholesale prices. In fact, they manufacture these themselves—thus "eliminating the middleman," creating affordable bedding for their customers, and generating more revenue for their charity.

You'll find two different lines, an economy set and a firmer luxury set. Either way, the prices are hundreds of dollars less than comparable brands at any department store. The deluxe queen-size set, for example, is only $329. Mattresses for cribs and bunk beds, too. Open seven days a week.

Salvation Army Thrift Store
- 1010 Fourth Ave. S, Seattle; 624-0205
- 12526 33rd Ave. NE, Seattle; 363-1606
- 422 S Third St., Renton; 255-0171

As with Goodwill, you're surely familiar with the nation's other thrift giant. But Mr. C does want you to know that their main store near the Kingdome is also among the largest he has ever seen; and that it includes "Antiques 'n Things," a separate section filled with furniture (fancier than you'd expect, though not always in the best shape) and collectibles. Mr. C found a Shaker style dresser for $199, and wine goblets from International Silver for $2.95 each. Tarnished, but remarkable.

Elsewhere around the store, you'll see some new clothing items (closeout deals), along with the usual selection of used clothes, luggage, large and small appliances, books, and toys. Store hours vary; the main branch is open Mondays through Saturdays from 9:30 A.M. to 5:30 P.M.

Shop 'n Save
- 1429 NW Market St., Seattle; 781-0641
- 10014 15th Ave. SW, Seattle; 762-8099
- 102 Cross St. SE, Auburn; 939-4245
- 16033 First Ave. S, Burien; 246-6608
- 4920-B Evergreen Way, Everett; 258-9347
- 6613 132nd Ave. NE, Kirkland; 881-0803

- 111 112nd Ave. S, Tacoma; 536-5444
- *And other suburban locations*

Back your '69 VW microbus up to one of these stores and, for less than $100, drive off with enough acceptable used tables, chairs, beds, toasters and telephones to furnish an entire empty apartment (as a pal of Mr. C's recently did). You'll still have enough dough left over to fill your closet with the finest fashions of 1975.

These huge commercial thrift stores are well-stocked with clothes, some better cared for than others—but all clean, and fanatically organized not only by type and size, but by color. Plus things like oak picture frames for a dollar, sporting goods, luggage, and more. Weekly and monthly specials cut 30% to 75% off these these already-minimalist prices. In fact, a little birdie told Mr. C that many vintage stores get *their* stuff here. Beat 'em to it—seven days a week, including every night (but Sundays) until 9 P.M.

Thangs 'n Stuff
- 1902 Second Ave., Second Floor, Seattle; no phone

On the mezzanine level of the Josephinium, an old residential hotel in the heart of downtown, one room is jam-packed with, well, the name says it all. It's like a cross between a thrift store and a vintage store, with racks of assorted clothing from jeans to leather motorcycle jackets to old suits and dresses. Most of these are under ten bucks (the jacket was $60). The rest of the tables are filled with dishes, jewelry, compact discs, audio and video tapes, clock radios, and just plain junk. A friendly gentleman presides over his domain from the front. It's open every day from 12 noon to 5 P.M.

This 'n That
- 8310 Greenwood Ave. N, Seattle; 789-1636

The Seattle Children's Home has spent the last century helping mentally ill youth with residential therapeutic care and independent living programs. Funds to continue this work come from a variety of sources, including this shop.

This 'n That is organized just like a retail store—men's, women's and children's clothing are grouped by style, then divided by size. The prices here are very low, the fashions recent; generally the quality is good, although some of the children's clothes look more worn. Men's dress pants are around $6, with most jackets priced at $20. Women's dresses generally range between $5 and $12; sweaters are even less. There are not a lot of things for infants, but there's a good selection for school-age kids. In the children's section, a jean skirt and pair of boy's shorts were seen for $2.50 each.

Other than clothes, This 'n That sells items like coffee mugs (50¢), silverware (15¢), and books (50¢ to $4). Stop by between 11 A.M. to 5:30 P.M. any day but Sunday.

ThriftKo

- 124 N 85th St., Seattle; 789-5357
- 12825 Des Moines Memorial Dr., Burien; 242-3918

Yet another big barn of bargains, ThriftKo mixes used clothing and housewares (by the truckload) with closeout deals on new merchandise from department stores and catalogs. There is, in fact, a "Catalog Corner," where Mr. C found Izod cardigans for $5 and kitchen curtains for $6.50. The quality and selection of used clothing is very good.

You need more incentives? Seniors (62 and over) get an extra 20% off, and everyone gets an extra 30% off any used merchandise on Sundays. Further sales may yield, say, 50% reductions on kids' stuff at back-to-school time. Open seven days a week.

Union Gospel Mission Bargain Centers

- 1321 First Ave., Seattle; 233-0429
- 6930 Martin Luther King, Jr. Way S, Seattle; 723-5700
- 2245 148th Ave. NE, Bellevue; 747-2787

Packed and busy, these charity shops carry a wide range of stuff: clothing, housewares and linens, furniture,

toys, books. Mr. C found a Harris Tweed blazer for $20, a silk dress from Nordstrom's for $8.99, and lots of children's clothing. Their Bellevue store, the **Eastside Bargain Center**, has the nicer digs and better selection. They'll even give you a map directing you to a dozen thrifts around the 'burbs.

Value Village

- 2929 27th Ave. S, Seattle; 723-5000
- 12548 Lake City Way NE, Seattle; 365-8232
- 131 SW 157th St., Burien; 246-6237
- 32945 Pacific Hwy. S, Federal Way; 874-3966
- 27241 132nd Ave. SE, Kent; 630-9885
- 17216 Highway 99, Lynnwood; 745-6603
- 16761 Redmond Way, Redmond; 883-2049
- 1222 Bronson Way N, Renton; 763-3285

Another commercial thrift chain, which donates a portion of its profits to various charities, Value Village is right up there with the best of 'em. Tons of merchandise, from clothing and shoes to household goods, furniture, and books, is neatly displayed and super-cheap. Even if you make clothing from scratch, you couldn't do it for so little money.

What's your taste? Classic wool suits from Nordstrom's for $25, fur wraps from the Bon for $22.99, Bandolino sandals for $6.99—and not all worn out, either. How about a pair of Levi's for $2.99? Also, VV frequently gets new clothing closeouts directly from the manufacturers. Not designer labels, but certainly nice-looking—rugby shirts for $10, or prom dresses in the spring for $25 and up. They even get in a stock of new Halloween costumes every year.

Check the color of each tag, since a different color is automatically reduced by 50% every day. Seniors (62 and over) get a 20% discount anytime. And, unlike many thrifts, the store takes returns—as well as personal checks. Open seven days a week.

Wise Penny
- 4744 University Way NE, Seattle; 524-8684

Most of these clothes have seen better days, but if you don't mind the "worn" look, great bargains can be found here. There are lots of men's button-down shirts, starting at $3.50, and women's sweaters starting at $4. There are also racks of children's clothes, but these seem to be the most obviously used. Of course, considering how fast kids grow, you may not mind spending $1.25 on a boy's tiger T-shirt—it's the wise thing to do. Bag-

gies pre-filled with small toys were marked 50¢ per bag; a Gerry highchair was seen for $5.50; and a Fisher Price three-wheel plastic bike was going for $10.

There's some furniture for the rest of us, too; a love seat, in fairly decent condition, was seen for $40. Wise Penny is open daily; proceeds benefit a variety of community outreach programs. Meanwhile, thrifty bookworms should check out the Wise Penny Annex next door for used books at very reasonable prices.

Here are a few more shops for the compulsively thrifty:

Children's Hospital Thrift Shop
- 15137 NE 24th St., Redmond; 746-3092

Aslan's
- 1175 NW Gilman Blvd., Issaquah; 392-4500

Aslan's Too
- 18827 Bothell Way NE, Bothell; 485-5401

The Butterfly
- 10216 NE 183rd St., Bothell; 486-3552

Eastside Community Aid
- 16112 NE 87th St., Redmond; 881-6100

St. Margaret's Thrift Shop
- 4228 128th SE Ave., Bellevue; 641-6830

COSMETICS AND PERFUMES

BJ Beauty Supply
- 2504 S Jackson St., Seattle; 325-7131

This friendly, neighborhood salon and store is hidden away in the Central District. Though it's small, the store has a good variety of cosmetics—mostly hair care, plus some nail and facial products. Exclusive brands like Aveda, L'anza, Nexxus, and Paul Mitchell can be found here, though not always at discount; plus lots of African-American products like Afro Sheen and Prosonique. For some brands, this store is the exclusive Northwest distributor.

When discounts are offered, they tend to be 10% to 30% off the retail price; you'll see lots of these signs among the shelves. BJ has been around

since 1981, and they clearly know their stuff. The store is open from 9 A.M. to 6 P.M. Mondays through Saturdays, and an hour later on Fridays.

Meanwhile, across the street in the Promenade shopping center, Western Beauty Supply at 2301 S Jackson Street (telephone 329-2582) offers some more discount opportunities on similar products.

Karin's Beauty Supplies
- 8314 Aurora Ave. N, Seattle; 526-5861
- 1007 Holman Rd. NW, Seattle; 782-0577
- Bellevue Square, Bellevue; 454-3443
- Loehmann's Plaza, Bellevue; 643-2121

- 26110 Pacific Hwy., Federal Way; 941-4009
- 1222 Bronson Way N, Renton; 271-7145
- *And other suburban locations*

Most cosmetics have prices set by the manufacturer, the same wherever they're sold; but, some beauty supply stores have different specialties, and are able to lower prices on specific items. Karin's has quite a good selection of the Revlon, Freeman, and KMS hair-care lines, at 10% lower prices than other retail stores. Most make-up, nail and skin care products are also at a 10% discount—find such names as Supernails, Orly, and La Femme on the shelves. While you can find several other well-known brands (Mr. C has promised not to say which ones) here, the prices are about equal to what any salon charges.

Karin's does offer one of the largest selections of salon products to the public. Also, there's a licensed cosmetologist at every branch to answer any questions you have. Stop by Mondays through Saturdays, from 10 A.M. to 5 P.M.

Perfumania
- Great Northwest Factory Stores, North Bend; 888-9494

Part of the Great Northwest Factory Stores shopping center, Perfumania is a national chain of 150 stores (and growing); their vast buying power enables them to sell top-name designer perfumes for men and women at cutrate prices. You can save big on names like Elizabeth Taylor's "Passion" and Cher's "Uninhibited," as well as colognes by Alfred Sung, Paco Rabanne, Ralph Lauren, Paloma Picasso, Halston, and many others. Price tags are color-coded to show you which bottles are selling at 20%, 40%, and 60% off.

Sample as many of these as you like; the staff is extremely knowledgeable and relaxed. The scents are sprayed onto special papers, which are then labeled for you with the respective brand; this way, you don't walk out of the store wearing ten con-

trasting fragrances.

The store also specializes in boxed gift sets which again are around half-off retail. In many cases, you can get a cologne set, with extras like matching lotion, shower gel (or whatever), for the same price as the perfume alone. Some even come pre-wrapped! There are cosmetic gift sets as well, such as eye shadow color kits. And you can always find a good selection of gifts here for under $10. The Great Northwest outlets are located directly off Exit 31 from Route I-90. Hours are daily from 10 A.M. to 8 P.M., except Sundays from 10-6.

Prestige Fragrance and Cosmetics
- Pavilion Mall, Tukwila; 575-3991

Here in Southcenter lies the Seattle area's only branch of this national chain. Owned by the Revlon company, Prestige is their clearance outlet for their products, as well as other batches of closeouts they acquire—designer fragrances and the like.

So, whether you go for a bottle of Revlon "Milk Plus 6" shampoo, marked down from $3.11 to $1.95, or Revlon earrings reduced from $12.95 to $8.95, plenty of various Revlon products are here at discount. Liquid nail wrap was seen here for $2 off at $1.25; and bottles of Ultima II facial base were reduced from $17.50 to $5.99. There are even boxes filled with hair care sampler sizes for as little as 33¢ each.

Plus Charles of the Ritz lip colors

marked down from $10 to $3, and Al-may Moisture Balance eye cream for half-price. On the cologne side, lots of favorite names are here—Armani, Polo, Halston, and more. A bottle of Oscar de la Renta eau de toilette was seen for ten dollars off at $42, while Perry Ellis cologne for men was knocked down from $30 to $22.50.

There are lots of gift sets here too; a Jean Naté after-bath set with a $13 combined value and a normal selling price of $9.95 was seen here for $6. Also, a set of manicure tools was reduced from $29 to $17.40. Prestige is open during mall hours, seven days a week.

Sally Beauty Supply

- Lake Forest Park Center, Seattle; 364-3390
- 2500 SW Barton St., Seattle; 938-1121
- 305 SE Everett Mall Way, Everett; 290-7276
- 19410 Highway 99, Lynnwood; 776-4237
- *And other suburban locations*

Sally Beauty Supply is a chain with over 1,500 stores nationwide; their parent company is Alberto Culver, the "VO5" folks. So they have a lot of factory-direct products, many of which are intended for salon use. This means high quality, large sizes, and good prices. A thirty-two ounce bottle of TRESemme European cleansing shampoo is just $2.59, while a fifteen-ounce bottle of "Volu-mizer" by Jheri Redding is $4.29. Sally also sells generic "copy" prod-ucts, made with exactly the same in-gredients as expensive name brands. Why pay extra just for someone's name?

There are also nail and skin care items—check out the $2.49 bottles of Nina nail polish—plus full lines of ethnic hair products, and discounted professional-grade hair dryers and curling irons. Be sure to check the "Reduced for Quick Sale" and "Cheaper by the Case" sections. Hours vary by store; most are open seven days a week.

DISCOUNT DEPARTMENT STORES AND LIQUIDATORS

These are some of Mr. C's favorite playgrounds. Keep an open mind about this vast subculture of places that have sprung up to sell any-thing that has not sold in retail stores. For basic necessities and splurges you'd never make at full-price, they can be lots of fun. And you may be amazed at what hidden, brand-name treasure may await you down the next aisle!

Before we go on, a word or two about membership warehouse clubs. You hardly need Mr. C to tell you about Costco, the local giant which has swept the nation. But please take them up on their offer to get a one-day "visitor's pass" and check the store out before you buy in. These mega-stores are not for all customers. You may not have the kind of storage area to take advantage of grocery deals by the case; there are some stores listed under "General Markets" in the "Food Shops" chapter which offer similar rates on smaller quantities without memberships.

For other kinds of merchandise, the discounts can be terrific, but the *selection* is often limited. Many of their televisions, computers, clothing, furniture, and even jewelry are closeouts; you can only choose from whatever deals they've been able to snap up from manufacturers. If you're looking for the best price on a particular model of refrigerator, they may only have a half-dozen of last year's leftovers. On the other hand, if you only care about the bottom line, this may suit you fine. Again, look before you leap.

Costco warehouses seem to be everywhere. Sam's Club, the arch-rival from the South, has also entered the region. Branches in the Seattle area include:

Costco
- 4401 Fourth Ave. S, Seattle; 622-1144
- 35100 Enchanted Pkwy. S, Federal Way; 874-0878
- 8629 120th Ave. NE, Kirkland; 828-6767
- 19105 Highway 99, Lynnwood; 775-2577
- 10000 Mickelberry Rd. NW, Silverdale; (360) 692-1135
- 3639 S Pine St., Tacoma; 475-2093
- 11013 Pacific Hwy. SW, Tacoma; 581-2081
- 1160 Saxon Dr., Tukwila; 575-3311

Sam's Club
- 13550 Aurora Ave. N, Seattle; 362-6700
- 3900 20th St. E, Fife; 922-1266

Now, on to the no-fee, low-price, anything-under-the-sun establishments:

Bargain Base
- 2401 Utah Ave. S, Seattle; 622-2264

Some of you may remember this as Bargain Bob's, in a new basement location. It's still a good place to check out for basic clothing, especially activewear and outerwear for men, women, and kids, as well as sporting goods and office supplies. Heavy cotton baseball jackets, for example, were recently seen for $29. Of course, you may prefer a textured powder-blue tuxedo jacket, with black velvet lapels—high style for a mere $9.99. Same price for racks of cool leggings and vests. And you can even get T-shirts by the pound (!) and sweatpants for $5.99.

Keep wandering around. You may find O'Brien snowboards in a variety of sizes (demo models) from just $49. Or a two-person nylon camping tent, reduced from $70 to $39, but not in size. Not to mention tennis racquets, bike helmets, and the odd kayak.

A far room is filled with office furniture closeouts, new and used. Basic foam-padded sofas were plentiful at $49 apiece, as were rattan swivel chairs for $39; but, as the sign overhead says, "Let's Talk!" Touch down at the Bargain Base seven days a week.

Big Mike's Factory Outlet
- 15226 First Ave. S, Burien; 248-6457

You gotta meet Mike Sanford. At well over six feet tall, he's a walking endorsement of truth in advertising. So is his store, which has really branched out in its two years or so of business. Mike is a wholesaler of garden supplies, and sells off his remainders, er, dirt cheap; get a 16-pound bag of Ortho plant food for a healthy $3.99. Mr. C also saw a bird feeder for $24.99 (this still bore a sticker from Eagle, where it was priced at $45.99).

Meanwhile, Mike now sells everything from toys and candy to factory-rebuilt power tools. Hardware and light bulbs. Nexxus hair care products for half-price. Generic aspirin and cough syrups, not expired. Framed art prints for your walls at $4.99 each. You name it, he's probably got it jammed somewhere into this small store. Just look for the giant gorilla outside. Closed Sundays.

The Bon Marché Warehouse
- 17000 Southcenter Pkwy., Tukwila; 575-2064

You say you like the Bon? You'll like it even better at up to 75% off regular prices, and that's what you'll find at their clearance center. It's filled with a constantly moving stock of furniture and bedding, rugs, electronics, and small appliances. These consist of everything from discontinued closeouts to refurbished returns, floor models, and some damaged items. But this is the place if you want to save $1,500 on a leather chair and ottoman set, or $500 on a 31-inch RCA color television.

There's lots of upholstered furniture to choose from, such as a contemporary "loose-pillow" style sofa and matching loveseat, reduced from $2,979 to $1,199. Mr. C found a 36" x 72" glass dining table, with a marble base, on sale for a remarkable $329. And lots of traditional looks in oak, pine, and cherry.

The home entertainment area was recently offering deals like a Panasonic stereo VCR, reduced from $379 to $249, and a complete Sony surround-sound system, with a five-CD changer, for $549. All sales are final, of course.

If it's home furnishings you're looking for, check out the Bon Marché Clearance Center in Northgate; see the listing under "Home Furnishings." Open weekdays from 10 A.M. to 9 P.M., Saturdays 10 A.M. to 6 P.M., and Sundays from 10 A.M. to 6 P.M.

Burlington Coat Factory
- 24111 Highway 99, Edmonds; 776-2221
- 10401 Gravelly Lake Dr. SW, Tacoma; 588-3595
- Pavilion Mall, Tukwila; 575-4269

Not content with being a popular clothing discounter for the entire family, Burlington Coat Factory stores have expanded from within to become something almost like actual department stores. They are quite large, and in each one, you'll not only find clothes, but also shoes, jewelry, linens, and infant furnishings.

You can outfit yourself from top to toe here, inside and out, in basic looks or the latest fashions. True to its name, you can find all kinds of outerwear here—like a Pierre Cardin lambskin bomber jacket, list priced at $300, for just $180; or racks of simulated fur coats for women. How about a faux fox, reduced from $200 to $120?

But there's more here than meets the elements. Underneath those coats, guys could be wearing a Harvé Benard double-breasted suit of 100% wool, discounted from $400 to $180. Or, creations by Ralph Lauren, Perry Ellis, Nino Cerruti, and Christian Dior at similar savings. For you female-types, perhaps a nifty black two-piece Oleg Cassini suit, not $270, but $150. A Jones New York turtleneck sweater, reduced from $140 to $90. Or 100% silk blouses for $12.95. Size selection is good here, from petite to plus sizes for women, as well as big and tall sizes for men.

Then, there are all the fashions for children, from tots to teens. Boys' Jordache ski jackets were recently seen reduced from $70 to $40; girls will look smart in dressy red coats by London Fog, marked down from $110 to $80. Both can save ten bucks or so off denims by Levi's, Guess?, and others.

You can also stock up on basics and accessories here, like ties, hats, and underwear (particularly Burlington hosiery, at $1 to $2 off all styles). There is also a small but serviceable jewelry counter, selling gold chains, bracelets, watches, and the like at permanent discounts of 40% to 50% off retail prices. And don't forget to look for the clearance racks in every clothing department!

Now, let's move on to the specialty stores-within-the-store. The Capezio Footwear Outlet extends these savings to all kinds of casual to classy shoes for men, women, and kids; it's not just for dancing anymore. Current styles in dressy shoes and boots are mostly sold at $10 to

$20 off list prices; for deeper discounts, though, look over on the long self-service racks, arranged by size. These are mainly close-outs and overstocks, all perfectly good. You may find a pair of red leather pumps by Bandolino, reduced from $72 to $39; men's dress loafers by Johnston and Murphy, marked down from $165 to $98; or Wrangler cowboy boots for $70 (not leather, obviously, but good looking). There is a more limited selection of sneakers, like ankle-high tennis shoes by Reebok for $49; plus kids shoes by Sesame Street, Fisher Price, and Hush Puppies.

Baby World sells discounted clothing, furniture, and accessories for newborns, small children, and moms. Along with good prices on infant and maternity wear, you can find things like a white crib set, complete with a Simmons mattress and colorful print sheets, reduced from $350 to $205. Not to mention plenty of soft and cuddly toys to fill those cribs. Also, such diverse items as a Little Tykes plastic table and chairs, for toddler tea parties; Graco strollers, like the "Elite" model, discounted from $140 to $99; and a Snugli car seat, reduced from $62 to $36.

Luxury Linens does the same deal for home furnishings, many by designers and name brands, at 20% to 50% below retail. Mr. C found things like Ardsley goose down comforters, in full or queen size, reduced from $140 to $90. Laura Ashley flat sheets were discounted from $32 to $12, along with names like Utica, Martex, and Bill Blass. Plus towels by Dundee, bed pillows (including orthopedic styles), shower curtains, decorative baskets, and more—all stacked from floor to ceiling.

It's all there in one place, seven days a week.

Chubby & Tubby

- 7906 Aurora Ave. N, Seattle; 524-1810
- 3333 Rainier Ave. S, Seattle; 723-8800
- 9456 16th Ave. SW, Seattle; 762-9791

Don't ask who's who. Do check C & T out if you're looking for good prices on hardware, flowers and gardening supplies, housewares, sporting goods, shoes and sneakers, and work clothes. Great closeout deals are mixed in with regular, first-quality goods, all at low prices. Mr. C found denim workshirts for $13.99; ranch boots for $70 and Avia cross-trainers reduced from $50 to $35 (look for the store's 25% off shoe sale, twice a year); baseball gear at 20% off during the season; a Coleman 7' x 7' dome tent on sale from $80 down to $60; a three-piece Lodge cast-iron skillet set for $19.88; and lots more.

Outside, the gardening center has flower bedding plants for 79¢, ceramic and clay pots in every conceivable size, lawn chairs from $7.99, huge bags of peat moss and potting soil, and various digging tools large and small. All stores are open daily from 9 A.M. to 9 P.M., Sundays 'til 6.

Direct Buying Service Discount House

- 915 Fourth Ave., Seattle; 623-8811

The Direct Buying Service Discount House is like an itty-bitty Costco—it has just about everything, including the kitchen sink. Literally. All you need to do is order it. Gadgets, appliances, things for the office, furniture—the motto here is, "You name it, we get it." All kinds of merchandise is crammed into the store, but the helpful staff will lead you to exactly what you're looking for. And, if whatever you want isn't in stock, peruse the name-brand catalogs and place an order—delivery takes two weeks. Flip through the Hoover catalog and find an upright "Encore" for $69.95—thirty dollars less than retail. The Minolta catalog shows an action zoom kit—camera, battery, film, and 2-year warranty—for $179.95, significantly less than the retail price of $249.

Although 70% of DBS's business is special-order, there's still a lot to choose from in the showroom. A Whirlpool 18-cubic foot refrigerator/freezer for a cool $549.95, a Sanyo juice extractor with its price squeezed down to $67.95, and a 35-inch RCA stereo home theater for a dramatically reduced $1,350. It's all new, directly from the catalogs, with full manufacturers' warranties. Fine jewelry, luggage, sporting goods, and toys can also be found here at super-low prices.

Shop at Direct Buying Service between 9:15 A.M. and 6 P.M. Mondays through Fridays, and 9:30 A.M. to 4 P.M. Saturdays.

Dollar$

- 1410 Third Ave., Seattle; 682-6545
- 4231 University Way NE, Seattle; 545-0724
- *And other suburban locations*

These places make Mr. C's job nice and easy: Everything here costs one dollar. That's it. You can find a vast selection of toys, stationery, cosmetics, kitchen gadgets, detergent; see for yourself. The stores are small, but they still manage to have lots of different types of merchandise on the shelves, in low- to mid-grade brands. Don't expect to recognize many of them, but the stuff will do in a pinch, or if you don't need it to last forever. This can be especially useful for the students in the vicinity of the U-District store. One thing's for sure—the stuff is inexpensive. Open seven days a week; hours vary at each location.

Another similar business, also with a "U" branch, is the 99 Cent Store chain, with in-town locations at 4341 University Way NE (telephone 633-3490), on First Hill at 109 Broadway E (328-6310), and other suburban locations. Same kind of stuff, and guess what? Lower prices!

Everything $3 Bucks or Less

- 1915 140th Ave. NE, Bellevue; 644-1145

Well, it *used* to be called "Everything $2 Bucks or Less," but that's inflation for ya. It's still a reasonable limit, right? And this closeout haven in the middle of a shopping center parking lot is certainly packed with all kinds of useful junk. Clothing, housewares, toys, even dented cans of food can be had for a song. On Mr. C's prowl, he found birthday

cards for 89¢, racks and racks of T-shirts in all sizes and designs from $1.49 to $3, cheap china for $1.19 a plate, compact discs by musicians you've never heard of for $3, Marge Simpson dolls, *Lion King* jigsaw puzzles, plus shampoo, lawn rakes, sunglasses....oh yes, and Mexican Jumping Beans (what kid didn't have a batch of *these* at some time?) for just a dollar. Fun stuff. Open from 9 A.M. to 8 P.M. on weekdays, 9-6 on Saturdays, and 11-5 on Sundays.

Liquidators Outlet

- 222 S Central Ave., Kent; 854-4390

The name says it all. Well, almost all; it was revealed to Mr. C that this is the authorized liquidator for a *very famous warehouse club based in the Northwest*. Naturally, Mr. C was sworn not to reveal the name in print, but you can probably guess—and if not, you're bound see it on tags around the store anyway. Now, that warehouse is famous for low prices; but get this—if it doesn't sell there, it winds up here, automatically reduced by 50%. Yowza.

Three dozen truckloads a week bring in clothing, jewelry, TV and stereo, lamps, furniture, packaged foods, toys, and more. Mr. C found such goodies as women's Reeboks for $15, men's Christian Dior bathrobes for $17.99, and a Sanyo boom-box (with AM-FM, cassette, and a six-CD changer built in) for $90.

Larger items included a Body Tech stairclimber slimmed down from $275 to $137, and even a Xerox copier, discounted from $1,799 to $899. Over in the food aisle, a 2 pound block of Wisconsin cheddar cheese was on sale for $4, and dented (but unopened) cans of Star-Kist tuna were reduced from $1.85 to 92¢.

All of these goods are new, or at least, unused; in fact, major items are still under full manufacturers' warranties, which begin when you make your purchase here, just as at any full-price store. Liquidators Outlet has been here for over five years; in fact, they recently increased their discount (it used to be "only" 25%) and their hours. They're open every day, including weeknights; call for recorded hours and directions.

The Salvage Broker

- 13760 Aurora Ave. N, Seattle; 365-7771

Way up north on Aurora, amid fast-food joints and superstores, this two-story wood-frame house seems almost out of place. But that's just the beginning of the surprises. These folks grab closeout deals on just about *anything* (although paper goods are, you might say, their calling card), and you really never know what you may find here at amazing discounts.

Mr. C grabbed a Samsonite "Accord" attaché case, originally $125, marked down to just $87.50; it can be you behind those Foster Grants, not for $12, but for $8.40; or, you may pick up a Texas Instruments calculator to help you figure out the discount when it's reduced from $45 to $32. Plus wall clocks, table lamps, college logo sweatshirts, cutesy gift coffee mugs....Fact is, most of what's in the store is brand-new, perfectly good, and cut by 30% from retail prices—except for a selection of remaindered books, which are sold at 50% off the cover prices (mainly reference books, like dictionaries and atlases).

Again, though, it's paper stuff—from office and art supplies to party goods—in which the Salvage Broker can keep you from going broke. Save big on reams of copier paper, legal pads, and business envelopes, as well as cocktail napkins, *101 Dalmatians* party plates, and packs of Hallmark invitations and greeting cards. They're all 30% off, open from 10 A.M. to 5 P.M. every day but Sunday.

Sears Outlet Store

- 76 S Lander St., Seattle; 344-4827
- 26020 104th Ave. SE, Kent; 854-9300
- 8720 S Tacoma Way, Tacoma; 584-8160

You all know what Sears carries. At these clearance centers, they liquidate a truly vast amount of furniture, appliances, home entertainment, and other

---

MR. CHEAP'S PICKS
Discount Department Stores

- ✔ **The Bon Marché Warehouse**—Off the selling floor and straight to Southcenter.

- ✔ **Chubby & Tubby**—No flab on these prices, from gardening supplies to the work clothes you'll garden in.

- ✔ **Direct Buying Service Discount House**—Order directly from manufacturers and save a bundle. DBS has a catalog for almost everything imaginable, *including* the kitchen sink.

- ✔ **Liquidators Outlet**—In Kent. Can't tell you who they liquidate *for*, but oh, you'll know.

---

items at discounts as high as 70%. Most goods are used (ever wonder where your trade-in goes?), but even these are fully warrantied to function properly. New items, in the minority, are clearly marked as such. These are usually discontinued models and floor samples.

On a recent visit, Mr. C found a brand-new plush leather rocker/recliner, declined in price from $500 to $350. A reconditioned 52-inch projection TV, with no box or remote control, was a *thousand dollars* off its original price at $998. In the appliance section, a refurbished, like-new Kenmore washer and dryer set was reduced from $1,199 to $899. Plus refrigerators, gas and electric ranges. Some of the furniture is also used, like a king-size SpringAir mattress set, marked down from $1,250 to $300. Some items are new but damaged; an oak-finish dining room table, scratched, was reduced from $560 to $200. Hey, just put some placemats on top.

It all goes to prove that there's a suitable price for everything. The downtown store, recently expanded, is on the third floor of the Sodo Center; all stores are open daily.

Six Star Outlets

- 4213 Wheaton Way, Bremerton; (360) 373-0153
- 166 SW 148th St., Burien; 242-5939
- 7601 Evergreen Way, Everett; 353-8771
- 1001 N Broadway, Everett, 259-4260
- 1207 13th St., Snohomish; (360) 568-0355
- 804 E 72nd St.,Tacoma; 475-8819
- 8722 S Tacoma Way, Tacoma; 588-7996

"NOTHING OVER $10" say the signs all around these stores, and it's true. Six Star liquidates a bit of everything, from clothing to housewares to packaged foods. It's easy to clothe your family with T-shirts at three for $10, six-packs of socks for $6.50, and leggings for $4.99. Plus lots of jewelry and hair accessories that, well, were never gonna sell for much anyway.

Tons o' toys include things like Looney Tunes coloring books reduced from $3.95 to a dollar, View Masters (loaded with "Little Mermaid" discs) for $6, and volleyballs for the same price. Household goods range from candles, greeting cards, and party supplies, to knock-off brands of cleaning products.

And Mr. C certainly appreciates Six Star's "Bonus Bucks" policy, which gives you a dollar of credit for every dollar you spend in the store; they can be redeemed on selected items only. Open seven days a week.

And *how* could Mr. C leave out. . .

Kmart

- 13200 Aurora Ave. N, Seattle; 363-6319
- 7345 Delridge Way SW, Seattle; 767-7004
- 15015 Main St., Bellevue; 747-4300
- 4210 Wheaton Way, Bremerton; (360) 377-3871
- 1207 S 320th St., Federal Way; 941-1752
- 8102 Evergreen Way, Everett; 353-8103
- 4800 W Valley Hwy., Kent; 852-9071
- 22511 Highway 99, Lynnwood; 774-7726
- 1414 E 72nd St., Tacoma; 531-6824

Mervyn's

- Southcenter Shopping Center, Tukwila; 439-1919
- 4126 124th Ave. SE, Bellevue; 643-6554
- Everett Mall, Everett; 353-8100
- 3301 184th St SW, Lynnwood; 672-7765

- Kitsap Mall, Silverdale; (360) 692-8898
- Lakewood Mall, Tacoma; 582-8844
- Sea Tac Mall, Tacoma; 627-0945
- Tacoma Mall, Tacoma; 474-8800

Target Stores

- 2800 SW Barton St., Seattle; 932-1153
- Factoria Square Mall, Bellevue; 562-0830
- 405 SE Everett Mall Way, Everett; 353-3167
- 2141 S 314th St., Federal Way; 839-3399
- 18305 Alderwood Mall Blvd., Lynnwood; 670-1435
- 3310 Meridian St. S, Puyallup; 840-2900
- 3201 NW Randall Way, Silverdale; (360) 692-3966
- 3320 S 23rd St., Tacoma; 627-2112
- Lakewood Mall, Tacoma; 581-7171
- 301 Strander Blvd., Tukwila; 575-0682

ELECTRONICS

There are lots of places to save money on appliances and electronics in Seattle. Some, unfortunately, are as far below repute as they are below retail. With merchandise that is imported from foreign countries, there is a greater possibility of shady deals, or inferior quality. Mr. C says this not with any kind of prejudice, but because he wants you to be careful. You should have no such worries with the stores listed here.

One of the best ways to protect yourself, if you have doubts as to *any* store's reliability, is to ask about their guarantee policy; make sure the item you want carries an American warranty. Since some stores deal directly with manufacturers in the Far East, their merchandise may carry a foreign warranty instead. Even for identical products, a foreign warranty can make repairs a hassle—unless you don't mind paying the postage to Japan! Remember, you are perfectly within your rights to inquire about this in the store.

AUDIO AND VIDEO EQUIPMENT

Adams TV
- 4411 Fremont Ave. N, Seattle; 632-4211

This small Fremont repair shop is crowded from floor to ceiling with used televisions. Some of the sets date back to the 1970s (does that mean they get first-runs of *The Brady Bunch*?), but all of them come with a 90-day limited store warranty.

Among the deals Mr. C found were a 25-inch RCA color TV from the late 1970s with a $135 price tag. A more recent, 19-inch cable-ready Magnavox, with remote, was seen for $179. Can't do color for much better than that.

The staff is very friendly and helpful, willing to answer any questions you may have. Adams TV's hours are Mondays through Fridays, from 9:30 A.M. to 5:30 P.M., and Saturdays by appointment.

Classic Audio
- 7313 Greenwood Ave. N, Seattle; 706-1561

Classic Audio is relatively new to Se-

attle, buying, trading, and consigning high quality, pre-owned stereo equipment. Some of the equipment can be as much as 15 to 20 years old, and anything in need of repair is fixed right at the store. Mind you, these are the kinds of components that were *built* to last.

Remember records? Some rock bands have actually gone back to putting out LPs, along with their CDs and cassettes. If you want to take part in this vinyl renaissance, or just dust off your old high school days, you don't have to feel left out—as you might in a department store. Here, you can find a good turntable for as little as $39, going up as high as $400. Of course, if you chucked all your records and now only play laser, no problem—CD players start as low as $59, and go up from there; they also have receivers, amplifiers, and speakers. Stop by and check out what's in stock Wednesdays through Sundays, 11 A.M. to 7 P.M.

Hawthorne Stereo

- 6319 Roosevelt Way NE, Seattle; 522-9609

This northern U-District shop specializes in high-end stereo components, the kind made mainly by British and European manufacturers, "from the affordable to the absurd." They've been at it for almost fifty years, offering top-notch service geared to keeping customers happy.

Though the prices on new equipment can be as high-end as the features, Hawthorne also sells used components taken as trade-ins or on consignment. Given the store's fussy clientele, according to one salesman, many fine pieces are traded in or sold "out of boredom." Well, their desire for the latest bells and whistles is your chance to get some fancy stuff for up to half-off the original price. And, unlike the models you see in department stores, these are usually high-quality components made to last a lifetime.

So, you may go for a pair of Apogee "Scintilla" speakers—a state-of-the-art, futuristic design—reduced from $4,000 to $2,000. If that's still too high-pitched, you may opt for a pair of Advents instead, marked down from $400 to $250. Being trade-ins, you will find a broader range of makers in the used department, such as a JVC receiver, originally $500, now $239—or a high-end Sony CD player, list priced at $1,800, now $800. There's also special equipment like reel-to-reel recording decks, amplifiers, and graphic equalizers.

All used items come with a 30- to 90-day store warranty, plus a 7-day money-back guarantee *and* a 30-day exchange policy for an item of equal value. And of course, you can trade in something of your own for credit toward either new or used equipment—another way to save big. Hawthorne's salespeople don't work on commission, and will spend plenty of time demonstrating whatever you'd like to hear in their clean, spare shop. They're open weekdays from 11 A.M. to 8 P.M., Saturdays from 10-6, and Sundays from 12-5.

Kane's Electronics

- 915 E Pike St., Seattle; 325-5513

Up on First Hill, Kane's is mainly a neighborhood service and repair shop; however, items never picked up by their owners are eventually sold off at reduced prices—and you'd be surprised at just how many such units there are. A twelve-year-old Zenith color TV, with 25" screen, was seen here recently for $300, while an eight-year-old Quasar, also with a 25" screen, was $230.

Every piece of equipment comes with a 90-day store guarantee, and delivery can be arranged for a small fee. The selection here is limited, but if you're not fussy and want a good deal, Kane's is worth a look. Stop by during the week between 9 A.M. and 5 P.M., or on Saturdays from 10 A.M. to 2 P.M.

Lee's Video-Audio-Fax

- 15625 NE Eighth St., Bellevue; 643-5555

Not the most creative name in the world, but it does tell you the facts (or is that "fax"?). All that's missing is the fact that you can save a ton of money here; but don't worry, signs bombard you with this point as soon as you walk in. The real fact is, Lee Tayebi ain't lying. His large store has the familiar walls of television monitors, VCRs, projection TVs, and (in a separate room) stereo receivers, CD players, tape decks, and speakers. Plus fax machines, 35mm cameras, cellular phones, and other portable electronics. Lee proudly proclaims that he is an authorized dealer for all major Japanese makers only; through a high-volume, low-overhead business, he can indeed offer low prices on all current models.

Most of these are mid- to high-grade lines. Among the good deals Mr. C found was an RCA 31-inch color television, with stereo surround sound, reduced from a list price of $799 to $679. JVC camcorders start from $649. In the audio room, an Aiwa auto-reverse cassette deck was on sale, marked down from an original $250 to just $99. And another closeout deal offered a high-end Mitsubishi office fax machine, meant to sell for $2,195 (!) now just $500.

What else does Lee do right? He promises to beat any advertised price by 70% of the difference, for up to one month *after* your purchase, or you get the item free. In business since 1982, he is a member of the nation's largest buying group—meaning low markup. The sales staff does not work on commission, creating a no-pressure atmosphere. The store also offers low-priced extended warranties, lasting up to five years; and they will exchange any item found to be defective within 30 days. The store is located in a shopping plaza across from the Crossroads Shopping Center in Bellevue. It's open seven days a week, including evenings.

The Old Technology Shop
● 7712 Aurora Ave. N, Seattle; 527-2829

Mr. C includes this Green Lake area shop more out of nostalgic interest than as a true bargain-hunting spot, although you can find some deals here on older pieces. Mainly, this is just a fascinating place for audiophiles to poke around in, a throwback to the radio repair shops of days gone by.

Proprietor Steve von Talge buys, sells, and restores vintage electronics of all kinds—radios, TVs, scopes, and many things Mr. C didn't even recognize. Not to mention cameras, bicycles, a few antiques, 78 rpm records, and sheet music, Heaven

---

┌─────────────────────────────────────┐

MR. CHEAP'S PICKS
Audio/Video Equipment

✔ **Lee's Video-Audio-Fax**—So, they don't win prizes for originality. Their prices will win you over.

✔ **Hawthorne Stereo**—Great deals on second-hand, high-end audiophile equipment.

└─────────────────────────────────────┘

---

knows, if you have any of these yourself, you need to know about this place. They've got vacuum tubes, parts, and manuals for all sorts of old-time gizmos, as well as information on swap meets and other events for collectors. And, you may snap up a rebuilt shortwave radio for $30, or a cool-looking black-and-white TV from the 1960s.

Everything is quite neatly organized for a store of this nature, though you may need some help finding exactly what you're looking for (if you *are* looking for anything in particular). But hey, take your time. Rumor has it, that's the way all stores used to be. Open Wednesdays through Saturdays from 12:30 to 6 P.M., and Sundays from 2-6.

COMPUTERS

Boeing Surplus Store
● 20651 84th Ave. S, Kent; 393-4060
See the listing under "Flea Markets and Emporia."

Bruno's Computer Superstore
● 510 Andover Park W, Tukwila; 575-8737

Bruno Santo is a driven man. You may catch him whizzing about the vast Southcenter store which bears his name. For ten years now, he's been gathering up overstocks, liquidation deals, and leftovers in every single aspect of computerdom—systems, components, software, books, manuals, the works. It really makes the store quite a resource. The software section alone carries current IBM and Mac packages, older versions, and even disks for Amiga and Commodore systems (remember those?). Some of these cost as little as $8 apiece. Look here if you need out-of-print manuals, too.

There are trade-in computers and peripherals; Mr. C found a WYSE 486 system (without a monitor) for $699, not that far into the reign of the 486. Current new models are also available at very competitive prices, and you can find accessories like a package of 50 bulk diskettes for $21.95. Call the above phone number, press 5, and you'll hear about weekly specials.

There are also tons of CD-ROMs, organized by genre, and many are displayed on bargain tables ("Everything 9% to 33% off"). Plus a special section devoted to children's software, including several stations where you can try programs out.

And then, there's the "Voodoo Corner." Techies, and any shoppers who remain undaunted by the scary name—and sometimes scarier look—of this area, can prowl around through shelves loaded with used parts and components. None of these items are guaranteed in any way, but who knows? You may come up with a hard drive for seven bucks. The staff knows their stuff, and can help advise you, but "no one knows if these work." There is a tech support hotline, if you should need it.

What else can Mr. C say? In all his travels, Bruno's is a unique find. It's open seven days a week, including weeknights until 7 or 8 P.M., and weekends until 6 P.M.

Compucare
- 19826 Aurora Ave. N, Seattle; 542-5434

Way up north in the Echo Lake area, Compucare offers deals on both new and used computers, along with upgrade options in their own lab. This allows you to save money by putting only the features you need into your present computer, or a new PC made from scratch. Either way, you can save a lot over the prices at the major chain stores. At a time when you could barely get a no-frills 486 model computer for just over $1,000 (prices change so rapidly, but this gives you an idea of the time frame), Compucare was offering a snazzy 486 SLC

package with a super-fast 66mhz clock speed for $1,099. That included, as all their new models do, a three-year warranty.

In the used division, Mr. C found an Intel 386 system, complete with monitor, for $629, at that same time; and a 24-pin dot-matrix Panasonic printer (old-fashioned, yes, but perfectly good) for $139. There were also some Macintosh finds among the used machines, such as a Performa 200 system for $599 complete. All used goods carry a 30-day store warranty on parts and labor. Open seven days a week.

Computers & Applications
- 10623 NE Eighth St., Bellevue; 451-8077

In business since 1981 (and how many of us had computers back then?), C & A is clearly well-established on the Eastside for new computers and accessories of all kinds. They are authorized dealers for many of the major brands, including Macintosh and IBM-type machines. They are also an authorized service center for many brands; and they can assemble components to your own specifications, another way to save.

It's almost pointless to mention prices for new computers, since these fluctuate; suffice it to say that, if you're in the market, you should price these guys. There's very little on display in their small showroom (much more space is devoted to their service department); but they have catalogs aplenty, and can order almost any configuration at good rates. Furthermore, they include one year of free classes with the purchase of any system, so that you're sure to get your money's worth *after* you buy. Open weekdays from 8 A.M. to 6 P.M., Saturdays 10-5, and Sundays 12-5.

Gemini Computers and Software
- 10331 Aurora Ave. N, Seattle; 524-0701

Gemini founder Howard Irby has a good idea. In addition to buying, selling, and upgrading new and used computers, he also buys and sells an extensive variety of software—in most formats, and again new or used. All of his software is priced at half or less of the current list price, and if used disks prove defective, you can return them within one week for a full refund.

This can be an unexpected way to save big bucks. After all, why spend $400 on WordPerfect for Windows, when you can buy a used set of the previous version for just $99.95? If you really know your software, you can decide whether "last year's model" has enough of the features you want—it usually does. If not, you can probably buy the old version plus the upgrade, and still come out ahead on cost. And if you're *still* not satisfied, you can return the software within two months and get a store credit for 50% of your purchase price. Whew!

Gemini also has lots of used CD-ROM disks; there are tons of games available, and most are $25 and under, around half of their retail prices. That even includes such hit titles as "Sim City" and "The 7th Guest." Some are in still-unopened packages. And then there are some 10,000 shareware disks for sale, all at $3 or less. They will also buy your old software, provided they consider it resellable.

You'll find some hardware here, including used IBMs and Macs; upgrades and service are available at very low rates (like the software, these can also be half the rates of other stores). Gemini has been around for over five years, though they just moved to their current location in '94. Open from 10 A.M. to 7 P.M., Mondays through Saturdays.

Plato's Pocket
- 17340 Southcenter Pkwy., Tukwila; 575-0939

Here's a unique looking store, located in a shopping plaza just south of the main mall area. Atmospheric lighting and music set the tone for a store poised to bring you the very latest high-tech accessories for your computer. Can such an artsy place be

MR. CHEAP'S PICKS
Computers

✔ **Bruno's Computer Superstore**—Near Southcenter, perhaps the area's biggest collection of new, used, and (you *thought*) bygone.

✔ **Gemini Computers and Software**—Second-hand and outdated versions of many popular software programs and CD-ROMS.

✔ **RE-PC**—Another warehouse packed with used hardware and components, for you do-it-yourselfers.

cheap? Well, folks who want to stay on the cutting edge have limited bargain options—the newest toys are always expensive. But Plato stays very competitively priced on all kinds of multimedia hardware and software.

That's their specialty; everything from hot new CD-ROM games and educational software to the sound cards and other add-ons you may need to use them. Lots of these disks are up and running, allowing you to test-drive them before purchasing. Some of the prices Mr. C scouted here were indeed below those at other stores; if you can't wait for the latest rage to die down, keep this store on your pricing list. Open seven days a week.

RE-PC
- 1565 Sixth Ave. S, Seattle; 623-9151

In a large industrial warehouse (formerly known as the PC Fixx Clearance Center), RE-PC specializes in, you guessed it, recycled computers and accessories. This can mean anything from a complete system to a spare monitor to the proverbial rat' nest of internal parts, on both th and Mac side of the game. Get an entire 386 system for as little as $650, ready to run; upgrade from there, if you wish. Or, for the technically-inclined, pick up just a 386 motherboard, loaded with 8 megs of RAM, for a mere $195—this part *alone* usually represents up to $500 worth of the price of an assembled computer.

As liquidators and salvage experts, these folks get tons of stuff from trade-ins, and all kinds of other sources—sometimes even directly from Microsoft! They're willing to bargain on some prices, and really seem to be having a fun time with it all. All used equipment carries a five-day warranty for defects: If you purchase any computer or peripheral that is defective, they will repair, replace, or exchange it at no cost.

This does not apply to "as is" items, which are another part of the RE-PC story. Toward the back of the large store, shelves and shelves are filled with—well, junk. At least it looks that way to the untrained eye. But again, if you're handy with electronics, you may very well be able to make use of a $5 monitor, a $35 printer, disk drives, empty cases, and the like. You may even find an entire system for $75. These are final-sale gambles; you get to find out whether they work or not. The thrill of the hunt, eh?

RE-PC is open from 10 A.M. to 7 P.M., Tuesdays through Saturdays.

Seattle Micro
- 2308 Fourth Ave., Seattle; 441-9111

This Belltown assembler and repair shop offers very competitive prices on new PCs in a number of high-powered configurations—or to any specs you desire. They use IBM-manufactured motherboards, which carry a three-year warranty (the rest of each system is warrantied for one year). It's a serious, no-frills store.

Meanwhile, they also have shelves ves of used older compo-
...uding monitors and printers
...up, as well as keyboards,
...nd cables. All used
...varrantied for 90 days,
...iod as you get with

such merchandise. Open weekdays only, from 8:30 A.M. to 5:30 P.M.

Software Etc.
- Bellevue Square Mall, Bellevue; 453-1696
- Sea Tac Mall, Federal Way; 941-2400
- Tacoma Mall, Tacoma; 472-2267

Software Etc. sells IBM and Macintosh software at discounted prices. These discounts can be small, especially on lower-priced items, or quite substantial, in the case of more expensive packages. A program like Quickbooks for Windows, retailing for $159.95, was seen here for just $99.99; and the Quicken/TurboTax bundle, regularly $139.90, for just $64.99. On the Macintosh side of things, you may find Aldus Super-Paint, originally $199, for $99.99—or Claris MacWrite Pro, regularly $249.99, for $189.99.

Of course, all work and no play makes Mr. C a dull boy. Games like "Prince of Persia," regularly $49.95, sell here for $39.99 (Mac) or $29.99 (IBM). The "Etc." includes accessories, like diskettes, mousepads, and so on; plus books and magazines, though these are not discounted. Hours are 9 A.M. to 6 P.M. on weekdays, Saturdays 10 A.M. to 5:30 P.M., and Sundays noon to 5:30 P.M.

Vetco
- 13029 Northup Way, Bellevue; 869-7025

Another haven for parts fiends, Vetco has two floors of used electronic parts for all kinds of computers. You can rummage around for monitors (mono from $39, VGA from $159), motherboards, hard disk and floppy disk drives, cables, keyboards, modems, and more. Most of these are neatly displayed on shelves or in glass cases; the staff is very knowledgeable, and can definitely help you save money, especially on upgrades.

There are also some complete systems, like a 386 DX with a monochrome monitor seen recently for $390. All used equipment carries a 90-day warranty. Open from 9 A.M. to 5 P.M., Mondays through Saturdays.

Not to mention (but we will) these well-known chains:

Ballard Computer
- 5424 Ballard Ave NW, Seattle; 781-7000
- 8525 120th Ave. NE, Kirkland; 822-7000
- 6111 Tacoma Mall Blvd., Tacoma; 471-0700
- 331 Tukwila Pkwy., Tukwila; 246-0700

Computer City Supercenter
- 12526 Totem Lake Blvd. NE, Kirkland; 820-1600
- 227 Andover Park E, Tukwila; 439-1600

Future Shop
- 13201 Aurora Ave. N, Seattle; 363-1955
- 14515 NE 20th St., Bellevue; 644-1984
- 802 SE Everett Mall Way, Everett; 348-8233

- 3326 S 23rd St., Tacoma; 572-2240

CompUSA
- 6007A 244th St. SW, Mountlake Terrace; 744-0165

Silo
- 809 NE 45th St., Seattle; 545-3506
- 10409 Aurora Ave. N, Seattle; 527-5000
- 14315 NE 20th St., Bellevue; 746-6080
- 811 SE Everett Mall Way, Everett; 355-7390
- 31621 23rd Ave. S, Federal Way; 941-6810
- 18833 28th Ave. W, Lynnwood; 771-2282
- 10796 Myhre Pl. NW, Silverdale; (360) 692-0775
- 17550 Southcenter Pkwy., Tukwila; 575-1012

FLEA MARKETS AND EMPORIA

Boeing Surplus Store
- 20651 84th Ave. S, Kent; 393-4060

No, you won't find cheap airplanes for sale here, though you may see plenty of their component parts—but that's not to say that this salvage liquidation store is only for aviation fans. Here in this vast warehouse, recycle-conscious Boeing sells off everything from scrap metal to metal desks. In fact, as much of the ever-changing stock comes from offices as from assembly plants.

So you may find, as one of Mr. C's expert bounty hunters did: Compaq computers for $175 and up, Epson printers from $40 and up, and IBM Selectric typewriters (remember those things we typed on before computers?) for $50. Plus desks for $10, and chairs for $5 apiece; flourescent bulbs at thirty for a dollar (!), hard hats and safety goggles for fifty cents to a buck;

and used drill bits in every size imaginable, for one dollar *per pound*.

Some items are new, though most, of course, are not. Salespeople are on hand in the computer area, to help you determine if items are compatible with your own systems. Needless to say, all sales throughout the store are final.

An adjacent outdoor yard sells sheet metal, and gives away scrap wood (which is often left out on the curb for anyone to take). And, speaking of curbs, good luck finding a parking space in the tiny lot—though people come and go pretty quickly, so if you're patient, you can grab a spot. Open from 10 A.M. to 5 P.M. Tuesdays through Fridays, and from 9 A.M. to 4 P.M. on Saturdays.

Capitol Hill Street Market
- Tenth Ave. E, Seattle; 860-8618

For a couple of summers now, this

happening area (of First Hill, really) has created a low-key, open-air market; it's the neo-hippie crowd's alternative to the yuppier Fremont Sunday Market (see below). Some fifty artists and vendors offer plenty to look at, from sterling silver jewelry at wholesale prices to tie-dyed T-shirts to fresh produce. Plus vintage clothing, books, and crafts. There's usually a few musicians jamming their way toward becoming a garage band. The market runs on Saturdays and Sundays from May through October; look for signs posted all over town for this year's actual dates.

Curbside Collectibles

• 12549 Lake City Way NE, Seattle; 363-3628

The proprietor here calls himself Antique Arnie, a salty character whose favorite phrase seems to be "Not a damn thing." Which may or may not also describe the result of your shopping experience at this tiny Lake City emporium. But then, these kinds of places are always hit-or-miss; that's part of the fun.

If your browsing taste includes vintage hats, you may do very well here; Arnie's got lots of styles, from turn-of-the-century straw boaters on up. These can be a bit pricey, but as Arnie said, "Make me an offer." Mr. C also found some cool 1950s toasters for $25, along with old typewriters, ashtrays, radios, and small furniture. For some reason, $42 seems to be a common price on many of these items. Go figure. Open Wednesdays through Saturdays from 11 A.M. to 6 P.M.

The Downtown Antique Market

• 2218 Western Ave., Seattle; 448-6307

Formerly the garage for Seattle's fire department wagons, this cavernous building now houses a collection of antiques displayed by over one hundred separate dealers. Each vendor rents a "space" on the floor, or a "case" in which they exhibit their treasures. Keep in mind that these are genuine antiques, often in fine condition—not everything here is inexpen-

sive. However, plenty of jewelry, hats, trinkets and more can be found for relatively low prices.

Many dealers have different themes, reflecting their individual tastes and collections. One may specialize in silverware or china, another in dolls, another in clothing. It would take quite a while to look at absolutely everything, but the Antique Market is very neatly arranged and inviting.

When Mr. C visited, several unique items were found at great prices, such as a little sterling silver salt and pepper shaker set ($15), an embroidered white bedspread ($22), and intricately designed perfume bottles ($5 and up). It just takes a little poking around to uncover some hidden bargain. The Downtown Antique Market is open Mondays through Saturdays, from 10 A.M. to 6 P.M., and Sundays from noon to 5 P.M.

Fletcher's General Store

• 12317 Lake City Way NE, Seattle; 364-4069

Down the road apiece from Curbside (see above), Fletcher's is the real find along this strip. A carpenter friend of Mr. C's reports that he's "never seen a better and cheaper selection of used tools in one place—and I've *looked*." Hammers for $2 or $3, rakes and shovels for $5, even some hardly-used power tools for one-half to one-third of their original prices. You get the idea.

Fletcher's also has things like used baseball gloves for $10 (hey, they're already broken in!) and golf clubs for $3 apiece; used compact discs, tapes and records; and some small furniture pieces. A browser's paradise. They're open from 11 A.M. to 5:30 P.M. Tuesdays through Fridays; weekends, 12 noon to 5 or 6 P.M.

Fremont Antique Mall

• 3419 Fremont Pl. N, Seattle; 548-9140

Downstairs from a doorway on Fremont's main street, this sprawling, winding store crams room after room with all manner of vintage collectibles. Clothing, jewelry, furniture, toys, comic books, trading cards, it's all here—the biggest and best selection of the many similar shops in this neighborhood. Mr. C found wool suits and dresses from the 1940s, still in good shape; authentic Levi's for $10 and up, with happy-face pins to accent any retro wardrobe; and a glass-top art deco coffee table for $75.

Of course, being antiques, many items are not inexpensive: Walk down another level, and be sure to check out the classic wood and aluminum soda fountain selling for $6,500—if it hasn't been purchased by some erstwhile drugstore pump jockey looking to reclaim his lost youth. The Fremont Antiques Mall is open from 10 A.M. to 6 P.M. daily.

Fremont Sunday Flea Market
• 600 N 34th St., Seattle; 282-5706
This weekly event takes place in the vast parking lot behind the stores "on the Ave." in Fremont. It brings together more than 100 vendors hawking everything from clothing to fresh produce to all-out junk. On any given Sunday, you're likely to find vintage clothes and furniture, crafts being sold by local artists, flowers and plants, books (which a gentleman was selling—literally—"by the pound"), used car parts, and other manifestations of the ever-popular bric-a-brac.

Given the nature of the Fremont area, there are plenty of booths selling artsy clothing—handmade sweaters, tie-dyed shirts, and the like. Also, there is usually live entertainment by local musicians to serenade you as you stroll about the two adjoining parking lots which this market can fill. It all runs on Sundays from 10 A.M. to 5 P.M., from May to Christmas.

And that's not all! This same parking lot is also home to the Fremont Almost Free Outdoor Cinema; see the listing under "Entertainment—Movies" for the story on *that*.

Lakeside School Annual Rummage Sale
• Seattle Center Exhibition Hall, 3131 Western Ave., Seattle; 440-2925
This absolutely gargantuan annual event recently celebrated its 45th anniversary, and it's still going strong.

MR. CHEAP'S PICKS
Flea Markets and Emporia

✔ **Boeing Surplus Store**— Construction materials *and* office supplies—and no need to cash in frequent flyer miles.

✔ **Downtown Antique Market**—A vast waterfront warehouse filled with buried treasures.

✔ **Fremont Antiques Mall and Sunday Flea Market**— Another building filled with ephemera, plus the city's best weekend flea market.

Run by the Parents Association at Lakeside, the money raised here goes toward student activities, scholarships, and LEEP, a six-week academic and athletic summer program for bright but disadvantaged young students.

The rummage sale is held for a good cause, but it's also a bargain-hunter's dream. Here are just a few different categories of things that you'll find: Clothing for everyone, in every size; sporting goods, toys, books, records, electronics, hardware, household goods, furniture, antiques, silver, china, jewelry, collectibles in the "French Room," and designer clothing and new merchandise in the "Boutique." Items are marked *up* 25% on the opening day of this four-day extravaganza (you're paying for "first-dibs," but still not a lot). The second day has "regular sale" prices, which are very cheap indeed. The third day goes to half of that price, and the last day is "Bag Day," when you can pay by the bagful for whatever's left. Start checking local newspapers in February to see when the next sale will be—they usually take place in early March.

FLOWERS AND PLANTS

Avant Garden
- 13510 Aurora Ave. N, Seattle; 361-0779

Okay, for starters, ya gotta love the name. This recent arrival (in a small block of shops in front of Sam's Club) covers a full range of cut flowers and artistic displays. Bouquets start as low as $2.98; a dozen roses go for $39.98, but they come arranged with a veritable forest of greens in a glass vase tied with a red ribbon. Or, for $16.98, consider an arrangement of gladiola and yellow roses in a bowl—very tasteful.

The store also deals in high-quality silk flowers and trees; old-fashioned chocolates, which can be sent with flowers; cards and balloons; all at very reasonable prices. It's a lovely shop, and it's open from 8 A.M. to 7 P.M. weekdays, 9 A.M. to 6 P.M. Saturdays, and 10 A.M. to 5 P.M. on Sundays.

Buckets
- 1329 Fourth Ave., Seattle; 954-2721

This shop is only slightly larger than a bucket—it's actually a wagon in downtown's Rainier Square, in front of Puget Sound Plaza. Lenny's been selling freshly cut flowers here for over six years. It should be obvious to any true bargain-hunter that a place like this costs less to rent than a full store; that means Lenny can sell at low-markup prices. So, the busy exec on the run can grab a dozen roses for as little as $22; someone heading to a lunch date can pick up a single long-stemmed rose, wrapped in greens, for a mere $1.50. Who says "romantic" has to be expensive?

Mixed bouquets, with flowers like daisies, lilies, and snapdragons, usually cost $4.95 or so. Some of these, too, are available as single blooms. As with so many things in Mr. C's book, cash-and-carry is always the least expensive way to go; however,

Buckets does take orders by phone, offering delivery in the business district for a $3 fee (there's also a $15 minimum for phone orders). Lenny's there from 7:30 A.M. to 4:30 P.M., weekdays only.

Central Flower Market
- 417 S Central Ave., Kent; 850-6000

South-enders should come in and see Gail for good prices. How about $16.95 for a dozen, wrapped, long-stemmed roses? Pretty good indeed. So are her carnations ($6.95 a bunch), and a limited variety of other flowers and plants. Plus cards and mylar helium balloons for those all-out greeting attacks. Open Mondays through Saturdays from 9 A.M. to 6 P.M.; Fridays 'til 7 P.M.

Chubby & Tubby
- 7906 Aurora Ave. N, Seattle; 524-1810
- 3333 Rainier Ave. S, Seattle; 723-8800
- 9456 16th Ave. SW, Seattle; 762-9791

See the listing under "Discount Department Stores."

Johnny's Flowers
- 4147 University Way NE, Seattle; 632-5400

Here's the place to go for anyone on a student's budget. Near UW, Johnny's offers all kinds of specials throughout the year. During the summer, for example (when flowers are more plentiful anyway), you may find deals like *two* dozen short-stemmed roses for $9.98. That's not a typo, folks. 'Course, these are the pre-wrapped variety, not necessarily the highest quality flowers in the shop, but who can argue with a price like that?

Johnny's also offers "Happy Hour Specials" that do not involve drinking vase water or such. Every day, from 3 P.M. to closing, a single long-stemmed rose costs $5; get a second rose for only $1 more. Same thing for the $3 medium-length roses. Meanwhile, cash-and-carry prices—on a full range of cut flowers—are always about a dollar per stem less than full-prices. Open weekdays from 8 A.M. to 8 P.M., Saturdays from 9 A.M. to 5:30 P.M.; Sundays during the school year only.

Kimura Nursery
- 3860 NE Bellevue-Redmond Rd., Bellevue; 881-6508

Well, here's a new one on Mr. C. He's written plenty of books detailing places to buy second-hand clothes, books, furniture, and the like; but in all his travels, he's never seen a second-hand *plant* store. Until now, that is.

This attractive shop amusingly refers to these as "previously enjoyed interior plants." Plucked from displays in shopping centers and offices—rescued might be a better word—plants in poor health are lovingly revitalized and sold here in a wide variety of types and sizes. They specialize in bonsai plants, among others. Mr. C was shown a slightly shopworn but healthy corn plant, eight feet tall, selling for $25; a lovely two-foot Chinese evergreen tree was $6.50. Its pot alone was worth twice that.

In fact, dozens of empty ceramic pots in many colors and sizes line an entire wall. Many are quite large, ranging from eight to twelve inches in diameter, and are priced around $5 each. Kimura Nursery is open from 9 A.M. to 5 P.M. daily.

The Rose Corner
- 10901 Aurora Ave. N, Seattle; 361-5051

Though it looks like little more than a roadside stand, closer inspection finds this to be a full-service shop—specializing in roses, but they don't stop there. The standard price for a dozen long-stemmed roses is $24.95, loosely wrapped, cash-and-carry; for ten dollars more, you can have these in a glass vase. Delivery is available, for an extra charge.

Rose Corner also sells carnations

MR. CHEAP'S PICKS
Flowers and Plants

✔ **Johnny's Flowers**—Would ya believe...Happy hour specials every afternoon?

✔ **Kimura Nursery**—A bonsai tree grows in Bellevue; many are available second-hand!

✔ **The Rose Corner**—Great deals on cash-and-carry roses, and more.

---

for $6.95 a dozen; mixed bouquets from $8.95; and all sorts of potted plants, in season, like chrysanthemums for $4.95. They also design and create wedding and party package deals, starting as low as $69.95. Open every day of the year but Christmas (a rarity!); daily from 8 A.M. to 7 P.M., Sundays from 10-6.

West Seattle Nursery
- 5275 California Ave. SW, Seattle; 935-9276

This full-service flower and garden shop is packed indoors and out with everything you need to beautify your home—plants, topsoil to put them in, and even books to show you how. In season, assorted ground covering plants are $1.98 a pot. Annuals in one-gallon pots, like geraniums, petunias, and marigolds, are $2.98. Mr. C also noted a "2-for-1" sale table of annuals toward the middle of the summer.

Out back, a huge area is devoted to fruit trees, large potted rose plants, tools, and soil. Everything is clearly labeled and explained throughout. Inside, the helpful staff will answer further questions, and sell all sorts of related decorative items. Prices are reasonable, and everything looks just great.

Down the road apiece, check out **Gatewood Floral Design** (6059 California Ave. SW, Seattle; 938-1376) for good rates on cut flowers. They're also known for offbeat specials, like their "Christmas in July Sale," when you can get special prices on decorated trees, centerpieces, and wreaths. Other frequent deals may include roses by the dozen for $24—wrapped, with ferns and baby's breath. Open weekdays from 9 A.M. to 6 P.M., Saturdays from 10-5.

Young Flowers
• 111 Third Ave., Seattle; 628-3077
Another downtown oasis, Young Flowers stakes out its corner with lots of blooms and plants out on the sidewalk—no doubt taking advantage of Seattle's natural watering system. This also means they can take advantage of working-folk passersby, the sort of foot traffic that keeps the flowers moving and costs low. Seasons

and holidays will affect the prices in any flower shop, but Young Flowers has better deals year 'round—like single long stem roses for just $2.95. Other places may charge $3.50 and $4. Young also offers a budget-rate alternative—same kind of rose, with a slightly shorter stem, for $1.75.

Among the deals Mr. C found were large seasonal bouquets of garden flowers for $8, and "Bells of Ireland" plants for $2. You can also find cacti, starting as low as $1.95 for an itty-bitty one. Oh, and if you're planning to buy a floral arrangement, bringing in your own vase will save you $5 to $10! Now, there's a fresh idea. Pick a stem or two for yourself, Mondays through Fridays only, from 7:30 A.M. to 5 P.M.

FOOD SHOPS

Quoting prices on fresh foods, like meat and produce, is about as smart as quoting politicians on their promises. Neither seems to keep very long. The prices mentioned herein, like everything else in this book, are simply examples which should give you some idea of each store's general pricing. It's worth noting, though, that the shops below were all visited at the same time of year; because of this, you can certainly use these descriptions for comparison with each other.

Finally, remember that many of the foods listed under individual categories can also be found at stores in the "General Markets" section of this chapter.

BAKERIES

Angus' Meat Pies Bakery Outlet
• 1206 N 155th St., Seattle; 362-6536
Just off of Aurora, this commercial bakery sells its first- and second-quality foods at a discount. There's quite a variety of these English-style delicacies, many of which are pre-packaged. Nine-ounce steak and kidney pies, or curried beef pies, are just $1.85 apiece; smaller Cornish pasties, filled with beef and vegetables or

smoked salmon, go for $1.40. There are also goods like beer biscuits, sausage rolls, and shortbreads. Many of these are also available in large quantities for even better values.

The retail shop opens only after the bakery is done for the day; that's weekdays from 3-5:30 P.M., and Saturdays from 10 A.M. to 1 P.M.

Ballard Baking Company Cafe

- 5909 24th Ave. NW, Seattle; 781-0091

See the listing under "Restaurants— North Area."

Entenmann's/Oroweat Bakery Outlet

- 1604 N 34th St., Seattle; 634-2700
- 7000 Greenwood Ave. N, Seattle; 634-4426
- 3310 Auburn Way N, Auburn; 939-3430
- 1405 134th St. NE, Bellevue; 641-3116
- 125 SW Everett Mall Way, Everett; 745-1669

Commercial bakeries crank out tons of baked goodies every day. When they put fresh boxes out on supermarket shelves all over town, any as-yet-unsold ones come back off—and go directly to these outlet stores. Such packages, though, have seldom reached their expiration dates; they're perfectly good for a few more days—and at prices far below those in the supermarkets.

The selection at these outlets is always large. You may find an Entenmann's fat-free fudge brownie cake, retail priced at $3.19, selling here for $1.09; and Oroweat premium breads selling at three loaves for $2.69. There are usually other related food products available as well; on his visit, Mr. C found half-dozen packs of Val's Bagels at three for $1.89, twelve-inch Boboli thin pizza crusts a dollar off at $1.89, and ten-pound sacks of Bob's Red Mill whole wheat flour for $2.62.

Unlike some bakery thrifts, Entenmann's also sells straight-from-the-oven merchandise at factory-direct prices. Thus, you can choose your level of discount, based on freshness. On top of that, senior citizens get a 10% discount on their total purchase. Store hours vary, but most are open Mondays through Saturdays.

Gai's/Langendorf Bakery Thrift Stores

- 1431 NW 49th St., Seattle; 782-4992

- 2906 Sixth Ave. S, Seattle; 682-2244
- 5980 First Ave. S, Seattle; 762-2186
- 2006 S Weller St., Seattle; 322-0931
- 13823 NE 20th St., Bellevue; 641-0293
- 2547 Perry Ave., Bremerton; (360) 377-6377
- 4800 Auto Center Way, Bremerton; (360) 373-8221
- 1515 E Marine View Dr., Everett; 252-6260
- 3931 Smith St., Everett; 252-6613
- 23009 Military Rd. S, Kent; 878-2242
- 430 164th St., Lynnwood; 743-5799
- 4804 212th St. SW, Mountlake Terrace; 774-4170
- 11216 Golden Givens Rd., Tacoma; 537-0749
- 8203 Durango St. SW, Tacoma; 584-4200
- 9112 E Marginal Way S, Tukwila; 762-6850

For as long as anyone can remember, these bakeries have provided Seattle with loaves, rolls, and pastries that are about as fresh as a huge commercial bakery can be. Here at their combination bakery/stores, you can get the goods straight from the oven at wholesale prices—before they are marked up at convenience stores and supermarkets.

Needless to say, people buy here in large quantities—whether they're supplying a school cafeteria or just picking up a box of fresh doughnuts for the office. Loaves of "Peasant Bread" cost $2.20 here; a one-pound loaf of sourdough goes for $1.89. Fresh miniature cookies are $1.69 a dozen, and a dozen gooey cinnamon buns are just $1.99. You can even get a cuppa hot coffee for a quarter.

There are also plenty of day-old loaves, in a variety of brands; how about two French baguettes for a dollar, or two packages of a dozen hamburger buns (each) for the same price. Mr. C also saw Archway cookies—two pounds of ginger snaps for $1.99—and Roman Meal oatmeal, $2.29 for a 16-ounce box. For the biggest selection, try Gai's Lynnwood branch, or the Langendorf on Sixth Avenue below the Kingdome. Store hours vary.

Greenwood Bakery Cafe

• 7227 Greenwood Ave. N, Seattle; 783-7181

The Greenwood Bakery Cafe is a tiny neighborhood bakery and sandwich shop. If you're on a tight budget, you can save some dough (oooh, sorry) by picking up some day-old baked goods. These are sold at half-price every Wednesday through Sunday. Some of the things you're likely to find are loaves of bread that go down to $1.50 each, and muffins reduced to 40¢ apiece—stock up and put a few goodies in the freezer. When they start out this good, who cares if they're a day old? GBC also serves up tasty (and cheap!) sandwiches; see the listing under "Restaurants—North Area" for details. The Greenwood Bakery Cafe is open from 6:30 A.M. to 9 P.M. Tuesdays through Saturdays, and Sundays from 7 A.M. to 6 P.M. Closed Mondays. Outside seating is available, weather permitting.

Hoffman's Fine Pastry

• 226 Kirkland Parkplace, Kirkland; 828-0926

See the listing under "Restaurants—Eastside."

John Nielsen Bakery

• 1329 Third Ave., Seattle; 622-1570

Ever wonder if there's a connection between that cheese danish you had for breakfast, and the actual country of Denmark? There is. From the outside, this place looks like any average city bakery. But John Nielsen makes excellent, authentic Scandinavian pastries that are very reasonably priced. These range from the standard small cookies ($3 a dozen) to things like apple strudels, cinnamon rolls, and those danish (all under a dollar), to the truly exotic—"baked potatoes" made from marzipan and custard ($1). They also make full-size cakes and pies, of course; and there are a few tables where you can sit over an espresso and something deliciously gooey. Open weekdays from 8 A.M. to 5:30 P.M.; they open an hour later on Saturdays.

Remo Borracchini's Bakery

• 2307 Rainier Ave. S, Seattle; 325-1550

For all kinds of Italian specialty foods, it doesn't get any better than this. Mr. C will hold Borracchini's up against the shops he's seen in the "Little Italy" of any major city, and the constant crowds only prove it further. So, get in line, and pick up some biscotti—never mind a buck (or more) apiece at Starbucks, get a *pound* of 'em here for $4.50.

A small round loaf of cracked wheat bread goes for 89¢. Plain, crusty rolls are a dime each; not to mention basil foccaccia bread and garlic bread loaves, and gooey doughnuts. If you're lucky, you'll get there in time for a day-old bag of these, still wonderful, just $1.80 a dozen. Open from 6 A.M. to 7 P.M. daily.

Roo's Market

• Pike Place Market, Seattle; 624-2945

Roo's carries two-day old goods from Brenner Brothers Bakery and Delicatessen, a New York-style bakery and coffee shop in Bellevue (see the listing under "Restaurants—Eastside"). The breads, muffins, and other goodies are only sold here for two days before they are removed from the shelves, so everything is still relatively fresh.

Assorted pastries are 75¢ each, or two for a dollar. A 16-ounce loaf of Russian rye bread can go for a mere 65¢, with French and Italian loaves just twenty cents more. For lighter breads, a pita bread six-pack is just 75¢. With prices this reasonable, it's easy to try something new. Live dangerously! Roo's is open from 9 A.M. to 6 P.M. daily.

Seattle Bagel Bakery

• 1302 Western Ave., Seattle; 624-2187

Although anyone from back East will probably tell you it's impossible to get a good bagel on the West Coast, even these curmudgeons seem to agree that there are none better in Seattle than the ones found at this shop just south of Pike Place Market. Certainly, few bakeries get more outrageous with their variations on the theme. Sure, they have sesame, wheat, onion, and the like; but have you ever tried a pesto bagel? Or, for that matter, jalapeño, apple raisin, and orange poppy?

Well, you can get 'em here, and they all cost the same as the good ol' plain. Bagels are 40¢ apiece, 35¢ if you get a dozen or more. They go so fast, it's not hard to find these hot out of the oven. And, if you're lucky, they'll have some bags of day-old (four bagels for a dollar). When they start out this fresh, one day is *nothing*.

SBB also makes up sandwiches, espressos (79¢!), and soups. There are a handful of tables if you want to stick around. Open seven days a week, from early mornings through late afternoons.

Standard Bakery Company
- 1835 Queen Anne Ave. N, Seattle; 283-6359

The Standard Bakery is your basic coffee shop, with comfortable seating inside and a seasonal patio out front. Among its shelves of yummies, the bakery also has a large selection of day-old pastries and bread, all selling for 50% off the original price. Pick up croissants for a light 55¢ each, and Danish for a mere 65¢ —the extra day doesn't hurt 'em a bit. For that matter, same-day breakfast items, like muffins, donuts, and scones, are reduced by 25% after 3 P.M. Standard Bakery is open from 6 A.M., and from 7 A.M. on Sundays.

Wonder-Hostess Thrift Store
- 14701 15th Ave. NE, Seattle; 364-1991
- 1924 S Jackson St., Seattle; 322-4247
- 14311 SE 16th St., Bellevue; 649-9628
- 310 Washington Ave. N, Kent; 852-7050

- 11729 124th Ave. NE, Kirkland; 820-7550

Like the Entenmann's bakery outlets described above, these shops are packed with returns from supermarkets and convenience stores—which usually have still not reached their expiration dates. And that means a lot more than Twinkies! Yes, those are here, at five packages for $2.15. But did you know that Wonder now makes corn flakes? An 18-ounce box is just $1.69. All varieties of Wonder breads and buns are here too, like three loaves of basic Wonder Bread for $1.50—Mr. C even saw a generic white bread for 27¢ a loaf (didn't know there *was* white bread more generic than Wonder).

Plus snacks like bags of potato chips and popcorn; boxes of macaroni and cheese mix (two for 89¢); even household goods, like aluminum foil and Spray 'n Wash. Most branches offer a "Bargain Day," with extra price reductions. All are open seven days a week.

CANDY

Dilettante Chocolates

- 2300 E Cherry St., Seattle; 328-1530

It's hard to believe, but these incredible, elegant candies—so often seen in pricey gourmet shops—are made in a rundown brick building in the Central District. And, by going right to the source, you can get some, er, sweet deals.

Mistakes will happen, after all, and they can save you money. When Mr. C and a pal visited, for example, the shop was discounting perfectly good milk chocolate candy bars—which happened to get put into "semisweet" wrappers. Other unique bargains included bags of chocolate scrapings, taken from the machines used to coat espresso beans; this is perfect for baking, and at a dollar a pound, there's an unlimited supply. The beans themselves sometimes come out misshapen; get a two-pound bag of these for $6.50, in all sorts of flavors.

In fact, Dilettante is quite well-versed in its resourcefulness; *nothing* is thrown away. They make wonderful chocolate-covered biscotti (get a half-dozen for $3); they then take the leftover crumbs and chocolate flakes, and melt them together into a kind of hasty cookie. It works.

Meanwhile, you can also get first-quality candies at factory-direct prices. A variety of melt-in-your-mouth truffles all cost $14.50 a pound here; that's half of the retail price. Tiramisu candy bars are 75 cents. This place is truly a chocaholic's dream, and it's open weekdays from 8 A.M. to 5 P.M. (Fridays 'til 6), and Saturdays from 10 A.M. to 4 P.M.

GENERAL MARKETS

Ballard Market

- 1400 NW 56th St., Seattle; 783-7922

You say you have to prepare meals for a small army? Maybe your campers are tired of the same old soup beans. Well, this place has over two dozen varieties of beans, selling in bulk for just 68¢ a pound. Lots of other bulk bins are filled with deals like unbleached flour for 28¢ a pound, or rolled oats for 49¢ a pound.

As you peruse the aisles of this folksy old-time grocery store *cum* supermarket, you'll see cooking recipes hanging from the shelves—recommending that you try one of the 150 varieties of bulk spices for a particular casserole, or something from the 40 kinds of nuts available for a special dessert. Plus all the things you'd find at any supermarket—seafood, fresh meats, even flowers and wines. And Mr. C never knew there were so many flavors and shapes of pasta. So, if you're in the market for twenty pounds of designer noodles, now you know which market to go to. The Ballard Market is open 24 hours a day, seven days a week—quite a selling point in itself.

Cash & Carry United Grocers

- 1760 Fourth Ave. S, Seattle; 343-7156
- 13102 Stone Ave. N, Seattle; 364-1733
- 2208 136th Pl. NE, Bellevue; 644-4638
- 2917 Cedar St., Everett; 339-2628
- 1628 S 344th St., Federal Way; 925-0550
- 21504 84th Ave. S, Kent; 872-7873
- 6412 204th St. SE, Lynnwood; 672-1886
- 6208 Tacoma Mall Blvd., Tacoma; 472-6879

Shop where the grocery stores shop. Cash & Carry is, a grocery wholesaler, the sort of distributor and warehouse that caters to the food store and restaurant trade; the difference is that *this* one allows the public to shop too, at the same wholesale prices.

And, unlike Costco—which pioneered this private/public approach—you don't need to become a member. Just walk in and shop.

For what kinds of things? Wow. Canned goods, frozen foods, meats, produce, eggs and milk, soda, coffee flavoring syrups, paper and party goods, household supplies, pots and pans, (professional) cooking supplies and appliances, the works. While many of these are sold in larger quantities than you might ordinarily want, you don't have to purchase by the case.

So, you may find a three-gallon jug of ice cream for $10.75. Huge avocados for 75¢. Lean ground beef for $1.12 a pound. Good prices on Tim's Cascade Potato Chips. A 32-ounce bottle of TRESemmé shampoo for $2.50. An eight-inch Wear-Ever stainless steel no-stick frying pan for $16.53. Commercial-grade blendors from Hamilton Beach and Waring. You get the idea.

The nice folks in here provide free cups of coffee (with flavorings!) at the front of the store. They even take personal checks. Hours vary, but all branches are open seven days a week.

Greenwood Market
- 8500 Third Ave. NW, Seattle; 782-1610

It looks like any standard neighborhood supermarket, which in many ways it is; but the Greenwood is also a haven for natural food fans and environmentally-conscious shoppers who may not want the upscale prices some specialty markets charge.

Bulk food bins offer a world of dried pastas from 99¢ a pound and up; along with quantity rates on grains, coffee beans, soup beans, cookies, and even flowers and plants. They're very big on recycling here; be sure to bring in your own containers and grocery bags. Open daily until 11 P.M.

Pike Place Market
- 85 Pike St., Seattle; 682-7453

Anyone who has been to this colorful, historic landmark knows that Pike Place Market vendors have some of the best food around. Founded at the turn of the century,

it's the oldest farmers' market in the country. The produce here is not the cheapest—but the quality is so high, and the variety so diverse, that above-average prices are easily justified. Consider it good value.

Browsing is just as much a feast for your eyes—everything is attractively displayed, and temptingly within an arm's reach. The only danger, besides buying more than you can afford or eating it all before you get home, is the flying fish at the Pike Place Seafood Market. Yes, these guys really throw fish around; don't worry, they have excellent aim.

If you can put up with the crowds, and respect the vendors who get nervous if you touch their perfectly-arranged produce, Pike Place Market is worth the trip to pick up something extra special. Or, just go for the people-watching. It's open from 9 A.M. to 6 P.M. Mondays through Saturdays, and from 11 A.M. to 5 P.M. Sundays.

Save U More
- 18715 E Valley Rd., Kent; 251-3922

Here's one you won't see on *Northern Exposure*. This grocery chain is in fact based in Alaska, but they also have this one store in the Seattle area—and it's huge, filled with huge savings. Often, that's because they carry lesser-known (but still national) brands; Mr. C noted a two-pound can of Chase & Sanborn coffee, for instance, selling for $4.99. Anywhere else, even Costco, it could be twice as much. You may also find deals like 69¢ for five pounds of raw potatoes. A six-pack of Pepsi was well-priced at $1.69, though you could also get a generic version for 99¢. Beer is sold at store cost; *nobody* can go lower. Plus all the usual packaged and frozen foods, household supplies, pet food, and the rest.

The store is strictly no-frills; but it's also no-membership. They even take coupons! If you live in or near the south end, this place will indeed save you more than most supermarkets. Open Mondays through Saturdays, from 9 A.M. to 6 P.M.

MR. CHEAP'S PICKS
General Markets

✔ **Cash & Carry United Grocers**—Like Costco, without memberships.

✔ **Pike Place Market**—Of course. Just *try* to find better quality, bigger selection, and a more festive atmosphere; popular with tourists and residents alike.

✔ **Save U More**—This discount supermarket in Kent will do what it says.

✔ **Sysco**—From this industrial district warehouse, you can get food-service packaging and prices.

Sysco
● 1242 Sixth Ave. S, Seattle; 447-9113

Nationally based in Kent, Sysco uses its warehouse in the industrial heart of downtown Seattle as a clearinghouse for all kinds of supplies for the food service business—meaning both food and the things to serve it on. It's open to the public as well, same stock, same prices.

Foods are sold in commercial, regular-folk, and individual-sale sizes. Many items are in damaged or discontinued packaging. You may find a 50-ounce dented can of Camp-bell's tomato soup for $1.71, or a 42-ounce box of Sysco's own brand of instant oatmeal for $2.18. Does your big family love French fries? Get a 30-pound case of frozen ones for $18.98. Or, check for "repacks"—if one of these boxes accidentally gets a hole punched in it, the one ripped bag of fries inside is removed, and the (perfectly good) rest of the case goes on sale for just five bucks.

Sysco also gets national brand sodas in by the truckload, with the high-volume prices you'd thus expect, like a case of Pepsi six-packs for $5.99. They also sell fresh milk, eggs, and produce at wholesale rates.

But food is only half of the story—and the store. Sysco has low prices on restaurant-grade cookware, from stainless wire whisks to appliances to pots large enough to make all the spaghetti sauce your family will ever need. Then, there are aisles and aisles of (basic) service stuff. Real china dinner plates for 50¢ each; cup and saucer sets for 20¢; stainless steel flatware for a quarter apiece. Plus a separate closeout area at the rear, where prices are cut in half *again*—wine glasses for 75¢, gravy boats for two bucks.

And we haven't even gotten to the paper and party supply section, where a 125-pack of 10" Chinet (microwaveable cardboard) dinner plates is only $14.91. Packages of fifty foam coffee cups for 45¢. Plus the obligatory wealth of plastic utensils, and cocktail napkins in a palette of colors.

Whew! Enough already. Sysco is open weekdays only, from 8 A.M. to 4:30 P.M.

HEALTH FOOD AND VITAMINS

Central Co-Op
● 1835 12th Ave. E, Seattle; 329-1545

Thrifty Northwesterners hardly need Mr. C to tell them what a co-op is all about. Suffice it to say, by joining this Capitol Hill grocery, you can save big on natural, macrobiotic, and vegan foods, organic produce, cruelty-free cosmetics, vitamins, and bulk items: grains, nuts, cooking oils, environmentally-safe cleaners, and more. Although anyone may shop here, members also get a newsletter, free parking, a say in company business, potential profit-sharing, and extra special discount deals. Non-members get a 15% markup. Which would you choose?

Novices are allowed insider prices on their first visit, however. To join, there is a $5 fee, which gets you in for real. Then, there are $2 monthly payments into an equity account; once you've pumped in $60, which is refundable if you resign, that's it. The fees help cover the co-op's overhead costs. Members may choose to get deeper discounts by volunteering to work at the store for as little as three hours a week, or by serving on a committee. The Central Co-Op is open from 9 A.M. to 9 P.M. daily; stop in for full information.

Pilgrim's Nutrition
- 4217 University Way NE, Seattle; 634-3430

Located at the back of a health food cafe called Ricardo's Juice Bar (see the listing under "Restaurants—University District"), this shop is well-stocked with vitamins, dietary supplements, cosmetic products, herbals, and other natural products.

The prices here are competitive; in fact, Pilgrim strives to match the advertised prices from any other local store, or they'll beat them by 5%. They also offer several discount options; for starters, there is a 10% discount card available to all UW students and staff. And anyone at all may sign up for a savings card which gives you 10% off the prices of vitamins and body care products after $100 worth of purchases. The store is open Mondays through Fridays from 10 A.M. to 7 P.M., Saturdays from 10 A.M. to 6 P.M., and Sundays from 12 noon to 6 P.M.

Puget Consumers' Co-Op
- 716 N 34th St., Seattle; 632-6811
- 6522 Fremont Ave. N, Seattle; 789-7144
- 6504 20th Ave. NE, Seattle; 525-1450
- 6514 40th Ave. NE, Seattle; 526-7661
- 5041 Wilson Ave. S, Seattle; 723-2720
- 2749 California Ave. SW, Seattle; 937-8481

MR. CHEAP'S PICK
Health Food and Vitamins

✔ **Puget Consumers' Co-Op—** Become a member for next to nothing, and get insider prices on upscale, all-natural foods.

- 9121 Evergreen Way, Everett; 742-1240
- 10718 NE 68th St., Kirkland; 828-4621

Like the smaller Central Co-Op (above), PCC is a full-service supermarket focusing on natural foods and health care products. And, like any co-op, you can save money on these often-expensive items by becoming a member. Beginning as a buyers' club in 1960, this has grown into one of the largest such chains in the country, thus able to keep prices down on everything from local organic produce and vegan cheeses to vitamins and all-natural cosmetics. There are all kinds of bulk dispensers; not only the usual variety, but even bottled water that is devoid of flouride, chlorine, sodium, and lead!

Membership rates are also similar to the Central. There is an $8 initial fee to join, which starts up your member account; you pay $2 each month into the account, and when it reaches $60, you are fully vested. The $60 is refundable if you leave the co-op. Member prices, of course, start as soon as you sign up; non-members pay a 14% markup over shelf prices, but anyone may get a one-day member pass the first time they visit.

Unlike many other co-operatives, PCC does not offer chances to save further by seeking volunteer staff. Also noteworthy, member prices are offered to certain people without joining and paying the $60 investment. This includes senior citizens, disabled persons, and anyone on food stamps or Women-Infant Coupons. There is just a one-time, $2 fee for a special card. Store hours vary by location, but all are open daily.

MEAT AND FISH

B & E Meats

- 15021 Ambaum Blvd. SW, Burien; 243-1900
- 22501 Marine View Dr. S, Des Moines; 878-3700

For thirty years, these shops owned by two brothers have paired up to offer folks to the south some incredible deals on fresh and frozen meats. On a recent visit, Mr. C found fresh, slow-cured corned beef for $2.79 a pound; homemade bratwurst for $2.99 a pound; and spare ribs for $1.49 a pound.

B & E can also save you a ton of money if you've got a large freezer. They make up about half a dozen different package deals, which can get you 25 pounds of assorted meats for as little as $39.95. Even that basic option—the "Dollar Stretcher"—includes marinated steak, pork loin, spare ribs, and more. They also accept food stamps. These guys really give you true, old-fashioned family butcher service. Open Mondays through Saturdays from 9 A.M. to 6 P.M.

A few blocks up the street from the Burien branch, check out **Tony's Market** at 14800 Ambaum Boulevard SW (telephone 431-0716) for fresh produce and prepared foods.

Jones Bros. Meats

- 5404 22nd Ave. NW, Seattle; 783-1258

In the heart of Ballard Square, these fellas have been butchering prices for years. You may find high-quality New York strip steak as low as $4.49 a pound, or lean ground beef for $1.39 a pound. Smoked bacon for $2.69. And uniquely Ballardian items, like Swedish potato sausage for $3.89 a pound (hmm...Jones... funny, they don't *look* Swedish).

The store also specializes in large quantity meat packs, for those of you who like to hibernate with a deep-freezer and a TV remote. A thirty-pound assortment with pot roast, sausage, ribs, chicken, ground beef, and steaks goes for $69.90—do the math, kids, that's an average of $2.33 per pound. Open from 9 A.M. to 5:30 P.M., Mondays through Saturdays.

Meat Distributors, Inc.

- 715 Eighth St., Kirkland; 822-6895

Not a fancy name for a not-too-fancy operation but...if you want meat, they've got meat! Pork, poultry, and beef, by the steak or by the case, are available to the general public directly from this wholesale butcher. Stroll up to the tiny window, tell the person what you'd like, and walk away with a steal. Lean hamburger and boneless/skinless chicken breast are usually priced under $3 a pound; they also have kosher meats if you wish.

The nice folks here (don't worry about the men wandering through in the background, their white lab coats splattered with red...) prefer that Mr. C not quote actual prices, since they fluctuate so much; but they do want you to know that every ounce is of the freshest, highest quality. And let's face it, this is about as factory-direct as it gets, so the prices must be good.

Meat Distributors is only open on weekdays from 6 A.M. to 3:30 P.M.; you can go there directly, or place orders by phone for pickup or delivery. Ask for their current price list.

Mutual Fish Company

- 2335 Rainier Ave. S, Seattle; 328-5889

For some fifty years, the Yoshimura family has operated a seafood market that is "mutually" considered among the best in the city. By whom? By chefs from the best restaurants in the city. You can spot them here any morning, gathering to pick out their day's supply, hanging out, chatting with each other and with the market staff.

It's a small shop, spotlessly clean and bright, with everything very well organized. And yet the prices are super-reasonable on fresh local clams and oysters, Dungeness crabs, perhaps some Maine lobsters flown in, salmon of course, and even sushi. They can also pack and ship it all to just about anywhere. The store is open Mondays through Saturdays, from 8:30 A.M. to 5:30 P.M.

Oberto Sausage Factory Outlets

- 9891 Aurora Ave. N, Seattle; 525-5701
- 1715 Rainier Ave. S, Seattle; 322-7524
- 26136 104th Ave. SE, Kent; 852-1219

Hey gang, ya like beef jerky? Did you know it's 97% fat-free? Did you know it also comes in flavors like pork, peppered turkey, and teriyaki? It does here.

Yes, Oberto is pushing the envelope of jerkydom, and these folks are justly proud of their exotic creations. You can try them all here at their factory stores—as many free samples as you like. Just put an extra layer of adhesive on your dentures first.

The shops offer reduced prices on irregular pieces, especially if you buy in bulk; the regular price is $15 per pound, but one recent deal offered a half-pound bag for $5.79. And why not? You can't get 'em any fresher—and they'll certainly keep.

Oberto also sells a variety of regular sausages; on sale recently were their "Hot Links" smoked sausages, just $1.50 a pound. In supermarkets, these can cost over a dollar more. Again, all prices here decline as you buy in larger quantities. They also sell sausage sandwiches, corn dogs,

---

---

and the like. Open Mondays through Saturdays from 10 A.M. to 6 P.M.

Torino Meats

- 1101 Madison St., Seattle; 623-1530
- 1024 Andover Park E, Tukwila; 575-9353

Since 1932, the Torino family has been making high-quality meats and prepared foods. Their retail shops near Virginia-Mason and at their Southcenter factory will save you money compared to the prices these meats command in fancier groceries. A pound of their coppacola, for example, costs $9.25 here; at Larry's Markets, the same delicacy can cost as much as $14 a pound.

Ditto for their "Hunter's Sausage" ($4.95 a pound), cotto salami, pepperoni, and the like. These shops also make up homemade minestrone, sausage lasagna, sandwiches, and more—to eat in, to go, or to heat up at home. Hours vary by location.

PASTA

Remo Borracchini's Bakery

- 2307 Rainier Ave. S, Seattle; 325-1550

As described in the "Bakeries" section above, for all kinds of Italian specialty foods, it doesn't get any better than this. Borracchini's is more than just a bakery, though. It's a full-service cafe and deli; they sell wines, olive oils, and imported packaged foods; and they make their own delicious pastas.

Most of these are frozen, ready for you to cook up at home. A pound of tortellini—filled with cheese, meat, or spinach—goes for about $3.50. For something that's definitely un-susual, try chicken-filled ravioli, just $2.89 a pound. Same price for the homemade gnocchi. It's all made fresh on the premises, with no preservatives. The store is open from 6 A.M. to 7 P.M. daily. *Mangia.*

PRODUCE

Rising Sun Farms
- 6505 15th Ave. NE, Seattle; 524-9741

Seattle, for all its cosmopolitan airs, is never far away from its more rural fields; the city's many farm stands are proof, like this one in the northern U-District. In season, you may find whole watermelons for 19¢ a pound, blueberries for $1.29 a pint, or five pounds of Walla Walla onions for a buck. Plus raisins and pistachios, dried black beans, fresh syrups and preserves, and some basic grocery items.

Rising Sun also sells flowering plants and herbs, such as violets, geraniums, and basil. Open seven days from 8 A.M. to 7 P.M.

Sunshine Produce
- 1831 E Madison St., Seattle; 324-4977

Here's another example of a fine city farm stand, this one located in the Central District. Here, in season, Mr. C found great deals on Rainier cherries, pineapples, lettuce, canteloupe, sweet onions, and more. Plus grocery basics like local milk, eggs, and juices. Fill your fridge for a buck or two. Open daily.

Valley Harvest
- 743-B Rainier Ave. S, Renton; 277-0221

This Filipino-owned supermarket excels in fresh fruits and vegetables, nuts, and grains. The store itself is rather run-down, having obviously been at least one other supermarket in its time; but the selection is amazing, and what it lacks in sparkle is made up for by a sense of local community.

The large produce section offers (in season, of course) everything from whole watermelons to more exotic Asian vegetables. There is even a "99¢" area, mainly for items that are closer to full ripeness. A group of bulk grain bins are filled with beans, rice, dried pastas, sugars, nuts, and edible seeds. Another area is for low-fat and fat-free foods. There's even, for some reason, a section of Mexican specialty items. The market is open from 7 A.M. to 6:30 P.M. daily.

PET SUPPLIES

Superstores have made high-volume, low-priced pet food almost universal. Smaller neighborhood pet stores, forced to compete, tend to match these same prices. The difference, of course, is that you get far better service and advice at the local shop on the corner, as well as fresher foods, since they don't have the room to stock as many of those monstrous bags. Mr. C will list some of the superstores here for you, but first he does want to mention one independent that caught his eye:

Pet Food Mart
- 140 SW 148th Ave., Burien; 241-6902

This tiny shop in Burien Plaza is packed with a surprising selection of product lines and variety in foods, supplies, and accessories only (You supply the pet). Along with such biggies as Science Diet, Iams, and Nutro, you'll also find veterinarians' brands like Vet-Kem, Flea Flea, and Wysong. There are some bird and fish supplies too, though it's mostly dog and cat time here. As noted above, all prices are competitive with the superstore chains; though you'll also find lots of unique items the giants don't even know about. PFM must be doing something right, hanging on with such a small store for nearly ten years. Open weekdays from 10 A.M. to 6 P.M., and Saturdays from 10-5.

Petco

- Aurora Square, Seattle; 364-3473
- 4732 42nd Ave. SW, Seattle; 932-1986
- 3832 124th Ave. SE, Bellevue; 746-3011
- 2004 S 314th St., Federal Way; 941-8562
- 17171 Bothell Way NE, Lake Forest Park; 364-3567
- 15011 NE 24th St., Redmond; 746-2939

- 17124 Redmond Way, Redmond; 881-6539
- 10583 SE Carr Rd., Renton; 271-8347
- 17614 140th Ave. NE, Woodinville; 481-5312

Pet Pros

- 7216 Aurora Ave. N, Seattle; 527-8766
- 10304 Lake City Way NE, Seattle; 525-4038
- 10610 NE Eighth St., Bellevue; 455-3797
- 13619 Mukilteo Speedway, Lynnwood; 348-5555
- 22 Highway 99, Lynnwood; 742-3388
- 3213 S 38th St., Tac
- 22 Highway 99, Lynnwood; 742-3388oma; 474-9392

Petsmart

- 1211 S 20th St., Federal Way; 839-0399
- 18820 Highway 99, Lynnwood; 672-4422
- 9588 Ridgetop Blvd. NW, Silverdale; (360) 692-1514

FURNITURE AND BEDS

This chapter combines stores selling new and used furniture, for the home as well as the office. Many of your favorite retailers operate clearance centers, where you can find leftovers and slightly-damaged models at drastic savings—if you're patient. While Mr. C found good deals all around greater Seattle, the Southcenter area is truly Furniture Discount Central.

A caveat to the cash-conscious: Be very careful when you're shopping for any leather products. The quality of leather used in making sofas can vary widely, and this can determine how durable your sofa will be in the long run. If you see lots of very obvious flaws in the grain of the leather, think twice before buying.

HOME FURNITURE—NEW

Abodio Clearance Center

● 790 Andover Park E, Tukwila; 575-2041

Trendy folks may know Abodio from its stores in Bellevue, Lynnwood, and other suburbs; the store carries those gleaming white, ultra-modern Scandinavian looks for bedrooms, kids' rooms, dens and in-home offices. There are some more traditional designs as well. Anyway, at the rear of their Southcenter store, you'll find Abodio's "Bargain Rack" of closeouts, floor models, and slightly damaged items at big savings.

It's a mix of furniture and household furnishings, mostly in good condition. On his visit, Mr. C found white Adirondack chairs, reduced from an original $119 each to $79, and again to $49; a queen-size white rail bed frame, $200 off at $399; same savings, same price on a plush white Bauhaus easy chair. And a natural-finish maple dresser was discounted from $699 to $499.

On the decorating front, lots of discontinued housewares were all 50% off—towel bars, shower curtains, colorful linen-woven placemats, and the like. Leaded crystal wine stems were reduced from $6 apiece to $3, and a 16-piece Wachterbach ceramic dinnerware set was marked from $59.95 down to $29.98.

There's usually a lot of fun stuff to browse through. Open daily from 10 A.M. to 7 P.M., Saturdays 'til 6, and Sundays from 12-5 P.M.

Alternative Futon Company

● 400 Minor Ave., Seattle; 979-7832

According to George Erroude, there's no magic to making that *chic* home furnishing, the futon mattress. "Hey, it's just like making a sandwich," he shrugs. Yet, he says, many futon manufacturers foster the illusion that these are exotic creations, and must therefore be expensive.

George's "alternative" is to make his own futons, as well as the frames, and sell them from his small Eastlake factory/shop himself. By making a limited range of styles, he and a few

assistants can "mass produce" enough sofas and beds to charge just over what most department stores *pay* for their versions—which they then mark up. He's been here for over fifteen years; must know what he's doing.

Sawdust and cotton batting drift across the floor of this industrial building. Lumber sits on sawhorses, waiting to be cut. Call it a no-frills boutique, or a high school wood shop all grown up; the ultimate in factory-direct. Wander around and pick out the elements: Choose the thickness of your mattress, and the type of frame. George uses no cheap pine, period; only solid oak and mahogany spoken here.

A tri-fold frame with a queen-size mattress costs—get ready—$139. A bi-fold sofa frame and futon costs $325, while a Mission-style platform bed and futon go for $350. Those are your basic options, cash and carry (delivery is available, for a fee). It all comes with a lifetime guarantee. Believe it! AFC is open weekdays from 11 A.M. to 8 P.M., Saturdays from 11 A.M. to 6 P.M., and Sundays from 12-5 P.M.

A-1 Furniture

● 1521 Second Ave., Seattle; 292-2121

What's odd about bargain-hunting at A-1 Furniture is that it doesn't *look* like a discount store. It's filled with fine, new furniture like any showroom. The list price is marked on each piece, and if you didn't already know what Mr. C's about to tell you, you might never give this place a try. The prices posted are *not* what you pay—in fact, you'll generally pay about half of what's on the tag. Great prices for names like Ther-a-pedic, Bassett, Douglas, Stanton Industries, Allied Furniture, and Michels and Company.

So, now that you won't be intimidated by large, ferocious numbers, take note of what Mr. C found: a sofa and matching love seat ($699 for the pair, down from $1,400), a Posturizer mattress and box spring ($250, down from $500), and kitchen table set with six chairs ($300, down from $600). A-1 is open Mondays through Saturdays, from 9 A.M. to 6 P.M.

B & D Unfinished Furniture
- 4449 35th Ave. SW, Seattle; 932-5751
- 826 S Third St., Renton; 271-5751

Actually, these two stores are independently owned; they used to be related, but both still carry a similar stock of your basic pine bookcases, bar stools, dressers, mirrors, and entertainment centers. Plenty of juvenile furniture, too. Everything here is solid wood; some pieces are in oak, and some are already stained. A variety of finishes may be added for an additional charge. Needless to say, you can also do this yourself, and really save a bundle. Both stores are closed Sundays.

Bald Bob's Mattress Outlet
- 13310 NE Bellevue-Redmond Rd., Bellevue; 643-7378
- 6500 Evergreen Way, Everett; 513-9114
- 17150 162nd St. SE, Monroe; 794-1137
- 15606 NE Wood-Duvall Rd., Woodinville; 486-1967

Yes, he really is. Low overhead costs and low-pressure salespeople make this a fine place for bedding bargains, whether you're looking for traditional mattresses or futon styles. Everything here is new and current, with a mix of major and lesser-known brands. Simmons and Serta are here, for example; but Englander queen-size sets start as low as $199. Many of these are priced at almost half of the suggested retail. Even better deals may await you among overstock sets, mattresses with incorrect labels, leftovers from wrong orders, and the like.

You'll find similar deals on futons and handsome, finished frames; a solid oak bi-fold glider frame was seen for $240. Futons themselves come in a good variety of thicknesses, and there is a wealth of printed covers in unusual designs for you to choose from. The atmosphere itself is no-frills, but the big place is nice and tidy. And, even at bottom-line prices, most of the mattresses carry a 20-year warranty. Open seven days a week.

Classic Home Furnishings Clearance Center
- 6415 32nd Ave. NW, Seattle; 783-1381

Not far from the rah-ther fancy Market Street store of the same name, Classic Home's clearance outlet is two rooms of closeout bargains in the otherwise sleepy Ballard neighborhood of Sunset Hill.

Although the store mainly deals in country and traditional looks, these are not always without some cute twists. Dining chairs with high backs in the shape of fish, for example. Among the items seen here recently were a "Wall-Hugger" leather recliner by Bradington-Young; with a list price of $1,520, it was first tagged at $1,220, and here reduced further to $922. A maple side table was marked from $475 down to $288, and a Shaker hutch from $2,000 to $899.

There are also lots of decorative pieces, like a copper wall pot for $9; framed mallard prints reduced from $118 to $98; woven couch throws for $18; and cane newspaper baskets for $12. All sales here are "as is" and final. The store is only open on Saturdays, from 11 A.M. to 5 P.M.

Crown Diamond Mattresses
- 1230 First Ave. S, Seattle; 623-0272

When you think about "factory direct," this is exactly the kind of store you're picturing. From a large warehouse just south of the Kingdome, Crown Diamond makes and sells mattresses for homes, hotels, and other purposes. A small showroom in the front displays samples of the Crown line, which even includes bedding custom made for boats and RVs. Most of their business is wholesale, but you can walk in off the street and buy the same products at just 15% above wholesale prices.

Everything sold here is first-quality, with manufacturer's warranties of up to 15 years. Buy in sets, or individual pieces. These folks make something for every budget level; full-size sets can cost as little as $185. A fancier 480-coil queen set goes for $525—easily a few hundred bucks less than the identical Sealy Posturepedic set.

This family business has been around for over fifty years. That's a lot of good sleep. The showroom is open weekdays from 8:30 to 5 P.M., and Saturdays from 10-4.

Dania Furniture Clearance Center

• 1251 Andover Park W, Tukwila; 575-1918

With showrooms throughout the Northwest, Dania is well-known for its upscale collections mainly focusing on the contemporary—in Danish teak, Italian leather, and Scandinavian white. Their Southcenter store, in addition to regular retail, also houses Dania's clearance center.

Here, Mr. C found lots of choices, although many were scratched or damaged. Many were simply discontinued or one-of-a-kind odd pieces. A gorgeous cherry wood oval dining table was reduced from $1,200 to $1,075. It had no damage; it also had no chairs. A dark mahogany "pencil post" queen-size bed frame, with a couple of minor scuffs, was $150 off at $549. And a single side chair, in Danish teak with a beige linen seat, was reduced from $229 to $169. All sales are final. Open seven days a week.

Denny's Concepts in Wood

• 1915 Rainier Ave. S, Seattle; 328-1915
• 5510-A Sixth Ave., Tacoma; 756-0998

Here's another store that primarily sells unfinished, solid wood furniture. Like B & D (above), the diverse selection leans mostly toward pine, with some oak mixed in. Denny's also has a number of catalogs, if you want to order something you don't see; and, though nothing is made in the store, they can arrange to have custom orders made to your specifications. Closed Sundays.

Discount Waterbeds

• 11010 NE Third Pl., Bellevue; 455-4314

It's tricky to find this little place, one of those older commercially-zoned houses in the heart of downtown Bellevue (hint: Head south on 111th Avenue, past NE Fourth). Yet, somehow, these friendly, laid-back guys have been here since 1976, not only offering great prices on waterbeds by Simmons, Boyd, and Somma (they're one of the largest Somma dealers in the Northwest, with prices $50 to $100 below major stores); but they also design and build their own uniquely functional platforms and related furniture.

Basic twin-size waterbeds, with platforms, start as low as $199; a special feature are mattresses with traditional exteriors, so that standard sheets will fit them. More interesting yet, though are the clever touches like telescoping, extra-deep drawers underneath, and headboards with popout snack trays. These folks really know what they're doing, and it's worth the fumbling around to find them. Open seven days a week, including weeknights 'til 8 P.M.

Don Willis Furniture

• 10516 Lake City Way NE, Seattle; 524-9944

Don Willis claims to offer Seattle's largest selection of unfinished furniture, and you just may believe it when you see this place. Three—count 'em—three floors are filled with both finished and unfinished pieces for indoors and out. It's a classy-looking, spacious store, and yet you can find some real bargains here. Mr. C fell in love with a Royola Pacific cherry-finish kitchen table with four chairs, priced at $259; a natural-finish version with painted white trim was $249.

Lots of patio furniture here too, which you'll see out front even before you enter the store. Chances are, whatever you're looking for, they've got: dressers, desks, butcher-block tables, bedframes, and the ubiquitous bookshelves. Much of the furniture is made locally, and most items carry a ten-year warranty. They can even create pieces from your own design. Open seven days a week, including weeknights until 8 P.M.

Elegant Furniture
- 15625 NE Eighth St., Bellevue; 747-6839

Next door to longtime electronics discounter Lee's Video-Audio-Fax (see the listing under "Electronics"), owner Lee Tayebi has opened a similar operation for highbrow, classically-styled European furniture. These are the sort of pieces that belong in large, tastefully appointed rooms, perhaps with a butler hovering just outside. Yet, thanks to volume purchasing, Lee can offer even this snooty seating at significant discounts off retail prices.

The small store displays half a dozen different ensembles, sold in sets or by individual piece. Mr. C saw an Italian sofa, in a white finish with gold trim and satin fabric, reduced from a retail price of $2,399 to $1,679. The matching loveseat was reduced from $1,999 to $1,399; a side chair from $1,249 to $879. And there are similar setups for French and British period looks as well, in mahogany, cherry, and other solid woods; they have dining tables and bedroom sets too.

There's little else in the Seattle area to compare this store with; suffice it to say, if this is your taste, you won't often find anyone taking the discount approach. It's located across from the Crossroads Shopping Center; open from 11 A.M. to 5 P.M., Mondays through Saturdays.

Everrest Mattress
- 1907 15th Ave. W, Seattle; 284-9531
- 21101 Highway 99, Lynnwood; 776-8180

"We Are the Factory," says Everrest, in a touching reminiscence of that all-star rock 'n roll anthem. Well, no, they've got nothing to do with Stevie Wonder, but you can have a brighter day when you wake up on a mattress that cost you half of department store

prices. That's because, for almost fifty years, this family business has made their own bedding—with prices that start as low as $99 *per set.* Of course, that's for your basic, it's-better-than-the-floor ensemble, twin-size; but even their top-grade "Elite" mattress and boxspring, in king-size, is only $459—and it carries a 20-year warranty. 'Nuff said. Both stores are open seven days a week, and offer free delivery/removal (and pillows!) with purchases over $165.

Futon Factory
- 13555 Aurora Ave. N, Seattle; 367-5575

Here's another small, personally owned-and-operated shop where they make their own futons—and make a nice departure from the hard-sell chain stores. Jeff and Tasha O'Day really do make their own futons; you can watch them climb over the stacks of rolled-up mattresses in this tiny shop. They don't make the frames, but they get wholesale rates on these, and can give you some good deals overall.

A tri-fold frame with a full-size futon (8" thick, not 6", as in many other stores) sells here for $199 complete with a solid-color mattress cover. All futons carry a two-year warranty, while frame warranties range from 2-4 years. Many designs have matching loveseats, coffee tables, etc. as well.

Occasional factory-seconds sales offer even better bargains, like oak gliders with futons from $299; watch newspapers for special advertisements. Closed Wednesdays.

Hardwick and Sons, Inc.
- 4214 Roosevelt Way NE, Seattle; 632-1203

Hardwick, a neighborhood hardware store and then some, also sells a combination of new, used, and unfinished furniture—all of it perfect for college dorm or first-apartment furnishing.

A five-foot tall, unfinished pine bookcase was seen here for $58.40. Used, solid mahogany headboards were just $39.95—a real deal. There are also a few children's items, rocking chairs and such, similarly priced. Everything is all jumbled together in a large storage area just off the main hardware room, to your right as you enter the store. Talk about no-frills shopping. Plan on taking some time to look everything over; there's a lot to see, some of which is tough to get at—but your hunt may reveal a treasure. Hardwick and Sons is open Tuesdays through Saturdays, from 9 A.M. to 6 P.M.

J.C. Penney Furniture Warehouse
- 17200 Southcenter Pkwy., Tukwila; 575-4792

Need Mr. C tell you about the illustrious world of J.C. Penney? *Not.* But you may want to check out their clearance center, filled with some decent deals for the home. A recent sale offered King Koil full-size mattresses and boxsprings for $139.50 per piece. Mr. C also found a Bassett "Cherry Hill" traditional-style sofa, a store return, selling for $539—$350 off its original price. And a leather easy chair by Lane, a special order that

was cancelled, was thus reduced from $949 to $569.

Plus headboards, desks, lamps, framed prints, and more. Some items are slightly damaged (and some are really gone), but there's a lot to see. Open Mondays through Saturdays from 9:30 A.M. to 5:30 P.M., and Sundays 11 A.M. to 5 P.M.

Krause's Sofa Factory
- 3930 196th St. SW, Lynnwood; 775-6127
- 2233 NE Bellevue-Redmond Rd., Redmond; 641-9573
- 2410 84th St. S, Tacoma; 588-1108
- 17740 Southcenter Pkwy., Tukwila; 575-1984

Take a seat. You'll have to wait a bit to get a sofa or chair from Krause's, but that's because everything here is made to order. They offer a choice of about one thousand different upholstery styles, including Ralph Lauren and Laura Ashley-imitation prints. Unfortunately, there's even more of a wait on the more tasteful and popular fabrics.

The deals you can end up with, however, are often worth the wait (it can take about a month for orders to arrive from Krause's manufacturer in California). The frames have a lifetime guarantee, and you can even save a bit more when the store holds frequent sales. Mr. C found a handsome leather sofa for $999, reduced from an original $1349; fabric-upholstered sofas run about $600, and chairs, about $349. They're very comfortable, too.

Many other kinds of items are available here to finish outfitting any room, such as coffee tables and lamps. These are not factory-direct, though, and the prices show it. Open daily.

Nationwide Warehouse & Storage
- 2525 W Casino Rd., Everett; 353-9494
- 3702 S Pine St., Tacoma; 472-9958
- 1004 Andover Park E, Tukwila; 575-1234

As the name suggests, Nationwide has stores all over the country—and it liquidates furniture and bedding for manufacturers all over the country.

The ever-changing stock is mostly in lower- and mid-grade quality—this is the sort of place where you can get a mattress for $18 (twin, on sale). Of course, they have better grades, but even their top-of-the-line pillowtop king mattress is only $149! It comes with a 25-year limited warranty.

In furniture, you may find a queen-size canopy bed frame, in "gunmetal" iron, for $148; a competitor's ad was taped to the wall beside it, listing the same bed for $398. And this is one of those hallowed places for deals like a sofa, loveseat, coffee table, and two end tables, all for $699 complete. The foam-filled padding may be a bit firm for your liking, but if you're looking to set up a house quickly and cheaply, this is it.

In fact, for an extra fee, you can have any item delivered the day you buy it. Free layaway is also available. Nationwide is open Mondays, Tuesdays, and Fridays from 10 A.M. to 8 P.M.; Saturdays from 10-6, and Sundays 12-6. Closed Wednesdays and Thursdays.

Oak Barn
- 17600 W Valley Hwy., Tukwila; 251-9345

Here's another of the many large furniture dealers in the Southcenter area. True to its name, Oak Barn sells (mostly) solid oak furniture for every room in the house, at competitive prices; but the rear third of their gigantic warehouse is also their clearance center, where you can snap up some fine deals.

Some of these pieces are damaged, and all are sold "as is." Mr. C found things like a Mission-style sofa, with an original retail price of $2,400, and a broken leg; it was now selling for $599. Fix it up yourself, or have the Oak Barn staff do it, and you *still* come out way ahead! Other bargains included an oak dresser reduced from $1,320 to $540, with a matching three-way mirror for $220; these were simply "last models." Same reason for a cherry roll-top writing desk being reduced from $1,799 to $899.

Mr. C also saw some Spring Air mattress and boxsprings, king-size, for $499 a set. And there are enough chairs, from rockers to dining table orphans, to seat the next Pacific Rim trade conference. Speaking of which, the staff here are sometimes willing to negotiate on clearance items. Open from 10 A.M. to 8 P.M. weekdays, until 7 P.M. Saturdays, and Sundays from 11 A.M. to 6 P.M.

Oak Warehouse
- 4815 California Ave. SW, Seattle; 933-0622

Owner Jeff Moffat works the lines nationwide to scoop up closeouts on furnishings for the bedroom, bathroom, living room, and dining room. Then, he packs them all into his deceptively small West Seattle store. Chairs hang from the ceiling, towel racks are mounted on the walls, and aisles are narrow, but do poke around.

OW carries a mix of solid wood and wood veneer stock. A solid oak roll-top desk, with a bit of scuffing, was on sale recently, "as is" for only $588 (Mr. C gazed longingly at this one for some time). An oak wardrobe was another hot sale item, reduced from $1,099 to $689. And a round, drop-leaf kitchen table, with two Windsor chairs, was just $249.

Plus entire bedroom ensembles, china cabinets, chairs and stools, mirrors, coatracks, shelves, and anything else you can imagine. Many items can also be specially ordered in configurations to suit your needs. OW also does a considerable business in mattresses and boxsprings, with sets available in three grades of firmness starting from $99 for a twin set. Delivery and removal of your old bed is free within West Seattle, extra beyond the area. Oak Warehouse is closed Wednesdays.

Oriental Furniture Warehouse
- 1111 Elliott Ave. W, Seattle; 286-3139

See the listing under "Home Furnishings."

Sansaco
- 5950 S 180th St., Tukwila; 575-0811

For over ten years, this family-run business has quietly been a high-volume, low-overhead, furniture heaven. They occupy a vast 35,000 square-foot warehouse in the heart of the Southcenter furniture district, filled with current, high-quality lines from Lexington, Bassett, Pulaski, and many other major and lesser brands. As one salesman put it, "We can sell you a dresser for $86, or for $3,000," and both would be good prices for the quality level.

Dining room ensembles are one specialty. All are configured in sets of nine pieces, complete with table, side chairs, and a matching china cabinet (though you may purchase by the piece). These start around $1,500; a handsome contemporary set in white-washed birch, which could cost up to $3,600 in department stores, goes for $3,197 here every day. Bedroom sets reach from one end of the warehouse to the other. These include mattresses from Englander, Simmons, and Restonic. Couches range from traditional wood-frames to contemporary leather.

Amazingly, although they can order anything directly from the factories, Sansaco has nearly every item in stock for you to take away instantly (delivery is available for a fee). "Cash-and-carry" keeps prices low; so does the fact that all sales are final. Lack of advertising is another cost-cutter—they don't even print up business cards! The store is located halfway along a block of warehouses and loading docks; ignore the "Private Road" signs and work your way in among the trucks. Sansaco is closed Wednesdays; otherwise, hours are from 10 A.M. to 8 P.M., daily, Saturdays from 10-6, and Sundays from 11-5.

The Seattle Design Center
- 5701 Sixth Ave. S, Seattle; 762-1200 or (800) 497-7997

Down in the industrial Georgetown area, the Seattle Design Center is where licensed interior designers get their goods. Until recently, they were the only ones allowed to tread this hallowed ground. It is now open, albeit for very limited hours, to the rest of us common folk.

Once on the inside, you'll find sixty showrooms featuring the latest looks in furniture, lighting, floor and wall coverings, decorative art pieces, and more—at prices that are about 20% off retail. Some 1,500 product lines are represented here, including McGuire, Karastan, Baker, Thomasville, Bassett, and Umphred. Mr. C isn't going to delude you into thinking that *anything* here is necessarily *budget*-priced; it's all high-end, high-quality home furnishings.

Basically, shopping here entitles you to the same discount that the interior design trade gets. Not good enough, you say? You want Mr. C to work harder for you? No problem. SDC also has a "Samples" room, where the dealers sell off their floor models at further savings of 40% to 60% off retail. And *all* of the lines carried here make their way to the samples room at one time or another. Obviously, you can't custom order samples; what you see is what you get. But that can be some fine items at substantial savings.

Cheap? No way. Less expensive than department stores and boutiques? Absolutely. The Seattle Design Center is only open to the public from 1-5 P.M., Mondays through Fridays. Your first visit will include a brief orientation to explain their purchasing system, in which professional designers do the ordering for you. Call the SDC for further details.

Sleep-Aire Mattress Company
- 6110 Roosevelt Way NE, Seattle; 523-3702

This locally based, family-owned company has been serving the Puget Sound area since 1952. Their brand-new merchandise can be purchased at 30% off retail prices here at Sleep-Aire factory's retail shop. In addition to mattresses, sleep-sofas, standard sofas and chairs are available too; these can even be custom-ordered at the same prices.

While visiting, Mr. C found an orthopedic queen-size mattress and boxspring set, with a fifteen-year warranty, for an impressive $399. A full-size sleeper sofa, with an all-wood frame, also looked especially good at $499. Free local delivery is available, with no minimum purchase. Sleep-Aire's hours are Mondays and Fridays, from 9:30 A.M. to 9 P.M.; Tuesdays, Wednesdays and Thursdays until 6 P.M., and Sundays from noon to 5 P.M.

Sleep King
- 8214 Greenwood Ave. N, Seattle; 782-3131

You sure won't lose any sleep over the prices at this discount mattress center. Sleep King actually makes its mattresses right there in its Greenwood store (well, the assembling takes place at their warehouse, but y'know, it's close enough).

Some of the deals Mr. C noted were a queen-size mattress and boxspring set for $199, while a complete day bed set was seen for $350. For those restless sleepers who want extra back support, Sleep King's "Ultra Rest Supreme" premium sleep system (you'll *need* a rest after saying that a few times) is available at just $250 for a full-size set, $330 for a queen set, and $430 in king. Local delivery is free with a purchase of $150 or more. Stop by any day of the week between 9 A.M. to 5 P.M., and from noon to 5 P.M. Sundays.

Underhill's Fine Wood Furniture
- 17034 Aurora Ave. N, Seattle; 364-4226
- 6020 Evergreen Way, Everett; 355-1960

The best deals at Underhill's are located underground—that is, in the bargain basement. Overstocks, discontinued items, and floor models can be found here, all reasonably priced and most in excellent condition.

Underhill's basement is not some dusty, piled-up hodgepodge of various pieces. It's clean, spacious, organized, and very easy to browse. Mr. C found a floral Bassett love seat marked down from $729 to $639, and a solid maple table with four chairs (assembly required) marked

down from $349 to $289. Bunk beds are always on sale here—for $349, you can buy one complete with basic mattresses. Underhill deals mostly in solid wood, with styles ranging from traditional to country, plus a few contemporary pieces mixed in.

When you've graduated from the first-apartment decorating mode, Underhill's is an easy step up—better quality, and with these savings, actually affordable. Open from 9:30 A.M. to 9 P.M. (8 P.M. at the Everett store) Mondays through Fridays, 'til 6 P.M. Saturdays, and from 11 A.M. to 5 P.M. Sundays.

United Buy & Sell Furniture
- 3849 First Ave. S, Seattle; 624-1292
- 4205 Wheaton Way, Bremerton; (360) 792-9366
- 133 128th St. SW, Everett; 290-7771
- 16929 Highway 99, Lynnwood; 745-2660
- 2902 NE Sunset Blvd., Renton; 227-9787

- 5950 N Ninth St., Tacoma; 565-8188
- 8726 S Tacoma Way, Tacoma; 581-2101

If this sounds like a trade-in kinda place, it did begin that way in Canada years ago. Nowadays though, United is a chain of vast showrooms filled with brand-new, first-quality home furniture and bedding. They "buy it by the boxcar" and thus can sell it at high-volume/low profit margin prices. UBS carries plenty of name brands, like Bassett, Shaw, Ashley, King Koil, and more, in what looks like a sea of sofas, chairs, and tables.

A Bassett motion recliner chair, list priced at $525, sells here for $349; a fashionable linen-covered couch by Gaines is reduced from $450 to $299, while a matching love-seat is $269. There are some leather looks, and plenty of contemporary styles. In bedding, Mr. C saw a pillow-topped king-size Englander "Posture Ultimate" set for $629, about half of the suggested retail price. Plus dinette tables and chairs, bookcases, computer furniture, even lamps and framed prints to complete any room.

The salespeople here don't work on commission, reducing the hard-sell as well as the prices. Store hours vary; the Seattle branch is open Mondays through Fridays from 10 A.M. to 9 P.M., Saturdays from 9-6, and closed on Sundays.

HOME FURNITURE—USED

Antique Liquidators

- 503 Westlake Ave. N, Seattle; 623-2740

Mr. C doesn't cover the subject of antiques, since these are unique items whose prices depend upon factors like rarity and age; you can't "comparison shop" a Louis XVI *armoire*. But one of Mr. C's experts told him he just had to see this place anyway, and it certainly deserves at least a mention.

Three floors of this huge industrial building near Lake Union are filled with furnishings of every shape, size, era, and quality; it's really a high-volume wholesaler for used furniture dealers throughout the Northwest. You can poke around too—they'll sell to anybody, and they're even willing to negotiate. Don't forget to check out the bargain basement. Open Mondays through Saturdays from 9:30 A.M. to 5:30 P.M., and Sundays from 12 noon to 5 P.M.

Cort Furniture Clearance Center

- 1230 Andover Park E, Tukwila; 575-4119

This national company leases basic furniture out to people who only need short-term furnishings; when it's no longer deemed lease-worthy, Cort sells it off from the rear of their Southcenter showroom. It's a mix of home and office stuff, from nice to merely functional, often at about half the initial prices.

One sofa Mr. C liked, with a "confetti" style linen weave, would have originally sold for $570; here, it was still in decent shape for $240. A cherry wood dining table, with four matching chairs, was reduced from a retail value of $1,100 to $550. And there are rows of cabinets, side tables, lamps, and even mattresses. Needless to say, all sales are "as is"; but everything has been cleaned and inspected.

On the office side, a mahogany secretary's desk with return was $1,770 new; here, it was $998. A nice drafting table was seen for $60, less than half its retail value. And all kinds of partition panels started from $80 per section.

Since leasing is their lifeblood, Cort will even lease out its used office furniture—perfect for those fly-by-night telemarketing scam operations (just kidding, folks, don't try this at home). And they do offer layaway plans on all used furniture. Open seven days a week.

Decorative Interiors
- 1919-A 120th Ave. NE, Bellevue; 641-1917

Here's another place that makes much of its profit from leasing, then sells off the furniture that comes back. Only in this case, you'd *never know it*. Reg and Mary Jo Lafaye buy high-quality furniture and lease it out to model homes. But such displays are changing all the time, and when pieces come back, it's time to liquidate. They've already made a portion of their money back, so they can afford to sell these barely-used goods for hundreds of dollars off.

Decorative Interiors only deals in solid wood furniture, mostly cherry; they buy traditional styles directly from manufacturers in North Carolina, such as Kincaid, Stanley, and Jamestown Heritage. Make no mistake, this is still pricey stuff: A solid cherry dining table with a pewter base and four matching chairs was reduced from $2,400 to $1,685. A Queen Anne period wingback chair, originally $695, was on sale for $295. And Mr. C was shown a gorgeous queen-size sleigh bed in wild black cherry, originally retailing for $985; here, it was available for $685.

Different styles, from Shaker dressers to more contemporary leather couches, also come and go; along with lamps, pictures, and other accent pieces. Further, with their factory connections, DI can even order new items for you—in your choice of finish, upholstery, whatever—at insider prices. But even their liquidation goods are warrantied for one year against any damages that may have gone unnoticed.

There is always a large selection in this cavernous warehouse. Purchases are cash (or credit cards) and carry. Decorative Interiors is only open Saturdays from 10 A.M. to 5 P.M., Sundays from 12 to 4 P.M., and by appointment; they also have a play area for the kiddies while you browse.

Dixon's Used Furniture
- 1528 12th Ave. E, Seattle; 322-0553

Dixon's sells used furniture in good condition. Lots of couches, tables and chairs fill the large, open, showroom up front. When Mr. C visited, he noted a shaker-style bedroom set with headboard, dresser, mirror, two nightstands, and a chest of drawers, all for $397. That's not bad, but get this—it was on sale that day for $299.95. Individual pieces like a cherry-wood china cabinet ($375), queen-size sofa bed ($299) and 30" x 60" desk ($69.95) caught Mr. C's eye. There are also a few new items here.

But wait, there's more. For really big savings, head back to the "Grunge Grotto," where a heap of slightly bruised tables, chairs, sofas, etc. awaits you. Want to furnish your entire living room for a hundred dollars? Just buy a comfy loveseat ($69) and an easy chair ($29) here, go pick up a used book somewhere with your remaining two bucks, and then sit at home and enjoy your worldly possessions.

Dixon's is open from 10 A.M. to 6 P.M. Mondays through Thursdays and Saturdays, 'til 8 P.M. Fridays, and from noon to 6 P.M. Sundays.

Foryu Furnishings

- 2299-A 140th Ave. NE, Bellevue; 865-9886

Okay, you all know about consignment clothing stores, where you can get used-but-like-new designer clothing for a song. Well, here's the same idea in furniture. Located in the Evans Plaza shopping center, this space might have been just another record store or bike boutique; instead, its two large rooms are filled with high-quality furnishings being sold for private owners.

You never know what you'll find, but Mr. C's visit revealed a French Provincial chair and ottoman for $579; Wassily chairs, easily $400 or $500 new, were just $195; and an Ethan Allen solid cherry entertainment center, once over $1,000, was seen for $549. Plus framed art prints, dishware, and occasional pieces.

Basically, everything here costs about half of its original price. And it's all in good shape, or the folks here won't take it in. Needless to say, you can arrange to sell your own items here as well; profits are split with the store, which has quietly made a name for itself for over five years now. Open Mondays through Saturdays from 10 A.M. to 6 P.M.

Pike Place Furniture

- 2200 Western Ave., Seattle; 441-0531

Just north of the Pike Place Market is the clearance center for Continental Furniture, a local leasing chain. Here, you can get deals on furnishings that have been used, sometimes heavily; but most of the stock is in good shape. They carry a mix of big names and lesser brands. Find used dressers from $49, lamps for half of their original prices, sofas, bedding, and all the rest.

Frequently, there are new pieces mixed in as well; Mr. C saw a Natuzzi leather chair, with a suggested retail of $1,000, selling here for $699. Two large floors offer plenty of selection, with new items coming in regularly. All sales are "as is" and final. Open daily from 9:30 A.M. to 5:30 P.M., Sundays from 12-4:30 P.M.

ReRuns Consignment

- 413 15th Ave. E, Seattle; 329-0549

See the listing under "Clothing—Used."

St. Vincent de Paul Retail Stores

- 17712 15th Ave. NE, Seattle; 364-1492
- 9835 16th Ave. SW, Seattle; 763-2130
- 13445 First Ave. S, Burien; 243-6370
- 2825 NE Sunset Blvd., Renton; 226-9426

See the listing under "Clothing—Used."

Spencer & Company

- 7216 Greenwood Ave. N, Seattle; 781-1378

Spencer aims to make antiques affordable, and it succeeds; but it also puts vintage jewelry and interesting odds and ends within a frugal shopper's reach. You will have to wind your way through a maze of beautiful furniture, many of which have further items displayed on top of them, but it's worth taking the time. Most things you'll find here are marked down 20% below list price, and the back room and bargain basement have even bigger savings.

Since antiques are collectibles, and cannot be comparison-shopped, Mr. C doesn't try to cover this territory; however, in the bargain basement, he did see a maple high-chair for $35, and a solid mahogany upholstered armchair for $45. Other noteworthy items were a Hobé bracelet and earring set seen for $75 (its list price would be $165), and a 19th-century Echt cobalt dinner set, containing eight dinner plates and fruit bowls, with twelve cups and saucers, all for $450.

The back thrift room contains far less expensive items, like salt and pepper shaker sets for $2, screwdrivers and hammers for $2, embroidered dresser scarves for a dollar, and mix 'n match cups and saucers, $1 each piece. Other cheap stuff here includes random clothing buttons, neatly arranged in a tiny set of drawers. Prices start at 10 cents.

Spencer's staff is very friendly and knowledgeable, and make shopping here a pleasure. Drop by between noon and 6 P.M. Wednesdays through Sundays.

Vintage Voola
• 512 E Pike St., Seattle; 324-2808
See the listing under "Clothing—Used."

OFFICE FURNITURE—NEW AND USED

Baywood Design
• 4216 Sixth Ave. NW, Seattle; 783-2613
Actually at the corner of 42nd Street and Leary Way, this commercial and residential design firm has turned its large garage space into a liquidation warehouse for factory seconds in office furniture. Some are slightly nicked and scuffed; often, it's only the carton that has been damaged. Some items require assembly (which the nice folks at this family business do for you). All of it is sold at 40% to 70% below retail prices.

Mr. C wandered around the cramped quarters and found a walnut credenza, originally meant to sell at $930, going for just $349. At that price, what's a side scratch here or there? A leather sofa, intended for some big-wig's suite, was reduced from $1,999 to $800. Other items included file cabinets ($48 and up), drafting tables, computer furniture, and more. New shipments come in every two weeks! Good place for you home-office entrepreneurial types to check out. Open weekdays from 8 A.M. to 5 P.M.

Budget Office Furniture
• 2244 First Ave. S, Seattle; 447-0393
Thrifty Office Furniture
• 2233 First Ave. S, Seattle; 622-6226
With names like these, this pair of stores naturally caught Mr. C's eye. Owned by the same company and located across the street from each other, one sells brand-new office furnishings, while the other sells "recycled" ones. Let's start there.

In our present economy, many companies are downsizing—while others are thriving and redecorating. Whatever the reason, when offices get rid of their old, perfectly good furniture, Thrifty snatches it up and resells it at half the price of new. The store itself ain't pretty—they sure don't put much money into decorating the place—but that's okay in Mr. C's book. Helps keep the prices low.

Among the big selection, Mr. C found a coffee table for $100, and a great looking hardwood desk for $350. Upstairs in the attic, they have a virtual ocean of office chairs: all types, all sizes, and all at low prices. You can get a simple metal task chair for $20, move up to one with arm rests for $49.50, or a fancier secretary's chair with caster wheels for $69.95. A musty basement, meanwhile, is filled with all the items that have definitely seen better days. These are *super* cheap.

Too shabby for your office? Back across the street, you can find good deals on new furniture at Budget. Find a stylish executive's chair in oak and cushioned cloth, list priced at $284, selling for $190; a Euromodern L-shaped desk by Hon with a laminated top, reduced from $920 to $630; plus modular panels and computer furniture and accessories. All of these are current season designs.

Both stores are open from 8:30 A.M. to 5:30 P.M. Mondays through Fridays, and Saturdays from 11 A.M. to 4 P.M. Closed Sundays.

Ducky's Office Furniture
• 1111 Mercer St., Seattle; 623-7777
Not only has this got to be the king

MR. CHEAP'S PICKS
Office Furniture

✔ **Budget/Thrifty Office Furniture**—Discounted new, dirt-cheap used, right across the street from each other.

✔ **Ducky's Office Furniture**—New and used deals by the ton, and a sense of humor into the bargain.

of new and used office furniture, they even have fun with it (how refreshing, in the business biz). "Duck! Low Prices!" say the signs all around this airplane hangar of a store. They sell, rent, buy, and repair enough furniture to start their own small country. And what have we learned by now, bargain-hunters? High volume means low prices.

Ducky's carries all the big names, like Hon, BPI, FireKing, La-Z-Boy, and dozens more. They sell everything from individual chairs to entire offices, including partitions and workstation setups. Yellow tags on new furniture indicate not only wholesale prices, but a 3% cash discount as well. And, if you're willing to wait three or four weeks for delivery, you'll get even lower prices on brand-new items.

Pink tags highlight closeout deals and used goods; freight-damaged items are clearly labeled to indicate the damage. Among the pink-tagged goodies, Mr. C found upholstered chairs as low as $15; an oak-veneer computer stand for $99; stacks of basic steel secretary's desks for $70; and file cabinets from $69. Some of these are pretty beat-up,

but you can have them reconditioned and still come out way ahead on the deal. The large sales staff is quick to serve you. Duck in any weekday from 8:30 A.M. to 5:30 P.M., or Saturdays from 10 A.M. to 4 P.M.

Secondary Office Furniture
• 2440 First Ave. S, Seattle; 682-2396
The merchandise at Secondary Office Furniture is anything but second rate. Even the showroom is classy—neatly arranged and very clean. The place itself is huge—the basement alone is 10,000 square feet, piled high with conference and computer tables, paneling systems, chairs, and other furniture.

A sturdy 30" x 72" folding table can have many uses in both the office and home; Mr. C spotted one here for only $50. Stacking chairs with arm rests and cushioned seats are $39 each, but if you buy more than ten, you can negotiate the price down a bit. Vertical and lateral file cabinets start at $60 and go as high as $400, depending on age, size, and quality. Four-shelf book cases in mahogany or oak are between $69 and $95.

Because Secondary Office Furniture is so large, they have many different styles and types of furniture in stock—let the staff know what you'd like, and they'll help you find it. Stop by Mondays through Saturdays between 8:30 A.M. and 5 P.M.

Just down the block, entrepreneurs should also check out **City Office Furniture** at 2412 First Avenue S, Seattle (telephone 587-5335). Here you'll find a smaller, scruffier selection including desks for as little as $35 (black metal), others from $100 to $200 (wood), file cabinets, chairs, and the like. Open Mondays through Fridays from 9 A.M. to 5:30 P.M., and Saturdays from 10 A.M. to 4 P.M.

HOME FURNISHINGS

This chapter covers all the other stuff for your home besides furniture: Linens, lighting, kitchen and bath furnishings, decorative items, and sundry hardware stuff. Whatever "sundry" means. . .

Abodio Clearance Center

- 790 Andover Park E, Tukwila; 575-2041

See the listing under "Furniture."

American Drapery, Blind & Carpet

- 1555 NW Market St., Seattle; 781-4993
- 31248 Pacific Hwy. S, Federal Way; 946-0413
- 20101 44th Ave. W, Lynnwood; 670-1270
- 7990 Leary Way NE, Redmond; 861-1804
- 700 S Third St., Renton; 255-3893

What began in 1946 as a drapery cleaning business blossomed over the years into a drape-making factory, also making blinds and shades; adding special-order carpeting and vinyl, American made further good on its name by building up a nationwide mail-order business. They're still big on service, coming to your home to clean your vertical blinds or to help design the perfect look for your living room.

In the stores themselves, you can get further consultations; you can also purchase factory surplus and closeout bargains in already-made items. Some are just plain "unclaimed." All of these are first-quality; if there's anything defective about these drapes and blinds, it's only that they were ordered in the wrong size. But, if they happen to be the right size for *you*, you may walk out with a steal. Some sale prices, Mr. C was told, are as low as five cents on the dollar!

Among the items recently available was a set of 88" x 44" woven-linen drapes. Though they had been marked down once to $59, they were further reduced to $24. There's a right price for everything, no? Several bins were filled with mini-blinds in a variety of sizes and colors. Any of these from 10" to 23" in length were priced at $7.99 apiece; from 24" to 42" were $12.99; and 58" to 74" were $29.99. Simple as that, and way cheap for this kind of quality.

Commercial and residential carpeting by Mohawk, Coronet, and other manufacturers, as well as vinyl floor covering from Armstrong and Congoleum, are available at competitive prices. Some of these can cost as little as $8.95 a square yard, installed. And all of their departments do a lot of business with hospitals, hotels, and schools.

The folks here are super-friendly, and ready to give you all the help you need without a lot of pressure. For the best selection of surplus bargains, check out the home-office branch in Renton, which is open seven days a week; other branches vary, with some closed on Sundays.

Annie's Affordable Art

- 2232 NW Market St., Second Floor, Seattle; 784-4761

Inside this mini-mall, Annie's is a dream come true for dorm denizens or first-apartment dwellers. The store is filled with posters and prints of every size and shape—with plenty of designs to choose from, whether your taste leans toward Rainier, Renoir, or *Ren and Stimpy*.

Furthermore, you can regulate your budget by purchasing your work of art fully framed, shrink-wrapped on cardboard, or rolled up and ready for Scotch tape. Annie's also sells premade frames in lots of sizes and colors, in addition to its reasonably priced frame-to-order service.

Mr. C found beautiful landscapes like the above-mentioned mountain, framed for $48; the print by itself costs $11.82. Many framed prints of various Impressionist works were seen in the $50-$80 range. Posters featuring TV shows like *Star Trek* and the Three Stooges were seen for $6. Small pictures with inspirational sayings, shrink-wrapped with a cardboard matte frame, were $5.50. Plus humor, cats, children's characters, and more. Open seven days a week.

The Beard Outlet

- 12005 NE 12th St., Bellevue; 451-9844

For folks on the Eastside, here's another opportunity to cover bare wall space cheaply. This small shop is the clearance center for Beard's three area framing stores, offering discounts on overstocked items. Like Annie's (above), the posters here range from Matisse to *Beavis and Butthead* (probably the first time in recorded history that those three have been mentioned in one sentence).

Framed pictures on Mr. C's visit included a Degas print, one of his classic ballet scenes; originally selling for $60, here it was reduced to $45. For the kids' bedroom, a framed Babar poster was only $30. And there are plenty of contemporary prints as well. Unframed posters are mostly $4.99 to $9.99.

Ready-made poster frames in wood and metal, along with standup photo frames, are sold here at half-price—as low as $5. There's also a selection of books on art (both instructional and ornamental), with an easy chair to sit in while perusing them; a large-size overview of Renoir's works, with color plates, was reduced from $75 to $35. The Beard Outlet is open seven days a week.

The Bon Marché Homeworld Clearance Center

- Northgate Mall, Seattle; 361-2121

Only the most devoted bargain-hunters seem to know that this branch of the Bon is where they clear out home furnishing overstocks. You can save big bucks on linens and towels, cook-ware, kitchen gadgets, and gift items. Sometimes you'll find clothing in here too. Most are sold at 50% to 75% off store prices.

On any visit, you may find things like Royal Velvet bath-size towels, reduced from $5.99 to $1.50; Utica down-filled comforters, once $170, now $85; a five-piece stoneware dish setting, marked down from $70 to $35; and a T-Fal no-stick skillet (say *that* three times fast) reduced from $32.99 to $16.50.

This is also the place where cutesy gift items go, after the craze dies down. Mr. C found Donald Duck coffee mugs, originally $18.99 each (!), now a more reasonable $4.75. And a Snoopy Waffle Baker was half-price at $20. Check it out! In the Bon, head down to the lower level, toward the rear of the store (the Fifth Avenue side). It's a single, small room. Even at these prices, items are returnable, with the receipt; Mr. C says always, *always* keep your receipts! Open regular mall hours, seven days a week. Diehard fans of the Bon should also check out the Bon Marché Warehouse in Tukwila. See the listing under "Discount Department Stores."

Bruning Pottery

- 2908 Sixth Ave. S, Seattle; 623-1007

Larry and Judy Bruning are just the nicest folks. And, for a family-run business, they run quite a large ceramics factory. They've been at it for a dozen years or so, recently moving to the industrial area south of downtown. They turn out very attractive dishware, coffee mugs, vases, and planters, which are sold in specialty stores and garden centers throughout the Northwest.

Of course, the more you make, the more you can mess up. And, here at their factory, the Brunings have filled a large retail shop with first- and second-quality products—though honestly, it's pretty hard to tell which are the seconds. There may be a small blemish in the glazing; a color may be slightly off; there could be a chip here or there, but Mr. C found surprisingly few broken items.

Clearly, their standards are very high. Yet these barely-seconds are sold at 20% to 80% off regular retail prices. Elegant dinner plates are $5 and $10 each. Mugs are as low as $2. Lots of four-inch planters and Bonsai pots go for $2.50, $3, and $4 apiece, while larger pots and vases are $7 to $20. They even have artsy refrigerator magnets for a buck or two.

The layered, swirling patterns seem to favor rich blues, reds, and purples, smooth and glossy. All dinnerware is lead-free, and safe for use in the microwave and the dishwasher. The store is open weekdays from 9 A.M. to 5 P.M.; Saturdays from 10-4, and Sundays from 12-4. The Brunings also host tours of the factory; see the listing under "Entertainment—Walks and Tours" for details.

Burlington Coat Factory
- 24111 Highway 99, Edmonds; 776-2221
- 10401 Gravelly Lake Dr. SW, Tacoma; 588-3595
- Pavilion Mall, Tukwila; 575-4269

See the listing under "Discount Department Stores."

C. Cutlery Center
- 2028 Second Ave., Seattle; 728-2730

For over 30 years, this tiny shop has outfitted Seattle's best chefs with professional-grade cooking knives and tools. You can shop here too, even if you're just a budding Frugal Gourmet. And CCC's budget brand, Dexter/Russell, offers you a less-expensive alternative that is still restaurant-quality—this New England company has been making knives since 1818.

A basic Russell three-piece starter knife set, with white plastic handles, goes for around $30 here; the same set by a top-line manufacturer like Henckels ("the Mercedes of cutlery," said the salesman) could cost up to $100. Yet they carry just as strong a warranty. If your kitchen just won't be complete without long-lasting, super-sharp chef's knives, check these out. Open weekdays from 9 A.M. to 5 P.M.

China, Silver & Crystal Shop
- 2809 Second Ave., Seattle; 441-8906

The name says it all. Except for the fact that this shop sells these ornate and expensive items at 25% to 40% off retail prices. They are authorized dealers for Wedgwood, Royal Doulton, Dansk, Spode, Mikasa, Noritake, Christian Dior...some forty or fifty designers in all. With so many items out on display, the shop simply dazzles.

So, a five-piece dinner setting by Noritake, which lists for $125, sells here for $74. A Mikasa crystal vase, elsewhere up to $75, is $53 here. And there are sometimes even better clearance deals; a Yamazaki 20-piece set of flatware, with a retail price of $240, was seen for an astonishing $80. All this, plus cutlery, photograph frames, and mechanical pens.

High-volume business allows CS & C to sell at discount. A few makers, such as Waterford, do not allow *any-one* to discount them; but to make up for it, the store offers free packaging and shipping on these, for which there is usually a fee. They also have a computerized bridal registry, and they can special order patterns that are not on display. Refunds are given (when you make purchases like this, does Mr. C even *have* to remind you to keep the receipt?) within 30 days; exchanges within 90 days. The store is open weekdays from 9 A.M. to 5:30 P.M., and Saturdays from 10 A.M. to 5 P.M.

Classic Home Furnishings Clearance Center
- 6415 32nd Ave. NW, Seattle; 783-1381

See the listing under "Furniture."

Cost Plus World Market
- 2103 Western Ave., Seattle; 443-1055
- 17680 Southcenter Pkwy., Tukwila; 575-0646

Much like the national chain Pier 1 Imports (below), Cost Plus sells an eclectic assortment of merchandise gathered from around the world. And they can do this at considerably good prices. In some cases, the prices are so low because the quality is not far behind; but most of the merchandise is fine, fun, and attractive.

Cost Plus is a great place for housewares, especially dishes and glassware. Mr. C found porcelain mugs from China for $3.99 each. Blue Willow dinnerware from England, no match for Wedgwood but handsome nonetheless, was just $17.26 for a four-piece place setting. You'll also find baskets by the hundreds, like a large woven picnic basket for $24.99. Many smaller baskets go for under a dollar.

Decorating your home? You'll find lots of nice things here. Mr. C found a colorful cotton 6' x 9' rug for $89.99. The always-popular *papasan* round bamboo chair was just $99, twin size, with cushion. Also, there's lots of framed art starting as low as $19.99.

Cost Plus also carries clothes, jewelry, and all kinds of international bric-a-brac. Recently, they had a selection of Moroccan jewelry as low as $19.99 and sterling silver and turquoise earrings for $14.99. Plus straw hats for $5.99, colorful rayon skirts for $12.48, and more.

This vast store imports packaged food items, too. There's a very good selection of teas, and tea accessories to go with them. Coffee beans are moderately priced; several are brewed up for you to taste, a nice touch. Imported gourmet cakes, in flavors like orange and kiwi, were also seen for $1.99 recently, and a liter of extra virgin olive oil from Italy was just $5.99—an incredible price anywhere. Open seven days.

Factory Direct Draperies
- 8300 Aurora Ave. N, Seattle; 525-7932

For over 40 years, this family-owned business has decorated homes all around the Seattle area—saving folks big money by making their draperies right here in town. They add to the value with attentive service; every house-call, from the first showing of samples to any necessary adjustments after installation, is included in the price. Sure, you can spend less at some department stores and buying-clubs,

but will they give you that kind of service? Even if those guys make their own drapes, it's often done out-of-state.

The selection of custom styles here is tremendous, from traditional pinch-pleated looks to the latest designer fashions out of Architectural Digest. Any given style may come in as many as fifty different colors. And, although they don't manufacture blinds and shades, FDD does offer plenty of these too, made to your order.

If you want to save more, the staff can work from their in-house stock of ready-made drapes. Periodic sales highlight selected lines, with extra discounts of up to 40% off regular prices. And it's always worth checking out the leftovers and unclaimed items, as much as half-off their original prices.

Their Aurora store has a separate phone number, 454-7909, for the Bellevue/Redmond area; they even save Eastsiders on telephone toll charges! In fact, FDD covers (excuse the pun) the entire Puget Sound area, from Tacoma to Arlington, Bainbridge to North Bend. Store hours are from 9:30 A.M. to 5:30 P.M., Mondays through Saturdays.

Far Fetched
- 2620 Bellevue Way NE, Bellevue; 827-3979

See the listing under "Clothing—Used."

Grand Central Mercantile Company
- 316 First Ave. S, Seattle; 623-8894

On the whole, this stylish kitchenware shop in Pioneer Square is not a discount store; however, you will find bargains upstairs in their loft. Damaged items, close-outs, and overstocks are drastically reduced in price; there's a good range of items, formerly sold on the main floor.

When Mr. C visited, coffee mugs with slight chips were on sale for just $1; portable hibachi grills by Le Creuset, originally $200, were marked down to $50, and novelty items, such as brass candlesticks, were marked at half-off the original $39.95 price. The discounted selection is limited, but then again, Mercantile sells high-quality and trendy kitchen stuff. For those of you who like to stock up on a few gifts for short-notice situations, this makes a good place to check out. Open Mondays through Saturdays, from 10 A.M. to 6 P.M., or Sundays, from 11 A.M. to 5 P.M.

Jen-Cel-Lite Factory Outlet
• 954 E Union St., Seattle; 322-3030
This small local manufacturer on First Hill also functions as its own discounter. And functionality is the name of the game here. Jen-Cel-Lite manufactures private label sleeping bags, polyester-filled comforters and pillows in all sizes; and they sell the seconds in this factory store at one-third to one-half off retail prices. You'll find a variety of full-size comforters as low as $30 (king-size for just $50).

JCL also sells some other manufacturers' goods at a discount. Lovers of down-filled comforters will be wooed by king-size quilts selling for $90 to $100. At the time of Mr. C's visit, the store was looking forward to adding backpacks, jackets, outerwear, and more. In addition to all of the finished products, sewing crafters will find this an unexpected source for discontinued fabrics, thread, and other supplies. When a retailer decides to discontinue a line, these leftover materials can often be had for a song. Hours are from 9 A.M. to 3 P.M., Mondays through Saturdays.

Laguna Pottery
• 5828 Roosevelt Way NE, Seattle; 523-4234
Along with its downtown branch at 609 Second Avenue, Laguna sells what it calls "20th Century American Art Pottery." This ranges from collectibles, like hand-painted ceramic tiles, to functional dinnerware—by such designers as Bauer, Fiesta, Franciscan, Winfield, and more. It's not, shall we say, cheap stuff. But, here at their U-District location, they do have a "Scratch-N-Dent Room" offering better prices on slightly damaged items. Although there's a lot on the shelves, Mr. C has to admit that much of it is a little further gone than he had

---

> # MR. CHEAP'S PICKS
> ## Home Furnishings
>
> ✔ **American Drapery, Blind & Carpet** and **Factory Direct Draperies**—Two businesses that offer well-priced custom service, plus amazing deals on orders that were never picked up.
>
> ✔ **The Bon Marché Homeworld Clearance Center**—At the Northgate Bon, a room packed with linens and cookware at 50% to 75% off.
>
> ✔ **Bruning Pottery**—Gorgeous, unique ceramics, and shelves of second-quality merchandise that looked just fine to Mr. C.
>
> ✔ **China, Silver & Crystal Shop**—Serious discounts on serious table settings.

---

hoped. Still, it's definitely worth a prowl; you never know what treasure you may unearth. Open Wednesdays through Saturdays from 12-6 P.M.

Lamps Plus
• 3611 196th St. SW, Lynnwood; 775-4320
• 16839 Southcenter Pkwy., Tukwila; 575-9110
Boasting the city's largest selection of lamps, track lighting, ceiling fans, chandeliers, and the like, Lamps Plus offers good prices indeed. Clearance items and special sales make for even better deals, like a ten-light contemporary chandelier, selling for half-price at $150. Most of the designs here, in fact, lean toward the modern. Another recent sale item was an architect's halogen floor lamp, with two joints for adjusting the position over a desk or chair; it too was reduced by half, to $49.95.

There are quite a lot of lesser-known brands mixed in with a few biggies. But, for folks on a budget, these may certainly fit the bill. LP is open seven days a week, including weeknights until 9 P.M.

Lechter's Homestores

- Everett Mall, Everett; 348-1273
- Kitsap Mall, Silverdale; (360) 698-8568
- Tacoma Mall, Tacoma; 474-2290
- Southcenter Mall, Tukwila; 244-6118

Well-established on the East Coast, Lechter's is making its way west with its stores chock full of goodies for the kitchen, bath, and other parts of the house, all discounted from retail. Some are closeouts, some just big-volume deals. A contemporary 18-piece boxed glassware set, meant to sell for $18, was recently seen here for $9. And a combination coffee, cappuccino, and espresso maker by Krups—originally $200—was on sale for $150.

A Bo-Nash hammered wok set, with a retail price of $45, was seen for $30. Other deals are smaller, both in price and relative importance to the kitchen. Find a wooden spice rack for $7.99, a Rubbermaid basting brush for $1.99, or a Pyrex measuring cup for the same price. All baking and cooking needs are quite fully addressed; you can even top it all off with an authentic chef's *toque* by Chef's Club for $6.99, and truly be the master of your kitchen.

For other rooms, you can find all sorts of "organizer" stuff, including sturdy plastic milk crates for $3.99; decorative hanging baskets, same price; and wooden 5" x 7" picture frames, two for ten bucks. Plus shower curtains, pizza-making boards, cutesy refrigerator magnets—they really seem to have a little bit of everything. And don't miss the clearance area in the back, for further bargains. Open seven days a week, including every evening but Sunday.

Oriental Furniture Warehouse

- 1111 Elliott Ave. W, Seattle; 286-3139

Given Seattle's proximity to Asia, you figure there *must* be places to get good deals on those distinctive kinds of furniture and decorative pieces. And here it is. OFW has been a direct importer of Oriental specialty items for nearly ten years; it certainly looks the part, a no-frills waterfront warehouse. Three or four times a year, huge containers arrive loaded with couches, tables, folding screens, vases, lamps, and more.

Many of these are by no means "cheap," but the prices are certainly better here than you may see elsewhere. A traditional Chinese black lacquer chest, with soapstone inlays, could cost as much as $400; here, it sells for $289. And a solid teak coffee table from Thailand was recently seen for a very reasonable $375. Cloisonné vases, the real thing, go for $149; there are also eclectic, modernized twists on some of these traditional items.

If you don't see that one exotic piece your living room cries out for, write it into the "wish list" book, and OFW's buyers will search for it. Get on the mailing list, too (as some 8,000 folks are) and you'll get advance notice of special arrivals and sales. The store is open Tuesdays through Saturdays from 10:30 A.M. to 6 P.M., and Sundays from 12-4 P.M. Look for the bright purple (this is Oriental?) facade—you can't miss it.

Pier 1 Imports

- 2815 Alaskan Way, Seattle; 448-4072
- 4345 University Way NE, Seattle; 545-7397
- Aurora Square, Seattle; 361-0984
- 905 Bellevue Way NE, Bellevue; 451-8002
- 1425 SE Everett Mall Way, Everett; 353-6345
- 3702 S Fife St., Tacoma; 472-5540
- 17197 Southcenter Pkwy., Tukwila; 575-4113

A favorite among yupsters, Pier 1 has nice things for literally every single corner and surface in your home. And, since they truly are direct importers from many of the producing nations on the other side of the globe, their prices are often quite reasonable. You can even see a chalkboard listing upcoming "arrivals."

The selection is vast, from major pieces of wicker furniture to tiny brass elephants. Not to mention glassware and dishware, rice-paper window shades, clothing and jewelry, candles and candleholders, throw pillows, rugs, posters and frames, dried flowers, and much more. Good place for gift shopping, too. Open seven days.

Rodda Paints
- 3633 Stone Way N, Seattle; 547-7405
- 5055 Fourth Ave. S, Seattle; 767-6043
- 1034 116th Ave. NE, Bellevue; 451-1666
- 4850 NE 24th St., Redmond; 861-7971
- 16717 Cleveland St., Redmond; 881-5583
- *And other suburban locations*

Rodda has good prices and a big selection on all the stuff for those projects around the house—and a lot more than just paint. Sure, there's plenty of that—their own semi-gloss latex goes for about five dollars a gallon less than comparable brands, with free custom color mixing. But they also have mill-direct wallpapers, at least 50% off retail; Mr. C saw one pre-pasted vinyl print reduced from $20.99 a roll to just $7.99. And a recent sale offered 20% off all Kirsch drapery and hardware.

Speaking of hardware, Rodda has everything else you'll need for the job: brushes, caulk, wood finishes, ladders, the works. Store hours vary by location.

Seattle Lighting Fixture Co.
- 222 Second Ave. Extension S, Seattle; 622-4736
- 14032 Aurora Ave. N, Seattle; 362-4444
- 12828 Bellevue-Redmond Rd., Bellevue; 455-2110
- 1811 Hewitt Ave., Everett; 252-4151
- 5611 196th Ave. SW, Lynnwood; 778-1124
- Tacoma Mall, Tacoma; 475-2110

- 349 Tukwila Pkwy., Tukwila; 431-8602

The Seattle Lighting Fixture Company is not a discount or bargain store; their specialty is in dealing with unique or unusual lighting fixtures. However, Mr. C had the illuminating experience of finding the back room, which was filled with reduced-price clearance stock.

Among the items that caught Mr. C's attention were a $211 Stiffel table lamp reduced to $97, and a $239 Casablanca ceiling fan marked down to $100. There is also usually a selection of assorted lamp shades at 60% off. Vanity lights for the bathroom, originally priced at $50 to $60, were an unbelievable $3. The merchandise changes constantly, so there's no telling what Seattle Lighting will have for clearance. Each store has a different selection, too. There's also a big sale every year in which list-price merchandise is marked down 15% to 20%. Watch the papers to see when the next sale will strike. Hours vary by store.

Tile For Less
- 2414 First Ave. S, Seattle; 623-7728
- 12305 120th Ave. NE, Kirkland; 820-4400
- 9990 Mickelberry St. NW, Silverdale; (360) 698-4052
- 1901 S 72nd St., Tacoma; 471-0271

A no-frills store for adding frills to your home. There's a goodly variety of granite, marble, terra cotta and glazed ceramics, and more to choose from here; some are even imported from Europe. Portuguese limestone, for instance, was seen here at $6.99 per square-foot tile. The section of discontinued and leftover lots offers the best bargains, some as little as 25¢ apiece (or per linear foot).

TFL also carries the supplies to install any tile and finish the job, along with as much free advice as you may need. In fact, if you leave them a deposit, they'll even let you borrow professional tools for a five-day period. No charge. Now, that's friendly! Open weekdays from 10 A.M. to 6 P.M., and Saturdays from 9 A.M. to 5 P.M.

Mr. C hasn't forgotten the big chains. You hardly need him
to tell you about Ernst, whose stores are more common
than coffee beans; here are the main locations for some
other good major chains.

Eagle Hardware and Garden
- 2700 Rainier Ave. S, Seattle;
  760-0832
- 11959 Northup Way, Bellevue;
  646-9031
- 4220 Wheaton Way NE,
  Bremerton; (360) 377-9052
- 2505 Pacific Ave., Everett;
  259-2017
- 35205 16th Ave. S, Federal Way;
  838-2233

- 101 Andover Park E, Tukwila;
  243-5470

Home Depot
- 2759 Utah Ave. S, Seattle;
  467-9200
- 7050 Tacoma Mall Blvd., Tacoma;
  474-9600
- 6810 S 180th St., Tukwila;
  575-9200

JEWELRY

Many of the stores in this chapter are located on upper floors of
downtown office buildings. This sometimes means getting past some
guy at a desk, but Mr. C has only listed businesses which do sell to the
public. Needless to say, without the expense of storefront showrooms,
these places can add a lower markup than those found at fancy boutiques.

Also, Seattle is home to more bead crafters than any other city
Mr. C has explored. You'll find bead and jewelry-making suppliers
noted under that section in the "Sewing and Craft Supplies" chapter.

Alexander's Bead Bazaar
- 920 NE 64th St., Seattle; 526-8909

Combining finished jewelry with
bead supplies of all kinds, Alexander's specializes in looks from
around the world. Beautiful turquoise
necklaces from China and Africa
range in price from as little as $9 up
to around $30; jade necklaces start
around $12. And a drop medallion of
hammered nickel, silver-plated, was
seen for $22. Islamic art is also a spe-
cialty. Open seven days a week.

Armadillo
- 3510 Fremont Pl. N, Seattle;
  633-4241

Here's a fun place for jewelry and
kooky gift items in all the latest
crazes. There are lots of earrings to
see, many of which are hand-crafted,

for $20 and up; meanwhile, sterling
silver and 14K gold earrings are
priced at $5, $7.50, $10, and $15 in a
wide selection of shapes and styles.
And don't forget the armadillo ear
studs, $2 apiece.

Other cute things on a recent visit
included stuffed frogs and lizards
from $5 to $12; simple leather and
bead bracelets, $5; and lots of nov-
elty T-shirts and greeting cards. Open
seven days a week.

Associated Gem and Jewelry Appraisal Service
- 1424 Fourth Ave., Suite 528,
  Seattle; 682-5548

Most of the jewelers in this building
deal exclusively in the wholesale
trade. However, Associated Gem and
Jewelry happily sells to the public.

Many items here are very high quality consigned or estate pieces. Several antique pieces are hand-made and unique, so they are more expensive; but beautiful gemstone jewelry can still be bought for under $200, like a 14-karat gold ring, with a sapphire surrounded by diamond chips, for $150. The specialty here is women's rings, with some pendants, necklaces, brooches and bracelets also on display. If you have any questions, Christina Harrington, the gemologist and accredited appraiser who runs the show, will gladly take the time to answer them for you. Associated Gem is open from 9:30 A.M. to 5:30 P.M. Mondays through Fridays; and on Saturdays by appointment only.

In the same building, on the fourth floor, you may also want to check out **Orogemma International** (telephone 382-1472). These importers and jewelers deal primarily in pearls, and again, do sell to the public.

Bayside Gold & Diamond Exchange

- 1425 Fourth Ave., Suite 725, Seattle; 624-1984

Entering this fortress of a building can take some doing—there is a guard posted in the lobby who seems rather opposed to people casually wandering through the corridors. You may want to call in advance to set up an appointment with Bayside. Once in the shop, though, you'll find a dazzling selection of diamonds, gold, silver, platinum, and estate jewelry. The folks here prefer not to commit specific prices to print, but these are estimated at being 40%-60% below retail—itself an elusive quantity in the jewelry biz. If you're looking for something specific, Bayside is a good place to get yourself an estimate.

True story (a well-disguised Mr. C took note of this candid endorsement): During the visit, a gentleman was there picking up a previously-ordered engagement ring. This man was quite happy with the beauty and quality of the ring, and commented to his buddy several times on the "great

---

MR. CHEAP'S PICKS
Jewelry

✔ **Jewelry Exchange Plaza**— Several dealers, sharing the hefty downtown rent, make this place a goldmine for fine jewelry at low prices.

✔ **Rhinestone Rosie**—At the opposite end of the spectrum, Rosie makes glass jewelry fun and elegant.

✔ **Robins**—This gem of a store has high-quality jewelry (custom-made if you like), outstanding service, and reasonable rates.

---

deal" he'd gotten. Decide for yourself—it can be worth jumping through a few hoops (no pun intended) for reasonable prices on fine jewelry. Open Mondays through Saturdays from 9 A.M. to 6 P.M.

D'Oro Jewelry Inc.

- 624 First Ave., Seattle; 682-7552

D'Oro deals mainly in gold, silver, and watches. A large selection of Seiko, Pulsar, and Citizen watches are always sold at a 25% discount off list prices. These watches still cost a lot more than a drugstore digital, but you're paying for quality and respectable brands. A man's Citizen watch was seen for $80, a man's Pulsar for $135, and a woman's Seiko for $275. Prices range according to style.

Gold and silver chains are priced by the gram—at the time of this writing, that's $3 for silver, $22 for 14-karat gold. D'Oro has a large selection of these, too. Open Mondays through Fridays, from 10 A.M. to 6 P.M.; Saturdays, from noon to 4 P.M. Closed Sundays.

Jewelry Exchange Plaza

● 1512 Fifth Ave., Seattle; see
   numbers below

A group of independent jewelry dealers share the space and rent at this
downtown location, allowing them to
pass high quality at low prices on to
you. They operate from rows of
counters, which also gives you a
chance to bounce from one dealer to
another and do some comparison
shopping under one roof. The plaza is
open Mondays through Saturdays,
from 10 A.M. to 6 P.M. Here are a few
jewelers that especially impressed
Mr. C during his recent visit:

   A & S Jewelry (telephone 340-
0866) deals in quality estate collections. All of these pieces are
genuine gold and silver; they sell no
costume jewelry, so although the
savings are great, the prices are still
high. A 14K gold ring with a 2-carat
cluster of diamonds was selling for
$999—less than half of its ap-
praised $2,700. A gold and diamond
watch, which could retail for
$2,900, was being sold here for
$850. Ring sizing is available.

   E & M Jewelry (343-0375) specializes in heavier chains and individual stones. A 14K gold necklace,
weighing 73 grams, was being sold
here for a remarkable $912. The
same necklace could retail for $1,600
elsewhere. Mr. C was also shown a
2.01-carat diamond for $3,100—the
same stone retails for $6,000.

   5th Avenue Time Shop (343-
0686) of course, does watches. There
were lots of Pulsars in stock when
Mr. C stopped by. There were also
other watches, like an upscale $110
Mickey Mouse style, and a gold and
diamond woman's watch for $150.
The prices here are estimated at
about 25% below retail. Lots of
bands and accessories, too.

   Image Fine Jewelry (292-8188)
specializes in cultured pearls and
"beautiful yet practical jewelry."

   Washington Gems and Jewelry
(622-9084) has hundreds of loose
stones, and a variety of settings,
ready to mix and match to your order.

   And finally, for more high-quality,

low-price jewelry, check **Swissa** just
up the block at 1518 Fifth Avenue;
telephone 625-9202.

Rhinestone Rosie

● 606 W Crockett St., Seattle;
   283-4605

Rosalie Sayyah is a woman after Mr.
C's own heart. "I can't bear to see
anything thrown away—not if it can
be repaired," she told him, and she's
built up an entire business around
that premise. Further, like your humble author, Rhinestone Rosie has created a professional monicker that
instantly tells you what her work is
all about. A lifelong fan of vintage
jewelry, Rosie has made an art of restoring, repairing, restringing, and
even re-designing pieces from the
1920s through the 1940s, the heyday
of ornate glass jewelry. People bring
in cherished family heirlooms, baubles they've discovered in the attic,
or some broken-but-interesting thing
they picked up at a yard sale. Rosie
can make them all like new again,
creating dazzling costume jewelry
with a minimal investment.

   In addition, she buys and sells jewelry in every color and size imaginable; her display cases are packed
with gleaming necklaces, rings,
brooches, earrings, and bracelets.
Talk about "all that glitters is not
gold"—with such beautiful examples,
you realize that it doesn't always matter. Meanwhile, a low rent (Rosie
shares her off-the-beaten-track location with a dress designer) means selling prices are cheap, even if the looks
are not. Much of the jewelry sells for
well under $20—and you'll have a
ball rummaging through the "$2.50
Shelf" of orphaned treasures.

   Some items are sold on consignment for their owners; Rosie keeps
up with what's out there by offering
estate appraisals. She also rents her
jewelry out, perfect if you've been invited to a costume ball but wouldn't
otherwise wear such vintage fashions. Rent any piece for 20% of the
selling price, per day. Meander
through the quiet sidestreets at the
top of Queen Anne Hill until you find

the store; it's open Tuesdays through Saturdays from 12 noon to 5 P.M.

Robins Jewelers
• 220 First Ave. S, Seattle; 622-4337

Since 1972, Robins Jewelers has been offering jewelry for 10% to 40% less than you'll find in other stores. The original owner still operates the business, and his in-house jewelry designer has been here almost as long. In short, Robins is established and experienced. They are also very friendly, and are determined to help you find the exact piece of jewelry you're looking for, even if that means custom-making it.

There are so many beautiful pieces on display. Mr. C loved a marquis-cut opal and diamond ring, cast in 14-karat gold, for $375; and a 16-inch, 14-karat gold rope chain for $198. You also have the option of choosing a ring mounting (starting around $300), and then selecting a stone.

Robins Jewelers is open from 10 A.M. to 5:30 P.M. Mondays through Fridays, and 'til 5 P.M. Saturdays.

The Sample Shop
• 613 Queen Anne Ave. N, Seattle; 282-8780

Surprisingly, this small clothing boutique (for more details, see the listing under "Clothing—New") has an absolutely enormous collection of costume jewelry to fit any occasion—and any budget. Jewelry displays cover about half the store, with most prices about 50% or more below retail value. A pair of classy sterling silver hoops was marked at $8, half of its original price, and an elegant 30-inch crystal necklace was seen for just $14.99, down from $40. With so much to choose from, in classic and modern designs, you're bound to find the style you're looking for. Stop by Mondays through Saturdays between 10 A.M. and 6 P.M.

LIQUOR AND BEVERAGES

The state of Washington regulates the sale of hard liquor, selling it only through state-run stores. As a result, the stores in this chapter highlight places to save money on beer and wine only.

Cash & Carry United Grocers
• 1760 Fourth Ave. S, Seattle; 343-7156
• 13102 Stone Ave. N, Seattle; 364-1733
• 2208 136th Pl. NE, Bellevue; 644-4638
• 2917 Cedar St., Everett; 339-2628
• 1628 S 344th St., Federal Way; 925-0550
• 21504 84th Ave. S, Kent; 872-7873
• 6412 204th St. SE, Lynnwood; 672-1886
• 6208 Tacoma Mall Blvd., Tacoma; 472-6879

See the listing under "Food Shops."

McCarthy & Schiering Wine Merchants
• 6500 Ravenna Ave. NE, Seattle; 524-9500
• 2209 Queen Anne Ave. N, Seattle; 282-8500

This company is not really a discounter; their small but well-stocked stores emphasize service and special ordering of select wines. However, they do offer something called the "Vintage Select Club," which may be worthwhile for fans of fine wines.

Anyone may join this club; there is a one-time fee of $100, but this is presumably good for life (M & S created the club in 1980, so it should be a worthwhile investment). Membership entitles you to a 17% discount on every wine purchase you make in

---

MR. CHEAP'S PICKS
Liquor

✔ **Pete's Supermarkets**—Three branches around town are a surprising source for a good variety of well-priced wines and beers.

✔ **Warehouse of Wine**—An even more careful selection including hard-to-find wines, yet still at discount. Plus free weekly tastings, in its own art gallery.

---

either store. You also receive a monthly newsletter, describing the newest special bottlings (sometimes before they reach the market), with a chance to order these early.

Considering how much some rare wines can cost, and especially if you purchase by the case, the club can wind up saving you a bundle. You must pay by cash or check; credit card purchases get 12%-14% discounts. The newsletter also tells you about special free wine tastings at the stores. The Ravenna store is closed on Sundays; the Queen Anne branch is closed Sundays and Mondays.

Pete's Supermarket
● 58 E Lynn St., Seattle; 322-2660
● 4036 E Madison St., Seattle; 325-2150
● 134 105th St. NE, Bellevue; 454-1100

Great liquor prices in a neighborhood grocery store? Yes, times three. Inside these otherwise unassuming shops, you'll find a surprisingly large selection of top-quality beers and wines at discount prices. Lots of microbrews, like Anchor Steam and Full Sail, are available; and there are always a few brands on sale, around $5.99 for a six-pack. Mass-market brands are even cheaper.

There are several aisles of fine wines and champagnes, many with printed descriptions or reviews taped beside them. Mr. C noted a '93 Georges DuBoeuf Beaujolais, selling elsewhere at the time for $7.99, priced here at $5.99. And a top-rated '90 Dominus Estate cabernet, usually $59.99, was on sale for $49.99. At the other end of the spectrum, he found a non-vintage label actually called "Cheap White Wine" (music to Mr. C's ears!) for $3.99 a bottle. Case prices offer good discounts, too. Pete's Supermarkets are open seven days and evenings a week.

Sav-On Beverages
● 14310 124th Ave. NE, Kirkland; 823-6246

Way up in the Kingsgate Plaza shopping center, this packed little store quietly sells a huge selection of beers from around the area and around the world. Local brews like Moss Bay and Maritime give you choices of Northwest micros well beyond Red Hook; other specialty beers from Europe and Australia include bottles in all sorts of unusual sizes and shapes.

Regular prices here tend to be lower than most everyday supermarket rates, and each month highlights a variety of special sale items. Good prices on cases and kegs, too. Sav-On also carries a limited selection of wines, also with case pricing; and they have nearly every kind of non-alcoholic beer and wine made.

This is a family-run business that's been here about a dozen years (they run the adjacent Zippy's Burgers, too). It's open every day from 9:30 A.M. to 10 P.M., closing at 8 P.M. on Sundays.

Warehouse of Wine
● 4530 Union Bay Pl. NE, Seattle; 525-6113

Some people are skilled at the art of matching wines with food. Here's a place that creates food for thought by matching wines with art. Warehouse of Wine sells a limited but unique selection of spirits not widely distributed in the Northwest, generally at below-market prices; it also houses the Lynne Gallery, which displays antiques and works by local artists.

In the shop, owner Rolla Halbert showed Mr. C a Dore white Zinfandel, rated in the 90s by the Wine Spectator, for $3.99; same price for a Chianti that would cost about twice as much in other stores; and vintage ports for $5-$10 less than their established prices. Bordeaux can be specially ordered at just 10% over cost, and cases are discounted by 10%—even if you wish to mix and match.

The adjacent gallery hosts a handful of shows through the year, in various media such as tapestries, oils, and photography, in a large room that's also filled with antique furniture. Each exhibition includes an opening reception with the artist, to which the public is invited.

This room is also the site for weekly wine tastings, which are also free of charge; each focuses on a type of wine or those of a particular cellar the store is carrying. Tastings take place from 5-7 P.M. most Thursdays; WW also sponsors other events and classes for oenophiles. Call or stop in to get on the mailing list for exhibits, tastings, and classes.

Quite a lot going on under one roof, eh? Next door, by the way, an unrelated shop called the **Brewers Warehouse** sells supplies for home beermeisters. Warehouse of Wine is open daily from 10 A.M. to 6 P.M., except Thursdays from 11 A.M. to 7 P.M. and Sundays from 12-4 P.M.

LUGGAGE

Bergman Luggage
- 1930 Third Ave., Seattle; 448-3000
- Northgate Mall, Seattle; 365-5775
- 881 Bellevue Way NE, Bellevue; 454-8689
- 18205 Alderwood Mall Blvd., Lynnwood; 774-9533
- 15116 NE 24th St., Redmond; 643-2344
- Kitsap Mall, Silverdale; (360) 698-0499
- 4020 S Steele St., Tacoma; 473-4855
- Pavilion Mall, Tukwila; 575-4090

With eight stores in and around the Seattle area, you could say that Bergman has the discount luggage market, er, well in hand. They've been around since 1927; thanks to expansion—and an affiliation with a California chain, the Luggage Center—they do a high-volume business which allows them to offer low-markup prices.

Everything they sell, from luggage to travel accessories, is discounted every day. Consequently, special sales are rare. Instead, you can walk in any time and find deals on current lines, like the latest Samsonite "Silhouette" suitcases at 30% below the retail price. If any of last year's models are still hanging around (and after all, how much can a suitcase change?), they may be marked at up to 50% off.

All the major brands are here: Not just Samsonite, but Andiamo, Skyway, Boyt, Tumi, and many others. In addition to luggage, the selection includes garment bags, briefcases, large and small duffel bags, day-planners, and more. It's all out on display for you to play with; they even post advertisements from other stores and catalogs, showing you how much lower Bergman's prices are for the exact same models.

Further, they have a "Baggage Claim" clearance department with one-of-a-kind pieces, mostly first quality. Here, Mr. C found garment bags for as little as $39.95 (!); and a Skyway "Executive Overnighter" briefcase, originally $90, first marked down to $45 and again to a remarkable $29.50.

The Southcenter store, in the Pavilion Mall, is the chain's largest, with the best overall and clearance selection. With most branches located in shopping centers, the stores are open during mall hours, seven days a week. The downtown store is open weekdays from 9 A.M. to 6 P.M., Saturdays from 9:30 A.M. to 6, and Sundays from 12-4:30 P.M.

T.W. Carrol & Co.
• 350 Upland Dr., Tukwila; 575-1064
Elsewhere in the Southcenter area, astute bargain-hunters can find more luggage deals by tracking down this tiny office in a business complex just off of Andover Park West. The small office is actually just the front of a 20,000 square-foot repair center, which does most of its work directly for airlines at nearby Sea Tac. When Fly-By-Night Airways mangles your suitcase, it's probably Carrol & Co. which fixes it for them.

And, when the damage is excessive, Carrol arranges to replace it. They have contacts and the latest catalogs from all of the biggies in bags, including American Tourister,

Samsonite, Delsey, Skyway, Halliburton, Andiamo, and the rest. But you don't have to own an airline—or even a frequent-flyer card—to shop here and get the same factory-direct prices. A 26-inch Delsey "Club" pullman, list priced at $150, sells for just over $100 here.

They offer similar savings on garment bags, luggage carts, briefcases, and even Thermos coolers. An attaché case by Avenues in Leather, meant to retail for $175, was seen here for $137.50. Carrol often makes its own off-price deals with manufacturers, allowing them to give even lower prices on selected models. But all prices are at least 25% off retail.

Big-volume as they are, this is still a friendly, family-owned business, going back a generation or two. Needless to say, if you *really* want to save on luggage, you might just ask about having them repair the stuff you've got now. Call first to inquire. Carrol & Co. is open weekdays from 8:30 A.M. to 5 P.M., and Saturdays from 9 A.M. to 12 noon.

MUSICAL INSTRUMENTS

Here's another category in which you can save money by "going used"—though many instruments actually increase in value as they age. Often, a top-quality used instrument which can repaired is a better investment than a cheaper, newer version. It will sound better and last longer.

Al's Guitarville
• 19258 15th Ave. NE, Seattle; 363-8188
Way up in a sleepy neighborhood at the north end of Seattle (and *not* in the U-District, as so many people misinterpret), Guitarville wakes everybody up with rock 'n roll bargains. Serious players find their way here early on, and then spend a lot of time hanging out. It's practically as old as rock itself—been here since 1958.

Al's began as a pawnshop for mu-

sicians; in fact, they still conduct loans. But the business grew. Now, these folks buy, sell, trade, consign, and repair just about *anything* with strings. Not just guitars and basses, but even banjos and mandolins—as well as amps and PA equipment.

New guitars are sold at considerable discounts. A Guild twelve-string, with a list price of $1,395, was seen here for $975; new electrics start around $350. Used models included an Ibanez "Les Paul" gold-top, selling for $249. At any given time, there are dozens to choose from. Mr. C was also shown a Martin bass, retail price $840, here selling for $588. Used guitars are not warrantied, but they're all carefully repaired before going on display.

Amplifiers can go for as little as $49 and up (most are in the $200-$300 range). Every accessory you can possibly need is here too; mike stands start under $20, and all strings are always sold at half of the list price. The friendly staff really knows what they're talking about, and they don't put a lot of sales pressure on you. So, next time you break a string on your ukelele, you know where to go. Open Mondays through Saturdays from 10 A.M. to 6 P.M.

American Music
- 4450 Fremont Ave. N, Seattle; 633-1774
- 14340 NE 20th St., Bellevue; 641 5005
- 5225 Tacoma Mall Blvd., Tacoma; 475-8360
- 17185 Southcenter Pkwy., Tukwila; 575-1970

The dominant (no pun intended) local chain in the music biz, American sells top lines of new and used musical instruments and related electronics. Rock 'n roll is the flavor here, with a large portion of the stock made up of guitars, drums, and keyboards, all at very competitive prices. New axes start around $250; used models may go as low as $150. You'll find all the biggies here—Fender, Gibson, Ovation, Guild, and the rest. Frequent sales offer good deals too, like 2-for-1 prices on strings.

Mr. C found a Roland JV-35 keyboard well-priced at just over $1,000; you can add all kinds of MIDI electronics and processors here, not to mention mixer boards, monitors, tape recorders, microphones, and more. Another recent deal slashed an extra $300 off their original *selling* price on a Tascam eight-track mixer.

Any of these kinds of instruments and equipment are welcome as trade-ins, too. Each branch hosts frequent

---

MR. CHEAP'S PICKS
Musical Instruments

✔ **Al's Guitarville**—Where guitar players really hang out.

✔ **American Music**—The big local chain, with an emphasis on rock.

✔ **Evans Music**—Don't dismiss their high-toned showrooms; you can find *relative* bargains among their used pianos.

✔ **Phil's Guitars**—Jazz heaven in Ballard.

(and free) seminars on music and recording, as well. All stores are open weekdays from 10 A.M. to 7 P.M., Saturdays from 10-6, and Sundays from 11-6 (except the Tacoma branch, which is closed on Sundays).

Aurora Music Center
- 18405 Aurora Ave. N, Seattle; 542-6311

As much an instruction center for musicians of all ages as a dealer of instruments, Aurora offers a 15% discount on everything in the store (except sheet music) to all students. They also rent out band instruments to local schools; and every summer, they sell many of these used models at 50% off. Even so, these all carry a one-year store warranty.

If you've been holding out for a good price on a trombone, this is the place for you. There are some regular discounts too, such as 2-for-1 guitar strings. Open every day but Sunday.

The Drum Exchange
- 4501 Interlake Ave. N, Seattle; 545-3564

The Drum Exchange buys, sells, consigns, and trades all different kinds of percussion instruments. Drum sets, cymbals, hardware, xylophones, and even electronic drum pads are all among the variety of stock here—though due to the nature of the business, not everything is available at all times.

When Mr. C visited, there was a mint condition, seven-piece Premier APK drum kit on display—with five cymbals, including a pair of hi-hats, for $2,000. If you bought this kit new, it would set you back between $3,000 or $4,000! There was also a set of six Ludwig maple shells for $395; expect to shell out about $800 elsewhere. Business is drummed up (ba-dum bum!) Mondays through Saturdays, from 10 A.M. to 6 P.M. Closed Sundays.

Evans Music

- 15003 Aurora Ave. N, Seattle; 363-6851
- 15575 NE 24th St., Bellevue; 643-2564
- 9960 Silverdale Way, Silverdale; (360) 698-2656
- 17430 Southcenter Pkwy., Tukwila; 575-1023

These attractive stores sell new and second-hand pianos at equally attractive prices. Mr. C was shown a used upright, less than twenty years old (that's nothing in piano years), selling for $1,695; new, it would cost at least $3,000. Another model, a Yamaha white baby grand, was only one year old (its resale was the unfortunate result of a divorce). Still gleaming like new, it was easily worth $16,000; the store price was $10,500.

All used models are completely serviced and tuned before going out on the selling floor, and carry a 90-day store warranty. Evans has competitive prices on new pianos too, as well as electronic keyboards and midi equipment. Open seven days a week.

The Folkstore

- 5238 University Way NE, Seattle; 524-1110

This small U-District music shop specializes in acoustic instruments—that's all they carry. Most are sold on consignment, with a broad selection of new and second-hand instruments. The day Mr. C visited, there was a 1960s Vega banjo with a soft-shell case for $495, and a new Goya classical guitar for $165. There was also a

decent selection of new Martin and Gibson guitars. For that really classical folk sound (be it in a Venetian gondola or a modern-day coffeehouse), the store had a mandolin on sale for $195, $70 off its original price. Stop by and pluck or strum any instrument you'd like to buy. The Folkstore is open every day but Sunday.

London Music and Studio

- 4519 University Way NE, Seattle; 720-4870

Elsewhere in the U-District, London Music carries enough instruments, equipment, and accessories to keep most economically-minded musicians (and really, isn't that all of them?) happy, from beginner to pro.

Although it was a little difficult nailing down specific prices for publication, Mr. C found used acoustic guitars going for $50 (they'd be $150 new), and used electric guitars for $100 ($195 new). Drum kits started around $500, and guitar amps at $150. Merchandise and prices change frequently, so if you're looking for something specific and are working with a limited budget, you may want to call first or check often. This smaller store is geared toward personal service—stop by 10 A.M. to 7 P.M. Monday through Saturday, 1 P.M. to 6 P.M. Sunday.

Phil's Guitars

- 5325 Ballard Ave. N, Seattle; 623-2780

Make no mistake—Phil Emerson is a jazz man. Mr. C knew it before he even entered this store, as melodious grooves could be heard up and down this otherwise deserted street late one summer afternoon. Phil had just moved his shop here from Pioneer Square, and he and two buddies were having an informal jam session. Beautiful stuff.

Phil's a serious player; he and his wife Judy are part of a group which can be heard Monday nights at the Five Point Cafe (see the listing under "Entertainment—Music"). He loves his guitars, and he carefully selects every model for sale here. They're all high-end American brands, and they're all second-hand, but not many are vintage styles. A handsome Les Paul model, for instance—which would be as much as $1,800 new—was selling here for $700. Not cheap, no, but chea*per*.

Other guitars start as low as $200-$300, like Guild and Epiphone solid-bodies. There are all kinds of beautiful ones to look at: steel guitars, archtops, some electrics. The new store is just as attractive, with hardwood floors and exposed brick walls. Part of the hip, "new" Ballard. Phil does repairs too, drawing not only on his longtime experience but on "30 years' worth of knobs, keys, and other parts." There is no store warranty on used instruments, but he'll make free adjustments if needed. "I'll jump through hoops to make people happy," he says, and you believe it. Phil's is open Tuesdays through Saturdays from 10 A.M. to 7 P.M.

Sherman Clay
- 1624 Fourth Ave., Seattle; 622-7580
- 10692 NE Eighth St., Bellevue; 454-0633

Okay, so no pianos are going to be *cheap*. However, you've got to admit that paying $2,500 for a used, top-condition piano sounds a lot sweeter than paying $5,000 or more for a new one. Sherman Clay has both new and used pianos in its large showrooms, including such names as Baldwin, Yamaha, and Wurlitzer. The price range on used instruments is generally between $2,000 and $4,000; since a good piano can last for decades, prices are based on condition, rather than age. There is a thirty-day store warranty, and delivery can be arranged (no pun intended). Open from 9:30 A.M. to 5:30 P.M. Mondays through Saturdays, and from noon to 5 P.M. Sundays.

Trading Musician
- 1512 NE 65th St., Seattle; 522-6707

Don't expect to unload five magic beans here, but still—the buying, selling, and trading here is just great. First of all, the place is larger than most used instrument stores. They do sell some new instruments to supplement their stock, so chances are they'll have *something* in what you're looking for, in a range of prices based on condition. Plenty of spare parts, too. Trading Musician covers the spectrum on stringed instruments: guitars, amps, violins, cellos, mandolins, autoharps, and banjos. Plus keyboards and drums, as well as rare and antique items. You name it, they've got it (just about—no kazoos).

Mr. C spotted such things as a Gibson J-40 acoustic guitar ($699), a Fender P-bass ($550), and a five-piece CB Percussion drum set, without cymbals ($450). Throw those together and you've got everything you need for a band except the players, all for about $1700. Not bad. Might even leave enough in the budget to add a two-year-old Roland W-30 keyboard for just $1000 more.

When Mr. C spoke with the head trader, plans were in the works to open another location around the corner at 1514 15th Avenue NE. The idea is to dedicate the newer shop just to TM's stock of drums; so be on the lookout for the **Trading Musician Drum Shop** to find even more deals. Currently, Trading Musician is open every day of the week between 11 A.M. and 7 P.M.

Western Pianos and Organs
- 13018 Lake City Way NE, Seattle; 363-2875
- 15015 Main St., Bellevue; 644-0155
- 10644 NE Eighth St., Bellevue; 454-5705
- 601 S Second St., Renton; 226-9515
- 3815 S Steele St., Tacoma; 839-0809

Established in 1890, WPO sells new and second-hand keyboards of all shapes and sizes. In fact, they furnish pianos to such institutions as the Seattle Opera, the Northwest Chamber Orchestra, and UW—surely, what's good enough for them is good enough for your living room. On a recent waltz around the showroom floor, Mr. C found a Kawai oak upright piano, list priced at $4,750, selling for $3,888; and a used Steinway baby grand ("one owner") for $13,595—half of its original price. Open weekdays from 10 A.M. to 7 P.M., Saturdays from 10 A.M. to 5 P.M., and Sundays from 12 noon to 5 P.M.

PARTY SUPPLIES

In addition to the stores listed below, don't forget to check out the liquidation stores listed in the "Discount Department Stores" chapter, as well as just about any "dollar" store you come across.

Ace Novelty Company

- 13434 NE 16th St., Bellevue; 644-1820

Hidden away like buried treasure in one of Bellevue's many industrial parks sits this enormous warehouse of toys, party supplies, stuffed animals, inflatables, and puzzles. At one end of the building, as luck would have it, there is a small store which sells this stuff to the public—even while trucks load up to haul these goodies coast-to-coast.

Ace carries those little toy favors for children's parties at prices starting from 50¢ a dozen. Five-inch diameter balloons sell for $4.80 a gross (!), while sizes up to eleven inches go for $15 a gross. Nothing gross about *those* prices. Plenty of supplies for more grown-up parties too. And, as any holiday nears—from New Year's Eve to Christmas—the stock takes on the appropriate look.

The company is also licensed to make and sell official T-shirts, toys, and other items relating to all of your favorite baseball, football, and basketball teams. Not to mention high-demand toys, like—yes—Power Rangers, or whatever the "Mommy, I want..." fashion of the moment is. These are still sold at discount prices, and are of better quality than imitation knockoffs. Ace is your ace-in-the-hole, open weekdays only from 9-5.

Cash & Carry United Grocers

- 1760 Fourth Ave. S, Seattle; 343-7156
- 13102 Stone Ave. N, Seattle; 364-1733
- 2208 136th Pl. NE, Bellevue; 644-4638
- 2917 Cedar St., Everett; 339-2628
- 1628 S 344th St., Federal Way; 925-0550
- 21504 84th Ave. S, Kent; 872-7873
- 6412 204th St. SE, Lynnwood; 672-1886
- 6208 Tacoma Mall Blvd., Tacoma; 472-6879

See the listing under "Food Shops."

Champion Party and Costume

- 124 Denny Way, Seattle; 282-8202

If your world came crashing down when *Star Trek: The Next Generation* aired its final episode, there is hope for you yet. In fact, the entire crew can join together once again—right in your living room. Champion Party and Costume sells life-size, cardboard cutouts of Captain Picard and the whole inter-galactic crew in various action poses. Bring home a Klingon for just $24.95—they make great dance partners and nifty coat racks! For that matter, they also have cartoon characters, movie stars, and—yes—Elvis has been sighted here as well.

Meanwhile, other fun stuff (including adult novelties) are all on display in this huge party supply store. Pick up those colorful, plastic Hawaiian lei for 38¢ each, or a plastic grave stone for just $2.59. Halloween costumes are available all year long; these range from a 79¢ Zorro mask to a child's complete Peter Pan outfit for $21.95. Lots of wigs are hair—er, here, too. The big, red "Peg Bundy" style is truly the modern fright wig at $29.95. Fake vomit and other little scientific accomplishments are in great supply, too.

Needless to say, Champion carries full lines of paper plates, drink cups, streamers, cartoon character tablecloths, mylar balloons—in short, the works. The selection is quite large, and the merchandise, no matter how unusual, is well-organized and easy to browse through. Open Mondays through Saturdays, from 9 A.M. to 7 P.M., and Sundays from 11 A.M. to 5 P.M.

Michaels Crafts
- 5959 Corson Ave. S, Seattle; 762-0900
- Crossroads Shopping Center, Bellevue; 747-1221
- 4205 Wheaton Way, Bremerton; (360) 479-8789
- 32061 Pacific Hwy. S, Federal Way; 946-1191
- 9755 Juanita Dr. NE, Kirkland; 821-4444
- 4027 198th St. SW, Lynnwood; 771-6600
- 4510 95th St. SW, Tacoma; 582-0314
- 17686 Southcenter Pkwy., Tukwila; 575-4352

See the listing under "Sewing and Craft Supplies."

The Paper Zone
- 1911 First Ave. S, Seattle; 682-8644
- 9423 Evergreen Way, Everett; 355-7703
- 3838 148th Ave. NE, Redmond; 883-0273

These everything-that's-fit-to-be-printed-upon stores put a funky spin on warehouse-type buying. They have a vast selection to choose from, whether you're looking for fine-grade stationery for the office or fun, decorative goods for Buffy's birthday party. And you don't have to be a member or a wholesale purchaser.

Among its aisles of party supplies, PZ has tons of plastic and heavy paper plateware, in artsy floral patterns and bold solid colors; plus disposable utensils, cups and goblets, tablecloths, fold-out gift boxes, streamers, and ban-

ners. They also sell invitations to just about any bash you can toss.

Volume pricing means you'll get good deals on all of this stuff, whether you're buying enough for your office banquet or a single punch bowl. Be sure to check out the "Sale Zone" clearance room, at the downtown store, for extra bargains. The staff is young and attentive, and ready to serve. Hours are 8 A.M. to 6 P.M. on weekdays, and 10 A.M. to 5 P.M. on Saturdays.

Party for Less
- 10015 NE 137th St., Kirkland; 820-4751

The best deal you're likely to find on greeting cards—anywhere—is here in this shopping center near Totem Lake. All cards are sold at 50% off the printed price, all the time. What's that? Not enough to make the trip worth it? How about plastic and latex balloons, from 59¢ to $2, depending on the size. Plus helium-filled balloons with hundreds of novelty prints and messages, tied up with a ribbon, for $1.99 each. There are also tons of picnic and party decorations, from printed paper and plastic tablecloths to plastic cups and cutlery, all sold at 30% off retail prices. PFL is open weekdays from 9 A.M. to 9 P.M., Saturdays from 9-6, and Sundays from 11-5.

The Salvage Broker
- 13760 Aurora Ave. N, Seattle; 365-7771

See the listing under "Discount Department Stores."

Sysco
- 1242 Sixth Ave. S, Seattle; 447-9113

See the listing under "Food Shops."

SEWING AND CRAFT SUPPLIES

Calico Corners
- 104 Bellevue Way SE, Bellevue; 455-2510
- 3225 Alderwood Mall Blvd., Lynnwood; 778-8019

Specializing in name-brand upholstery and drapery fabrics, these suburban stores boast 50% savings over retail and private designer costs. Mr. C found bolts of Waverly fabrics selling at $13-$15 a yard, as well as Kaufman and Robert Allen designs. Though this is an upscale kind of place, much of Calico's inventory is made up of big-name second-quality and end-of-the-bolt clearance deals. The cash you save with these should, um, "cover" the cost of custom labor to finish your project—or, do it yourself and pocket the savings. Hours: Mondays through Saturdays from 10 A.M. to 6 P.M., and Sundays from 12 noon to 5:00.

Craft Supply
- 14603 NE 20th St., Bellevue; 624-4929
- 14911 Fourth Ave. SW, Burien; 243-9360
- 25414 104th Ave. SE, Kent; 854-0150

This chain of craft stores is especially proud of its custom frames—as well it should be. A 16" x 20" metal frame, complete with glass and matte, all cut and mounted for you, costs a mere $24.68. They also do a good job with off-the-shelf frames. Most of the other kinds of items here are sold at standard, competitive prices, but Mr. C did find some unusual bargains. Eleven-ounce cans of Weekend spray paint are available in 18 colors for $1.88 each; acrylic colors by Delta, in over 200 hues, are 98¢ for a two-ounce bottle. And a plethora of wicker and straw baskets, in all shapes and sizes, start under $3 each. Open seven days a week.

Famous Labels Fabric Outlet
- 17810 West Valley Road, Tukwila; 251-0067

How famous is famous? How 'bout L.L. Bean flannels for $4.99 a yard? Plus Jantzen, Speedo, OshKosh, Liz Claiborne....ah, that's gotten your attention. This large, warehouse-style store gets overruns from the factories that make fabrics for all of these designers and then some. Most sell at 30% to 40% below retail prices. Most are first-quality, too; some are seconds, sold at even better discounts.

Recent deals included cotton/lycra print fabrics for $7.99, 100% cotton twills for $4.99, and sweatshirt fleece for $3.99. Nylon, lycra, and cotton/lycra blends are the store's forte, with literally hundreds of bolts to choose from in a wide range of styles, basic to bold. Fun novelty prints for kids' bedrooms, lycra with foil accents, nylon for windbreakers, plus all kinds of trim and accessories at similarly rock-bottom prices. And don't miss the "Fabric by the Pound" bins, filled with remnants of all kinds. Anything you find is yours for $3.20 a pound!

Famous Labels offers senior citizens a 10% discount every Sunday. Groups making large purchases can get extra discounts, too. The store also hosts sewing classes; once or twice a month, these are given free of charge. With titles like "Create Easy Aerobic Wear in Less Than an Hour," these focus on short cuts (no pun intended) for using whatever's on sale that month. Stop in or call for their monthly newsletter. The staff is friendly and very knowledgeable. With all this going on, it's no wonder folks come here from as far away as Canada. Open Mondays through Saturdays from 9:30 A.M. to 5:30 P.M., Sundays from 12-5 P.M.

House of Fabrics
- 14510 Aurora Ave. N, Seattle; 363-0430
- 2217 NW 57th St., Seattle; 782-6242

Outrageously high fabric prices may mean that a store is in an expensive location; but on the other hand, with fabrics, super-cheap prices can also mean poor quality. House of Fabrics is a national chain, and their prices fall somewhere in the middle. Lots of fabric, in several different designs and textures, is on display, plus lace, crafts, and jewelry supplies.

Most larger stores like this have discount or clearance tables, usually loaded with remnants or leftovers. The quality and selection in this department were especially impressive the day Mr. C dropped by; home decorating fabrics were marked 50% off. Mr. C saw a bolt of beautiful, thick, 100% cotton tapestry fabric selling $17.50 per yard—half its original price. Not all the fabric costs that much—bolts of 100% cotton calicos were selling for an every day price of $3 per yard. Open from 9:30 A.M. to 9 P.M. Mondays through Fridays, 'til 7 P.M. Saturdays, and from noon to 6 P.M. Sundays.

In the Beginning
- 8201 Lake City Way NE, Seattle; 523-8862
- 14125 NE 20th St., Bellevue; 865-0155

Quilting is the specialty here. Everything you'd ever need to design and put them together, including books and classes, is available. There is a high-quality assortment of fabrics and patterns, from vintage Americana to fun stuff for the kiddies—all at excellent prices. According to Mr. C's

---

expert, who clued him into this favorite of hers, cottons that cost $7.95 a yard here would easily cost $10 or more in other stores—if you could find any which carried as good a selection. They're even clever with their remnants: Rather than selling ends of bolts in odd lengths, these are cut up into six-inch squares and sold in bundles, ready to be made into patchworks. Smart, huh?

There is a fee for classes, but none for ITB's regular newsletter, which not only lists schedules but includes tips, patterns, events, and other chat stuff for quilters in the area. The stores are open seven days a week, including Wednesday and Thursday evenings until 9 P.M.

Michaels Crafts
- 5959 Corson Ave. S, Seattle; 762-0900
- Crossroads Shopping Center, Bellevue; 747-1221
- 4205 Wheaton Way, Bremerton; (360) 479-8789
- 32061 Pacific Hwy. S, Federal Way; 946-1191
- 9755 Juanita Dr. NE, Kirkland; 821-4444
- 4027 198th St. SW, Lynnwood; 771-6600
- 4510 95th St. SW, Tacoma; 582-0314
- 17686 Southcenter Pkwy., Tukwila; 575-4352

Taking the superstore approach to fabrics and craft supplies, Michaels' vast selection is hard to beat. This national chain can offer everything from drafting tables to silk ficus trees, acrylic paints to ready-made picture frames, beads to baskets. They're all at high-volume, low prices.

They seem to have anything required by artists (pre-made 16' x 20' canvases, two for $5 on a recent sale), latch-hook rug makers, knitters, quilters, and dried flower arrangers. "Blank" T-shirts, sneakers, and baseball caps await appliqués and liquid rubber paint. And at Christmastime, there are miniature wooden sleighs to fill, ornament kits, stencils, and all the rest. The party supplies section discounts Gibson greeting cards by 40%; made-to-order wedding invitations are also discounted by that much (during special sales); not to mention wrapping paper, latex and mylar balloons, and candles.

Frequent sales knock anywhere from 30% to 50% off the store's regular prices ("30% off all custom framing orders"). They also feature free classes and demonstrations, which vary by store. Open seven days.

Jen-Cel-Lite Factory Outlet
- 954 E Union St., Seattle; 322-3030

See the listing under "Home Furnishings."

Nine Lives
- 1656 E Olive Way, Seattle; 325-6530

Nine Lives is a vintage store, and quite frankly, Mr. C thinks it's the cat's pajamas. The reason why it's listed in this chapter is because it is one of the few shops that sells vintage cloth scraps and buttons. Now, if you really want vintage fabric, you could buy an old garment and cut it up. At Nine Lives, it's already done

for you, so you don't have to feel guilty about destroying someone's prom gown. The scraps here start at 50¢ per piece. Rich velvets, satins, calicos—the pieces aren't large, but perfect sizes for crafts, patches, or making small items like hats, headbands, or purses. There's a wide selection of old buttons for sale too—most of which are under 50¢ each.

For even more cheap, unique buttons, see the listing for Spencer & Company under "Furniture—Used." Nine Lives is open from 11 A.M. to 6:30 P.M. Mondays through Saturdays, and from noon on Sundays.

Pacific Fabrics & Crafts Outlet Stores
- 2230 Fourth Ave. S, Seattle; 628-6237
- 4214 Wheaton Way, Bremerton; (360) 479-4214

Overstocks and remnants pour into Pacific's outlets from its dozen stores stretching as far north as Alaska. Mr. C visited the outlet just below the Kingdome, where tables are piled high with bolts, large remnants, and all kinds of accessories.

Plunge into any one and you're likely to find black velvet for $6.99 a yard, decorator fabrics as low as $4.99 a yard (including Kaufman, Waverly, and Mill Creek!), country-style wallpaper rolls at 50% off, sewing patterns from 25% to 50% off, and much, much more. Lots of cartoon novelty prints, like Snoopy and the Flintstones, for children's room projects. All notions are always 10% off, throughout the store; plenty of craftmaking supplies, too. Open seven days a week, including weeknights until 9 P.M.

BEAD AND JEWELRY-MAKING SUPPLIES

Alexander's Bead Bazaar
- 920 NE 64th St., Seattle; 526-8909

See the listing under "Jewelry."

The Bead Factory
- 621 Broadway E, Seattle; 328-7047

With so many different kinds of beads out there, it can be difficult to

compare prices between these popular kinds of stores. However, the Bead Factory offers a bit of price protection: If you do find the same item in another store for less, BF will beat the price by 5%. Other ways to save money here include showing a jewelry maker's license, which entitles you to wholesale prices. Or, you can join their Bead Club for $3, allowing you to attend workshops at a 20% savings, receive a monthly newsletter with coupons, and get $10 worth of free beads with every $100 you spend.

Of course, you can always just walk in and find inexpensive beads. Most charms, porcelain, wood, and metal beads cost between 35¢ and $2.95, depending on the intricacy of the bead's pattern. Indian glass beads range in price from 3¢ to 15¢. When Mr. C visited, Indonesian sterling silver beads, normally 35¢ to $6.50, were half-price in a clearance sale. Check in during February for the storewide anniversary sale, too. The Bead Factory is open from 10 A.M. to 9 P.M. Mondays through Saturdays, and from 11 A.M. to 6 P.M. Sundays.

TSI Beads

- 101 Nickerson St., Seattle; 282-3046

Just across the bridge from Fremont is a veritable haven for all jewelry makers. If that's you, then you need to know about TSI. May not look like much from the outside, but artisans rave about the treasures found within. Far more than just beads—at wholesale prices—they also carry everything you'll need to make your creations. Mallets, vise grips, setting pliers, Dremel bits, and wire cutters go for about half the price you'd see in most other bead and wire stores. Plus every imaginable FIMO product, for making your own beads.

Being a no-frills dealer, TSI offers quantity discounts on most of its merchandise. The more you buy, the more you save. And, for an added convenience, the whole kit and caboodle is listed in a handy catalogue, with pre-printed order forms. The friendly folks here are ready to help you with any problems. Open Mondays through Saturdays from 9 A.M. to 5:30 P.M.

World Beads

- 98 Virginia St., Seattle; 441-7022
- 233 Broadway E, Seattle; 323-4998

What makes World Beads a crafter's dream? You can buy beads at wholesale prices *without* a jewelry-maker's license. You do have to buy in large quantities—most beads are sold in packages of tens or hundreds—but if you make a lot of jewelry, then it's perfect. Here, you order your beads wholesale; the order takes about two weeks to come in, but you get a 75% discount! Ongoing monthly sales also make for good deals, like 20% taken off already-created jewelry.

The store itself is very shopper-friendly; beads are grouped by style, then arranged by color from light to dark. Tiny beads, arranged by the same system, are contained in vials. Since it can be difficult to visualize how long fifty or one hundred beads can be, World Beads has "crafted" a simple solution. Strings of each kind of bead are on display. By seeing how long the various strands are, it's easier to select the right size vial. All kinds of "findings" (the parts which hold jewelry pieces together) are in stock here; and if you don't know exactly what you need, there's plenty of help available. It's even possible to walk in as a novice, and walk out with a piece of self-created jewelry. Open daily; hours vary at each location.

SHOES AND SNEAKERS

Athletic Supply Company Outlet
- 224 Westlake Ave. N, Seattle; 623-8972

See the listing under "Clothing—New."

Burlington Coat Factory
- 24111 Highway 99, Edmonds; 776-2221
- 10401 Gravelly Lake Dr. SW, Tacoma; 588-3595
- Pavilion Mall, Tukwila; 575-4269

Not content with being a popular clothing discounter for the entire family, Burlington Coat Factory stores have expanded from within to become something almost like actual department stores. They carry big names at good prices; some are very good bargains indeed. You can outfit yourself from top to toe here, inside and out, in conservative or stylish looks.

The Capezio Footwear Outlet extends these savings to all kinds of basic and classy shoes for men, women, and kids; it's not just for dancing anymore. Current styles in dressy shoes and boots are mostly sold at $10 to $20 off list prices; for deeper discounts, though, look over on the long self-service racks, arranged by size. These are mainly close-outs and overstocks, all perfectly good. You may find a pair of red leather pumps by Bandolino, reduced from $72 to $39; men's dress loafers by Johnston and Murphy, marked down form $165 to $98; or Wrangler cowboy boots for $70 (not leather, obviously but good looking). there is a more limited selection of sneakers, like ankle-high tennis shoes by Reebok for $49; plus kids shoes by Sesame Street, Fisher Price, and Hush Puppies. And it's a good place to stock up on stockings and socks; Burlington Hosiery is sold here at $1-$2 off all styles. Open seven days and evenings.

Loehmann's
- 3620 128th Ave. SE, Bellevue; 641-7596

Loehmann's means low prices on fancy women's clothing and shoes, simple as that. These folks practically *invented* the designer closeout store, years ago in New York; suave Manhattanites still shlep out to Brooklyn for their famous deals.

Among the racks of fine designer shoes seen recently were a pair of dressy heels by Larry Stuart, meant to sell for up to $98, reduced to $60. Leather moccasins by JP Tod, originally retailing for $180 (?!) were seen here for a more comfortable $70. And there were lots of choices priced at $29.99, including flats and heels by Caressa, Bandolino, Evan-Picone, and others. To borrow that famous Robin Williams quote, "Imelda Marcos, *come on down!*"

Loehmann's is the anchor store for the shopping plaza of the same name, across from Factoria Square. It's open from 10 A.M. to 9 P.M. on weekdays, 10-7 on Saturdays, and 12-6 on Sundays.

Nordstrom Rack
- 1601 Second Ave., Seattle; 448-8522
- 3115 Alderwood Mall Blvd., Lynnwood; 774-6569
- 17900 Southcenter Pkwy., Tukwila; 575-1058

Mr. C hardly needs to tell you about this local legend—but would a book like this be complete without it?

Sure, you know about Nordstrom's always-enticing selection of clothing bargains, but don't forget that they're also a fantastic place to shop shoes for everyone in the family. And "the Rack," combined with the Shoe Pavilion (described below) and the Burlington Coat Factory (above), makes Southcenter's Pavilion Mall a particular magnet for footwear fans.

Women will love bargains like a pair of classy heels by Donna Karan, with a suggested retail price of $340 (ouch!) reduced to $109 (now *that's* a better fit). Mr. C found pumps by Via Spiga and Ellen Tracy, both retailing around $150, both half-price at $74.90. And casual loafers by Rockport, Bandolino, and Nine West were all seen for $30 a pair.

For the guys, a pair of Cole-Haan dress shoes were recently reduced from $200 retail to $130 here. Lower-priced options included leather shoes by Dexter reduced from $65 to $35, and about the same for a pair by Nunn Bush. On the athletic side, Nike "Air" sneakers which retail for $78 can sell here for $57; Reeboks were trimmed from $63 to $50. There are similar deals for women, too, like Asics "Gel" shoes, elsewhere as much as $70, here $32.

And, lest the kiddies be left out of this footwear frenzy, Mr. C saw girls' Birkenstock sandals for $19, classic patent leather party shoes by Buster Brown for $12.90, and teens' Nike sneakers for $20; boys bargains included Wildcat hiking boots reduced from $30 to $19.90, and Reebok basketball shoes, once $45, here $30.

All sales at the Rack are final, so try everything on and make sure they fit. It's strictly self-serve; at these prices, you won't mind. Open seven days a week; hours vary with each location.

Shoe Pavilion
- 1501 Fourth Ave., Seattle; 382-0258
- 830 NE Northgate Way, Seattle; 368-0719
- Aurora Square, Seattle; 367-8716

- Loehmann's Plaza, Bellevue; 643-3828
- 14339 NE 20th St., Bellevue; 747-3620
- 3225 Alderwood Mall Blvd., Lynnwood; 672-0322
- Pavilion Mall, Tukwila; 575-0196

With branches in all the right spots (i.e. Factoria, Aurora Square, and of course, the Pavilion Mall) this regional chain offers major discounts on name brand shoes for men, women, and kids. Most are in the range of 30%-40% off, but look carefully and you can find some pairs marked down as much as 60% or 70%.

On a recent scouting mission, Mr. C found good deals on shoes by Anne Klein, Pappagallo, Naturalizer, Zodiac, Dexter, and many others. A pair of Bandolino sandals were marked from a list price of $65 down to $39; Evan-Picone flats were reduced from $100 to $60. And a set of Western boots by Vittorio Ricci, listed at $105, were on sale for $39.95.

For men, leather dress shoes by Nunn Bush ($40) and Stanley Blacker ($60) were each $30 off list price. Loafers by David & Joan (the flip side of Joan & David, natch) were reduced from $149 to $79. There is also a small selection of sneakers, like women's aerobic shoes by Avia, marked down from $75 to a trim $40.

How do they do it? Shoe Pavilion buys large quantities of popular models for stores up and down the West Coast, and sells them in a no-frills manner. In other words, everything's out on racks, and you have to stand there and try them on by yourself. But hey, for these deals, it's worth it. Sizes are fairly well represented: Women's shoes range from 5-10, and men's from 7-12. Open seven days a week, mall hours.

SPORTING GOODS

Bargain Base
- 2401 Utah Ave. S, Seattle; 622-2264

See the listing under "Discount Department Stores."

Big 5 Sporting Goods
- 1740 NW Market St., Seattle; 783-0163
- 4315 University Way NE, Seattle; 547-2445
- Aurora Village, Seattle; 546-4443
- 2500 SW Barton St., Seattle; 932-2212
- Factoria Square Mall, Bellevue; 747-5230
- 125 SW 148th St., Burien; 246-2707
- 1916 S 320th St., Federal Way; 941-9991
- 24216 104th Ave. SE, Kent; 852-2524
- 12520 120th Ave. NE, Kirkland; 821-4366
- 18600-A 33rd Ave. W, Lynnwood; 771-8066
- 508 S Third St., Renton; 271-6900

This major West Coast chain has a little bit of everything, for the most solitary exercise nut or any size of team. The prices are, well, competitive; better yet, items in every department are reduced in weekly sales. You're sure to find something you need here.

One such sale recently featured 30% off on all skiwear in stock, and during the height of the skiing season! At the same time, citybound daredevils could save $80 on Ultra-Wheels "Zephyr" in-line skates. Tennis enthusiasts, meanwhile, could find a Wilson "Cobra 95" graphite racquet marked down from $110 to just $49.99. Big 5 has plenty of home fitness equipment, from Everlast training bags to Weider home gym systems to electronic stairclimbers by Voit and others. Plus savings on golf, baseball, camping, basketball. . .not

to mention the appropriate clothing and footwear for all of these activities. Save anywhere from $10 to $40 on select models of Reebok, Nike, Asics, Pony, Saucony, and many others. Play ball at all branches seven days a week.

Bikesmith
- 2309 N 45th St., Seattle; 632-3102

This tiny but busy Wallingford shop sells and services new, used, and consignment bicycles of every shape and size from the latest mountain hybrid to some really rusty old classics. Owner Val Kleitz's neatly coiffed handlebar moustache *alone* shows the careful and loving attention to detail that makes many of his customers longtime devotees.

Among new bikes, Mr. C found mountain bikes by Motiv starting from around $250, and from just $135 in kids' sizes (of course, some would say *all* such bikes appear to be kid-sized...). Second-hand bikes are fully tuned up before being put out for sale, and even so, they come with a 30-day store warranty in case any further adjustments are needed. You can get a Raleigh road bike for as little as $75 this way! Models being sold by the store on consignment included a Trek 360 road bike for just $400 during Mr. C's visit.

Bikesmith also claims to offer the "least expensive, most comprehensive standard tune-up in Seattle," and in 24 hours, to boot. Mr. C makes no attempt to compare services in his books (just scouting discount buys is a full-time job!), but these folks will indeed show you a long list of the parts they check. The store is open seven days a week, but no evenings.

Capitol Hill Camping & Surplus
- 910 E Pike St., Seattle; 325-3566

This small "Mom and Pop" operation carries only merchandise that comes from close-outs, damaged boxes or the like, and passes on the savings to you. Except for Mom and Pop, there are no other employees, and this also helps to keep down costs.

Some of the good deals you may find include backpacker stoves, with fuel, for $5.98; generic combat boots for $25; sleeping bags starting at $19.98; and tents starting at $29.98. As an additional service, tent poles can be customized here. There's plenty of clothing, too; European military surplus, "Mom's Recycled Chic," (told you) plus good quality new and secondhand garments are available at very reasonable prices. Gently used cotton kimonos and toasty winter robes were seen for $15-$20, and no-name canvas high-top sneakers for $20.98. Hike in for a visit, Mondays through Saturdays between 10 A.M. and 5 P.M.

Encore Sports and Fitness
● 16389 Redmond Way, Redmond; 883-7900

Along with its lines of new sporting goods and fitness equipment, what makes this store interesting to Mr. C is its extensive selection of exercise machines that are looking for *second* owners. He saw three treadmills, for instance—an Active Sport 77, and a pair of Power Fit 3001 models—each priced at $439, far less than the prices for comparable new versions. Why give your checkbook a harder workout than your cardiovascular system?

There's also a good variety of stationary exercise bicycles and rowing machines; and, for the duffer, golf clubs that are still decent looking, even though they've seen some duty on the back nine. They usually have some used regular bicycles as well; the gem on Mr. C's visit, in fact, was a tandem bike with drum brakes for a piddling (or is that pedaling?) $199. Two seats for the price of one! Second-hand equipment does not carry a store guarantee here, but it is all carefully checked out before going out on the sales floor. Encore is open Mondays through Thursdays from 10 A.M.

to 7 P.M., Fridays and Saturdays from 10-6, and Sundays from 12-5.

Federal Army & Navy Surplus
● 2112 First Ave., Seattle; 443-1818

Army/navy surplus stores used to be synonymous with cheaply priced, sturdy clothing. With the emergence of superstores, outlets, and all sorts of other discount opportunities, that's not so much the case anymore. However, you can still find some good deals at a place like Federal.

Second-hand, and slightly flawed merchandise offer the best bargains, along with stock overruns. Mr. C found an Aurora sleeping bag for $75 that'll keep you nice and warm down to fifteen degrees above zero. Put it on a Therm-a-Rest self-inflating sleeping pad ($32-$70 depending on thickness) and it'll feel just as comfy as your own bed, if not better! And lastly, even though it's never, ever, ever wet in Seattle (yeah, and Cleveland winters are balmy too), hooded jacket and pants rain slicker sets start at $35. Federal Surplus is open Mondays through Saturdays from 9:30 A.M. to 6 P.M.

Koppel's Army-Navy
● 16119 Redmond Way, Redmond; 881-3501

Will you see Ted in here, suiting up for a Nightline assignment from the battlefront? Well...no. But you will see lots of new and used clothing, as well as camping gear, for your own rough and ready outings. Mr. C found several good used items, such as camouflage jackets and wool pants, for under $12; other noteworthy deals included GI jungle boots under $30, and nylon sleeping bags from $19.88. Open weekdays from 9 A.M. to 6 P.M., Saturdays 9-5, and Sundays 11-3.

Montlake Bicycle Shop
● 2223 24th Ave. E, Seattle; 329-7333
● 10047 Main St., Bellevue; 462-8823
● 514 Central Way NE, Kirkland; 828-3800

For over a dozen years, these guys have been keeping Seattle rolling on all sorts of fine-quality wheels. They claim to be the biggest Cannondale dealer in the whole state of Washington, for instance; and they certainly have quite a few—not to mention Diamond Back, Bianchi, Mongoose, and more.

Many of these brands can really set you back financially; how to save a buck on a bike? Montlake has a couple of options. For starters, consider one of last year's models. Usually, all that changes is the color scheme. August tends to be the best time of year for closeout deals, like a Cannondale mountain bike reduced from a list price of $2,000 to $1,500. The original Eastlake store, by the way, is the biggest of the bunch and tends to have more selection than its suburban siblings.

Option number two: Buy a rental bike. Montlake rents out all kinds of models, and they are perfectly happy to sell *any one* of these at *any* time. Each rental is noted in a log book; and the more times a bike has been used, the more they shave off its selling price. This rarely results in all-out giveaways, but you can certainly save some dough; for example, a Diamond Back cross-country bike, $285 new, might be reduced to $200 after about fifteen rentals. That's not exactly heavy usage; any avid cyclist might put that much mileage on in just a few weeks. Furthermore, if you rent a bike yourself and decide to purchase it, you can apply the rental fee to the current selling price; what a great way to save money *and* make sure it's the right bike for you.

One final bonus under this scheme: Technically, if you buy a rental bike, you are still its first owner. That means you get the full manufacturer's warranty, from day one, just as though you'd bought the bike brand-new off the showroom floor. Nice, huh? Montlake offers full servicing, by the way, and usually promises a 24-hour turnaround; many smaller repairs are done while-u-wait. All branches are open seven days a week.

Outdoor & More
- 510 Westlake Ave. N, Seattle; 340-0677

Beginning with 10,000 square feet (not to mention thirty years of buying experience) and expanding from there, Steve Hess has created a no-frills paradise in the Lake Union area. He's filled his own store with both sporting goods and the necessary clothing, much (but not all) of it closeouts. See the listing under "Clothing—New" for the scoop on that side of the business.

And where to show off such hot (thermally speaking) fashion? How 'bout inside a Stansport "Odyssey" dome tent for two. Identical to a $200 model from The North Face, this one goes for a cozier $60 here. Add a portable roll-up eating table, $40 elsewhere, for $25. O & M has every season covered, offering deals on just about anything from cross-country skis and snowboards to kayaks and vinyl boats—not to mention a full selection of sundry camping, fishing, and backpacking gear. Everything, even the tents, is out on display, and all at good prices; and it all carries a 30-day refund (with receipt) or exchange policy. Open seven days.

Play It Again Sports
- 10738 Fifth Ave. NE, Seattle; 365-6226
- 14339 NE 20th St., Bellevue; 643-2599
- 10121 Evergreen Way, Everett; 356-2776
- 1320 S 324th St., Federal Way; 946-2029
- 19513 Highway 99, Lynnwood; 343-5722
- 9702 163rd Pl. NE, Redmond; 869-2153
- 17622 108th Ave. SE, Renton; 227-8777
- 2941 S 38th St., Tacoma; 472-0551
- 17301 140th Ave. NE, Woodinville; 481-8676

From humble beginnings in Minneapolis, this has grown into a national chain of some 400 suburban stores—all buying, selling, and trading new and used sports equipment. The merchandise gets swapped around between stores, insuring a large, balanced selection in every branch. PIAS gets good deals on new items that have been discontinued (but hey, how much can a baseball glove change?). Among these, Mr. C saw an Alpine Tracker exercise machine, reduced from $160 retail to a *svelte* $99.95. A pair of Ultra Wheels in-line skates was $25 off at $150. And a Mizuno baseball mitt, worth over $100, was selling here for $59.

About 60% of the stock consists of used equipment. Seen recently were a boy's mountain bike for $69.95, a pair of K2 downhill skis for $89.95, billiard cues from $11.95, and a set of Tommy Armour .845s golf irons, valued at $1,000, selling for $399. Plus hockey sticks, basketballs, baseball bats, footballs, shoulder pads for linebackers of all ages, tennis racquets, and lots more. Best of all, you can trade in your old stuff toward anything in the store—even new items. Good excuse for cleaning out the garage! Open seven days a week.

Pro Golf Discount

- 10746 Fifth Ave. NE, Seattle; 367-3529
- 14121 NE 20th St., Bellevue; 641-6766
- 19125 33rd Ave. W, Lynnwood; 771-2131
- Tacoma Mall, Tacoma; 473-4290
- 301 Tukwila Pkwy., Tukwila; 431-0100

High-volume sales make for under-par prices on new golf equipment, from club to cleats. The sales staff, clearly experienced duffers themselves, are ready to help you choose from the walls of club sets, which on Mr. C's visit included things like a set of eight Wilson 1200 midsize irons, list priced at $600, selling for to just $290. An Allied Classic 17-piece bag and club set was marked down on a special sale from $320 to $199. And, you can save even more with used clubs, like a set of three Spaulding "Centurion" drivers for $60; or, perhaps something from the $5 club bin.

There are lots of sale-priced shoes;

MR. CHEAP'S PICKS
Sporting Goods

✔ **Capitol Hill Surplus**—Not the biggest, but the Mom & Pop staff will take good care of you.

✔ **Encore Sports and Fitness**—As in second-hand treadmills and exercise equipment—much better than sending your money off to those TV info-mercials.

✔ **Montlake Bicycle Shop**—You can purchase their rental bikes at *any* time; the more they've been rented, the lower the price.

✔ **2nd Base** and **Second Bounce**—Don't get 'em mixed up, now. Both score big savings in used sports equipment, on everything from tennis balls to kayaks.

one example was a pair of Nike "Air Classics," retailing for $120, on sale for $80. Plus similar discounts on balls and accessories, and clothing. There's even a demo area in the store, where you can try out your swing with that new Titleist you've been eyeing. Open seven days a week.

REI

- 1525 11th Ave., Seattle; 323-8333
- 15400 NE 20th St., Bellevue; 643-3700
- Gateway Center Plaza, Federal Way; 941-4994
- 4200 194th Ave. SW, Lynnwood; 774-1300

To answer your first question, it stands for Recreational Equipment, Incorporated. This is a rather unusual sporting goods store, focusing not on team sports, but outdoor activities—bicycling, running, skiing, rock climbing, camping, and more. It's also unusual in that it's actually a membership cooperative; anyone may shop here, but if you become a member, you'll get all kinds of extra discounts and benefits.

Membership costs a one-time-only fee of $15. That gets you early notification of special sales, some of which are for members only, as well as discounts on equipment rentals and repairs. It also means that you're involved in company profit sharing, which includes an annual dividend—around 10% of whatever amount you've spent during the year. The stores also offer free clinics and demonstrations in various sports.

Meanwhile, about the merchandise itself: REI carries only what it considers to be high-quality stock—brands like Patagonia, Woolrich, Helly-Hansen, Specialized bicycles, and others. These are all competitively priced, even before the dividend you get back. And there is a special "Clearance Corner" section, where you can get big discounts on close-out items. Mr. C found a pair of Nike bicycling shorts reduced form $65 to $45, and Oxford-style leather casual shoes by Rockport marked down from $135 to $99. They even offer bridal registry, for the couple on the go! Open seven days a week.

R + E Cycles
- 5627 University Way NE, Seattle; 527-4822

No, it's not "Recycles," selling used bikes, as the sign seems to indicate from a distance; the "R + E Cycleplex" is actually quite an unusual place. It's really three stores in one; Mountain Bike Specialists and Seattle Bike Repair are a pair of the tenants in this two-level shop, and certainly worth looking into. But it's R + E proper, entered from around the side of the building, that will most interest dedicated Cheapsters.

Here, you can stock up on closeouts on all kinds of bicycling accessories; some are end-of-season remainders, others are of second-quality, and it's all laid out in bargain bins on shelves and tables.

The place is so no-frills and no-pressure, in fact, that a nearby sales clerk wouldn't even venture into this part of the store; she pointed to a sign overhead that read "Customers Only Beyond This Point." Go wild.

Tumbled into various boxes were lycra cycling shorts, originally $35, selling here for $15 (or two for $28); Cycross gloves, half-price at $15 (two pair, $25); Giro helmets, once $80 each, here for $50; and lots more. Fanny packs for six bucks. Specialized brand bike seats for $19.99. InSport nylon windbreakers for $30. Ya just never know what'll be here, but you can rummage through for yourself seven days a week, including weeknights until 8:00 P.M.

2nd Base
- 1101 E Pine St., Seattle; 325-BASE (2273)

Big as a Texas League double, 2nd Base has more used sports equipment than you can shake a stick at—hockey stick, that is. One downstairs wall is loaded with vintage sporting equipment, some of which has even been rented out to TV, theater, and film crews. While this equipment is not for sale, here's some stuff that is: Wilson tennis rackets ($20), cleats (children to adults, $8-$20), tennis balls and softballs (four for a dollar), plastic and metal weights (20¢/lb., 40¢/lb.), hiking boots ($15 and up), and diving flippers ($25). If these prices are still a bit out of reach, please feel free to negotiate, as a sign in the store says.

Is all this somewhat overwhelming? You'll get a 2nd wind when you see all the clothes, skis, boots, bikes, clothing, and team pennants on sale upstairs. 2nd Base is open from 10 A.M. to 7 P.M. Mondays through Fridays, from 9:30 A.M. to 6 P.M. Saturdays, and from 11:30 A.M. to 5 P.M. Sunday. Batter up!

Second Bounce
- 513 N 36th St., Seattle; 545-8810

This is a relatively new addition to the hopping (literally and figuratively) Fremont scene, populated as it is with active folks who want to get out there and play. As the name implies, the store deals in second-hand sporting goods, and it's packed from floor to ceiling with stuff that will not only excel in a second bounce, but a third and a fourth at least.

Owner John Bolivar scours the area for deals and consignments, snapping up everything from manufacturers' closeouts to garage sale goodies. Thus, you may find used softballs for $2, and aluminum bats to slug them with for $8; tennis and squash racquets, in great shape, for less than half their original prices; bicycles of all types; hiking boots for $20, and Goretex "Anorak" ski parkas, made for The North Face, half their original prices at $95.

The range goes all the way up to a year-old Northwest "Cadence LP" kayak, selling for $1,650; still looking like new, that price included a complete package with paddle and life jacket, all of which had originally retailed for $2,350. Just add water. John has lots of stuff for water sports, in fact, including kayak racks for your car, as well as fly-fishing clothing and gear. For those who seek their thrills closer to home, Mr. C noticed a Nordic Track exercise machine reduced from a list price of $650 to just $350. Some items in here are new, such as a bin filled with factory overstock Gecko sports sandals. This current-look footwear was marked down from $65 to $39.50 a pair.

Second Bounce is open Wednesday through Sunday from 12 noon to 6 P.M., and a bit later in summer. Indeed, *everything* about the place is casual; a sign in the window begs earlybird customers for patience. "This is a one-man show," it reads, "and sometimes the show is a bit late."

Sports Exchange
- 2232 15th Ave. W, Seattle; 285-4777

Just south of the Ballard Bridge, as they put it, Sports Exchange deals in new and used gear for bicycling, water sports, and snow sports—whichever is appropriate for the season. Owner Ron Fisher is one

enthusiastic salesman; not so much for the merchandise, but for just getting out there and doing it. He'll eagerly, but carefully, explain the latest safety technology in sit-on-top kayaks, or make sure a bike is just the right size for you or your child. He's been "doing it" himself for years; he's got the know-how.

Sports Exchange can save you money in several ways. First, much of the equipment is available for rental, at cheap rates; also, you can purchase rental units, especially toward the end of their season (how 'bout a Cypress Gardens "knee board" demo model, made to sell for $175, for a mere $60). Second, Ron gets factory closeouts, new items that are simply being cleared out by their manufacturers. Mr. C saw a new kayak by On the Edge, originally listed at $499, selling here for $350; same deal on a Diamond Back mountain bike, reduced from $375 to $299. And a batch of unused "shorty" wetsuits were well-priced at $49 each.

Then, there are used items being sold on consignment. These recently included a girl's bicycle for $25, or a men's Miyata reduced from $600 to $100; plus lots of skis and bindings, some as low as $40-$50. Finally, the store also offers low-cost repairs; bicycle tires, for example, come in three price ranges—"Cheap," "Average," and "Deluxe." Take your pick. Sports Exchange is open from 10 A.M. to 6 P.M., seven days a week from October through March; during summer months, they're closed on Tuesdays and Wednesdays—presumably, to get out there and enjoy the elements themselves.

Sportmart
- 1901 S 72nd St., Tacoma; 572-9900
- 17500 Southcenter Pkwy., Tukwila; 575-2100

South-enders can save big at these branches of this national chain, where clothing, sneakers, and some gear are predominant. Replica jerseys for NFL, NBA, NHL, and MLB teams by Champion, Russell and other "makers to the pros" can often be found at discounted prices, not to mention caps from knock-offs to the real thing. At the other end of the body, save on sneakers like a pair of men's mid-rise Converse All-Stars for $39.95, women's Avia aerobic shoes for $29.95, and kids' soccer cleats by Adidas for $18.95.

Many of these are closeout deals, but first-quality, and lots of 'em. Meanwhile, Wilson tennis racquets have been seen here for as little as $29, Jansport backpacks with leather bottoms for $24.95, and treadmills from $250 or so. Open seven days a week, plus every night but Sunday.

Tom Wells Golf Company
- 8914 Aurora Ave. N, Seattle; 523-7124

For over twenty years, Tom Wells has been a name to reckon with in the Seattle area for golf equipment and supplies. The store may have changed locations a few times—but their customers follow them from green to green, since these prices can save you a lot of greenbacks.

Much of their stock of clubs are custom-built, mimicking the features of more famous (and more expensive) heads. TW refers to these as "generic emulations"; call them what you will, a set of irons which could cost up to $600 elsewhere sells for under $200 here. These component-built clubs use Tru-Temper shafts, as well as graphite varieties; lots of different grips are available, and any set will be custom-fitted to your swing. Service—from in-store to mail-order—is the name of the game here. Wells also has below-par prices on bags, head covers, balls, hand-carts, and more. One bag Mr. C found was marked down from $79 to $49. There are also used and consignment clubs and sets, a further way to hit the fairways more cheaply (how about a *full* set for $230?). Most of these have an in-store guarantee of a week or so for you to try them out. On custom-built sets, there is a 30-day refund or exchange policy, plus a one year parts and labor warranty at no charge. Closed Sundays.

Velo Stores
- 1535 11th Ave., Seattle; 325-3292
- 421 E Pine St., Seattle; 325-1958
- 4560 University Way NE, Seattle; 632-3955

Like many bicycle stores, Velo sells at retail prices. However, what Velo will do is match anyone's prices on the identical bike, if it is in stock. Also, if within fourteen days of purchase your bike goes on sale someplace else, Velo will refund you the difference. Of course, that other store must have your exact color, size, and model in stock; well, that's only fair. There is a large selection to check out. Velo stores are open seven days a week.

Winters Surplus
- 6169 Fourth Ave. S, Seattle; 763-2722

Camped out in the heart of industrial Georgetown, Winters has a little bit of everything for the budget-priced outdoorsman (or woman). The place is packed from floor to ceiling with new stuff, closeouts, and genuine army/navy surplus clothing from various genuine armies and navies (see the listing under "Clothing—New"). Meanwhile, Winters has every kind of rod, reel, lantern, stove, paddle, and whatever you'll need to stow these in. Backpacks in all sizes and configurations start from $14.95; Coleman sleeping bags were spotted for $32.95; and there was even a section of used cross-country skis for—get ready—$9.95. Mr. C wasn't sure if that's *each*, or per pair; at that price, does it matter?

Oh, and finally—walk around behind the main store, and you'll find a warehouse (you mean, Mr. C, we weren't in the warehouse *already*?) stuffed to the gills with Winters' other surplus—office furniture. Most of this is well-worn, and some is downright junk; however, if your timing is right, you may unearth a steal, like a Global ergonomic office chair or a Hon filing cabinet. The vast Winters empire is open weekdays from 9-6, and Saturdays from 9-5.

Here are some more chains and superstores to equip you weekend warriors:

Nevada Bob's Discount Golf and Tennis
- 9445 Silverdale Way NW, Silverdale; (360) 692-995
- 6409 Tacoma Mall Blvd., Tacoma; 474-8288

Olympic Sports
- 10700 Fifth St. NE, Seattle; 363-3007
- 14404 NE 20th St., Bellevue; 747-7990
- 10429 NE Fourth St., Bellevue; 455-4855
- 32225 Pacific Highway S, Federal Way; 941-5600
- 4918 196th St. SW, Lynnwood; 775-3535
- Lakewood Mall, Tacoma; 582-0202
- 6015 Tacoma Mall Blvd., Tacoma; 471-1010
- 300 Andover Parkway W, Tukwila; 575-3799

Sports Authority
- 800 156th Ave. NE, Bellevue; 747-6112

STATIONERY, OFFICE, AND ART SUPPLIES

The Complete Line
- 2741 152nd Ave. NE, Redmond; 885-6360

Nestled away in an office park just off of Route 520 is this modest art supply store with a huge inventory, amazing prices, and the most helpful salesfolk you'll ever meet. Art and design students, in fact, show up here at the start of each semester, list in hand. Even if they're not sure what the heck they're asking for, they know they'll get it at the best possible price.

Regular rates are 20% to 25% off manufacturer's list; each month, special items get knocked down further...a *lot* further. Mr. C found a seven-pen set of Koh-I-Noor technical pens recently for a mere $50; this can cost up to $125 in other stores. X-Acto knife were seen here for $7.50, half their retail price. Plus, well, "complete lines" of Letraset transfer lettering, Berol design templates, and foam core in all thicknesses; plus names like Scotch, Stadtler, Pentel, Formatt, and the rest.

No prices are marked on the items, so you'll have to ask; don't worry, it's all on the up-and-up. Free delivery is available anywhere in the Seattle area. Oh, and try not to show up near the beginning of a semester. Open weekdays only, from 8:30 A.M. to 5 P.M.

The Paper Zone
- 1911 First Ave. S, Seattle; 682-8644
- 9423 Evergreen Way, Everett; 355-7703
- 3838 148th Ave. NE, Redmond; 883-0273

These everything-that's-fit-to-be-printed-upon stores put a funky spin on warehouse-type buying. They have a vast selection to choose from, whether you're looking for fine-grade stationery for the office or fun, decorative goods for Buffy's birthday party. And you don't have to be a member or a wholesale purchaser.

On the office supply side of things, PZ stocks name brand and lesser-known stationery and copier paper, in every conceivable blend, including recycled. Plus harder-to-find goods like copier inks and chemicals, laser-compatible blank business card stock, shipping cartons, and more.

Volume pricing means you'll get good deals on all of this stuff,

---

MR. CHEAP'S PICK
Stationery, Office, and Art Supplies

✔ **The Complete Line**—Buried treasure in a Redmond office park. Where art students get their stuff.

One of the city's oldest and most comprehensive art supply houses, Seattle Art has just completed a major renovation of its store. Here, whether you're a professional artist or you're learning from that guy on public television, you can find great prices on a tremendous selection of materials.

All the "p's" are well-represented: paint, paper, pens, and pencils (paints by such makers as Winsor Newton and Liquitex are always discounted off their list prices). Not to mention good prices on easels, drafting tables, graphic supplies, books, and more.

How else does Seattle Art save thee? Let Mr. C count the ways. They offer a 10% discount to all students and teachers—even those who are not in the arts! Senior citizens get 10% off, too. There is a corporate discount program, and *anyone* can save when buying most items in quantity. Finally, there are featured monthly sales, with a different department highlighted each month. Recently, for example, the book section offered markdowns of 20% to 80% on selected titles.

Seattle Art is open seven days a week: Mondays through Saturdays from 9 A.M. to 6 P.M., and Sundays from noon to 5 P.M.

whether you're buying ten reams of stationery or just a handful, priced by weight. Be sure to check out the "Sale Zone" clearance room, at the downtown store, for extra bargains (occasional tent sales here, too). The staff is young and attentive, and ready to serve. Hours are 8 A.M. to 6 P.M. on weekdays, and 10 A.M. to 5 P.M. on Saturdays.

The Salvage Broker
- 13760 Aurora Ave. N, Seattle; 365-7771

See the listing under "Discount Department Stores."

Seattle Art, Inc.
- 1816 Eighth Ave., Seattle; 223-ARTS (2787)

Of course, sometimes you've just *got* to have fifty-seven cases of paper clips. . .

Arvey Paper and Office Products
- 2930 First Ave. S, Seattle; 622-9232
- 1910 132nd Ave. NE, Bellevue; 643-4333

Office Depot
- 1751 Airport Way S, Seattle; 587-2582
- 13501 Aurora Ave. N, Seattle; 364-2404
- 100 108th Ave. NE; Bellevue; 453-2900

- 5710 196th Ave. SW, Lynnwood; 771-2582
- 3330 S 23rd St., Tacoma; 572-6595
- 290 Andover Park E, Tukwila; 248-2582

OfficeMax
- 2401 Utah Ave. S, Seattle; 467-0071
- 14515 NE 20th St., Bellevue; 641-1418
- 18420 33rd Ave., Lynnwood; 775-7510

TOYS AND GAMES

The world of retail toys is a very competitive one; fun 'n games are a far more serious business than you may think! They all tend to keep pace with each other, and so there aren't many places to save money beyond the well-known retail giants. In addition to the stores listed below, don't forget to check out the liquidation stores listed in the "Discount Department Stores" chapter, as well as children's resale clothing shops for used toys.

Ace Novelty Company
- 13434 NE 16th St., Bellevue; 644-1820

Hidden away like buried treasure in one of Bellevue's many industrial parks sits this enormous warehouse of toys, party supplies, stuffed animals, inflatables, and puzzles. At one end of the building, as luck would have it, there is a small store which sells this stuff to the public—even while trucks load up to haul these goodies coast-to-coast.

Ace carries those little toy favors for children's parties at prices starting from 50¢ a dozen. Five-inch diameter balloons sell for $4.80 a gross (!), while sizes up to eleven inches go for $15 a gross. Nothing gross about *those* sizes. Plenty of supplies for more grown-up parties too. And, as any holiday nears—from New Year's Eve to Christmas—the stock takes on the appropriate look.

The company is also licensed to make and sell official T-shirts, toys, and other items relating to all of your favorite baseball, football, and basketball teams. Not to mention high-demand toys, like—yes—Power Rangers, or whatever the "Mommy, I want..." fashion of the moment is. These are still sold at discount prices, and are of better quality than imitation knockoffs. Ace is your ace-in-the-hole, open weekdays only from 9-5.

Play It Again Toys
- 16003 Redmond Way, Redmond; 881-6920

Here's a novel idea: A consignment shop for second-hand toys and games, just like all those resale shops devoted to clothing and such. This small, unassuming storefront in a Redmond shopping plaza is tidy, with plenty of ever-changing inventory in good condition. The stock is mostly geared to toddlers; brand names like Fisher Price, Sesame Street, and Little Tykes abound at half-off their original prices—or better.

Along with these toys, there are lots of children's books and videos, many priced under $5; as well as Nintendo games for around $15 for the slightly older crowd. And, for when you take the rug-rats outside, Play It Again has a selection of strollers, car seats, and related items at far below retail prices. Mr. C even saw one stroller designed for twins—just $25 (or $12.50 per child.) This fun store is open from 10 A.M. to 5 P.M. daily

---

MR. CHEAP'S PICK
Toys and Games

✔ **Play It Again Toys**—Just like consignment clothing stores, only for—you guessed it—toys.

(plus Thursdays until 8 P.M.), and Sundays from 12-5.

Top Ten Toys

• 104 N 85th St., Seattle; 782-0098

No, it's not a David Letterman gag. This Greenwood store is simply a kid's paradise, in which winding aisles are filled with toys, games, costumes, and more—and playing is definitely encouraged. Moms and dads will find this a haven as well, since TTT is big enough for its prices to reflect a low markup. The store also pleases parents by taking an educational angle as much as possible; focusing on safety and good value; and carrying no action figures or violence-oriented toys.

Near the front, rows of colored bins are filled with tiny toys, all priced at a buck or two. It's your classic collection of animals, plastic insects, wind-up cars, spinning tops, etc. They're like year-round stocking stuffers. Further in, one row offers a menagerie of stuffed animals, many under $10 (including those all-important dinosaurs). Another displays puzzles and magic tricks; yet another features ready-to-assemble model kits.

For older kids, there are chemistry sets, art supplies, learn-the-states-and-countries games, and lots of other alternatives to the standard fare seen at the mega-chains. Plus a section filled with books for *all* ages. Top Ten Toys is tops with Mr. C. It's open from 10 A.M. to 6 P.M. Saturdays through Tuesdays, and from 10 A.M. to 9 P.M. Wednesdays through Fridays.

And when your kids yearn to roam freely across seventeen aisles of the latest action figures and computer games . . .

Kaybee Toys

• Sea Tac Mall, SeaTac; 839-4434
• Kitsap Mall, Silverdale; (360) 692-3527
• 10509 Gravelly Lake Dr. SW, Tacoma; 588-6082
• Tacoma Mall, Tacoma; 474-3730
• Southcenter Shopping Center, Tukwila; 248-2215

Toy Liquidators

• Centralia Factory Outlet Center, Centralia; (360) 330-2150

Toys "R" Us

• 103 110th Ave. NE, Bellevue; 453-1901
• 1325-A SE Everett Mall Way, Everett; 353-8697
• 31510 20th Ave. S, Federal Way; 946-0433
• 3567 Randall Way NW, Silverdale; (360) 698-1882
• 4214 Tacoma Mall Blvd., Tacoma; 472-4568
• 16700 Southcenter Pkwy., Tukwila; 575-0780

UNUSUAL GIFTS

This is Mr. C's "catch-all" chapter, in which he's put some of the stores which just don't fit anywhere else in the book. Many of the stores below are places to find truly nice gifts, while others fall more into the realm of the fun and decidedly offbeat. Don't forget to check the "Flea Markets and Emporia" chapter for other unique gift ideas.

Armadillo

• 3510 Fremont Pl. N, Seattle; 633-4241

Here's a fun place for jewelry and kooky gift items in all the latest crazes. There are lots of earrings to see, many of which are hand-crafted, for $20 and up; meanwhile, sterling silver and 14K gold earrings are priced at $5, $7.50, $10, and $15 in a wide selection of shapes and styles. And don't forget the armadillo ear studs, $2 apiece.

Other cute things on a recent visit included stuffed frogs and lizards from $5 to $12; simple leather and bead bracelets, $5; and lots of novelty T-shirts and greeting cards. Open seven days a week.

Art/Not Terminal Gallery
• 2045 Westlake Ave., Seattle; 233-0680

Just a few blocks from downtown's Westlake Center, in an otherwise dull area of motels and bars, this co-operative gallery livens things up considerably. Formerly located across from the Westin Hotel, A/NT moved to more spacious digs a few years ago, giving its member artists—who run it as a non-profit—more room to display all kinds of bright, colorful, and sometimes risqué works.

This guarantees viewers the chance to see an incredible range of items and approaches, from sculptures to handicrafts, most of which are for sale. Visits at various times will yield different selections; Mr. C found wildly creative earrings, using all kinds of materials, ranging from $15-$20; bead necklaces from $10-$12, with fancier stone necklaces around $35; tote bags with artistic silk-screened designs for $12; and reproductions of postage stamps from around the world, enlarged and made into refrigerator magnets, two bucks each. Plus eye-catching notecards to go with your gifts, some of which were original prints and sketches, for $1.50 apiece.

A/NT also hosts free gallery openings once a month; see the listing under "Entertainment—Art Galleries." Hours are Mondays through Saturdays from 11 A.M. to 6 P.M., and Sundays from 12-6.

Bruning Pottery
• 2908 Sixth Ave. S, Seattle; 623-1007

See the listing under "Home Furnishings."

Folk Art Gallery
• 4138 University Way NE, Seattle; 632-1796

Owner and art collector Leslie Grace travels the world to pick out unique handicrafts for her two-floor U-District shop. Mostly, that means the Third World, for things like masks, unusual instruments, dolls, jewelry, and other traditional items; but works by many American artists are also represented. You may find sterling silver earrings for $20 a pair, and other kinds for $12; leather necklaces strung with a single agate stone for $25; blank notebooks with hand-embroidered covers for $14; and handsome carved wooden boxes, in all shapes and sizes, from $15.

For more exotic tastes, there are Native American "spirit rattles" ($20), Chilean rainsticks (which imitate the sound of a tropical downpour, $14), Indonesian "Fishing Frogs" ($20), Peruvian dolls ($14), and brightly colored tapestries from Guatemala ($8-$14 a yard). Suffice it to say, if you bring one of these gifts to a party, you needn't worry about someone else giving the same thing.

Folk Art Gallery can also ship its goods anywhere in the U.S. and Canada; and—closer to home—they offer free parking validation in two nearby lots. Open Mondays through Saturdays from 10 A.M. to 5:30 P.M., staying open until 9 P.M. on Thursday evenings.

Great Western Trading Company
• Pike Place Market, Seattle; 622-6376

The name conjures up images of cowboys and cracker barrels; what you'll find on display, however, are such things as African masks ($30 or so) and Chinese flats ($2.99 a pair). This small, winding store, located on the mezzanine level of the Main Arcade, is just packed with interesting and offbeat things. Beaded belts were seen for $4, and wooden soldier nutcrackers (yes, exactly the kind that Clara gets for Christmas in a certain ballet) for $3.70. Not everything thing here is inexpensive, but there are enough great prices to make the Great Western Trading Company worth a trip. Stop by between 10 A.M. to 5:30 P.M. during the week, 'til 6 P.M. Saturdays, and from 11 A.M. to 5 P.M. Sundays.

Hand in Hand

• 129 Park Lane, Kirkland; 822-7332

Similar to the Folk Art Gallery (above), this not-for-profit store sells attractive crafts made by cultures from Mexico, Peru, Haiti, the Philippines, and around the world. Want a pet for the apartment, without the muss and fuss of caring for it? How about a Mexican papier-mache parrot sitting on a perch that hangs from your ceiling. It's only $9—and no birdseed costs. Tiny animals made from straw were seen for only $1.25 apiece.

Clothing and jewelry seen on Mr. C's visit included a turquoise and painted-bead necklace from Nepal, for $32, and a colorfully embroidered baby's sweatshirt for $17. Plus musical instruments, like maracas from Ecuador ($6.25 apiece), brass, pottery, and delightful greeting cards. The store also sponsors live arts events on a regular basis; call or stop in for a schedule. Open Tuesdays through Saturdays from 10 A.M. to 6 P.M., and Sundays from 1-5 P.M.

Istanbul Imports

• 623 Queen Anne Ave. N, Seattle; 284-9954

After being in the wholesale gifts business for three years, this husband and wife team has expanded into retail. Some of the more interesting objects you'll find are "Blue Eyes" trinkets, which supposedly ward off evil spirits or curses. They come in several different shapes and sizes, ranging in price from $1.50 to

$5.95—not a bad investment to become curse-free.

Besides unique ornaments and jewelry, hand-woven articles are also a specialty here. Tribal kilim throw pillows ($9 and up), handmade Uzbeki hats ($6 and up), and flat-woven rugs ($300 and up, depending on age, size and condition) are also available in many bright, colorful designs. Travel to Istanbul Mondays through Saturdays from 10:30 A.M. to 7:30 P.M., and Sundays from 11 A.M. to 6 P.M.

Kong Sun Company

• 676 S King St., Seattle; 223-1474

Sun May Company

• 672 S King St., Seattle; 624-1467

To find gifts with a real Asian flavor, these International District shops are good places to try. At Kong Sun, tea sets (complete with a tray, pot, and six cups) can be found for just $11; brass incense burners start at $2.77; and painted iron balls, used for relaxation and hand exercises, are $8.50. Embroidered slippers and women's Chinese flats are $3.45 and $5.50 a pair, respectively. And, if you seek laughing Buddhas, search no more— you can find them here starting at $10.88.

Next door, Sun May offers a different line of gifts and housewares. Fancy painted sauce dishes are $3.50, incense is 80¢ a stick, and bamboo flutes start at $5.25. Women's cotton Chinese flats are not sold here, but men's are for some reason, and for only $4.50 a pair. Genuine glass Coca-Cola bottles (are these Oriental?), some never opened, are available for just a few dollars a "pop."

If you're wandering through the area in search of the exotic, perhaps a souvenir of your visit to the Pacific Rim, it's worth a few minutes to stop into these shops. Generally, both are open seven days a week.

Pharaoh's Treasures

• Pike Place Market, Seattle; 622-3582

This is twenty-five-year-old family operation, still based in Egypt; not exactly as old as the kings, but a good start. Artists and craftspeople create extraordinary and beautiful items over there, and the store imports these pieces to Seattle to be sold at near-wholesale prices. Where else can you find a new lambskin leather jacket for $175? Or a sheet of papyrus, printed with a design containing 14-karat gold ink, for only $4.95?

Delicate, hand-made perfume bottles, also painted with 14-karat gold, start at $10 for a small one, $16 for two. A wide variety of charms and rings starts at just a few dollars apiece. For the more exotic purchase, a complete line of belly dancing accessories and costumes is available, starting at $150 and going up to $2,000 (the expensive ones have real diamonds in them).

Check out the Treasure on the second level of the Main Arcade between 11 A.M. to 5:30 P.M. during the week, and 10 A.M. to 6 P.M. on weekends.

Pyramid Imports
- 106 Pine St., Seattle; 448-8447

While we're on the subject of Pharaohs, Pyramid Imports has jewelry fit for Cleopatra at prices that would make a snake charmer smile. When Mr. C visited, exotic-looking earrings were selling for $5 a pair, or three pairs for $10. Depending on how much piercing you've had done, you may *need* all three pairs. Matching earring and necklace sets are also cheaper in quantity—$8.95 for one set, $15 for two.

Other interesting items, such as tambourines ($48 for a large one), *gamer* scarabs ($8 and up) and hand-carved, hand-painted wooden dolls ($4.99) make Pyramid great for window shopping, or buying a gift for the person who has everything. Pyramid is open from 10 A.M. to 7 P.M. Mondays through Saturdays, from noon to 5 P.M. Sundays.

Stampola
- 607 N 35th St., Seattle; 548-1010

This tiny shop in the heart of Fremont specializes in one thing only: rubber stamps. Oh, but they don't just rubber stamp the same old thing over

and over—these are strictly for fun. Just about any image you can think of, and many you never have, is available on the packed display shelves. Every state in the union is represented; so are the Marx Brothers, Australian postage stamps, wacky sayings (many of which cannot be printed here), and vintage designs that call to mind those crazy Monty Python animations.

Most of these are priced between $4 and $7 apiece. Ink pads are here too, in a wide variety of colors, from $3.50. Definitely different. Stampola is open daily from 11 A.M. to 6 P.M.

Tatonka Traders
- 2909-A E Madison St., Seattle; 323-8546

From humble beginnings with a pushcart in the Broadway Market, these folks have moved on and moved up to a full shop in this trendy Madison Park neighborhood. It's filled with beautiful and fascinating decorative items from Southwest American cultures.

An actual feather from a great horned owl (it's bigger than you think!) is a unique item, and it costs $7.50. Beaded charm necklaces start around $6. And Native American handicrafts, like those cool "dream catchers" are $25. Plus silver and turquoise jewelry, incense, teas, traditional and new-age music tapes, drums, and more. It's all interesting and much of it is affordable. Open Tuesdays through Saturdays from 10:30 A.M. to 6 P.M., Sundays from 11 A.M. to 3 P.M.

Trinkets and Treasures
• 517 15th Ave. E, Seattle; 325-5942
At first glance, this appears to be a rather ordinary thrift shop, with a rack of well-worn clothing outside the door. But looks can be deceiving! Sure, you can find $3 blue jeans and $4 dresses, and the store's profits help run the Epiphany Episcopal Church's local programs for the homeless; but there are other kinds of things here that are not usually found in a thrift store.

T & T also displays crafts by local artists, many of which are functional as well as decorative—not to mention affordable. Mr. C found ceramic bowls, featuring elegant designs of horses, priced at $5 and $8 each; an equally creative casserole pot and cover for only $16; plus hand-blown glassware, costume jewelry, paintings, and many other unique items. And as Christmas approaches, the store adds lots of holiday gifts, such as ornaments and candles. Always worth a quick browse. Trinkets & Treasures is open Tuesdays through Saturdays from 12 noon to 4 P.M.

Uzuri Gifts
• 401 Broadway E, Seattle; 323-3238
Between the burning incense, lively African music, and jam-packed shelves, tables and walls, trying to decide what to look at first here can be a bit overwhelming. Uzuri's staff encourages browsing and questions, so feel free to take your time and ask about various pieces. Tribal silver earrings cost $4.99, or three pairs for $12; and sparkly, dangling anklets (try saying *that* three times fast) cost $6.99, or two for $10. Beads, rings and other trinkets cost even less, while bags, clothes, and wallhangings can be significantly more.

Authentic antiques are also sold here, and although they may be out of Mr. C's price range—like $500 for a century-old tribal mask—it costs nothing to stand there admiring them. Open from 10 A.M. to 9 P.M. Mondays through Fridays, 'til 10 P.M. Saturdays, and from noon to 6 P.M. Sundays.

The Window
• 6401 32nd Ave. NW, Seattle; 706-8432
Just opened (excuse the pun) in late '94, Jana Balliet and Pat Eskenazi have created a marvelous little shop in the quiet area of Ballard near Sunset Hill.

It's filled with all sorts of baubles and bangles, not all of which are necessarily in Mr. C's price range; but plenty of pretty items are priced under $20, much of which is made by local artists, and sold on consignment. Native American woven "dream catchers" start as low as $5 for small sizes, ranging up to $12 and $16. A tiny, decorative angel ($5) sits at the end of a stick, meant to adorn potted plants. Garlands of dried flowers sell in any length for $8 per foot.

Plus stationery supplies, jewelry in the $5-$10 range, candles, candies, *potpourri* and miniature boxes, and lots of hand-made greeting cards. Store hours are from 11 A.M. to 6 P.M. Tuesdays through Saturdays, and 11-3 on Sundays.

ENTERTAINMENT

All area codes (206) unless otherwise noted.

Seattle has so much to see and do, and it seems there is more coming along all the time. Lots of entertainment is inexpensive and often free. Movies, concerts, theater, museums, nightclubs . . . you name it, there's a way to enjoy it on the cheap.

Of course, sometimes you're looking for that special night out—a splurge at the opera or the Intiman—but you still want a bargain (otherwise, how could you afford dessert afterward?). Well, Mr. C can help with this, too. Some of the listings in this section are more expensive, but significantly discounted from their full prices. Hey, there's no reason why a limited budget should keep anyone from enjoying the arts.

Meanwhile, the city's best overall deal is Ticket/Ticket, described fully in the "Theater" chapter. In fact, this service offers day-of-performance bargains on dance, music, and comedy. Often, it's your cheapest way into some of Seattle's biggest halls.

ARTS AND CULTURAL CENTERS

These centers present a variety of fun and inexpensive activities under one roof (whether actual or administrative). Many of the programs and classes are designed for adults, children, or both; they often involve active participation.

ArtsWest

- 4734 42nd Ave. SW, Seattle; 938-0963

This community organization states its goal as "Making West Seattle a Work of Art!" They seem to be doing a pretty good job, with generous helpings of chamber music, visual arts, literature, and plans for live theater, too.

The ArtsWest Concert Series presents ensemble chamber music by the likes of Beethoven, Mozart, Bach, Debussy, and more. Single ticket prices are $11 for adults, $9 for students and seniors, and $6 for children ages five to fifteen. Subscription plans make these prices even cheaper. Concert locations vary around the West Seattle area, so call for info.

Also popular is "Lively, Local, and Free," a weekly community arts series that includes visual arts, poetry, music, and more. One recent week, they presented Native American poetry; another week featured local folk musicians. Locations for this series also vary, and include **Bonvechio's Book & Bean** at 4554 California Avenue SW, and the **Alki Bakery** at 2738 Alki Avenue SW. Both of these are good places to pick up flyers for upcoming events.

ArtsWest runs a gallery in Jefferson Square (at the main address above) where they exhibit the work of local and Northwest area artists. Exhibits change monthly, and a free public reception in honor of the artist is held on the first Wednesday of each month.

Bainbridge Performing Arts Cultural Center

- 200 Madison Ave. N, Bainbridge Island; 842-8578

The Bainbridge Performing Arts Cultural Center is the sort of place you may not think of first for live theater, dance, music, and more—but it certainly makes for a lovely destination.

Ticket prices are $12 for adults, and $9 for seniors (65 and over) and students (6-18). Occasional special events may be a bit more. Now what do you get for such short change? Take your pick. How about the "Main Stage Series," which recently included local productions of *The Sound of Music, A Midsummer Night's Dream*, and a stage adaptation of Arthur Miller's television drama, *Playing for Time* (about a group of women musicians at Auschwitz). Most ambitious indeed. Or, speaking of orchestras, perhaps you'd like to take in a Saturday evening performance by the Bainbridge Community Orchestra. There's also a children's event series, the annual "Independent Theatre Festival," and lots more. Call the number above for a complete list of upcoming events.

BPACC also sponsors a late-night improvisational comedy series, starring its very own "BPA Second Stage Improv" troupe. The laugh-fest takes place on weekends, "almost monthly." Tickets are just $8 apiece, and each weekend features two or three different performances. And they conduct classes in improv comedy, taught by Second Stage performers. All in all, it's a hopping place, and a fun one—especially if you, like the majority of Seattleites, include the ferry ride to the island and back!

Bellevue Regional Library
● 1111 110th Ave. NE, Bellevue; 450-1775

See the listing under "Children's Activities."

Broadway Performance Hall
● 1625 Broadway, Seattle; 323-2623

Located on the campus of Seattle Central Community College, Broadway Performance Hall is at the corner of Pike Street on Capitol Hill. The school rents out this space to a variety of independent dance and arts troupes. The **Allegro Dance Series** calls BPH home, presenting everything from traditional to contemporary choreography. During a season running from September to June, many local and international dance troupes dazzle students and the public alike.

Plays and films are also presented; the Seattle Film Festival and the Fringe Theatre Festival are just two more events which make use of the hall. BPH has 300 seats, all offering clean, unobstructed views. Generally, tickets are $10 or less, with a few "pay what you can" performances mixed in. And, once each year, you can catch a free dance performance by the Cornish College of the Arts. Call for upcoming events, or stop into the lobby anytime to browse the tables cluttered with flyers and newsletters.

Carco Theatre
● 1717 Maple Valley Hwy., Renton; 277-5536 or 277-5559

The Carco Theatre has a great lineup of live local theater and music, with ridiculously low ticket prices. The regular ensembles here include the Renton Parks Concert Band and the Valley Community Players. The RPCB is a 60-piece band that plays selections ranging from Handel and Haydn to Gershwin, Sondheim, Duke Ellington, and others. Tickets for these concerts are usually a suggested donation of $2. Music admirers can also enjoy performances by the Renton Youth Symphony Orchestra; tickets to RYSO concerts are $4 for

---

MR. CHEAP'S PICKS
Arts and Cultural Centers

✔ ArtsWest—Rounding up the thriving and eclectic arts scene in West Seattle.

✔ Seattle Center—Of course. The one, the only; home to dozens of concerts, exhibitions, and family events each *month*.

---

adults, and $2 for students and senior citizens.

If the play's the thing for you, check out the productions of the Valley Community Players, who present a four-show season. The VCP's slant is definitely a comedic one; recent shows have included Paul Rudnick's off-Broadway hit *I Hate Hamlet*, and Kaufman and Hart's classic comedy *You Can't Take It With You*. Ticket prices are a bargain: $10 for adults and $9 for students and seniors, on Friday or Saturday nights. Go on Thursdays or Sundays, and you'll save $1 per ticket. What's more, because the season only has four plays, subscriptions are *way* cheap. Season tix for one adult are $34 for Friday/Saturday shows, or $30 for Thursday/Sunday. A definite deal. For more info about VCP, call 226-5190.

Other offerings at Carco include their award-winning "Summer Teen Musical" and "Fall Family Concert" series. A recent teen presentation of *Fiddler on the Roof* cost just $6 for adults, $4 for students and seniors—and $17 for a family of four. The concert series includes music, stories, and more, again tailored to outings by the entire family. Tix are $1 each, by donation. Call Carco Theatre for a complete list of upcoming events.

New City Theater
● 1634 11th Ave., Seattle; 323-6800

See the listing under "Theater."

Seattle Center

• Denny Way and First Ave. N,
Seattle; Information, 684-8582

Originally the site of the Seattle
World's Fair, held in 1963 (residents,
please pardon the history lesson), the
Seattle Center continues to provide
much of the city's cultural life. The
Space Needle and the Monorail look
just as futuristic as they did thirty years
ago; that's either a tribute to their designers back then, or a comment on
how far we have yet to go. In any case,
they are just part of a complex that includes an amusement park, a newly
renovated professional basket-
ball/hockey arena, nationally renowned
theaters and museums, plus restaurants
and stores. In all, there are some two
dozen performance areas alone.

These spaces host a busy schedule
of public events all year 'round, and
many are free and open to everybody.
They range from concerts to children's events to car shows, some of
which are described throughout this
book. The center is also home to
weekend-long festivals, like the annual "Bite of Seattle" food frenzy,
which do charge admission. The diversity of activities is too great to describe here; there can be literally over
a hundred each month. Pick up an
events calendar at visitor information
centers all over town, or call SC's
automated events line at the number
above. For more detailed info from a
human being, call their customer service number, 684-7200.

Seattle Public Library

• Downtown Branch, 1000 Fourth
Ave., Seattle; 386-4636

True Cheapsters already know that
the library is one of any city's first
stops for cultural bargains. Read the
day's newspapers, borrow a compact
disc or a classic film on video, all for
free—and that doesn't even get to the
books! But wait, there's more. Seattle
area libraries sponsor free concerts,
workshops, lectures, book discussion
clubs, author readings, and more,
throughout the year.

Confused about how to use the In-
ternet? Take a workshop called "Drivers' Education on the Information Super-
highway." Want to draw your family
tree? Attend the "Genealogical Research" workshop with a lecture, orientation, and walking tour of research
facilities. SPL even offers assistance
with taxes, earthquake preparedness, job
hunting, and much more.

Literature fans have enjoyed recent poetry readings by Margaret
Hodge; Hortense Calisher, winner of
four O. Henry awards, has read from
her novel *In the Palace of the Movie
King*. Travel programs take you (by
slide-show) halfway across the world.
And a lecture especially close to Mr.
C's heart featured author Andy Dap-
pen with ideas from his book *Cheap
Tricks: 100s of Ways You Can Save
1000s of Dollars*. There's live music,
too; recently the Thornton Creek
String Quartet performed classical
music by Mozart and Schubert. Melodious souls should also check out the
regular "Ladies Musical Club Brown
Bag Concerts." Who says libraries
have to be silent places?

And of course, the library is a
great place for children's activities.
See a separate listing in the "Children's Activities" chapter for more
ideas on that front. Events vary by
branch; some require pre-registration.
Call the branch nearest you to get a
complete list of upcoming happenings. The SPL branches are:

• **Ballard**, 5711 24th Ave. NW,
Seattle; 684-4089
• **Beacon Hill**, 2519 15th Ave. S,
Seattle; 684-4711
• **Broadview**, 12755 Greenwood
Ave. N, Seattle; 684-7519
• **Columbia**, 4721 Rainier Ave. S,
Seattle; 386-1908
• **Douglass-Truth**, 2300 E Yesler
Way, Seattle; 684-4704
• **Fremont**, 731 N 35th St., Seattle;
684-4084
• **Green Lake**, 7364 E Green Lake
Dr. N, Seattle; 684-7547
• **Greenwood**, 8016 Greenwood
Ave. N, Seattle; 684-4086
• **Henry**, 425 Harvard Ave. E,
Seattle; 684-4715
• **High Point**, 6338 32nd Ave. SW,
Seattle; 684-7454

- **Holly Park**, 6805 32nd Ave. S, Seattle; 386-1905
- **Lake City**, 12501 28th Ave. NE, Seattle; 684-7518
- **Madrona Sally Goldmark**, 1134 33rd Ave., Seattle; 684-4705
- **Magnolia**, 2801 34th Ave. W, Seattle; 386-4225
- **Montlake**, 2300 24th Ave. E, Seattle; 684-4720
- **North East**, 6801 35th Ave. NE, Seattle; 684-7539
- **Queen Anne**, 400 W Garfield St., Seattle; 386-4227
- **Rainier Beach**, 9125 Rainier Ave. S, Seattle; 386-4227
- **Southwest**, 9010 35th Ave. NE, Seattle; 684-7455
- **University**, 5009 Roosevelt Way NE, Seattle; 684-4063
- **Wallingford Wilmot**, 4423 Densmore Ave. N, Seattle; 684-4088
- **West Seattle**, 2306 42nd Ave. SW, Seattle; 684-7444

Furthermore, such programs are not limited to libraries within Seattle; whichever town you live in, chances are they have something like this as well. Check 'em out (and pardon the pun).

ART GALLERIES

Most city dwellers know that browsing through art galleries is one of the truly enlightening and (best of all) *free* cultural activities around. For no more than the price of an espresso at a nearby cafe—you have to do that, right?—you can while away a fine afternoon or early evening.

Some galleries may require you to buzz in, only for security purposes. Don't fear that you're being kept out because of an annual income below that of, say, a certain software CEO; go on in! After all, the richer people are, the less they have to care about their appearances—for all the gallery owners know, you could be an eccentric millionaire in those torn jeans. Be sure to sneer at one or two paintings, as though you *could* buy one if it were any good.

Pioneer Square is the heart of Seattle's established, "blue-chip" art dealers; yet they co-exist, cheek-by-jowl, with trendy young upstarts in the same area. Sample a bunch of these during a Pioneer Square "Art Walk," or one of the others around the Seattle area; these are described further in the "Walks and Tours" chapter.

Animation, USA
- 104 First Ave. S, Seattle; 625-0347

Animation, USA is a gallery for the kid in all of us—filled with contemporary and vintage animation art. What is animation art? you ask. Well, all those cartoons you loved as a kid (and maybe still do) are made up of "cels," short for "celluloids," the clear plastic sheets on which animators draw and paint. Even the animators themselves must never have realized that these would become fine art, but it seems that every major city now has at least one such gallery.

You'll find all your favorite characters here, from classic Disney and Warner Bros. characters to more recent phenomena like the Simpsons and Ren & Stimpy. All of them are for sale, of course, as hot a "collectible" as baseball cards and comic books. But there's no charge—and plenty of fun—to walk in and look around.

Animation, USA hosts lots of special events, too. A recent Disney show included one of that studio's current animators giving a demonstration of animation technique. Beats a stuffy wine-and-cheese *soiree* any day. Open from 10 A.M. to 6 P.M. Mondays through Saturdays, and 12 P.M. to 6 P.M. on Sundays.

Art/Not Terminal Gallery
• 2045 Westlake Ave., Seattle; 233-0680

Just a few blocks from downtown's Westlake Center, in an otherwise dull area of motels and bars, this cooperative gallery livens things up. Formerly located across from the Westin Hotel, A/NT moved to more spacious digs a few years ago, giving its member artists—who run it as a nonprofit—more room to display all kinds of bright, colorful, and sometimes risqué works.

The gallery is not limited to these members, however; any artist can pay a fee, put up his or her work, and sell it (with a small commission going to the gallery). It's a great opportunity for up-and-coming types who haven't broken into the established gallery circuit yet; it also guarantees viewers the chance to see an incredible range of items and approaches, from large canvases and sculptures to smaller handicrafts.

Gallery openings usually take place on the first Saturday evening of each month, and these events include refreshments and live music, all free and open to the public. This is also a cool place to shop for that special trinket; see the listing under "Shopping—Unusual Gifts." Regular hours are Mondays through Saturdays from 11 A.M. to 6 P.M., and Sundays from 12-6.

Bremerton Art Galleries
• Various locations; see below

Not to be outdone by Bellevue, Kirkland, and other suburbs, Bremerton has attracted a sizable arts community. The whole area is great for browsing and strolling, and galleries pop up in various parts of this happy 'burb, too. A few that you shouldn't miss include:

Amy Burnett Gallery, 412 Pacific Ave., (360) 373-3187, open Tuesdays through Saturdays from 10 A.M. to 5 P.M., Sundays from 10 A.M. to 4 P.M.

Windrose Gallery, 301 Pacific Ave., (360) 792-0995, open Mondays through Fridays from 10 A.M. to 5 P.M.

Gallery Semanas, 2009 Harkins St., (360) 377-2930, open Mondays through Fridays from 9 A.M. to 5 P.M., and Saturdays 10 A.M. to 3 P.M.

Carolyn Staley Fine Prints
• 313 First Ave. S, Seattle; 621-1888

This gallery holds more than 8,000 fine and rare prints, dating from the 16th century to the present. Specialties include old and modern master prints, antique botanical and natural history subjects, maps, *ukiyo-e* and modern Japanese prints, Northwest historical views, and more. The collection of Japanese prints includes the work of Hashiguchi Goyo, noted artist of the 1920s. These selections are very different from the usual contemporary art fare, making Carolyn Staley a great place to browse. The gallery is open Mondays through Saturdays from 10:30 A.M. to 5 P.M.

Center on Contemporary Art
• 1309 First Ave., Seattle; 682-4568

Directly across First Avenue from the Seattle Art Museum is a very different artistic venue that strays far, very far, from the traditional. Unless you're a regular *habitué* of the *avant-garde*, odds are that you may have never seen anything even close to what goes on at the COCA.

Don't be surprised to hear, for example, of strangely titled exhibits (that are always as interesting as their names) such as *Cult Rapture*, featuring the art and propaganda of various cults; or the coin-operated *Sim-Sex Arcade* (not to worry, it's clean enough for all). Speaking of which, though, it's often noted that the COCA sits next door to an art house of a rather different nature: the "Lusty Lady" porn theater. Yet, they seem to be good-natured neighbors— the LL's marquee offers such quips as "Our Art is Well Hung."

COCA shows, changing over about five times per year, usually in-

corporate a lineup of live performances as well, from panel discussions
to sound-art performance interactions
to new-wave music concerts. They
even held a recent screening of *It
Came from Outer Space* (in terrifying
3-D, of course). Call or stop by for a
schedule.

Rates for all this are pretty fair:
General admission is around $7, de-
pending on the exhibit. Students, seniors, and artists can get a membership
for $15, which knocks a couple of
bucks off the entry fee. Special
events usually cost from $2-$5 for
the public, and are always free to
COCA members.

Evergreen Gallery
- 15167 NE 24th St., Redmond;
  747-6758

Gallery hopping in itself can be an en-
joyable sport. But when you mix it in
with your coffee, the combo can really hit the spot. The Evergreen Gallery, specializing in representational
Northwestern watercolors, brews up
a great cup of java at their coffee
bar/espresso lounge located in the
Overlake Square shopping center. Relax over a cappuccino and pastry
while discoursing over works by
some of the region's most recognized
artists. You may even be inspired to
consider a purchase; you're on your
own from there, though, says Mr. C.

The Evergreen Gallery opens at
9:30 A.M. daily. Sipping and browsing
ends promptly at 6 P.M. on weekdays
and 5 P.M. on Saturdays.

Evolution Gallery
- 317 NW Gilman Blvd., Issaquah;
  392-6963

Situated upstairs in the old Feed and
Farm building of the Gilman Village
shopping center, the Evolution Gallery is a showplace for many of the
art world's most contemporary crea-
tors. The Gallery's eclectic collection
is a constantly progressive gathering
of mixed-media, photography, sculpture, and painting—always with a
twist of some sort. Recently, the gallery has featured the works of many
award-winning and internationally acclaimed artists. The Evolution Gallery

---

MR. CHEAP'S PICKS
Art Galleries

✔ **Center on Contemporary
Art**—Across from the Seattle
Art Museum's famous
"Hammering Man," some
truly hard-hitting art.

✔ **Henry Art Gallery**—On the
UW campus, impressive
collections from traditional to
avant-garde.

✔ **Museum Associates Gallery
of Planetary Art**—Here's
your big chance to make up
for all those science classes
you slept through.

✔ **Sacred Circle Gallery**—
Check out the Puget view
from the Daybreak Star Arts
Center, then wander through
this gallery of Native
American art.

✔ **The Toaster Museum**—This
kitschy place is actually part
of a Pioneer Square building
filled with young, happening
galleries.

---

is open Mondays through Saturdays
from 10.00 A.M. to 6:00 P.M., and
Thursdays until 8:00 P.M. Sunday
hours are from 11:00 A.M. to 5:00 P.M..

FireWorks Fine Crafts Gallery
- Westlake Center, 400 Pine St.,
  Seattle; 682-6462
- 210 First Ave. S, Seattle; 682-8707

With branches in Westlake Center
and Pioneer Square, it's difficult to
describe FireWorks Gallery—each location is as different from the other
as those neighborhoods themselves
are. Like Animation, USA (see
above), these are shops masquerading
as galleries, but what does Mr. C
care? They're filled with fun, fascinating, and often beautiful items. Brows-

ing here is a delightful way to spend some time.

The stores specialize in one-of-a-kind American crafts, including *trompe l' oeil* furniture, sculpted earrings, ceramic vessels, functioning timepieces, children's toys, and animal-inspired teapots. Pieces run the gamut from fanciful to elegant, living up to their slogan, "sophistication with a spirit of whimsy." FireWorks features regionally and nationally acclaimed artists, about a third of whom are from the Pacific Northwest. Both galleries are open seven days a week.

Foster/White Gallery

- 311 Occidental Ave. S, Seattle; 622-2833
- 126 Central Way, Kirkland; 822-2305

Founded in 1969, Foster/White Gallery represents some of the region's best-known artists, including Mark Tobey, Morris Graves, and Kenneth Callahan. They also represent artists from the internationally acclaimed Pilchuck School of Glass, including Dale Chilhuly and William Morris. In fact, they have an entire room filled with Chilhuly glass work. At either of these two locations, you can also see contemporary paintings, sculpture, and ceramics.

Exhibits change regularly, and Foster/White participates in both Seattle and Kirkland art walks (described in "Walks and Tours"). Recent exhibits included Priscilla Maynard's "Wild & Free: African Journal" and William Turner's "On The Road: The Imagined Landscape."

The Seattle gallery is open Mondays through Saturdays from 10 A.M. to 5:30 P.M., and from 12 noon to 5 P.M. on Sundays. The Kirkland branch is open Mondays through Fridays from 11 A.M. to 9 P.M., Saturdays from 10 A.M. to 9 P.M., and Sundays from 10 A.M. to 6 P.M.

Freighthouse Art Gallery

- 440 E 25th St. #49, Tacoma; 383-9765

If you see something here you're not crazy about, you may want to make your criticisms quietly—it's possible that the artist who created it is standing nearby. Freighthouse is run by local artists, ready to chat about the works on display. Ruth, the staffer who gave Mr. C the low-down on the place, described the gallery as "stressing pictorial images in loose realism, with some contemporary visual interpretation." Make what you will of *that*.

The 3,000-square foot space has a high ceiling with skylights, to let you see the true colors of these canvases. Watercolors, acrylics, pastels, and batiks are hung on walls and free-standing panels, allowing lots of room to wander and ponder. There is some pottery on display too, plus a small, but dazzling collection of blown and fused glass.

Freighthouse Art Gallery is open daily, from 10 A.M. to 7 P.M. Mondays through Saturdays, and from 12-5 on Sundays. Admission is free.

Also among the unique boutiques and ethnic restaurants of this city is the **American Art Company—Tacoma**, located at 1126 Broadway (telephone 272-4327).

Fremont Foundry

- 154 N 35th St., Seattle; 632-4880

There's more to art in Fremont than the Troll. Visit this collection of studios, attached to a genuine metal foundry, just a west of the Red Hook Brewery. The facility includes a spacious, two-level gallery, a stone yard, and of course, the vast foundry room itself, quite an impressive indoor sight. There are also private art studios, which you can sometimes visit to see the artists at work; classes in the fine arts are also offered. Gallery hours are Tuesdays through Saturdays from 9 A.M. to 5 P.M., and from 6-9 P.M. as well. Call for more info on open studios and classes.

Linda Farris Gallery

- 320 Second Ave. S, Seattle; 623-1110

The Linda Farris Gallery has been a fixture in Pioneer Square for about 25 years, exhibiting contemporary Northwest and American art. The gallery represents over twenty artists from all around the country, including the creative meccas of New York and California. Linda Farris Gallery is open Tuesdays through Saturdays from 11 A.M. to 5:30 P.M., and Sundays from 1 P.M. to 5 P.M.

The Lynne Gallery
• 4530 Union Bay Pl. NE, Seattle; 525-6113
See the listing for "Warehouse of Wine" under "Shopping—Liquor."

Kirkland Arts Center
• 620 Market St., Kirkland; 822-7161
The Kirkland Arts Center has two main occupations: they sponsor art classes and workshops for adults and children, and they present exhibitions in their gallery. The classes are reasonably priced, and there are even a few free workshops; but Mr. C is most interested in the gallery itself. The focus here is on contemporary art and craft, mostly by local artists. Many of the shows feature works by artists-in-residence at the center, often getting a lot of media attention. One recent example is "The Bridge," featuring work by some 25 local artists exploring the relationship between Seattle and its suburbs. Call for a brochure with info on classes, workshops, and exhibitions.

Metropolis Gallery
• 105 University St., Seattle; 682-6077
Right across the street from the Seattle Art Museum, but hardly dwarfed by it, the Metropolis Contemporary Art Gallery offers several winding rooms filled with paintings and sculpture by some of the nation's finest modern artists. Exhibits change monthly, with a public reception usually offered during the first week. The bright, comfortable space makes a nice, low-key alternative to the SAM; add a visit to the Center on Contemporary Art (see listing above), which also faces the museum across First Avenue, and you can have yourself a full dose of artistic contemplation even if you can't afford to tie up a whole day in the more formidable museum. Metropolis is open from 12-5 P.M., Tuesdays through Saturdays.

Moss Bay Gallery
• 128-A Park Lane, Kirkland; 822-3630
Tucked away in that oft-forgotten area between Kirkland Parkplace and the waterfront, Moss Bay Gallery displays original works of art in a variety of media, including paintings, sculpture, glass, and pottery. The works are done mostly by local, emerging artists. Recent shows included "His and Hers," paintings and photographs by Leonard and Lucille Berkowitz, and a show of sculpture by Phil Montague. Moss Bay is a prominent gallery in downtown Kirkland, taking part in the monthly art walks and other collective activities. It's open seven days a week.

Museum Associates Gallery of Planetary Art
• 1013 First Ave., Seattle; 621-1693
The Gallery of Planetary Art, one of only a few of this type in the world (this one, at least), is truly a gallery of the gods. Filled with a dazzling array of exotic crystals and fossils ranging in age from one thousand to billions (!) of years old, its collection is virtually unsurpassed.

Among the awe-striking artifacts you may encounter are a 4,000-pound quartz cluster from Arkansas, fish imprint fossils unearthed from the dry plain of Kansas, gems from Africa, and even a 1,000-year-old egg. Pieces come and go as they are purchased and discovered, so stop in every once in a while; you may find that perfect Eocene fossil for the coffee table.

The gallery is open every Wednesday through Friday from 11:00 A.M. to 8:00 P.M., as well as Saturdays from 12 P.M. to 5 P.M. Admission is free; furthermore, there is no minimum purchase—good thing too, considering that many pieces cost upward of $100,000.

Pacific Arts Center
• Seattle Center, 305 Harrison St., Seattle; 443-5437
See the listing under "Children's Activities."

Phoenix Rising Gallery

- 2030 Western Ave., Seattle; 728-2332

Phoenix Rising is a happening gallery. Don't just take Mr. C's word for it; this was voted the best gallery in Seattle by the readers of *Seattle Weekly*, and is listed as one of the top ten in the nation by the American Craft Council Board. The Phoenix focus is on "functional, affordable, and exquisite" art.

Of course, Mr. C wouldn't dare begin pricing unique works of art—this place is fascinating simply to explore. The works are done in a variety of media: mostly glass, clay, metal, fiber, and wood, representing the works of over 400 artists. Phoenix Rising Gallery is open Mondays through Saturdays 10 A.M. to 6 P.M., and Sundays from 11 A.M. to 5 P.M.

Pratt Fine Arts Center Gallery

- 1902 S Main St., Seattle; 328-2200

The primary purpose of Pratt Fine Arts Center is *teaching* the fine arts. Classes are offered in glassblowing, painting, jewelry making, welding, bronze casting, and more. In addition to all this, though, Pratt has a gallery which exhibits works by instructors, students, and working artists in the community. As part of its educational mission, Pratt also offers public lectures and craftwork demonstrations. The gallery is open Mondays through Fridays from 9 A.M. to 5 P.M.

Public Art at the Convention Center

- Eighth Ave. at Pike St., Seattle; 447-5000

With its commitment to making art accessible, the Washington State Convention and Trade Center boasts an extensive art gallery that's free and open to everyone. No need to wonder if someone in a dark suit will want to see you wearing one of those plastic name badges with a blue ribbon dangling from it.

The center's "Galleria" is home to temporary exhibits that encompass a broad range of artistic styles and techniques. The works seen here are on loan from museums, corporations, arts organizations, and private collectors; the majority are loaned by the Northwest's wealth of professional artists. Past exhibits have included works by the North Coast Collage Society, the Contemporary QuiltArt Association, and the Seattle Metals Guild. Institutions which have lent pieces to the convention center range from the Rosie Whyel Museum of Doll Art to the Museum of Flight.

And, along with all of these visual displays, the WSCTC also offers a regular slate of free concerts and lectures. Call the number above for a bimonthly calendar of events. The center itself is certainly "accessible" enough: It's open from 6 A.M. until 10 P.M. every day of the week.

Sacred Circle Gallery at Daybreak Star Arts Center

- Discovery Park, Seattle; 285-4425

Hidden inside Magnolia's Discovery Park, the Sacred Circle Gallery is the Daybreak Star Arts Center's contribution to the world of public art—in other words, it's free and open to all. Atop a scenic bluff overlooking Puget Sound, the gallery houses works by Native Americans from all over the continent, displaying as many genres as there are tribes represented (360, in case you were wondering). From glasswork to weaving, these artists have taken their traditional crafts to new heights, discovering modern themes and taking advantage of contemporary media to elaborate upon ancient ideas.

Dance performances, as well as videos, photography, and other visual arts, all praise nature, traditional cultures, and harmony; it all makes for a fascinating look at the American experience.

The Daybreak Star Arts Center is itself worth the trip, the park is a sight to see, and the gallery is a must. Gallery hours are Wednesdays through Saturdays from 10 A.M. to 5 P.M. and Sundays from 12 noon to 5 P.M.; and admission, as noted above, is free.

154

The Toaster Museum

- 416 Occidental Ave. S, Second Floor, Seattle; 624-9737

"A museum for toasters?" you're thinking. "C'mon, Mr. C, you've gotta be kidding." Nope. This small gallery, upstairs in a building full of galleries between Pioneer Square and the Kingdome, is for real. It's jam-packed (excuse the pun) with hundreds of toasting contraptions from the turn of the century to the present day. Top-loaders, side-loaders, conveyor models, cartoon character styles, they're all here.

Many bear very little resemblance to anything you'd have around the house—that is, unless you're like proprietors Eric Norcross and Kelly Godfrey. Norcross began collecting these babies while running an art gallery and cafe, which featured working old-fashioned toasters on every table. Alas, the cafe is gone, but the toasters (some 300 by now) remain. There isn't even room enough to display them all; but those on view provide a fascinating, angle on mechanical design, as well as social customs. Souvenirs for sale help the museum expand its collection, and will help you describe this wacky place to the folks at home. Open Thursdays, Fridays, and Saturdays from 11 A.M. to 5 P.M., and by appointment.

Other galleries on both floors of this building include **Art Mavens**, telephone 682-7686; the **In*Sights Gallery**, telephone 624-6411; and the **Seattle Clay Studio**, telephone 682-2325. These present somewhat more traditional works in different media; hours vary for each space.

CHILDREN'S ACTIVITIES

See also the "Museums" and "Outdoors" chapters for listings of other activities suitable for children and families.

Barnes & Noble Booksellers

- 626 106th Ave. NE, Bellevue; 451-8463
- Crossroads Shopping Center, Bellevue; 644-1650
- 300 Andover Park W, Tukwila; 575-3965

This growing national chain is fairly new to the Northwest book scene. They've wasted no time establishing themselves not only as major stores, but as good places to frequent for book-related events as well, including many which are designed for various younger audiences.

Recent events have featured readings of Shakespeare for teenagers; a "Brown Bag It" lunch with a King County executive, talking about his job in government; and, of course, lots of storytelling hours for the little ones. B & N has also created a young reader's circle, for children ages eight to twelve. Naturally, the store's interest in young readers is somewhat mercenary, in their desire to create a new market for the future; but, if they help expand literacy and knowledge in the meantime, Mr. C says, more power to them.

For a full listing of upcoming events, stop into any branch and pick up a flyer. And, for info about more grownup literary activities, see the listing under "Readings and Literary Events." B & N locations are open seven days a week, usually into the late evening.

Bellevue Regional Library

- 1111 110th Ave. NE, Bellevue; 450-1775

Like Seattle's library system (see the listing under "Arts and Cultural Centers"), the Bellevue Regional Libraries have lots of fun activities to keep the little ones amused through the "what do we do now?" summer months. In past summers, kids learned how to yo-yo, make paperfold frogs, shoot off model rockets, and more.

Of course, there are storytimes galore, scheduled at various times during the week, throughout the year. BRL has a monthly story corner with professional storytellers. The main purpose for most of these activities is getting youngsters to read more. Other events the whole family can enjoy include jugglers, puppeteers, theater, and live music. Happenings vary by season; for a full schedule of upcoming events, call or stop in. There is also plenty to do at other King County regional libraries. The system has 39 branches; for the number of the branch nearest you, see the government section in the white pages of your phone book.

Borders Books and Music
• 1501 Fourth Ave., Seattle; 622-4599
Another fast-growing national chain, Borders presents a packed schedule of readings, live music, and more. Kids aren't left out; they'll enjoy the weekly storytelling hour, which includes more than just readings. One recent hour explored the life and art of Pablo Picasso, and participants got to create a Picasso-inspired collage. Another featured David Gordon, author of *Field Guide to the Slug*, exploring the hidden world of slugs and their kin—complete with a terrarium full of these slimy creatures (it may sound gross to you, but you know how kids love *that*). Sing-a-longs, arts and crafts, and more are all part of the weekly fun. To get a full listing of upcoming programs, pick up a copy of their newsletter "FootNote." For more info on adult activities, see the listing under "Readings and Literary Events."

Children's Activities at Bumbershoot
• Seattle Center; Information, 684-7200
Four days of music, arts, food, and more make Bumbershoot perhaps the most popular of Seattle's annual festivals, held every Labor Day weekend.

While much of the entertainment is geared toward adults, there is plenty to keep the little ones (and not-so-little ones) happy and amused.

Almost anything available for grownups, in fact, is also offered in a kiddie version. There's live music (like Toy Box, a G-rated rock 'n roll band comprised of two sisters aged eight and six), theater, art exhibits, dance, storytelling, and magic shows. Many of the "Taste of Seattle" food vendors even offer kid-sized portions!

Children will have no problem finding stuff to fuel their imagination, as well as their energy. In the past, Bumbershoot has had a "Lego Construction Zone" with thousands of Lego pieces to delight future engineers, and a "Billboard Art-in-Progress" to entertain blossoming artists. There's a dizzying amount to see and do here. Mr. C suggests getting a listing of the events so you won't miss your faves. Call the number above or the Bumbershoot hotline at 682-4FUN (4386); or pick up brochures in a variety of area restaurants for a full listing. For more info on Bumbershoot's main activities, see the listing under "Festivals."

Carnation Farm
• 28901 NE Carnation Farm Rd., Carnation; 788-1511
Located in a small town west of Redmond, Carnation Farm is a real working dairy, where you can take a free self-guided tour. It makes a fun (and definitely different) family outing. The farm has about sixty head (or 240 feet?) of cattle for you to see; show your own little heifers how cows are milked and fed.

The farm also has a kennel, a garden, a gift shop and more. The tour is free, but be warned—no visit would be complete without some farm-fresh ice cream! Visitors are welcome Mondays through Saturdays from 10 A.M. to 3 P.M. Carnation is about 40 minutes' drive from downtown Seattle; take the Redmond-Fall City Road (Route 202 East) to Route 203 North.

The Children's Museum

- Seattle Center, 305 Harrison St., Seattle; 441-1767

Filled with exhibits that encourage visitors to touch, explore, and pretend, the Children's Museum is popular with kids of all ages (including the grownup ones who bring them there). Way-cool displays include "The Neighborhood," a whole child-size town complete with doctor's office, store, fire engine, and bus; "Playstage Theater," where participants create their own productions, from lights to costumes to action; and "The Bubbles Area," in which children create gigantic bubbles—learning about viscosity and surface tension in the process. Kiddies have so much fun here, they hardly notice how educational it all is! The museum even has an area for infants and toddlers called "Little Lagoon," and a drop-in art studio, "Imagination Station."

Admission is an amazingly reasonable $3.50 for all ages. The Children's Museum is open Tuesdays through Sundays from 10 A.M. to 5 P.M.

The Elliott Bay Book Company

- 101 S Main St., Seattle; 624-6600

Long-established in Pioneer Square, the Elliott Bay Book Company looms large amidst Seattle's literary scene—in terms of both book selection and public events. While most of these events are for adults, there are also lots of things for kids. EBBC sponsors a monthly "Young Readers Book Group," geared toward ages eight to twelve. It's described as "a flexible, informal gathering to talk about books." For kids who'd rather be read to, there are two monthly storytelling sessions, one for ages two to eight and another for ages eight to twelve.

Recent special events have included a sing-along, a "Teddy Bear Picnic," and a bookmark-making workshop. Kids' events are free (no tickets are necessary), and are held in the Children's Readings & Activities area of the store. Stop in for a copy of the EBBC newsletter, "Voices By Water," to get the full scoop on up-coming activities. For more info about their literary happenings for adults, see the listing under "Readings and Literary Events."

MR. CHEAP'S PICKS
Children's Activities

✔ **Carnation Farm**—This real, working dairy offers free, self-guided tours.

✔ **The Children's Museum** and **The Pacific Science Center**—Your kids want to have fun, you want them to learn. These Seattle Center museums let you *all* win. Just don't tell them it's e-d-u-c-a-t-i-o-n-a-l.

✔ **Seattle Public Library**—It's not just for books anymore! SPL branches host free storytimes, magic shows, movies, and more. Just bring your library card—'cause you won't *need* American Express.

Forest Park Animal Farm

- Forest Park, 802 Mukilteo Blvd., Everett; 259-0303

Each summer, Forest Park Animal Farm is hopping with all types of barnyard babies, including bunnies, ducklings, chicks, piglets, llamas, lambs, and more. Visitors are welcome to wander through and pet these cuddly creatures; and for 25¢ you can get a handful of feed and give them a snack. The staff does bottle feedings three times daily, which are also fun to watch. There are pony rides for the kiddies, too.

The farm is open everyday from 9 A.M. to 5 P.M., but only in the summer (May through Labor Day). Admission is by a donation of your choice. Oh, and if you're looking for a pet, the farm sells adult goats to good homes. Could be a cheap alternative to the lawnmower.

Eastsiders should also check out **Kelsey Creek Farm and Park** at 13204 SE Eighth Street, Bellevue; telephone 455-7688. Kelsey Creek is another petting farm, with lots of baby animals. Admission is free. It's open from 8 A.M. to 4 P.M., 365 days a year.

Fun Forest Amusement Park
- Seattle Center, 305 Harrison St., Seattle; 728-1585

Here's a popular place to keep the kids entertained for hours without going broke. Located right off the monorail in the Seattle Center, admission to the amusement park is free; but you do have to buy tickets to get onto the rides. Tickets are 85¢ each; save money by buying a batch of eight for $5.50, or eighteen for $15. Most rides require two tix, while you'll need four to get on the really good rides like the "Wild River" flume and the "Windstorm" rollercoaster.

Fun Forest also has special days when you simply pay one price (usually $12 to $15) for a full day of unlimited rides. These tend to be weekdays during the summer, and weekend days in the off-season. From June through September, Fun Forest is open Mondays to Thursdays from 12 noon to 11 P.M.; Fridays and Saturdays from noon to midnight; and Sundays from noon to 10 P.M. In the off-season, it's open on weekends only.

Island Books
- 3014 78th Ave. SE, Mercer Island; 232-6920

Once upon a time, there was a bookstore called Island Books, which held weekly storytelling events at 11 o'clock every Saturday morning. During the school year, dozens of children would gather to hear professional tale-spinners from the Seattle Storytelling Guild read yarns and fables of their own creations. Adults as well as kids listened intently, oh-so-eager to find out what goblin or gopher lurked or burrowed just ahead in the mind of the storyteller. But nobody knew what to expect; the stories were all so new, untested, and free for all. And guess what? The storytelling was sooooo popular, that it continues to this very day! The end.

Lynnwood Wonder Stage Summer Series
- Lynndale Park Amphitheater, 18927 72nd Ave. W, Lynnwood, 771-4030

The Lynnwood Wonder Stage Summer Series offers children's performances every Wednesday at noon throughout the summer. Events include music, theater, magic shows, puppet shows, and more. Best of all, they're completely free!

Past performances have included the Carter Family Marionettes, the Island Time Steel Drum band, basketball magic with Magic Charlie, and the Adefua African Music and Dance Company. Bring a lawn chair or a picnic blanket and make yourself comfy. Shows start at noon, but you're encouraged to arrive early.

Pacific Arts Center
- Seattle Center, 305 Harrison St., Seattle; 443-5437

The main focus of the Pacific Arts Center is arts education for kids—in particular, those kids who might not otherwise have a chance to experience them. That means both looking at art, and getting into it (literally). PAC's educational activities include classes taught by professional artists, a summer arts camp, and an outreach program to underfunded schools. PAC also provides resources for educators who want to use the arts to enrich their own teaching.

In addition, PAC has an exhibition space, the **Anne Gould Hauberg Gallery**. This shows works that are by, or of special interest to, children. One recent exhibit, "Wings: Children's Expressions of the Russian Soul," included paintings, drawings, and folk art all made by Russian children. Another, "Alphabet Land: The Imaginary Garden" took kids on a walk through a three-dimensional alphabet created by artist Rod Stuart. Admission to the gallery is by a suggested donation of $2 for adults, $1 for seniors, and free for children under sixteen. On Tuesdays, the gallery is free for everyone.

The Anne Gould Hauberg Gallery at the Pacific Arts Center is open from 10 A.M. to 5 P.M. Tuesdays through Saturdays, and from 12 noon to 5 P.M. on Sundays.

Pacific Science Center
- Seattle Center, 200 Second Ave., Seattle; 443-2001

This is definitely not a ho-hum, aren't-those-nice-exhibits-behind-the-glass museum. Take a child (for their educational enlightenment, of course— surely not because *you* want to play) and plan on spending the better part of the day. There are so many excellent hands-on exhibits to experiment with that kids may forget they're learning, and grownups may forget they're, well, grown up.

Try riding a bike on a narrow, circular rail, which also happens to be about twenty feet in the air. Of course there's a safety net beneath you—otherwise, you might fall into the reflecting pool! Disorient yourself walking down an uphill slope, or vice versa (the way the scenery is constructed, an optical illusion tells your brain the opposite of what your eyes actually see).

Learn about dinosaurs, robotics, meteors, and how well your body works. For a really big show, check out what's playing at the larger-than-life IMAX movie theater. Museum admission is $3.50 for pre-schoolers, $5 for juniors (up to age 13), $6 for adults, and $5 for seniors. Add on $2 more per person to see the laser and IMAX matinees.

Parkplace Book Company
- 348 Parkplace Center, Kirkland; 828-6546

Parkplace Book Company offers terrific children's activities—especially in the summer months when parents are desperate to entertain the little tykes. Story times include arts and crafts projects to keep four- to eight-year-olds happy. Parkplace tries to tie the project in with the story; a reading of Mary Calhoun's *Henry the Sailor Cat* added a drawing session in which kids created a "porthole picture." What a great way to get kids to fall in love with reading!

PBC also hosts a Young Readers' Book Discussion Club, for ages eight through twelve. The group discusses books they've read, just like the adult groups, and sometimes gets to meet with the authors. Most discussions are accompanied by a project. When the group discussed *Spirit Quest* by Susan Sharpe, they also tried their hands at mask making; and when they considered *Tales of the Egyptian Princesses*, they learned how to write with hieroglyphs. Most children's events are held in the afternoon or on Saturdays; stop in for a calendar of events to get exact dates and times.

Seattle Children's Theatre
- Charlotte Martin Theatre, Seattle Center, Second Ave. N and Thomas St., Seattle; 441-3322

See the listing under "Theater."

Seattle Public Library
- Downtown Branch, 1000 Fourth Ave., Seattle; 386-4636
- *And other branches throughout Seattle*

True Cheapsters know that the library is a great place for fun, *free* children's activities. The many various branches of the SPL sponsor magic shows, workshops, movies, artist demonstrations, and, of course, lots of storytelling.

These programs often feature more than just books. For the recent "Fascinating World of Reptiles" program, Scott Peterson, a zoologist and educator, brought along some real reptilian friends. Other kids' events have included origami classes, a puppet-mask show from Indonesia, and a special Pacific Science Center workshop demonstrating robots and computers. Also popular are the "Family Fun Nights," evenings of stories, games, songs, puppets, and films.

But wait, there's more! The library offers just as many treasures for grown-ups, too. See the listing under "Arts and Cultural Centers" (there you'll also find a full listing of SPL branches). All events differ from branch to branch; some require pre-registration. Call the outpost nearest you to get a complete list of upcoming happenings.

COLLEGE PERFORMING ARTS

The college campuses of the Seattle area offer a wealth of music, dance, theater, and films which don't require much personal wealth to attend (unlike colleges themselves). Many events are free to students, of course; don't forget your ID! Most are open to the general public as well, also for free or a very small charge. If you want to put culture into your life on a regular basis, this is a great way to do it.

Art Institute of Seattle
• 2323 Elliott Ave., Seattle; 448-6600
They say you can't get something for nothing, but what do "they" know? At this acclaimed art school, there is plenty to be gotten (eight different exhibitions every year) and it costs not a thing to see them. Works by Emmy Award-winning graphic designers, pictures from the Pacific Northwest's most acclaimed photographers, and even high-fashion creations have all been seen recently in the Art Institute's gallery.

No sooner does one of these displays leave than it is replaced by some other show of modern work, such as computer-generated art or manual illustration. There's always something new and interesting! Being part of a school, this gallery's hours are different from most. It's open from 8:00 A.M. to 8:00 P.M. Mondays through Thursdays; from 8 A.M. to 5 P.M. on Fridays; 8 A.M. to 3 P.M. on Saturdays; and closed on Sundays.

Cornish College of the Arts
• 710 E Roy St., Seattle; 323-1400
Atop Capitol Hill, what was once the Cornish College of Music has spread its wings more fully—and become one of only four schools in the nation to offer training in all of the performing and visual arts. This gives a unique advantage to both students and spectators.

Throughout the season, running from November to April, the college hosts a wide range of events, featuring visitors from the professional circuit, local celebrities, and of course, Cornish students and faculty. Many dance and music concerts are free to all, with some ranging up to $6; theater never runs you more than $5 a ticket. The Cornish's professional concert series tops the list, maxing out at $10.

Also, fine art exhibitions are always free at the school's **Fisher Gallery,** open Monday through Saturday from 12 noon to 5:00 P.M. For performance schedules and specific ticket prices, contact the public relations department at the above phone number, extension 467.

Pacific Lutheran University
• 121st St. and Park Ave., Tacoma; 535-7430
Jazz buffs know all about KPLU-FM, that cool radio station at the beginning of the FM dial. Well, for a cheap and hearty dose of Music Appreciation 101, head down to the source—the campus of Pacific Lutheran University, just south of downtown Tacoma. The school's renowned music program offers plenty for listeners of all stripes. With fourteen performing ensembles on PLU's campus, there is bound to be something for everyone: orchestras, opera and choral groups, chamber ensembles—and, of course, jazz bands.

There are as many as ten concerts each month of the school year, many of which are free or very inexpensive ($1-$8 at the door). Why, at those prices, you can even afford to take a chance on something outside of your usual musical boundaries.

In addition to music, PLU's theater department presents shows ranging from William Inge's *Bus Stop* to Gilbert and Sullivan's *Pirates of Penzance*. Or, maybe you would rather just listen to actor Barry Williams (Greg) rap about his "Brady Bunch" days. Yup, he's dropped by. The number to call for music info is 535-7601; for theater, call 535-7761.

Seattle Pacific University
- 3307 Third Ave. W, Seattle; 281-2205

All who enjoy the arts will want to make the small but busy Seattle Pacific University on Queen Anne Hill a regular stop. SPU's School of Fine and Performing Arts is known for its dedication to the spiritual nature of art, as a personal and sacred expression.

Throughout the academic year, the campus's galleries, theaters, and churches host dozens of events. These feature student groups, faculty recitals, and even alumni presentations. Mainstream plays, as well as more independent creations in the visual and performing arts are always open to the public, and nothing costs more than $10—indeed, most shows cost substantially less. Call the number above for a schedule.

University of Puget Sound
- 1500 N Warner St., Tacoma; 756-3329

Established in 1888, the University of Puget Sound has long served the surrounding community through education, social service, and the arts. There's no need to tell locals about Puget's ambitious theater, art, and music departments. Each month, UPS hosts around ten different events in various art forms, ranging from wind ensemble recitals to full symphony concerts; exhibits in Kittredge Gallery; lectures that are open to the public; and theater classics like a recent adaptation of C. S. Lewis's *The Lion, the Witch, and the Wardrobe.*

Most events are free; for some performances, admission may only consist of a donation of canned goods to help local charities. However, certain

---

MR. CHEAP'S PICKS
College Performing Arts

✔ **Pacific Lutheran University**—They're big on music at this Tacoma campus. As many as ten concerts a month: jazz, pop, classical.

✔ **University of Washington**—A "NoteCard" general pass (students $21, public $35) to over 100 different concerts may be Seattle's best arts bargain. Theater deals, too.

UPS events, like the holiday "Sounds of the Season" concert featuring the Madrigal Singers and Adelphian Concert Choir, do charge still-reasonable ticket prices—always less than $10. Performances take place all around the beautiful Puget Sound campus; check with the Information Center in the foyer of the Student Union Building, or call 756-3329 for all the info you need.

University of Washington
- NE 41st St. and 15th Ave. NE, Seattle; 543-4880

The University of Washington, home to 35,000 students (and seemingly as many faculty and staff), offers a plethora of entertainment for anyone operating on a student's budget—whether you're enrolled or not. Some events feature big-name stars along with the up-and-comings, and there are always discounts for students, senior citizens, children, and UW faculty. Who says college doesn't pay off? Ticket prices, showtimes, and locations vary greatly, so educate yourself by calling ahead to ask about discounts and schedules. And be sure to bring along the appropriate ID!

The UW School of Music presents concerts in several auditoriums around this vast campus, including the Brechemin, the Walker-Ames

Room, Kane Hall—and, largest and most acoustically acclaimed, Meany Theater. Fresh from a major renovation inside and out, the Meany is host to student recitals and opera productions, faculty concerts, and myriad other musical events. In fact, over 100 concerts take place each year. Tickets for these are all but given away to students, senior citizens, and U-Dub employees, while the rest of us pay only a few dollars more.

If you plan to see more than one or two concerts, Mr. C says it makes sense to purchase an annual pass. "NoteCards" cost $35 to the public; students, senior citizens and faculty pay between $21 and $25—remember, these prices get you into over *a hundred* shows for less than the price of one ticket to, say, the Seattle Opera! It may just be the best arts value in town. Month-by-month music calendar information is available by calling 685-8384.

With nine mainstage shows and two "Fringe Season" productions each year, the UW School of Drama keeps its actors and audiences busy. Best buys are, as always, along the season ticket route, where the whole slate can cost around $60—about five bucks a show. Productions range from classics for the intellectual types to cutting-edge performance art. Individual tickets cost between $3 and $8, depending on the show. As with the music department, special discount passes are sold to students ($21 for six admissions) and the public (the "Crazy 8" card, eight plays for $48).

If you hanker for a hunk o' really big-name entertainment, call in spring or summer for a subscription to any of the four overlapping University of Washington World Series showcases—which have nothing to do with baseball—also at the Meany. Subscribers save between 25% and 33% per ticket, and the discounts get bigger for students and elders. Recent events have included a Venezuelan dance interpretation of the classic *Don Quixote*, a British Film Institute/Matrix Ensemble performance art collaboration, and a concert by the Wynton Marsalis Septet.

Rush tickets are another bargain opportunity for students and senior citizens. Check in at the box office a half-hour before the show; you may come up empty-handed, but if the show isn't sold out, rush tix cost a mere $8 apiece. Makes it worth the gamble. Ultimately, no amount of price cutting can make a Yo-Yo Ma concert *cheap*; regular ticket prices hover around $25. But these deals can make it *cheaper*, so don't be shy, ask!

Fine arts and natural history get no less attention on this campus, by the way. Both the Henry Art Gallery and the Burke Museum host temporary exhibits as well as permanent collections (see the listings under "Museums"). But a lesser-known local favorite is the Suzzallo and Allen Libraries, which house small-scale exhibitions on a variety of subjects from mountaineering to Christopher Columbus. It's located directly across the plaza from Meany Hall.

Most events, including the World Series, run from mid-September until early May. Some performances and exhibits also take place during the summer months. Tickets for just about everything may be purchased at the UW Ticket Office located at 4001 University Way NE—or you can call at 543-4880. Once you get hooked on the UW arts scene, check into getting an Arts Bonus Card for further discounts on many of these offerings—sort of a "frequent-flyer" deal for patrons of the arts. Any way you go, UW offers a lot for a little.

COMEDY

For standup comedy, the best cost-cutter in the biz remains the "Open Mike" night, when you can get in for a very low cover charge to see up-and-coming "stars of tomorrow." Guaranteed, there'll be plenty of klunkers (does the name Rupert Pupkin ring a bell, DeNiro fans?), but the shows are hosted by headliners, so you're sure to get plenty of good laughs no matter what. Many clubs, some of which are listed here, have open mike shows; they tend to be early in the week. Call your favorite venue to see what they offer.

Atlantic Street Pizza
- 9041 Holman Rd. NW, Seattle; 783-9698

See the listing under "Music."

Bainbridge Performing Arts Cultural Center
- 200 Madison Ave. N, Bainbridge Island; 842-8578

See the listing under "Arts and Cultural Centers."

The Comedy Underground at Swannies
- 222 S Main St., Seattle; 628-0303

This Pioneer Square club offers lots of comedy, with some of the lowest cover charges in town. The best deals, as with most nightclubs, are found early in the week. Monday and Tuesday nights, come down for the "Seattle Comedy Showcase." You'll see fifteen to eighteen local comics for $3—that's less than 20¢ per comic! Oh, sure, a few of these folks are bound to bomb, but it's all part of the adventure. Never know who you may "discover."

Wednesday nights feature more experienced, still-getting-known comics at the also-reasonable price of $5. On Thursdays, the Underground presents their own improvisational sketch troupe, "Improv is Comic;" again, 'tickets is $5.'

Weekends feature comics from the national circuit, along with higher cover charges; Friday and Saturday tix are $7.50. Still not bad, especially since there's never a food or drink minimum. But, if $7.50 is too steep for you, go instead on Sunday, a.k.a. "bargain hunter's night." You'll see the *same* show for just $5! Talk about Mr. Cheap's night out.

The Comedy Underground has featured some heavy-hitters in its time, including Jerry Seinfeld, Dana Carvey, and Harry Anderson. These days, those guys are too expensive, but the current lineup may just showcase the Church Lady of tomorrow.

The Eastside Comedy Club
- Kirkland Roaster & Ale House, 111 Central Way NE, Kirkland; 827-4400

Need to put a little mirth into your weekend? The Kirkland Roaster & Ale House, near that town's picturesque waterfront, doubles on weekends as the Eastside Comedy Club. The club features both regional and nationally-known comedians. Tickets are $7.50 for a show which generally includes two warm-up acts and a headliner. The top of the bill consists of well-established veterans who've been seen on television showcases like "A & E's Evening at the Improv" and others.

A single performance starts at 10 P.M. every Friday and Saturday night; the line begins to form around 9:30, so don't dawdle. For an easy (and cheap) night out, Mr. C also recommends the restaurant itself, which offers good, relatively inexpensive

MR. CHEAP'S PICKS
Comedy

✔ **The Comedy Underground at Swannies**—The Seinfelds and Carveys of tomorrow can be seen here today, at far less than they'll charge when they hit the big time.

✔ **Theatersports**—The funniest thing since "American Gladiators"—competitive improvisational comedy.

dinners or late-night appetizers, along with over a dozen microbrews on tap. See the listing under "Restaurants—Eastside."

Giggles Comedy Nightclub
● 5220 Roosevelt Way NE, Seattle; 526-5653

Located in the University District (where would comedy be without college campuses?), Giggles Comedy Nightclub presents mainstream comedy at a reasonable admission price. Shows on Fridays and Saturdays (starting around 8 P.M. and again at about 10:30 P.M.) cost $8—not bad. The better deal, of course, is found on Wednesday and Thursday nights, when tickets are just $6. There's only one show on these mid-week nights, at 8:30 P.M. You won't find superstar names here, especially at these prices; but Giggles is a national chain of comedy clubs, bringing in up-and-coming talent from around the country. Call ahead for the week's schedule.

Jet City Improv
● Belltown Theatre Center, 115 Blanchard St., Seattle; 781-3879

Jet City Improv specializes in audience-inspired comedy, with shows every weekend at this Belltown club. For those who aren't familiar with improv, a style of comedy that has its roots in Chicago's Second City troupe, here's a brief explanation: These comic actors ask for elements of a scene (a locale, character types, etc.) and then immediately create sketches based on those suggestions. That means that you can become a part of the show! In fact, JCI *really* likes to get the audience involved—at least once a night, some lucky (?) audience member winds up on stage. Not that you should feel pressured.... The troupe even incorporates live music, improvising songs and musical theater numbers on the spot.

You can join in the fun every Friday and Saturday night at 10:30 P.M. Tickets are a reasonable $7, and $5 with a student ID. But here's a great tip: half-price, day-of-show tix to Jet City Improv are often available at Ticket/Ticket (see the listing under "Theater"). In any case, you're sure to get your money's worth from this hard-working comedy ensemble.

Theatresports
● Market Theatre, 1428 Post Alley, Seattle; 781-9273

Comedy-as-spectator-sport, a new format that's popped up in cities all across America and Canada, is the idea behind Theatresports. The group divides into two teams and performs improvised sketches based on audience suggestions; that's true of any improv troupe, but this time, there are points awarded to the side that gets the most laughter and applause. The team with the most points at the end of the night wins! No wagering, please....

Admission is $8 on Friday and Saturday nights. Ardent Cheapsters should go on Sunday nights, however, when admission is only $5. Now, if you prefer more non-competitive comedy, then the Market Theater is also the place to be on Wednesday nights—when "Cream of Wit," a long-format improv sketch group, takes over for the evening. The fun starts at 7 P.M., and tickets are $5.

DANCE

Co-Motion Dance

• 206 First Ave. S, Seattle; 382-0626
This acclaimed, small dance company presents a handful of concerts each season in their combination studio/theater. Each show tends to be varied in style, ranging from traditional masterworks to new, experimental pieces. Tickets are around $15, but half-price discounts are sometimes available at the Ticket/Ticket stand (see the listing under "Theater").

Co-Motion also performs a tribute to Martin Luther King Jr. each January, and tickets to this concert are just $5. The troupe's season runs from September to May. Call for a season schedule.

Dance Centre Seattle

• 704 19th Ave. E, Seattle; 322-3733
Dance Centre Seattle is primarily an arts service organization; professional dance classes are taught in these studios, and studio space is available for rent by small troupes. Performances are given on an irregular and informal basis.

There is a series of sorts called "Informance," a showcase for local, independent choreographers. Tickets are just $5, even for shows that run on Friday and Saturday nights. In fact, most performances here are on weekends, and rarely is the admission more than five bucks. It's a low-tech, studio setting, but the work is top-notch—and you certainly get to see it up-close, unlike large concert halls. Aside from "Informance," the Pat Graney Company presents works-in-progress on a regular basis, with admission by donation.

DCS has one other regular (though still informal) series, called "The Jam." This is not just a show to watch; this is one you can join in on. Every Tuesday night, open movement improvisation is held from 7:30 to 9:30 P.M. Tickets are sold on a sliding scale, from $3 to $5. Call for more details on how to join the fun.

Olympic Ballet Theatre

• Various locations; Information, 774-7570
The Olympic Ballet Theatre is known for popular classics such as *Swan Lake*, *Giselle*, and *The Nutcracker*. Despite the high quality of their work, OBT tickets can be snapped up for just $12 to $16. Quite a deal, especially considering that comparable tickets to see the Pacific Northwest Ballet sell for $20 to $60 a pop.

Occasionally, Olympic Ballet also presents choreographer's workshops of new works, with tickets for $15; and some programs offer children's tickets for $8 to $12.

OBT doesn't have a permanent home; performances can be at a number of venues, anywhere from the Everett Community Theatre to Moore Theatre in downtown Seattle or the Meydenbauer Convention Center in Bellevue. Call for a full schedule.

On the Boards

• 153 14th Ave., Seattle; 325-7901
Even if you think you're open-minded to everything that art has to offer, you may be a little thrown off by such ensembles as the Cranky Destroyers or Holy Body Tattoo. No, Nirvana is not regrouping under a new name; these two dance troupes are part of a typical lineup organized by On the Boards in its ongoing series of contemporary dance performances. Yes Virginia, that means no *Nutcracker* this Christmas; instead, you may get an opportunity to see Amanda Miller's Pretty Ugly Dance Company. And, to fans of cutting-edge dance, this is *not* the equivalent of a lump of coal in their tights.

Don't let the names scare you, folks. On the Boards brings some of

MR. CHEAP'S PICKS
Dance

✔ **Olympic Ballet Theatre**—
Classical dance doesn't mean
ticket prices have to be lofty.
OBT features first-rate dance
at cut-rate prices.

✔ **On the Boards**—Their "12
Minutes Max" series offers
experimental choreography,
with tickets only $5.

✔ **Pacific Northwest Ballet**—
Students and senior citizens
are eligible for half-price rush
tickets, at the box office an
hour before the show.

the world's most offbeat, yet established, professional troupes to Seattle—and best of all, especially
compared to some other big-time
stuff, it's cheap! Tickets for most
shows go for $14-$16, and that
doesn't even include the $2 discount
for senior citizens and students.

The *real* On The Boards bargain,
though, is "12 Minutes Max," an experimental series held about seven
times a year. The show is sort of an
"open-mike" for choreographers and
troupes, in which anything goes. Newcomers can strut their stuff for a little
exposure, while veterans can test out
whatever dance/music/video/etc.
pieces they happen to be developing.
Tix are a snappy $5, and these shows
take place about once every month
and a half—usually on a Sunday or
Monday, the so-called "dark nights"
in show biz terms (i.e., the major
halls have nothing booked). Locations vary; call to find out how you
can get in on the act.

Pacific Northwest Ballet
● Seattle Center Opera House, 301
Mercer St., Seattle; 441-2424
Seattle's premier ballet company

keeps the classics alive, while insuring that newer stuff also has its place.
This company, fifty dancers strong,
mixes up classics by Stravinsky and
Tchaikovsky with the top-notch choreography of Kent Stowell, PNB's artistic director. The innovative design
of the sets and costumes, along with
critically acclaimed dancing, make
for a can't-miss evening of ballet.
And of course, look to the PNB for
the definitive annual holiday production of *The Nutcracker.*

Now, tickets can pirouette as high
as $60 apiece; but, with others start-
ing as low as $10, there is indeed a
seat (somewhere) for everyone. Do
try to grab these plebeian tix well in
advance, though. Ah, but here's another idea: Students and senior citizens can often nab great seats for
half-price by waiting in line for rush
tickets, sold one hour before the show.
These are almost always available; be
sure and bring the appropriate ID.

Spectrum Dance Theater at Madrona
● 800 Lake Washington Blvd.,
Seattle; 325-4161
A presenting organization as well as a
performing troupe, the Spectrum
Dance Theater Company is one of
those that covers, well, all ranges of
the spectrum. They bring into Seattle
renowned groups from across the nation, to grace the stages of the Meany
Theater on the University of Washington campus four or five times a year.
You may see things like the That's
Jazz dance company whooping it up
to the music of Bing Crosby, or Chicago's Hubbard Street Dance Company's re-interpretation of the tango.
When Spectrum's not hosting these
troupes, its own company of profes-
sionally-acclaimed dancers travels
the U.S. and the Seattle area showing
off ethnic and stylistic diversity.

Tix for the national acts and mainstage Spectrum Dance Company productions can get up to around $20 for
adults, $15 for seniors, and $10 for
students. That's not so much, when
you may get to see a world premiere
directed by Ann Reinking or the Spec-

trum company dance the night away.

Lower-key studio performances, lecture-demonstrations, and open rehearsals take place at Spectrum's Madrona Dance Studio, a renovated lakeside bathhouse—for a lower price. Not all of these are open to the public, but when they are, its only $5-$7 a pop. Call to find out their upcoming schedule.

FESTIVALS

Seattle's tendency for dry weather in the summer makes this prime time for about a gazillion outdoor festivals, appealing to families, arts fans, and folks for whom "summer camp" takes on a whole new meaning. Herein are most of the city's best:

Bumbershoot Festival

• Seattle Center; Information, 684-7200

Four days of music, arts, food, and more make Bumbershoot perhaps the most popular of Seattle's annual festivals. Held every Labor Day weekend, Bumbershoot (a quaint British term for umbrella) is probably so named in anticipation of the rainy winter ahead. Unlike many other festivals, you must pay admission to Bumbershoot. Tickets are $9 for adults and $1 for kids and seniors. But, considering the line-up of national and international stars who perform here, $9 is a steal. Furthermore, admission is free on Friday, the first day of the fest.

Predictably, the most famous acts are saved for the "pay" days. In the past, these have included musicians Joan Baez, the Neville Brothers, Jackson Browne, Bruce Hornsby, and Bonnie Raitt. Theater and dance offerings have included the Seattle Shakespeare Festival, the Seattle Mime Theater, and Russia's St. Petersburg Ballet.

Bibliophiles will love "Bookfair," with readings by notables from Tom Robbins to Robert Bly. And, don't miss "ArtMarket," with arts and crafts to purchase or merely peruse. See? All this for $9! Bumbershoot is also the home of "Taste of Seattle," representing restaurants all over the city. The food isn't free, but it's certainly a cheaper way to sample some of these eateries than going to each one for a full meal.

There's a dizzying amount to see and do here. Mr. C suggests getting a listing of the events so you won't miss your faves. Call the number above or the Bumbershoot hotline at 682-4FUN (4386); or pick up brochures in a variety of area restaurants for a full listing. There's also a lot of stuff especially designed for kids; see the listing under "Children's Activities" for more details.

Free Summer Concerts at Bellevue Botanical Gardens

• 12001 Main St., Bellevue; 462-2749

The Bellevue Botanical Gardens, in conjunction with the City of Bellevue Parks and Recreation Department, sponsors a series of free concerts throughout the summer. Here, you can enjoy music in a beautiful natural setting. Performers that have been part of this series include the Prevailing Winds Trip, the Foggy Bottom Jazz Band, and acoustic duo Eric Tingstad and Nancy Rumel. At the time of this writing, concerts take place on Sunday afternoons and Wednesday evenings. Call for a complete schedule. Of course, Bellevue Botanical Gardens is a great place to visit anytime; see the separate listing under "Outdoors" for more info.

Free Summer Concerts at Chittenden Locks

- 3015 NW 54th St., Seattle; 783-7059

Ballard's Hiram Chittenden Locks are a diverse place for all kinds of free fun, especially during the summertime. That's when the locks become a music mecca, featuring free concerts most Sundays from June through the beginning of September. The music offered here tends toward jazz and pop. You won't find any big stars, but plenty of accomplished local groups. The names alone give a sense of fun: The Ballard Sedentary Sousa Band, the W. T. Preston Hard Aground Jazz Band, and the Seattle Navy Rock Band have all been among the performers.

Concerts start at 2 P.M. on the lawns across from the Visitor Center. Stop in there or call for an up-to-date schedule. For more information on the Chittenden Locks see the listing under "Outdoors."

Free Summer Concerts in Edmonds

- City Park, Third and Pine Sts., Edmonds; 771-0228
- Frances Anderson Center Amphitheatre, 700 Main St., Edmonds; 771-0228

For north-enders, the Edmonds Arts Commission sponsors free summer concerts through July and August in City Park. The concerts are held on Sundays at 3 P.M. and embrace a broad range of musical styles, including folk, jazz, bluegrass, brass bands, and ethnic music—featuring groups like Oomph, performing traditional European *klezmer* music, and others.

In addition, the EAC also sponsors a family concert series during July. These are held at the Frances Anderson Center Amphitheatre on Thursdays at noon. Past performances have included puppeteers, storytellers, and music.

Free Summer Concerts in Kent

- Kent-Kherson Peace Park, Second and Gowe Sts., Kent; 859-3991
- Mill Creek Canyon Earthworks Park, 742 Titus St., Kent; 859-3991

To the south, meanwhile, a variety of summer concerts in Kent entertain flocks of families, with free admission. Head to Kent-Kherson Peace Park on Thursdays, from 12 noon to 1 P.M., for "LunchBreak Performances," where you'll hear everything from jazz and blues to reggae and calypso. On Wednesdays, bring the kids to "Picnic Performances" from 12 noon to 1 P.M. at Mill Creek Canyon Earthworks Park. These concerts are geared to the young 'uns, and have included the Gentlemen Jugglers, the Rockaroos, and the Banana Slug String Band. Gotta love a name like that.

There's also a "Friday Night Live" series at Earthworks Park from 7 to 8:30 P.M. The performers in this series lean toward jazz sounds, with some blues, bluegrass, and ethnic sounds thrown into the mix. Concerts in Kent usually run throughout July and August. Times and dates will vary; call the number above for more info. While admission is free, donations to keep the concerts going are gladly accepted.

Fellow Cheapsters will also want to know that Mill Creek Canyon Earthworks Park doubles as the site of the **Canterbury Faire** in mid-August. The fair assembles two days of music, theater, dance, crafts exhibits, and more; and admission is only $1.

Free Summer Concerts at Mural Amphitheatre

- Seattle Center, 305 Harrison St., Seattle; 684-7200

The Seattle Center is the scene for lots of entertainment all year long, especially in the summer. One of the most popular programs is the outdoor summer concert series at the center's Mural Amphitheatre. The concerts are completely free and open to the public, featuring an eclectic mix of music styles from R & B, gospel, rock, and jazz, to international sounds.

Concerts are scheduled almost every Friday, Saturday, and Sunday from the middle of June until the end of July. Most last for several hours, with more than one band usually on the bill. The performers hail from all over the region, though you will see the occasional national act mixed in. Of course, every concert gives you an opportunity to relax on the lawn or dance the day or evening away.

Ivar's Family Concert Series

- Coulon Beach Park, Renton; 587-6500

Maintaining the late Ivar Haglund's commitment to the Seattle-area public, Ivar's sponsors a series of free outdoor concerts in this south-end park. The concerts take place on Thursday nights (generally every other week) at 6 P.M., from June through August.

The music covers a broad range of styles, including Latin percussion, Broadway show tunes, country and bluegrass, folk, rock, jazz, and more. Whatever your musical tastes, you're sure to find *something* that will interest you. Call the number above for a complete list of dates and times.

Jetty Island Days

- Jetty Island, Everett; Information 259-0300

More than just a few days of mirth and merriment, Jetty Island Days extend from the first Wednesday after Independence Day to the first weekend in September—sort of a northern Seafair festival. Each day (except Mondays and Tuesdays) is filled with family activities like puppet shows, arts and crafts, storytelling, sandcastle contests, and more.

Twice each day, park rangers take visitors on a nature walk. These walks will introduce you to the unusual plant and animal life that inhabits the island. You can request special group tours, too, with names like "Hug a Bug" and "Squirmy, Squiggly, & Squishy" (held during low tides only). Kinda says it all, huh? There are several music events scheduled throughout, as well.

Even if you don't take part in the festivities, Jetty Island is a fun place to hang out. A narrow two miles of sandy beach and upland dunes are home to some 45 species of birds alone! Everett Parks and Recreation provides a ferry, free of charge, to

---

MR. CHEAP'S PICKS
Festivals

✔ **Bumbershoot**—Music, theater, literature, and dance with some of the hottest artists around. Add the "Taste of Seattle" and you get the city's best-loved festival.

✔ **Jetty Island Days**—Ferry rides, nature walks, arts and crafts—the "Seafair" of the north.

✔ **Out To Lunch Concert Series**—Various downtown spots become outdoor concert stages each summer.

✔ **Pacific Northwest Arts & Crafts Fair**—Artists, artisans, and art lovers travel from far and wide to Bellevue each summer.

✔ **Seafair**—The grandaddy of 'em all, all summer long.

---

and from the island—which is open Wednesdays through Sundays from 10 A.M. to 5:30 P.M. The island is accessible to the public year-round; but the ferry only runs in the summer, and off-season use is sometimes restricted to protect the wildlife. If you plan on sailing over, call the Parks Department before you set out. There are four late night programs each summer, complete with campfires, when the island stays open until 9 P.M. Call the number above for further details.

Kirkland Festival of the Arts

- Parkplace Center, Kirkland; 822-7066

For one weekend every summer, this arts and crafts fair completely takes over the parking lot of this popular Eastside shopping center. A smaller-scale cousin to the Pacific Northwest

Arts and Crafts Fair in Bellevue (see listing below), this event is no less a tradition—it's been going for almost 25 years.

Sponsored by the Kirkland Arts Center, the family-oriented festival opens on Saturday morning with a "clown parade." Meanwhile, booth after booth fills the parking lot with hundreds of artists selling handmade clothing, jewelry, and crafts; regional recording companies hawk CDs of local musicians; and there's plenty of food, live music, dancing, and face painting for the kids. The fest usually takes place in mid-July; keep an eye on the papers for info, or stop by the arts information center in a storefront at Parkplace (open weekdays from 9 to 5) for more details on this and other arts events all around Kirkland.

Kirkland Jazz Festival
● Various locations; Information, 822-5158

Every August, Kirkland becomes the place to be for jazz *aficionados*. The Kirkland Jazz Festival attracts mostly regional players, with a few national acts mixed in. There's also a children's area with its own music, crafts, and carnival games. In addition, downtown restaurants, cafes, coffee shops, and such get into the act by hosting small local jazz groups in their establishments.

Most of the 'round-the-clock happenings are found in Kirkland's Marina Park and Carillon Point, both along the scenic waterfront. Tickets are $20 for a two-day pass, $12 for a Saturday-only pass, and $10 for a Sunday-only pass; with six to ten acts playing each day from noon until early evening, you certainly get your money's worth. For more info or a schedule of performers, call the Downtown Kirkland Association at the number above anytime during early summer.

Mostly Music in the Park
● Luther Burbank Park, 2040 84th Ave. SE, Mercer Island; 236-3545

Here's one for the island folks. The Mercer Island Arts Council brings you a summer of free music in

Luther Burbank Park. Through July and August, "Mostly Music in the Park" presents two concerts each week, ranging from classical, jazz, and country/western groups to ethnic music and even barbershop quartets! The series is called "Mostly Music," though, because they do offer the occasional non-music event, such as a recent performance of *Much Ado about Nothing* by the Shakespeare Theatre. Regardless of type, events are held on Tuesdays at 7 P.M. and Sundays at 6 P.M.

The Mercer Island Arts Council sponsors other events throughout the year, including literary readings and a "community spotlight" program. MIAC is also home to an art gallery that displays works by Northwest artists, along with traveling shows from heavy-hitters like the Smithsonian Institute. The art gallery is located at the Mercer Island Arts Council community center, 8236 SE 24th Street. Call them at the number above for more info and a complete list of their programs.

Northwest Folklife Festival
● Seattle Center, 305 Harrison St., Seattle; 684-7300

In these politically correct times, "diversity" is a word that gets tossed around rather freely. Well, at the Northwest Folklife Festival, this word doesn't even *begin* to describe the range of activities you and your family can enjoy. The festival is four days filled with music, dance, arts and crafts, and food from over one hundred different nationalities. By the end, you'll feel like a world traveler—without spending a penny on airfare. Admission and events are all free (except for the food, which is reasonably priced).

There is so much to see and do here. Music and dance performances over the years have included swing dancers, old-time fiddlers, barbershop quartets, reggae bands, and gospel choirs. Poetry and storytelling are always a staple; especially popular is the "Tall Tales Contest." All this, plus children's games, art demonstrations, symposiums, and more. The festival is held every year over the Memorial Day weekend.

Meanwhile, at this same spot each November, you'll also find the Festival of World Traditions. Held during the three days following Thanksgiving, this festival solely emphasizes international arts and crafts. Great opportunity to get a jump on Christmas shopping, direct from the artists!

"Out To Lunch" Concert Series

• Various locations; Information, 382-7827

Produced by the Downtown Seattle Association, "Out to Lunch" is a series of free lunchtime concerts held in a variety of outdoor locales. The music ranges from jazz to classical, country to pop, showcasing a diverse mix of local and national talent. Concert locations include the Rainier Square Roof Garden, between Fourth and Fifth Avenues; the Seattle Art Museum; City Hall Park (near Pioneer Square); Piers 55/56; and others.

This well-attended series runs from mid-June through mid-September, with several concerts scheduled each week. All concerts take place from 12 noon to 1:30 P.M. Days and dates vary, call the above number, or the Downtown Seattle Association at 623-0340, for details. Get out (to lunch), bring a brown-bag, and grab yourself some of that fine summer weather!

Pacific Northwest Arts & Crafts Fair

• Bellevue Square Mall, Bellevue; 454-4900

For some fifty years, the Pacific Northwest Arts & Crafts Fair has been a major event on the summer calendar, much anticipated by Eastsiders, Seattleites, and art fans from far and wide. Hosted by the Bellevue Art Museum (see their listing under "Museums"), the fair sprawls from inside this shopping mall out to several surrounding parking lots. Over 300 booths display creations in wood, ceramics, glass, textile arts, jewelry, and more. Many prominent regional artists got their start at this fair (including Dale Chihuly, who once blew glass here). If you're serious about buying unique crafts, try to get there on Friday, the opening day.

But this is more than just a big crafts sale. Inside, the museum shows its annual Pacific Northwest juried exhibition. There are lots of performing arts here, too, from the Bellevue Philharmonic Orchestra, African and Latin bands, and folk singer/songwriters.

Going on at the same time is "Kids' Fair at Bellevue Place," featuring hands-on activities like making and painting pottery, children's music, and other family entertainment. Bellevue Place is located diagonally across the street from the Bellevue Square mall. And, you'll get a "Taste of Bellevue" with food concessions at both sites, representing area restaurants. No wonder this fair attracts hundreds of thousands of visitors each year.

The Pacific Northwest Arts and Crafts Fair is generally held on the last weekend of July. Call the number above for specific dates and times, or look for a special supplement in the *Eastsideweek* newspapers.

Redmond Arts in the Parks

• Various locations, Redmond; Information, 556-2350

The Redmond Arts Commission and the Parks and Recreation Department team up each summer to present a full slate of free outdoor concerts for the family. Throughout July and August, on selected weekdays at noon and Sunday evenings at six, folks gather to enjoy the good weather and good music.

Bands come from all over the area, and even around the West Coast; each week brings something entirely different, with an emphasis on various ethnic groups. One week may offer reggae, the next *klezmer*, the next good ol' Dixieland jazz. The concerts take place at such locations as diverse as Anderson Park, the Overlake Fashion Plaza shopping center, and even the campus of Microsoft. Bring a lawn chair or a blanket, something to nibble, watch your kids cavorting in the sunshine, and relax. All locations are handi-capped-accessible. Pick up a calendar in early summer at stores in the area, or from the Parks Department.

Seafair
• Various locations; Information, 728-0123

If you're anywhere *near* Seattle dur-ing Seafair, you'll know it. Each July and August, the entire city partici-pates in a family-oriented frenzy of parades, food festivals, crafts fairs, road races, and more. These may be cultural in theme, ethnic or religious, or just the coming-together of a par-ticular neighborhood from the U-Dis-trict to Alki Beach. It's all in the name of good will, and the general celebration of Seattle's diverse com-munities.

Seafair has been going on for nearly half a century, and nobody's had enough of it yet—indeed, the fes-tival seems to get bigger every year. When summertime rolls around, look for stacks of the *Seafair Schedule of Events* or the *Official Festival Pro-gram* at stores and cafes all over town—you'll need it if you're plan-ning on attending any of the dozen or more parades, myriad cultural com-munity festivals, daredevil airplane exhibitions, the world's most famous hydroplane race, or the ongoing array of clowns, contests, and costumes. The best thing about Seafair is that it's full of free fun. But you'll have to check the schedule for specifics.

University Village Courtyard Music Festival
• University Village Shopping Plaza, NE 45th St. and 25th Ave. NE, Seattle; 523-0622

Mr. C was quite delighted, one sum-mer afternoon, to happen across a genuine, honest-to-goodness big band, swinging like a house afire in the middle of this huge shopping cen-ter. The sounds of classic Count Basie and Glenn Miller tunes had toes tapping among old and young folks alike. What a surprise!

And that was just the beginning. Each Wednesday through August and September, the Courtyard Music Fes-tival brings hot sounds to this other-wise unlikely setting of quiet boutiques and upscale shops. From alternative rock to R & B to jazz to *a capella* doo wop, all kinds of bands hold forth from 5 to 7 P.M.— and it's all free, in a lush, semi-cov-ered atrium setting. Plenty of food shops around the plaza, too.

MOVIES

Unfortunately, there's not much to be done about the ever-rising prices of first-run Hollywood movies. But don't despair! There are lots of alternative options for the budget moviegoer—as long as you're will-ing to go a bit out of your way, or at some time other than a weekend night. You probably know that most cinemas offer a bargain matinee or "twilight" discount showing, even on current hits; not only can you save money this way, but you can also see the newest releases without the has-sle of huge crowds. That's worth it right there.

Some theaters extend this deal to all shows before 6:00 P.M., such as the **General Cinemas** chain, with branches in North Seattle, Everett, Renton, and Federal Way. Others, such as the **Crossroads Cinemas** in Bellevue, discount all of their Monday shows. Check the papers or call your local 'plex for details.

Meanwhile, there are all kinds of other options:

AMC SeaTac 12
- 31600 20th Ave. S, Federal Way; 839-3050

Generally speaking, this is your basic full-price, first-run movie complex. The SeaTac 12 does, however, have lower-prices and better discount rates than most others in the metro area. At the time of this writing, the top ticket price is $5.75. Matinees, before 4:00 P.M., are always $3.50 for adults; that's also the price for children and senior citizens at all times. And the standard late-afternoon discount shows—between 4:00 and 6:00 P.M. daily—are a mere $2.75 for all tickets.

Fremont Almost Free Outdoor Cinema
- 600 N 34th St., Seattle; 282-5706

From mid-May to October, a strange cult of men, women, and children gather in the large parking lot behind Fremont's main street to celebrate a bi-weekly ritual. No, there are no pagan sacrifices. At dusk, on the first and third Saturdays of the month, some 400 to 500 people garbed in outlandish costumes (strictly optional) come together to worship campy B-movies, old-time serials, cartoons, and truly classic flicks.

It's been said that art imitates life; here, life imitates art. Elvis impersonators gyrate to a screening of *Viva Las Vegas*. Modern-day maidens-in-distress scream along with Fay Wray during *King Kong*. And *Rocky Horror Picture Show* dress-alikes, perhaps befuddled by the title, enjoy Bogart nevertheless at a showing of *The African Queen*. All presented on the outside of an ordinary building in the parking lot, painted white and outlined with a grand old (painted) "curtain."

Gate prizes for best (and worst) costumes, shadow puppetry, food, and comedy surround this movie madness. Seating is strictly BYO. Participants say that rarely-seen films and the interesting crowd bring them to this sacred Fremont plot, but Mr. C suspects the "pay what you can" policy may also have something to do with it. The suggested admission fee is $5, and the folks who run the show request that you kindly pay if at all possible. For all you get, on screen and off, it's well worth it.

Grand Illusion Cinema
- 1403 NE 50th St., Seattle; 523-3935

Taking its name from Jean Renoir's classic film, the Grand Illusion carries on the art-house mantle for Seattle. This small, cozy theater in the U-District is known for premiering avant-garde, political documentaries like *Sex Drugs & Democracy*, the recent underground hit detailing law and morality in present-day Holland. Tickets are $6, which puts this cinema just barely under the average citywide rates; however, tix are always just $4 for any show before 6:00 P.M. And you certainly won't find *these* films playing at your local mall. Before or after the film, the adjoining Grand Illusion Café is a comfortable place for inexpensive yet creative light food. It's open days and evenings.

Klondike Gold Rush National Historical Park
- 117 S Main St., Seattle; 553-7220

See the listing under "Museums."

911 Media Arts Center
- 117 Yale Ave. N, Seattle; 682-6552

There's no telling *what* you're bound to see at the 911 Media Arts Center, a combination screening room and learning facility for underground film-making. Located in the industrial area between Eastlake and First Hill, the 911 (whose name comes from a former address, not the emergency squad) offers seminars and workshops conducted by professional filmmakers from nearby and as far away as Europe.

Screenings by these guest artists are quite frequent and take on a variety of themes, from serious to downright scandalous. Themes of intoxication, mayhem, and subversive sex have been known to dot the monthly schedule; other programs highlight films by women, live performance artists, festival prize-winners, and the like. Most ticket prices range from $3-$6. Alternate Mondays (year-round except in August) feature "Open Screenings," sort of a video version of poetry slams. These start at 8 P.M. and only cost a dollar for admission. Bring your reel.

Becoming a member of the 911 entitles you to discounts on admissions, lectures, and workshops. Students can join for $25, $35 for adults, and $50 for the family (not that this could be considered family fare, in the Jesse Helms sense). Some of the programs take place in other locations, so call for the monthly newsletter and schedule. This will also give you a resource page of classified ads detailing job and grant opportunities, festivals to enter, and more.

Pike St. Cinema

• 1108 E Pike St., Seattle; 682-7064
Dennis Nyback—owner, CEO, program director, and head popcorn popper at the Pike—asserts that he is un-funded, un-advertised, under-attended, and unrepentant; but that's not the whole picture. In reality, he gets all the advertising a budding theater could ever want—every time this tiny storefront on First Hill screens another controversial film. $5 gets you in to see all kinds of wacky, unusual stuff, though you won't always walk out with a smile. Enlightenment, not escapism, is on the bill here; past programs have included unmainstream pics with titles like *Bad Bugs Bunny: The Dark Side of Warner Brothers* and *Dada From Z to A*. There is room for entertainment along the way, as with the recent "Festival of Cult Television," featuring shows like *Mod Squad* and *Land of the Giants*, complete with "vintage" TV commercials. Gotta have fun sometimes.

Dennis often programs the theater from his own personal collection, which includes some true rarities. The Pike yields to none, so if you're not too easily offended or shocked,

stop in for a showing of indies like *Just Cause He's Dead Doesn't Mean It's Wrong to Hate Nixon*—or whatever anti-Hollywood is ranting about this week. By the way, as schedule flyers point out, the Pike St. Cinema "is not in the Pike Place Market." One visit, and you'll have no trouble remembering this point.

Seattle Art Museum Film Series

• Seattle Art Museum Auditorium, 100 University St., Seattle; 654-3100

For true film-lovers, the Seattle Art Museum offers a refined alternative to shopping mall cinemas. Film series run throughout the year, organized around a variety of subjects. Past themes have included French and American *film noir*, Caribbean films, the works of François Truffaut, and the Asian-American Film Festival.

General admission tix cost $6; if, however, you plan on spending a lot of time watching this particular silver screen, subscription tickets are a better good buy. Prices are also discounted for SAM and 911 Media Arts Center members; annual memberships to these organizations range from $20-$30.

Call for information on lectures (like film score composer Toru Takemitsu), special programs, and previews.

Seven Gables Discount Card

• **Broadway Market Cinema**, 401 Broadway E, Seattle; 323-0231
• **Crest**, 16505 Fifth Ave. NE, Seattle; 363-6338
• **Egyptian**, 801 E Pine St., Seattle; 323-4978
• **Guild**, 2115 N 45th St., Seattle; 633-3353
• **Harvard Exit**, 807 E Roy St., Seattle; 323-8986
• **Metro**, NE 45th St. and Ninth Ave. NE, Seattle; 633-0055
• **Neptune**, NE 45th St. and Brooklyn Ave. NE, Seattle; 633-5545
• **Seven Gables**, 911 NE 50th St., Seattle; 632-8820
• **Varsity**, 4329 University Way NE, Seattle; 632-3131

It's a deal already: Nine theaters under the name of seven! Now, here's the real deal. All of these houses accept the Seven Gables discount pass. Pick up a pass for $22 at any of the above cinemas; it's good for any five admissions. You can use more than one at a time, for up to six months. The pass is accepted at any showing Mondays through Thursdays, or Friday and Saturday shows before 6:00 P.M. only (except at the Varsity, where the pass is honored for any repertory show). Just ask at the box office for details.

University of Washington Film Series

- Husky Union Building Auditorium, University of Washington; 543-3456

All you over-the-hill types—y'know, anyone over 25—should brush back a tear of regret that you are no longer a student...specifically, that you are not a UW student, and therefore not allowed admittance to UW's Tuesday Night film series. Unless you carry a UW student ID card, see, you just can't take advantage of the house deal here: A double feature of recent hit films for only $2.50. Who says college is expensive?

Okay, Mr. C will let you in on a little secret: each UW cardholder *is* entitled to bring one guest into the Husky Union Building's Auditorium—at the same price! So, if you don't possesses one of these sacred cards, wait outside the HUB before 6:30, make a new friend, and you'll be all set. Schedule info on this and other, more obscure campus films can be found by calling 543-7663.

Valley 6 Drive-In Theaters

- 401 Auburn Ave. N, Auburn; 854-1250

It seems you just can't beat the drive-ins (those few that remain) for bargains on current movies. Perhaps it's because of the element of inconvenience—and "elements" is the right word—or, because these places now tend to cram half a dozen smaller screens into the same size parking lots that used to hold one big screen. Hmm, just like the indoor cinemas.

Anyway, the Valley offers six current double-features every night at dusk, with an admission price of only $5 for adults, and $3.50 for seniors and kids ages 12-15. Admission is free for children under age 11. The place opens at 8:00 P.M., with shows beginning at dusk (usually about an hour later—call for exact times). One other important note: These totally modern drive-ins use no speakers. The movie soundtrack is broadcast over your car's AM radio. If your radio is on the fritz, bring a portable—or you'll be watching a silent movie!

Folks in the north end can find similar deals at the **Puget Park Drive-In**, 13020 Meridian Ave. S, Everett; telephone 338-5957.

Varsity Cinema

- 4329 University Way NE, Seattle; 632-3131

Seattle's premier repertory house, the Varsity programs short runs of everything from mainstream art flicks like a Brit double-bill of *Shadowlands* and *Remains of the Day* to such leftwing stuff as *Coming Out Under Fire*, the story of gays in the military during World War II. Somewhere in between these are foreign films, Hollywood big-screen classics, animation fests, and more. The Varsity is also Seattle's weekly home of *The Rocky Horror Picture Show*, with a live cast accompanying the film—among other midnight weekend offerings.

Tickets are $6.50 for adults, and $4 for children and senior citizens;

same price for the repertory double-features, though, making them a "reel" bargain (sorry, couldn't resist). Further, the first show of the day is usually discounted, with tix $4 for everyone. And don't forget, the Seven Gables Discount Card (see the listing above) is accepted at all Varsity repertory shows, any time, any day.

SECOND-RUN DISCOUNT CINEMAS

Second-run movies are the same Hollywood releases that you see in the shopping malls and downtown cinemas, after they've finished their "first runs" in those major venues. Well before they make their way to pay-per-view and videocassettes, they often show up at some of the theaters listed below. Not only do you get one last chance to see recent hits you may have missed—still on the big screen—but the tickets usually cost less than half of those at the big-deal houses.

Admiral Twin Theater
- 2347 California Ave. SW, Seattle; 938-3456

All shows $2.00? Aye aye sir! Two screens, each with double-features daily.

Alderwood Village 12
- 3815 196th Ave. SW, Seattle; 771-6194

Purchase a membership for a one-time fee of $2.00, and admission for all will be only $1.50 for Monday through Thursday shows; a whopping $2.00 on Friday, Saturday, and Sunday. Needless to say, you get a dozen or more recent cinematic choices.

Crest Cinema
- 16505 Fifth Ave. NE, Seattle; 363-6338

Actually in Ridgecrest, just north of the Seattle city line. All seats $2.00, no questions asked.

Liberty Cinema
- 114 W Main St., Puyallup; 845-1038

Pierce County's favorite family theater, specializing in shiny, happy films, and prices that the whole family can enjoy. Normal evening shows are $3 for adults and $2 for kids and senior

citizens. Before 6 P.M., everyone gets in for two dollars, even ma and pa.

North Bend Cinema
- 125 North Bend Blvd. N, North Bend; 888-1232

In the shadows of Mt. Si (well, not at night, of course), this place is another throwback to the old days of family moviegoing. There is one showing a night, at 8:00 P.M., of a recent hit; the booking changes each week. The adult ticket price is $3.50, while anyone under age 17 gets in for $2.50. For extra entertainment in the minuscule lobby, there's usually a batch of signs taped to the wall which say things like "Free kittens, see Harry."

Roxy Cinema
- 504 S Third St., Renton; 225-5656

All seats, all shows $1.50. Period.

U.A. Discount Cinema 150
- 2131 Sixth Ave., Seattle; 443-9591

Unlike most theaters in this category, Cinema 150 is located right in the heart of downtown Seattle. Old, comfortable rocking seats and the biggest screen in the city. Up to four recent hits at a time. The name says it—tickets are $1.50, every seat, every show, every day.

MUSEUMS

Mr. C firmly believes that *all* museums are bargains. Consider how many treasures you can see, for less than the price of a movie! If you really enjoy a particular museum, by the way, consider becoming a member. This gets you free admission anytime, including perhaps your family, for the price of a couple of visits. It's a money-saver, and it helps out your beloved institution at the same time.

Bellevue Art Museum
• Bellevue Square Mall, Bellevue; 454-6021

An art museum in a mall? Well, we *are* talking about Bellevue Square, dahling. And, unlike just about everything else at this upscale shopping center, the Bellevue Art Museum is cheap (there are two other surprising bargains here, the Overlake Service League Thrift Shop and the Zoopa restaurant; see those listings under "Shopping—Clothing—Used" and "Restaurants—Eastside").

Found up on the third level of the mall, BAM tends to feature arts and crafts by Pacific Northwest artists, with some of national and international repute. BAM also hosts the Pacific Northwest Arts & Crafts Fair, an annual event some fifty years in the running. For more information, see the listing under "Festivals."

Though the fair sprawls all around the mall's parking areas, the jewel at its center is the juried art show held upstairs in the museum itself. Here, you can see the top fifty works of art in a variety of media produced by area artists during the past year; just outside the galleries, another juried show features the best works by children and students through high school age. During the three-day weekend run of the fair, museum admission is free to all.

During the rest of the year, admission is just $3 for adults, $2 for students and seniors, and free for children under 12. And, for true starving artists who want to see the work of their peers, the museum is free to all every Tuesday! It even stays open an extra two hours on Tuesday, so you can take full advantage of the free time. The Bellevue Art Museum is open Mondays through Saturdays from 10 A.M. to 6 P.M. ('til 8 P.M. on Tuesdays), and Sundays from 11 A.M. to 5 P.M. It's closed between exhibitions, and on major holidays.

Burke Museum
• NE 45th St. & 17th Ave. NE, Seattle; 543-5590

Permanent exhibits at the Burke Museum take visitors on a fantastic voyage through time and history, pausing to see fully re-constructed dinosaurs, fossils, and other prehistoric artifacts. Bringing it all up to the present, though, a touch-screen computer puts the entire museum's vast holdings at your fingertips. And, while parents fiddle with these sophisticated mechanisms of information, kids can enjoy the "Discovery Room" where they can interact with all sorts of wonders of the Pacific Rim—and touching is definitely allowed!

So don't get the idea that the Burke is your run-of-the-mill, dry, history museum; to complement their renowned permanent collection, the museum hosts a number of widely popular and often unusual exhibitions throughout the year. One recent show, "Darkened Waters: Profile of an Oil Spill," offered a topical and first-hand encounter with the ecological effects of shipping disasters. The

Burke is even known for its flights of scientific fancy; in Ray Troll's whimsical multimedia exhibition "Planet Ocean," you could have seen such evolutionary possibilities as "sabretooth salmon."

Now, how much does it cost to enter so many exotic worlds? A measly three dollars!!! Better yet, students and folks over 65 save a dollar; and kids age 6 to 18 pay only $1.50. Best of all, UW students and staff don't even pay a dime. The Burke Museum is located on the northwest corner of the University of Washington campus. Parking is available, free from Saturday afternoon through Sunday; the fee ranges from $2.25 to $4.50 on weekdays, but is less for carpools—an extra tip from Mr. Cheap!

Center for Wooden Boats
• 1010 Valley St., Seattle;
  382-BOAT (2628)
See the listing under "Outdoors."

Charles and Emma Frye Art Museum
• 704 Terry Ave., Seattle; 622-9250
Charles and Emma Frye spent the early part of this century collecting some two hundred oil paintings from all over the western hemisphere. Then, in their wills, they provided for the creation of a public art museum to show their collection, for free, to anyone and everyone. The canvases survey a variety of painting styles, from French naturalists to German and American expressionists. Though considered by some to be rather conservative in its tastes, the Frye holds works by Edouard Manet, Adolphe Monticelli, Sören Emil Carlsen, Alexander Max Koester, and Gabriel Max.

In addition to its permanent collection, the museum has regular exhibitions of contemporary works by regional artists. The museum sponsors the annual Puget Sound Area Exhibition, and new paintings are being purchased to this day by the Frye's successors.

The Frye Art Museum is open Mondays through Saturdays from 10 A.M. to 5 P.M., and Sundays from 12 noon to 5 P.M. To get on their mailing list and receive a copy of the monthly newsletter *Frye Vues*, leave your name and address at the counter. Groups can arrange guided tours by calling the number above.

General Petroleum Museum
• 1526 Bellevue Ave., Seattle;
  323-4789
Housed in a Capitol Hill industrial building which had been a Ford distributorship in the 1920s, the General Petroleum Museum is a nostalgia fan's dream—filled with assembling pumps, signs, display cases, oil and gas cans, uniforms, advertising materials, and other "petroliana." The focus is on artifacts that were common as courtesy during the era between World War I and World War II; some are now the last of their kind in existence. With over 18,000 pieces, owners Jeffrey and Susan Pederson believe this to be the largest collection of its kind in the country...and it would be hard to doubt them.

Best of all, you can view it all for free. Jeff and Susan are really *caters* by trade; they also own the nearby Museum Cafe (see the listing under "Restaurants—Capitol Hill"). A primary function of the museum itself, y'see, is to be a function-room for weddings, birthdays, and other catered events. Now, since *this* is the main gig, the museum does not have standard operating hours; call ahead, though, and you can make an appointment to see this vast treasure trove just about any time it's not otherwise, er, engaged. GPM is usually open Monday through Friday from 9 A.M. to 3 P.M., but due to the rather unorthodox nature of the place, *always* call ahead to be sure it's open. If they're around on the weekends they'll let you in, but this is infrequent.

Gilman Town Hall Museum
• 615 SE Andrews St., Issaquah;
  392-3500
The structure standing on Lot 13 of Block 7 in Inglewood, King County, Washington Territory, has gone through the somewhat predictable evolution of any late-19th century pioneer building. It no longer houses

wild animals, and it has been equipped with modern plumbing facilities (whew!); but the two-cell cement jail still stands behind the original structure. The Gilman Town Hall has served as the site of gala balls, a library, a religious center, fire station, and private residence. Today, it houses the artifacts of all these—the history of the past 120 years, organized into special exhibitions from mining to brewing to the daily life in 19th century Washington.

Seeing the exhibits may require a bit of schedule juggling, since the museum is open only on Saturdays from 12 P.M. to 4 P.M. and Mondays from 10:30 A.M. to 2:30 P.M. Do feel free to call for an appointment, though; guided tours, and special programs sponsored by the Issaquah Historical Society can be arranged. Admission is free to all, but donations are always appreciated (and certainly encouraged—Mr. C says, there is such a thing as being *too* cheap!).

Henry Art Gallery
• 15th Ave. NE and NE 41st St., Seattle; 543-2280
Not far from the Burke Museum (above) sits the Henry Art Gallery, the state's oldest public art museum, and home to the University of Washington's collection of 19th and 20th century artwork. The fine art, photography, ceramics, "ethnographic textile," and Western clothing collections are among the best in the region—and acclaimed by experts from all over.

Yet, the Henry is even better known for the special caliber of its temporary exhibitions. Many highly progressive shows pass through here for a lengthy stay, like Gary Hill's multimedia video sculpture installations. A visit to the Henry is bound to be more than your average museum visit—and an intellectual experience available to all for just $3.50.

Better yet, on Thursdays, admission is by a donation of any size; the Henry stays open later that night too, until 9 P.M. Otherwise, gallery hours are from 11 A.M. to 5 P.M., Tuesdays

through Sundays (closed Mondays). Of course, UW folks get in for free at any open time.

King County Historical Museums
• Various locations; see below
History has been well-preserved in many of the towns surrounding Seattle, where pioneer structures dating back to the mid-1800s still stand in the exact locations where they were constructed. Each of these museums displays the history of its area through objects left behind by the original pioneers and the generations that followed.

Some offer unique exhibits that are not to be found elsewhere in the U.S., while others dedicate themselves to the historical development of the Pacific Northwest, tracing the evolution of agriculture, manufacturing, and the waterways.

Admission is usually by donation, suggested as a buck or two, and well worth it. Hours and days of operation vary from museum to museum and can be limited to a few days a week, especially during the off-season; so it's best to call ahead of time. And be sure to inquire about special programs, lectures, and new exhibitions. The museums themselves include:
• **Black Diamond Depot Museum,** 32627 Railroad Ave., Black Diamond; 886-2142
• **Island County Historical Society Museum,** 908 NW Alexander St., Coupeville; (360) 678-3310
• **Maple Valley Historical Museum,** 23015 SE 216th Way, Maple Valley; 432-3470
• **Renton Historical Society and Museum,** 235 Mill Ave. S, Renton; 255-2330
• **Snoqualmie Valley Historical Museum,** 320 North Bend Blvd. S, North Bend; 888-3200
• **White River Valley Historical Museum,** 918 H St. SE, Auburn; 939-2783

Klondike Gold Rush National Historical Park
• 117 S Main St., Seattle; 553-7220
In many ways, Seattle became the

thriving city it is today as a direct result of the Klondike Gold Rush. Prospectors in search of fame and fortune headed to the Yukon via Seattle, creating opportunities for businesses that were previously unknown. The Klondike Gold Rush Museum, run by the National Park Service, preserves the history of that fast-moving time. What's more, admission is free. If that doesn't make history fun, Mr. C doesn't know what does.

Near Pioneer Square, these exhibits and activities recreate turn-of-the-century Seattle. There are short movies, like *Seattle: Gateway To The Goldfields* and *Hiking the Chilkoot Trail*, shown in a miniature replica of an old-fashioned music hall; park rangers give talks and gold panning demonstrations.

In the summer, they'll take you on free walking tours of Pioneer Square, the heart of the gold rush; many buildings from that era still stand in this historic district. The Park Service offers these tours on Sundays at 10 A.M. from June through September. And here's a further extra: On the third Sunday of each month, the Klondike Museum shows Charlie Chaplin's silent comedy classic, *The Gold Rush*, in their movie theater—free of charge to all. What a perfect match! The museum is open from 9 A.M. to 5 P.M. every day of the week.

Marymoor Museum
● 6046 W Lake Sammamish Pkwy. NE, Redmond; 885-3684

Located in a one-time hunting lodge, turned farmhouse, turned museum, the Marymoor—located in the heart of what is now one of the Eastside's largest and finest parks—recollects the history of this area from the 1870s to the present day.

As a farmhouse, the estate was well-known for its rare collection of Morgan horses and Hillshire cattle; today, its renown comes from an extensive collection of Native American and pioneer artifacts, including logging and shipping paraphernalia and the history of local ferry service—an essential aspect of life, east and west

of Seattle, to this day.

The Tudor-style Marymoor Museum is open from 11:00 A.M. to 4:00 P.M., Tuesdays through Thursdays, as well as Sundays from 1-5. Admission is $3 for adults and $1 for kids.

Museum of Flight
● 9404 E Marginal Way S, Seattle; 764-5720

It seems fitting that the finest aviation museum outside of the Smithsonian be located in what some call "the city that Boeing built." It is a fine museum indeed, and a vast one; exhibits trace the entire history of flight from its earliest attempts to the most recent advances in space travel.

The oldest "wing" (pun intended, sorry) is the "Red Barn," the Boeing Company's original manufacturing plant. In here, you can see an authentic recreation of an aircraft wood shop (!) and a working replica of a wind tunnel actually used by the Wright Brothers (who must've invented the first non-stop from North Carolina to Seattle). In the Great Gallery, the museum's huge steel-and-glass exhibit hall, over fifty full-size aircraft are on display; more than a dozen of these are suspended from the ceiling, as if caught in mid-flight.

Special programs include films, lectures, and hands-on workshops. During the summer, the museum hosts an annual air show, the Emerald City Flight Festival. Parents will be interested in the museum's educational programs, which encourage children's interest in math, science, and technology. The museum library houses the largest aviation archives on the West Coast.

Admission to the Museum of Flight is $6 for adults, $3 for children under 15, and free for children under 6. That top price just about "pushes the envelope" as far as Mr. C is concerned, but you certainly do get plenty for your dollar. For a cheaper (as in *free*) aviation-related outing, consider a visit to the Boeing factory in Everett; see the listing under "Walks and Tours." Hours at the museum are from 10 A.M. to 5 P.M. daily (and Thursdays until 9 P.M.). It's open every day except Christmas.

The Nordic Heritage Museum

- 3014 NW 67th St., Seattle; 789-5707

There are two ways to explore the rich history of the Pacific Northwest's Scandinavian settlers. One, of course, is to walk through Ballard. For something a little more complete, though, make its Nordic Heritage Museum your destination. Housed in a three-story elementary school built in 1907, the museum's displays reflect the cultures of Norway, Denmark, Finland, Iceland, and Sweden. Exhibits incorporate everything from historical artifacts and documents to contemporary arts and crafts. And there are frequent special events too, including performance art, films, lectures, concerts, children's programs, and more.

Admission is $3 for adults, $2 for students and senior citizens, and $1 for children ages six to sixteen. Children under six are admitted free. The museum is open Tuesdays through Saturdays from 10 A.M. to 4 P.M., and Sundays from noon to 4 P.M.

Pacific Science Center

- Seattle Center, 200 Second Ave., Seattle; 443-2001

See the listing under "Children's Activities."

Puget Sound Maritime Historical Society

- 901 Fairview Ave. N, Seattle; 624-3028

Working to remind us of Seattle's strong ties to the sea, the Puget Sound Maritime Historical Society maintains an impressive collection of ship models, rare photos, books, and artifacts which show the development of seagoing vessels from the 18th century onward to the present day.

In fact, the PSMHS has so much of this neat stuff, there's not nearly enough room to display it all. And so it organizes two exhibits a year at the Seattle Museum of History and Industry, not far away (see the listing below). The permanent exhibit is on view at the Chandler's Cove location.

MR. CHEAP'S PICKS
Museums

✔ **Bellevue Art Museum**—A museum in a mall? Well, it's not just *any* mall. BAM has a lot to offer for a minimalist admission; and on Tuesdays, it's free.

✔ **Burke Museum**—At UW, explore the exciting worlds of natural history—from prehistoric times up into the future.

✔ **General Petroleum Museum**—For fans of automotive nostalgia, this free collection is truly a gas.

✔ **Seattle Art Museum** and **Seattle Asian Art Museum**—Two for the price of one! Admission to either one of these spectacular museums gets you into the other. What's more, both are free the first Tuesday of each month.

Admission to the Puget Sound Maritime Historical Museum is always free, and the hours are from 11 A.M. to 7 P.M. Mondays through Saturdays, and Sundays from 12 noon to 5 P.M.

If the small size of the gallery sounds like it's not worth a trip in itself, Mr. C reminds you that this southern edge of Lake Union is laced with related activities. Just a few blocks down are the Center for Wooden Boats and the Northwest Seaport Maritime Heritage Center (see the listings under "Outdoors" and "Walks and Tours," respectively), featuring the *Wawona*, a 19th century schooner which is open to the public for tours. And you can always round out your nautical outing with lunch or dinner at a variety of seafood restaurants along the way. Mr. C recommends Benji's, the outdoor fish and chips version of the more expensive Benjamin's Restaurant. See the listing under "Restaurants—Eastlake Area."

Rosalie Whyel Museum of Doll Art

- 1116 108th Ave. NE, Bellevue; 455-1116

For anyone who loved dolls as a child, not to mention those who still do as adults, the Museum of Doll Art is a must-see. It's dedicated to preserving and exhibiting a wide range of dolls, with literally hundreds of examples from all over the world. More than just a random display of collectibles, these exhibits put dolls—not to mention teddy bears, miniatures, and other toys—into an historical, cultural, and artistic context. The names of the special exhibits alone do this: "What Shall I Wear? Dressing Ourselves and Our Dolls."

The permanent collection includes rare 18th and 19th century pieces, original Barbies and G.I. Joes, and contemporary doll sculptures. While this museum is clearly popular with the kiddies, the majority of the exhibits are strictly "no-touch," due to their fragile nature. But the museum staff works hard to create educational programs and events that will appeal to children of all ages.

Admission is $5 for adults, $4.50 for senior citizens, $4 for children under 17, and free for children under five. The Rosalie Whyel Museum is open from 10 A.M. to 5 P.M. Mondays through Saturdays, and from 1 P.M. to 5 P.M. on Sundays. Doors stay open 'til 8 P.M. on Thursday nights, too.

Seattle Aquarium

- 1483 Alaskan Way (Pier 59), Seattle; 386-4320

As far as museums go, the Seattle Aquarium is a whole 'nother kettle of fish. Instead of quiet corridors with lots of paintings and sculptures, you'll find exciting, living exhibits of fish, octopuses, and all sorts of other fascinating sea creatures.

The aquarium's dome offers visitors a true "underwater" experience,

where you can walk around amidst the permanent residents, as they swim in a giant tank which surrounds you. And, if you wander over to the tide pool exhibit, you can even play with little crabs and sand dollars.

The fee for all this finny fun is a whopping $6.75 for adults—at the top end of Mr. C's range, but you do get a lot for your dollars (the paper kind). Admission is $5.25 for seniors and disabled citizens, $4.25 for children and youths aged six to eighteen, $1.75 for kids three to five years old. What's more, King County residents get an extra discount, just for paying taxes. That'll reel 'em in! The Seattle Aquarium is open seven days a week; hours are from 10 A.M. to 8 P.M. Memorial Day through Labor Day, and 10 A.M. to 6 P.M. the rest of the year.

Seattle Art Museum

- 100 University St., Seattle; 654-3165

Did you know that admission to the Seattle Art Museum is free on the first Tuesday of each month? That's when you can stroll throughout this spacious, four-story building to your heart's content, and not pay a dime. SAM's permanent collection contains some 20,000 objects, specializing in ancient and recent art from Africa, China, Japan, Korea, and Europe. Naturally, they also have an extensive collection of Northwest Native American works.

SAM's rotating exhibitions include the recent "Chiefly Feasts," ceremonial works of art from the Kwakiutl people, natives of Vancouver Island. Accompanying this and many other SAM exhibits is an activity booklet designed for children, with pictures to color, questions to answer, and puzzles relating to the displays—a very nice touch.

The museum sponsors a wealth of special events for the public, from artist demonstrations, workshops, and lectures, to storytelling for children, and more. Many of these are free with regular museum admission, though some do charge an additional fee. Admission to the Seattle Art Museum is $6 for adults, $4 for seniors and students, and free for children under twelve. SAM is open Tuesday through Sunday from 10 A.M. to 5 P.M.; they're open late on Tuesdays (to 7 P.M.) and Thursdays (to 9 P.M.).

In the summer of 1994, the **Seattle Asian Art Museum** opened as an extension of SAM; it's housed in the original SAM building in Volunteer Park, and admission to either branch includes entry for the other. See the listing below for more details.

Seattle Asian Art Museum

- 1400 E Prospect St., Seattle; 654-3100

When the Seattle Art Museum moved into its big downtown digs, it left behind a handsome art-moderne building in Volunteer Park. The facility has now been reopened as the Seattle Asian Art Museum, filled with beautiful and historic objects from all over the Far East. SAAM is poised to become a world leader in the display and study of Asian art—as well it should, given Seattle's Pacific Rim status.

The depth and breadth of the collection is extraordinary; yet, you can easily "do" this museum in an afternoon. SAAM displays funerary art, metalwork, and decorative arts from China; Buddhist art from China and Japan; sculpture and ceramics from Southeast Asia; and textiles, ivory and jade pieces from Muslim India. Perhaps the most popular display, as it was when Asian art was only one of many exhibits at the old Seattle Art Museum, is the Chinese snuff bottle collection, a marvel of miniatures. The museum also hosts lectures, concerts, and other special events relating to Asian art in its downstairs auditorium.

Admission is $6 for adults, $4 for students and seniors, and free for children under twelve. The best news, however, is that you can get into both SAM and SAAM for one price! First, admission to one museum gets you into both—good for two days. Since both are open weekends and some Monday holidays, this can be a great deal, especially for tourists and art

students. Further, membership in either museum includes the other, a great way to double your benefits. Hours (the same for both museums) are 10 A.M. to 5 P.M. Tuesdays through Sundays (until 9 P.M. on Thursdays). On the first Tuesday of each month, the museums are open from 10 A.M. to 7 P.M.—and admission is free to all.

Seattle Museum of History and Industry (MOHAI)

- 2700 24th Ave. E, Seattle; 324-1126

Located just across the ship canal from Husky Stadium, the Museum of History and Industry collects, preserves, and exhibits all manner of historical objects gathered from Seattle, King County, and the Pacific Northwest region. One of the best deals around, says Mr. C, is on Tuesdays, when admission to this fascinating center is by donation of any amount. Throw a few bucks in the pot and stroll through the permanent and changing exhibits that include photographs, books, maps, documents, textiles, fine art, and more.

MOHAI is a great place for children's activities, too. Check out the "Family Funtivities" program, a fun way for families to learn about history together through interactive, hands-on activities. These, as well as many other programs, are free with museum admission.

Over 100,000 people visit MOHAI annually, and at least part of the reason must be the low admission fees. Other than Tuesdays, general admission is $3, senior citizens ("only" 55 and older) and children ages six to twelve get in for $1.50, and children under six are admitted free. The museum is open from 10 A.M. to 5 P.M. every day.

Tacoma Art Museum

- 1123 Pacific Ave., Tacoma; 272-4258

So, you want to see important works of art, but you don't want to pay huge admission fees? Well, here's one solution. The Tacoma Art Museum has a well-renowned collection, and—unlike its big brother in Seattle—the admission here is just $3 for adults, $2 for students and senior citizens, and $1 for children ages six to twelve. What's that ya say? Not cheap enough for you yet? No problem. Just come in on any Tuesday, when admission is free for all ages, all day.

The permanent collection concentrates on 20th century American art, particularly paintings and works on paper. Artists exhibited here cover the gamut from Andy Warhol to Keith Haring to good ol' Walt Disney. TAM's special collections show a more wide-ranging taste and sense of history, including European impressionism, Japanese woodblock prints, 19th century Chinese textiles, and a retrospective installation of Dale Chihuly glass. In addition to regular exhibitions, the museum presents lectures, tours, concerts, films, and special festivals, most of which are free with regular admission. And, at the ArtWORKS gallery, you can even try your hand at making some art of your own.

TAM is open Tuesdays through Saturdays from 10 A.M. to 5 P.M. (Thursdays 'til 7 P.M.), and Sundays from 12 noon to 5 P.M.

While you're in the area, don't miss the nearby Chihuly at Union Station, a special installation of Chihuly glass found at 1717 Pacific Avenue. It's open Mondays through Fridays from 10 A.M. to 4 P.M., and admission is free at all times. Tours are available Tuesdays through Fridays at 1 P.M.; for more info, call 572-9310.

Washington State Historical Society
• 315 N Stadium Way, Tacoma; 593-2830

And, while we're hanging out down south: Washingtonians who are interested in the evolution of their own backyard will love this museum. The Washington State Historical Society is dedicated to the preservation and presentation of the history of the Evergreen State.

Its featured permanent exhibit, "Washington: Home, Frontier, Crossroads," has some 700 artifacts depicting the cultures, locales, and events

that shaped the development of the state to the present day. Changing exhibits highlight more specific elements of state history. The museum also sponsors special programs, including lectures and workshops. It is the site of several annual conferences, including the Northwest History Conference and the Washington Heritage Conference.

Admission to WSHS is just $2.50 for adults, $2 for senior citizens, and $1 for children ages six to eighteen. Better yet, if you're bringing the whole brood, take advantage of the special family admission price of just $5. One price fits all! Hours are Tuesdays through Saturdays from 10 A.M. to 5 P.M., and Sundays from 1- 5.

Wing Luke Asian Museum
• 407 Seventh Ave. S, Seattle; 623-5124

On a smaller scale than the Seattle Asian Art Museum, this International District museum displays many aspects of Pacific American culture, history, and art. The exhibits here highlight a diverse mix of Asian communities, including Chinese, Japanese, Filipinos, Koreans, Vietnamese, Cambodians, and Laotians.

The permanent centerpiece exhibit, "One Song, Many Voices," focuses on the 200-year history of Asian immigration and settlement in the Pacific Northwest. Recent temporary exhibits included "The First 100 Years: Reflections of Seattle's Chinese Americans" and the award-winning "Executive Order 9066: 50 Years Before and 50 Years After," which examined the internment of Japanese-Americans during World War II.

The Wing Luke is open free to all every Thursday. Obviously, that's the best deal, but regular admission is also a bargain: $2.50 for adults, $1.50 for students and senior citizens, and just 75¢ for children five to twelve. The museum is open Tuesdays through Fridays from 11 A.M. to 4:30 P.M., Saturdays and Sundays from 12 noon to 4 P.M.

MUSIC

Seattle abounds with live music of all kinds—far beyond the national reputation it's garnered for "grunge" rock 'n roll (yes, that's still what they call it everywhere else). There are lots of opportunities to hear tunes in the clubs for free, or a very low cover charge; and even the big classical institutions offer ways around their high ticket prices.

CLASSICAL MUSIC

ArtsWest Concert Series
- 4734 42nd Ave. SW, Seattle; 938-0963

See the listing under "Arts and Cultural Centers."

Bellevue Philharmonic Orchestra
- Westminster Chapel, 13646 NE 24th St., Bellevue
- Meydenbauer Convention Center, 11100 NE Sixth St., Bellevue
- Information; 455-4171

Each year from October to June, a mere twelve dollars can take you on a ride through the music of Holst's *The Planets*, orchestral interludes from Wagner operas, and even such "modern" composers as George Gershwin—all performed by the Bellevue Philharmonic Orchestra, under the direction of R. Joseph Scott.

The Meydenbauer Chamber Series is an opportunity to hear the classics on a somewhat smaller scale (pardon the pun), with such works as Vivaldi's *The Four Seasons*, Handel's *Royal Fireworks Music*, and Mozart's *Requiem* among the repertoire. The Chamber Orchestra performs in the intimate Meydenbauer Convention Center, which only seats about 400 people. Tickets for this series go fast, so buy them well in advance.

But if $12 or $13 is still too expensive for a concert, then wait around for the totally free Summer Pops Series. Hear more of these works in some of Puget Sound's most scenic outdoor settings, such as the Chateau Ste. Michelle and Snoqualmie Wineries. For details on these Bellevue Philharmonic Orchestra concert series, dates, and general admission tickets, call the number above.

The Esoterics
- Plymouth Congregational Church, 1217 Sixth Ave., Seattle; 525-8486

This highly unconventional chorus, 24 voices strong, strays far from the territory of your basic church choir. Bringing 20th century *a cappella* choral music to the forefront, the Esoterics present seven or eight concerts a year, concentrating on the works of local composers along with more established names such as Gyorgy Ligeti (of *2001* soundtrack fame), Shostakovich, and minimalist Philip Glass. The Esoterics make the claim that classical music is no longer the toy of the elite, but for the enjoyment of all (even Generation Xers). And they've got the following to back it up.

Tix to these concerts cost $10 for students and senior citizens, and $12 for other folks. Series subscriptions, though, can bring prices down to about $10 for anyone. Call the number above for more info.

Seattle Choral Company
- Various locations; Information, 363-1100

The Seattle Choral Company boasts a high degree of professionalism, offering world premieres and even CD releases; yet it remains a popular and accessible group, enjoyed by many. And, even as it grows in fame and fortune, tickets are still only $13 for adults, $10 for students and senior citizens.

The 100 voices of the Seattle Choral Company and its accompanying orchestra reproduce Latin sounds (chants, not cha-cha), the opuses of J.S. Bach, and works by the very latest American and European composers.

Since most concerts offer unreserved seating, it's a good idea to show up early, ticket in hand, to insure a good spot. However, if you're the more spontaneous type, fear not; concerts are generally held in such large halls as the Meany Theater on the UW campus, and St. Mark's Cathedral on First Hill (1245 Tenth Ave. E) where you can usually slide in at the last minute and still hear a wonderful concert amplified by vast acoustics. Do call the number above, at least, for a schedule of upcoming appearances.

Seattle Opera
- Seattle Center Opera House, 321 Mercer St., Seattle; 389-7676

As far as highbrow entertainment in this town goes, the Seattle Opera is probably the *créme de la créme*—a fact, alas, reflected in the prices. Generally, these tickets don't come cheap (full-price tickets can cost as much as $65...and that's for *one* person!); but if you time your purchase carefully (say, for a Wednesday night early in the run of any show), then a decent seat within good sight of the stage may be gotten for around $15. Now, that's a bargain already. However, there is an even lower-priced option, if you're willing to take a chance and wait in line at the last minute.

Mr. C suggests you show up at the box office at least half an hour before curtain time, when any remaining tix may be available at half-price. Of course, you never know *which* seats, if any, will be offered; the lower-priced ones may be gone, and there's no guarantee that couples can get two seats together—but there's usually

something there, and at such savings, it's certainly worth considering. (You can meet in the lobby after each act and trade critiques—or, better yet, save them for later on, over coffee and dessert.) In any case, for a chance to experience the most-acclaimed opera in these parts, it's well worth the risk.

An average season consists of five or six productions, ranging from well-known warhorses (the Seattle is widely renowned for its quadrennial mountings of Wagner's "Ring Cycle") to Gershwin's *Porgy and Bess*, as well as lesser-known discoveries. Call the box office for a schedule of upcoming programs.

Seattle Symphony
- Seattle Center Opera House, 321 Mercer St., Seattle; 443-4747

The granddaddy of Seattle's classical music scene, the Seattle Symphony has over ninety years of performance under its belt. Each season offers a parade of special series and distinguished artists, including such international stars as violinist Nadja Salerno-Sonnenberg and pianist Bella Davidovich. Music ranging from Handel to Brahms to Stravinsky, as well as contemporary composers, have highlighted many a season at the Opera House.

Ticket prices here can climb several octaves, but fear not—there are always ways to save, and Mr. C has found them for you. At most concerts (there are more than 15 series per year) tickets range from about $10 to $42. Naturally, a high-up seat can beat the higher prices in this acoustically excellent house. You'll hear every note perfectly, even if the conductor looks like an ant with a baton. Better deals await patient students who can show up one hour before any concert (with a student ID) for half-price tickets even in the good areas.

Another good discount opportunity is season tickets. Series subscriptions include all sorts of wonderful perks to go along with a reserved seat for as many as 18 concerts: discount cards for area restaurants and hotels, local parking, and *NO LINES*. Best of all, you get a discount off the full, single-ticket prices. For most series, the savings is equivalent to one regular ticket; in some cases the savings can be as much as several tickets' worth. For those who want to enjoy the symphony on a regular basis, it's a great way to save.

The Seattle Symphony season runs almost all year long, with its Pops and Mozart series, special holiday performances like Handel's *Messiah* or "Prairie Home Companion" host Garrison Keillor, and regular-season concerts. Call for a free brochure and go from there.

Seattle Youth Symphony
- Seattle Center Opera House, 321 Mercer St., Seattle; 362-2300

Mr. C has already introduced you to the concept of taking in art at colleges because of lower ticket prices (see the "College Arts" chapter for details). In a similar manner, tickets to the Seattle Youth Symphony are significantly less expensive than those for their adult (and professional) counterparts. But don't be fooled into thinking you're getting inferior performances; these youngsters are highly talented indeed, and most certainly on their way to being pros themselves. Their concerts feature works by Beethoven, Brahms, Rachmaninoff, Sibelius, Berlioz, Copland, and others.

As with most orchestras, ticket prices vary depending on seating. Seats for the general public range from $7 up to $25, while seats for students and senior citizens go from $5 to $17. Far less than the prices for major symphony orchestras. There are discounts for subscriptions, and student rush tix are sometimes available 15 minutes before curtain.

Tudor Choir
- St. James Cathedral, 804 Ninth Ave., Seattle
- St. Mark's Episcopal Cathedral, 1245 Tenth Ave. E, Seattle

MR. CHEAP'S PICKS
Classical Music

✔ **Bellevue Philharmonic Summer Pops Series**—Free concerts in glorious outdoor settings.

✔ **Seattle Choral Company**— One hundred heavenly voices fill various venues.

✔ **Seattle Opera** and **Seattle Symphony**—Half-price rush tix, when available, make these high-class but high-priced institutions accessible to just about anyone.

- Information: 633-5018

The Tudor Choir does a little bit of everything in the choir music canon. Full choral, *a capella*, 16th century Tudor, early American "shape-note" music, 20th century British song, and more are all part of their repertoire. Specializing in high-treble singing, the eighteen members of the Tudor Choir perform about six concerts per year at the two locations listed above.

Three-concert series subscriptions are a discount option, though even ticket prices at the door are pretty reasonable: $12 for general admission and $8 for students and senior citizens. St. James Cathedral calls its admission price a "suggested donation," so if you can't quite afford it, pay what you can— but do pay full-price if you can. Mr. Cheap is never stingy about fine art. Perhaps the best deal of all, though, is to attend a Sunday morning service at St. James, in which the Tudor Choir participates weekly.

FOLK MUSIC

Conor Byrne's Diddley Arcade
- 5140 Ballard Ave. NW, Seattle; 784-3640

Conor Byrne's features a steady stream of live Irish bands, and cover charges are generally just a few dollars. Friday and Saturday are the big nights here; there's usually a band playing Irish ballads or dance music or both, for a cover of around $3. On Sundays, there's an informal Irish jam session, and there's no cover charge. Wednesdays have been reserved for traditional Irish folk dancing (except in the summer months), also with a live band. It's free and very casual; lessons are available on a rather informal basis. Call for more details.

Coyote Coffee Company
- 111 Main St., Kirkland; 827-2507

Coyote Coffee Company is a popular venue for jazz, acoustic folk, and spoken word performances. Regularly scheduled events include Sunday morning jazz, Friday night acoustic folk, and Monday night open-mike poetry. Other events occur on a more informal basis. There's never a cover charge, so stop in for a cuppa coffee and some mellow music. What's more, since the Coyote serves no al-

cohol, the shows are open to all ages. Call ahead for more current schedule information.

Globe Cafe & Bakery
- 1531 14th St., Seattle; 324-8815

See the listing under "Readings and Literary Events."

Kell's Restaurant and Pub
- 1916 Post Alley, Seattle; 728-1916

Once the basement crematorium of the Butterworth Mortuary (oooh), Kell's is now a popular Irish pub in Pioneer Square. Perhaps the Irish bands which play here derive inspiration from that morbid history. Whatever the secret, it seems to work. Kell's features live music every Wednesday through Saturday night. You may find sing-alongs, acoustic artists, or, of course, traditional Irish bands.

Now, here's something of interest to fellow Cheapsters: Kell's books its bands to play all four nights, for two weeks in a row. What does this mean to you? Well, you can hear the same band on Wednesday and Thursday night, when there's *no* cover charge, that you'd hear on Friday and Saturday, when there *is* a cover. Of course the cover charge is usually no more than $3, so there's really no way to lose. Bands are generally Northwesterners, with some from other parts of the United States and Ireland.

The restaurant/pub serves up hearty portions of (what else?) Irish food, at reasonable prices. The kitchen closes at 9 P.M., but the place stays open until 1:30 in the morning.

Murphy's Pub
- 1928 N 45th St., Seattle; 634-2110

In the heart of Wallingford, Murphy's Pub features a steady stream of live Irish music (what did you expect?). The true bargain is found each Wednesday, which is open-mike night. Admission is free, and in a place like this, the odds are pretty good that even these unpaid musicians know what they're doing.

Weekends are a deal, too, featuring Irish or blues bands for a cover that's usually around $2. At one time,

---

MR. CHEAP'S PICKS
Folk Music

✔ **Kell's Restaurant and Pub**— Don't let the fact that Kell's was once a mortuary deter you. The calendar includes live Irish music, and the cover is never more than $3

✔ *Wawona* **Concert Series**— There are certain things that make Seattle unique, and this is one of them: A tall ship and a little music to steer her by, all for seven bucks.

Murphy's featured live music every weekend; but they've cut back in order to concentrate on the better local bands around town. Good food, too. Call ahead to find out what's coming up.

Rendezvous
- 2320 Second Ave., Seattle; 441-5823

The Rendezvous is a popular Belltown watering hole, but the real news is in the back at the Jewelbox Theater. It is in here that you'll find live music and poetry readings on a regular basis, costing you very little. The schedule here isn't as regular as at some other clubs, but you'll generally find something going on at least three weekends out of each month; cover charges for these are usually around $4. The music varies, so it's impossible to say for sure what you'll see at any given time. Call for a complete list of upcoming events.

Wawona Concert Series
- 1002 Valley St., Seattle; 447-9800

If you happen to hear Irish fiddle

tunes coming from the *Wawona*, the 19th century schooner docked at the Northwest Seaport Maritime Heritage Center, don't be surprised. It is not a convention of leprechauns, but part of the Heritage Center's "Folk and Maritime Concert Series."

For only $7 ($5 for students/senior citizens, $3 for kids), you too can climb aboard—perhaps for an evening of sea-chanteys from all over the world, blues from down south, or just plain ol' country music—all on the upper deck of the boat. If it happens to rain, you will be taken to the Fore Castle to hear the show (or to the brig if you misbehave).

Concerts take place about once a month throughout the year and sometimes sell out, so Mr. C recommends that you get your tickets in advance. The *Wawona* is also open to public tours during the daytime, for only a dollar; see the listing for the Northwest Seaport Maritime Heritage Center under "Walks and Tours."

JAZZ, BLUES, AND CABARET MUSIC

Atlantic Street Pizza
- 9041 Holman Rd. NW, Seattle; 783-9698

Why isn't this on Atlantic Street? Who knows? Anyway, up in the Crown Hill section of Ballard, Atlantic Street Pizza serves up hearty helpings of jazz, blues, and comedy. There's no cover charge and no minimum, though Mr. C warns that you may not be able to resist the inexpensive gourmet grub (see the listing under "Restaurants—North Area").

The schedule generally runs this way: Blues on Sunday, jazz on Wednesday, open-mike comedy on Thursday, and a mixed bag on the weekends. The musicians are generally local, and the comedians are from all over. Now, you can't expect top-name, national stars for free, but it's definitely a fun time out. Most shows start at 9 P.M.; call the number above for a complete schedule.

Beatnix
- 518 E Pine St., Seattle; 322-0679

In the tradition of the original beat generation, this First Hill club offers an eclectic lineup of good, cheap entertainment, while carefully avoiding restrictive labels like "grunge," "sports," "gay," etc. As a result, it has become a popular spot in a relatively short amount of time.

There's something going on here every night of the week. Monday is "Game Day," featuring your favorite board games, including Risk and Monopoly, plus ping-pong, darts, and free pool. Take advantage of this opportunity to perfect your bank shot, because on Tuesday night there's a pool tournament at 8 P.M. (entrance fee is $4). On Wednesdays, shift gears and enjoy open-mike acoustic music. There are no cover charges for these early-in-the-week nights.

If you're a fan of spoken word, come in on Thursdays. Nothing like a little poetry to help wind down the week, and the cover charge is just $1. Music is on tap each weekend, when the cover is still only $3 to $5. Each night has a slightly different sound. On Friday, it's time for the blues; Saturdays, mix it up with a little reggae and salsa; and on Sundays, relax with some jazz. Beatnix is open until 2 A.M. every night. Oh, and tell "Mama" Chuck that Mr. C sent you.

Chicago's
• 315 First Ave. N, Seattle; 282-7791
Taking its name from a city synonymous with the blues, this family-style Italian eatery is located just outside of the Seattle Center. Befitting its name, the bar area of the restaurant hosts rhythm and blues shows. On Friday and Saturday nights throughout the year, you can hear live bands perform with absolutely no cover charge. Shows begin around 9:30 P.M., playing until 2 A.M. or so; such local artists as Swamp Mama Johnson and Little Bill & the Bluenotes are among Chicago's regulars. Makes a good place to stop in for a nightcap after an event at the Center.

The Cloud Room
• 1619 Ninth Ave., Seattle; 682-0100
Coming to you live, from high atop downtown Seattle's Camlin Hotel, we bring you the melodious sounds of Xavier Coochy and his Rumanian Rumba Band....Well, the band is fictitious, but the room isn't. Indeed, from the eleventh floor of this elegant, older hotel, you can feast on sumptuous views of the city while various pianists tickle the ivories and croon popular tunes. The Cloud Room is an expensive restaurant, but their adjacent piano bar features live jazz Tuesday through Saturday evenings with no cover charge. There's no minimum either, but you do have to order *some*thing—even if you nurse it along. Be sure to save a buck to toss into the pianist's glass jar. Music takes place from 9 P.M. to midnight. The Cloud Room also has a happy hour every weeknight, from 4:30 to 6:30.

Earshot Jazz
• Various locations; Information, 547-6763
Earshot Jazz isn't a place; rather, it's an organization whose aim is to support and present jazz in Seattle. The idea is to make jazz reasonably affordable and accessible to all, creating a greater appreciation for this truly American art form. One of their gigs is the weekly "Living Spirit of Jazz" at Dimitriou's Jazz Alley (Sixth Avenue and Lenora Street, in downtown Seattle; telephone 441-9729). Every Sunday, Living Spirit showcases some of the Northwest's rising talent in Seattle's foremost jazz club—one which is out of Mr. C's price range on most other nights. Admission is $5 for Earshot members, $7 for non-members.

Earshot also presents the "World Jazz Festival" every fall, attracting some of the hottest jazz talent in the country for a month of concerts, jam sessions, and more. The festival features over 20 different events, and tix to most are around $12 or so. Call the main number above for more details.

Finally, don't miss the "Earshot Jazz Eastside Showcase," part of the Crossroads Late Night in the Market series. These free, all-ages performances generally happen on the last weekend of each month from July through November. For more info about free music at Bellevue's hoppin' shopping mall, see the listing under "Rock and Pop" below.

True jazz *aficionados* should consider becoming a member of Earshot Jazz. Membership will get you discounts to various shows, while helping to support Earshot's programs. For more info, call the number above.

The Five Point Cafe
• 415 Cedar St., Seattle; 448-9993
Sitting in the shadow of Chief Seattle at the junction of Fifth, Cedar, and Denny, the aptly named Five Point is a cool little joint—an old-time luncheonette down one side, and a lounge on the other. The scene gets even more cool on Monday nights, when a jazz combo inserts itself into a corner

of the tiny establishment, and plays laid-back guitar jazz. Sit on one of the lunch counter's classic round metal stools, or squeeze yourself in at a table (even on a Monday, this place fills up). Order up a bottomless cuppa java, a sandwich, or dessert, and hang out. There's no cover charge; the music grooves from 7 to 11 P.M.

Julia's Park Place
- 5410 Ballard Ave. NW, Seattle; 783-2033

This popular Ballard restaurant, serving a reasonably priced menu of health-oriented, also serves up free jazz and blues music on weekends. Each Friday and Saturday from 9 to 11:30 P.M., a different local ensemble takes the stage in this large and comfortable room; the calendar is as varied as the menu, ranging from swing and cabaret jazz to R & B and funk. There is no cover charge, and you can just sit at the bar if you wish. Reservations are recommended for dinner, which is served from 5 to 10:30 P.M.

Larry's Greenfront Restaurant & Lounge
- 209 First Ave. S, Seattle; 624-7665

You won't have to spend a lot of green at Larry's to enjoy local and national rhythm and blues bands seven nights a week. The cover is generally $5 during the week, going only up to $7 on Friday and Saturday. Larry's is also part of the Pioneer Square "joint cover" alliance (see the listing below), meaning that you can get in for free if you've already paid the cover at another participating club. Bands that have played here recently include the legendary Junior Walker and the All-Stars. The kitchen closes at 8 P.M., but the music jams on 'til 2 A.M.

New Orleans Creole Restaurant
- 441 First Ave. S, Seattle; 622-2563

The New Orleans cooks up Creole food in the kitchen, and jazz and blues in the front room. Styles range from Dixieland to reggae to Cajun zydeco, and just about everything in between. Regular acts include groups with names like the Filé Gumbo Zydeco Band, Sweet Talkin' Jones and the Muscletones, and Swamp Mama

---

MR. CHEAP'S PICKS
Jazz and Blues Music

✔ **The Cloud Room**—Not the expensive restaurant, but its no-cover piano lounge, with romantic nighttime views of the city.

✔ **Earshot Jazz Programs**—Inexpensive (sometimes free!) jazz all over, from downtown's Jazz Alley to Bellevue's Crossroads Mall.

✔ **The Five Point Cafe**—Free Monday night jam sessions in a retro luncheonette may be the coolest deal in town.

Johnson. Kinda says it all, *n'est pas*? On weekends, the cover is a mere $7 (they're also part of the Pioneer Square joint cover deal, see below) and many weeknights are free. Stop by for a full listing of upcoming acts.

Rosebud Espresso & Bistro
- 719 E Pike St., Seattle; 323-6636

Every Thursday night from 8 'til 11, you can relax to the sounds of live, contemporary "Java Jazz," performed in the cozy dining room of this elegant coffeehouse. Two rooms separated by an archway give you a choice of watching the musicians respectfully, or sitting just around the corner for mellow conversation.

Each week presents a different local soloist or small ensemble from a rotating corps. Coffees and pastries are available at the bar. The show itself is free; come early to get a good seat. You have to be 21 to be in the bistro side, but there's no age restriction on the espresso bar side. For more details about inexpensive dining here, see the separate listing under "Restaurants—Capitol Hill."

Salute! In Città

• 612 Stewart St., Seattle; 728-1611

This fancy downtown *ristorante* offers live jazz with no cover charge, as many as seven nights a week. The ever-varying schedule includes regular Sunday night jam sessions, featured local musicians, and some occasional guests from the national circuit. It's all straight-ahead jazz. The restaurant itself is handsome and cozy, with its red-checked tablecloths and Italian cinema posters; the menu, though, is rather expensive. Instead of dining, you can sit at the blond wood bar and enjoy the music with just a two-drink minimum per person. This can get pricey too, but don't forget the area—laced with glitzy hotels—and the talent, which is first-rate. In all, this is still a good deal. Music generally takes place from 8 P.M. to midnight on weekday evenings, and from 9 P.M. to 1 A.M. on weekends. Call to see who's coming up.

Starbucks Coffee Company

• 102 First Ave., Seattle; 382-2656
• 4512 University Village Ct. NE, Seattle; 522-5228
• *And other locations in the city and suburbs*

On it's way to taking over the world of coffee (and possibly the world in general), Starbucks has realized that some people want more than a stirrer with their java. They want something stir-*ring*. In an attempt to give a little more of that coffeehouse feel, Starbucks has recently begun to expand some of their stores to offer more seating, a food menu, and cultural events.

At the time of this writing, the entertainment is rather limited—but it is free, and the trend seems to be moving toward expanding in this area as well. At the Pioneer Square location, you can enjoy jazz music every Saturday night (and occasional Fridays) from 8:30 P.M. to 11 P.M. At the newly renovated store in University Village, you'll find live jazz every Friday night from around 8 P.M. to 11 P.M. Starbucks is looking to add more music and also poetry readings to the above offerings. Keep your eyes peeled; with all that caffeine, this should be no problem.

Serafina

• 2043 Eastlake Ave. E, Seattle; 323-0807

A hidden gem of a restaurant, this classy place describes itself as a "rustic Euro-Italian restaurant and bar." The dark-wood decor sure is handsome, though it gives rustic looks a *nouvelle* twist—just as the kitchen does with the food. They use organic produce and smoke their own meats and cheeses on the premises.

The menu is moderately priced, though a bit above Mr. C's range; meanwhile, Serafina also hosts live jazz six nights a week with no cover charge. If no tables are available inside or on the garden patio (frequently true at this popular spot), there is a small bar where you can sip, tap your feet, and take in the *chic* atmosphere. The styles range all over the place: traditional jazz and vocalists, South American rhythms, perhaps even a duo of accordion and mandolin. Music runs from 8-11 P.M. Tuesdays through Thursdays, from 9:30 to 12:30 Fridays and Saturdays, and from 7-10 on Sundays.

Wild Ginger

• 1400 Western Ave., Seattle; 623-4450

This trendy waterfront spot is an Asian restaurant and bar, with a lively singles scene and dramatic contemporary decor. It also offers live jazz on Monday nights with no cover charge. Even though that's a weeknight, the joint was jumpin' when Mr. C dropped in. Smart-looking thirtysomethings lined the bar area, filled the dining tables, and spilled out onto the sidewalk (it was a mild and dry evening). They were all chattering away while a quintet played straight-ahead jazz inside the front windows.

It's certainly not a scene for true jazz devotées, but this is a classy hangout and a chance to hear some good local music. Sit or stand by the bar if you wish; the menu is a moderate, but not inexpensive, mix of Chinese, Thai, and Vietnamese dishes. The music happens on Mondays from 9:30 P.M. to 1:30 A.M.

ROCK AND POP MUSIC

Brass Connection
- 722 E Pike St., Seattle; 322-7777

If you seek the hottest in techno-pop dance music, but don't want to spend a fortune on cover charges, look no further than this First Hill club. At the Brass Connection the cover charge is rarely more than $2, and you'll find plenty to keep you amused.

As you might guess from its location, BC has a largely gay following—but overall, the crowd is mixed and the atmosphere is comfortable. During the week, the club presents lots of special events, from a lip sync contest known as "It's Never a Drag," to a karaoke night, to a best-body contest. Weekends feature lots of hot dance music. Open seven nights a week, until 2:30 A.M.

Cafe Paradiso
- 1005 E Pike St., Seattle; 322-6960

This popular First Hill coffeehouse only brings in live bands occasionally (about twice a month), but the cover charges are so low (usually just $2 to $3) and this place is such a favorite among Seattle's hip crowd, that Mr. C felt compelled to include it. The music featured here tends to be from local bands; it's usually all-out rock, with some jazz thrown in for good measure.

There was also an open-mike night with spoken word stuff going on, but that seems to come and go. Shows at Cafe Paradiso are open to all ages. Call ahead for a current schedule. Good food, by the way (see the listing under "Restaurants—Capitol Hill"); and photography by local artists line the walls.

Captain Cook's Pub
- 1414 Alaskan Way, Seattle; 223-9467

Located near the Aquarium along Seattle's waterfront, Captain Cook's Pub is a laid-back sort of hangout, catering to the older end of the Generation X spectrum. Most come to enjoy the live music Thursdays through Saturdays.

On Thursdays, there's no cover to hear local acoustic musicians. On Friday and Saturday nights, pay just $3 to hear alternative rock bands, that kind that have made the "Seattle sound" a national phenomenon. But don't shy away on Wednesday or Saturday night when Captain Cook's offers free pool (usually 75¢ a game), darts, and video games. And, don't miss the full menu of burgers, sandwiches, nachos, and more. Cook's is open from 11 A.M. until 2 A.M. daily; music is generally heard from 10 P.M. to 1 A.M.

Casa U-Betcha
- 2212 First Ave., Seattle; 441-1026

This Casa may be a colorful, mild-mannered Mexican restaurant by day, but on Friday and Saturday nights, watch out! At 10 P.M., dinners stop being served, and the tables are cleared away for dancing. The fiesta begins at 11 P.M., with a DJ spinning disco and Top-40 tunes until 2 A.M. There is no cover charge. U-bet this is one wild way to spend a night out.

Colourbox
- 113 First Ave. S, Seattle; 340-4101

This prominent Pioneer Square nightclub has top local groups rocking the joint nearly every night. Not familiar with some of the names? Colourbox thoughtfully lists all the bands for the week on a large board at the club's entrance, with a brief description of the kind of music each group plays. For example, if you haven't heard of the Lemons, their bio blurb would've told you that they play a Ramones-style pop punk. So, if you're looking to mellow out with a lovely cup of herbal tea and hear an acoustic guitar being strummed quietly, this would not be the show for you.

Not that acts at the Colourbox would fit such a description anyway; this is a place for some real head-banging. Ticket prices hover around $5 or $6. Colourbox is also part of the Pioneer Square "joint cover" alliance (see the listing below). Open until 2 A.M.

Crocodile Cafe

- 2200 Second Ave., Seattle;
  441-5611

The Crocodile rocks nearly every night of the week—live bands perform in the "Funky Voodoo Snake Pit" adjacent to the cafe. The type of music varies—rock, acoustic, and country rock groups have all performed here on various nights. Shows generally start around 9 or 10 P.M., and the cover can be as low as $2—call for details about this week's schedule, then come and rock around the Croc.

Crossroads Shopping Center

- 15600 NE Eighth St., Bellevue;
  644-1111

Recently renovated into a mall for the 21st century, Bellevue's Crossroads Shopping Center is a forty-acre shopping extravaganza with plenty of activities to complement the retail side. Most of the entertainment is free of charge. The popular "Late Night in the Market" series features a diverse mix of musical performers, including the Jet City Jazz Band with swing and big band sounds; Freylakh with Jewish *klezmer* music; contemporary rockers Bananafish; and world music with Urban Bushmen. Late Night happens every Friday and Saturday from 7:30 P.M. to 10 P.M. (well, that's "late" for suburban shopkeepers, anyway). It's free and open to all ages.

On Thursdays, enjoy their open-mike night, featuring acoustic folk, instrumentals, singer/songwriters, blues, jazz, and even classical music. If you want to get in on the act, sign up at the MarketStage. Open-mike goes from 6 P.M. to 9 P.M., again, free of charge. There's also a children's concert one Sunday each month, and there are plans in the works for some literary offerings as well.

Furthermore, annual events here include a family fair, a jobs and careers fair, an arts and crafts festival, and other kinds of special happenings. A full slate of holiday music is featured throughout December. Call the number above for a complete listing of events, or pick up a flyer next time you pass through.

Highliner

- 3909 18th Ave. W, Seattle;
  283-2233

Part of the Fisherman's Terminal complex, this regular-Joe bar and grill offers live, down-and-dirty rock and blues every weekend. Shoot a game of pool, watch sports on the large-screen TV, and boogie to the sounds of local bands every Friday and Saturday night from 9 P.M. on. There's a modest $3 cover charge; musicians can join in the Saturday night blues jam sessions and get in for $2. A full bar and plenty of pub food will fill out the evening nicely.

Hunan Chef

- 425 116th Ave. NE, Bellevue;
  451-8398

Rock 'n roll in an Eastside Chinese restaurant? Sure! Live bands play in the bar every weekend, catering (sorry about the pun) to a thirtysomething suburban crowd. Hey, these folks aren't over the hill—they dance up a storm to their favorite tunes from the '50s and '60s, thank you very much.

Bands also play here on Tuesday through Thursday nights, with a chance for audience members to get up and sing or play along in a jam-session set. There are no cover charges for any of this excitement—and better yet, no MSG. The music starts at 9 P.M., running as late as 2 A.M. on weekends.

Latitude 47

- 1232 Westlake Ave. N, Seattle;
  284-1047

Weekend nightclubbing just got a whole lot cheaper. Cover charges at this Lake Union club are just $3 on Friday and Saturday nights. The DJ will keep you moving with a steady stream of top-40 dance tunes. Three bucks too steep? Then bop over on Monday or Tuesday nights—same music, no cover.

If you prefer salsa and Latin tunes, come by on a Wednesday or Sunday night; the cover is $3. Oh, and Thursday is Disco Night (will it *never* go away?). There's no cover charge, and Mr. C is told that it's very popular, attracting a mixed crowd. Go figure. The fun starts every night at about 9 P.M.

Mo'Roc'caN Cafe
● 925 E Pike St., Seattle; 324-2406
For a rockin' good time, "Moe" has live, loud and fast music performed nearly every night of the week. The bands are mostly local, though this has become a drop-in spot for some nationally known artists like Michelle Shocked and Ministry's Cris Connelly. Most shows usually cost between $4 and $7, jumping up to $10 or so for big names. Avoid long lines by dining at Moe's cafe first (see the listing under "Restaurants—Capitol Hill"), but be sure to tell your server you're going to the show.

On Sunday nights, you can catch a jazz quartet in the bar area, midway between the restaurant and the main dance room. And, even though these guys may be blowin' the roof off the place, they have little effect on the enormously popular acid jazz dance party in the main dance room around the corner. That's how big and rambling this place is. DJ-hosted with live percussion accompaniment, the acid jazz parties are way "moe" crowded and hotter than the bar. Do the quartet, the dance thing, or wander between both; whatever you decide, it's just $4 on Sundays. The club is open nightly until 1:30 A.M.

Neighbors
● 1509 Broadway E, Seattle; 324-5358
Check your hang-ups at the door and come have a *fab*-ulous time! Near East Pike and the college area of First Hill, Neighbors has DJs spinning your favorite tunes for a cover charge of just a dollar or two on most nights. And on off nights, like Wednesdays or Sundays, it's free. There's something here for every taste, including drag-queen lip sync contests, "Retrovenge," featuring '70s and '80s music, and lots of dancing. The crowd, as you might imagine, is a mixed lot: gay, bi, straight, and whatever.

Definitely try to stop in on Friday or Saturday night when the nominal cover (around $3), includes a food buffet. Neighbors is closed on Mondays.

Off Ramp Cafe and Lounge
● 109 Eastlake Ave. E, Seattle; 628-0232
Hmm...wonder where they came up with the name? Yes, this alternative rock institution sits in the shadow of Route 5, right at the Denny Way exit. The interior is a wacked-out mix of psychedelic colors, old-time pinball games, wooden booths—and a shopping cart hanging from the ceiling, for good measure.

Rock rules here every night, featuring three or more different bands. Some come in from the national scene, like Boston's punk sensation, Morphine; others hail from the local circuit. Meanwhile, cover charges vary from $3-$5; some weeknights have no cover charge at all. Music usually starts around 9:30 P.M., until 1 A.M. or so; the cafe opens for food and beverages at 5 P.M. daily. If you're really watching the budget, have a "Poverty Burger," just a dollar—"a small little burger with a few fries added for color." Or, show up for the 5-6 P.M. happy hour, with $1 well drinks.

The OK Hotel Cafe
● 212 Alaskan Way S, Seattle; 621-7903
It's not really a hotel anymore, though the creaky old wooden staircase in the middle of this joint must have led to upstairs rooms at one time. Judging by this neighborhood of old, industrial, waterfront warehouses, near Pioneer Square it's probably just as well. The seedy look outside, however, gives way to a funky coffeehouse on the inside— serving up huge breakfasts and lunches (see the listing under "Restaurants—Downtown Area"), even bigger art canvases on the two-story walls, and hot music on weekend nights.

The OK has several microbrews on tap, such as Black Butte Porter, with many other potent potables in bottles. On Wednesday through Sunday nights, taped Dylan gives way to live bands ranging from progressive rock to jazz to stompin' rhythm and blues to the occasional "Madcap Cabaret."

The music starts around 8:30 or 9:00 P.M., usually running to midnight. Cover charges are in the $5-$6 range. The OK is also OK for younger audiences, as one of the few all-ages rock clubs in town, and proud of it.

The Owl 'N Thistle

● 808 Post Ave., Seattle; 621-7777
A touch of the blarney stone in downtown Seattle! The Owl 'N Thistle is a neighborhood-type Irish pub with atmosphere and food befitting a groggery in downtown Dublin. This means it's a sure bet for cheap eats (see the listing under "Restaurants— Downtown Area"), but it's also a sure bet for cheap music. The house band, Harvest Home, plays Wednesdays through Sundays with a mix of rock 'n roll and Irish folk. On Tuesdays, the sound shifts gears when Urban Jungle Tribe takes over with African and reggae tunes. A cover is only charged on Friday and Saturday nights, and even then, it's a mere $2. The house jams 'til 2 A.M.

Pioneer Square Joint Cover

● Various locations; see below
Here's a deal, not a place. Or rather, it's a bunch of places. These clubs, all in Pioneer Square, have banded together (sorry about the pun) to make pop music fans a great offer. Pay the cover charge at any one of the clubs below, and get into any of the others at no extra charge! This is available every night of the week. On Fridays and Saturdays, the cover is $7 (not bad even for one club); during the week, it may go even lower.

Some of these clubs are described in more detail elsewhere in this chapter; for current lineups, check newspaper listings or call the numbers below. And with nine different joints, you can go club-hopping several times without even seeing the same place twice. Nightclubs are, by their

nature, volatile places, so some of these may close or change names from time to time; Mr. C *always* recommends calling ahead before making an out-of-the-way trip.

● **Bohemian Cafe**, 111 Yesler Way, 447-1514
● **Central Cafe**, 207 First Ave. S, 622-0209
● **Colourbox**, 113 First Ave. S, 340-4101
● **Doc Maynard's**, 610 First Ave., 682-4649
● **Fenix Aboveground and Fenix Underground**, 323 Second Ave. S, 343-7740
● **Larry's Greenfront Restaurant and Lounge**, 209 First Ave. S, 624-7665
● **New Orleans Creole Restaurant**, 441 First Ave. S, 622-2563
● **Old Timer's Cafe**, 620 First St., 623-9800

RKCNDY

● 1812 Yale Ave. N, Seattle; 623-6651
No, Mr. C didn't break all the vowel keys on his computer. It is pronounced "rock candy" and it is one of the hottest clubs in town. Live music is the staple; you can see local grunge acts and some from the national circuit, usually for just a few bucks. Yes, Mr. C knows that "grunge" is already passé, but no one's come up with a name for the stuff that's replaced it. Let's call it "post-grunge" for now.

Anyway, Friday night shows can cost as little as $1 to get in. Even national acts are affordable, like $10 for a recent Joan Jett and the Blackhearts date. RKCNDY is a pretty large and popular place, so perhaps they can afford to charge lower covers. (In other words, how do they do it? VOLUME!!) Check local alternative papers like *The Stranger* for announcements of upcoming shows.

Romper Room

● 106 First Ave. N, Seattle; 284-5003
Hey kiddies, here's an artsy, wild sort of bar in Queen Anne, with DJ-hosted dancing or live performances nearly every night. Playtime begins with a

happy hour from 4 to 7 P.M.; be daring and try different local brews, or stick with your favorites—whatever combination you choose, it's "3 Beers for 3 Bucks." Shoot some pool, or just take a seat and soak up the wacked-out scenery—there's a gigantic bronze face propped in the corner, stuffed animals (teddy bears *and* taxidermy) hanging from the ceiling, and Cabbage Patch dolls smoking cigarettes.

As for the sounds, "versatility" is the key: Mondays are live acoustic nights, Wednesdays are "Dead (but Grateful)," Thursdays offer house-funk dance parties, and Fridays and Saturdays are devoted to what one local newspaper refers to as "genre music." In other words, it's a toss-up, but Mr. C guesses basic techno-pop. Open weeknights until 2 A.M., Fridays and Saturdays until 3 A.M. Mmm . . . nice 'n late.

Scarlet Tree
- 6521 Roosevelt Way, Seattle; 523-7153

This U-District restaurant and lounge features live music from local bands. On any given night, you may hear rock, rhythm and blues, or pop music. Recent acts seen here include Soul Kiss, Apollo Creed, and Tour de Force. The cover charge is generally $2 to $4 on weekends, usually free on weeknights. ST presents live music every night, except Sunday, and the action starts around 9:30 P.M.

Scarlet Tree also has a full menu of relatively cheap eats. You can have dinner here for about $10; less for burgers, salads, soups, and such. What's more, if you eat dinner, you don't pay a cover charge. This could be your one-stop place for weekend food and entertainment.

Sit & Spin
- 2219 Fourth Ave., Seattle; 441-9484

Remember all the fun you had twirling around on your "Sit-n-Spin" until you felt like you were gonna lose it? Well, this is the more grown-up version (at least, for the twentysomething set). It's just as sensory-overloading, but without the likelihood of becoming sick to your stom-

---

MR. CHEAP'S PICKS
Rock and Pop Music

✔ **Colourbox**—A good place to keep up with local bands—they'll even describe the week's acts for you. Part of the **Pioneer Square Joint Cover** deal, a bar-hopper's dream come true.

✔ **Crocodile Cafe** —From the stuffed reptile over the front door to the "Funky Voodoo Snake Pit" dance area, this place will never leave you cold.

✔ **OK Hotel Cafe**—Just a few bucks to see top-notch rock 'n rollers, including some national acts? Okay!

✔ **RKCNDY**—Live rock shows as low as a dollar. Must be because they didn't spend any money to buy a vowel.

✔ **Mo'Roc'caN Cafe**—First in First Hill's heart.

---

ach—unless, of course, you haven't done your wash in four months.

That's right, kiddies, Sit & Spin is part cafe, part laundromat, allowing Belltown apartment dwellers to tackle two vital human needs at the same time. S & S is decorated in a boisterous, neo-1950s style, with a string of lone, escapee socks along the walls of the laundry room, and old black-and-white television sets spewing forth snowy pictures around the cafe. Board games further enhance the hang-out experience.

This is also a fun place to catch some free, live rock and roll. Every Wednesday and Thursday evening, starting at 9 P.M., groove to the sounds of the "Acoustic Jelly Session," presenting two different bands each night. And, on Tuesday evenings, the comedy improv group "Off Limits" cracks the place up, also starting at 9. You can catch poetry slams here, too. Meanwhile, a sign on the wall proudly proclaims: "No Cover Ever!"

The cafe portion opens later and closes earlier than the laundromat. Food is served from 11 to 11 early in the week, and until 1 A.M. Thursdays through Saturdays. For more info about the food offered, see the listing under "Restaurants—Downtown Area."

Sports Bar & Grill
● 5260 University Way NE, Seattle; 526-1489

It really says something about Seattle that even the bars with "sports" in their names have live music on Friday and Saturday nights; you'd never see that in New York or Chicago. It's only rock 'n roll, but the Emerald City likes it. And the college crowd likes it here at the Sports Bar & Grill, where cover charges range from just $3 to $5, even for popular local bands like Blind Tribe, Speakeasy, and Running With Scissors. Live bands play Friday and Saturday nights from roughly 10 P.M. to 2 A.M.

Tractor Tavern
● 5213 Ballard Ave. NW, Seattle; 789-3599

The name of this club doesn't contain any deep, hidden meaning: the founders just liked the name because it gave the impression of movement, and they felt it'd be somehow easy to remember. What's even more memorable is the low-priced live music, and the eclectic mix of entertainment.

Cover charges range from $5 to $8, though many are as low as $3 or $4. The staple here is local alternative rock music, with some acoustic and jazz music thrown in on occasion. The Tractor is trying to move toward more unusual stuff, however, and has recently featured ballroom dancing, *klezmer* music, Gaelic music, contra dancing, and more. You never know *what* will be happening next; evidently, that's the way these folks like it. Call them to get a calendar of events.

Under the Rail
● 2335 Fifth Ave., Seattle; 448-1900

Under the Rail (the Monorail, that is), one of Seattle's more prominent rock clubs, is a dark, cavernous room. That's about it for decor—the way-cool atmosphere comes from the crowd and the big-name bands that play here.

The music is loud and diverse. Besides Northwest bands like Beads of Mercury, Thread, and 212, "rock legends" David Lee Roth and Air Supply (yes, Air Supply) have performed. The San Francisco band Zero and Grammy-winning reggae group Inner Circle have also had shows here; R & B, jazz, and "polyethnic Cajun slamgrass" are just a few other kinds of music you may hear.

An admission price of $6 or $7 will get you in to see lesser-known bands, but the big, national acts can cost as much as $17.50. Tickets are generally a few dollars less when bought in advance. Music plays until about 1:30 A.M. most nights.

Vogue
● 2018 First Ave., Seattle; 443-0673

Another of-the-moment, trendy club, Vogue is where scads of twenty-somethings come to see and be seen. Can Cheapsters afford such hipness? Well, when cover charges are rarely more than $5, the answer is yes, and with attitude to spare.

Entertainment at Vogue consists mostly of DJs spinning rock, alternative, and industrial tunes—while voguers and *voyeurs* do their thing on the dance floor. The cover can be as low as $2 to $3 during the week, generally $5 on weekends. Thursday is "Ladies Nite," when women get in for free, all night! Most nights, the cover is reduced or free before 10 P.M., but *no one* goes out before 10 P.M., do they?

Waldo's
● 12657 NE 85th Street, Kirkland; 827-9292

Where's Waldo's? You won't have to look too hard—it's right in the heart of Kirkland. Not the trendy water-front area, that is, but to the east, along the shopping strip that crosses Route 405 and *then* becomes Central Way. And what will you find when you get there? A huge tavern, lots of great rock 'n roll, and low cover charges.

Popular local bands are generally seen here on Wednesdays, Fridays, and Saturdays. Midweek is cheapest, around $3; weekends aren't much higher at $5. Here's an extra tip from Mr. C: Most nights, Waldo's doesn't charge a cover until about 7:30 P.M., so arrive early and get in free! Of course, you then have to find something to do until the music starts at 9:30 P.M. Have something to eat, shoot a rack or two of pool, and socialize. Waldo's rocks until 2 A.M.

The Weathered Wall
● 1921 Fifth Ave., Seattle; 448-5688
This popular Belltown club features an ever-changing, eclectic blend of music, literature, and more. On any given night, they may offer punk rock, jazz, flamenco, or whatever. Most entertainment here has a distinct edge to it: For example, recently WW presented a night of "gothic industrial music," for which "deviant dress" was required. Proceed at your own risk. It has also been home to the "Lollapalooza Poetry Slam." Cover charges are rarely more than $5 or $6, sometimes they're as low as a buck. Stop by or check the local alternative weeklies to get the full scoop on upcoming events.

OUTDOORS

Seattle ain't called the "Emerald City" for nothing. It is blessed with over 300 parks and playgrounds, taking up some 5,000 acres of parkland. Not to mention, of course, its various waterways. Unlike many other major metropolises, you can barely take a step here—even from downtown—without seeing greenery or blue water. So much to do, so much of it free. . .

Arboretum Waterfront Trail
● Foster Island, Seattle; Information, 325-4510
Take a hike! That is, a thirty-minute hike through the largest wetland area in Seattle, just across the Ship Canal from UW. Park in the lot for the Museum of History and Industry; at the edge of the lot, you'll see the path leading to Marsh and Foster Islands, with a map posted at the entrance. Soon you'll be walking along a wood-chipped path, up and over floating footbridges, winding your way through tall grasses, and mingling with all sorts of wildflowers and waterfowl.

There are plenty of benches along the way, as well as little floating docks to pause for views of Union Bay (and from some, cars zipping by

on the elevated Route 520). These also make for good fishing spots. Continue east along the paths, and you'll reach an open park area on Foster Island, popular during the summer for picnicking, and as a destination for canoe paddlers from the UW Waterfront Activities Center (see the listing below). From here, you can turn around and head back, or cut south into the Washington Park Arboretum and extend your journey.

Free trail guide maps are available at the Arboretum Visitor Center and MOHAI; dogs, bikes, and joggers are not permitted on the paths. The trail is open every day from dawn to dusk. By the way, another interesting walk starts north from the museum lot to the Ship Canal, and underneath the Montlake Bridge to Portage Bay.

Plenty of nautical activity to see along here.

Bellevue Botanical Gardens

● 12001 Main St., Bellevue; 462-2749

Imagine that you could enjoy 36 acres of hills, woods, meadows, streams, and walking trails, flush with flora, without leaving the city (well, barely). Now, imagine that none of this will cost you a cent. It's real! The Bellevue Botanical Gardens are filled with native plants and wildlife, and it is open to the public free of charge all the time.

Take a stroll and enjoy an artist's palette of perennials, a Japanese rock garden, and more. The BBG's docent staff is on hand to lead special tours if you want to find out more about what you're seeing. There are other opportunities to learn more about horticulture, too: gardening classes, cooking classes (using herbs they can teach you to grow!), and lectures. Many of these classes are free, though some charge a modest fee for supplies.

Other special events include the "Mother's Day Tea," a summer concert series (see the listing under "Festivals"), and the "Garden D'Lights Holiday Open House," two weeks of holiday music and related workshops each December. For more info check in with the Visitor's Center which is open seven days a week from 10 A.M. to 5 P.M. The grounds themselves are open sunup to sunset, everyday.

Center for Wooden Boats

● 1010 Valley St., Seattle; 382-BOAT (2628)

At the very southern tip of Lake Union, between the Naval Reserve and a Burger King (ugh), the Center for Wooden Boats is still a great urban secret to many Seattleites; not only is it a "living museum" of classic sailboats and rowboats, but it's an amazingly peaceful—and free—oasis right in the heart of the city. It costs you nothing to walk along the gently bobbing docks; through the boathouse, where you may hear a free lecture by a real captain or a deep-sea diver (and

maybe even get a bite to eat); or past the painstakingly careful restoration-in-progress of the *Wawona*, a schooner originally built in 1897.

You can volunteer to do some work yourself, too; surprising again is the fact that, for all the people seen puttering around here, there are only four full-time staffers. Literally hundreds of others volunteer their time in a variety of ways. You can even learn how to help with the restoration. And, for every three hours given, volunteers are entitled to one free hour of boat rental on the lake.

Yes, more than half of these nifty-looking vessels can be rented, to the general public as well. Sailboats ranging from 12 to 20 feet in length rent for $10-$15 per hour, while smaller rowboats of various shapes and sizes cost even less. The best deal for the nautical enthusiast is an annual membership, which costs $25; it's only $10 for students, and $40 for an entire whole family. It's easy to pay off the cost of membership with the 25% savings you'll then get on every rental.

So, imagine this deal: You go with three or four pals, rent an antique rowboat for a few hours, and still pay only a few bucks per person. Bring a picnic lunch, and you're set for a whole day of adventure. If you do plan to rent a sailboat, there is a one-time-only trial run, just so the folks can make sure you know what you're doing. This costs five bucks, but that's better than accidentally sinking a 100-year-old dory, isn't it? Full-fledged sailing courses are also offered here.

A final note: The Center for Wooden Boats is privately run. That means donations of time and of dollars are the only funding they receive. With so much to take advantage of, for so little cost, do consider dropping a few bucks in the till. The Center is open from 11 A.M. to 7 P.M. daily (closed on Tuesdays), with rentals starting no later than 6 P.M. The nearby Northwest Seaport Maritime Heritage Center is another great place for boat-lovers; see the listing under "Walks and Tours."

Chittenden Locks

- 3015 NW 54th St., Seattle; 783-7059

Ballard's Hiram M. Chittenden Locks area is one of Seattle's most popular attractions—for both tourists and locals alike. It's no wonder why, with so much to see here, and all of it free! The locks allow ships to pass from the fresh-water Lake Union into salt-water Puget Sound (or vice-versa), and each run finds big commercial vessels side by side with tiny pleasure boats. Not unlike the big-fish-little-fish world of the sea, eh? (Said in Mr. C's best Jacques Cousteau.)

Speaking of which, Chittenden is also home to Seattle's famous "Fish Ladder." This 21-step waterway lets sockeye, Chinook, trout, and other finny friends migrate to Lake Washington and its tributaries. In the fish viewing room, six lighted windows give you a chance to see different parts of their journey, while learning to identify the various species.

The real place to start for all of this is at the Visitor Center, on your way into the park. Educational films are shown in a small cinema, special exhibits are on display, and the expert staff can answer all of your questions. From June through September, the center is open seven days a week, from 10 A.M. to 7 P.M.; during the October to May off-season, it's open Thursday through Monday from 11 A.M. to 5 P.M.

The Visitor Center offers free tours, too. These take place at 1:00 and 3:00 P.M. daily in the summer, and on weekends only during the rest of the year (at 2 P.M.). The grounds themselves, meanwhile, are open year-round from 7 A.M. to 9 P.M. daily. And if all this fishy fun whets your appetite for some seafood, have a nibble at the Lockspot Cafe (see the listing under "Restaurants—North Area") next to the parking lot. The Chittenden Locks are also a great place to enjoy free summer concerts and lectures; see separate listings under "Festivals."

English Botanical Garden

- 3015 NW 54th St., Seattle; 783-7059

On your way to the Chittenden Locks, you'll pass along the Carl S. English Jr. Botanical Garden—home to over 500 plant species from around the world. The garden is named for a member of the Army Corps of Engineers, who transformed the barren lawns of the Locks into this garden of unsurpassed beauty. Some of the many plants you'll see here include the Chinese witch-hazel, heather, azaleas, rhododendrons, magnolias, Japanese flowering cherries, crab-apples, oaks, and maples. Most interesting, perhaps, is an eighteen-foot fan palm. They claim it was literally grown from a seed, planted in the garden some 35 years ago!

A great place for having a picnic, reading the paper on a park bench, or taking a relaxing amble, the English Garden is open daily from 7 A.M. to 9 P.M. year-round. Admission is free.

Fresh and Saltwater Fishing

- Department of Fish and Wildlife; 16018 Mill Creek Blvd., Mill Creek; 902-2200 or 775-1311

Sometimes, you just need a break from the hustle and bustle of city life—and Mr. C knows a great way to unwind on those occasionally sunny weekends. With over 4,000 rivers and streams, 7,000 lakes, 208 reservoirs, plus numerous bays, straits, and islands (and not *too* far away, one major ocean), Washington is a fishing fanatic's paradise. Washington boasts eight different varieties of trout alone—not to mention the bottomfish, flatfish, and five different types of salmon. We're talkin' *way* beyond Chinook here. Year-round fishing is allowed in many bodies of water around the Seattle area; others have strict seasons and catch limits, especially in the salty seas.

How to know which is which? Glad you asked. The Washington Department of Fish and Wildlife publishes an annual booklet outlining opening dates, recent regulations, and current license fees. For residents of

201

Washington, an $8 fishing license is a great bargain since it lasts all year. Non-residents pay $20 for the same full-year pass; or, if you're just a visitor, you can get a special $5 permit good for two days of angling.

Here's an extra tip from Mr. C: Whether you intend to do a little fishing or a lot, call one of the above numbers to order a copy of the *Washington Fishing Guide*. It only costs a couple of bucks for postage, and gives you lots of helpful info on fishing statewide. It's sure to help make any trip pay off.

Gas Works Park
- N Northlake Way at Meridian Ave. N, Seattle; 684-4075

Everyone in Seattle seems to have their own favorite view of the city; Mr. C casts his vote for Fremont's Gas Works Park Viewpoint. Once a filthy old industrial site, the area was cleaned up in 1956—and is now pleasant, serene, and even picnicable. In fact, folks with an appetite for the surreal will enjoy looking at these monuments of industry—which still remain intact, and are now painted in glorious Technicolor.

Across Lake Union, meanwhile, lies the modern skyline of Seattle. The day view is an impressive sight, but to really appreciate the panorama, you've got to see it at night. Of course, sunset (when there is one) is really nice too, with sunlight glinting off of skyscrapers. Aw heck, the view is fabulous just about anytime. The park itself is open from 6 A.M. until 11 P.M. daily.

Green Lake Boat Rentals
- 7351 E Green Lake Dr. N, Seattle; 527-0171

Green Lake is a much-cherished landmark for Seattleites who enjoy jogging, biking, rollerblading, and people-watching. It's also a notorious *rendezvous* for "personals" introductions. Naturally, it's also popular for various water activities, including boating. Head over to the boathouse on the northeast side, where you can rent a variety of vessels for just a few dollars. Rates run from a low of $8

per hour for paddle boats, row boats, kayaks, and canoes, to a high of $12 an hour for windsurfers and sailboats.

These are not the cheapest boat rentals in town, but it's still quite reasonable—especially if you're splitting the cost with your partner. Boat rentals are available seven days per week, in season. Hours are from 10 A.M. to dusk from Memorial Day through Labor Day, and from 11 A.M. to dusk the rest of the year.

Of course, you don't have to spend a dime to enjoy Green Lake itself. Along with the aforementioned activities, visitors also take part in volleyball, baseball, Frisbee, and swimming. Grab a friend and a picnic basket; what more do you need?

Eastsiders whose sense of adventure does not include a trip over the bridge needn't feel left out. You folks can rent canoes and kayaks from the City of Bellevue Canoe and Kayak Boat Rentals at Enatai Beach Park on Lake Washington. The address is 3519 108th Ave. SE; telephone 451-7518. Rates are comparable to those at Green Lake. Meanwhile, the *cheapest* canoe deal around is right in between these locales; see the listing for "University of Washington Boat Rentals" below.

Kubota Garden
- 55th Ave. S and Renton Ave. S, Seattle; 684-4584

The Kubota Garden was created in the 1920s by Fujitaro Kubota, a man who wanted to produce Japanese-style gardens using native Pacific Northwest plants. Today, the garden has "grown" to some twenty acres of hills and valleys, waterfalls, ponds, rocks, and a rich variety of plants. The Kubota Garden Foundation invites the public to enjoy the beauty and tranquillity of this botanical paradise, free of charge. Grab a map and follow one of the many trails, or take a seat by a pond and watch everyone else work for their fun. The garden is open everyday during daylight hours.

Northwest Outdoor Center
- 2100 Westlake Ave. N, Seattle; 281-9694

A kayaking excursion doesn't have to be a task worthy of Jack London. This sport has become one of the easiest and most popular around the Seattle area. Kayakers can enjoy the relatively calm blue waters of Lake Union all year 'round—yes, even in the dead of winter—by checking out the Northwest Outdoor Center's kayak rental depot. With up to forty different types of kayak to choose from, built for one or two people, such an excursion can be rewarding, relaxing, and even inexpensive. For only $8 to $10 per hour (prices vary depending on the size of the craft) you can enjoy the freedom of boating. And, if you make your voyage on a weekday, ask about the "four hours for the price of two" deal. A tip from Mr. C.

Pacific Rim Bonsai Collection
- 33663 Weyerhaeuser Way S, Federal Way; 924-5206

Hidden within the campus of Weyerhaeuser's corporate headquarters, you'll find a living outdoor museum filled with over fifty examples of bonsai art from Japan, Korea, China, Taiwan, Canada, and the United States. Weyerhaeuser built the collection to honor its trade relations with Pacific Rim countries, and in tribute to the Washington State Centennial. Cheapsters will be happy to find they can enjoy the collection free! Wander through and marvel at miniature crabapple trees and Chinese juniper. Pop into the conservatory, too, which houses the more tropical bonsai trees.

In season (March through May), the collection is open from 10 A.M. to 4 P.M. every day except Thursdays. From June through February, it's open from 11 A.M. to 4 P.M. every day except Thursdays and Fridays. For information about group tours call 924-3153.

Pacific Water Sports
- 16055 Pacific Highway S, Sea Tac; 246-9385

If you're into canoeing or kayaking, Pacific Water Sports has some of the best equipment and greatest prices around. A whole day (10 A.M. to 6 P.M.) for a one-person boat is only

---

MR. CHEAP'S PICKS
Outdoors

✔ **Center for Wooden Boats**— A serene oasis in the heart of the city. The "volunteer work for free rentals" deal is perfect for sailing fans with a wealth of time.

✔ **Chittenden Locks**—The "Fish Ladder" makes this one of the city's most popular tourist attractions, and it's completely free—as is the adjacent **English Botanical Garden**.

✔ **Seattle Singles Yacht Club**— One organization fills two important needs: Singles who seek activities and skippers who seek passengers.

✔ **UW Waterfront Activities Center**—You don't have to be a student to get the city's best deal on canoe rentals—though if you are, the deal is even better.

✔ **Washington Zoological Park**—A small, up-close-and-personal zoo where animal preservation is the emphasis.

$27. Pacific also rents double kayaks as well as double and solo canoes for long weekends ($60-$90), overnight ($34-$55), or for a couple of days ($43-$65). Some of these rates work out to a few bucks per hour! Be sure to bring a credit card or some extra cash for a fully refundable deposit. But be warned that there is no body of water near Pacific Water Sports—Mr. C suggests bringing along a car with some sort of boat carrying capacity.

The professionals at Pacific also lead guided tours for all levels from whitewater to scenic lake paddling.

And if you're thinking of buying, try the rent-to-own plan. Store hours are 10 A.M. to 6 P.M., daily, except Sunday.

Point Defiance Zoo and Aquarium

- 5400 N Pearl St., Tacoma; 591-5337

Point Defiance is home to some 5,847 animals, representing over 300 species. These critters show a definite Pacific Rim bent, encompassing everything from the Arctic tundra to Southeast Asian rainforests—and, of course, the Puget Sound coastline. Favorite exhibits include "Sharks: The Survivors," with over ninety sharks from ten species, and "Rocky Shores" with sea lions, harbor seals, walruses, sea otters, and beluga whales. Point Defiance is dedicated to research and conservation projects, too.

Admission is $6.50 for adults, $6 for seniors and disabled citizens, $4.75 for children ages five to seventeen, $2.50 for ages three to four, and free for toddlers under two. There are discounts available for organized groups of twelve or more; call the above number for info and reservations. Open seven days a week during the long summer season from 10 A.M. to 7 P.M.; the rest of the year, it closes at 4 P.M.

Public Art in Seattle

- Various locations; see below

Enlightened metropolis that it is, Seattle is famous for its public displays of artworks. Anywhere you turn, it seems, you'll see sculptures of one variety or another, from local to internationally renowned artists. Jonathan Borofsky's "Hammering Man," looming (and hammering) over the entrance to the downtown Seattle Art Museum, is probably the most widely recognized, while the best-loved may well be Richard Beyer's "People Waiting for the Interurban," at the north end of the Fremont Bridge. Mr. C has even seen these terminally patient bus riders gaily decorated with streamers and party hats. Meanwhile, a few blocks north, underneath the Aurora Bridge, a larger-than-life troll devours a real VW Beetle.

One of Seattle's most popular sculptors is George Tsutakawa, known especially for his fountains. Children of all ages love the 15-foot-high fountain at Sixth Avenue and Seneca Street, and Seattle University is blessed with a cascade of its own. At Fourth and Pike, in front of the Westlake Center, there's a "wall of water" you can walk through. Other local faves include sculpture giant Henry Moore's "Vertebrae," downtown at Fourth Avenue and Madison Street; "The Itinerant," the sculpture of a newspaper-draped man sleeping on a bench in Capitol Hill's Broadway District; and nearby, "Dancer's Series: Steps" is set into either side of Broadway between East Pine and East Roy Streets (Mr. C warns you, however, that trying to do the outlined rumba will brand you as a tourist immediately). Take a look around and see those tax dollars hard at work—pleasing people.

Seacrest Boat House

- 1660 Harbor Ave. SW, Seattle; 932-1050

So you wanna go fishin' but you don't have a boat. No problem. Take your tackle over to this scenic spot around the point from Alki Beach, where you can rent a seaworthy (well, at least Sound-worthy) vessel for only $15 a day. Alas, there is a catch: You have to row. If you prefer to go in style, propelled by a massive six-horsepower engine, then you'll have to pay the full rate of $11 an hour, or $9 if you're a senior citizen. Still pretty reasonable, especially if you're not going out for the whole day.

The Seacrest Boat House hours are from 5:30 A.M. 'til 6 P.M. every weekday, and 4:30 A.M. to 7 P.M. on weekends. For your convenience, you can get bait, tackle, hot-dogs, donuts, and coffee—all the things a hearty fisherman needs—at their Seacrest Cafe.

Seattle Department of Parks and Recreation Community Centers

- Various locations; Information, 684-4075

Especially during the summer vacation months, community centers are great places to send your kids when they begin watching more than ten hours of TV a day. Aside from camps, there are also all sorts of traditional family activities like picnics, swimming pools, sports facilities, and the oh-so-famous arts and crafts.

But nowadays, community centers aren't just for kids; many offer computer training courses, ethnic dancing, and drawing—all intended specifically for grownups. And since community centers are publicly funded, you don't have to pay a lot for their offerings. Go out and learn something new—batik, pottery, yoga; or maybe you want to perfect your pickleball game with some neighborhood friends. Don't hesitate, the cost is minimal. Here are some of the locations, spread out all over the Seattle area:

- **Ballard Community Center,** 6020 28th Ave. NW; 684-4093
- **Ballard Pool,** 1471 NW 67th St.; 684-4094
- **Bitter Lake Community Center,** 13040 Greenwood Ave. N; 684-7524
- **Evans Pool and Green Lake Community Center,** 7201 E Green Lake Way N; 684-4961
- **Loyal Heights Community Center,** 2102 NW 77th St.; 684-4052
- **Magnolia Community Center,** 2550 34th Ave. W; 223-7061
- **Queen Anne Community Center and Pool,** 1901 First Ave. W; 386-4240
- **Rainier Community Center,** 3701 S Oregon St.; 386-1919
- **Southwest Community Center and Pool,** 2801 SW Thistle St.; 684-7438

Seattle Singles Yacht Club

- 2040 Westlake Ave. N, Seattle; 233-8511

Okay gang, get this. If you're single and over 21, you can go on all kinds of sailing trips in and around Seattle—*practically for free.*

The SSYC is a social organization dedicated to introductions and just plain having a good time. Among its members are over fifty skippers of boats large and small, looking for folks to take out for day or evening sails on Lake Washington, Elliott Bay, and beyond.

To get in on the fun, all you have to do is attend one of their Monday night meetings—open to any single adult—held at the China Harbor restaurant (the address above). It costs $4 to attend. At the meeting, all of that week's activities are announced; sign up for anything you like. There are no further charges. Just meet your boat at the appointed time and place, bring along food for a potluck meal, and whatever you want to drink. That's it!

Some of the boats are large enough to take two dozen singles at a time for a short trip. Other voyages last for several days—still free, mind you—and they often participate in "raft-ups." In these outings, one large boat drops anchor, and several smaller boats then hitch up in all directions; the result is one big party, with people wandering around from boat to boat.

Sailings take place year-round, though there are fewer in the winter. SSYC sponsors lots of other activities: dinners, dances, tennis, and skiing trips, usually with reasonably-priced deals on lodging and lift tickets. Events are well-attended, with plenty of turnover among the crowd. The age range runs from twentysomethings up to folks in their sixties; unmarried couples can participate too.

People who attend meetings and activities often may find it more economical to join officially. Membership costs $100 a year per person, which gives you free admission to the Monday gatherings and discounted rates on major activities. One recent late-season ski trip included lodgings in condos with an indoor pool and spa: The member cost was a total of $50 for two weekend nights. Drop by any Monday, or call the number above for more information.

Another group that offers boating activities for singles is the **Northwest Riggers Yacht Club**; call 324-5104 or 365-6222 for their information.

University of Washington Observatory

- NE 45th St. & 17th Ave. NE, Seattle; 543-0126

Right across from the Burke Museum, on the University of Washington campus, a live presentation of nothing less than the entire universe is open to the public, and free of cost. Sound too good to be true? Read on.

Two nights a week, anyone—whether a member of the university community or not—is welcome to peer through UW's six-inch refractor telescope. That's pretty big, in telescope terms; and your journey through the heavens will be guided by an expert on the subject (a university staffer—sorry, Carl Sagan is too busy). Even if the weather is cloudy, don't despair—a fully-narrated slideshow of heavenly sights is always ready to go in a pinch. Not only is this worth the price of admission (and how much *was* that, folks?), but it's good preparation for a return visit on a clearer night. The observatory is open every Monday and Thursday night; times vary by season, so call ahead.

University of Washington Waterfront Activities Center

- Montlake Blvd. NE, Seattle; 543-9433

The best boating bargain in all of Seattle can be found in the shadow of Husky Stadium. To get to the Waterfront Activities Center, walk through the stadium's parking lot, or down from the north end of the Montlake Bridge, and head toward the water. Within moments, you're sure to stumble over one of the center's 90 watercraft, stacked up on the docks.

At just $3.50 per hour, the WAC charges less than half the hourly rate of rentals on Green Lake, with the more varied scenery of Union Bay into the bargain. And you need not be a student to get this microscopically small price; this facility is for use by students *and* the general public—one of Seattle's best open secrets. Of course, if you *are* a UW student, you'll pay a mere $1.60 an hour. Discounts for faculty, staff, and UW alumni, too.

Choose a canoe or a rowboat for a voyage across the mouth of the ship canal (no, you can't go in there) to Foster Island, or duck under the footbridge (no pun intended) and drift through the Arboretum. Take a boat out any day of the week, from February through October; the center is closed on all major holidays. Hours vary through the season, but during the prime months of summer, rentals run from 10 A.M. to 9 P.M. on weekdays, and they start an hour earlier on Saturdays and Sundays (no starting after 7 P.M.). An extra tip from Mr. C: During summer weekends, if the weather is especially nice, you should try to arrive before noon—or all the boats may be taken!

Volunteer Park Conservatory

- 1400 E Galer St., Seattle; 684-4743

Near Capitol Hill, the 45-acre Volunteer Park has been a haven of relaxation for over eighty years. Plant-o-philes in particular know that the Conservatory is a colorful oasis in the center of the city. A short walk from the newly re-opened Seattle Asian Art Museum, this indoor botanical garden was completed in 1912, and has maintained an impressive collection of flora from all over the world ever since.

Outside the greenhouse is a monument to William Seward (of Folly fame), not to mention shaded and open fields, picnic tables, pathways for quiet strolls, a wading pool, and the above-mentioned museum. Also nearby is one of Seattle's original water towers, which you can climb inside for a commanding view of the city. All of this outdoor stuff is free.

The conservatory is open all year 'round. A visit to the palm or the cactus rooms makes for a balmy respite from a raw winter's day—a cheap getaway for those who can't afford a trip to warmer climates.

206

If you do have some dough to spare, look into becoming a Friend of the Conservatory, and help the continual process of restoring and maintaining this historic landmark—or just buy a plant at one of the conservatory's seasonal garden sales. Hours are from 10 A.M. to 4 P.M. after the beginning of October and from 10 A.M. 'til 7 P.M. when the weather is warm.

Washington Park Arboretum
- 2300 Arboretum Dr. E, Seattle; 543-8800

Prize flower of Seattle's many arboreta, described throughout this chapter, the Washington Park Arboretum is the city's largest, spreading across over 200 acres from the Floating Bridge entrance south to Madison Park—and you can explore it all for free.

This sixty-year-old living museum is filled with over 5,500 different plants, most of which are native to the area. Enjoy the bright colors of "Azalea Way"; a promenade lined with flowering cherries, azaleas, and dogwoods; "Rhododendron Glen"; and the rock garden. For a picnic, a peaceful stroll near the heart of the city, or a family outing, you can lose yourself in here all day. You can even walk underneath Route 520, to connect with walking trails along Foster Island; see the separate listing at the beginning of this chapter.

What's more, admission to all of this splendor is free, with one exception. The Japanese Tea Garden, located in the middle of the arboretum, does charge an admission of $2 for adults, and $1 for children and senior citizens; it's free for children under twelve. Laden with red maples and bonsai trees, this is also the site for a formal Japanese tea ceremony, held on the third Saturday of each month at 1:30 P.M.

If you'd like to learn a little more about the arboretum, a free public tour is offered every Sunday at 1 P.M. (except in December). Horticulture classes and group tours are also available. Call the Visitor's Center at the number above, or stop in during your stroll, for more information. The arboretum is open from dawn to dusk; the Visitor's Center is open on weekdays from 10 A.M. to 4 P.M., and weekends from 12 noon to 4 P.M.

Washington State Ferries
- Seattle Ferry Terminal, Pier 52, Seattle; 464-6400

Why spend a fortune on expensive boat tours, when the State of Washington operates commuter ferries for a fraction of the cost? After all, they ride the same water, and you get the same spectacular views...at least, when the weather cooperates. Every day from dawn until after midnight, a fleet of passenger/car and passenger-only boats makes frequent runs between the Ferry Terminal in downtown Seattle and various landings on the other side of Puget Sound.

Sail across to Winslow on Bainbridge Island, or south to Vashon, in about 30 minutes; to Bremerton in an hour. Similar ferries make connections both north and south of the city, including routes from Anacortes to the San Juan Islands. Pick up a current-season schedule at any terminal.

The standard fare for the downtown Seattle ferries at the time of this writing is $3.50 per person, plus an extra 50¢ if you're carrying a bike along. Children ages 5-11 pay half-fare. If you're in a car, a vehicle-and-driver ticket is $5.90; drivers over 65 get a reduced rate, and extra passengers pay the walk-on rate. In many cases, fares are only collected in one direction. All the rest of the details and minutiae are explained in the schedule brochures.

By the way, as a friend of Mr. C's always insists: Sailing into the downtown Seattle terminal at dusk or nighttime, when the skyline lights sparkle, is one of the grandest sights the city has to offer.

Washington Zoological Park
- 19525 SE 54th St., Issaquah; 391-5508

The Washington Zoological Park specializes in the care of threatened and endangered animal species. It's a teaching zoo, fostering the appreciation of wildlife through education, research, captive breeding, and conservation. Therefore, your admission fee goes toward helping out some pretty cute creatures. These include many varieties of birds, including parrots, ducks, bald eagles, geese, and cranes. Non-avian animals include cheetahs, deer, wallabies, and some primates. The grounds are designed so that you can experience a close encounter with the animals; and, since it's a teaching zoo, there is special emphasis on educational activities for all ages.

Admission is $4.50 for adults, $4 for senior citizens, $3.50 for children ages four to fifteen, $2.50 for children two and three, and free for kids under two. Group rates are also available. The zoo is open Tuesdays through Saturdays from 10 A.M. to 5 P.M., and Sundays 11 A.M. to 5 P.M. Gates close an hour earlier November through February.

Woodland Park Zoo
- 5500 Phinney Ave. N, Seattle; 684-4800

Admission to Woodland Park Zoo is a bit more than Mr. C would normally recommend you spend. Still, Mr. C can't help but tell you about this delightful place. Besides, when given a choice between spending $6.50 on a two-hour movie or a day at this fine zoo, which is the better bargain?

Highlights include the elephant forest, home to one African elephant and three Asians (can you tell the difference?); the raptor center, with such birds of prey as eagles, hawks, falcons, owls, and more; and the "Tropical Rain Forest," which exhibits the plant and animal life found at every level of a rain forest, from floor to canopy.

Fascinating stuff, and yet there are big improvements on the way. The zoo is being redeveloped into eight "bioclimatic zones" to mimic natural environments found all over the world. This major renovation will take several years, but there are still plenty of exhibits to enjoy in the meanwhile.

Admission to the zoo is $6.50 for adults, $4 for kids ages six to seventeen, and $1.75 for children three to five; also $4.75 for seniors, and $4 for disabled citizens. Because they are helping to pay for the new zoo with their taxes, King County residents get a discount of a dollar or so on tickets. Children under age two—regardless of county of origin—are admitted free. The zoo opens at 9:30 A.M., 365 days a year. The exhibits close at 6 P.M. from March 15 to October 14, and at 4 P.M. from October 15 to March 14. Visitors are allowed to stay on the grounds, though, until dusk.

READINGS AND LITERARY EVENTS

Barnes & Noble Booksellers
- 626 106th Ave. NE, Bellevue; 451-8463
- Crossroads Shopping Center, Bellevue; 644-1650
- 300 Andover Park W, Tukwila; 575-3965

This growing national chain is fairly new to the Northwest book scene. They've wasted no time establishing themselves not only as major stores, but as good places to frequent for book-related events as well. Along with the major author-on-a-book-tour-visitations, bringing in such literary luminaries as Erica Jong and J. A. Jance, B & N presents lots of lesser-knowns, too, offering readings, lectures, workshops, and children's activities. Recently, nature writer Ann Saling presented a workshop, "Ten Secrets Every Nature Writer Should Know," and Gun Agell discussed his book *Strengthen Your Immune System*.

Barnes and Noble is also a terrific place to get kids involved in literature. See the listing under "Children's Activities" for more info. B & N locations are open seven days a week, usually into the late evening.

Bonvechio's Book & Bean
- 4554 California Ave. SW, Seattle; 935-1003

Bonvechio's Book & Bean has everything you could want in a bookstore/cafe: A nifty name, good books, plenty of literary events, and of course, ever-ready cups of espresso. Regular offerings include the "Meet Me at Bonvechio's" series, in which local authors read and sign their latest releases; children's storytelling sessions on Saturday mornings; and "Lively, Local, and Free," script and literary readings co-sponsored with ArtsWest (see the listing under "Arts and Cultural Centers").

Stop in to BB&B for a calendar of events.

Borders Books and Music
- 1501 Fourth Ave., Seattle; 622-4599

Another fast-growing national chain, Borders presents a packed schedule of readings, live music, and more. The topics are, to say the least, eclectic. Events have included appearances by cookbook author Bunny Cameron (complete with samples!), a discussion of environmentalism for consumers with Deborah Dadd-Redalia, and a slide show with Scott McCloud, author of *Understanding Comics: the Invisible Art*. There's even a weekly chess night; Borders once sponsored a "Chess Challenge" with international grand chess master Yasser Seirawan.

But wait, there's more: Since they sell recordings as well as books, Borders also hosts regular live music events. Folk-rocker Fran Marranca recently performed here, joined by guitarist Jeff Ford and sign language interpreter Kris Arnett. Other performances have featured classical guitarist Charles Solbrig, among various local classical music guests at the "Sunday Tea at the Borders" series.

To get a full listing of upcoming programs, pick up a copy of their newsletter "FootNote." Borders has lots of kids' events, too. See the listing under "Children's Activities," for more info.

Central Saloon Poetry Slams
- 207 First Ave. S, Seattle; 622-0209

One of the many establishments claiming to be "Seattle's Oldest" something or other, this cavernous Pioneer Square bar and grill is home to a pair of regular weekly poetry series. "Slammin' in the Square" takes place every Monday night at 7 P.M., while a newer series, "A Word to the Wired" happens on Fridays at 8 P.M.

Both offer a variety of poets, musicians, and other entertainers—ranging from professional *laureates* to aspiring writers who've signed up that evening (poets who bring two guests get in free). On Mr. C's visit, the bill even included the Saloon's short-order cook, taking a break from the kitchen. The quality varies accordingly. Speaking of food, there's a fairly varied menu of "Starving Poet" food and drink specials.

The Elliott Bay Book Company
- 101 S Main St., Seattle; 624-6600

Long-established in Pioneer Square, the Elliott Bay Book Company looms large amidst Seattle's literary scene—in terms of both book selection and public events. There's something going on here almost every day—sometimes twice a day!

Writers who've appeared here run the gamut from local celebs like novelist Sondra Shulman to such nationally-acclaimed scholars as Paula Gunn Allen, author of *Voice of the Turtle: American Indian Literature 1900-1970*. The topics discussed can be as diverse as the authors themselves; recent subjects have ranged from journalism and travels in the South Pacific to baseball fiction. With a few exceptions, events at EBBC are free, but since the room fills up fast, you do need tickets to reserve your place. Call or stop in to make your arrangements in advance.

Can't make it to the appearance of your all-time fave writer? No problem!

Elliott Bay broadcasts some of these readings on radio station KCMU (90.3 FM) on Sunday mornings from 8:30 A.M. to 9 P.M. These have included Seattle poet Bernard Harris Jr. reading from his work Visions, and author Nelson Perry with Black Fire.

Elliott Bay also has plenty of events for children as well; see the separate listing under "Children's Activities." Of course, some of the cognoscenti consider a cup of coffee or a light meal downstairs in the cafe to be a literary event in itself. Whatever brings you in, be sure to pick up a copy of the store's lengthy newsletter, Voices By Water, to get the full scoop on all of the upcoming activities.

Globe Cafe & Bakery
● 1531 14th Ave. E, Seattle; 324-8815
The Globe Cafe features a variety of Saturday night poetry readings and music events to tickle almost anyone's fancy. The first and third Saturdays of each month feature local poets reading from their own original writing, along with the work of other poets who've strongly influenced them. This is not an open-mike, as found in so many other venues; each event is fully programmed in advance.

Of course, you can have your poetry and read it too: The second Saturday of the month is an open-mike, acoustic songwriters' night, bridging the gap between literature and music. Finally, on the fourth Saturday, enjoy "Accordionist's Night Out." Would Mr. C make this stuff up? Could he? This is also an open-mike event, so be sure to bring your accordion. All of these events are free and begin at 8 P.M.

The Green Room Cafe
● 4026 Stone Way N, Seattle; 632-6420
Proclaiming itself to be "Seattle's Theatrical Coffeehouse," Wallingford's Green Room Cafe presents readings on a semi-regular basis. Unlike so many poetry slams and such, the work here leans toward longer pieces. These performances generally alternate between short stories one week, and script-in-hand readings of plays the next. Admission is free: and, as an added bonus, all you brave readers get free coffee!

Head on down with your sure-to-be-a-Tony-winner and join in the fun. Readings begin at 7:30 P.M., usually on Monday or Thursday nights. The schedule varies, so do call ahead.

Killing Time Mystery Books
● 2821 NE 55th St., Seattle; 525-2266
It doesn't take much of a sleuth to figure out the specialty of this bookshop. Just as the shelves are lined with volumes of suspense, the calendar is filled with appearances by today's hottest mystery writers. With one or two events scheduled each week, you're almost certain to see your favorite page-turner represented. Authors who've appeared recently include David Linsey, author of An Absence of Light; Steve Martini with Undue Influence; and Julie Smith, winner of the Edgar Award, with New Orleans Beat. Event times vary; check KTMB's newsletter, Deadline (get it? get it?), for a full listing.

Killing Time is open Tuesdays through Saturdays from 10 A.M. to 6 P.M. (Thursdays 'til 8 P.M.), and Sundays from 12 noon to 5 P.M.

Parkplace Book Company
● Parkplace Center, Kirkland; 828-6546
The calendar at Parkplace Book Company is jammed with literary events for both adults and kids. There's an event just about every week, sometimes more than one, even in the relatively slow summer months. Mostly, you'll find authors reading and signing their latest creations; but there are also other kinds of happenings, like reading circles and book clubs.

Parkplace does a good job of presenting lesser-known writers from small presses—a chance perhaps for you to catch tomorrow's bestselling star today. All of the events at Parkplace are free and open to the public. Most activities are at 7:30 P.M.; PBC has a great variety of activities for young readers, too. For more info, see the separate listing under "Children's Activities."

The Play's the Thing

● 514 E Pike St., Seattle; 322-7529

All the world's a stage, especially at this First Hill bookstore specializing in the world of drama. The Play's the Thing schedules frequent readings of both new and previously published works. About five times each season, The Northwest Playwrights Guild comes in to read their latest scripts-in-progress; and, every other Tuesday, there are readings of well-known plays like *Glass Men*, *Sleuth*, or *The Lion in Winter*.

The Play's the Thing stays open late on Monday and Tuesday nights for readings and meetings of other local playwrights' groups. Give them a call to find out what's coming up. Hours are Mondays and Tuesdays from 10 A.M. to 10 P.M., and Wednesdays through Sundays from 10 A.M. to 5 P.M.

Red and Black Books Collective

● 432 15th Ave. E., Seattle; 322-READ (7323)

Advertising "good books for a change," Red and Black Books presents readings that look toward a variety of utopias. Like the books on the shelves, the authors who make appearances here reflect a multicultural world, expressing comment, celebration, and critiques of the world we live in.

Red and Black hosts readings several times each month, depending on the season; most start at 7:30 P.M., on various days of the week. Recently, R & B presented Ursula LeGuin reading from *Buffalo Gals, Won't You Come Out Tonight?*, a story based in Native American traditions; and Margarethe Cammermeyer reading from *Serving in Silence*, about her life in the military and subsequent dismissal because of her sexual orientation. Pick up the Red and Black newsletter at the store, which contains a calendar as well as reviews of new books.

Seattle Arts and Lectures

● 1308 Fifth Ave., Seattle; 621-2230

MR. CHEAP'S PICKS
Readings and
Literary Events

✔ **Bonvechio's Book & Bean**— Part of the arts scene in West Seattle, BB&B pitches in with poetry and literary readings.

✔ **The Elliott Bay Book Company**—EBBC has something happening almost every night of the week.

✔ **The Green Room Cafe**— Instead of poetry, try a reading of new plays or short stories.

✔ **University Bookstore**— Along with Elliott Bay, the other literary landmark in town for a packed slate of big-name author appearances.

The Seattle Arts and Lectures' six-part author series puts interested readers in touch with many of the greatest American authors of our generation. Toni Morrison, Wallace Stegner, Amy Tan, and Gary Trudeau have been among the guests at one of Seattle's most popular intellectual venues. At only $14 per event for general admission (better yet, half-price for students), almost anyone can afford to rub elbows with the glitterati of the literati. Subscriptions offer another opportunity for anyone to get good discounts, about $10 per reading.

These bi-monthly lectures encompass a variety of subjects and are always followed by Q & A sessions. But you may have to speak up if you want to be heard by the approximately 2,000 other listeners who assemble at the downtown events, held in the 5th Avenue Theatre—more typically home to big-scale Broadway musicals.

Tower Books
- 20 Mercer St., Seattle; 283-6333
- 10635 NE Eighth St., Bellevue; 451-1110
- 2501 S 38th St., Tacoma; 473-3362

See the listing under "Shopping—Books."

University Bookstore
- 4326 University Way NE, Seattle; 634-3400
- 990 102nd Ave. NE, Bellevue; 632-9500

You'd expect Seattle's largest independent bookstore to have an exciting lineup of literary stars, and University Bookstore does not disappoint. Heavy-hitters who've done readings and signings here include

Gloria Steinem, Allen Ginsburg, humorist Dave Barry, space pioneer Alan Shepard, and that politics-*really*-makes-strange-bedfellows couple, Mary Matalin and James Carville.

There can be as many as a dozen events each month. Readings are generally held at 7 P.M. on weeknights, or on Sunday afternoons; most take place in Kane Hall on the UW campus. Check local papers, or stop in to get on the mailing list.

The University Bookstore is also a great place to browse. Both the Seattle and Bellevue locations have good selections of full-price and bargain remainder books, along with academic fare from supplies to sweatshirts.

SPORTS AND PLAY

No, Mr. C can't get you into the Kingdome for free—though don't forget that many professional sports ticket prices start around $10. Cheaper alternatives include minor leagues and colleges, where lower prices don't necessarily mean fewer thrills.

Meanwhile, why not consider some other kinds of sports—the kind in which your participation means more than just raising a bottle of beer? Mr. C's got it all.

SPECTATOR SPORTS

Everett Giants
- Everett Memorial Stadium, 2118 Broadway, Everett; 258-3673

Strike-anguished baseball fans recently discovered what many hardcore types have known for years: Minor-league baseball has all the same thrills, without the big names—or the big prices—as the majors. For that matter, you also don't have to put up with artificial turf, nosebleed seats, or downtown parking.

The Everett Giants are the "single A" affiliate for the parent club in San Francisco. That means these guys are *way* down on the farm, with three

more levels to advance before making it to the big leagues; but hey, everybody has to start somewhere. And who knows, you may spot the next Griffey, years before Nike does.

Tickets, even the best seats in the house, are only $4.50; they may be more expensive on the "Famous Chicken Night," but even then—as of this writing—prices stay under $8. Meanwhile, in such a small stadium, you can't be far from the action—and it's all outdoors, the way baseball was meant to be seen. These Giants play some forty home games from June 'til August; call or check the sports pages for schedules.

Seattle Mariners
- The Kingdome, 201 S King St., Seattle; 296-3111

It's no news to baseball devotees that, in more than a dozen seasons, the Mariners have yet to win their division—despite such future Hall of Famers as Ken Griffey, Jr. and Randy (Big Unit) Johnson. Still, even with such unfortunate interruptions as player strikes and ceiling tile woes, the M's can be fun to watch—and since games rarely sell out, tickets are as easy to score as you'll find anywhere around the big leagues. Good for those spur-of-the-moment outings.

Top-price tix were $15 during the '94 season, but they ranged down to a mere $6 for the cheap seats. Once inside, you may be able to move around a bit for a better view—though security gates divide the bowl more or less in half, so "bleacher bums" can't wind up behind home plate.

Call Ticketmaster at 622-HITS (4487) for all the details. Ceiling permitting, the Mariners play 81 games from April to early October. Oh, and check for special promotional dates—when, for example, all seats may be half-price. Talk about a steal!

Seattle Supersonics
- Seattle Center Coliseum, First Ave. N; 283-DUNK (3865)

Seattle has not missed out on the NBA mania that has swept the nation. Breaking records and leading their division with stars like Shawn Kemp have made the Sonics a hit. Tickets at the completely spruced-up Coliseum at the Seattle Center can jump as high as $65; but, surprisingly, you can get a piece of the action for as little as $7 a ticket, as of this writing. The NBA season runs from November to April; better show some quick moves to get those low-priced tix, though.

Sure, you could go for the front row; but Mr. C would rather just bring binoculars and save some cash for the overpriced snacks.

Seattle Thunderbirds
- Seattle Center Coliseum, First Ave. N, Seattle; 448-7825

Pushing is allowed, and body-check-

ing may even be encouraged, among loyal Thunderbirds fans. They gather by the thousands each September through March to cheer Seattle's entry in the Western Hockey League, a minor-league to the NHL. Hockey in Seattle is more than a passing interest (as you'd expect, this close to Canada, eh?). The T-birds have held the league attendance record, and the team has boasted many top players—but you would never know it by the ticket prices.

A good, full-price seat will only set you back $12; kids, seniors, and members of the military pay about a buck less. Games can get very crowded, so you may want to call ahead for reserved seats. Also, there is a Non-Alcohol Family Section if you want a little distance from those particular—um, *enthusiastic* Thunderbird fans.

Tacoma Tigers
- Cheney Stadium, 2502 S Tyler St., Tacoma; 752-7700

As it did for the Everett Giants (above), the dreaded baseball strike turned out to be a boon for minor league teams like the Tigers of the Pacific Coast League—who, in spite of their name, are the "AAA" affiliate of the Oakland Athletics, not the club in Detroit. Unlike the rookies in Everett, though, these guys are just a phone call away from The Show; they may find themselves in the majors at any time. Makes for some very competitive play. Tickets at the intimate, 10,000-seat Cheney Stadium range from about $4 for general admission to $8, which will put you in a box seat. And there are around 75 games each season, running from April through August. Hardcore fans may opt for the ten-game coupon book ($30), which allows you to see whichever games you want, whenever you prefer, for—you guessed it—three bucks a pop. And *that's* no fly-out.

University of Washington Huskies
- Various locations; Information, 543-2200 (basketball and football) or 543-2279 (all other sports)

The pros are the pros, but high-intensity competition can be found at a fraction of the price if you know where to look. For less than $15, all sports fans (not just students) can attend a Pac-10 football game at 72,000-seat Husky Stadium, the alleged birthplace of "The Wave." Garb yourself in purple and gold, and hit the tailgate parties a couple of hours before the game with U-Dub loyals; if you're *really* into it, follow the crowds after the game to the Edmundson Pavilion Addition for the famous "Husky 5th Quarter."

Now, if football's not your game, there are many other sporting options around this sprawling campus. UW women's basketball, for example, has been known to draw sellout crowds. Admission to these and other non-football events tend to be around $5 and under, with tickets almost always available. Campus parking areas surround the stadium and gymnasium areas, accessible from Montlake Bridge and Pacific Street or from NE 45th Street, near the University Village shopping center.

PARTICIPATORY SPORTS

Belltown Billiards
- 90 Blanchard St., Seattle; 448-6779

Not your average, old-style pool hall, Belltown Billiards brings a stylish new look to the genre. This combination billiard room and upscale Italian restaurant/bar is a marvel of post-industrial chic, with an atmosphere that's dark and refined, not dark and smokey. You'll want to shoot pool in your double-breasted sharkskin suit here, y'know?

Rates for the dozen or so tables range from $6 an hour during the day, up to $14 on weekend evenings. For better deals, come in during BB's "Chardonnay Happy Hour," weekdays from 4 to 7 P.M., when rates are cut to half-price, and wine prices are reduced as well. Wednesday is Ladies' Night; any all-female groups can play for free. Belltown Billiards is open from 11:30 A.M. to 2 A.M. every day (weekends from 12 noon to 2 A.M.).

Cascade Family Billiards
- 17056 116th Ave. SE, Renton; 228-7424

A smoke-filled pool hall full of drunken hustlers is no place for family entertainment. Thank goodness, then, that Cascade Family Billiards is no such place. Even kids and non-smokers can enjoy the fun of pool and billiards here. A professional staff and great deals make a winning combination at this joint, where pool-sharks-to-be can get lessons from the world's 42nd-ranked shooter (just consider it an investment).

From 11 A.M. until 12 midnight, Sundays through Thursdays, you can play as long as you like for only $7.50 per person. And if you want to step out for a snack, no problem—get your hand stamped, and come back later for more. Hourly rates for Friday and Saturday evenings run $3 per person, per hour.

Eastlake Zoo
- 2301 Eastlake Ave. E, Seattle; 329-3277

Seattle Weekly's Critic's Choice for "Best Real Pool Joint" hasn't changed much despite the publicity. They just keep serving up dollar

Pabst Blue Ribbons and emptying the quarters out of the 50¢ pool tables. True bargain hunters, though, will want to take advantage of the free pool special, offered from 11 A.M. to 3 P.M. daily. That, with a glass of water, makes for the possibility of a good old-fashioned afternoon of fun without spending one red cent. Well, maybe that's pushing this "Cheapster" thing a bit too far. Anyway, you get the idea: Nothing fancy here, just a pool hall, pure and simple. The Zoo closes up at 2:00 A.M., and is open every day of the year—even on Christmas.

Grand Slam USA
- 3848 148th Ave. NE, Redmond; 861-SLAM (7526)

Batting cages in a business park? Why not. The Lakeridge Business Park, Building B, to be precise—just above Route 520 on the Bellevue/Redmond border. Oh, and it's all the way in the back. Okay, now that you've found it, what do you get? Plenty of brand-new batting cages, basketball half-courts, and video games. And, with its low-rent, out-of-the-way location, you get major league facilities at minor league prices.

A token costs $1.75, which lets you whack at twenty (rubber) baseballs; you can get three tokens for $5. But here's the best deal of all: Step up to the plate any weekday from 11 A.M. to 4 P.M., and all rates are reduced to half-price. Now *that's* worth finding. Same deal applies to basketball, which is normally $3 per person for half an hour, $5 for one hour. Again, it's half-price until 4:00.

Team or group rentals can be arranged; this is also a great place for birthday parties and private functions. You can even buy a "Gold Card" offering extra discounts and privileges for one year. Call or "swing" by for details. Grand Slam is open Mondays through Saturdays from 11 A.M. to 9 P.M., Sundays from 12-5.

Imperial Lanes
- 2101 22nd Ave. S, Seattle; 325-2525

Okay, so maybe a bunch of old guys

with personalized bowling balls isn't your idea of cool pins. In this age of roller discos and laundromat cafes, you want something more for your bowling dollar. Well, just minutes from downtown at these Central District lanes, you can "Rock and Bowl" the night away from 10:00 P.M. to 1:30 A.M. every Thursday. It's an all-you-can-bowl deal: strings all night, shoe rental, rock music, even pizza—for only $10 a person!

"Rock and Bowl" isn't for everyone; but the average bowler can check out daily and seasonal specials. A normal string costs around $2 per person before 6 P.M.; evening hours kick the price up to about $3. For newcomers to the sport, Imperial Lanes has bumper bowling at the same price as regular lanes.Other amenities include automatic scoring on all bowling lanes, as well as a restaurant serving up American and Asian grub; not to mention a video game room. Imperial is open from 7 A.M. to 12 midnight during the week, and 'til 2 A.M. on weekends.

Jazwieck's Golf & Train
- 7828 Broadway, Everett; 355-5646

Miniature golf *and* a miniature railroad? Not the most predictable combination, but it works. Putter around on Jazwieck's challenging 18-hole mini-golf course for $3.75 a game, then take a 15-minute put-put trip, oohing and aahing over replicas of America's most famous landmarks. Think of it as a whirlwind geography lesson. Kids love this place, and it makes for a campy cheap date. Special deals are available for frequent duffers, and of course, if you hit the clown's mouth on the 18th hole, you get the traditional free game. Jazwieck's Golf & Train is open from mid-March through October. Hours can vary, but the place is generally up and running from 11 A.M. to 10 P.M. daily.

Jillian's Billiard Club
- 731 Westlake Ave. N, Seattle; 223-0300

If you think Belltown Billiards is classy, here's the toast of the town.

Two spacious floors of activities—pool and billiards, snooker, darts, and more—are elegantly set out, complete with a dark wooden cafe area and full bar. All with floor-to-ceiling plate glass windows overlooking Lake Union. Fancy? Yup. Cheap? Nope. So, what's it doing in Mr. C's book?

Take Mr. C's advice. Go during the day. Sure, it's not as classy, but...instead of paying as much as $12-$14 an hour, you'll only pay $6 an hour—no matter how many players share the table. Bring a few pals, split the tab, and you'll actually have enough left over to buy some expensive drinks. Plus, Jillian's is not as crowded during the day—when Mr. C visited, he practically had the place to himself. Naturally, he won every game. Open until 2 A.M.; on Fridays and Saturdays until 3 A.M.

Kenmore 50 Lanes
- 7638 NE Bothell Way, Bothell; 486-5555

Yes, 50 lanes, count 'em, 50; and they're only 75¢ per game. With footwear renting at $1.85 a pair, this makes a pretty cheap way to entertain yourself for a few hours. You can even treat your friends; with prices like these, anyone can afford to be generous. Friday and Saturday night rates do go up to $2 a string.

Along with inexpensive bowling, Kenmore 50 Lanes also has a card room, a huge game room, and a restaurant/lounge offering prime rib for $9 or a plain ol' burger and fries for under $4, along with many other low-priced snack items. Kenmore is open seven days and nights a week for your bowling pleasure.

Roxbury Lanes
- 2823 SW Roxbury St., Seattle; 935-7400

For kids, adults, birthday parties, or a night out, Roxbury Lanes—near White Center—is another great place to bowl. The rates are good ($2.16 a game—any day, any time), the hours make the 24-lane establishment convenient (9 A.M. to 1 A.M., seven days a week), and the computers make scoring a breeze.

But, if you're one of those people who can't seem to keep the ball out of the gutter, check out the other gaming facilities. Try the blackjack table, video-game room, or, better yet, get a lane lesson from one of the staff professionals and impress your friends the next time around. Roxbury's in-house restaurant offers a full menu with bargains of its own: A burger runs you a mere $2.65 with chips, cole slaw, and beans, while an authentic Polish sausage (do they bowl in Poland?) costs less than a five-spot.

Seattle Funplex
- 1451 15th Ave. W, Seattle; 285-8007

Remember when you visited arcades as a kid, spending all your money on junk food, pinball, and the batting cage? Well, grown-ups can still enjoy modern-day fun—and you won't even have to keep running back to Ma and Pa for another buck. Funplex, a vast indoor amusement park, offers such classics as go-carts, miniature golf, and a kiddie play area—all at minimal cost.

A whole day's worth of this excitement runs about $11 per adult. Shorter humans (and students, of any size) get the same deal for a slightly lower $10. Bargain packages, such as the "Miniplex" (which limits you to certain areas, and includes less of the good stuff) are also available. Play the 18-hole mini-golf course alone for under $5 a game, or just check out the video game room. You and your family can enjoy the alcohol- and tobacco-free atmosphere of the Funplex for an all-day indoor outing. Open seven days a week, all year 'round.

2-11 Billiard Club
- 2304 Second Ave., Seattle; 443-1211

"Strict Pool" is the motto of the 2-11, and they take the "no-whistling" rule rather seriously here. This Belltown joint is for serious cue-wielders who appreciate a good game more than fancy ambiance.

Weekday rates are hard to beat. Between 11 A.M. and 4 P.M., Mondays through Fridays, two people can shoot for a total of $4.20 an hour. Prices jump by about two bucks on evenings and weekends. Beers and wines are reasonably priced, and that's about the extent of the refreshments offered. Hours are 11 A.M. to 1:30 A.M., Mondays through Saturdays; and Sundays from 3 P.M. to 12 midnight.

Village Bowling Lanes
- 4900 25th Ave. NE, Seattle; 524-4800

This University District "entertainment center" has much more to offer than its name reveals. Oh sure, they have bowling, 32 lanes of it; ah, but that's only one of the attractions. Behind the pins-and-balls exterior lies a plethora of playtime activities: half a dozen pool tables, pinball and video games, a lounge, and a restaurant where hungry players can procure breakfast for $1.95 or lunch for $3.95.

Prices for everything are well in line with these low rates. Bowl a string for between $1.75 and $1.95, depending on the time and day (it's cheapest on weekdays, natch, before 6 P.M.). Village Bowling Lanes, open seven days a week from 9 A.M. to 1 A.M., even accepts competitors' discount coupons.

Zones Entertainment Complex
- 2207 NE Bellevue-Redmond Rd., Redmond; 746-9411

Hidden in the parking lot of an Ethan Allen furniture store, Mr. C discovered yet another great place for parents to spend a few quality hours with their brood on a rainy afternoon. Of course, we big kids are welcome too.

Among the amusements contained within the walls of this gigantic room are an 18-hole mini-golf course, which costs $4 per person

---

($3.50 for groups of four or more); two batting cages, each with a choice of softballs or baseballs, tossing 15 pitches for 75¢; plus skee-ball, video games, and one of those "moon walk" bouncing bubbles for the kiddies.

Mr. C and his companions had their biggest thrills, though, on the recently added bumper cars. At $2 a person for four minutes, all your aggressions will be gone in no time—call it cheap therapy. A snack bar serves up pizza, hot dogs, milkshakes, and of course, espresso (*that'll* make the bumper cars more fun). And, if you're thinking birthday party, you're right—Zones offers two different party packages, at $6.95 or $8.95 per child, for groups of six or more. Zone out from 11 A.M. to 10 P.M. Sundays through Thursdays, and until midnight on Fridays and Saturdays.

THEATER

Didja know? Seattle has more Equity (professional actors' union) theaters than any other city outside of New York. In all, by a recent count, there are more than 150 troupes of all sizes and stripes around town. That's a lotta drama.

Theaters in Seattle are also unusually dedicated to "outreach"—allowing as many lower-income audiences to see their work as possible. Many offer at least one "pay what you can" performance during the run of each show; yes, you literally decide the price of your ticket. Don't be *too* stingy, now. . . most theaters are poor, too.

Another way to save money on theater is a little-known option: **Volunteer ushering.** Many houses use regular folks to help rip tickets, hand out programs, or guide people to their seats. In exchange for your services, you can watch the show for free. Responsibilities are light; dress nicely, arrive a bit early to learn the layout of seats, and then go to it. As soon as the doors close, find a seat for yourself and enjoy the show—you're all done. Ushering can even make a fun cheap date—it's a guaranteed conversation starter afterwards! Best of all, you'll save yourself some cash *and* help that theater out at the same time. Call ahead to find out if a show you've been eyeing uses volunteers; many of the following troupes do, as noted.

A Contemporary Theatre
- 100 W Roy St., Seattle; 285-5110
- *Volunteer ushering*

The cleverly named A Contemporary Theatre (look at the initials) recently celebrated its 25th anniversary. In that time, it has grown into one of Seattle's leading professional troupes. Their season, which runs from April to December, brings six plays to their fully outfitted open stage, with comfortable seating on three sides. Plays presented here include many world premieres, funny and serious, from both new and established authors. In one summer alone, they went from Jane Martin's *Keely and Du*, a hard-hitting drama about abortion, to the latest comedy by Britain's Alan Ayckbourn, *Man of the Moment*.

With success comes higher prices. Tickets range from $12-$25, not as cheap as they once were here; you can certainly head for those $12 tix, sold at preview (first) performances; and subscriptions are also a good way to save cash. See all six plays for as little as $57.50, less than $10 each. Student subscriptions, for teens up to 18 years old, cost only $38. ACT also offers rush tickets, if a performance is not sold out; side section seats go for half-price to anyone, first-come-first-served, half an hour before the show. That can be as little as $6 or $7.50 each.

A Contemporary Theatre plans to move from Queen Anne into new downtown digs in late 1995; their new home will include two cozy 375-seat auditoriums. No doubt prices will go up again, but the relative options described here should remain the same. Call the box office for their latest season calendar.

Annex Theatre
- 1916 Fourth Ave., Seattle; 728-0933
- *Volunteer ushering*

"We have a tendency to produce theatrical events, rather than just plays," said a representative of the Annex, entering its seventh year in downtown Seattle. "We get a young audience, and we focus mostly on new works that are experimental and raucous." Certainly, this would describe their recent production of Clare Booth Luce's classic *The Women* (picked up by Hollywood in the 1930s with Jean Harlow, as well as the 1990s with Julia Roberts). The Annex version was partially cross-cast, with half of the all-female roles played by men. And *this* was a Christmas show!

A company of 110 actors, directors, playwrights and designers all "own" the theater, working in various combinations to generate most of their own work. Writer members create plays for actor members, for example, developing them through two-week workshops in their "Playwrights Kitchen." These shows are open to the public, along with the mainstage shows. And, as this book was going to press, plans were in the works to do exchanges with alternative theater troupes in New York City.

In all, the Annex produces over a dozen plays during its year-long season. Tickets are $7 for Thursday and Sunday evening performances, and $9 for Friday and Saturday shows. In addition, the first Wednesday preview of each play is usually a "pay what you can" deal. Tix to the readings of new plays are all $7.

Also, look for their monthly late-night cabaret, "Up Past Your Bedtime." Described as a "curated open-mike," this show is almost like modern vaudeville—combining everything from comedy to interpretative dance. UPYB takes place one Saturday a month at 11 P.M.; call for current dates.

The Annex's intention is to keep prices as close as possible to movie prices. Even so, they claim, "If someone wants to come in and they really can't afford it, we'll work something out."

Bathhouse Theatre
- 7312 W Green Lake Dr. N, Seattle; 524-9108
- *Volunteer ushering*

The name is a literal one; this building was put up in 1927 as a public changing facility for the adjacent beach in Green Lake Park. Today, the Bathhouse Theatre is dedicated to bringing high-quality theater to as many people as possible, especially those who wouldn't ordinarily have access to live plays.

This troupe seeks to give a fresh twist to venerable classics, along with a mix of contemporary plays and original musical revues. Such twists can mean Shakespeare updated to an unusual setting or time period. It can also mean giving an old play a new layer of interpretation in the modern world; the Bathhouse presents many plays that overtly or subtly deal with gay themes. And, for an Equity professional theater with a strong reputation, tickets are reasonably priced at $13 to $20.

But there are lots of ways to get into the Bathhouse at a discount. First, each mainstage production offers one specially designated "pay what you can" performance. Tickets to this performance are made available, in advance, to seniors and low-income families. To get in on this deal, call the Parks Department Senior Program at 684-4951 or the Recreation Division at 684-7186. Remaining tickets are available to the public, at the door, on the afternoon of the performance. If any are left, you can truly name your price.

Whenever possible, the Bathhouse sells $7 rush tickets, also based upon availability at around ten minutes before curtain time. On the weekends (Friday, Saturday, and Sunday), rush tickets are available to students and seniors only.

Last but not least, BT has outreach programs that help bring theater to those who are least likely to see any at all. "Literacy-in-Stages" uses live theater to enhance the skills of adults learning to read. There's also the "Shakespeare Education Program," which brings the Bard to students;

and "Classical Connections," helping
to translate the values and ideas of
classical theater to school kids. The
"Bathhouse, Stage Right" program
even offers unsold tickets for free,
through community service organizations. To get more info about any of
these innovative programs, call the office at 783-0053.

Book-It Repertory Theater
- 1219 Westlake Ave. N, Seattle;
  216-0833
- *Volunteer ushering*

Book-It is a troupe of actors who
take non-dramatic texts—novellas,
short stories, poems, whatever—and
turn them into stageworthy pieces.
Book-It has brought to life the works
of many famous authors, ranging
from Eudora Welty to Raymond
Carver. At the time of this writing,
they were planning to do their first
full-length novel.

Book-It's season generally consists of four shows, with tickets at
$10 to $12 ($8 for seniors and
groups). Keep your eye out for special works-in-progress performances,
too; tickets to these are $5, by dona-
tion. There are even occasional opportunities to see (or hear) Book-It for
free! They've been known to make an
appearance at the Bumbershoot, and
they do an annual Halloween radio program, in that Orson Welles tradition.
Call the number above for a complete
list of upcoming performances.

Empty Space Theatre
- 3509 Fremont Ave. N, Seattle;
  547-7500
- *Volunteer ushering*

There's just too much to say about
this theater to leave an empty spot
here. Celebrating its 25th anniversary
in 1995, Empty Space carries on the
tradition of presenting Fremont fans
and other Seattleites with an "amazing and astounding experience of a
theatrical kind."

Among the shows lined up for the
October-to-May anniversary season
were *The Salvation of Iggy Scrooge*,
a rock musical version of Dickens.
Of course, the first ghost to visit him
is that of his former partner, *Bob* Mar-

ley, mon. Certainly not your traditional holiday treacle. Yet, the troupe
is just as comfortable offering shows
like *Oh Mr. Faulkner, Do You Write?*,
a one-man show about the genteel
Southern novelist. They also run playwriting labs, which lead to workshop
readings of experimental scripts.

The cozy theater seats 150 people,
and because the rows are tiered, virtually every seat has a great view.
There is a range of ticket prices: $10
to see a preview show, $12 for mati-
nees and Sunday performances, $15
for Tuesday through Thursday shows,
and $20 for Fridays and Saturdays.
Rush tickets are half-price, if available, and sold just ten minutes before
each show. Call for info about their
"pay what you can" matinees, too.

Fringe Theatre Festival
- Various locations; Information,
  325-5446

Seattleites may not have coined the
term "fringe theater," which in fact
has its origins in Edinburgh, Scotland
(where small troupes give performances on the periphery, literally, of
their prestigious international festival); but the Emerald City has definitely developed one of the most
active local theater communities in
the United States. This year-round activity culminates in the annual Seattle
Fringe Theatre Festival—two weeks
of cutting-edge, experimental, and
just-plain-out-there productions grac-
ing several stages around town.

Each year, the festival features
some 75 different companies; most
are from Seattle and its environs,
but others hail from New York, Chicago, St. Louis, and California. During the course of the fest, seven
venues present as many as 300 inexpensive performances. So much
fringe, so little time!

Here's the best news: Tix to all
shows are just $8 each, and half-price
for students and seniors. SFTF also
offers festival passes: $25 for a five-
show pass and $75 for the super-du-
per all-festival pass. You won't be
able to see everything on the schedule, but you'll certainly get your

money's worth—as many plays as you can stand. Sure, some of these may be flops, or just not your cup of latté; part of the fun, though, comes from catching the first viewing of next year's hit. For more info on the festival, and Seattle fringe theater in general, call the League of Fringe Theaters (LOFT). Their hotline (637-7373) lists performances, auditions, classes, and workshops. Call the number in the heading if you prefer to speak with a human.

The Group Theatre
- Seattle Center, 305 Harrison St., Seattle; 441-1299
- *Volunteer ushering*

Newly relocated to the Seattle Center, the Group Theatre specializes in challenging dramas which address current social issues. They're dedicated to nurturing a diversity of voices in the theater arts. Recent shows have included Lorraine Hansberry's *To Be Young, Gifted, and Black*, as part of Black History Month; *Harvest Moon*, a world premiere by Jose Cruz Gonzalez, which was developed in the Group's "Playwrights Lab Workshop"—and so popular it was revived just two years later; and *Undesirable Elements/Seattle*, an experimental piece by avant-garde performance artist Ping Chong. Generally, the company's season consists of five plays and some special events. Their annual holiday show, *The Voices of Christmas*, includes celebrations of the winter holidays from more than the standard European roots.

Regular ticket prices are just $12 to $19; you can do even better with season subscriptions. Meanwhile, senior citizens can get half-price tickets anytime, and students can get half-price tickets on the day of the show. There are also discounts available for groups of ten or more.

Intiman Playhouse
- Second Ave. N and Mercer St., Seattle; 626-0782
- *Volunteer ushering*

Now well-established as part of the Seattle Center, the Intiman was created in 1972—and has grown into the third largest theater in the state. Taking its name from the same root as "intimate," this cozy, 400-seat theater has maintained an emphasis on playwriting over stage spectacle. Does that mean shows here are dull? Hardly. The heart of their 1994 season was no less than Tony Kushner's Broadway mega-hit, *Angels in America*. The Intiman has also offered major world premieres, such as Robert Shenkkan's *The Kentucky Cycle*, which went on to win a Pulitzer Prize.

In that case, the question becomes: Can such highbrow art come cheaply? Yes it can. While standard ticket prices range from $16 to $34, there are several discount options. If tickets are available *anytime* on the day of a show, students and senior citizens can get half-price tix at the box office. Anyone else can get the same deal, if seats remain, ten minutes before the curtain. There are also standing room tickets for $8, also sold just before showtime. And, if that seems like taking too much of a chance for you, attend a "pay what you can" performance, usually the first Thursday of each play. There is a $1 minimum.

But wait, there's more! For a fee of just $10 for the entire season (five or six shows, from May to December), you can be a "staff" volunteer usher. This covers the cost of a handbook and special newsletter mailings; apart from that, you'll see *all* the shows at no further cost. And finally, the Intiman also offers its "New Voices" series of script-in-hand readings of brand-new plays. See 'em before they become hits, and stick around for a discussion with the playwright; tickets are just $6, or $18 for a subscription of four readings. Again, students and seniors can get half-price tix earlier in the day.

Whew! Call the box office for more details and brochures about all this exciting drama (and dramatic savings).

New City Theater
- 1634 11th Ave., Seattle; 323-6800
- *Volunteer ushering*

Located in an old railroad house on

First Hill, the New City Theater is an alternative contemporary arts center. The building dates back to 1904, when it contained four apartments; today it houses a 60-seat cabaret, a 75-seat black-box (flexible seating) theater, and a 150-seat black-box. The works presented here lean toward somewhat abstract (and often risqué) contemporary works by American playwrights. And these folks like to cook up a few surprises—literally: One recent play, set in Louisiana, included servings of Cajun food for the audience after the show. With all this, tickets are just $7 to $12. As if that weren't cheap enough, NCT also includes one or two "pay what you can" performances in each run. There's no excuse not to take a chance on these experimental works.

New City also sponsors two annual festivals: The "New City Actors and Directors Festival," held each August, and the "New City Playwrights Festival," in November. Each marathon features some forty to fifty works, generally by new, emerging artists. They also present the "R^3 Literary Series," featuring writers from Seattle, San Francisco, and Canada. R^3 is held on the first Tuesday of every month. The facility also houses a three-room art gallery for works by local artists. Quite a lot packed into one old building! Call the box office to find out the schedule of upcoming events.

Northwest Asian American Theatre
• 409 Seventh Ave. S, Seattle; 340-1049
• *Volunteer ushering*

With its Pacific Rim location, Seattle is filled with artists of Asian heritage. Yet, up until about twenty years ago, there was no single place for these folks to practice and present works with this identity. Born on the UW campus, the NWAAT quickly outgrew its first home, and moved to a permanent space in the International District.

Now, the primary focus is on thea-

ter; such major Asian-American playwrights as David Henry Hwang, Wakako Yamauchi, and Philip Kan Gotanda have been represented here. Four main shows are produced in the "Theatre Off Jackson," a 140-seat black-box space, during the October-to-June season. Each January, NWAAT hosts its annual "WinterFest," four weeks of other cultural offerings from dance to music to solo performance art, from all over the country.

Ticket prices for most shows are $12 for general admission, $9 for students, senior citizens, and the physically challenged; and $6 for children and any fellow artists. At Thursday evening performances, tix are $6 for all but general admission. Subscriptions, which can save you a few bucks off these rates, are available in six- or three-show deals, allowing you to select from all mainstage and WinterFest offerings. The space is also rented out to independent troupes (including non-Asian) throughout the year, which are not part of this price structure.

Be sure to stop in to the **Wing Luke Asian Museum** next door, too; see the listing under "Museums" for more details.

The Play's the Thing
• 514 E Pike St., Seattle; 322-7529
See the listing under "Readings and Literary Events."

Seattle Children's Theatre
• Charlotte Martin Theatre, Seattle Center, Second Ave. N and Thomas St., Seattle; 441-3322
• *Volunteer ushering*

With 15,000 subscribers and an operating budget that makes many "grownup" theaters envious, the Seattle Children's Theatre is the second-largest children's theater in the country—but these are no kiddie rides. Most of the productions are new works created by some of Seattle's most gifted artists, leading to an audience that is 43 percent adult; clearly, the appeal spreads farther than the kindergarten set. These shows have ranged from adaptations of Rudyard Kipling's *Just So* and

Other Stories to *The Hardy Boys in the Mystery of the Haunted House* (complete with real motorcycles on-stage for the chase scenes!).

Tickets to SCT plays are not cheap, though reasonable for such professional, glitzy fare: $16 for adults and $10 for children. Rush tickets are not offered (shame!), but half-price deals are sometimes available at Ticket/Ticket (see entry below). There's also a special program for school groups that gets kids in for just $7 each. Call the number above for more details.

Seattle Repertory Theatre

• Bagley Wright Theatre, Seattle Center, 155 Mercer St., Seattle; 443-2222

Broadway hits, world premieres, experimental workshops; you'll see all of these at the nationally known, Equity-professional Seattle Rep. A recent season included the world premiere of Neil Simon's *London Suite*, as well as the Broadway smash *The Sisters Rosensweig* by Pulitzer Prize- and Tony Award-winning playwright Wendy Wasserstein. The latter was directed, as it was in New York, by the SRT's own Daniel Sullivan (who got his own Tony nomination).

Can all of this star talent come cheaply? Well, yes and no. Tickets can reach for the stars themselves, as much as $34 a pop; but Mr. C has found plenty of ways to save. For instance, seats that are a bit further from the stage are much less pricey—even on opening night. Further, Seattle Rep offers preview performances for all shows; the same ticket that costs $34 on opening night is just $19 a couple of nights earlier. Folks who are more spontaneous can try to get half-price rush tickets, sold (if available) at the SRT box office two hours before curtain. Students, seniors, and hearing- or visually-impaired individuals are entitled to these same rush tickets for only $7; and anyone who is strong of back can opt for standing room tix at the rear for $8.

But wait, there's more—as in other,

MR. CHEAP'S PICKS
Theater

✔ **A Contemporary Theatre**—Steady quality has made this one of Seattle's pre-eminent troupes. Catch them during low-priced previews, or volunteer to usher.

✔ **Annex Theatre**—Daring versions of classics, new scripts-in-progress, and none of it over $10.

✔ **Book-It**—Whether you like your theater to be literary or your literature to be theatrical, this group offers a unique approach.

✔ **Northwest Asian American Theatre**—From a grassroots start, this has grown into one of the country's premier ensembles, ethnic or otherwise.

✔ **Ticket/Ticket**—No, not double, but half-price tickets to Seattle's myriad theatrical offerings—not to mention music, comedy, dance, and other events.

---

less-expensive plays. The "Stage 2" series, held in the PONCHO Forum, has lower prices overall. Stage 2 preview tickets are just $16.50 and weekend evening performances are a reasonable $22.50. And, don't miss the New Play Workshop Series, where works in progress can be seen for $9, all seats. You can even get a subscription to this series, which may offer some real diamonds-in-the-rough: the aforementioned *The Sisters Rosensweig* was in the Rep's workshop series before it went on to its successful Broadway run.

There are even more ways to save, including group discounts and a variety of subscription deals, usually sold prior to the fall season. Call to get more info.

Seattle Shakespeare Festival
- Various locations; Information, 467-1382
- *Volunteer ushering*

The Seattle Shakespeare Festival doth present top-notch productions of—what else?—Shakespeare's plays, along with works by his fellow Elizabethan chums. In addition to full-length works, this troupe likes to re arrange the Bard into its own concoctions, such as "When Love Speaks," a four-person romantic comedy compiled from Elizabethan love poems. The SSF is currently contemplating a series of modern works as well; but have no fear, hard-core Bard buffs: as they told Mr. C, "we will *always* do Shakespeare."

Tickets are usually $15 each ($12 for students and seniors). If that's too high for you, the festival also offers several "pay what you can" performances and, when possible, they make half-price tix available at Ticket/Ticket (see entry below). In addition, they offer a half-price discount for all theater artists; if you're in show biz yourself, call ahead for details. The SSF also presents free outdoor shows during the summer, at locations around the city; they are trying to move toward having a completely free summer season in the tradition of the New York Shakespeare Festival. Call the number above to get a calendar of their current season with times and locations.

Tacoma Actors Guild
- Theater-in-the-Square, 915 Broadway, Tacoma; 272-3107
- *Volunteer ushering*

Here's one for you southerners. The Tacoma Actors Guild is a resident professional theater in South Puget Sound. They present six shows per season, plus a holiday show, ranging from classic works to peppy musical revues. Recent productions have included Shakespeare's *The Comedy of Errors*; the Cabaret du Paris in *World's Fair Cruise*; and Charles

Dickens' holiday chestnut, *A Christmas Carol*.

The important question, for the Scrooge in all of us, is: Are the tickets cheap? Yes they are, and that's no humbug. Single ticket prices range from $15 and $16 for preview performances to $26 and $27 for weekend evenings and opening nights. In between, at $18 to $20, you'll find matinee and weekday evening tickets. The preview tix are obviously the best value, and they're even available by subscription.

TAG also offers rush tickets. Students and seniors can begin snapping up these half-priced gems as early as noon on the day of the show. Other folks can take advantage of this deal a half-hour before curtain, for any remaining seats. In any case, you must show up in person at the box office to get them.

Theater Schmeater
- 1500 Summit Ave., Seattle; 324-5801

The name says it all. There are no pretensions at this tiny, grassroots theater in First Hill; the space is nothing more than a blacked-out garage. Sets and costumes are minimal, but then, so are the ticket prices. What *do* you get? A troupe that isn't afraid to take risks. This is the kind of company that will put on a bare-bones production of *Othello*, and cast a woman in the role of the evil Iago.

Another frequent offering even shows an ability to poke fun at themselves—the ongoing late-night "Twilight Zone Marathon" series. These stage adaptations of Rod Serling's now-campy scripts, complete with the original theme music, are already an unusual choice. On top of that, the cast also breaks character to add their own live commercials ("Hi! I'm not the devil, but I play one on TV..."). Certainly not your traditional approach.

Theater Schmeater does take at least one thing seriously: They want young audiences to see live plays, ensuring the future of the art form. Anyone under the age of 18 gets in for free, any time. Good going. For the rest of us, tickets are a modest $7 for most shows, and $4 for the late night series. TS also produces an annual summer show, performed outdoors at various locations free of charge, during its year-round season.

Theatre Babylon

- Eastlake Studio, 601 Eastlake Ave. E, Seattle; 624-2931
- *Volunteer ushering*

Next to the Eastlake Cafe, cut off from the rest of the artsy-gritty First Hill area by scenic Route 5, Theatre Babylon produces four to six plays each year in its downright (downscale?) cozy space. Tickets for this low-tech lair are just $6 to $8. The focus is really on the acting and writing, be it a pair of one-act plays by David Mamet or an evening of original ten-minute plays titled "Nine Holes."

The best deal is the monthly late-night showcase, "Cabaret Babylon," usually held on the second weekend of each month. It's an unpredictable mix of comedy, music, performance art, poetry, and more. Admission is simply "by donation." Toss a few bucks in the pot and have a rollicking good time.

Theatre Babylon also rents its space, the Eastlake Studio, to other theater companies. TB does not set the ticket prices for these outside organizations, but they tell Mr. C that most tend to stay in the $6 to $10 range. Some recent visitors have included Descending Productions with *The Mechanics of Human Love* and the Northwest Shakespeare Ensemble with Samuel Beckett's *Endgame*.

Enter through the Eastlake Cafe, which is also a great and grungy place for cheap eats (see the listing under "Restaurants—Eastlake Area"). Theater seating is limited, so reservations are recommended.

Ticket/Ticket

- Broadway Market, 401 Broadway E, Seattle; 324-2744
- Pike Place Market Information Booth, First and Pike Sts., Seattle; 324-2744

This is not a theater itself, but rather your way in to many of the area's finest venues at discounted prices. Ticket/Ticket has two locations, in the Capitol Hill area and in the Pike Place Market; both sell half-price tickets to shows which have plenty of unsold seats for that evening (or afternoon, as the case may be).

You take a chance, of course, that the show you're interested in will be "on the board"; alas, Ticket/Ticket will not give out this info over the phone. Mr. C advises you to be flexible—have a few shows in mind, and then go with the flow. With all that Seattle and its environs have to offer, many of which are profiled in this book, you should certainly be able to find *something* that fits your tastes.

These deals, by the way, are not limited to theater: T/T regularly gets tix for the top music, comedy, and dance performances in town. Some of the places that regularly make discounted tickets available here include the Seattle Symphony Orchestra, Pacific Northwest Ballet, Seattle Children's Theatre, the Jazz Alley nightclub, and the Seattle Opera House.

Ticket/Ticket is a cash-only, walk-up-only operation. All tickets are sold at exactly half the face value, plus a service charge (usually about $2). Tickets for matinee performances are available the day before or the morning of a show; evening performances are sold during that day only. The Broadway location is open Tuesdays through Sundays from 10 A.M. to 7 P.M.; the Pike Place Market site is open Tuesdays through Sundays from noon to 6 P.M. (tickets for Monday events are available on Sundays). Both branches have the same offerings. Unlike its relatives in other major cities, Ticket/Ticket does not sell any full-price advance tickets.

The Velvet Elvis Lounge

- 107 Occidental Ave. S, Seattle; 624-8477

For something that's sure to be different, check out this hip house just off Pioneer Square. You'll know it's unusual the moment you walk in—and across the stage. Yes, the seats are actually on the far side of the cavernous space. And "Far Side" is an appropriate pun. Looking up, you'll see that they've given new meaning to "theater lights": Not only actual stage lights, but also 1950s table lamps are suspended from the ceiling. Wacky. Behind the audience risers, a refreshment area includes more velvet—as in red velvet comfy chairs—and a snack bar that includes cocktails.

Okay, enough about the building. The shows themselves reflect a similarly eclectic attitude, ranging from a well-received one-man portrayal of Jack Kerouac to live music and late-night comedy shows. There's always something new and daring here. Tickets tend to be in the $5-$10 range. Of course, you also get the wackiness of Pioneer Square at nighttime; for those of you who prefer your adventure confined to the stage, do take this into consideration.

WALKS AND TOURS

This section is designed as much for "tourists in their own home town" as for out-of-town visitors. There's a lot to see out there!

Arboretum Waterfront Trail
• Foster Island, Seattle; Information, 325-4510
See the listing under "Outdoors."

Art Walks
• Various locations; see below
Anyone who enjoys looking at the fine arts should set aside his or her Thursday evenings—that's the time to see the latest on the gallery scene. In order to increase viewership, art galleries in several areas in and around Seattle have coordinated their exhibit openings to be held on the same day, encouraging more people to go gallery hopping—truly a Cheapster's night out.

The first Thursday of each month is the time to visit the high-toned, ritzy galleries of Pioneer Square. "First Thursday" has become an institution, as hordes of art-lovers stroll through at a leisurely pace—enjoying the walk as much as the art. The rooms stay open into the evening, to accommodate working folks. Many of the retail stores in the area have seen the potential in this monthly ritual and keep their doors open later, too. Discuss your interpretations and recharge your batteries over a cup of cappuccino at one of the ubiquitous cafes.

More recently, Kirkland has gotten into the act with—guess what—"Second Thursday." The galleries in this burgeoning arts community near the Marina Park waterfront feature special artist receptions and rotating shows. And Tacoma, falling right in line, hosts its "Art Walk" on the third Thursday of each month.

There are no set hours for these Art Walks. Things generally get going around 5:30 or 6 P.M., and most places stay open until at least 8:30 or 9 P.M. Participating galleries can change from time to time; if you have questions, your best bet is probably to call one of the more established galleries in each area. **Linda Farris** in Seattle, **Foster/White** in Kirkland and Seattle, and the **Freighthouse Art Gallery** in Tacoma are good places to start. All are described in more detail in the "Art Galleries" chapter.

Bill Speidel's Underground Tour
• Doc Maynard's Public House, 610 First Ave., Seattle; 682-1511
Well, technically, it's a ground level tour—but maybe they thought nobody would go to something that sounded so dull. Modern-day Pioneer Square is actually one story above

the original ground level, and these fun folks will take you on a walk beneath the present streets, buildings, and sidewalks of this historic district. Onward! Or should that be, "Downward!" Whatever...

Did you know that, back in the early days of Seattle, some people may have taken only one bath in their lifetime? This treat cost ten cents for a tub filled with hot, clean water. If *Mr. Cheap's Seattle* had been around back then, it would have noted that, for the bargain price of five cents, a bath could still be had—however, the water would be lukewarm and, er, used. Yuck.

These fascinating facts and other tasteless tidbits are told in abundance throughout the tour. All, however, will teach you more about Seattle than you ever thought you wanted to know (be sure to ask about the tide schedule and its effect on the sewage system, and the brilliant fire-fighting strategies employed by the citizens as early Seattle went up in smoke).

This educational and entertaining tour is frequented by visitors and locals alike. Tickets are $5.50 for adults, $4.50 for seniors, $4 for students, and $2.50 for children six to twelve. Dress for the weather (yes, if it's raining above, it rains underneath), and consider wearing closed-toe shoes. The whole thing takes about 90 minutes; many tours sell out, so make reservations at 682-4646, and do arrive at least 20 minutes early to pick up your tickets.

Bruning Pottery
- 2908 Sixth Ave. S, Seattle; 623-1007

Larry and Judy Bruning are just the nicest folks. And, for a family-run business, they run quite a large ceramics factory. They've been at it for a dozen years or so, recently moving to the industrial area south of downtown. They turn out very attractive dishware, coffee mugs, vases, and planters, which are sold in specialty stores and garden centers throughout the Northwest.

Here at their factory, they sell seconds (though you can hardly tell) at 20% to 80% off regular retail prices. For more information on the pottery, see the listing under "Shopping—Home Furnishings."

Meanwhile, they are also interested in hosting group tours of the facility. You can see, up-close-and-personal, the entire operation—from throwing soft clay on a spinning wheel, through dyeing, baking, and glazing. Families, horticultural groups, community centers, schools, and just about anyone else are all welcome to observe this fascinating look at the process.

The tours are free; they'll even provide coffee and snacks. Bruning Pottery is open weekdays from 9 A.M. to 5 P.M.; Saturdays from 10-4, and Sundays from 12-4. Tours can be arranged for almost any time, with advance notice.

Columbia Seafirst Center
- 701 Fifth Ave., Seattle; 386-5151

For just $3.50—about half the price of the Space Needle—you can enjoy the view from the twelfth tallest building in the world. For children and senior citizens, admission to the Columbia Seafirst Center, Seattle's tallest skyscraper, is a mere $1.75. A small price to pay, indeed, to be whisked to the observation deck on the 73rd floor, and gaze out at the beauty of Seattle. It doesn't offer a full 360-degree view, but it comes close—about 280 degrees, according to the person with whom Mr. C spoke.

The other catch? Columbia Seafirst Center's observation deck, being part of a business building, is only open from 8:30 A.M. to 4:30 P.M. Mondays through Fridays. It's not open at all on weekends. Still, for tourists, school groups, and even office folks who want a dramatic lunch break, this is a fine view.

The Cascade Wine Country
- 14030 NE 145th St., Woodinville; 488-2776

Washington State, as you probably know, produces award-winning wines; it is one of the largest wine regions in North America. Unfortunately, the side of the Cascade Mountains that is closest to Seattle doesn't get enough sun to ripen the grapes (is anyone surprised?). Therefore, you can visit several *wineries* close to town, tour their winemaking operations or enjoy samplings, but the *vineyards* themselves are not near the Seattle area. Those places are still worth a visit, if you're planning a longer trip. Either way, you'll find places to stroll or picnic, and enjoy beautiful scenery. Wineries close to Seattle include:

Chateau Ste. Michelle, at 14111 NE 145th Street in Woodinville (telephone 488-3300) offers guided cellar tours and complimentary tastings from 10 A.M. to 4:30 P.M. daily. The grounds include trout ponds and an arboretum, making this a lovely place to spend the day and explore.

Columbia Winery, nearby at 14030 NE 145th Street in Woodinville (488-2776) offers free tours on weekends and free tastings daily. Tours are given on Fridays through Sundays from 10 A.M. to 4:30 P.M. Tastings are held every day from 10 A.M. to 7 P.M.

French Creek, at 17721 132nd Ave. NE in Woodinville (486-1900) has tours and tastings from 12 noon to 5 P.M., every day except Tuesday. Pack a lunch and enjoy their creekside picnic area.

Silver Lake Winery, at 23712 Bothell-Everett Highway in Bothell (485-2437) has a tasting room at the Country Village Shopping Center which you are invited to visit at no charge. Hours are Mondays through Saturdays from 12 noon to 6 P.M., and Sundays from 12 noon to 5 P.M.

Snoqualmie Winery, at 1000 Winery Road in Snoqualmie (888-4000) has a great view overlooking Snoqualmie Valley, the perfect setting for a lunch *al fresco*. Tours and tastings are available daily from 10 A.M. to 4:30 P.M.

Evergreen State Volkssport Association

- 10228 29th St. E, Puyallup; 840-1776

"Volkssporting," loosely translated from German, means "sport of the people." The ESVA is part of a national organization which sponsors walking tours and other activities, many of which take place in and around the Seattle area. The idea is to complete various mapped-out courses, for credit within the club— sort of like earning Boy Scout merit badges. But it's really a social group, intended to get you up and out, meeting friendly people, and participating in non-competitive sports.

Dozens of local clubs each set up a handful of routes. There are four clubs in Seattle; plus others in Bellevue, Lynnwood, Federal Way, Tacoma, and lots more.

Now, here's the best part: You don't have to be a member to take these walking tours. Better still, if you *are not* a member, the tours don't even cost you a penny! Slight fees ($2-$3) are only charged if you want official ESVA credit for your achievements (there is a whole system of log books, lapel pins, and so on).

With a bit of advance preparation, in fact, even tourists can take these free guided walks. Just call the main number above to find a chapter in any particular area; call that group to find out its starting point; then go there to sign up and walk, any time from sunrise to sunset, any day of the year. At the start point (usually a hotel or restaurant), you'll get a brochure outlining the exact path, and a start card. Registration is important to the ESVA, even if you're not paying or getting credit, just for their own records.

Meanwhile, the brochure will tell you how long the walk is, how strenuous, how much time to allow, and where to find food and restrooms along the way. It also describes your sightseeing in the kind of detail only natives could know; the trips direct you to historic sites, grand views, and little-known points of interest. In Seattle, for instance, a club called the "Family Wanderers" offers one trail along the waterfront and one up Queen Anne Hill. Elsewhere, a club called the Yakima Valley Sunstriders guides you along Mt. Rainier.

For more information on the whole shabang, including group walks, call the central office (listed above) for a copy of their monthly newsletter, *The Pathfinder*.

Kingdome Tours

● 201 S King St., Seattle; 296-3126
Did you know that a crew of fifteen people can transform the Kingdome from a football field to a basketball arena in fewer than five hours? This is just one of the many facts you'll learn on a tour of the King County Stadium, better known as the Kingdome. You'll see a genuine locker room, the press box, VIP areas, and walk across the Astroturf—all while guides explain the history and daily operations of the stadium. Sports fans are sure to enjoy this one-hour, behind-the-scenes look at the home of the Seahawks and the Mariners.

It costs far less to tour the place than to see some of those games: $4 for adults and teens, $2 for kids age six to twelve and seniors over 65, and free for children under six. For an even better deal, arrange a group tour. You'll get a small savings on each ticket and, more importantly, the tour can be tailored to meet the needs and interests of your group. You must have at least 25 people, and make arrangements at least ten days in advance. Tours are given year-round (they even continued during the 'Dome's unexpected renovations), but times vary; call ahead to verify the schedule and availability.

Klondike Gold Rush National Historical Park

● 117 S Main St., Seattle; 553-7220
See the listing under "Museums."

Northwest Seaport Maritime Heritage Center

● 1002 Valley St., Seattle; 447-9800
At the southern tip of Lake Union, the Northwest Seaport Maritime Heritage Center is the home of the *Wawona*. Completed in 1897, this is the largest three-masted sailing schooner built in North America; in 1970 it became a National Historic Site, the first ship to be so designated. Though it's currently under restoration, you can take a self-guided tour of this grand old ship for just $1—across the deck, through her vast hold, and into the sail loft with its antique sewing machine.

The Maritime Heritage Center also includes the **Center for Wooden Boats**, a working shipyard with other smaller boats, marine artifacts, and ship restorers at work. At the time of this writing, plans were under way to open two more historic boats, the tug *Arthur Foss* and the lightship *Relief*, to the public.

The NW Seaport is open every day, except Thanksgiving, Christmas, and New Year's. Summer hours are from 10 A.M. to 5 P.M. Mondays through Saturdays, and 12 noon to 5 P.M. on Sundays. It closes an hour earlier every day in the fall and winter.

NW Seaport also sponsors concerts aboard the *Wawona*. For more info, see the listing under "Music." At the nearby Center for Wooden Boats you can rent a vessel and take off for the open waters. For more information see the listing under "Outdoors."

Pike Place Market Tours

● Pike Place Market Information Booth, First Ave. and Pike St., Seattle; 682-7453
Feeling a bit swamped by the press of the crowd at this popular spot? Afraid you'll miss some of the more fascinating elements of its history? For a mere $5, you can take a guided tour of the oldest farmer's market in the country. The tour lasts for about an hour and a half, beginning with a complimentary continental breakfast, where your guide will give a preliminary talk. Then you're off and shopping—er, touring.

There are basic Market tours, along with special theme walks for Christmas and other holidays, the various seasons, and so on. Tours are generally given on Wednesday mornings in the summer and Saturday mornings the rest of the year. Individual times can be arranged for groups; call for details. For all tours, you do need to make reservations at least three days in advance.

Rainier Brewery Tours

- 3100 Airport Way S, Seattle;
  622-6606

Seattle has gained quite a reputation for its beers both large and small; for a contrast to the folksy microbrewing operation at the Red Hook Ale plant (below), beer fans will want to check out the older, larger Rainier Brewing Company tour. This factory is located south of the Kingdome; you pass right by it heading south through the city on Route 5.

Tours are given Mondays through Saturdays, from 1 P.M. to 6 P.M., on the half-hour. You'll take a stroll through the vast Rainier cellars, and watch a video program which explains the history of beer, brewing, and the wonderful world of Rainier. Of course, the tour concludes with free samples. The whole presentation lasts approximately 30 minutes, and it's all free of charge; no reservations are required, except for large groups.

Red Hook Brewery Tours

- 3400 Phinney Ave. N, Seattle;
  548-8000

First you drink, then you tour, then you go and drink some more! If this isn't the official slogan for the Red Hook Brewery tour, then gosh darn, it oughtta be. On Mr. C's visit, the merry guide poured four generous rounds of Red Hook's finest before the tour even *began*. In fact, groups assemble in RH's Trolleyman's Pub, adjacent to the brewery (see the listing under "Restaurants—North Area"). It's all quite a sociable experience.

As much as any of Seattle's suds, Red Hook Ale has gotten increased national exposure recently as part of the microbrew craze, though it hasn't yet reached the marketing heights of the Samuel Adams sort (although they've just opened an East Coast branch). Brewski *aficionados* are sure to find this an enlightening—and yes, educational—experience. The beer-making process is explained in its entirety, with live demonstrations and plenty of photo-ops. After being led throughout the small but bustling factory, the group winds up once

again in the pub (how convenient!) to sample more of this wondrous elixir.

This tour costs only a dollar, making it economically feasible to go visit the Red Hook Brewery again and again (now, let's not support any habits here). And with every tour, you get a free Red Hook glass! Tours are offered seven days a week in summer, weekdays only during the off-season. Call ahead for the current schedule, but no reservations are needed.

Seattle Times Production Plant Tour

- 19200 120th Ave. NE, Bothell;
  489-7000

With a background in newspapers himself (no, not sleeping under them), Mr. C *loves* newspaper tours. Unfortunately, the *Seattle Times* tour doesn't let you peek into the newsroom or any of the editorial offices. Still, for less than the price of a paper—in other words, absolutely free—you can tour the *Times*'s production plant in Bothell.

From a spectator's point-of-view, this is the more exciting part anyway. Makes you think of all those movie transitions where a headline comes hurtling out at you from a background of whizzing papers. During the hour-long tour, you'll see the pressroom with all its machinery, and learn about the intricate process of printing a daily newspaper (it has changed a bit since the days of *The Front Page*).

This is fascinating fun for groups of any age. Tours are available Mondays, Wednesdays, and Fridays at 9 A.M., noon, and 1:30 P.M. It's free, but you do need to make reservations. Groups can be no larger than forty people. Call the number above for information or reservations.

Seattle Waterfront Streetcars

- Various locations, Seattle;
  Information, 553-3000

A fleet of authentic 1920s streetcars klickety-klack their way along a two-mile downtown path leading from the International District to Myrtle Edwards Park, along the Elliott Bay waterfront, and back again. Big enough for fifty people, these give you a sense of history—as well as a chance for walked-out tourists to rest their feet for a while. And best of all, it's cheap enough—merely the price of a bus fare.

Yep, just 85¢ (or a bus pass) gets you on board at any of nine stops; pick up a map on the trolley, or at most visitor information centers. Rush hour fares are $1.10; this is, after all, an official part of Seattle's public transit system. Ask for a transfer when you pay, and you'll be allowed to get on and off as much as you like for 90 minutes. The entire route itself takes about 20 leisurely minutes in each direction, starting from the Metro Tunnel Station (Fifth Avenue S and S Jackson Street), running along S Main Street to Alaskan Way, and then along the waterfront up to Pier 70.

Streetcars get pretty crowded at peak times, especially during the summer; be prepared to wait, and possibly ride standing up. The cars and stations themselves are handicapped-accessible; for more details, the number above is Seattle Metro's 24-hour info line.

Smith Tower

• 506 Second Ave., Seattle; 622-4004

Well before a certain needle came along (built in 1914, to be exact), the Smith Tower rose above Seattle as the tallest structure in the city—and for that matter, in all the West. Since then, many other skyscrapers have been added to the skyline; but the pointed, Italian-style Smith Tower at the southern end of the city remains one of the most famous and recognizable. For a time, it was even caught up in a "high stakes" rivalry with a building around the corner built by the Hoge family. History tells us that Mr. Smith won this round by a good twenty stories. By the way, this fella was no ordinary Smith: If some tour guide hasn't told you already, L.C. Smith was associated with both a Mr. Wesson of firearm fame, and a Mr. Corona of typewriter fame. Anyway, according to residents and visitors

---

---

alike, it still offers a fine view of Seattle from its "mere" 42 stories.

For only $2 per adult and $1 for kids (as opposed to a stratospheric $6.50 for the Space Needle), you will be carried to the top of the Smith Tower in its original, manually operated elevator; check out the view, bring a bag lunch if you like, and enjoy your savings while gazing at the spectacular panorama of downtown and the surrounding waterways. In order to accommodate the office folks who actually work here, the elevator operates for visitors only from 9 to 11:30 A.M., 1:30 to 4:30 P.M., and 5:30 to 10 P.M. every weekday. Weekend hours are simpler: 9 A.M. to 10 P.M., inclusive.

The Space Needle

- Seattle Center, 219 Fourth Ave. N,
  Seattle; 443-2111

Being an icon certainly has its privileges. The Needle is no longer the tallest building around, the restaurant at the top is reputed to be just so-so (at the very least, overpriced), and admission is a tad more expensive than the other observation decks around the city. Despite these shortcomings, people flock to the top because it is, after all, *the* Space Needle. Like the monorail train that whisks you there from only one other spot in town, it is the physical manifestation of everything that makes Seattle the kitschiest place on the planet.

All kidding aside, Mr. C does recommend the $6.50 ride up. The spectacular, 360-degree view is breathtaking; and you can stay up there as long as you want, to get your money's worth. The inside observation deck has detailed maps that point out noteworthy Seattle sights, while the outdoor deck allows you to enjoy the city scene *au naturel* (bring a jacket or something—it's chilly up there, even in summer!). All in all, it's not that hefty a price for such a popular spot. Don't shy away if you're anti-tourist, however; the Needle is very popular with locals, too. In fact, it was once voted "Best Place to Get Engaged" in *Seattle Weekly*.

Admission is reduced for senior citizens ($5.75), and children five to twelve ($4). Children under four are admitted free. Speaking of out-of-towners, by the way: Residents who often have company may want to check into annual membership. $36 gets you unlimited visits with up to four guests. Sounds expensive, but two rides up with a few friends, and you're already way ahead of the normal prices. Special rates for groups and school field trips are also available; call during weekday business hours for more information.

RESTAURANTS

All area codes (206) unless otherwise noted

For the dining chapters of the book (which many Cheapsters consider to be its main course), Mr. C decided not to dig in alphabetically, but rather by geographical area. After all, when you're hungry, you want to eat *now*—no matter how appetizing some place halfway across town may sound. The city has been divided into broad sections, so that you can just pick up the book and find the cheap choices in your area—or, the area where you're *going* to be. Use this section with the "Entertainment" chapters to plan out a whole day or night on the town!

All of the restaurants in this book are places where you can eat dinner for under $10 per person (in many cases, far less), not including tax and tip. Lunch prices, of course, can be even lower. Even so, most of these eateries serve "real" food, not phony fast-food junk.

That $10 limit also does not include alcohol, which is going to be expensive just about anywhere. In fact, many of these places can afford to serve good, cheap food *because* they make their money on the drinks. If you're really tight on cash, you can always nurse one beer or an overpriced soda, eat well, and still come out ahead on the deal. And check out Mr. Cheap's special "Tip-Free" list for establishments where you can safely save an extra buck or two in *that* department. Enjoy!

TIP-FREE RESTAURANTS

Yes, the truly budget-conscious can even save an extra buck or two by frequenting some of these restaurants. Mr. C is not suggesting that you sneak out and stiff your waiter; these are places which are self-service or take-out establishments. Here's to 'em.

Capitol Hill
The Bagel Deli
Cafe Paradiso
Capons Rotisserie Chicken
Dick's Drive Ins
Macheezmo Mouse Mexican Cafe
Magic Dragon
My Favorite Piroshky
Nueva Cocina
Pizzeria Pagliacci
Rocket Pizza
Rosebud Espresso & Bistro
Surrogate Hostess

Downtown Area
Bagel Express
Bakeman's Restaurant
Bangkok Hut
Bruno's
Burrito Express
Casa D's
Duffy's
du jour
The Elliott Bay Book Company Cafe
Gourmet Salad House
The Green Turtle
Ivar's Acres of Clams
La Vaca
Macheezmo Mouse Mexican Cafe
The Palomino Cafe Express
Panchito's Restaurant
Sit & Spin
Sound View Cafe
Taco Del Mar
Three Girls Bakery
Todo Loco
World Class Chili

Eastlake Area
Benji's Fish and Chips
Eastlake Cafe

Eastside
Big Time Pizza
Brenner Brothers
Capons Rotisserie Chicken
Casa D's
Fresh Choice
Hoffman's Fine Pastry
La Cocina del Puerco
Macheezmo Mouse Mexican Cafe
Pasta Nova
Sunshine Baking Company
Zoopa

North Area
Ballard Baking Company Cafe
The Buzzorium
Capons Rotisserie Chicken
Dick's Drive Ins
Fresh Choice
Fresh on the Go
Greenwood Bakery Cafe
Kidd Valley
La Vaca
Macheezmo Mouse Mexican Cafe
Pizzeria Pagliacci
Still Life in Fremont Coffeehouse
Taco Del Mar
Teahouse Kuan Yin

Queen Anne Area
- Dick's Drive Ins
- Kidd Valley
- La Tazza
- Little Chinook's
- Macheezmo Mouse Mexican Cafe
- Maybe Monday Caffé
- Pizzeria Pagliacci
- Taco Del Mar

University District
- Atlantic St. Pizza
- Big Time Brewery and Alehouse
- Black Cat Cafe
- Chin Viet Thai Restaurant
- Grand Illusion Cafe
- Kidd Valley

- The Last Exit
- La Vaca
- Pizzeria Pagliacci
- Poco Loco
- Ricardo's Juice Bar and Espresso Cafe
- Shultzy's Sausage

West Seattle
- Alki Bakery
- Bangkok Shack

Outer Suburbs
- Fresh Choice
- King's Table
- Macheezmo Mouse Mexican Cafe
- Zoopa

CAPITOL HILL
(including Central District, First Hill)

The Bagel Deli
- 340 15th Ave. E, Seattle; 322-2471
- *Tip-free*

Hailing from Boston, Mr. C *knows* bagels. For some reason, you just can't get that kind of genuine, authentic bagels on the West Coast; however, First Hill's Bagel Deli offers a pretty good facsimile thereof, and these are the basis for a number of interesting sandwich variations. Many have names straight out of NYC, like the "Manhattan," made with corned beef, pastrami, Swiss cheese, cole slaw, and Russian dressing on an onion bagel; or the "Bronx," roast beef and cream cheese on a plain bagel. Also falling into the cute name category is the "Gobbler," with turkey and Swiss on a plain bagel. Each of these bagel sandwiches are a tasty handful for only $2.37.

If you can't quite get your mouth around all that, Bagel Deli has more combos served on breads like caraway rye or honey wheat. Again, you won't quite feel like you're in Times Square, but the "New Yorker" (a "Manhattan" on rye), gets you close. These sandwiches are all $3.99.

The Bagel Deli serves food in a traditional deli manner: order your food at a counter and take it back to a table in this bright, cheerful room. They also do a big take-out business. Open seven days a week for breakfast and lunch.

Cafe Paradiso
- 1005 E Pike St., Seattle; 322-6960
- *Tip-free*

Definitely one of the hip and happening hangouts in the Capitol Hill/First Hill area. The black walls of this two-level cafe are festooned with fliers for upcoming events, as well as local artwork for sale. Speaking of art, the far walls both up and downstairs are actually chalkboards waiting for creative patrons—ask for colored chalk at the counter. There's an additional espresso bar upstairs, so no matter where you are, you won't have to hike great distances for a refill.

Downstairs, you can find more of substance, like one of the daily specials. On Fridays, for example, the snack *du jour* is pesto, cream cheese, tomatoes, and sprouts on a bagel (if you can find it under all that) for $2.00. For something more filling, order a calzone for $4.50; or a tomato, cucumber, hummus, and toasted almond *chapati* ($2.95), a sort of rolled-up veggie sandwich.

Mr. C was amused by the style of service here; although you order at a counter and give your name, you don't have to pick up your own food. Just tell them if you'll be upstairs or downstairs, and they'll come and find you. This leads to the frequent sight of aproned staffers wandering around the dining area with plates of food, almost mindlessly chanting, "John...John..."

Live music is periodically performed here, too; see the separate listing under "Entertainment—Music" for more details. Cafe Paradiso is open from 6 A.M. to 1 A.M. Mondays through Thursdays, and all the way to 4 A.M. on Fridays. Weekend hours are 8 A.M. to 4 A.M. Saturdays, and 8 A.M. 'til 1 A.M. Sundays.

Caffé Minnie's
- 611 Broadway E, Seattle; 860-1360
- 101 Denny Way, Seattle; 448-6263

This newer Capitol Hill branch joins the original Caffé Minnie's in Belltown as one of the few Seattle joints that is truly open 24 hours. That alone gets a big thumbs up from Mr. C. Even better, the food is fabulous.

Lunch is served starting at 11 A.M.,

but you can still order a plate of $4.75 pecan nut pancakes, or the $6.95 "Frank Sinatra" omelette, filled with Italian sausage, garlic, black olives, scallions, pepper jack, and cheddar cheese. Who could sing after downing all that? Matter of fact, breakfast is served all day. If you've got the time and the sweet tooth, go for the Dutch babies—especially light and eggy pancakes topped with sweet things. They take about twenty minutes to prepare, and are worth the wait. Try the $5.95 "Fruit Baby," an oven-baked masterpiece topped with hot apples, strawberries, blueberries, or raspberries, served with syrup and whipped cream.

Lest you get the impression that lunch and dinner are any less enticing, Mr. C especially recommends the hearty bowl of black bean soup with cheddar cheese—nice and spicy—for $3.50. Made with skim milk, it's more like chili than soup. Minnie's tortellini salad ($6.95) mixed with fresh garlic, prosciutto and crisp bacon, is also very good. Burgers and sandwiches start at $4.75. For something even more filling, pasta dishes, like smoked salmon tossed with fresh garlic pasta in a hazelnut cream sauce ($11.95), are served with soup or salad and hot rolls.

Capons Rotisserie Chicken

- 605 15th Ave. E, Seattle; 726-1000
- 1815 N 45th St., Seattle; 547-3949
- 3615 128th Ave. SE, Bellevue; 649-0900
- 17122 Redmond Way, Redmond; 882-4838
- *Tip-free*

Rotisserie chicken has become the hottest (no pun intended) fast-food craze of the '90s. This is probably because chicken is one meal that can be made as efficiently as any fast-food fare, yet still be whole, real, and recognizable; it's as close to home cooking as you'll find in any chain. Every major city seems to have spawned a local version, and this is Seattle's.

Service is cafeteria-style. Grab a tray and choose your main dish and side items along the counter. Even so,

Capon's is comfortably decorated with tiled kitchen walls, earthy colors, and lots of plants. Also, as in the coffeehouses, daily newspapers are usually lying around for you to read if you wish. Nice touch.

As for the food, well, the name says it all. The chicken is quite good; you can order it *a la carte* (quarter, half, or whole); or as a complete dinner, which adds cornbread muffins and a choice of two side dishes. These include mashed potatoes and gravy, seasonal vegetables, sage stuffing, or a tossed green salad. A half-chicken dinner goes for $5.95, while a complete dinner for a family of four is $19.95. A child's chicken dinner is available for $2.95.

Capons also offers salads, sandwiches, soups, and other specialties, like a tasty chicken pot pie, individually sized at $3.95. Couple of sweets for after dinner, too. Open daily from 11 A.M. to 10 P.M.

Deluxe Bar and Grill

- 625 Broadway E, Seattle; 324-9697

On Capitol Hill, at the very beginning of the entire restaurant stretch of Broadway, you'll find the Deluxe, a popular tavern known for big portions of good, cheap eats. Adding to the popularity of this boisterous neighborhood spot are the 17 microbrews they keep on tap.

As they should be at any bar, burgers are always a good bet; here they're priced from $5.45 to $6.95, served up hot and juicy with hand-cut French fries. If red meat's not your thing, how about a ground turkey Reuben, with fries, for $6.25? More substantial dishes include linguini in clam sauce ($6.95); three-cheese ravioli with salad ($7.95); and New York steak, with a baked potato and soup or salad ($9.95). If you're looking for a quick snack, or just want to nibble something while watching the game, appetizers include deep-fried ravioli ($2.95), and potato skins filled with cheese, diced avocado, ground beef, and black olives ($3.75).

The Deluxe offers plenty of weekday lunch and dinner specials, too.

Mondays through Fridays from 11 A.M. to 4 P.M., you can get a burger (beef or veggie), a half-order of fettucine Alfredo, a honey ginger stir-fry, and other choices—with salad and bread—each for $3.99. You could spend more than that at a McChain and get less for your money. Dinner specials vary nightly, but usually include things like burgers for $3.99; a six-ounce top sirloin and fettucine, with salad and bread, for $5.99; and more.

Microbrew fans, take note as well: All micros on tap are just $2 a pint every Tuesday and Thursday. The Deluxe Bar and Grill is also well-known for its equally deluxe, homemade desserts—large slabs of homemade cakes, pies, and more. Chocolate mousse pie ($3.50) is worth every penny. Open seven days a week, serving food until midnight.

Dick's Drive Ins

- 115 Broadway E, Seattle; 323-1300
- 500 Queen Anne Ave. N, Seattle; 285-5155
- 12325 30th Ave. NE, Seattle; 363-7777
- 111 NE 45th St. Seattle; 632-5125
- *And other suburban locations*
- *Tip-free*

No book on cheap (priced) Seattle restaurants would be complete without mention of this longtime landmark. Burgers, fries, shakes, and a see-and-be-seen atmosphere have made Dick's a favorite spot for decades. The food may not be first rate, but hey—it's classic all-Americana. 75¢ burgers and 90¢ cheeseburgers will fill you up and never break the bank. Even the quarter-pound "Deluxe," made of two patties, cheese, and a few extra fixin's, is only $1.60. Of course, no burger here should be eaten without fries—buy a greasy bagful for 85 cents. And, for the full heartburn effect, wash it all down with a nice, thick shake ($1.10). Your cholesterol level may go through the roof; but remember, Dick's is better for your soul than your heart. Drive in from 10:30 A.M. to 2 A.M. anyday.

El Greco

- 219 Broadway E, Seattle; 328-4604

Things are always changing at this bright, cozy cafe, from the artwork on the walls to the fine cuisine. El Greco offers both daily and weekly specials, so no matter how often you stop by, you can probably try something new. When Mr. C visited, the weekly special was *dolmas*; these folks stuff their grape leaves with rice, pine nuts, and currants, top them with coriander-yogurt sauce, and add a Greek salad on the side—all for $5.95.

Each dish is so artistically arranged on the plate that dining here is a feast for the eyes as well as the stomach. Other regular menu features of note include fresh mozzarella *panini*, or Italian grilled bread sandwiches, for $4.95. Special pasta dishes are also served daily, representing that *other* part of the Mediterranean. El Greco is open from 8 A.M. until 9:30 P.M. during the week, and 8 A.M. until 10 :30 P.M. on the weekends.

General's Bar-B-Que

- 2023 E Madison St., Seattle; 328-2414

If good ol' down-home barbecue is your thing, you had better go see the General. Long established in the Central District, this casual spot cranks out all the standard favorites, and slathers them in its own homemade sauce (you can take home a jar, too). And, like all good barbecue joints, they're geared to massive quantities.

The dining room may be a bit tattered around the edges, but then, soul food wouldn't taste right at the Ritz, would it? The place is comfortably done up with potted plants and a big fish tank. Everyone here is friendly, too, and the big tables are ready to be filled with enough food to take care of any size appetite or group. Oh sure, you can have a single order of pork ribs for $6, or a half-chicken for $4.95; but you can also choose from several special platters designed for two people ($15.95), six ($39), and so on, up to sixteen people (!). In each case, you'll get a mixed variety of things like ribs, chicken, hot links, baked beans, and potato salad—and they always work out to around $8 per person.

There is a selection of lunch specials as well, all priced at $6.95. Of course, none of these include dessert, but with home-baked pecan pie, yam pie, and peach cobbler all around $2.50, you'll want to leave room. Open daily from 10 A.M. to 8 P.M. (Sundays from 1-8 P.M.); they even have their own parking lot, always a valuable commodity in the city.

Gravity Bar
• 415 Broadway E, Seattle; 325-7186
The decor of this Broadway Market eatery is a sort of industrial/exploded Tinman, while the food is ultra-vegetarian. Somehow, Gravity Bar pulls off this weird combination of widget-meets-wheatgrass successfully.

The juice bar serves up exotic-tasting and quite filling concoctions. Have Dan-o book you a "Hawaii Five-O" (pineapple, papaya, banana, yogurt, and coconut, $3.95), and you'll practically get a meal in itself. However, if you want something a bit more substantial, sandwiches and salads range between $4 and $7. Mr. C especially enjoyed the $5.25 "Gravity Club Sandwich," made on buckwheat sunflower toast, filled with olive tapenade, cucumber, tomato, lettuce, sprouts, avocado, and provolone cheese. Blue corn chips are served on the side.

Gravity Bar opens at 9 A.M. everyday, closing at 10 P.M. during the week, 11 P.M. on the weekends.

Hana Restaurant
• 219 Broadway E, Seattle; 328-1187
Even though Hana has lots of tables jammed in close together, you still may have to wait for a seat. This little Japanese restaurant always seems to be very busy, and no wonder; they serve delicious and inexpensive meals for those who know it'll be worth the wait.

Mr. C ordered the salmon teriyaki ($6.25). This scrumptious dish came with a cup of miso soup, salad, and cooked vegetables—along with a pair of chopsticks. If you are unaccustomed to this method of eating, don't fret; forks are just a request away. And—not that this will help your co-

---

MR. CHEAP'S PICKS
Capitol Hill/First Hill

✔ **Cafe Paradiso**—Where the cool, the chic, and the insomnia-prone ease their late-night angst.

✔ **General's Bar-B-Que** —Terrific soul food, by the bucket if necessary.

✔ **Hana Restaurant**—Looks can be deceiving; this small, plain cafe will satisfy your yen for tasty and inexpensive sushi and tempura.

✔ **Surrogate Hostess**—Elegant food and pastries in a summer-camp atmosphere of long tables and sacks of flour.

---

ordination—beer is available, too.

It may not look like much from the outside, but this is a surprisingly bountiful storefront restaurant. It's open Mondays through Saturdays from 11 A.M. to 10:30 P.M., and Sundays from 4 P.M. to 10 P.M.

Jalisco Mexican Restaurant
• 1467 E Republican St., Seattle; 325-9005
• 122 and 129 First Ave. N, Seattle; 283-4242
• 8517 14th Ave. S, Seattle; 767-1943
• 12336 31st Ave. NE, Seattle; 364-3978
• 115 Park Lane, Kirkland; 822-3355
A shop owner of Mexican extraction told Mr. C to be sure to include Jalisco, for truly authentic regional food. Named for one of that country's more scenic states, this restaurant upholds that tradition of beauty—at least one branch sports a wall mural depicting a village center, complete with guitarist serenading a dancing couple by a fountain. Piñatas and plants are perched high above, and high-backed booths provide a secluded dining experience.

Try one of the huge "Especiáles de la Casa," like the chimichangas or enchiladas rancheras, for $7.55 each. All of these specialties are served with rice and beans, making for a gigantic plateful. For the lighter appetite, a single tamale ($2.65) or taco salad ($4.50) will do you right.

Be sure to try something with Jalisco's homemade *mole* sauce; usually made from unsweetened chocolate (yes, for dinner), these folks make it as a nifty peanut sauce instead. If you're not entirely familiar with such native culinary terms, there's a helpful glossary on the back of the menu.

The First Avenue location, just outside Seattle Center, has recently spawned a quicker-fare "taqueria" right across the street; the Lake City location adds a cocktail lounge. All branches are open daily from 11 A.M. to 10 P.M., and to 11 P.M. on Fridays and Saturdays.

Kokeb Restaurant
- 926 Twelfth Ave., Seattle; 322-0485

Seemingly in the middle of nowhere sits this popular Ethiopian restaurant. The rather desolate stretch of the Central District makes entering Kokeb seem like finding an oasis in the desert. The interior is cozy and exotic-looking, decorated with large plants and African masks; it's somewhat formal, but not heavily so.

After all, how fancy can any place be that asks you to eat with your hands? That is the standard style for most Ethiopian cuisine—in which crêpe-like pieces of *injera* bread are used to scoop up wonderfully aromatic stews and meats. You don't have to do it this way, but it is kinda fun.

Try the *eyeb begomen*, for example: a seasoned cottage cheese blended with collard greens. Or perhaps a spicy lentil stew. There are plenty of chicken and beef dishes as well, all priced between $7 and $10 (vegetarian entrees are in the $5-$7 range). The menu also features lamb and seafood dishes, but these are somewhat more expensive. Combination dinners, which include soup and a salad, start as low as $9.95 per person.

There's a limited cocktail bar, with house wines and bottled beers. This is not a particularly spicy cuisine, but it sure is flavorful, and beer complements it very well. Ethiopian dining is a unique experience if you've never tried it; definitely worth going out of your way for. Kokeb serves dinner only, from 5 to 10 P.M. daily.

Macheezmo Mouse Mexican Cafe
- 211 Broadway E, Seattle; 325-0072
- 701 Fifth Ave., Seattle; 382-1730
- 1815 N 45th St., Seattle; 545-0153
- 425 Queen Anne Ave. N, Seattle; 282-9904
- 2028 148th Ave. NE, Bellevue; 746-5824
- 3805 196th Ave. SW, Lynnwood; 744-1611
- *Tip-free*

The '90s mean that even Mexican fast food has gone health-conscious. In fact, Macheezmo Mouse is so serious about it that they print up pamphlets on weight management, diabetic exchanges, heart health— and how their food fits in. Every item on the menu is accompanied by nutritional information: The chicken burrito, for example, has 580 calories, 17% from fat—while the veggie power salad has 200 calories, 1% from fat. Make your informed decision.

Mr. C was a bit put off by a display of sample platters at the Queen Anne location. It's nice to see the choices before you order, but this food sits out all day, and looks a bit um, *faded* after a few hours. Is this the best way to tout healthy food? Well, most branches just show you photos, a better idea. After ordering and paying at the counter, give your name, and they'll call you once your order is ready.

Most burrito, enchilada, and taco plates are $4, including rice and beans on the side. There are also salads, quesadillas, and a children's menu as well; and nothing on the menu tops $5.25. To add a little kick to your meal, stop by the fixin's bar and try a unique but delicious concoction of spicy-sweet citrus barbecue sauce called Boss Sauce. Beer is available too—draft pints are $2-$3, while a bottle of Bud is $1.75.

Macheezmo Mouse restaurants are spacious, clean, and done up in a brightly colored Southwestern motif. Most have tables both inside and out. These features, plus a few children's items on the menu, make it a good bet for families, as well. Open for lunch and dinner, seven days a week.

Magic Dragon
- 420 Broadway E, Seattle; 726-9776
- *Tip-free*

Puff would never be able to fit in here. Almost the entire length of this long, narrow restaurant is counter space, loaded with heaping bins of mouth-watering Chinese dishes. As their menu proclaims, "hot & fresh" and "big portions" are what you'll find. Every half hour the bins are stoked with new goodies, to ensure the freshness and quality of what you'll eat.

Business is evenly divided between take-out and eat-in customers; there is a small dining room in the back, and along one wall is a countertop with a few chairs. Wherever you dine, you can enjoy such standard treats as honey sesame chicken or Cantonese beef and broccoli, both available in $1.75 and $3.95 sizes. Check the daily specials to see what's cookin'—open 11 A.M. to 10 P.M. everyday.

Mo'Roc'caN Cafe
- 925 E Pike St., Seattle; 323-2373

"Moe" to its friends, this First Hill restaurant/rock club serves up almost as much chic atmosphere as food. The menus are printed on cardboard discs in record album sleeves; curved, pea green booths surround kidney-shaped tables in neo-1950s style; and there's some kind of huge coil with dangling droplets overhead. Most of the other artwork, for whatever reason, is of a circus motif. A bar is located in the back, which winds you into one of Seattle's hottest live music clubs; but minors are allowed in the front cafe section.

The breakfast LP lists such hits as all-you-can-eat homestyle potatoes

for $2.95, and omelettes from plain ($2.95) to extravagant (leeks, spinach, tomatoes, mushrooms and roasted pine nuts, $4.95). Lunch and dinner albums share many of the same tracks, like hearts of palm Alfredo ($7.50), a hot turkey and Havarti sandwich ($5.95), and burgers from $4.95. Dinnertime adds extras like vegetarian marsala for $4.95, broiled halibut steak for $8.95, and other nightly specials.

Moe spins out great food from 11 A.M. during the week, 9 A.M. on the weekends. Closing time varies depending on the day—generally the cafe shuts down around 10 P.M. during the week, and 1 A.M. on the weekends. Considering the trendy environs, and the well-prepared *nouvelle* cuisine, prices here are quite reasonable—if not the cheapest around.

Live bands perform most nights of the week, usually something loud, fast, and great for dancing or going wild. See the separate listing under "Entertainment—Music" for um, moe details.

Museum Cafe
- 321 E Pine St., Seattle; 621-8580

What a nice, bright little eatery this is. Why, it's enough to give gas a good name—and it's not often you can say that as a compliment. Mr. C refers, actually, to the General Petroleum Museum (see the listing under "Entertainment—Museums"), and its ode to the history of oil-based products. Their cafe is decorated with vintage gasoline pumps, signs, and other nostalgic artifacts from the early days of automobilia.

The food, while definitely not derived from petroleum, is enough to keep you well-fueled for some time. Nothing on the menu costs over $6; and the entrees, like quiche and meatloaf, come with two side dishes (choose from cottage cheese, applesauce, fries, and garlic bread, just to name a few). Sandwiches and burgers can come with a small salad for 50¢ more. Breakfast is also served, rounding out the all-American fare with omelettes and pancakes.

Primarily a breakfast and lunch spot, as well as a catering company, the Museum Cafe is open from 9 A.M. to 6 P.M. Mondays through Fridays only.

My Favorite Piroshky
- 122 Broadway E, Seattle; 322-2820
- *Tip-free*

Is it just Mr. C, or does this sound to you like a TV sitcom about Russian dumplings? Well, that's not all that makes this tiny Capitol Hill eatery stand out. Their fillings definitely take a *nouvelle* turn, putting a new spin on what has traditionally been a very plain and heavy food. These breaded meat pies offer a variety of fillings that, to Mr. C's knowledge, have never been put into piroshky before—like turkey, almonds, and cheese (that's all one dumpling, folks). As you can see in the storefront window, many of these are baked into fun shapes, like a fish or a hambone, to indicate the filling inside. Cute!

These make a wonderful meal for bargain-hunters, because they are not only cheap but also very filling. Piroshky stuffed with vegetables, like carrots, broccoli, onion, or potatoes in various combinations, are $2.25 each. Piroshky filled with beef, chicken, or turkey, are a mere $2.50. One or two of these will keep you going for a long while.

Having a party? Order a dozen bite-size piroshky for $7.80. And these hearty handfuls are not just for lunch anymore; MFP has plenty of sweets, too, like blueberry or cherry piroshky, along with apple cinnamon rolls, almond twists, and raspberry walnut rolls. Open daily, 8:30 A.M. to midnight.

Nueva Cocina
- 401 Broadway E, Seattle; 328-7634
- *Tip-free*

Nueva Cocina, brought to you by the owners of Poco Loco and Burrito Express (see separate listings), offers that same kind of quick, basic Mexican fare. However, one big difference is that Nueva Cocina adds fried treats to its menu, like taco salads in crispy shells and deep-fried chimichangas, each for $4.95. All burritos are $3.75, whether you want ground or shred-

ded beef, chicken, or vegetarian filling. Tostadas and crispy tacos are $3, while soft tacos are $3.50. Stop by for tasty take-out or claim one of the tables. The kitchen is open Mondays through Saturdays from 9:30 A.M. to 9 P.M., and Sundays 9 A.M. to 7 P.M.

Pizzeria Pagliacci
- 426 Broadway E, Seattle; 324-0730
- 2400 Tenth Ave. E, Seattle; 632-1058
- 550 Queen Anne Ave. N, Seattle; 285-1232
- 4003 Stone Way N, Seattle; 632-1058
- 4529 University Way NE, Seattle; 632-0421
- *Tip-free*

Pizza is not the only supper you'll sing for on this menu. Calzone, soup, and pastas—both hot dishes and unique salads—are also served fresh daily. The atmosphere is casual, but nicer than your average pizzeria; fresh flowers in recycled juice bottles adorn every table, while artsy black and white photos and sketches decorate the walls. The most exciting thing you'll see is the occasional Frisbee of dough being flung up in the air by the chef behind the counter. All pizza dough is made fresh daily and tossed in this manner—"no rolling pins or sheeters to take the life out of the dough," as the menu boasts. This attention to quality definitely results in a superior pie.

Ordering takes place after you've viewed everything in the glass display cases. Mr. C particularly enjoyed a delicious $3.95 pesto and artichoke pasta salad; the basics, such as the "extra-pepperoni" pizza, are always on hand, either by the slice or the whole pie. Pizzeria Pagliacci is open from 11 A.M. to 11 P.M. Sundays through Thursdays, and 'til 1 A.M. Fridays and Saturdays.

Red Robin
- 1600 E Olive Way, Seattle; 323-1600
- 3272 Fuhrman Ave. E, Seattle; 323-0918
- Pier 55, 1101 Alaskan Way, Seattle; 623-1942

- 1100 Fourth Ave., Seattle; 447-1909
- Northgate Mall, Seattle; 365-0933
- 11021 NE Eighth St., Bellevue; 453-9522
- 2390 148th Ave. NE, Bellevue; 641-3810
- 1305 SE Everett Mall Way, Everett; 355-7330
- Sea Tac Mall, Federal Way; 946-TOGO (8646)
- *And other suburban locations*

Red Robin is a popular chain where families, business types, mall creatures, and others all come together for standard American fare. The atmosphere is bright, lively, and convivial. Separate bar areas, fully outfitted for beers and cocktails, include televisions showing various ball games.

The menu is dominated by the "Gourmet Burgers" (the world's greatest, in their humble opinion), in more than a dozen varieties. Try the "Banzai Burger," marinated in teriyaki sauce and topped with grilled pineapple and cheddar cheese ($5.95), or the "Lone Star Burger," with jalapeño jack cheese, salsa, and guacamole ($5.25). Non-carnivores may want to try the "Amazing Meatless Burger," made with veggies and grains ($5.25). In fact, you can have any style made with a meatless patty.

The one-size-fits-all menu also includes soups and sandwiches, entree-sized salads, pastas, and plenty of bar-food appetizers. Red Robin is a safe bet for bringing the gang to munch on wings and nachos. And save room for desserts like mud pie, cheesecake, brownie sundaes, shakes, and root beer floats. There's also a kiddie menu, with half a dozen meals all priced at $2.99 each. Most Red Robins serve food daily until midnight.

Rocket Pizza
- 612 Broadway E, Seattle; 329-4405
- *Tip-free*

This popular Capitol Hill pizza parlor is sure to send your tastebuds into orbit. Business here is about half take-out and half eat-in; more than most pizzerias, the room is comfortable enough to hang in for a while. Speaking of half-and-half combinations, try one of Rocket's three-topping pizza slices (a mere $1.85), or veggie combo calzone ($3.25).

Whole pies start at $8.25 for a 14" cheese pizza, going all the way up to $17.20 for an 18" with ricotta, artichoke hearts, and sun-dried tomatoes. For a couple of dollars more, a "create your own" approach can be applied to either the pizzas or the calzones (do allow up to half an hour for calzones; they're made to order, and worth the wait). Summer squash, feta cheese, and pesto are just some of the exotic extras to toss in or on. Gourmet pizza at down to earth prices! Rocket is open seven days a week, 'til midnight on Fridays and Saturdays.

Rosebud Espresso & Bistro
- 719 E Pike St., Seattle; 323-6636
- *Tip-free*

This inviting cafe offers three different places to eat, drink and be merry: a back patio, a cozy dining room, and a sort of living room with sofas, coffee tables, and paintings by local artists on the walls. Wherever you alight, it's a nice place to sit back and relax. Stop by between 8 and 11 on a Thursday night, and you'll also be treated to free live jazz (see the listing under "Entertainment—Music").

If you plan on visiting the Rosebud frequently, pick up a Rosebuddy card. Each time you order an espresso drink, the card gets stamped. With every ten stamps, you receive a free drink. Not a bad deal, eh? And another good deal is the food itself; everything on the lunch menu is under $5, from sandwiches to a soup and salad combo for $4.75. Mr. C enjoyed the large ham and Swiss sandwich, and the vegetable beef soup really hit the spot. Brunch offers treats like pecan waffles ($3.75), cheese baked eggs ($3.50-$5.50), and "breakfast pastas"—linguine with scrambled eggs in a cream sauce ($4.25).

Happy hour occurs *twice* each weekday here, from 7:30-9 in the morning, and 6-8 in the evening. What makes folks so happy? On Mondays, Wednesdays and Fridays, you get a free extra espresso shot; on Tuesdays and Thursdays, you get double stamps on your Rosebuddy card. Even Charles Foster Kane could be happy here. Open daily; lunch is served from 11-3, weekend brunch from 10-2; espressos and light fare all day from 7:30 A.M. until 1 A.M. (to 3 A.M. Fridays and Saturdays).

Siam on Broadway
● 616 Broadway E, Seattle; 324-0892
This yupscale Thai restaurant at the top of the Broadway restaurant crawl is quite popular, no doubt due to its extremely good food, prompt service, and laid-back-but-trendy atmosphere. The decor includes traditional Asian art, parasols, and masks, all lit in a dramatic style. The long, narrow dining room is partitioned down the middle by fish tanks.

But enough of painting the scene—what about the food? Well, the mixed crowd of Asians and non-Asians alike attests to its authenticity. Siam's serves up large portions of yummy Thai treats at prices that are suprisingly low. Garlic prawns are a bargain at $7.50, as is chicken sauteed with ginger, mushrooms, onions, and peppers ($5.75).

The adventurous may want to try one of the "Siam choices," half a dozen combinations of vegetables, nuts, and sauces with your choice of meat for just $5.75. Vegetarian dishes are all priced under $6. Mr. C loved Siam's "Garden Delight," veggies topped with peanut sauce, for $5.75.

Siam also serves up inexpensive lunch dishes, most for under $5. It's open seven days a week; lunch and dinner are served on weekdays, dinner only on the weekends.

Surrogate Hostess
● 746 19th Ave. E, Seattle; 324-1944
● *Tip-free*
Not far from Volunteer Park, Surrogate Hostess is a longtime Capitol Hill institution. The name is certainly accurate, since they take good care of your appetite here—but this is far from a dainty, mannered hostess. It's a boisterous, convivial sort of place, where you order at the counter, pick up your food on a tray, and take it to a long, wooden, communal table. A friend of Mr. C's has likened the experience to summer camp; rest assured, that's where the resemblance ends.

After all, did you ever go to any camp that served up mushroom-walnut paté, or a Havarti, pesto, and red pepper sandwich? At lunch, either of these may be on the daily-changing menu for a thrifty $4.25. Or, you may opt for a bowl of curried squash with carrots and ginger ($2.85) or a cup of soup, a bean salad, and a hunk of freshly baked bread, all for $4.15.

Baking is the primary specialty here, by the way—evidenced by the fifty-pound sacks of flour and other provisions which serve as decor all around the big, open room. They do make wonderful breads and pastries here, perfect for a quick bite with tea or a big latté. Go for a slice of Black Bottom cake, a mere $1.75.

At breakfast, you can have a heaping platter in which two eggs are scrambled and baked into a dish with bacon, cheese and *crème fraiche*; it's served with fresh fruit, and your choice of such pastries as pineapple coffee cake or a Scottish oat scone—all for $5.25. Cholesterol readings are not included.

Dinner, served until 9 P.M., offers different specials daily—like salmon cakes with garlic and smoked Gouda cheese ($7.95). Beers and wines are available from about $2 each. Evenings may also pair the food with live music, usually folk or jazz, no cover charge.

Helping make up a bit for character (or lack thereof) is a mild sense of humor around the place. A hot water tap bears the punning sign, "Like Water for Tea." Another, more cautionary sign reads "Napkins=Trees." And Surrogate Hostess is as friendly to vegans as it is to the environment; you can even add soy milk to your coffee, if you prefer. Open from 6 A.M. for breakfast, seven days a week, including weekend brunch.

Taqueria Express
• 219 Broadway E, Seattle; 329-8675
This cozy, red brick Mexican restaurant is tucked away in the back upstairs corner of the Alley. There's plenty of seating in the quiet dining room—in spite of the fast-food-sounding name, you can actually hang out over a relaxing meal. Try a chicken burrito for $3.50, or a soft taco for $2.40; the food is no-frills, but the charming atmosphere and friendly staff more than makes up for the limited menu.

No alcohol is served; as Mr. C's fans know, this is one way for restaurants to keep prices down—no expensive liquor license to pay for. Stop by Taqueria Express Mondays through Saturdays between 11 A.M. to 10 P.M., or Sundays noon to 9 P.M.

Torrey's Eggs Cetera
• 220 Broadway E, Seattle;
  325-EGGS (3447)
Seemingly out of place along First Hill's punk-ish main stretch, this old-time coffee shop serves up more than just eggs; however, the egg specialties and omelettes listed on the first two pages of the menu may sound so good, you won't even look at the rest.

Most of the egg dishes, which are served all day, cost between $4 and $6 (including toast and hash browns or grilled red potatoes). An egg-cellent choice (sorry, couldn't resist) is the three-egg "Danish Modern" omelette, loaded with sauteed mushrooms, diced ham, onions, and cheddar cheese.

Moving on to the "cetera" part: Waffles (under $4), burgers, sandwiches, and salads (under $6), fill out the rest of this inexpensive menu. The oatmeal waffle is especially yummy; if you're not interested in breakfast, the cashew turkey salad sandwich, or a mushroom burger (with mushrooms sauteed in sherry) will easily fill you up.

Dedicated Cheapsters will want to stop by on Tuesday nights and enjoy the $5.95 all-you-can-eat spaghetti special, offered from 5 to 9 P.M. Beers ($1.75 to $2.50) and wines ($2.50 per glass) are also served. Torrey's Eggs Cetera is open from 6:30 A.M. to 9 P.M. Monday through Friday, and from 7:30 on the weekends.

DOWNTOWN AREA
(including Belltown, International District, Pioneer Square, the Waterfront)

Bagel Express
• 205 First Ave. S, Seattle; 682-7202
• *Tip-free*
In Pioneer Square, here's a businessman's (or woman's) delight—quick, cheap, and healthy. Order a hummus, cucumber, sprouts, and tomato bagel sandwich; or a roast beef, Swiss, cheddar, and horseradish version; or one of the many other varieties. Stacked though they are, all bagel sandwiches are priced at $3.05. And, for just $2.50 more, add a bowl of soup to your sandwich.

Bagel Express whips up some of its own flavored cream cheeses, like lox spread or olive and pimiento, to add some pizzazz to your bagel experience. These special blends are also sold in little cartons to bring home. Bagel Express is open Mondays through Fridays, from 7 A.M. to 3 P.M.

Bakeman's Restaurant
• 122 Cherry St., Seattle; 622-3375
• *Tip-free*
Located below street level, Bakeman's is down a flight of stairs directly from the sidewalk. The left side of the restaurant looks like a

school cafeteria, complete with flourescent lighting and large tables; the remaining quarter, set off by a partial wall and flight of stairs, is a bar.

The restaurant, sparse but large, serves up hefty sandwiches made on its homemade bread. Try the $2.70 meatloaf sandwich, or the $2.30 egg salad. Speaking of eggs, Bakeman's serves up breakfast until 10:30 A.M.— a three-egg omelette with cheddar, served with hash browns and toast, will run you a paltry $3.25.

Hang out with the morning newspaper—there's plenty of room to spread out, and you certainly don't have to worry about spilling your coffee, or suavely dipping your sleeve in it, at a joint like this. Bakeman's is open from 8 A.M. to 3 P.M. Mondays through Fridays; the bar and lounge are open until 7 P.M. only. It's all closed on weekends.

Bangkok House
• 606 S Weller St., Seattle; 382-9888
Bangkok House's menu is very large, covering a wide variety of Thai dishes from salads to seafood. The menu helpfully rates its food from mild to very hot, so you'll know whether you should order extra rice (you do know that drinks do nothing to calm down a fiery tongue, don't you?).

Try the panang for $6.50—chicken or beef sauteed in a thick red curry sauce, coconut milk, and basil. The house specialties are also quite interesting, like the yen ta four ($5.95), a hot-and-sour noodle soup loaded with prawns, calamari, pork, deep-fried tofu, and spinach, in tomato sauce. Plenty of vegetarian dishes are available, too. "Swimming Angel" tofu— deep-fried on a bed of spinach, and topped with peanut sauce ($5.50)— was especially yummy.

This International District eatery is open from 11 A.M. to 10 P.M. Sundays through Thursdays, and until 11 P.M. Fridays and Saturdays.

Botticelli Cafe
• 101 Stewart St., Seattle; 441-9235
Lowish prices, good food, and lots of it—that's Botticelli Cafe in a nutshell. And, speaking of nutshells,

that's just about the size of the cafe, too. If you're one of the lucky few to grab a seat, try the $5 seasoned pork with parsley sauce on rustico bread. Just around the corner from Pike Place Market, Botticelli is open during the week from 7:30 A.M. to 5 P.M., and Saturdays from 11 A.M. to 5 P.M.

Bruno's
• 1417 Third Ave., Seattle; 622-3180
• *Tip-free*
This cafeteria-style joint serves up both Mexican and Italian food in generous portions. The dining room inside is quite nice; both fresh and silk flowers adorn the tables, brightening the darker exposed-brick walls and archways.

Pasta dinners, such as lasagna and manicotti, are $5.59 a la carte—but adding just a dollar more gets you salad and garlic bread, too. The Mexican dishes include a "Banderilla" enchilada and chimichanga with beef or chicken for $4.85 and $6.25 respectively. Now, a *banderilla* is a dart used in bullfighting; what this has to do with the food is beyond Mr. C. It's certainly not beyond his price range, though. Beer and wine available, too. Bruno's is open from 11 A.M. to 7 P.M. Mondays through Fridays, and from 11:30 A.M. to 4 P.M. on Saturdays.

Burrito Express
• 1429 First Ave., Seattle; 623-3619
• *Tip-free*
Owned by the same folks who run Nueva Cocina and Poco Loco (see separate listings); this popular branch offers similar Mexican basics. One difference, however, is that Burrito Express isn't exactly a restaurant— merely a take-out window near Pike Place Market, with no seating to speak of. If you can't find it, even with the festive Mexican paintings on the Burrito Express staff door, just look for long line of people standing patiently. The $3.35 burritos, $2 tostadas, and $1.50 crispy tacos are clearly worth the wait. Open daily from 10 A.M. to 5 P.M.

Casa D's
• 2429 Second Ave., Seattle; 448-6678

246

- 102 Bellevue Way NE, Bellevue; 462-8410
- *Tip-free*

Casa D's portions are *muy grande*, while the prices are *pequeño*. The menu accurately boasts that every item is a meal. And, even though some items on the menu (like the taco salads, $5.45) may be fried, Casa D's is at least nominally concerned for your health. Select an apple or orange from a basket on the counter for your dessert.

Mr. C especially enjoyed a picadillo burrito, stuffed with shredded beef, Monterey jack cheese, rice, beans, fresh tomato salsa, green salsa, and sour cream. Saying all that is a mouthful—imagine eating it! The whole thing costs $4.25, plus 50 cents extra if you want to add some guacamole. A super burrito, rolled with two flour tortillas, is just $5.95.

Seating inside looks like an upscale fast-food joint, but there's plenty of room if you do want to sit and eat there. Otherwise, it's a good take-out place. Open seven days, from 11 A.M. to 8 P.M.

Common Meals
- 1902 Second Ave., Seattle; 443-1233

Now here's something Mr. C is very happy to talk about: An inexpensive meal that is not only fancy, but also helps people out at the same time. Common Meals is a not-for-profit restaurant which employs homeless men and women, giving them skills for a transition into a more normal life. But this is no soup kitchen! Once a week, full-course dinners are presented by major chefs from the area, who volunteer to design the menu and oversee its preparation.

Every Thursday, a chef from a different restaurant or hotel whips up his or her favorite creations. Dinner is served in a formal dining room (though it has seen better days) from 5:30 to 8:30 P.M. For a set price of $12.50 per person, you may find yourself dining on something like thyme roasted chicken and vegetables, along with wild greens in vinaigrette, a starter of carrot-tomato-rosemary soup, and a dessert of cheesecake topped with fresh blueberries. What a meal—and what a deal.

More casual breakfasts and lunches are available from 7:30 A.M. to 2 P.M., any weekday; and these too are incredible bargains. Have a coupla flapjacks for $1.75, or an omelette with your choice of filling (sausage, smoked ham, Swiss cheese), plus hash browns and an English muffin, all for $3.50. Add a tall double latté for just $1.85. At lunch, a quarter-pound cheeseburger is $3.25; for another buck, add an order of "Josee Fries," seasoned potatoes pan-fried with the skins on. Grilled breast of chicken Dijon, served over fresh greens and vegetables, is $4.95. And a cup of chili with hot corn bread is only $1.95. Plus lots of other sandwiches, soups, salads, and desserts.

Everything is made on the premises, and just delicious. Best of all, some 80% of the graduates of Common Meals' twelve-week course are successfully placed into the restaurant business. That's as heartwarming as any hot meal.

Crocodile Cafe
- 2200 Second Ave., Seattle; 448-2114

The smiling crocodile over the door welcomes you to a casual, yet colorful diner-style restaurant. Large green and white tiles checker the floor, while fanciful birds are suspended from the ceiling.

Fortunately, the reptilian theme does not extend to the menu. Instead, good choices include things like the $4.50 "Belltown Bite," made up of two eggs, jack cheese, and ham or bacon on an English muffin. Like McD's, only with real ingredients—and bigger. Lunch and dinner menus both feature the same food at the same prices: cheeseburgers are $5-$6, as are a variety of sandwiches; fettucine Alfredo, with soup or salad, is $6.95. Beer and wine are served as well.

Live music is performed almost nightly in the "Funky Voodoo Snake Pit" adjacent to the cafe. See the listing under "Entertainment—Music" for details. The Crocodile Cafe serves food Tuesdays through Saturdays, from 8 A.M. to 11 P.M., and Sundays until 3 P.M. Closed Mondays.

Cyclops
- 2416 Western Ave., Seattle; 441-1677

Inside this boldly purple and green building is an eatery that is about as typical of Seattle's trendy cafe scene as you'll find. Inside, an artsy post-industrial decor is warmed up by 1950s-style lamps at each booth and table (not to mention other kitschy pieces, including a Virgin Mary). Though it's laid out like other coffeehouses, Cyclops is a full restaurant with table service—whether you're here for just dessert or a meal.

Not everything here is super-cheap, and you'll stretch your dollar further at lunch rather than dinner; but considering its popularity, near-waterfront location, and fancy food, this is a pretty reasonable place. Espressos are just 75¢, and desserts like tiramisu are $3.75; if you're lucky, they'll have a batch of white chocolate brownies, one dollar apiece.

Lunch offers a world of entrees, like polenta pizza, bruschetta, baba ghanoush, and chicken pesto, all priced around $5-$6; Mr. C loved a sweet potato open-faced sandwich, smothered with smoked mozzarella, artichoke, red peppers, basil, and pesto. Filling, yummy, and very messy.

During the dinner hours, many of these items become appetizers ($4-$5), while larger dishes are added, such as penne with fresh garlic, sausage, chicken, leeks, and gorgonzola cheese ($7.95) or empanadas filled with vegetables and served with black beans ($7.50). There's also a selection of beers and wines, with one of each chosen as a daily special for $2.50 (beer) and $16 (bottle of wine).

Just look for the hubcap outside, looming like a large eye over the front door. Open for weekday lunch from 11 A.M. to 4 P.M.; on weekends, Cyclops serves brunch from 9 A.M. to 2 P.M. Dinner is served seven nights a week from 5-11 P.M. Call ahead; this place fills up quickly at peak times.

Duffy's
- 319 Second Ave. S, Seattle; 622-6458
- *Tip-free*

Duffy's feels kind of like an upscale cafeteria—trays, glass counters, paying-then-eating, that sort of thing. The only difference is that the place probably looks a lot nicer than what you remember from school days; oh yes, and the food is definitely better.

Duffy's makes up hot and cold deli sandwiches, salads, and vegetarian fare. They've gotten into the baked, stuffed potato craze; hot spuds with a choice of different toppings, like chili and cheddar, or assorted vegetables with cheese sauce. A baked potato *a la carte* costs about $4; with soup, it's $4.80; and with salad, $5.20. The salads start as the fresh, leafy kind, then are transformed into Caesar, shrimp, or taco salads, to name a few, all around $5.50. Sandwiches come in half- or full-sizes (if you can't take leftovers away with you, the half-sizes may be more convenient, but are not the better value). Ham, tuna, roast beef and more are stuffed into the different sandwiches—all under $5. At dinnertime, an 8-inch personal pizza is $7, with pepperoni or black olives and mushrooms. A more full-size version, with up to five toppings, is $12.95.

Open for breakfast and lunch every day but Sunday; Mondays, they're open 'til 4 P.M., Tuesdays through Saturdays to 7 P.M., and they stay open 'til midnight during the summer. This Duffy's is unrelated, by the by, to a place of the same name in Bellevue.

du Jour
- 1919 First Ave., Seattle; 441-3354
- *Tip-free*

From the outside, you may not expect *du jour* to have a beautiful view of Elliott Bay, let alone any place to sit. However, this narrow cafe opens up to a spacious dining room in back, with a large picture window revealing a gorgeous waterfront view. Surprise!

Aside from bringing your food to the table via plastic tray, this is a fairly classy joint for the business and tourist crowd. The cuisine is a smattering of European and American favorites, to be eaten in, taken out, or delivered. The antipasto plate and *du jour*'s "Petite Lunch"—half a chicken salad sandwich on a sourdough baguette, plus soup or salad, and fruit—are both good choices at $4.95 each.

There are also reasonably priced daily specials, such as *paella* with a salad and roll ($6.95), or a New Orleans-style muffaletta sandwich plate ($4.35). Open from 7 A.M. to 6 P.M. during the week, 8 A.M. to 5 P.M. on Saturdays, and closed on Sundays.

The Elliott Bay Book Company Cafe

- 101 S Main St., Seattle; 682-6664
- *Tip-free*

Downstairs in Pioneer Square's literary landmark, Elliott Bay Books pairs food for the soul with food for your tummy. The simple menu leans toward the quick and healthy "S" fare: soups, salads, and sandwiches. Start with a cup of soup (miso, gazpacho), or a small salad, each $1.75. Add a slab of (for example) mushroom-dill-ricotta quiche for $3.75. Other daily specials may include such hot plates as cheese enchiladas ($3.95). And there are always sandwiches (half $2.75, whole $4.60) like natural smoked turkey, double cheese, hummus, and more.

Not to mention all kinds of delectable pastries, espresso drinks, and teas, as well as wines and beers; linger over these as you read the day's newspapers in the warm and cozy confines of the exposed-brick cellar. Open every day from morning through early evening (the kitchen closes at 9:30 P.M., though drinks are available for an hour or so longer.) EBBC is also one of Seattle's busiest book havens, both for selection and for readings by local and national authors; see the listing under "Entertainment— Readings and Literary Events."

Emmett Watson's Oyster Bar

- Pike Place Market, Seattle; 448-7721

MR. CHEAP'S PICKS
Downtown

✔ **Common Meals**—Fancy, three-course dinners for under $15—and it helps the homeless.

✔ **Gourmet Salad House**— Salads from around the world, sold by the pound.

✔ **Mama's Mexican Kitchen**— Enjoy the colorful, fiesta-type atmosphere; and pay a visit to the Elvis shrine.

✔ **Palomino Cafe Express**— Faster, cheaper side of this ritzy rooftop restaurant and bar.

✔ **Sit & Spin**—As in, do your laundry while you drink your cappuccino, play Trivial Pursuit, or listen to live rock.

It can be a bit tricky to find, tucked into a Pike Place alley, but once you get inside, the interior of Emmett's is very homey—blue wooden booths and checkered curtains create a pleasant country-style atmosphere. The courtyard outside, encircled by a lattice-work fence, has potted trees and flowers for more charm. Take your pick; either place makes a great setting for a tasty and affordable meal.

As the name implies, Emmett's is famous for its oysters. The prices of most shellfish entrees can be high, as they fluctuate with the market. But there are some standards, such as six broiled oysters with parmesan cheese and bacon sauce for $7.95, and the oyster bar special—two oysters on the half shell, three shrimp, a cup of chowder or gazpacho, and bread—all for $5.65. Emmett's house specialties include fish, oysters, or clams 'n chips, each priced under $5. Smoked salmon, served with Havarti cheese and bread, is just $5.95. Such food, at such prices, in such a popular location!

End with a slice of cheesecake for $2. Oh—and absolutely, positively, no credit cards. During the summer, Emmett's is open Mondays through Saturdays, from 11:30 A.M. to 9 P.M., and 'til 6 P.M. on Sundays. Winter hours are from 11:30 to 7 P.M. Mondays through Saturdays, and from 11-5 on Sundays.

The Five Point Cafe
• 415 Cedar St., Seattle; 448-9993
Sitting in the shadow of Chief Seattle at the junction of Fifth, Cedar, and Denny, the aptly named Five Point is a cool little joint—an old-time luncheonette down one side, and a lounge on the other. This makes it somewhat identical to Queen Anne's Mecca Cafe, both of which have been owned by the same family since 1929. The (smaller) wooden Indian behind the cash register seems to have been there just as long.

What makes it so cool? Mr. C can list five points: 1) Breakfast all day. 2) Open all night. 3) Genuine luncheonette counter, stools, and black-and-white tiled floor. 4) Wacky, "we're here to have fun" staff. 5) See the very end of this write-up. Meanwhile, the food is homemade and hearty. Order up a stack of hotcakes and a fried egg, all for $3.75, or an omelette filled with green peppers, zucchini, tomatoes, ham, and three cheeses for $5.95.

Homemade turkey noodle soup, laced with carrots and celery, comes to you in a bowl carved from a loaf of sourdough bread (!) for $4.25. A "Fajita Chicken Burger" ($5.95) is something you won't see every day. There are plenty of regular burgers, grilled cheese sandwiches, and even a meatloaf special (a lean $3.95). Great bottomless cups of coffee, too—but then, you'd expect that here, wouldn't you?

The Five Point is a popular place, and competition for a table can be fierce at times; but everyone manages to scrunch in somehow. Especially for the free, live jazz on Monday nights; see the listing under "Entertainment—Music" for details.

Four Seas Restaurant
• 714 S King St., Seattle; 682-4900
Four Seas, one of the larger and more elegant of the International District's Chinese restaurants, serves up delicious Cantonese and Mandarin dishes. Roasted duck ($5.25), *kung pao* prawns ($9.25), and Mongolian beef ($8.25) are among the fine dishes you'll find on their extensive menu. There are quite a few vegetable dishes too, ranging between $6.50 and $7.25; for that matter, most other entrees can be prepared without meat—just ask. Four Seas is open Mondays through Saturdays, from 10:30 A.M. to 2 A.M., and until midnight on Sundays. Also, *dim sum* is served up daily between 10:30 A.M. and 3 P.M.

Gourmet Salad House
• 621 Third Ave., Seattle; 623-9770
• *Tip-free*
There's a lot more than just lettuce and a sneeze guard here. This salad bar is a parade of tempting treats like teriyaki chicken, beef or spinach lasagna, and potato and pasta salads; plus your basic greens and fresh fruit. These choices change every day, though; don't be surprised if you find something different from the above-mentioned preparations.

The way it works is simple: You pay $3.99 per pound, no matter what you pile on your plate—from Japanese *yaki soba* noodles to black bean chicken, to fresh pineapple. If you'd rather have homemade soup and half a sandwich, that's available too, for $2.99. Check the listing on the wall for the daily menu.

And, even though this place looks small, you don't have to do take-out rather than wait for a table. There's plenty of seating in the loft space upstairs. Catering primarily to office worker bees, Gourmet Salad House is open Mondays through Fridays from 7 A.M. 'til 4 P.M.; it's closed on weekends.

The Green Turtle
• 99 Yesler Way, Seattle; 621-0000
• *Tip-free*
Contrary to whatever its name may suggest, The Green Turtle serves up

cheap Asian cuisine in a hurry. Most people order their food to go from this cafeteria-style restaurant, but there are a few tables if you'd like to stay there.

For $4.95, you can get barbecued beef or pork, an egg roll, fried rice, and beef with broccoli. Or, for $3.95, try the sweet and sour pork or chicken, fried rice, and salad. The Green Turtle is open from 10 A.M. to 8 P.M. Mondays through Saturdays.

Ho Ho Seafood Restaurant
● 653 S Weller St., Seattle; 382-9671
The seafood served at this International District spot is not only fresh, it's alive. It doesn't reach your plate that way (unless you want a new pet—Ho Ho is very accommodating with personalized orders), but you can see the tanks filled with lobsters and other sea critters on your way in.

There are two dining rooms here, both casual but nice. Plenty of bigger tables equipped with lazy-Susans, too, to make large-group dining convenient.

The best deals here are the lunch specials, which include soup and rice with any of several main dishes, each for $4.25. Choose from Mongolian beef, vegetable chow mein, and *kung pao* chicken, among others.

Seafood, of course, is the specialty here. Prices fluctuate with the seasons, but a few remain more or less constant—such as cashew shrimp, oysters sauteed with ginger and scallions, or fresh squid in black bean sauce. These, like most of the regular-menu seafood, range between $8 and $10.

Ho Ho is open Sundays through Thursdays from 11 A.M. to 1 A.M., Fridays and Saturdays, all the way to 3 A.M.

House of Hong
● 409 Eighth Ave. S, Seattle; 622-7997
For some 35 years now, House of Hong has been an International District landmark— a family-run business cooking up tasty and fairly reasonably-priced Chinese cuisine.

The menu includes Hunan and Szechuan dishes, like sesame chicken ($7.95) and spicy *ma pou* bean curd

($5.95). Other Chinese specialties—Peking royal spareribs ($7.50), sea cucumber with black mushrooms ($9.50) and Mandarin crispy beef ($8.50)—are also fine choices, and not that expensive, considering the fact that you're likely to share them anyway.

House of Hong is lavishly decorated, with Chinese arches separating each booth—a nice touch for more private dining. It's open daily, from 11 A.M. to 10 P.M. during the week, and until midnight on the weekends.

Ivar's Acres of Clams
● Pier 54, Alaskan Way, Seattle; 624-6852
● *Tip-free*
Sure Ivar's is (are?) everywhere now. If you stand still long enough, they'll probably build one around you. But this is where it all started back in 1938, folks, and it still offers one of the best deals in town. Not the restaurant itself, that is—where most entrees are well over $10—but the take-out windows along the side.

If you're sightseeing along the waterfront, and looking for an alternative to all those pricey, touristy restaurants, Ivar's take-out is Mr. C's pick. You can walk up to the window, carry away an order of wonderful fish and chips for just $4.29, add a soda for a buck, and still get your choice of indoor or outdoor seating with a waterfront view.

Other choices on the menu include fried salmon and chips, for something a little different, at $4.69; Ivar's trademark fried clams or oysters, served with more of those great fries (each $4.49); and super-fresh clam chowder ($1.39/cup, $2.49/bowl). Indeed, everything Mr. C and his companions tasted was fresh, light, and delicious. You can see by watching the busy kitchen that everything is fried up to order—none of it is made in advance.

As for the seating, there is a permanent covered area filled with picnic tables right next to the take-out stand; but, if you really crave a front-row seat, walk alongside the restaurant (on the left-hand side of the building) and see if any tables are available there. You'll be right out on the water. Oh, and if you can't finish your fries, do what Ivar Haglund himself, founder of the Seattle Gull Society, always preached—feed the seagulls.

Ivar's Salmon House at 401 NE Northlake Way (632-0767), also features an outdoor fish bar. This restaurant is a little different, though—done up in the style of an early Native American trading post, with further salmon choices on the menu. A more convenient, less expensive version of that touristy Tillicum Village thing.

King Cafe
- 723 S King St., Seattle; 622-6373

King Cafe is hardly a royal palace. It may look more like a pauper than a prince on the inside; but, as Mr. C so often points out, don't let appearances deceive you—some of the best Cantonese-style *dim sum* the International District has to offer can be sampled here. For something really exotic, try the *yee chee gow* (shark fin and pork), *gin dau* (deep-fried sweet rice balls with lotus paste), or the *ha gow* shrimp ball; each comes in a small dish of three servings for $1.40. Chow mein ($5.25), won ton and noodle dishes ($2.60 to $5) are also good bets here. King Cafe is closed on Wednesdays, but otherwise it's open from 11 A.M. to 5 P.M. daily.

La Vaca
- 613 Third Ave., Seattle; 622-0154
- 4129 University Way NE, Seattle; 632-4909
- 7910 Green Lake Dr. N, Seattle; 517-2949
- *Tip-free*

That's "The Cow," for those of us not fluent in Spanish. Don't take it personally—go ahead and um, pig out. This busy little take-out joint serves Mexican food in *gigante* portions at low prices. Burritos are $3.25; choose from vegetarian, beef, chicken, or beans and cheese. Large enchiladas and tacos are $1.25, tostadas $2.50. Ordering by number speeds up the process—this is a good pit stop for a cheap, quick, and filling lunch. Stop by between 11 A.M. and 5

P.M., during the week; La Vaca on Third Avenue is closed on the weekends, and the University location is closed Saturdays. The Green Lake restaurant is open seven days.

Macheezmo Mouse Mexican Cafe
- 701 Fifth Ave., Seattle; 382-1730
- 211 Broadway E, Seattle; 325-0072
- 1815 N 45th St., Seattle; 545-0153
- 425 Queen Anne Ave. N, Seattle; 282-9904
- 2028 148th Ave. NE, Bellevue; 746-5824
- 3805 196th Ave. SW, Lynnwood; 744-1611
- *Tip-free*

The '90s mean that even Mexican fast food has gone health-conscious. In fact, Macheezmo Mouse is so serious about it that they print up pamphlets on weight management, diabetic exchanges, heart health—and how their food fits in. Every item on the menu is accompanied by nutritional information: The chicken burrito, for example, has 580 calories, 17% from fat—while the veggie combo salad has 200 calories, 1% from fat. Make your informed decision.

Mr. C was a bit put off by a display of sample platters at the Queen Anne location. It's nice to see the choices before you order, but this food sits out all day, and looks a bit um, *faded* after a few hours. Is this the best way to tout healthy food? Well, most branches just show you photos, a better idea. After ordering and paying at the counter, give your name, and they'll call you once your order is ready.

Most burrito, enchilada, and taco plates are $4, including rice and beans on the side. There are also salads, quesadillas, and a children's menu as well; and nothing on the menu tops $5.25. To add a little kick to your meal, stop by the fixin's bar and try a unique but delicious concoction of spicy-sweet citrus barbecue sauce called Boss Sauce. Beer is available too—draft pints are $2-$3, while a bottle of Bud is $1.75.

Macheezmo Mouse restaurants are spacious, clean, and done up in a brightly colored Southwestern motif. Most have tables both inside and out. These features, plus a few children's items on the menu, make it a good bet for families, as well. Open for lunch and dinner, seven days a week.

Mama's Mexican Kitchen
- 2234 Second Ave., Seattle; 728-MAMA (6262)

A quick glance through Mama's doorway can be deceptive—the plain room with its tiny booths may seem unappealing. But venture in, and you'll discover a colorful labyrinth of rooms, decorated to the hilt in a blend of retro and "south of the border" styles. You can dine like royalty in "The Elvis Room"—a walk-in shrine filled with artwork dedicated to the King; some has even been contributed by patrons in the form of napkin sketches. Viva Las Vegas!

This fun and festive atmosphere is livened up further by the spicy food (not dangerously so) coming out of the kitchen. Chips and salsa arrive before you even see the menu. The average prices for basic entrees stick around $6.50-$7.50; combination platters, starting at $7.25, come with rice, beans, and salad. Choose from such traditional fare as enchiladas, tacos, tamales, tostadas, and burritos. Mexican plates, starting at $5.50, include the same selections but only a single serving, and come with rice and beans. And try a "Screamer" ($4), a mild cheese and sour cream enchilada in a tomato-vegetable sauce. There's quite a lot on Mama's menu, with a variety of single orders and combinations to satisfy any appetite.

Cocktails, wine and beer are available too, ranging from cheap to expensive. A happy hour, from 4 to 6 P.M. Mondays through Fridays, offers well drinks and lime margaritas for $1.75. Mama's is open from 11 A.M. to 10 P.M. Mondays through Thursdays, 'til 11 P.M. Fridays and Saturdays, and from 9 A.M. to 9 P.M. Sundays.

Merchants Cafe
- 109 Yesler Way, Seattle; 624-1515

MR. CHEAP'S PICKS
Pike Place Market

✔ *du jour*—Today's special: Quick, inexpensive continental fare on plastic trays—but with a classy waterfront view.

✔ **Emmett Watson's Oyster Bar**—You don't have to hock the family pearls to get fresh and fabulous seafood here.

✔ **The Pink Door**—Here's a hidden-away Italian gem, with another great view of the bay.

For good food, atmosphere, and a side order of history, Merchants Cafe in Pioneer Square is a must. In one form or another, this pub has been around since 1890, just a year after Seattle burned to the ground (oops). Enjoy dining upstairs by the bar, or downstairs in the arched brick cellar. Remember, this is an old building, so if it's raining out, beware of the skylights—an occasional drop of rain may spice up your order.

A lunch special called the "Square Meal" is just that—very filling and worth the money. For $4.20, you get soup, salad, and half a sandwich. The dinner menu has lots of good values, too, like the $7.95 chicken Dijon with vegetables and cream sauce—served with rolls, more vegetables, and baked potato or pasta. The $5.25 Philly steak sandwich is also a tasty deal—sliced beef, onions, and peppers are piled over cheddar cheese. Soup, salad, or potato chips accompany each sandwich.

Merchants Cafe is open with espressos every morning at 10 A.M., closing at 3 P.M. Sundays and Mondays; 4 P.M. Tuesdays; and 8 P.M. Wednesdays through Saturdays. The hours later in the week tend to vary a bit; be flexible, or call ahead.

Nitelite Restaurant & Bar
- 1926 Second Ave., Seattle; 448-4852

This coffeeshop is the flip-side of a hip late-night hang-out lounge in Belltown. The bar is classic Seattle cool—dark, laid-back with plenty of vinyl-seated booths for secluded conversation. A menu of basic appetizers is served daily until midnight. On the restaurant side next door, you can chow down on classic American diner food for breakfast, lunch, or dinner. And, in the tradition of diner food, it's all good 'n cheap.

Start your day off right with two eggs, two hotcakes, and two strips of bacon or sausage for $3.95. Not enough for ya? Lasso yourself the "Cowboy"—country-fried steak, two eggs, potatoes, and toast for $4.75. And, of course, there's your standard selection of omelettes and pancakes.

Lunch and dinner choices are both available after 11 A.M. These include sandwiches (all under $5), burgers, soups, salads, steaks, seafood, and more. Get a breaded veal cutlet with gravy for $5.25 or a four-piece chicken dinner for $5.75. Each dinner plate includes soup or salad, as well as mashed potatoes, French fries, or hash browns. Another good deal is "George's Famous Fish & Chips," served with fries and cole slaw, for a mere $5.25. Whether you're looking to eat, drink, or just be merry, the Nitelite Restaurant & Bar is open 24 hours a day.

The OK Hotel Cafe
- 212 Alaskan Way S, Seattle; 621-7903

It's not really a hotel anymore, though the creaky old wooden staircase in the middle of this joint must have led to upstairs rooms at one time. Judging by this neighborhood of old, industrial, waterfront warehouses, near Pioneer Square it's probably just as well. The seedy look outside, however, gives way to a funky coffeehouse on the inside—serving up huge breakfasts and lunches, huge art canvases on the two-story walls, and hot music on weekend nights.

The food here is all homemade in a tiny but efficient kitchen right behind the lunch counter (there are spacious booths in the rear half of the restaurant). The menu is an eclectic, world-beat collection of all-American omelettes and sandwiches, mixed with international and vegetarian dishes. Breakfast is served daily until 3 P.M.; have a mushroom, onion, and jack cheese scramble for $4.95, or French toast on thick slices of Italian bread for $3.85.

For lunch or dinner, the OK Burger ($4.95) is a big, juicy handful, topped with lettuce, tomato, and onion on a fresh roll; the price includes your choice of home fries, homemade soup, or a garden salad packed with vegetables. The same price gets you a well-stuffed chicken burrito, served with chips and salsa; add a salad for a total of $5.75. Or, try the Thai fried rice heaped with vegetables and topped with peanut sauce (again $4.95, $5.50 with salad). For lighter appetites, homemade soups are just $2.95 with fresh bread.

The OK has several microbrews on tap, such as Black Butte Porter, with more in bottles. Hoist a few while shooting a game of pool and listening to Dylan; the weekday happy hour, from 4-7 P.M., offers $2 pints in all varieties. On Wednesday through Sunday nights, taped music gives way to live bands (see the listing under "Entertainment—Music"). The OK Hotel Cafe serves food daily from 8 A.M. until 4 P.M. only.

The Old Spaghetti Factory
- 2801 Elliott Ave., Seattle; 441-7724

Here's a rare combination: good value along the waterfront tourist trail. For quality *and* quantity, the Old Spaghetti Factory ranks up there with the best of 'em. It's a big, boisterous, family-oriented restaurant, and feeding the kids here won't gouge a hole in their college fund. The menu, of course, consists of pasta dishes—from spaghetti with mushroom sauce to ravioli to fettucine Alfredo. All the entrees are well under $10, with most in the $6 to $7 price range. The best deals by far are located under the "complete meal" selection; each choice includes salad, fresh baked bread, coffee, tea or milk, plus a spumoni dessert. Basic beers, wines, and cocktails are also available.

The decor in the restaurant is a story in itself. The booths are actually made from the head- and foot-boards of brass and wrought-iron beds. Tiffany-style, fringed fabric lampshades hang close overhead and give a soft light to the otherwise dark dining room; you may *almost* miss the cable car sitting in the middle of the room, which offers additional seating in an even more unlikely setting. This entire, wacky (and hearty) approach has given rise to a national chain of Spaghetti Factories—but this is the original.

It's open Mondays through Thursdays, from 11:30 A.M. to 2 P.M. for lunch, and 5 P.M. to 10 P.M. for dinner (Fridays 'til 11 P.M.). Weekend hours are from noon to 11 P.M. Saturdays, and from noon to 10 P.M. Sundays.

The Owl 'N Thistle
- 808 Post Ave., Seattle; 621-7777

The Owl 'N Thistle is your good ol' neighborhood Irish pub, where "there are no strangers, only friends you have not met." (Insert *Cheers* theme here.)

The menu consists of local and traditional Irish favorites. The most expensive items are eight-ounce steaks ($12.95), like the "Gaelic Steak" made with a flaming Irish whiskey cream sauce. Potatoes (of course), fresh vegetables, salad, and brown bread come with it—you'll certainly be getting your money's worth. Like so many pubs, profits from the bar help keep the food prices low.

Most of the other items, meanwhile, range between $4 and $6. Try the wonderful homemade cottage pie, filled with ground beef, lamb and veggies, and topped with browned mashed potatoes for $4.95; or fish and chips, made with Red Hook beer batter, for $6.25. Playing a game of pool or tapping your feet to live music are after-meal options; stick around and enjoy the fun. See the list-ing under "Entertainment—Music" for more info about the live bands. Open from 11 A.M. to 2 A.M. Mondays through Saturdays, and from noon to 2 A.M. on Sundays.

The Palomino Cafe Express
- 1420 Fifth Ave., Third Floor, Seattle; 623-5752
- *Tip-free*

For a quick, "open-air" version of its parent restaurant, the Palomino, "The Cafe" is a noteworthy alternative. Most importantly, it's less expensive, too. Cafe Express serves its tasty lunches on the top floor of the chic City Centre Building, complete with all the ritzy atmosphere and cool attitude true Cheapsters lust after.

The room consists simply of a counter with tables scattered about the area. Try a $4.95 individual pizza, or a variety of sandwiches, all priced around $5-$6. If you're not here on a lunch break and have some time, relax with a beverage; coffee and a slice of tiramisu, or perhaps something from the Palomino bar, just across the hallway.

The Express is open Mondays through Fridays, from 11:15 A.M. to 3 P.M. only.

Panchito's Restaurant
- 704 First Ave., Seattle; 343-9567
- *Tip-free*

Near Pioneer Square, Panchito's is a pleasant little Mexican restaurant—not just another take-out—with red brick walls and plenty of tables. Order your food in back, sort of fast food style, and bring it to your table. These meals are anything but mass-produced, although they are made quickly, all day long.

All of Panchito's prices are nice and low; the special combinations are truly the best deals. Choose from the "Mini Chimi" and hard taco combo, enchiladas, and tostadas, to name but a few. Any one item is $4.75, two are $6.25, and three are $7.25—and a combo counts as a single item! Each of these combinations comes with rice, beans, and salad. Panchito's is open from 11:30 A.M. to 9 P.M., seven days a week.

Pho Hoa

- 618 S Weller St., Seattle; 624-7189
- 4406 Rainier Ave. S, Seattle; 723-1508

Many of the International District restaurants look their part—but Pho Hoa looks as though it were transplanted here from some trendy, artsy district in New York. Its towering windows reach up to the high ceiling, modern art on the walls is the only decoration, and the food is served in those trendily huge pasta bowls.

Decor aside, Pho Hoa is an authentic Vietnamese restaurant, with prices and food that are equally impressive. Entrees of marinated prawns or grilled pork slices are each $4.25, as is the beef stew with rice noodles. Pork chops grilled with ground lemon grass costs just 25 cents more.

Chopsticks and plenty of sauces are kept on each table. The downtown branch is newer and fancier than its Rainier Valley counterpart; both are open daily from 9 A.M. to 9 P.M.

The Pink Door

- 1919 Post Alley, Seattle; 443-3241

Recipient of many awards (check 'em out in the window), this Italian restaurant in the Pike Place Market could easily go unnoticed, tucked away as it is without even a sign to point folks in its direction. For those who do discover it, this place is a treat.

While the dinner prices hover around Mr. C's $10 per person budget—the most expensive entree is the $14.95 beef tenderloin—pasta dishes sneak in under $10 each. In particular, the spinach lasagna ($9.50) is fabulous. Dining with a view of Elliott Bay is available outdoors on the deck; or, for that old-world European atmosphere, the dining room is decorated with stone cherubs, gilded mirrors, and a gurgling fountain with fresh flowers.

In short, let's call this a Mr. C splurge—because even Cheapsters want something nicer once in a while—say, a restaurant that doesn't use plastic forks. Walk through the Pink Door for lunch or dinner, any day of the week.

Red Robin

- Pier 55, 1101 Alaskan Way, Seattle; 623-1942
- 1100 Fourth Ave., Seattle; 447-1909
- 1600 E Olive Way, Seattle; 323-1600
- 3272 Fuhrman Ave. E, Seattle; 323-0918
- Northgate Mall, Seattle; 365-0933
- 11021 NE Eighth St., Bellevue; 453-9522
- 2390 148th Ave. NE, Bellevue; 641-3810
- 1305 SE Everett Mall Way, Everett; 355-7330
- Sea Tac Mall, Federal Way; 946-TOGO (8646)
- *And other suburban locations*

Red Robin is a popular chain where families, business types, mall creatures, and others all come together for standard American fare. The atmosphere is bright, lively, and convivial. Separate bar areas, fully outfitted for beers and cocktails, include televisions showing various ball games.

The menu is dominated by the "Gourmet Burgers" (the world's greatest, in their humble opinion), in more than a dozen varieties. Try the "Banzai Burger," marinated in teriyaki sauce and topped with grilled pineapple and cheddar cheese ($5.95), or the "Lone Star Burger," with jalapeño jack cheese, salsa, and guacamole ($5.25). Non-carnivores may want to try the "Amazing Meatless Burger," made with veggies and grains ($5.25). In fact, you can have any style made with a meatless patty.

The one-size-fits-all menu also includes soups and sandwiches, entree-sized salads, pastas, and plenty of bar-food appetizers. Red Robin is a safe bet for bringing the gang to munch on wings and nachos. And save room for desserts like mud pie, cheesecake, brownie sundaes, shakes, and root beer floats. There's also a kiddie menu, with half a dozen meals all priced at $2.99 each. Most Red Robins serve food daily until midnight.

Saigon Gourmet

- 502 S King St., Seattle; 624-2611

According to So Luu, the friendly woman who owns the place, this humble gem of a Vietnamese cafe may be changing hands. Hopefully, whoever takes over will keep up the tradition of serving delicious, filling, Vietnamese dishes that are super-cheap.

Atmosphere at this tiny storefront is practically non-existent; half a dozen tables with an open kitchen at the rear. Ms. Luu, a former Boeing employee who decided to run her own (considerably smaller) operation, seems to comprise the entire staff—dashing back and forth between taking folks' orders and the clanging of pots and pans. Of course, this no-frills approach is also reflected in the low prices.

Menu prices start at $3.75 for appetizers (like three fried shrimp rolls with peanut sauce), and go as high as $6.45 for such entrees as broiled pork meatballs. Mr. C especially enjoyed the beef noodle soup with brisket for $3.95. This is a meal in itself—so filling, he could hardly finish it!

End your meal with a cup of strong Vietnamese-style coffee, sweetened with condensed milk for that after-dinner rush. Saigon Gourmet is open Tuesdays through Sundays, from 10 A.M. to 8 P.M. If So Luu is still there, be sure to say hello!

Sit & Spin
- 2219 Fourth Ave., Seattle; 441-9484
- *Tip-free*

Remember all the fun you had twirling around on your "Sit-n-Spin" until you felt like you were gonna lose it? Well, this is the more grown-up version (at least, for the twentysomething set). It's just as sensory-overloading, but without the likelihood of becoming sick to your stomach—unless, of course, you haven't done your wash in four months.

That's right, kiddies, Sit & Spin is part cafe, part laundromat, allowing Belltown apartment dwellers to tackle two vital human needs at the same time. S & S is decorated in a boisterous, neo-1950s style, with a string of lone, escapee socks along the walls of the laundry room, and

old black-and-white television sets spewing forth snowy pictures around the cafe. Board games further enhance the hang-out experience.

The front counter serves up sandwiches—regular, bagel, and focaccia—for under $5, in such varieties as salami pesto, cashew chicken tarragon, and black bean pita. Plus "made from scratch" soups and vegetarian chili from $1.95, and all kinds of "Yum Yums," like warm strawberry shortcake for $2.25. Espresso drinks and teas, as well as fresh-squeezed juices, are also served, along with beer and wine.

The cafe portion opens later and closes earlier than the laundromat. Food is served from 11 to 11, and until 1 A.M. Thursdays through Saturdays. Sit & Spin also presents free live music, comedy, and poetry; see the listing under "Entertainment—Music" for more info.

Sound View Cafe
- Pike Place Market, Seattle; 623-5700
- *Tip-free*

One wall of this cafe is comprised entirely of windows—no, not the Bill Gates variety—and guess what you get a view of? You guessed it. Of course, it's *really* Elliott Bay rather than Puget Sound, but a waterfront view is a waterfront view. And at these prices, who's complaining?

When you first walk in, you'll encounter a salad bar just loaded with greens, fruit, tabouli, *pasta alla Caesar*—lots of nifty choices like that. The small bowl is $2.50, the large is $5. Skilled salad-pilers can make that small bowl go a long way! The hot stuff, meanwhile, is served cafeteria-style just to the right of the salad bar. Homemade soups ($3.95), are created daily, and dished out alongside of entrees like Mexican vegetarian lasagna ($3.75). You can get breakfast here, too. Try a stack of pancakes ($3.75), with a few links of turkey sausage ($1.75).

Sound View is open from 7 A.M. to 5 P.M., Mondays through Saturdays, and from 9 A.M. to 3:30 Sundays.

257

Szechuan Noodle Bowl

- 420 Eighth Ave. S, Seattle; 623-4198

This cozy, American-looking cafe in the International District serves big, heaping bowls of Szechuan noodle dishes at prices that will warm every Cheapster's heart (as well as tummy). Most of the noodle dishes, like their "original" beef noodle with soup, and shredded chicken noodle with soup, are priced at $4.25 for a substantial bowl. Cold dishes include such choices as cold noodles with sesame sauce and vegetables, for a mere $3.95.

Dumplings ($3.95 to $4.50) and hand-made pancakes ($1.95) are also wonderful; ordering both together enhances the flavor and texture of each. Szechuan Noodle Bowl is open from 11:30 A.M. to 8 P.M. Tuesdays through Sundays.

Taco Del Mar

- 705 Madison Ave., Seattle; 467-0603
- 1301 Alaskan Way, Seattle; 233-9457
- 615 Queen Anne Ave. N, Seattle; 281-7420
- 3526 Fremont Pl. N, Seattle; 545-8001
- *Tip-free*

These places are hardly bigger than a taco themselves, but if you're visiting, say, the Queen Anne location, you'd never know it from looking at the large beach scene mural inside—complete with frolicking dinosaurs, an opera diva, mermaids, and a dude named Ray. The crew working here is enthusiastic, the music is loud, the deals are good, and the food is even better.

Batches of guacamole and salsa are made fresh throughout the day. The Jumbo Burrito is filled with beans, rice, salsa, onions, and either chicken, pork, or beef; at just $2.95, your wallet will yell *"Olé!"'* The vegetarian burrito may cost slightly more, but it's still a bargain at $3.50. Nachos, tacos, and all of the other standard Mexican fare are also available, at prices that make it easy to fill up. Taco del Mar is open every day.

Three Girls Bakery

- Pike Place Market, Seattle; 622-1045
- *Tip-free*

You can't sit down and eat at this place; in fact, to paraphrase Gertrude Stein, there's not even a "place" there—unless you count the market itself. Three Girls looks more like one of those drive-up photo developing booths, but it happens to turn out great "to go" food at low prices through its window. Try a Reuben sandwich for $4.60, or a bowl of halibut chowder (!) for $2.15. The breads are great, of course; and their wide assortment of pastries, such as 75¢ cookies, are also especially good. They all make wonderful accompaniments for strolling through the market.

Three Girls is open from 7 A.M. to 6 P.M., seven days a week. Sandwiches are not made past 5:30.

Todo Loco

- 1000 Second Ave., Seattle; 386-7301
- 1501 Fourth Ave., Seattle; 343-0435
- 2101 Fourth Ave., Seattle; 448-2459
- *Tip-free*

There's nothing crazy about making healthy Mexican food, and that's exactly what Todo Loco does. These three small downtown cafes run a take-out business for the most part; but if the weather is nice, you can sit at one of the few tables out front. Try the chicken, veggie, or calimari wraps for $3.59 each. The wraps are whole wheat tortillas, filled with brown rice, lettuce, sprouts, veggies, and salsa—plus your choice from above, and a special peanut sauce or yogurt-cucumber-lime dressing. Whew!

Another satisfying meal is the $4.99 "Maui Burrito." This special burrito consists of a whole wheat tortilla filled with snap peas, shredded carrots, red cabbage, onions, tomatoes, cilantro, and cheddar jack cheese, topped with a warm avocado sauce, and it's all served with brown rice and black beans. Just describing this burrito is a mouthful.

Being a downtown office crowd

kinda place, Todo Loco is open from 7 A.M. to about 4 P.M. Mondays through Fridays. Weekend hours, if any, vary from store to store.

Trattoria Mitchelli

• 84 Yesler Way, Seattle; 623-3883
The owners of this sidewalk cafe/pub-style restaurant believe that good Italian food should be available just about any time of the day or night. Their schedule accommodates this belief, as you can see below.

Not all of Mitchelli's dishes are truly inexpensive—veal marsala, for example, goes for $11.95—but you can do well here on a budget. To get your money's worth, order pizza or calzone—prices range between $5.75 and $7.75. A plate of four-cheese ravioli for $8.75 is also a good choice. There are two dining areas—and children are welcome anywhere but the bar.

Trattoria Mitchelli is open from 7 A.M. all the way to 4 A.M., Tuesdays through Fridays; they open at 8 A.M. on Saturdays and Sundays, and close early, at 11 P.M., on Mondays. Keep in mind that this is Pioneer Square; the later the hour, the wilder the area gets.

Two Bells Tavern

• 2313 Fourth Ave., Seattle; 441-3050
Located in the heart of Belltown, this appropriately named pub serves up a fine selection of beers and wines. But, no sports bar this; the food menu, while limited, offers no chicken fingers or potato skins. Instead, have a bowl of chicken-lime soup for $3; or a hot sausage sandwich ($5.25), a spicy number with mustard and melted Jarlsberg cheese on sourdough bread. Or, perhaps an egg salad-and-almond sandwich with a side of Tim's Cascade chips ($4.95).

They do have burgers here; go for the special, topped with bacon, grilled onions, lettuce, and tomato, all for $5.25. But these are balanced by health-conscious choices like Caesar salads ($4.50 for a large bowl) and a fruit and cheese board (same price). The beers, meanwhile, include such serious micros as Widmer Hefe-weizen and Pike Place Pale Ale, on tap and in bottles. Plus a handful of house wines.

MR. CHEAP'S PICKS
The Waterfront

✔ **Ivar's Acres of Clams**—The take-out stand beside the original restaurant practically gives away its fish 'n chips.

✔ **The OK Hotel Cafe**—Funky spot for breakfast and lunch by day, rock 'n roll by night.

✔ **The Old Spaghetti Factory**—Families love to twirl their forks here, again the home base for a popular chain.

The atmosphere at Two Bells is clean-cut and laid-back, somewhat more refined than some of its grunge-era neighbors. Live music is offered on Monday nights at 9 P.M.; live poetry readings take place on the second and fourth Sundays of the month. There is no cover charge for any of the entertainment. Now, *that's* music to Mr. C's ears.

Union Square Grill

• 621 Union St., Seattle; 224-4321
The Union Square Grill is definitely "suited" to this ritzy, downtown locale; professional types completely fill this vast restaurant around the noon hour. If you show up looking for a quick lunch, it may take a moment to get over the feeling you've walked in on a convention of power-tie purveyors.

No, the Union Square Grill isn't cheap—burgers are $6—but if you're down here doing the corporate thing, this classy and crowded place will at least fill you up for under $10, and give you your money's worth (in food as well as flash). It's a good bet for impressing your peers without going too far beyond your means.

Mr. C especially enjoyed a cup of the soup of the day, which was broccoli and cheddar, along with a ham and Havarti cheese half-sandwich. This combo was $6.75, and a basket of warm sourdough bread came with it. Keep in mind that these are lunch prices—dinners generally are even more expensive. But you do get a good amount of food. And besides, if you come here for dinner, you'll miss all that networking fun.

During the week, Union Square Grill is open for lunch from 11 A.M. to 3 P.M., then dinner from 5 P.M. to 10 P.M. (to midnight on Fridays). On the weekends, only dinner is served, starting from 4:30 P.M.

VICI Galleria-Caffe
● 2218 First Ave., Seattle; 443-0707
Not just another take-out joint, this Belltown establishment is a full-scale pizza restaurant. The walls are decorated with locally-produced artwork, eye-catching displays such as torn-paper collages or photography, which changes every couple of months.

VICI serves up a pretty big deal on Tuesdays, when all pizza slices are just $2 each. That's one price, no matter how many toppings you request. However, if you crave a whole pie, hold out for the Thursday take-out special—order a large three-topping pizza, and pay only $10.99. And these pies are good stuff, too. Come, see, and conquer, Mondays through Thursdays from 7 A.M. to 9 P.M.; Fridays, 7 A.M. to 2

A.M.; and Saturdays, 11 A.M. to 2 A.M.

World Class Chili
● 1411 First Ave., Seattle; 623-3678
● *Tip-free*
Many Seattle dining critics have praised World Class Chili, as evidenced by the reviews on display; well, here's one more endorsement. This chili is indeed delicious, filling, suprisingly healthy, and—most important to Mr. C—relatively inexpensive.

Their stew of the gods comes in several different styles. "Texas" is comprised of beef with five kinds of chili peppers; "Cincinnati" has beef and pork with a touch of chocolate and cinnamon; and, not to leave anyone out, there's a vegetarian blend, too.

Served over your choice of tiny shell pasta, brown rice, pinto or black beans, or any combination of these, portions come in three sizes—and this may get confusing: "Texas" for $3.92 (just under a pint), "Alaska" for $6.88 (just over a pint), and a quart for $13.76. Sorry, quarts don't qualify for statehood.

Plain old, straight-ahead chili—just meat and sauce—costs a bit more: The same sizes are $6.88, $13.76, and $27.52, respectively. Buying in quantity doesn't always mean paying less! World Class Chili is open from 11 A.M. to 6 P.M., Mondays through Saturdays; it's closed on Sundays.

EASTLAKE AREA
(including Lake Union, Madison Park, Montlake)

Attic Alehouse & Eatery
● 4226 E Madison St., Seattle; 323-3131
Given the primarily yupscale surroundings in Madison Park, you might not expect to find a place like the Attic, which feels like a college hangout for the upper half of the twentysomething crowd. There are 17 drafts on tap (lots of local micros

and imports), 15 more in bottles, plus darts, and half a dozen TVs around the room. The joint itself *looks* like an attic, with its big wooden ceiling beams and plenty of clutter collected over the forty years it's been here.

Meanwhile, there is a decent-sized menu of pub-style food: burgers, sandwiches, and salads, all of which will keep you full for a good long time. And yet these are inexpensive, with nothing on the menu topping $8. Try "The Attic," their basic burger, for $4.95 or, for heartier appetites, "The Cluttered Attic," topped with grilled onions, Havarti, bacon, and homemade guacamole for $6.75.

Other sandwiches include a BLT on sourdough ($5.45); grilled pastrami and Swiss on rye ($5.95); and a vegetarian sandwich with Havarti, cucumber, lettuce, tomato, and guacamole ($4.95). These big, homemade sandwiches get nice and messy. They're served in a basket with the always wonderful Tim's Cascade Potato Chips. And don't miss out on another bar staple, chili—homemade and hearty at $4 a bowl.

The Attic also has nightly dinner specials which are great values. Mondays offer all-you-can-eat spaghetti, with salad and garlic bread, for $4.95; on Wednesdays, you can get a New York steak with potatoes and salad for $8.95. During the warm and dry summer months there's a handful of tables on the sidewalk in front of the restaurant, a good idea if the bar is too crowded. The place also opens up for breakfast on weekends, with lots of brunchy stuff starting under five bucks. The kitchen serves food until 11 P.M. on weekdays, 'til midnight on Fridays and Saturdays.

Benji's Fish and Chips

- 809 Fairview Pl. N, Seattle; 624-5709
- *Tip-free*

Why dine on pricey seafood at Benjamin's, when you can go around the back to their take-out stand, and be even closer to the boats on Lake Union? Well, it could be raining, for one thing. But, especially in summer, this is a fine way to dine *al fresco* as well as *al cheapo*.

A tugboat-shaped booth serves up terrific fried foods in various quantities. A "single" order of fish and chips is only $2.99, ranging up to $5.19 for a triple. Inside at Benjamin's, a standard F & C plate goes for nine bucks! There are also a few interesting variations here, like Cajun

popcorn (fried crawfish) and chips for $4.49. Add a cup of clam chowder for $1.89; wash it all down with Thomas Kemper root beer, Starbucks coffee, or Red Hook beer.

Benji's offers a patio of umbrella-covered tables for your dining pleasure. But why not stroll around the lakefront a bit, and find a quiet spot on a dock somewhere. Watch the crew restoring the *Wawona* at the Center for Wooden Boats, right next to the restaurant. Gaze wistfully at the expensive sailboats in the marina, comforted by the knowledge that your tasty-yet-thrifty meal will get you to your first million that much sooner. Benji's is open from 11:30 A.M. to 8 P.M. daily.

Eastlake Cafe

- 601 Eastlake Ave. E, Seattle; 621-9811
- *Tip-free*

With a gigabyte's worth of coffeehouses in Seattle (most of which seem to be in the Capitol Hill area), Mr. C is hardly about to evaluate them all; most have similar offerings and prices, anyway. So, what makes the Eastlake an exception? How about espressos for 85¢ ("all our shots are doubles"), plus muffins, scones, and brownies at a dollar apiece. Ah, *that's* gotten your attention.

Yep, those are the going rates at this prototypical grunge den (sure, we've moved on from grunge in our minds, but we still have it with our coffee). Cut off from the rest of the Hill by good ol' Route 5, this cafe boldly stakes out its own territory, undaunted by its relative inaccessibility. A steady clientele finds its way here not just for sweets, but for hearty food as well: $2 Caesar salads, or a bowl of homemade soup for $1.35. A full slate of well-stacked deli sandwiches ranges from $1.75-$4.75, with your choice of breads and extras.

There are also a few bigger specialty items. Would you believe, a plate of salmon-filled ravioli, served with garlic bread and a salad, all for $7? This menu takes "eclectic" to a goofy new high. "Hotdogs—the infamous meat-filled tuber," it proffers.

The coffee itself is said to be "great with cigarettes." It all fits in perfectly with the grubby charm of the place, with the requisite mismatched couches, old magazines, games, etc.

The Eastlake Cafe even delivers in the Lake Union area (which it technically belongs to; it just *feels* more like East Pike than Eastlake). And, one Saturday a month, they host an open-mike cabaret at 9:30 P.M., with a $5 cover charge. *Now* you see why Mr. C is making all the fuss. The cafe opens on weekdays at 7:30 A.M., weekends at 10 A.M.; it closes at 10 P.M. Sundays through Thursdays, and at midnight on Fridays and Saturdays.

Through the cafe, you'll also find the entrance to **Theatre Babylon**, which offers shows of its own; see the listing under "Entertainment—Theater" for the full scoop.

14 Carrot Cafe
● 2305 Eastlake Ave. E, Seattle; 324-1442

Okay yupsters, gather 'round, and get yourself over to this Eastlake spot, if you haven't tried to fight your way in already. It's an extremely popular place, and with good reason. You get a ton of food here; big portions of comfort food that you'll have trouble finishing, but you won't have much trouble paying for. The atmosphere here is certainly not refined by any stretch. It's fun and raucous, and worth the wait.

The hardest time to get in is weekend brunch—especially on Sundays, when folks bring the newspaper and pig out on omelettes, waffles, and all kinds of other heavy treats. You can get two eggs with bacon and a bagel on the side for $4.75. Or, build your own omelette: the basic price is $4.50, to which you may add a variety of fillings for 50¢ to $1.25 each. All omelettes come with grilled potatoes and bread.

Truly an update on the classic coffee shop, many of 14 Carrot's breakfast offerings are available throughout the day. If you prefer something more closely associated with the noon hour, the lunch menu includes huge salads, soups, and big-time sandwiches. Mr. C likes the "Cranberry Turkey," fresh sliced turkey topped with cranberry sauce, cream cheese, tomatoes, and sprouts. At $4.95, it's all of Thanksgiving between two slices of bread. Other sandwich choices include grilled ham and Swiss; and pita chicken, also $4.95. The 14 Carrot Cafe is open for breakfast and lunch seven days a week; they close up at 3 P.M. weekdays, 4 P.M. on weekends.

Grady's Pub & Eatery
● 2307 24th Ave. E, Seattle; 726-5968

The roast beef *au jus* sandwiches once served up at a place called Kelly's on this Montlake corner are the stuff of legend—especially to thousands of baby-boomers who attended UW or who grew up in the area. Grady's carries on the tradition, having acquired the recipe for Kelly's "secret" dipping sauce. It's part of a varied menu of tavern fare available at this comfy neighborhood joint.

Alas, prime rib is "dear," as folks used to say; at $10.95 (or $6.95 for a half-sandwich), the Kelly special is good, but not exactly cheap. Fresh burgers are a better deal, starting at $4.75 (plus $1.25 for a heap of hand-cut fries). There are even lamb and vegetarian burgers, not to mention whole chicken breast, salmon and Alaskan halibut; all of these are in the $5-$6, served with potato chips unless you ask for the fries.

There are lots of salads and home-made soups, unusual for a pub; but then, Grady's is much more clean, spacious, and laid-back than your average watering hole—as befits this gentrified locale. Plenty of appetizers, of course, from nachos and salsa ($5.95) to "Jalapeño Poppers" ($4.95), mild deep-fried pepper halves with a cheese filling. And there's a goodly variety of brews to wash it all down—a dozen local micros on tap (even Ballard's rarely-seen Maritime Ale), plus Blackthorne cider, and much more in bottles from around the world. Also several non-alcs, as well as Kemper's root beer

on tap; and an extensive wine list
(save 20% off bottle prices on Mondays and Tuesdays!).

What more could anyone ask?
Well, how about free pool (two tables, free from 2-5 P.M. daily) and big-
screen TVs for sports. With UW right
across the bridge, Grady's is a popular spot indeed. And yet, it gets couples and families too, with big, a
non-smoking area, and a separate
children's' menu (kids are welcome
until 7 P.M.).

Pazzo's
- 2307 Eastlake Ave. E, Seattle;
  329-6558

Next door to the 14 Carrot Cafe (see
above), Pazzo's is the creation of several chefs from the ever-popular
Cucina! Cucina! who sought a place of
their own to serve more casual Italian-
style food. Basically, that means pizzas
and calzones, but with a twist: exotic
toppings and fillings like marinated
chicken, pesto, and artichoke hearts.
And it worked—Pazzo's is a big hit.

Calzones, all priced at $6.95,
come with a green salad or a pasta
salad. Try the "Vatican," filled with
pepperoni, salami, artichoke hearts,
tomatoes, ricotta, provolone, and parmesan cheeses; or the "Caruso" with
hot Italian sausage, green peppers,
red onions, ricotta, mozzarella, and
gorgonzola cheeses. The pizzas range
from simple, like the "Margharita"
with fresh basil, roma tomatoes, fresh
mozzarella, and sauce ($8.25), to
complex, like the "Prato" with pesto,
artichoke hearts, tomatoes, mozzarella, feta, and parmesan cheeses
($8.75). Mmmm.

European-style focaccia sandwiches, antipasta, and salads round out
the menu. It's all in a friendly, lively atmosphere that characterizes this yuppie
Eastlake enclave. Pazzo is open seven
days; hours vary, so call ahead.

Red Robin
- 3272 Fuhrman Ave. E, Seattle;
  323-0918
- 1600 E Olive Way, Seattle;
  323-1600
- Pier 55, 1101 Alaskan Way, Seattle;
  623-1942

**MR. CHEAP'S PICKS
Eastlake Area**

✔ **The Attic**—Great burgers,
dinners, and beers, near the
water in Madison Park.

✔ **Eastlake Cafe**—Vast amounts
of food for almost no money,
and "every espresso shot is a
double."

✔ **14-Carrot Cafe**—Popular
yuppie hangout, especially for
weekend brunch.

- 1100 Fourth Ave., Seattle; 447-1909
- Northgate Mall, Seattle; 365-0933
- 11021 NE Eighth St., Bellevue;
  453-9522
- 2390 148th Ave. NE, Bellevue;
  641-3810
- 1305 SE Everett Mall Way,
  Everett; 355-7330
- Sea Tac Mall, Federal Way;
  946-TOGO (8646)
- *And other suburban locations*

Red Robin is a popular chain where
families, business types, mall creatures, and others all come together
for standard American fare. The atmosphere is bright, lively, and convivial. Separate bar areas, fully outfitted
for beers and cocktails, include televisions showing various ball games.

The menu is dominated by the
"Gourmet Burgers" (the world's
greatest, in their humble opinion), in
more than a dozen varieties. Try the
"Banzai Burger," marinated in teriyaki sauce and topped with grilled
pineapple and cheddar cheese
($5.95), or the "Lone Star Burger,"
with jalapeño jack cheese, salsa, and
guacamole ($5.25). Non-carnivores
may want to try the "Amazing
Meatless Burger," made with veggies
and grains ($5.25). In fact, you can
have any style made with a meatless
patty.

The one-size-fits-all menu also includes soups and sandwiches, entree-sized salads, pastas, and plenty of bar-food appetizers. Red Robin is a safe bet for bringing the gang to munch on wings and nachos. And save room for desserts like mud pie,

cheesecake, brownie sundaes, shakes, and root beer floats. There's also a kiddie menu, with half a dozen meals all priced at $2.99 each. Most Red Robins serve food daily until midnight.

EASTSIDE
(including Bellevue, Kirkland, Mercer Island, Redmond)

Beach Cafe
- 1270 Carillon Point, Kirkland; 889-0303

Part of the sprawling complex which includes the pricey Yarrow Bay Grill and the Woodmark Hotel, the Beach Cafe is the less expensive dining alternative on the block—yet it's no less picturesque. Situated right on Lake Washington, you get spectacular water and sunset views (assuming, of course, that there is a sunset to see...), whether you're inside or on the deck which juts out into the marina.

So, you can feel like you're part of the sailor set here, even if you can barely afford a down-payment on a dinghy. The cafe is a lively restaurant-and-bar which attracts a handsome singles scene—especially with a happy hour that offers all appetizers at $2.25, along with various cocktail deals. Times vary by season; call them for details.

The menu itself ranges from big sandwiches like sliced turkey breast and Havarti with French fries, or a "Thai Tuna Burger" (each $6.95) to full seafood entrees like pan-fried oysters ($9.95). Most of the latter will put you well over Mr. C's $10 limit, though. Pasta dishes provide a happy medium: Smoked salmon fettucine and seafood linguine are both available in half portions for $8.95, or full portions for $10.95.

Meat entrees are also at the higher end of the menu, though you can lin-

ger over "Santa Fe Chicken Stew" ($6.95)—sauteed pieces of chicken breast, potatoes and corn in a tomato-jalapeño sauce. Mmmm. Plenty of soups and salads, too, as well as sinful desserts.

In other words, while this is not the least expensive joint in Mr. C's book, there are certainly enough budget-priced choices (to help offset the exorbitant drink prices), and the gorgeous setting just can't be beat. Carillon Point can be found just off of Lake Washington Blvd., north of Route 520. Open for lunch and dinner seven days a week, as well as breakfast on Sundays from 9 A.M. to noon.

Big Time Pizza
- 7281 West Lake Sammamish Pkwy. NE, Redmond; 885-6425
- *Tip-free*

Here's a real find in the pizza biz. These are no ordinary pies; they are hand-thrown, with homemade sauces, and an unusual range of fresh toppings from smoked chicken to artichoke hearts. Yet, it's all casual and affordable, tucked away in a strip mall just off Route 520.

Pies are made in two sizes, starting as low as $6.50 for an eight-inch individual pizza with three cheeses. Fourteen-inchers start at $12. But why stick with the basics? Try the "Smokehouse Sizzle," topped with smoked pork loin, peppers and onions, and a tangy barbecue sauce. Or, head for "The Caribbean," made with Jamaican jerk-style chicken, garlic, cashews, fontina cheese, and mango salsa.

You get the idea—pizza doesn't just mean tomato and mozzarella anymore. There are two dozen exotic varieties on the menu, which maxes out at $19.95 for a large "Pacific Rim," topped with prawns, sun-dried tomatoes, two cheeses, garlic and ginger oil. The large sizes are easy enough for two people to split, especially with all that stuff on top. There are salads to fill out a meal, as well as house wines and microbrew beers. They even have draft root beer on tap—and all sodas include free refills!

The decor calls to mind an old-time ice cream parlor, rather than a pizza parlor; it's bright and lively, with a covered patio at the rear. Open for lunch and dinner daily.

Brenner Brothers
- 12000 Bellevue-Redmond Rd., Bellevue; 454-0600
- *Tip-free*

This Eastside bakery and delicatessen will almost make you feel as if you've been transported to the Lower East Side of New York City. Half the place is a food store, with breads baked on the premises, meats, and Jewish specialty groceries. At the other end, traditional delicacies like matzoh ball soup and chopped liver sandwiches on rye bread are served up in an otherwise charmless coffee shop with cafeteria-style service and Formica tables (*that's* New York!). Basic sandwiches at $4.85, including corned beef, pastrami, liverwurst, and more.

For hearty appetites, the "Big Macher" ($6.95) doesn't quite match the mile-high sandwiches at Manhattan's Carnegie Deli, but it comes darn close. Other sandwiches to try: "Saucy Big Bird, " turkey and coleslaw with Russian dressing ($5.25); and the "Brenner's Club Sandwich" with corned beef, pastrami, and turkey ($6.95). And don't miss the cheese or apple blintzes (two for $3.35). Brenner's is not bad for a simple and quick breakfast or lunch, on the way to or from downtown Bellevue. They're open from early

morning until 6 P.M., seven days a week.

Brief Encounter
- 2632 Bellevue Way NE, Bellevue; 822-8830

Contrary to what some newcomers may think, Bellevue isn't all glass-and-steel. It's origins are much humbler, and these can still be found once you get away from downtown and the sprawling shopping centers. Take this strip-mall coffee shop, for example.

Despite its cutesy name, Brief Encounter is your basic luncheonette, small and cozy, with lace curtains for a bit of country-style decor. They serve up hearty homemade soups (Mr. C loved a bowl of turkey rice and vegetable soup, just $1.75), simple sandwiches, and blue-plates. Rustle up a country-fried steak or a boneless veal platter, each $4.95, including salad or soup. Burgers are the basic flat griddle variety, from $2.95. And the pasta special on Mr. C's visit was fettucine, $4.25 with soup or salad.

Do save room for a slice of homemade boysenberry pie and coffee afterwards. This may be the only place in all of Seattle that *doesn't* serve espresso—and probably proud of it. They cook up standard breakfasts, too. Open every day but Sunday, from 6 A.M. to 3:30 P.M.; they close up a little earlier on Saturdays.

Capons Rotisserie Chicken

- Factoria Square Mall, Bellevue; 649-0900
- 17122 Redmond Way, Redmond; 882-4838
- 605 15th Ave. E, Seattle; 726-1000
- 1815 N 45th St., Seattle; 547-3949
- *Tip-free*

Rotisserie chicken has become the hottest (no pun intended) fast-food craze of the '90s. This is probably because chicken is one meal that can be made as efficiently as any fast-food fare, yet still be whole, real, and recognizable; it's as close to home cooking as you'll find in any chain. Every major city seems to have spawned a local version, and this is Seattle's.

Service is cafeteria-style. Grab a tray and choose your main dish and side items along the counter. Even so, Capon's is comfortably decorated with tiled kitchen walls, earthy colors, and lots of plants. Also, as in the coffeehouses, daily newspapers are usually lying around for you to read if you wish. Nice touch.

As for the food, well, the name says it all. The chicken is quite good; you can order it *a la carte* (quarter, half, or whole); or as a complete dinner, which adds cornbread muffins and a choice of two side dishes. These include mashed potatoes and gravy, seasonal vegetables, sage stuffing, or a tossed green salad. A half-chicken dinner goes for $5.95, while a complete dinner for a family of four is $19.95. A child's chicken dinner is available for $2.95.

Capons also offers salads, sandwiches, soups, and other specialties, like a tasty chicken pot pie, individually sized at $3.95. Couple of sweets for after dinner, too. Open daily from 11 A.M. to 10 P.M.

Casa D's

- 102 Bellevue Way NE, Bellevue; 462-8410
- 2429 Second Ave., Seattle; 448-6678
- *Tip-free*

Casa D's portions are *muy grande*, while the prices are *pequeño*. The menu accurately boasts that every item is a meal. And, even though some items on the menu (like the taco salads, $5.45) may be fried, Casa D's is at least nominally concerned for your health. Select an apple or orange from a basket on the counter for your dessert.

Mr. C especially enjoyed a picadillo burrito, stuffed with shredded beef, Monterey jack cheese, rice, beans, fresh tomato salsa, green salsa, and sour cream. Saying all that is a mouthful—imagine eating it! The whole thing costs $4.25, plus 50 cents extra if you want to add some guacamole. A super burrito, rolled with two flour tortillas, is just $5.95.

Seating inside looks like an upscale fast-food joint, but there's plenty of room if you do want to sit and eat there. Otherwise, it's a good take-out place. Open seven days, from 11 A.M. to 8 P.M.

Coco's Family Restaurant

- 530 112th Ave. NE, Bellevue; 453-8138
- 14804 NE 24th St., Redmond; 746-7510
- 17535 Ballinger Way NE, Lake Forest Park; 364-8910

Even though this looks like the sort of place you'd find in the lobby of a Holiday Inn anywhere in America, Coco's does make a lot of its own food and they bake their own scrumptious desserts. Mr. C wasn't terribly impressed with the fast-food-type lunch and dinner items, which were also not particularly cheap. Breakfasts, along with those desserts, are the standouts here.

Morning choices run the gamut from traditional, artery-clogging platters of eggs and bacon to healthier choices like oatmeal and fresh fruit. Weekdays from 6 to 11 A.M., a mere $2.99 will get you two eggs any style, sausage, and two pancakes—with free orange juice refills! Health-conscious morning folks will want "Coco's Low Cholesterol Breakfast" with a choice of hot or cold cereal, fruit or juice, whole wheat toast, and coffee or tea, all for $4.49. Omelettes can be made with three eggs or an egg substitute. Coco's even has a selection of "Senior Breakfasts," for those 55 and older, all priced under $4.

Now, let's skip over lunch and dinner and go straight to the pies. The various incarnations include the traditional fruit fillings (apple, cherry), the traditional whips (banana cream, lemon meringue), and the seasonal favorites (key lime, pumpkin). Also available are specialty pies like pecan, tollhouse, double chocolate silk, and chocolate truffle crunch. *Yum.* A slice of pie runs $2.25 to $3.25, or 80¢ more *a la mode.* Whole pies are also available; Coco's will bake one for you in an hour. Open seven days a week from early morning through late evening.

Fresh Choice
- 1733 Northup Way, Bellevue; 822-2548
- Northgate Mall, Seattle; 440-8136
- Sea Tac Mall, Federal Way; 941-3860
- *Tip-free*

One of the cleanest, brightest, and spiffiest of the shopping center buffet restaurants, these are (as of this writing) the only Northwest outposts of this California chain. But, before you give it the la-la-land snub, give it a try. You'll find food that is both fast and healthy—an overwhelming choice of salads, soups, pastas, and fixings. It's the G.C. (Gastronomically Correct) answer to the King's Table chain.

Everything here is "made from scratch" using all natural ingredients; many items are available in low-fat or non-fat versions, with color-coded name tags (everything here is clearly labeled, with ingredients listed out). And one price, $7.25, covers all the food you want—including seconds. Children pay half of that, and kids under five eat free.

Grab a tray! The first display is the lengthy salad bar, which includes prepared salads such as Caesar and Chinese almond. Or, make up your own creation from literally dozens of fresh vegetables, dressings, and toppings. This could be enough for some

appetites, but oh, there's more! Move on to the baked potato bar for a spud heated up with your choice of stuffings; the pasta bar, where you can slather sun-dried tomato cream sauce on linguine or cheese tortellini; the soup bar, with different homemade selections daily, like Southwestern corn chowder and Cajun black bean; and the bread/muffin table, which even has crispy slices of cheese pizza (we need this too?). Oh yeah, and you can help yourself to desserts, from fruits to "Chocolate Decadence" brownies.

Needless to say, it's not hard to get your money's worth; it's just hard to finish it all. Empty tables with lots of food left behind show folks' tendency to order with dazzled eyes. How can the place stay in business with so much waste? Well, they do get you with the drinks, which cost extra—how 'bout $1.75 for a bottle of apple juice—but, if you're a hearty eater, things should still work out in your favor. Those drinks include bottled wines, wine coolers, and beers, by the way.

The atmosphere is as refined as you'll see at any shopping mall. The large dining room is carpeted. White walls are decorated with framed art prints. Classical music plays in the background. A busy staff keeps the place spotless, bussing tables promptly (if you get up for seconds, there's a "Be Right Back" card). In all, this could be the healthiest pig-out you'll ever have. Open daily, with mall hours.

Hoffman's Fine Pastry
- 226 Kirkland Parkplace, Kirkland; 828-0926
- *Tip-free*

For a simple, quick meal while shopping in this popular Eastside mall, Mr. C recommends Hoffman's not just for its pastry and coffee—worthy of a pit stop or a whole trip—but for light breakfasts and lunches.

There are several specials daily. In the morning, it may be two steamed eggs with herb butter, along with fresh fruit, yogurt, and a croissant, all for $4.50. In the afternoon, you may opt for a turkey and cheddar cheese sandwich on sourdough bread ($3.75), or a bowl of soup and a fresh roll (wild rice, for example, $2.75). Plus quiches and salads, all fresh and homemade daily. One gripe: The quiche (a yummy spinach, Swiss cheese, and red onion during Mr. C's visit) is sliced up in advance and heated in the microwave for a fast but mushy result. Shame!

No such fumbles, though, with the pastries—from biscotti (only 60 cents apiece!) to big croissants (95¢) to gooey "Pecan Triangles" ($1.25). Loaves of whole wheat bread are $1.75. There's also a "day-old" basket by the door, which may yield even better bargains. It's all in a sedate, refined atmosphere, with bus 'em yourself tables; a quiet oasis if you've overdosed on shopping. Hoffman's is located around the side, across from the QFC. Open daily until 8 P.M., closing earlier on Sundays.

Hunan Garden

- 11814 NE Eighth St., Bellevue; 451-3595

Just east of downtown Bellevue, in an area (literally) on the other side of the tracks, you'll find this fabulous Chinese restaurant. Unassuming from the outside, in a parking lot shared with an older strip-mall and the Pumphouse pub (see below), Hunan Garden is in fact rather elegant on the inside. The glassed-in dining room looks a bit like a greenhouse. The formally dressed waiters are extremely attentive, and quick to serve you; yet the prices here are quite reasonable. You'll *feel* like you spent much more—and isn't that the idea? says Mr. C.

Most entrees are under $8; try sliced chicken with broccoli ($7.75), Hunan-style pepper steak ($7.95), or sweet and sour pork ($7.50). Specialty dishes and seafood entrees are a bit more expensive, but still not outrageous. If you feel like a splurge, try sliced lamb Hunan-style, sauteed shrimp with in wine sauce (each $8.95), or "Camphor Wood and Tea Smoked Duck" ($9.50).

Three- or four-course complete dinner specials, priced for groups, start as low as $10 per person—and no one should go hungry. Hunan Garden's quick lunch specials are only $4.95 and include soup, fried wontons, fried rice, and an entree. Even if you aren't interested in the specials, you'll save by eating before 3:00; all the lunch dishes are about two bucks cheaper than the dinner versions. Hunan Garden is open seven days a week.

Izzy's Pizza

- 12301 120th Ave. NE, Kirkland; 820-9279
- 10117 Evergreen Way, Everett; 355-3207
- 20500 108th Ave. SE, Kent; 859-0950

Buffet restaurants have become big business in the suburbs around Seattle. This chain, spreading throughout Washington and Oregon, offers a new twist: pizza meets salad bar. There is a brief menu, from which you can choose your pie (starting as low as $2.95 for an individual pan pizza); the menu also includes a couple of sandwiches, soups, and pastas. Then, there's a salad bar, brimming with greens, vegetables, fruits, dressings, prepared salads, soups, and even desserts. Finally, there is also a hot buffet of pizza slices, fried and barbecued chicken, side dishes like baked beans and roasted potatoes, and Izzy's very popular warm cinnamon buns.

Confusing? Mr. C thought so, too. But wait—here come the dining options and combinations! Now. . . . You can have a pizza. You can have the salad bar, once through or in unlimited trips. You can have one pass through the salad bar and all the pizza you can eat. You can have just the chicken and potatoes. Or, for the total pig-out, you can have the hot buffet, which includes pizza and chicken, plus unlimited trips to the salad bar. And this doesn't even get to the different *kinds* of pizza, like Five-Cheese, Western BBQ Chicken, and Hawaiian Supreme, each in three sizes.

Talk about one-restaurant-fits-all. Well, it seems daunting, but apparently it works, especially with the family crowd. The prices sure help: The hot buffet/salad bar deal, which offers the most diversity, costs $5.95 per person at lunch and $6.95 at dinner. In fact, no buffet option here costs more than that—just add the drinks (sodas and beers are both available by the glass or pitcher). Made-to-order pizzas, of course, go higher; most range from about $6 to $16, depending on the toppings and size. For chain restaurant pizza, they're not bad.

Whichever way you go, you can feed an army—or anybody who eats like one—without increasing the defense budget. Open daily for lunch and dinner.

Jalisco Mexican Restaurant
- 115 Park Lane, Kirkland; 822-3355
- 1467 E Republican St., Seattle; 325-9005
- 122 and 129 First Ave. N, Seattle; 283-4242
- 8517 14th Ave. S, Seattle; 767-1943
- 12336 31st Ave. NE, Seattle; 364-3978

A shop owner of Mexican extraction told Mr. C to be sure to include Jalisco, for truly authentic regional food. Named for one of that country's more scenic states, this restaurant upholds that tradition of beauty—at least one branch sports a wall mural depicting a village center, complete with guitarist serenading a dancing couple by a fountain. Piñatas and plants are perched high above, and high-backed booths provide a secluded dining experience.

Try one of the huge "Especiáles de la Casa," like the chimichangas or enchiladas rancheras, for $7.55 each. All of these specialties are served with rice and beans, making for a gigantic plateful. For the lighter appetite, a single tamale ($2.65) or taco salad ($4.50) will do you right.

Be sure to try something with Jalisco's homemade *mole* sauce; usually made from unsweetened chocolate (yes, for dinner), these folks make it as a nifty peanut sauce instead. If you're not entirely familiar with such native culinary terms, there's a helpful glossary on the back of the menu.

The First Avenue location, just out-

side Seattle Center, has recently spawned a quicker-fare "taqueria" right across the street; the Lake City location adds a cocktail lounge. All branches are open daily from 11 A.M. to 10 P.M., and to 11 P.M. on Fridays and Saturdays.

King's Table
- 4111 Wheaton Way, Bremerton; (360) 377-7044
- 137 SW 160th St., Burien; 244-1883
- 3802 Broadway, Everett; 252-6555
- 12120 NE 85th St., Kirkland; 828-3811
- 1545 NW Market St., Seattle; 784-8955
- *Tip-free*

Perhaps the lowest in overall quality of the Seattle area's many buffet restaurants, King's Table nevertheless offers a ton of food for the money. Dinners cost $6.99 per person (lunches about a dollar less), payable at the beginning of what is basically a cafeteria line. KT also offers a "Gold Card" for $1, allowing you to then save 50¢ on every visit; and Thursday is "Family Night," when kids under 12 pay just 39¢ for every year of their age.

The food is adequate, centering on such entrees as fried chicken, fish and chips, and hand-carved roast beef; along with these are a salad bar, side dishes, taco shells and fillings, and basic desserts, including a do-it-yourself soft ice cream machine. They also serve a breakfast buffet, priced at $4.99. King's Table cer-

269

tainly fits the bill for families and for
seniors, who can have a fixed-income
night on the town. Open daily.

Kirkland Roaster & Ale House
- 111 Central Way NE, Kirkland;
  827-4400

A big, rambling neighborhood-style
bar and pub, the Kirkland Roaster &
Ale House is a boisterous weekend
hangout near the Kirkland marina. The
full bar offers 19 taps with various microbrews, like Oregon Honey Beer and
Rogue Saint Red Ale—including price
breaks on four different beers daily.
The bar's big special (literally) is its 34-
ounce mug of beer for $6.50.

Like so many restaurants that have
a happening bar scene, the money
made on liquor allows Kirkland
Roaster to sell the food at reasonable
prices. While this place is not as inexpensive as many other restaurants in
this book, their prices are moderate
for this popular waterfront locale.
And you do get a lot of wonderful
food for your money.

The menu goes on and on, mostly
"revolving" around their Vertical Spit
Roaster chicken. The house specialty,
"Flav'r Gusto Classic Chicken
Roast" is $10.75 for a half-bird,
served up with honest mashed potatoes and steamed veggies. Then there
are things like roast pork and top-
grade sirloin, all with the same sides.
There are also a number of barbecue
plates to choose from, as well as
soups, salads, and sandwiches. Something for everyone.

The Roaster also offers "Skin-
nies," entrees made with reduced fat
and calories. "No-Fat BBQ Chicken"
($8.25) and "No-Fat Teriyaki Tur-
key" ($7.85) are among the high-
lights. What's more, everything's
available for take-out. They claim
that their containers keep food warm
for up to one hour.

On weekends, the Kirkland
Roaster & Ale House is home to the
Eastside Comedy Club with plenty of
"cheap" laughs (see the listing under
"Entertainment—Comedy"). Open
seven days.

La Cocina del Puerco
- 10246 Main St. NE, Bellevue;
  455-1151
- *Tip-free*

An Eastside copycat of Pike Place's
popular El Puerco Lloron, this downtown Mexican eat-in-or-take-out spot
looks like a permanent fiesta.
Mariachi music plays through the
speakers, piñatas (some in the shape
of beer cans) hang from the ceiling,
and the whole place is ablaze with
bold Southwestern colors.

Order your food at the counter and
find a table. "Tres Taquitos" ($5.89)
is a platter of three corn tortillas
topped with beef or chicken, diced onions, tomatoes, and peppers, with rice
and beans on the side. A similar vegetarian burrito plate is $4.99. Add a bas-
ket of guacamole and chips for $2.99.
The food is made up fresh ("We have
no microwaves," reads a sign), with
low-fat ingredients wherever possible.

Beer drafts are just $1.25; several
south-of-the-border varieties are also
available, including Tecate and Paci-
fico Claro. It's open daily, until 10 P.M.

Macheezmo Mouse Mexican Cafe
- 2028 148th Ave. NE, Bellevue;
  746-5824
- 211 Broadway E, Seattle; 325-0072
- 701 Fifth Ave., Seattle; 382-1730
- 1815 N 45th St., Seattle; 545-0153
- 425 Queen Anne Ave. N, Seattle;
  282-9904
- 3805 196th Ave. SW, Lynnwood;
  744-1611
- *Tip-free*

The '90s mean that even Mexican
fast food has gone health-conscious.
In fact, Macheezmo Mouse is so serious about it that they print up pamphlets on weight management,
diabetic exchanges, heart health—
and how their food fits in. Every item
on the menu is accompanied by nutritional information: The chicken burrito, for example, has 580 calories,
17% from fat—while the veggie power
salad has 200 calories, 1% from fat.
Make your informed decision.

Mr. C was a bit put off by a display of sample platters at the Queen

Anne location. It's nice to see the choices before you order, but this food sits out all day, and looks a bit um, *faded* after a few hours. Is this the best way to tout healthy food? Well, most branches just show you photos, a better idea. After ordering and paying at the counter, give your name, and they'll call you once your order is ready.

Most burrito, enchilada, and taco plates are $4, including rice and beans on the side. There are also salads, quesadillas, and a children's menu as well; and nothing on the menu tops $5.25. To add a little kick to your meal, stop by the fixin's bar and try a unique but delicious concoction of spicy-sweet citrus barbecue sauce called Boss Sauce. Beer is available too—draft pints are $2-$3, while a bottle of Bud is $1.75.

Macheezmo Mouse restaurants are spacious, clean, and done up in a brightly colored Southwestern motif. Most have tables both inside and out. These features, plus a few children's items on the menu, make it a good bet for families, as well. Open for lunch and dinner, seven days a week.

O'Char
- Loehmann's Plaza, Bellevue; 641-1900
- Gilman Village, Issaquah; 392-2100

No, you won't find corned beef and cabbage here. Though it sounds Irish, O'Char serves up traditional Thai cuisine. The atmosphere is quite elegant, with its pink linen tablecloths and napkins; it's cozy and mellow with scrumptious food. Yet, the place is inexpensive. And, with locations in two popular shopping centers, O'Char is convenient, too.

Lunch specials offer the biggest bargains. $4.95 gets you a spring roll, salad, and your choice of an entree, like pad Thai, beef pepper steak, or green curry. Many of the entrees are available in vegetarian versions, bringing the price down to $4.50.

Dinners are very reasonable, as well. Start off with an order of those spring rolls ($3.95), deep-fried and dee-lish. Several wonderful entrees

---

MR. CHEAP'S PICK
Mercer Island

✔ **Rene's**—Cheap eats on Mercer Island? Yes, it's true, when the place is a big catering kitchen with a restaurant at the front.

---

are priced in the $5.50 to $7 range, including a mix-and-match section of eight preparations (sweet and sour, ginger and vegetables, etc.), to which you add your choice of meat; Mr. C also recommends the char-broiled pork (or beef) marinated in garlic, pepper, and coriander; it's served with hot chili sauce. Quite a potent combination of flavors.

One unique dish which has brought O'Char a lot of attention is its "Red Wine Angel Wings" ($5.95), deep-fried chicken wings marinated in garlic and vegetables, and served in a red wine sauce. You won't find *these* wings in any sports bar. O'Char is open daily.

Pasta Nova
- Loehmann's Plaza, Bellevue; 644-4400
- *Tip-free*

A few doors down from O'Char, this cozy storefront serves up hearty portions of fresh pastas, sandwiches, and salads for notta lotta *lire*. Clearly geared to the take-out crowd, it's nevertheless a comfortable place to hang out—assuming you can get one of the four tables or handful of window stools. Jazz music and classical paintings set an upscale tone—even though it's self-serve.

The menu changes daily, with all food cooked right there in full view behind the counter. For about $5.25-$7.25, you can mix-and-match fresh pastas and sauces, like angel-hair pasta with marinara or spinach fettucine with Alfredo sauce. But wait—

these prices *include* a full-size Caesar salad, or a bowl of soup (minestrone, zucchini dill...)! There are usually a couple of other hot dishes; Mr. C raved over wild mushroom ravioli ($6.95). Individual pizzas ($4.95, with salad) get even wilder—how 'bout Thai chicken, goat cheese, or barbecue?

Moving to cold foods, PN offers a wide range of prepared salads priced by the pound; again, not only can you find chicken salad in a creamy basil sauce, but also non-Italian creations like Oriental chicken and broccoli. Experiment with a "Three Salad Sampler" for $6.95. Pastas and sauces can also be purchased by the pound, by the way, for fancy meals at home.

Pasta Nova is also a fine place to sit over lattés and biscotti after a bargain matinee across the street at the Factoria cinemas. Open for lunch and dinner until 8 P.M., Sundays from 12-6 only.

The Pumphouse
- 11802 NE Eighth St., Bellevue; 455-4110

Downtown Bellevue can be pretty ritzy, but you don't have to get far from the glass-and-steel to find simpler stuff. This cozy neighborhood-style sports bar is just that. What do they pump here? Large beers, for one thing. There are nine microbrews on tap, including unusual varieties like Hale's Honey Wheat and Kemper Weizenberry.

The atmosphere in the Pumphouse is LOUD, LOUD, LOUD. This is the kind of place where local softball teams like to hang out after their games, buying pitchers of beer and generally cavorting and having a great time. More games are pumped out of the television monitors located up above, all around the room.

The Pumphouse claims to serve the Eastside's biggest burger. Mr. C wasn't entirely convinced of that, but with one-third of a pound of beef, you certainly won't go away hungry. Get a basic model for $5.25, or a bacon and cheddar burger for $6.50. All of these are served with fresh-cut fries. Of course, any burger joint

worth its ketchup in this part of the world must offer a non-meat alternative. The Pumphouse garden burger is a grilled veggie patty served with a salad for $6.50. If none of these options appeal to you, the menu also has seafood, chicken, hot and cold sandwiches, and salads. Most everything is under $7.

Lunch and dinner deals are offered daily; during Mr. C's visit the dinner special was teriyaki chicken, with a salad and baked potato, all for $9.75. There are nightly drink specials as well. And, even in a city where espresso drinks are served everywhere from gas stations on upward, it still seems kinda funny for a sports bar to be pushing its lattés almost as aggressively as its beers. But they do. The Pumphouse is open weekdays from 8 A.M. to midnight; they open an hour later on Saturdays, and are closed on Sundays.

Red Robin
- 11021 NE Eighth St., Bellevue; 453-9522
- 2390 148th Ave. NE, Bellevue; 641-3810
- 1600 E Olive Way, Seattle; 323-1600
- 3272 Fuhrman Ave. E, Seattle; 323-0918
- Pier 55, 1101 Alaskan Way, Seattle; 623-1942
- 1100 Fourth Ave., Seattle; 447-1909
- Northgate Mall, Seattle; 365-0933
- 1305 SE Everett Mall Way, Everett; 355-7330
- Sea Tac Mall, Federal Way; 946-TOGO (8646)
- *And other suburban locations*

Red Robin is a popular chain where families, business types, mall creatures, and others all come together for standard American fare. The atmosphere is bright, lively, and convivial. Separate bar areas, fully outfitted for beers and cocktails, include televisions showing various ball games.

The menu is dominated by the "Gourmet Burgers" (the world's greatest, in their humble opinion), in more than a dozen varieties. Try the "Banzai Burger," marinated in teriyaki sauce and topped with grilled pineapple and cheddar cheese ($5.95), or the "Lone Star Burger," with jalapeño jack cheese, salsa, and guacamole ($5.25). Non-carnivores may want to try the "Amazing Meatless Burger," made with veggies and grains ($5.25). In fact, you can have any style made with a meatless patty.

The one-size-fits-all menu also includes soups and sandwiches, entree-sized salads, pastas, and plenty of bar-food appetizers. Red Robin is a safe bet for bringing the gang to munch on wings and nachos. And save room for desserts like mud pie, cheesecake, brownie sundaes, shakes, and root beer floats. There's also a kiddie menu, with half a dozen meals all priced at $2.99 each. Most Red Robins serve food daily until midnight.

Rene's
- 7660 SE 27th St., Mercer Island; 232-6607

Cheap eats on Mercer Island? Yup—and here's why: Rene's is a catering company which runs a storefront cafe along with its spacious kitchen. Furthermore, it's tucked away in a rather sleepy shopping plaza instead of a snooty location. All of this adds up to lower operating costs, hence, lower prices.

Soft jazz, framed prints, and a country-style decor awash in flowers and indoor trellises do much to relieve the otherwise faded and cavernous space. At night in particular, the lights are dimmed and the atmosphere is mellow. Alas, dinner prices stretch Mr. C's $10-a-person limit, though not by much. And, consider what fancy food you can get: Daily specials may include grilled fresh red snapper with garlic ($11.95), boneless breast of chicken in a Dijon cream sauce ($9.50), or sauteed prawns with peppers and mushrooms ($12.95). And all dinners include homemade soup (such as egg-lemon-rice) or a big, fresh salad. So, you can do very well indeed.

Lunch offers even better deals, with more casual food. An array of

---

MR. CHEAP'S PICK
Redmond

✔ **Big Time Pizza**—Hidden away in a strip-mall near the freeway, this pizza is *ready* for the big time.

---

mountainous sandwiches, made on thickly sliced home-baked bread, all go for $5.95 or $6.95. Again, there are big, leafy salads. And Mr. C was amazed by the soup and sandwich combination—noted on the menu as a half-sandwich and cup of soup, it was more like a *whole* sandwich and a *bowl* of soup, all for $4.95!

There are a few lunchtime entrees as well, around $7-$8—including pot roast and a pasta of the day, served with vegetables. House wines start at $2.95 a glass. Service is extremely attentive. Great desserts, too. Open from 11 A.M. to 9 P.M. weekdays; 10 A.M. to 3 P.M. on Saturdays, and until 2 P.M. on Sundays.

The Roanoke Inn
- 1825 72nd Ave. SE, Mercer Island; 232-0800

And here's the other cheap choice on Mercer Island. The Roanoke is truly the stuff of local legend, a country-style tavern and communal meeting spot since 1916. It is, in fact, a state landmark; but, in spite of history and posh surroundings, there's no need to put on airs here. Not over such simple, hearty fare as chili burgers ($4.50), grilled ham and cheese sandwiches ($4.25), and taco salads ($6.25).

These are primarily lunch choices; dinner switches to items like nine-inch pizzas with your choice of toppings ($6.20-$7.45) and Roanoke Steaks—$7.95 for a slab of top sirloin with potatoes, warm bread, and a salad. Thursday evenings add a spaghetti special: A heaping plate served with garlic cheese bread for $5.95

($6.75 with salad). Can't beat that.

There is a full bar, of course, including beers, wines, and champagnes; plus plenty of finger food if you'd rather nibble on "Wings of Fire," pepperoni sticks, or a cup of warm pistachio nuts. Hang out in the dimly-lit interior, or try for a table on the inn's wraparound front porch. Lunch is served from 11 A.M. to 2 P.M., and dinner from 6-10 P.M. daily; The Roanoke also serves breakfast on Sundays from 9 A.M. The bar is open throughout the day and evening, until 2 A.M. (10 P.M. on Sundays).

Sunshine Baking Company

- 14625 NE 20th St., Bellevue; 641-6121
- *Tip-free*

More than just a place to fill up while doing Overlake errands, this rather charming spot has become a favorite among the power-tie-over-the-shoulder corporate lunch set. The food at this bakery/restaurant is largely homemade, and yummy with a capital yum. A sign dubs this place as the "originator of Seattle sourdough" (hmm...didn't it start in San Francisco?)—a tall claim, but it's good stuff.

Breakfasts are noteworthy here; before 11 A.M., you can get two eggs any style, home fries, toast, and coffee for $2.95. Or, if you prefer, have them whip that sourdough into French toast for $3.95. Oh, and the coffee refills are free. At lunch or dinner time, the casual menu includes sandwiches like veggie burgers ($4.95), as well as chicken Caesar salad ($7.50) and Chinese chicken salad with crispy rice noodles, honey roasted almonds, and sesame dressing ($6.50). Most items are under $6.

The setup is cafeteria-style, but the ambiance goes beyond your standard fast-foodery, decorated as it is with baking implements, pots, and pans. The tables sit among showcases filled with scones, muffins, breads, pies, and cakes—plus shelves displaying imported dried pastas, olive oils, spices, and marinades to take home. Sunshine is open daily from 7 A.M. to

9 P.M., except Sundays from 9 A.M. to 3 P.M. only.

The Yankee Diner

- 13856 Bellevue-Redmond Rd., Bellevue; 643-1558
- 5300 24th Ave. NW, Seattle; 783-1964
- 6812 Tacoma Mall Blvd., Tacoma; 475-3006
- *And other suburban locations*

This place is tailor-made for families of any size, as the usually packed waiting room will attest. You may hang out there as long as an hour before getting a table; yet, no one leaves. If you can manage to keep the kids quiet long enough, you won't be disappointed. This place is BIG: big on portions, and big on old-time, American-style foods. These go beyond the trademark Yankee pot roast, to include steaks, roast turkey, pot pies, and more. Best of all, you can get the whole brood in and out and still have enough money for the violin lessons.

The aforementioned pot roast, for instance, is just $8.75. Even cheaper is meat loaf ($7.95) or chicken fried steak ($7.45). Of course, it's the side dishes that make these entrees such a great value: Each one comes with a cup of soup or a green salad, vegetables, a choice of potato (including homemade mashed!), and biscuits baked from scratch. If you do have little ones to feed, a kids' menu includes turkey and pot roast dinners for under five bucks.

Folks with (slightly) lighter appetites can go for one of 35 different sandwiches, hot and cold, at lunch or dinner. Most of the dinner entrees are also available for lunch, at two or three dollars less. Come in midday and enjoy breaded veal cutlets or hickory smoked ham, with all those trimmings, for $5.95. At night, these go for $8.45.

Early risers aren't left in the cold, either. Mr. C *has* seen lower-priced breakfasts, but then, you won't need to eat again all day. The "Diner Special," for example, includes juice, fresh fruit, three eggs, bacon, ham or sausage, fried potatoes and toast or pancakes. Even at $6.25, it's a bargain—if you can finish! French toast made with the Yankee's home-baked cinnamon bread is another winner. Speaking of sweets, the diner is also popular for its desserts, malted milkshakes, and home-baked goodies. Open seven days a week.

Zoopa

- Bellevue Square Mall, Bellevue; 453-7887
- 393 Strander Blvd., Tukwila; 575-0500
- *Tip-free*

Along with Fresh Choice, described elsewhere in this book, Zoopa is swooping down upon the suburban Northwest, putting a new spin on shopping center dining. Of all the buffet restaurants encircling Seattle, these two chains are clearly ahead of the rest—in terms of quality and sheer quantity of offerings.

Zoopa also starts you off with a salad bar, consisting not only of a zillion fresh greens, vegetables, and fruits, but specially prepared salads like "Turkey Taco" and "Confetti Couscous" as well. There's also a "Kidstall" buffet which adds bins of Froot Loops and such among the veggies—clever strategy, eh, moms?

Meanwhile, it's off to the pasta counter next, for your choice of noodles and sauces—marinara, pesto, Alfredo. Soups, on Mr. C's visit, included minestrone, hearty onion, and chili. Add a few hunks of fresh bread, along with sodas, juices, beers, and wines, and it's a full meal.

Not to leave out the most important part—dessert. Help yourself to brownies, muffins, and/or soft-serve ice cream machines with a toppings bar of nuts and candies. Whew! Somewhere along the way, maybe they should add an Alka Seltzer counter, too. Eat as much as you can stand for $7.35, or $6.35 at lunch. Children (ages 5-11) are half-price at all times; and for kiddies up to age four, it's all-you-can-throw, absolutely free. Seniors over 60 get a 10% discount, too.

The atmosphere at Zoopa is a lively one; it rocks, while Fresh Choice rolls along to classical music. Potted trees reach up to the mauve-painted air ducts along the high ceilings. The place gets noisy, but one thing's for sure—no one walks away hungry. The Tukwila branch is in Southcenter Plaza, across Strander from the main Southcenter Mall. Open seven days a week.

NORTH AREA
(including Ballard, Fremont, Greenwood, Lake City, Northgate, Wallingford)

Atlantic Street Pizza

- 941 Holman Rd. NW, Seattle; 783-9698
- 5253 University Way NE, Seattle; 524-4432

This large and cozy restaurant seems to be especially popular with families looking for pizza as the easy way to please the kiddies (and avoid cooking). Atlantic may not have a large rodent for a mascot, like a certain national chain; but the pizza is better here any-

way, made with a gourmet flair. The special dough is all-natural, made without sugar or yeast. Also, there are five homemade sauces to choose from, including five-cheese, and a mild, sweet crushed tomato sauce.

Toppings...there are so many, they've been broken down into categories like seafood, vegetables, and cheese. Peppers get their own heading. If you're feeling particularly indecisive, plenty of combinations are laid out for you—for example, the "Cinque Formaggi" ($10.75) with mozzarella, parmesan, Havarti, Swiss, and feta. The "Delaurenti's" ($12.75—named for movie mogul Dino?), smothered in green peppers, black olives, mushrooms, and tomatoes, is also just fabulous. The prices quoted here are for the 12" medium size; the 15" larges are a few dollars more. If it's just you eating, try the 7" small size, starting at only $3.40. Beers ($1.75 and up) and wines ($2 per glass and up), plus a full bar, are available, too.

While this is a family restaurant, the kiddies must be out by 9 P.M. They won't turn into pumpkins, but because there is live entertainment, everyone here past 9 P.M. must be at least 21. See the listing under "Entertainment—Music." Both locations are open daily; hours vary at each. Note also that the U-District location is for take-out only.

Ballard Baking Company Cafe

- 5909 24th Ave. NW, Seattle; 781-0091
- *Tip-free*

Half bakery, half cafe, the "BBC" is no half-baked notion of either. Some shops import foods from across the seas; these folks have imported a hearth baking oven from France, in order to make their own wonderfully crusty creations. While some of these loaves can be pricey, they also serve as the outsides of some wonderful sandwiches.

These are stacked tall, and so are available in whole or half-sizes. Mr. C wrapped his mitts around a club sandwich made with freshly roasted chicken slices, melted Swiss cheese, and bacon, on organic six-grain bread—served with red cabbage cole slaw and Tim's Cascade potato chips on the side. All that for $5.50!

Most sandwiches are in the $5-$6 range, with half-sizes about $3-$4. Add a cup of Italian vegetable rice soup for $2; this comes with its own slab of bread. There are also things like vegetable-filled croissants, quiche Lorraine, and a slew of fabulous pastries. Try an apple *beignet* for 95¢, a huge and gooey chocolate eclair for $1.25, or a slice of cherry custard coffee cake for $1.50.

An espresso to sip with your dessert is only 85¢, and other drinks include apple cider and hot chocolate. The interior of this small, cozy establishment is simple; take your food to a table, along with plastic utensils. There's room for another table or two on the sidewalk of this quiet neighborhood, as weather permits. The BBC Cafe is open Tuesdays through Saturdays from 6:30 A.M. to 7 P.M.; Sundays from 7 A.M. to 5 P.M.; closed Mondays.

Beeliner Diner

- 2114 N 45th St., Seattle; 547-6313

Here's a fine example of the "nouveau diner" rage. Beeliner is a tiny stainless-steel-counter-and-booths place in the heart of Wallingford. They serve up all-American comfort foods like meatloaf, country-fried steak, and pot roast. One waitress covers the joint, and she sings out each order to the busy cooks. "One *blue* plaaaaate!" When she's not singing, someone like Ray Charles is, on the way-hip sound system. Yet, they put a modern twist on these classics; sure, you can get a basic burger and fries, but they also offer a "Notta Nut Burger"—the vegetarian alternative.

Everything has a creative touch. Start off with a red cabbage salad, topped with hot creamy bacon dressing, for $4.25. Move on to "Paulo's North End Sausage Linguine" ($8.50), or an order of "Sweetwater Sea Tacos" ($8.75), soft tortillas stuffed with grilled gulf fish. Side dishes include real mashed potatoes and fantastic homemade biscuits. Add an IBC soda, beer, or some "cheap white wine" (how could Mr. C not love this place?).

Weekends offer "Blunch" dishes like "Red Flannel Hash" ($5.75) and "Toad in the Hole" ($4.75)—cheddar cheese, eggs, and potatoes tucked into grilled sourdough bread, with Canadian bacon over the top. Beeliner is open from 8 A.M. to 11 P.M., seven days a week. Getting in at peak times can be difficult; fortunately, there are lots of other good choices in this neighborhood.

The Breakfast Club
- 12306 Lake City Way NE, Seattle; 361-2582

True to its name (more or less), this Lake City joint is only open for breakfast and lunch. It's strictly a no-frills, damn-the-arteries-full-speed-ahead kind of establishment. If that's your style, read on. Naturally, eggs are the specialty of the house; get 'em any way you want, from basic preparations to Florentine, Welsh, and Benedict. Such platters are about as fancy as these folks get, complete with toast and greasy hash browns for $5-$6 each. Pancakes and French toast go for about $2-$4, and sandwiches (weekdays only) for $3-$5.

So, if you're expecting to find Molly Ringwald and her fellow yuppie brat-packers, guess again. Strangely enough, there is a picture from "I Love Lucy" on the wall, along with some old-fashioned washboards and other homey touches. But, for you fans of hearty breakfasts all day, check it out. Open from 6 A.M. to 2 P.M. Sundays through Wednesdays, and from 6-6 Thursdays through Saturdays.

The Blue Planet
- 2208 N 45th St., Seattle; 632-0750

For the vegetarian, Blue Planet offers a large menu filled with delectable homemade treats. All meals are individually prepared, using organic ingredients as much as possible.

Tofu fajitas ($7.85) are grilled with peppers and onions, all stuffed into a whole wheat *chapati* (or corn tortilla) with guacamole, salsa, and sprouts. Blue corn chips and salsa are served on the side. The $7.25 marinated teriyaki tempeh sandwich also comes with blue corn chips and salsa, or salad. Garden burgers ($7.25), soups ($3.10), and salads ($7.25) are also available.

There is also quite a variety of specialty juice drinks to go with these—$3.25 for 12-ounce glass, $3.75 for a 16-ouncer. Be daring and try some "Jitterbug Perfume," a mixture of beet and carrot juice. Or, thwart rainy-season colds with "Oh, Say Can You C," a tasty blend of orange, grapefruit, lemon, apple, and cranberry juices.

Frequent visitors to this planet should be sure to pick up Blue Planet cards—after nine entrees (at a minimum of $5.75 each), these healthy souls receive the tenth for free, thus enhancing the vitality of their wallets. Beam down between 8 A.M. and 10 P.M. during the week; from 9 A.M. on weekends.

Buddy's Homesick Cafe
- 8420 Greenwood Ave. N, Seattle; 784-6430

If the eccentric 1950s decor doesn't remind you baby-boomers of the home you grew up in, or *somebody's* comfy home (courtesy of "Nick-At-Nite" sitcoms), the menu certainly will—with enough comfort food to take care of any case of homesickness.

The good ol' American cooking that Buddy's serves up includes treats like "Super Duper Meatloaf" for $6.95, and "Northwest Cranberry Pot Roast" (bit of revisionist history there) for $7.95. Dinners come with real mashed potatoes, homemade gravy, fresh vegetables, a buttermilk biscuit, and soup or salad. Various hand-formed hamburgers, served with fries, cole slaw or potato salad, are around $5.95. And your mother always said you need calcium for strong bones; so she'd surely approve of adding a chocolate shake for $2.75.

Buddy's Club House Lounge is found at the same location, serving

---

MR. CHEAP'S PICKS
Ballard

✔ **Illiterati**—What the new Ballard is all about.

✔ **Scandies**—What the old Ballard is all about.

---

up cocktails to go with this hearty fare. It's the kind of corner bar Dad always stopped into on the way home from work, though we never actually *saw* such a place on the show. Say, pal, why not stop in to Buddy's yourself, between 11 A.M. and midnight during the week, and from 8 A.M. on weekends.

The Buzzorium

- 8548 Greenwood Ave. N, Seattle; 784-7451
- *Tip-free*

With enough coffeehouses to turn Puget Sound into one big latté *grande*, Mr. C isn't about to rate every cafe in town. Especially, those which don't serve food. But the Buzzorium scores with low beverage prices—and besides, this joint *jumps*. When Mr. C visited, hard rock was blasting over the sound system, funky artwork was rattling against the walls, and people were shooting pool on a mustard-colored billiard table. Seating is a bit limited, but if you're lucky, you can grab a spot on the comfy, black vinyl sofa.

The couple that owns the place was justifiably proud of the fact that they did not raise prices after the '94 coffee bean freeze—a single shot of espresso was still going for a mere 80 cents. Added flavorings are free on Fridays; at other times, they're just 25¢ more. Soda is cheap, too—70¢ gets you a twenty-two ounce *small*.

The Buzzorium is open Monday 9 A.M. to 6 P.M., Tuesdays through Saturdays, from 8 A.M. to 6 P.M., and Sundays 10 A.M. to 4:30 P.M.

Capons Rotisserie Chicken

- 1815 N 45th St., Seattle; 547-3949
- 605 15th Ave. E, Seattle; 726-1000
- 3615 128th Ave SE, Bellevue; 649-0900
- 17122 Redmond Way, Redmond; 882-4838
- *Tip-free*

Rotisserie chicken has become the hottest (no pun intended) fast-food craze of the '90s. This is probably because chicken is one meal that can be made as efficiently as any fast-food fare, yet still be whole, real, and rec-

ognizable; it's as close to home cooking as you'll find in any chain. Every major city seems to have spawned a local version, and this is Seattle's.

Service is cafeteria-style. Grab a tray and choose your main dish and side items along the counter. Even so, Capon's is comfortably decorated with tiled kitchen walls, earthy colors, and lots of plants. Also, as in the coffeehouses, daily newspapers are usually lying around for you to read if you wish. Nice touch.

As for the food, well, the name says it all. The chicken is quite good; you can order it *a la carte* (quarter, half, or whole); or as a complete dinner, which adds cornbread muffins and a choice of two side dishes. These include mashed potatoes and gravy, seasonal vegetables, sage stuffing, or a tossed green salad. A half-chicken dinner goes for $5.95, while a complete dinner for a family of four is $19.95. A child's chicken dinner is available for $2.95.

Capons also offers salads, sandwiches, soups, and other specialties, like a tasty chicken pot pie, individually sized at $3.95. Couple of sweets for after dinner, too. Open daily from 11 A.M. to 10 P.M.

Charlie's Bar & Grill

- 7001 Seaview Ave. NW, Seattle; 783-8338

You'd hardly expect to find Mr. C hanging with the navy-jacket-and-white-pants set. Yet here he is, enjoying a high-up view of Puget Sound, over good food that is not as outrageously priced as the offerings of many other waterfront restaurants. Located on the second floor of the yacht club at Shilshole Bay Marina, Charlie's Bar and Grill is a comfortable, casual alternative to places like Hiram's just up the road.

Early-bird dinner specials, a permanent part of the menu, offer particularly good deals daily from 4 to 7 P.M. The standard price of $8.95 gets you a complete dinner from appetizers through to dessert, with several choices including London broil, fresh king salmon, and vegetable lasagna.

The regular menu options also fall well within Mr. C's budget—even seafood, not always known for its affordability. Enjoy Japanese Panko sole, with a baked potato and fresh vegetables, for just $6.95; or seafood skewers, made with prawns, salmon, and Alaskan cod (plus the same sides), a bargain at $9.95.

If seafood doesn't float your boat, even in this salty setting, don't worry. There's London broil, chicken Dijon served with a baked potato and veggies (each $6.95), plus soups, salads, and sandwiches. Salads are entree-sized, and priced accordingly; a seafood Caesar is $9.95. Sandwiches are a better bet for value, with burgers ($4.95 and up), grilled Reubens ($6.25), or a good ol' BLT ($4.95). All of these are served with thick-cut French fries.

The atmosphere at Charlie's is laid-back and rather hotel-like; it seems more like an upscale lounge with food. This makes it good for a variety of crowds. The indoor seating features floor-to-ceiling glass windows; there are also plenty of tables on the balcony outside, perfect when the weather cooperates. Either way, the restaurant is positioned for spectacular sunsets over the water. Open weeknights until 10 P.M., Fridays and Saturdays until 11 P.M.

Dick's Drive Ins

- 12325 30th Ave. NE, Seattle; 363-7777
- 9208 Holman Rd. NW, Seattle; 783-5233
- 111 NE 45th St. Seattle; 632-5125
- 115 Broadway E, Seattle; 323-1300
- 500 Queen Anne Ave. N, Seattle; 285-5155
- *And other suburban locations*
- *Tip-free*

No book on cheap (priced) Seattle restaurants would be complete without mention of this longtime landmark. Burgers, fries, shakes, and a see-and-be-seen atmosphere have made Dick's a favorite spot for decades. The food may not be first rate, but hey—it's classic all-Americana. 75¢ burgers and 90¢ cheeseburgers

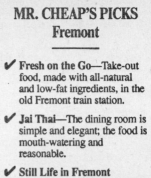

MR. CHEAP'S PICKS
Fremont

✔ **Fresh on the Go**—Take-out food, made with all-natural and low-fat ingredients, in the old Fremont train station.

✔ **Jai Thai**—The dining room is simple and elegant; the food is mouth-watering and reasonable.

✔ **Still Life in Fremont Coffeehouse**—One of best in Seattle, if not the whole *genre*.

will fill you up and never break the bank. Even the quarter-pound "Deluxe," made of two patties, cheese, and a few extra fixin's, is only $1.60. Of course, no burger here should be eaten without fries—buy a greasy bagful for 85 cents. And, for the full heartburn effect, wash it all down with a nice, thick shake ($1.10). Your cholesterol level may go through the roof; but remember, Dick's is better for your soul than your heart. Drive in from 10:30 A.M. to 2 A.M. anyday.

Dubliner Pub

- 3405 Fremont Ave. N, Seattle; 548-1508

There is certainly no shortage of watering holes in Fremont, thanks no doubt to the presence of the Red Hook Brewery nearby. For cheap pub food right in the heart of the hopping Fremont scene, check out the Dubliner, which serves a slightly more expanded menu than one usually finds at the average bar. For starters, a green salad with a hunk of "peasant bread" is just $2 (or $3 for a large size); add an order of toasted cheese and tomato sandwiches—five small sandwiches stacked on top of each other for $3.75. How British.

If you're looking for something more substantial, go for the "Dublin

Cod" fish and chips ($4.95). It's probably been caught closer to home, but why fuss? You get three large, batter-dipped pieces. The traditional corned beef and cabbage dinner ($7.50) is about as pricey as it gets here, and that includes red potatoes and a side salad. More unlikely is the curry chicken breast salad ($6.25), and other eclectic choices.

Needless to say, there is also a world of brews available on tap, soccer on the telly, and live Irish music on Wednesday nights. Lunch is served from 11:30 A.M. to 3:00 P.M. daily, and dinner from 5-10 P.M.

Right next door, meanwhile, the more upscale Red Door Alehouse at 3401 Fremont Avenue N (547-7521) does much the same sort of thing, at somewhat higher prices.

El Tapatio
- 8564 Greenwood Ave. N, Seattle; 782-7545

Way up north on Greenwood is where you'll find El Tapatio, and yes, it is worth the trip from just about any part of town. El T has a truly authentic Mexican feel to it, complete with a huge, colorful mural, mariachi music, and of course, great food.

Expect to leave the table full (you, that is, not the table). Most entrees come with rice and beans; enchilada dishes can be ordered singly or doubly, the pair costing a little over a dollar more than the $5 basic. Most of the tostada plates are $5, too. Stop by for a lunch special Monday through Friday between 11 A.M. and 3 P.M., when all dishes are $4.25. Choose from chimichangas, burritos, and enchiladas, among others—again, with rice and beans on the side. Wine ($1.75 per glass) and beer ($1.60 domestic, $2.25 imported) are available, too. Open from 11 A.M. until 10 P.M. Mondays through Saturdays, and from 1 P.M. to 9:30 P.M. on Sundays.

Fresh Choice
- 301 NE Northgate Way, Seattle; 440-8136
- 1733 Northup Way, Bellevue; 822-2548

- Sea Tac Mall, Federal Way; 941-3860
- *Tip-free*

One of the cleanest, brightest and spiffiest of the shopping center buffet restaurants, these are (as of this writing) the only Northwest outposts of this California chain. But, before you give it the la-la-land snub, give it a try. You'll find food that is both fast and healthy—an overwhelming choice of salads, soups, pastas, and fixings. It's the G.C. (Gastronomically Correct) answer to the King's Table chain.

Everything here is "made from scratch" using all natural ingredients; many items are available in low-fat or non-fat versions, with color-coded name tags (everything here is clearly labeled, with ingredients listed out). And one price, $7.25, covers all the food you want—including seconds. Children pay half of that, and kids under five eat free.

Grab a tray! The first display is the lengthy salad bar, which includes prepared salads such as Caesar and Chinese almond. Or, make up your own creation from literally dozens of fresh vegetables, dressings, and toppings. This could be enough for some appetites, but oh, there's more! Move on to the baked potato bar for a spud heated up with your choice of stuffings; the pasta bar, where you can slather sun-dried tomato cream sauce on linguine or cheese tortellini; the soup bar, with different homemade selections daily, like Southwestern corn chowder and Cajun black bean; and the bread/muffin table, which even has crispy slices of cheese pizza (we need this too?). Oh yeah, and you can help yourself to desserts, from fruits to "Chocolate Decadence" brownies.

Needless to say, it's not hard to get your money's worth; it's just hard to finish it all. Empty tables with lots of food left behind show folks' tendency to order with dazzled eyes. How can the place stay in business with so much waste? Well, they do get you with the drinks, which cost extra—how 'bout $1.75 for a bottle of apple juice—but, if you're a hearty eater, things should still work out in your favor. Those drinks include bottled wines, wine coolers, and beers, by the way.

The atmosphere is as refined as you'll see at any shopping mall. The large dining room is carpeted. White walls are decorated with framed art prints. Classical music plays in the background. A busy staff keeps the place spotless, bussing tables promptly (if you get up for seconds, there's a "Be Right Back" card). In all, this could be the healthiest pigout you'll ever have. Open daily, with mall hours.

Fresh on the Go

- 1100 N Northlake Way, Seattle; 545-1905
- *Tip-free*

Most people believe that healthy food can't possibly taste good, and that fast-food can never be healthy. Well, this recently-arrived take-out spot, housed in the historic Fremont train depot building, proves all these nay-sayers wrong. Fresh on the Go serves up hearty meals that are quick, delicious, *and* healthy. Everything here is made from low-fat or no-fat ingredients and many dishes are vegetarian or vegan.

That must mean this food is no fun, right? Wrong again! The compact menu manages to include a few choices each from Italian, Mexican, and Indian cuisines, as well as basic American favorites. Everything here seems to be a new twist on old ideas. Instead of a burger, try a turkey "Pro-Patty," blended with fresh garlic and parsley ($5.50, with a side dish). That side dish could be fat-free home fries, with steamed onions and green peppers—a truly guilt-free treat ($2.75 alone, 75¢ as a side). Other sides include baked yams or wild organic greens ($3 each).

The "Big Boy Burrito" ($5.50) is filled with shredded chicken breast, black beans, vegetables, and salsa. Nothing unusual, just made with all-natural, low-fat ingredients. Add your choice of a dozen hot sauces. Of course, FOTG offers salads, such as tuna or pasta ($2.75 each). Breakfast

---

MR. CHEAP'S PICK
Green Lake

✔ **Mae's Phinney Ridge Cafe**— Longtime luncheonette, now lovingly done over completely—and they mean *completely*—in cow motif.

---

dishes, available anytime, include "Baby Cakes," mini-pancakes made with ten-grain flour and egg whites ($2.50 for four, $3.50 for six).

Whatever you decide on, it will taste good and be good for you. Fresh on the Go promises "Food for fitness/Food for fun." And fast. Although there are no tables, you're just a few steps away from the ship canal, a fine place to take your food and sit. FOTG is also expert at setting you up with full meals ready to go into the microwave. These friendly folks are open Mondays through Fridays from 8 A.M. to 9 P.M.; Saturdays and Sundays from 8 A.M. 'til 7 P.M.

Greenwood Bakery Cafe

- 7227 Greenwood Ave. N, Seattle; 783-7181
- *Tip-free*

Another bakery doubling as a cafe, this tiny neighborhood spot makes some terrifically tasty sandwiches. The $5.95 "Club Special" is filled with fresh roasted chicken, Swiss cheese, and bacon, and served on six-grain bread. All specialty sandwiches come with potato chips and a side salad. There's not a lot of seating in the cafe, alas—you may be better off just picking up something to take with you. Outside seating is available, weather permitting.

And, if you're on a tight budget, the counter is frequently bedecked with low-priced pastries; day-old baked goods are sold at half-price every Wednesday through Sunday. See the listing under "Shopping—

Food Shops" for more info. Greenwood Bakery Cafe is open from 6:30 A.M. to 9 P.M. Tuesdays through Saturdays, and Sundays from 7 A.M. to 6 P.M. Closed Mondays.

Greenwood Mandarin Chinese Restaurant
● 7303 Greenwood Ave. N, Seattle; 783-6426

Saying that the Buddha on the cover of this menu is laughing would be an understatement. In fact, he's just about the most deliriously ecstatic Buddha ever to endorse a restaurant. Maybe it's because he's found paradise on Earth—the food is really superb, and the prices are fantastic.

A $15 combination dinner includes egg drop soup, egg rolls, almond chicken, sweet and sour pork, and rice—for *two* people. Or, you may opt for such individual dishes as crab Shanghai for $6.95, Mongolian beef for $5.95, and sauteed bean sprouts for $4.95.

As for atmosphere, the Greenwood Mandarin Chinese is spacious and nicely decorated in your basic Asian motif, just right for a pleasant evening out. It is only open for dinner, in fact—from 4 P.M. to 10 P.M. Sundays though Thursdays, and until 11 P.M. Fridays and Saturdays.

Illiterati
● 5327 Ballard Ave. NW, Seattle; 782-0191

Here's a fine example of the hip, "new" Ballard. This storefront eatery is decorated with gumball machines, Bozo the Clown, outlandish paintings, and giant fish that swim overhead. Illiterati may wish to sound dumb, but they clearly know what's going on in the cafe business.

Open only for breakfast, lunch, and brunch, Illiterati offers the latest in trendy dining—with morning starters like breakfast burritos ($4.75) and cappuccino eggs ($4.50)—three steamed eggs made with cheese and fresh herbs. Brunch adds such treats as bread pudding French toast ($5.50) and shrimp Benedict ($6.95). Plus the *de rigueur* espresso drinks and pastries.

The luncheon menu switches to equally creative sandwiches, all served with the unbeatable Tim's potato chips. Mr. C raved over a grilled Italian pork sandwich, bulging with provolone cheese, roasted peppers, onions, and olives on terrific fresh bread. It's all yours for $4.95, or $3.50 for a half-size. There are also soups, salads, and a stew of the day. And, you can save a buck off the price of any small salad or soup when it's purchased with any sandwich, large salad, or large soup.

Illiterati serves breakfast weekdays from 9 A.M. to 12 noon, and lunch Mondays through Saturdays from 10 A.M. to 5 P.M.; brunch is served from 9 A.M. to 2 P.M. on Saturdays, and 9-3 on Sundays.

Jack's Farm Fresh
● 5900 15th Ave. NW, Seattle; 781-JACK (5225)

Though claiming to be open 24 hours, Jack's in fact closes around 3 A.M., but late is late and Mr. C isn't about to shave points for this. The mood here is fun, beginning with the parking lot where every spot is "reserved" with the name of a famous celebrity named Jack—Kerouac, Kennedy, Nicholson, and even Cousteau, to name a few. Inside, the theme continues, with portraits and photographs of the above named Jacks and many others, including the playing card variety. This decor competes with a pastoral cow motif featured on giant wall murals, emphasizing the "farm fresh" part of the name. The interior is cozy and pleasant with a lunch counter up front and several separate rooms filled with booths, perfect for late-night hanging out.

Breakfast and lunch at any hour is the deal here. The all-American menu offers plenty of eggs, omelettes, pancakes, soups, salads, and burgers. Bargains include two eggs with potatoes, fruit, and toast for $2.95. Get a stack of banana nut or apple-oat flap"jacks" (get it?) for $3.75.

If you're interested in having lunch with Jack, you'll have even more choices. Try a "BLT & J" (J is for Jack cheese, of course) for $4.75. Sandwiches and burgers come with a heap of French fries or a salad. Roast turkey plates go for $6.75, and chicken Dijon for $6.85; each comes with soup or salad, sweet molasses bread, vegetables, and mashed potatoes or fries. Dinner offerings are the same, with slightly higher prices.

Given the menu, the nostalgia, and the Ballard location, Jack's is a rather sedate place, popular with older folks. In fact, seniors, take note: Show your ID and get 11 percent off anytime, or get 20% off between 4 P.M. and 5 P.M. Why 11 percent? Who knows? Oh, that Jack, what a crazy guy.

Jai Thai
- 3423 Fremont Ave. N, Seattle; 632-7060

Here's a very pleasant, quiet Fremont cafe—right on the main stretch—that cooks up wonderful Thai food and serves it in a relaxed and pretty dining room. Fresh flowers brighten each table, while Eastern artwork, musical instruments, and stick puppets adorn the walls. The atmosphere is a step above most Oriental eateries in this price range, not to mention most eateries in this neighborhood, period.

The dishes are prepared individually; spices can be adjusted from tame to flaming, as you prefer. Mr. C especially enjoyed the $5.50 "Swimming Rama"—sauteed chicken served over spinach with a creamy peanut sauce. The priciest items on the menu are the $7.25 *tom yum talay* (salad), and *yum talay* (soup), both containing prawns, scallops, and squid. Most of the dishes fall into the $5 to $6 range, in good-sized portions.

A limited selection of beer ($2 and up) and wine ($3 and up) is available, too. Jai Thai is open from 11 A.M. to 9:30 P.M. Sundays through Thursdays, and until 10:30 P.M. on Fridays and Saturdays.

Jalisco Mexican Restaurant
- 12336 31st Ave. NE, Seattle; 364-3978
- 1467 E Republican St., Seattle; 325-9005
- 122 and 129 First Ave. N, Seattle; 283-4242
- 8517 14th Ave. S, Seattle; 767-1943
- 115 Park Lane, Kirkland; 822-3355

A shop owner of Mexican extraction told Mr. C to be sure to include Jalisco, for truly authentic regional food. Named for one of that country's more scenic states, this restaurant upholds that tradition of beauty—at least one branch sports a wall mural depicting a village center, complete with guitarist serenading a dancing couple by a fountain. Piñatas and plants are perched high above, and high-backed booths provide a secluded dining experience.

Try one of the huge "Especiáles de la Casa," like the chimichangas or enchiladas rancheras, for $7.55 each. All of these specialties are served with rice and beans, making for a gigantic plateful. For the lighter appetite, a single tamale ($2.65) or taco salad ($4.50) will do you right.

Be sure to try something with Jalisco's homemade *mole* sauce; usually made from unsweetened chocolate (yes, for dinner), these folks make it as a nifty peanut sauce instead. If you're not entirely familiar with such native culinary terms, there's a helpful glossary on the back of the menu.

The First Avenue location, just outside Seattle Center, has recently spawned a quicker-fare "taqueria" right across the street; the Lake City location adds a cocktail lounge. All branches are open daily from 11 A.M. to 10 P.M., and to 11 P.M. on Fridays and Saturdays.

Kidd Valley
- 4910 Green Lake Way N, Seattle; 547-0121
- 14303 Aurora Ave. N, Seattle; 364-8493
- 135 15th Ave. NE, Seattle; 328-8133
- 5502 25th Ave. NE, Seattle; 522-0890
- 531 Queen Anne Ave. N, Seattle; 284-0184
- *And other suburban locations*
- *Tip-free*

Kidd Valley is Seattle's own answer to McDonald's, though most locals would argue that Kidd Valley is better. And they're right. There's more of a selection, and your order is prepared while you wait. The classic hamburger is $2.29; the cheeseburger is $2.44. These burgers are juicy and delicious; 'nuff said.

For those who may be suffering from burger burn-out, there are also quite a few sandwiches to choose from, like a BLT ($2.49), broiled chicken ($3.54), and grilled ham and cheese ($2.99). The homemade onion rings ($1.19) and specialty shakes ($1.49) should not be missed, though only the strong of stomach will want to have both in the same sitting.

Kidd's atmosphere is strictly early-American fast-food joint—kinda sparse, a few prominent colors, and lots of booths. Open seven days a week.

King's Table
- 1545 NW Market St., Seattle; 784-8955
- 4111 Wheaton Way, Bremerton; (360) 377-7044
- 137 SW 160th St., Burien; 244-1883
- 3802 Broadway, Everett; 252-6555
- 12120 NE 85th St., Kirkland; 828-3811
- *Tip-free*

Perhaps the lowest in overall quality of the Seattle area's many buffet restaurants, King's Table nevertheless offers a ton of food for the money. Dinners cost $6.99 per person (lunches about a dollar less), payable at the beginning of what is basically a cafeteria line. KT also offers a "Gold Card" for $1, allowing you to then save 50¢ on every visit; and Thursday is "Family Night," when kids under 12 pay just 39¢ for every year of their age.

The food is adequate, centering on such entrees as fried chicken, fish and chips, and hand-carved roast beef; along with these are a salad bar, side dishes, taco shells and fillings, and basic desserts, including a do-it-yourself soft ice cream machine. They also serve a breakfast buffet, priced at $4.99. King's Table certainly fits the bill for families and for

seniors, who can have a fixed-income night on the town. Open daily.

La Vaca
- 7910 Green Lake Dr. N, Seattle; 517-2949
- 613 Third Ave., Seattle; 622-0154
- 4129 University Way NE, Seattle; 632-4909
- *Tip-free*

That's "The Cow," for those of us not fluent in Spanish. Don't take it personally—go ahead and um, pig out. This busy little take-out joint serves Mexican food in *gigante* portions at low prices. Burritos are $3.25; choose from vegetarian, beef, chicken, or beans and cheese. Large enchiladas and tacos are $1.25, tostadas $2.50. Ordering by number speeds up the process—this is a good pit stop for a cheap, quick, and filling lunch. Stop by between 11 A.M. and 5 P.M., during the week; La Vaca on Third Avenue is closed on the weekends, and the University location is closed Saturdays. The Green Lake restaurant is open seven days.

Left Coast Cafe
- 5228 Ballard Ave. NW, Seattle; 706-0361

Part of the Olympic Athletic Club, in this yuppified section of lower Ballard, the Left Coast Cafe is way cool, dude. It's a rather *chic* tavern, with its exposed brick walls, natural wood tables, and hanging plants everywhere—and you don't have to be a member of the gym to eat here. Whether you've just worked out or not, park yourself on a couch and leaf through a collection of magazines and newspapers.

The simple menu consists of light fare, as you'd expect—sandwiches and salads, mainly. You can build your own sandwich for $4.25; choose from a selection of meats, cheeses, fixings, and put it all on your choice of rye, nine-grain, sourdough, or a sub roll. Speaking of subs, they have a bunch to choose from, each in two sizes, six-inch and foot-long. Health-conscious types will like "Please No-Meat" with lettuce, tomato, mayo, mustard, provolone, cheddar, Swiss, onion, and cucumber ($2.75 small/$5 large). Or, perhaps a Caesar salad, $5.95, with fresh bread.

The Left Coast Cafe of course has the requisite lattés, mochas, cappuccinos, and what-have-you. They also have a wide assortment of fruits and vegetables for custom fresh-squeezed drinks or frozen yogurt smoothies: Honeydew, strawberry, kiwi, carrot, zucchini, and many others. The cafe is open Mondays through Fridays from 6 A.M. to 9 P.M. (they serve breakfast, too), and Saturdays from 8 A.M. to 9 P.M.

Lockspot Cafe
- 3005 NW 54th St., Seattle; 789-4865

Near the entrance to the English Gardens and the Chittenden Locks (see these described under "Entertainment—Outdoors"), this salty restaurant is a bit of old Ballard. The insides are done up in full naval dress, with dark wood tables, brass lanterns, porthole windows, and other nautical touches. Some of the guys at the bar look as if they've been there since the days of Captain Ahab themselves.

Seafood is the specialty here (how did you guess?). Choices like grilled trout and blackened halibut (each $8.75) are served with soup, rice, and cooked vegetables. Fish and chips also comes with soup, available in two sizes at $5.95 and $7.75.

Or, start with a cup of clam chowder ($1.50), and shift over to fried chicken ($5.95) or a double-patty hamburger ($4.75). And a huge, 18-ounce New York prime rib plate is a good value at $12.95. There's a full bar, including basic beers and wines.

Lockspot also serves breakfasts (steak and eggs, $7.95), just the thing to stoke your furnace for a day at sea or a day at the locks. Open daily from 5 A.M. (that's right, folks); the kitchen closes around 9 or 10 P.M., depending on the season, although the bar remains open until 2 A.M. every single night.

Macheezmo Mouse Mexican Cafe
- 1815 N 45th St., Seattle; 545-0153
- 425 Queen Anne Ave. N, Seattle; 282-9904
- 211 Broadway E, Seattle; 325-0072
- 701 Fifth Ave., Seattle; 382-1730
- 2028 148th Ave. NE, Bellevue; 746-5824
- 3805 196th Ave. SW, Lynnwood; 744-1611
- *Tip-free*

The '90s mean that even Mexican fast food has gone health-conscious. In fact, Macheezmo Mouse is so serious about it that they print up pamphlets on weight management, diabetic exchanges, heart health—and how their food fits in. Every item on the menu is accompanied by nutritional information: The chicken burrito, for example, has 580 calories, 17% from fat—while the veggie power salad has 200 calories, 1% from fat. Make your informed decision.

Mr. C was a bit put off by a display of sample platters at the Queen Anne location. It's nice to see the choices before you order, but this food sits out all day, and looks a bit um, *faded* after a few hours. Is this the best way to tout healthy food? Well, most branches just show you photos, a better idea. After ordering and paying at the counter, give your name, and they'll call you once your order is ready.

Most burrito, enchilada, and taco plates are $4, including rice and beans on the side. There are also salads, quesadillas, and a children's menu as well; and nothing on the menu tops $5.25. To add a little kick to your meal, stop by the fixin's bar and try a unique but delicious concoction of spicy-sweet citrus barbecue sauce called Boss Sauce. Beer is available too—draft pints are $2-$3, while a bottle of Bud is $1.75.

Macheezmo Mouse restaurants are spacious, clean, and done up in a brightly colored Southwestern motif. Most have tables both inside and out. These features, plus a few children's items on the menu, make it a good bet for families, as well. Open for lunch and dinner, seven days a week.

Mae's Phinney Ridge Cafe

• 6412 Phinney Ave. N, Seattle;
  782-1222

If you're one of those people who can eat until the cows come home, well, this is where they live. Each section in Mae's winding maze of rooms features a different, grandly overdone decorating scheme—most of which have to do with cows. Just about every available surface, it seems, is festooned with big black and white spots, including the tables. It's like living in a Far Side cartoon.

Not to ignore, of course, the Elvis room—decked out with enough memorabilia of the King to rival the Hard Rock Cafe. Yet, this is no flashy downtown tourist spot; just a cozy, folksy, neighborhood luncheonette. Only in Seattle...

Owner Jeanne Mae Barwick took the place over a few years back, but an eatery has existed here—on a slope overlooking Green Lake—since the turn of the century. Mae wanted to keep that old-time feeling, right down to the soda fountain and counter, but still have some fun with it.

Thus, you can sit yourself down in front of a "Cow Pie Sundae" ($3.75), two scoops of vanilla ice cream on a chocolate brownie, topped with the works; or a good ol' "Black Cow" (a.k.a. root beer float) for $2.25. Meanwhile, breakfast is served all day—huge three-egg omelettes like shrimp Creole and chili cheddar (each $5.75), served up with toast or a biscuit. Or, for a dollar more, have one of Mae's mountainous homemade cinnamon rolls on the side. In fact, you can never get too far from the sweets, even at an early hour: "Shake & Eggs" ($6.25) combines two eggs with hash browns and a milk shake. A breakfast of champions.

Lunch kicks in at 11:30, offering sandwiches, soups, and salads. A bowl of *chili con carne*, with cornbread, goes for $2.75. Burgers start at $4.50, with fries. Specialties include things like chicken almond pot pie, $5.95 with a salad. And of course, there's a hot meatloaf sandwich, served with real mashed potatoes and gravy,

same price. Finish off with a slab of Mae's own fruit pie and ice cream, $3.25; the sweet tooth strikes again.

The portions are as outlandish as the decor, and it's all homemade and wonderful. Mae's is open from 7 A.M. to 3 P.M. every day.

The New York Cafe

• 1605 N 45th St., Seattle; 548-1134

This cozy Wallingford spot won't make New York transplants feel exactly like you're back at home; in fact, from the outside, this humble woodframe building looks more like a New England clam shack. Inside, skyline shots of the Big Apple and a Yankees baseball shirt make a good Gotham try.

Breakfasts (served all day) are hefty, whether you order a full plate or a sandwich version, which is available for many basic items. A plate of two eggs any style, for example, with home fries and toast, runs you $3.75; but you can have just the eggs on a roll or grilled toast for $2.75. French toast is yummy at $3.50; for a dollar more, top it with sliced bananas or diced apples and raisins in cinnamon. And the "Kids Special" offers three small pancakes, two slices of bacon, and milk or orange juice, all for $3.75.

There is a whole menu page entitled "Fourteen Great Omelettes," all of which are made with four eggs and a wide variety of fillings. Try the New York corned beef, which also contains onions and Swiss cheese; or the Neapolitan, the Pizzaola, or the American Veggie. Most are priced around $6-$7, including home fries and toast. Coffee is always free with any breakfast, by the way, including refills. Gotta love a place where they ask, "Some caffeine for you?" as you walk in the door.

Big hamburgers start at $4.50 a plate; wrap your hands around a corned beef Reuben sandwich for $5.25, or an "Italian-style" cheese steak sandwich for $5.50. Now, that's an East Coast kind of thing. Soups are homemade here, as well. Obviously, the NY is a popular breakfast spot—especially for weekend brunch, when you may have to wait for a table. It's only open from 6 A.M. to 4 P.M., Tuesdays through Sundays.

Nikolas Pizza & Pasta

• 1924 N 45th St., Seattle; 545-9090
Another of the many attractive and affordable dining options in Wallingford, Nikolas—from the same folks who brought you the Costas restaurants—straddles the Mediterranean with a mix of Greek and Italian cuisine.

Pizzas, the house specialty, are therefore of the thick, doughy variety. They come topped with everything from garlic to gyros. Among the other interesting options are Canadian bacon and pineapple, and the "Venetian," topped with artichoke hearts and almonds. There are four sizes available, ranging in price from $6.25 for a small basic, all the way up to $21.95 for the works—but you'll either be splitting this or living off it for days.

Pasta is the other side of the picture here: Dishes like spaghetti with mushrooms and broccoli, baked lasagne, and fettucine with chicken. Most of these are $7.95 or $8.95, which includes a cup of homemade soup or a side salad. Nikolas also has a decent menu of burgers and sandwiches in the $4-$5 range, as well as individual pizzas from just $2.95. They've recently added a breakfast menu, with big omelettes from $5.50, and several weekday morning specials (two eggs and toast, $1.99).

The restaurant is large, modern, and very handsome; the walls feature oversized exposed brick, and booths are upholstered in a country print fabric. There are plenty of potted plants and other yuppie accouterments, making a very pleasant atmosphere. Open seven days a week from 8 A.M.

Patty's Eggnest

• 7717 Greenwood Ave N, Seattle; 784-5348
Recipient of the national Golden Egg Award (who knows? They're very proud of it) and home of the gigantic all-day breakfast, Patty's Eggnest has many different claims to fame—be-

sides being a friendly, cozy, "working people's" establishment.

All of the egg dishes and omelettes are made with three eggs (or, just egg whites if you're watching your cholesterol), and are served with homemade hash browns, toast, and natural, all-fruit jelly. The $5.95 chef's omelette is just loaded with ham, onions, mushrooms, and cheese, while the $6.25 vegetarian version overflows with tomatoes, mushrooms, onions, green peppers, and cheese. The steak-and-eggs price fluctuates, but at the time of this writing it was $8.95; remember, that's an eight-ounce steak, cut fresh in-house, plus three eggs any style, hash browns, and toast. Yowza.

Patty's hamburgers are just as filling as her breakfast items. Weighing in at one-third of a pound and under six bucks, the bacon cheeseburger and the chili burger with cheese and onions are both large and delicious choices. All burgers and sandwiches are served with your choice of French fries, soup, or a salad.

Settle into the Eggnest any day between 7 A.M. and 3 P.M., and be sure to bring a huge appetite.

Pizzeria Pagliacci

• 4003 Stone Way N, Seattle; 632-1058
• 550 Queen Anne Ave. N, Seattle; 285-1232
• 4529 University Way NE, Seattle; 632-0421
• 426 Broadway E, Seattle; 324-0730

- 2400 Tenth Ave. E, Seattle;
  632-1058
- *Tip-free*

Pizza is not the only supper you'll
sing for on this menu. Calzone, soup,
and pastas—both hot dishes and
unique salads—are also served fresh
daily. The atmosphere is casual, but
nicer than your average pizzeria;
fresh flowers in recycled juice bottles
adorn every table, while artsy black
and white photos and sketches decorate the walls. The most exciting
thing you'll see is the occasional Frisbee of dough being flung up in the air
by the chef behind the counter. All
pizza dough is made fresh daily and
tossed in this manner—"no rolling
pins or sheeters to take the life out of
the dough," as the menu boasts. This
attention to quality definitely results
in a superior pie.

Ordering takes place after you've
viewed everything in the glass display cases. Mr. C particularly enjoyed a delicious $3.95 pesto and
artichoke pasta salad; the basics, such
as the "extra-pepperoni" pizza, are always on hand, either by the slice or
the whole pie. Pizzeria Pagliacci is
open from 11 A.M. to 11 P.M. Sundays
through Thursdays, and 'til 1 A.M. Fridays and Saturdays.

Red Robin

- 138 Northgate Plaza, Seattle;
  365-0933
- 1600 E Olive Way, Seattle;
  323-1600
- 3272 Fuhrman Ave. E, Seattle;
  323-0918
- Pier 55, 1101 Alaskan Way, Seattle;
  623-1942
- 1100 Fourth Ave., Seattle; 447-1909
- 11021 NE Eighth St., Bellevue;
  453-9522
- 2390 148th Ave. NE, Bellevue;
  641-3810
- 1305 SE Everett Mall Way,
  Everett; 355-7330
- Sea Tac Mall, Federal Way;
  946-TOGO (8646)
- *And other suburban locations*

Red Robin is a popular chain where
families, business types, mall creatures, and others all come together

for standard American fare. The atmosphere is bright, lively, and convivial. Separate bar areas, fully outfitted
for beers and cocktails, include televisions showing various ball games.

The menu is dominated by the
"Gourmet Burgers" (the world's
greatest, in their humble opinion), in
more than a dozen varieties. Try the
"Banzai Burger," marinated in teriyaki sauce and topped with grilled
pineapple and cheddar cheese
($5.95), or the "Lone Star Burger,"
with jalapeño jack cheese, salsa, and
guacamole ($5.25). Non-carnivores
may want to try the "Amazing
Meatless Burger," made with veggies
and grains ($5.25). In fact, you can
have any style made with a meatless
patty.

The one-size-fits-all menu also includes soups and sandwiches, entree-
sized salads, pastas, and plenty of
bar-food appetizers. Red Robin is a
safe bet for bringing the gang to
munch on wings and nachos. And save
room for desserts like mud pie, cheesecake, brownie sundaes, shakes, and
root beer floats. There's also a kiddie
menu, with half a dozen meals all
priced at $2.99 each. Most Red Robins
serve food daily until midnight.

Scandies

- 2301 NW Market St., Seattle;
  783-5080

For those who don't already know
(and yes, there are some), Seattle has
a strong Scandinavian community,
and Ballard is the heart of it. And
Scandies is like the heart of Ballard.
Homey and casual, it's decorated
with hanging lamps and white lace
curtains. Stop in here for a plate of
authentic Swedish pancakes ($3.95),
eggier than your standard IHOP variety, laced with tangy lingonberries,
and topped with whipped cream.
Same price for an egg and smoked
sardine sandwich—no, it's not for
everyone.

A Danish chef's salad is made
with—what else?—Havarti instead of
Swiss cheese ($6.50), and a Norwe-
gian hamburger ($5.50) is something
more like meatloaf, served with sau-

teed onions, stewed peas, and potato salad. Finish off with an egg custard caramel (the Spanish call it *flan*) or a slice of apricot-filled cake. Not a menu for those on a diet, but then, Scandinavians do know how to store up for those long winters. Open weekdays from 7 A.M. to 4 P.M. only, and weekends from 8 A.M. to 4 P.M.

74th Street Ale House
- 7401 Greenwood Ave. N, Seattle; 784-2955

Either the 74th Street Ale House encourages people with tastebuds of steel to eat here, or it merely wants everyone to *think* that they do. Everywhere you look, you'll find "Bottled Hell," a hot pepper sauce that will ignite your burger, gumbo, and perhaps the table top. Mercifully, plenty of food in this neighborhood corner pub is tame by comparison.

Appetizers here are a perfect way to begin your meal if you're with friends; they will also fill you up if you're dining solo (you parties of one may also enjoy various sports being shown on TV). The "74th St. Ploughman's Plate" ($6.50) is fancier than any farmer could imagine—composed of sliced pepperoni, double Gloucester cheese, onion marmalade, and a small salad topped with raspberry-Dijon vinaigrette. Bread is served on the side. Other standard pub favorites, like burgers ($4.50), sandwiches (around $6.50), and chips with salsa ($2.50) are also available. But don't forget, even if you're just grabbing a bite to eat—and not interested in the $2.75 pints of beer—you must still be 21 to come inside. Food is served daily from 11:30 A.M. to 12 midnight.

Still Life in Fremont Coffeehouse
- 709 N 35th St., Seattle; 547-9850
- *Tip-free*

Is there still life in Fremont? You bet there is, and at almost any given hour, most of it seems to have jammed into this popular cafe. Serving more than just coffee, Still Life is the social center of the neighborhood. Artists sit and sketch. Students pore over their books as they pour milk

---

---

into their java. Young professionals make the place a tight squeeze at lunchtime. While you're waiting in line, you can leaf through stacks of alternative newspapers and flyers advertising galleries and lectures.

The food mainly consists of salads, sandwiches, and soups, all fresh and homemade. Many choices vary from day to day, and are as creative as the crowd. Southwest chicken salad incorporates chicken, rice, vegetables, chili, and corn, served with a slice of crusty bread for $5.75 ($3.50 for a smaller portion). Chilled puree of spinach soup, blended with potatoes and leeks, is $3.95 for a bowl, $2.50 for a cup. Mr. C enjoyed a huge slab of vegetable pie, sort of like a quiche, filled with tomato, spinach, asiago, and mozzarella; it's filling at $4.75, but you can add a salad for a total of $6.

Breakfasts include choices like kippered salmon on a bagel ($4.95), with cream cheese, avocado, and a slice of red onion; not to mention Still Life's wonderful and big pastries. These can be pricey, but if you're lucky, you may be able to grab a day-old bargain at half-price.

When pastries start out this good, one day is nothing! Add a cuppa coffee for 83¢, which *includes* one refill; a second refill costs 25¢ more.

Unlike many cafes, this one offers as much variety in its teas as in its coffees. Loose tea leaves are set out in glass jars; fill your own infuser and drop it into your cup. The condiments table offers more than just milk—there are white and brown sugar, honey, and several jams for your bread. If you're just sipping, make your way to the big windows at the front of the room, settle into a couch beside the large coffee table, and lose yourself in a newspaper.

Still Life is open every day, from 7:30 A.M. to 10 P.M., closing an hour later on weekends. Thursdays usually offer free live music from 8-10 P.M., except in summer. Food, food for thought, music, coffee—is it any wonder why everybody hangs here?

Taco Del Mar

- 3526 Fremont Pl. N, Seattle; 545-8001
- 615 Queen Anne Ave. N, Seattle; 281-7420
- 705 Madison Ave., Seattle; 467-0603
- 1301 Alaskan Way, Seattle; 233-9457
- *Tip-free*

These places are hardly bigger than a taco themselves, but if you're visiting the Queen Anne location, you'd never know it from looking at the large beach scene mural inside—complete with frolicking dinosaurs, an opera diva, mermaids, and a dude named Ray. The crew working here is enthusiastic, the music is loud, the deals are good, and the food is even better.

Batches of guacamole and salsa are made fresh throughout the day. The Jumbo Burrito is filled with beans, rice, salsa, onions, and either chicken, pork, or beef; at just $2.95, your wallet will yell *"Olé!"* The vegetarian burrito may cost slightly more, but it's still a bargain at $3.50. Nachos, tacos, and all of the other standard Mexican fare are also available, at prices that make it easy to fill

up. Taco del Mar is open every day.

Thai Food

- 8530 Greenwood Ave. N, Seattle; 784-1830

Decorated with Asian artwork on its walls, and tall plants in its center, this *chic* yet casual restaurant makes for a nice kick-back-and-relax sort of dining experience.

The reasonable prices are just as relaxing—most dishes range between $5.50 and $7.50, for filling platters like *tom yum talay* ($7.50)—a hot and sour soup brimming with seafood, mushrooms, lemon grass, *kaffir* leaves, and a touch of chili paste. The ever-popular pad Thai, just $5.75, is a winner. Also especially good is the "Swimming Tofu" (not in a bathing suit, but a yummy peanut sauce) for $5.25.

The name of the restaurant may not be quite as imaginative as that dish, but that's hardly a concern of Mr. C or fellow Cheapsters. Thai Food is open weekdays from 11:30 A.M. to 2:30 P.M. for lunch, and from 5 P.M. to 9:30 P.M. for dinner; Saturday and Sunday hours are from 4 to 9:30 P.M. only.

Teahouse Kuan Yin

- 1911 N 45th St., Seattle; 632-2055
- *Tip-free*

Leave it to Wallingford to boast the one teahouse in all of coffee-crazed Seattle. As you may guess, this place is a relaxing alternative indeed, brewing up three dozen varieties of tea—along with an international array of finger foods and desserts.

There's a lot more here than Lipton. Teas come in several kinds of black, green, oolong, and house-blended flavors. Many are herbal, but don't be mistaken; some pack quite a caffeine kick. A detailed brochure describes each one in those laboriously vague terms found in wine magazines: "A fully-fermented, well-finished, complex tea..." "As close to imbibing Spring as one may hope for..." and so on. Better yet, just ask the folks behind the counter for advice; they know their stuff.

Whichever you choose, $1.75 gets you a large pot draped in a tea cozy and filled with two or three cups' worth. (A tip from Mr. C: Weekdays from 10 A.M. to 2 P.M., Kuan Yin offers its "T-4-2" deal, when the same price gets you a pot large enough for two people to share.)

Now, what to have with your tea? The assortment of eats rotates daily, but usually includes several Asian delicacies: Chinese noodles in a spicy peanut sauce ($2.75), Vietnamese spring rolls ($3.75 for three) or *hum-bow*, round buns filled with pork or vegetables ($1.75). Or, spin the globe and go for Italian quiche ($2.95). Each item comes on a small plate; combine two or three, and you have a meal—kind of like a world-beat *dim sum*. If you've left room for—or skipped directly to—dessert, there is a world of choices here as well, from Pakistani shortbread cookies to hazelnut torte. Or, keep the theme going with a dish of green tea ice cream ($1.50).

Kuan Yin is an attractive place, appropriately decorated with Japanese calligraphy paintings, shoji screens, and all kinds of tea-serving paraphernalia. Background music takes the same world-tour approach as the food. There are plenty of small tables, with a couple outside; as with coffeehouses, it's a fine place to read the paper or write in your journal. You can also purchase any tea by the ounce; many are blended just for this teahouse, and they do a brisk (no pun intended) mail-order business. Open daily from 10:00 A.M. to 11:00 P.M., to midnight on weekends.

Triangle Tavern
- 3507 Fremont Pl. N, Seattle; 632-0880

Even if the Triangle Tavern were named something like "Doug's Musk Ox Heaven," the three-sided motif would still be impossible to ignore. Take for example, their "wall of fame"—if you're a triangle and have really made it in the world, your picture is up here. The dollar bill's pyramid, Superman's chest symbol, that Bermuda death-trap, and various others are all on display. The ceiling, too, is covered with the geometric figure of choice. No doubt these all take their inspiration from the flat-iron shape of the building itself. The rock music is loud, the bar area by the door is happening (microbrews on tap start at $2.25), and the seating outside—when weather permits—is hard to come by. Got a clear enough picture? It's a hit.

Now for the grub; like so many yuppie trough 'n brews, TT matches *nouvelle* cuisine with its micros for a winning combination. Entrees are not all that cheap, but moderately priced, and tasty. Pizza of the day ($5.75) is especially good and unique—when Mr. C visited, the lineup consisted of spinach, mushrooms, leeks, provolone, onions, and pepperoni, piled on top of an Alfredo sauce base. Roast pork loin served over Vietnamese noodles ($7.95) and bruschetta of the day with soup ($5.75) also looked good. Give 'em a tri—er, *try*. Open seven days a week.

Trolleyman's Pub
- 3400 Phinney Ave. N, Seattle; 548-8000

Part of the Red Hook Brewery in Fremont, the Trolleyman's Pub makes a fine start or finish to a tour of the brewing factory (see the listing under "Entertainment—Walks and Tours") or just a day in the Fremont area. The attractive interior, with its bright white walls, track lighting and cozy fireplace, epitomizes the modern appeal that microbrews have over the old-time, mass-produced stuff. But, if you think that the food in such an eatery will be as upwardly priced as the upwardly mobile folks who eat here, guess again. The Trolleyman is yuppified, but the fare is simple and casual, which keeps prices reasonable.

A hearty bowl of gazpacho, just the thing for a summer's day, might seem pricey at $4.50—but it comes with a garden salad and fresh bread. Also on the light side, the ploughman's lunch ($5.50) keeps this place in line with pub traditions—sliced bread, cheese, and vegetables, served here with potato salad to boot. For more substantial meals, daily specials may include such 'round-the-world treats as tandoori chicken, served with couscous; or sausage lasagna, with bread and salad. Both were recently on the board for $6.50, which is about as high as these entrees get.

Of course, there are plenty of Red Hook potables on tap to wash this fine food down with; even these are reasonably priced (well, after all, you are buying factory-direct). An 11-oz. glass of Red Hook ESB is $1.75; pints are just $2.50. The pub is open daily, with food served only until 8:00 P.M. (though the bar stays open later).

Vera's Family Restaurant

- 5417 22nd Ave. NW, Seattle; 782-9966

This Ballard eatery is a "family" restaurant in every sense of the word. First, they serve big portions of hearty Italian food. Not too many fancy twists here; mainly, the menu consists of the basics. And, with plenty of big-sized tables and booths, you can really bring along the entire brood. Owned and run by a family, the folks at Vera's are clearly proud of their restaurant and their service.

What about the food? Vera's serves up basic Italian foods that range from *nouvelle*-sounding entrees like spaghetti with artichokes, fresh mushrooms, basil, sun-dried tomatoes, and parmesan cheese ($8.50) to old standbys like lasagna and fettucine Alfredo (each $7.50). All pasta dishes are served with soup or salad, and warm bread. Chicken and veal entrees, including veal with lemon sauce ($9.95) and chicken marsala ($8.95) are served with soup or salad, pasta, vegetables, and bread. You could make a meal out of just the side dishes.

Or, let the family sink its teeth into one of Vera's pizzas. A large (16") is just $9.95 plain, $11.95 with pepperoni. There's also a big selection of sandwiches: Reuben and Monte Cristo are each $5.95. Each comes with soup, salad, or French fries. Wash it all down with an eclectic selection of beer and wine, or end your meal with a little *dolci* and the ever-present espresso; give the tiramisu a

try for $2.95. Vera's is open Fridays and Saturdays from 4:30 P.M. to 10 P.M., and Sundays, Wednesdays, and Thursdays from 4:30 P.M. to 9:30 P.M.

Wingdome

- 1501 N 45th St., Seattle; 634-WING (9464)

The summer of '94 brought the roof down in the Kingdome, and a "hot" new restaurant to Wallingford, the Wingdome. With a new wave approach to the traditional sports bar, the Wingdome features a decor that could just as easily be some trendy modern art gallery.

Along with all this are lots of beers and plenty of everyone's favorite appetizer: chicken wings. These come in a dizzying choice of flavors and spiciness, from "5-Alarm Flame Throwin' Wings" to "Training Wings for Real Chickens." Special varieties include "Kamikaze Wings" with teriyaki sauce and "Rasta Wings" with Jamaican-style sauce. Once you've made a choice, the prices are pretty simple: $4.95 for ten wings, $9.95 for twenty-five, $17.95 for fifty, $24.95 for seventy-five, and $30.95 for, yes, one hundred wings—great for those team chowdowns after the softball game. Tack on about a dollar more for an order of specialty wings.

But then, man does not live by wings alone. There *are* other options, most following the hot and spicy theme. Spicy burgers are a bargain at $5.95, with fries. Pep 'em up even more with toppings like jalapeños or chili for 50¢, or your favorite wing sauce for a quarter. Salads are served as only the Wingdome could: with mouth-burning wings, of course.

Cool off your tongue with a cold brew; domestic, imported, or micro. Non-imbibers can opt for a tall glass of soda or lemonade. And save room for a frosty dessert—ice cream, what else? Open seven days; the Wingdome stays open 'til 1 A.M. on Fridays and Saturdays for late-night nibbling.

The Yankee Diner

- 5300 24th Ave. NW, Seattle; 783-1964

- 13856 Bellevue-Redmond Rd., Bellevue; 643-1558
- 6812 Tacoma Mall Blvd., Tacoma; 475-3006
- *And other suburban locations*

This place is tailor-made for families of any size, as the usually packed waiting room will attest. You may hang out there as long as an hour before getting a table; yet, no one leaves. If you can manage to keep the kids quiet long enough, you won't be disappointed. This place is BIG: big on portions, and big on old-time, American-style foods. These go beyond the trademark Yankee pot roast, to include steaks, roast turkey, pot pies, and more. Best of all, you can get the whole brood in and out and still have enough money for the violin lessons.

The aforementioned pot roast, for instance, is just $8.75. Even cheaper is meat loaf ($7.95) or chicken fried steak ($7.45). Of course, it's the side dishes that make these entrees such a great value: Each one comes with a cup of soup or a green salad, vegetables, a choice of potato (including homemade mashed!), and biscuits

baked from scratch. If you do have little ones to feed, a kids' menu includes turkey and pot roast dinners for under five bucks.

Folks with (slightly) lighter appetites can go for one of 35 different sandwiches, hot and cold, at lunch or dinner. Most of the dinner entrees are also available for lunch, at two or three dollars less. Come in midday and enjoy breaded veal cutlets or hickory smoked ham, with all those trimmings, for $5.95. At night, these go for $8.45.

Early risers aren't left in the cold, either. Mr. C *has* seen lower-priced breakfasts, but then, you won't need to eat again all day. The "Diner Special," for example, includes juice, fresh fruit, three eggs, bacon, ham or sausage, fried potatoes and toast or pancakes. Even at $6.25, it's a bargain—if you can finish! French toast made with the Yankee's home-baked cinnamon bread is another winner. Speaking of sweets, the diner is also popular for its desserts, malted milkshakes, and home-baked goodies. Open seven days a week.

QUEEN ANNE AREA
(including Magnolia, Seattle Center)

Brelundi Restaurant
- 1919 Queen Anne Ave. N, Seattle; 281-9055

Brelundi is a quaint little restaurant that, along with its gourmet pizzas, Italian pastas, and Greek entrees, serves breakfast items as well. Among the start-your-day-off-right breakfasts are the "Russian" omelette, filled with bacon, hash browns, green onions and sour cream for $5.95; the stack of blueberry pancakes, $4.50, is also hearty.

For later in the day, the 8" individual pizzas are especially good deals at $6.95. The "Three Cheese" pizza

includes generous portions of mozzarella, feta, and gorgonzola cheese. The popular Greek dish, *moussaka*, and Italian classics such as fettucine primavera, are also priced at $6.95. Brelundi is closed on Mondays.

Caffé Ladro
- 2205 Queen Anne Ave. N, Seattle; 282-5313

Here's the sort of laid-back coffeehouse with which Seattle—and Queen Anne—are packed. Differentiating it somewhat from the beverage-and-pastry-only crowd are its weekend breakfasts. A limited number of selections are cooked up each Saturday and Sunday between 7 A.M. and 1 P.M. Among the choices, Mr. C liked Ladro's eggs Benedict ($5.25); French toast, made with three thick slices of challah bread ($4.95); and Italian-style scrambled eggs, prepared with garlic, roma tomatoes, fresh basil, capers, and parmesan, served on bruschetta ($5.25). Caffé Ladro is open everyday between 6 A.M. and 10 P.M.

Caffé Minnie's
- 101 Denny Way, Seattle; 448-6263
- 611 Broadway E, Seattle; 860-1360

Rounding the corner at Denny and First, along with a new Capitol Hill location, Caffé Minnie's is one of the few Seattle joints that is truly open 24 hours. That alone gets a big thumbs up from Mr. C. Even better, the food is fabulous.

Lunch is served starting at 11 A.M., but you can still order a plate of $4.75 pecan nut pancakes, or the $6.95 "Frank Sinatra" omelette, filled with Italian sausage, garlic, black olives, scallions, pepper jack, and cheddar cheese. Who could sing after downing all that? Matter of fact, breakfast is served all day. If you've got the time and the sweet tooth, go for the Dutch babies—especially light and eggy pancakes topped with sweet things. They take about twenty minutes to prepare, and are worth the wait. Try the $5.95 "Fruit Baby," an oven-baked masterpiece topped with hot apples, strawberries, blueberries, or raspberries, served with syrup and whipped cream.

Lest you get the impression that lunch and dinner are any less enticing, Mr. C especially recommends the hearty bowl of black bean soup with cheddar cheese—nice and spicy—for $3.50. Made with skim milk, it's more like chili than soup. Minnie's tortellini salad ($6.95) mixed with fresh garlic, prosciutto and crisp bacon, is also very good. Burgers and sandwiches start at $4.75. For something even more filling, pasta dishes, like smoked salmon tossed with fresh garlic pasta in a hazelnut cream sauce ($11.95), are served with

soup or salad and hot rolls.

Chicago's
- 315 First Ave. N, Seattle; 282-7791

Boasting itself to be "a nice, neighborhood Italian place," Chicago's is part family restaurant, part bar, and on weekends, a rhythm and blues club (see the listing under "Entertainment—Music").

The restaurant section is spacious and bright; in the daytime, light pours in through skylights high above and through a huge, stained-glass window with a contemporary design. The menu consists of (what else?) Italian favorites. Pizzas start at just $3.95 to $5.95 for a single; pasta dishes, such as eggplant parmigiana and tortellini, range between $6.95 and $9.95 a plate. Soup, or a trip to the salad bar, accompanies each entree. For simpler meals, go for a meatball or Italian sausage sandwich, each $5.95.

The bar and weekend R & B shows are only for people 21 years and older; there's no cover charge, another plus in Mr. C's opinion. Chicago's is open Mondays through Thursdays from 11:30 A.M. 'til 9 P.M., Fridays and Saturdays 'til 2 A.M., and Sundays from 4 P.M. to 9 P.M.

Chinook's at Salmon Bay
- Fisherman's Terminal, 1900 W Nickerson St., Seattle; 283-HOOK (4665)

As bargain priced dining spots go, Chinook's at the Fisherman's Terminal is quite a "catch." You wouldn't expect a restaurant of this size, with so many fancy features and a gorgeous view of the canal, to be inexpensive. But, surprise of surprises, it is! The vast menu features dozens of seafood, meat, and poultry specialties, very few of which are priced over $10.

Salmon, obviously, is the specialty of the house, and though prices vary according to market rates, some of these entrees start as low as $7.95 (for a homemade salmon pot pie). There's also a good selection of shellfish, including Penn Cove mussels and Discovery Bay littleneck clams, both $7.95. If you like pasta and seafood, indulge in seafood marinara: clams, mussels, ling cod and Dungeness crab in marinara sauce served over linguine ($8.95). The best bargain of all, though, has to be the Monday night "all-you-can-eat" fish and chips deal for $7.95. Don't be surprised if you have to wait for a table, on this "off" night. There are beef and chicken dishes too, by the way. Even at these prices, most entrees include potatoes and a side order of vegetables.

Desserts are also homemade, and beer and wine are served at moderate prices to match those of the food. The spacious interior has enough upscale touches to make this a perfect restaurant for a special evening out. Large plate-glass windows along one entire side of the restaurant face out to the ship canal and Ballard, offering plenty of salty views to go with the seafood.

Outside and around the corner, **Little Chinook's** is the take-out-stand version of big Chinook's. Fish and chips is the main item here; an order, made with ling cod, is just $3.99. Clam strips and chips go for $4.99, and several varieties of chowder are $1.39 to $2.39. Pick up your food, find a bench, and enjoy an even closer view of the nautical activity on the canal. It's open year-round, serving until dusk.

Also just outside the restaurant is the **Bay Cafe**, a breakfast and lunchtime coffee shop, which primarily serves the folks who work around Fisherman's Terminal. Needless to say, you are just as welcome, for inexpensive diner fare. It's open daily from 6:30 A.M. to 2:30 P.M. only.

Dick's Drive Ins
- 500 Queen Anne Ave. N, Seattle; 285-5155
- 111 NE 45th St. Seattle; 632-5125
- 115 Broadway E, Seattle; 323-1300
- 12325 30th Ave. NE, Seattle; 363-7777
- 9208 Holman Rd. NW, Seattle; 783-5233
- *And other suburban locations*
- *Tip-free*

No book on cheap (priced) Seattle restaurants would be complete without mention of this longtime landmark. Burgers, fries, shakes, and a see-and-be-seen atmosphere have made Dick's a favorite spot for decades. The food may not be first rate, but hey—it's classic all-Americana. 75¢ burgers and 90¢ cheeseburgers will fill you up and never break the bank. Even the quarter-pound "Deluxe," made of two patties, cheese, and a few extra fixin's, is only $1.60. Of course, no burger here should be eaten without fries—buy a greasy bagful for 85 cents. And, for the full heartburn effect, wash it all down with a nice, thick shake ($1.10). Your cholesterol level may go through the roof; but remember, Dick's is better for your soul than your heart. Drive in from 10:30 A.M. to 2 A.M. anyday.

Emerald Diner
- 105 W Mercer St., Seattle; 284-4618

Picture a diner. Y'know, your classic, downtown, hash-slinging diner. Got it? Well, forget about it, 'cause *this* one's different. This little gem is no truck stop; rather, it is perhaps the heart and soul of Queen Anne's busy cafe scene. It's dark and atmospheric inside, done up more like a nightclub, with eye-catching local artworks hanging on the wall. The back lounge is well-known for its poetry slams, though these tend to come and go. Give 'em a call to see if any entertainment is going on these days.

The Emerald does keep with diner traditions in two respects—you get a lot of food, and the prices are reasonable. Mr. C especially enjoyed a club sandwich served with a cup of delicious, creamy turkey soup, all for $6.95. If soup's not your thing, you can substitute French fries or salad as your side dish. Their freshly prepared, batter-dipped fish and chips is also $6.95 and also delicious. Plus all your other diner favorites. See? Told ya it was a diner. Open from 8 A.M. to 10 P.M. Mondays through Thursdays, 'til 11 P.M. Fridays and Saturdays.

5 Spot
- 1502 Queen Anne Ave. N, Seattle; 285-7768

What is it that makes 5 Spot such a hip and happening place? Could it be the flamingos perched high above coat racks made to look like palm trees? Or the sign that points you "To the beach" for their patio? It must be just the whole beach party atmosphere, that Frankie and Annette thing.

Lunch and dinner specialties include comfort food choices like a tall turkey sandwich and chips ($5.75) and "Pasta Gardenia" ($8.50): spinach, mushrooms, tomato and calamata olives are sauteed in garlic and olive oil, then tossed with linguini and pesto.

On Saturdays and Sundays until 3 P.M., the 5 Spot serves something it affectionately calls "blunch," a breakfast/lunch menu combo. The plates are piled so high that you'll spend quite a while eating before you actually find the dish. Mr. C especially enjoyed (for the good part of an hour) a Swiss cheese and spice omelette, priced at $5.50 with a side of home fries. Other delicious and very filling treats include a stack of three huge, fluffy pancakes for $4.50.

The 5 Spot is open from 8:30 A.M. 'til 10 P.M., Sundays through Thursdays; Fridays and Saturdays 'til 11 P.M. On Saturdays and Sundays, it's closed between 3 P.M. and 5 P.M., just after blunch and before dinner. Got it? Don't worry about bringing the sunblock—but remember what your momma told you, and wait thirty minutes after eating before you can swim. At this place, better make that sixty.

Floyd's Place
- 521 First Ave. N, Seattle; 284-3542

From the moment you see the gleefully jigging cow and pig doing a two-step above the door, you know that Floyd's is smokin'—they serve the best zing-your-tastebuds, melt-in-your-mouth barbecue west of the Mississippi, or at least west of the Seattle Center.

Floyd's is a bar, so no one under 21 can be served; the young'uns will have to be satisfied with eating your leftovers, which you will almost certainly have. That said, try a mouth-watering beef brisket sandwich for $6.50, or an order of baby back ribs for $7.95. To make room for the three side dishes (corn bread, baked beans, and potato salad, for example) that are included with these meals, mosey on back to the game room, past the animal heads on the wall (gorilla, rhino, fish, y'know, the usual) and play a round of shuffleboard or pinball. Wash everything down with one of Floyd's 26—count 'em, 26—draft beers, including three always-changing regional microbrews.

Finally, a note to particularly messy eaters: each table comes equipped with a roll of paper towels, and the floor is—what else—barbecue-sauce red. Floyd's may not be a good choice for a first date—but there's no denying that the food is first rate. Floyd's is open from 3 P.M. 'til 2 A.M. during the week, and from 12:30 P.M. on the weekends.

Guadalajara Hacienda
- 1531 Queen Anne Ave. N, Seattle; 283-0788
- 5923 California Ave. SW, Seattle; 932-2803

Guadalajara Hacienda strives to create the illusion that you're eating in a grand old Mexican plantation house; music, natural light, and murals all help to complete this effect. Of course, what good are the murals, if the cooking reminds you more of Air Mexico? Not to worry—the food is as splendid as the decor, and you won't have to spend too many pesos either.

Fajitas are the house specialty—each platter comes with rice, beans, sour cream, guacamole, and tortillas. Mr. C recommends the prawn fajitas ($9.75) with sauteed peppers, onions, zucchini, tomatoes, and mushrooms. A variety of deluxe enchiladas (you get two of them) are topped with cheese and served with rice and beans. All but one are $6.95; the chile verde enchilada, spicy and filled with pork, is $7.45.

Lunch specials, as always, are the best buys; all entrees are $4.75, with refried beans and rice. You can choose a pair of beef enchiladas, or the chile-colorado burrito (flank steak in a mild sauce, with rice, beans, and sour cream), or any of the other thirteen lunch selections. Also good to know, Guadalajara Hacienda will gladly make vegetarian versions of any dish upon request. The restaurant is open from 11:30 A.M. daily until 9:30 P.M. during the week; 'til 11 P.M. Fridays, 10 P.M. Saturdays, and 9 P.M. Sundays.

Hilltop Ale House
- 2129 Queen Anne Ave. N, Seattle; 285-3877

Hilltop Ale House is, obviously, a pub. What should that also mean? Good pub food. Well, this place fits the bill, and then some. Along with standard grub, their menu is filled with items like chicken liver paté ($5); a sausage sandwich smothered with grilled onions, red, yellow and green peppers, and mozzarella ($6); and Hilltop halibut cakes ($7.50).

As this is a bar, you do need to be 21 to come inside, even if you just want a Coke and a burger. Sorry, kids. Hilltop is open from 11 A.M. to midnight during the week, and 'til 2 A.M. Fridays and Saturdays.

Hoyt's Pub
- 1527 Queen Anne Ave. N, Seattle; 284-2656

Hoyt's is your classic, neighborhood bar: dark interior, pool tables, dart boards, and of course, good ol' fashioned pub food. Burgers and sandwiches are all priced around six bucks—Hoyt's basic chili burger is a particularly tasty example. Hot and spicy chicken wings ($5.25) and fried mozzarella sticks ($4.95) are perfect finger foods to snack on. Hoyt's has over twenty beers on tap, so you won't have any problem finding something to wash it all down. You will have a problem if you're under 21—Hoyt's doesn't serve minors.

Stop by for a snack and round of darts between 11:30 A.M. and 11 P.M. during the week, and until midnight on the weekends.

MR. CHEAP'S PICKS
Queen Anne Area

- ✔ **Cafe Minnie's**—Great food, "Dutch Babies," and coffee, 24 hours a day.

- ✔ **Chinook's**—Fascinating views of the canal, plus all-you-can-eat fish 'n chips on Monday nights.

- ✔ **5 Spot**—Festive "beach party" bar and restaurant, at the top of the Hill.

- ✔ **Floyd's Place**—Near Seattle Center, this *sssmokin'* pub serves up tangy barbecue— and rolls of paper towels at each table.

- ✔ **Jalisco**—Authentic Mexican food served in a charmingly decorated dining room.

Jalisco Mexican Restaurant
- 122 and 129 First Ave. N, Seattle; 283-4242
- 1467 E Republican St., Seattle; 325-9005
- 8517 14th Ave. S, Seattle; 767-1943
- 12336 31st Ave. NE, Seattle; 364-3978
- 115 Park Lane, Kirkland; 822-3355

A shop owner of Mexican extraction told Mr. C to be sure to include Jalisco, for truly authentic regional food. Named for one of that country's more scenic states, this restaurant upholds that tradition of beauty—at least one branch sports a wall mural depicting a village center, complete with guitarist serenading a dancing couple by a fountain. Piñatas and plants are perched high above, and high-backed booths provide a secluded dining experience.

Try one of the huge "Especiáles de la Casa," like the chimichangas or enchiladas rancheras, for $7.55 each. All of these specialties are served with rice and beans, making for a gigantic plateful. For the lighter appetite, a single tamale ($2.65) or taco salad ($4.50) will do you right.

Be sure to try something with Jalisco's homemade *mole* sauce; usually made from unsweetened chocolate (yes, for dinner), these folks make it as a nifty peanut sauce instead. If you're not entirely familiar with such native culinary terms, there's a helpful glossary on the back of the menu.

The First Avenue location, just outside Seattle Center, has recently spawned a quicker-fare "taqueria" right across the street; the Lake City location adds a cocktail lounge. All branches are open daily from 11 A.M. to 10 P.M., and to 11 P.M. on Fridays and Saturdays.

Kidd Valley
- 531 Queen Anne Ave. N, Seattle; 284-0184
- 4910 Green Lake Way N, Seattle; 547-0121
- 14303 Aurora Ave. N, Seattle; 364-8493
- 135 15th Ave. NE, Seattle; 328-8133
- 5502 25th Ave. NE, Seattle; 522-0890
- *And other suburban locations*
- *Tip-free*

Kidd Valley is Seattle's own answer to McDonald's, though most locals would argue that Kidd Valley is better. And they're right. There's more of a selection, and your order is prepared while you wait. The classic hamburger is $2.29; the cheeseburger is $2.44. These burgers are juicy and delicious; 'nuff said.

For those who may be suffering from burger burn-out, there are also quite a few sandwiches to choose from, like a BLT ($2.49), broiled chicken ($3.54), and grilled ham and cheese ($2.99). The homemade onion rings ($1.19) and specialty shakes ($1.49) should not be missed, though only the strong of stomach will want to have both in the same sitting.

Kidd's atmosphere is strictly early-American fast-food joint—kinda sparse, a few prominent colors, and lots of booths. Open seven days a week.

La Tazza
- 1503 Queen Anne Ave. N, Seattle; 284-8984
- *Tip-free*

La Tazza is an itty-bitty sandwich shop that makes some pretty huge Italian sandwiches. In fact, the joint is almost as small as the Italian cup for which it's named. You can eat here if you'd like—grab a stool along the front window if there's one available—but this is mainly a take-out sort of place.

La Tazza has a list of sandwiches, all priced at $4.25, to choose from: Mr. C picked the "Mistro," stuffed with Italian fontina and fresh mozzarella cheeses, artichoke hearts, and roma tomatoes on focaccia bread. Yummy! There are also daily specials. You're certainly not going to find these kinds of choices in any fast-food sandwich chains.

La Tazza is open from 6:30 A.M. to 7 P.M. during the week, 7:30 A.M. to 2 P.M. Saturdays, and 8:30 A.M. to 7 P.M. Sundays.

Macheezmo Mouse Mexican Cafe
- 425 Queen Anne Ave. N, Seattle; 282-9904
- 211 Broadway E, Seattle; 325-0072
- 701 Fifth Ave., Seattle; 382-1730
- 1815 N 45th St., Seattle; 545-0153
- 2028 148th Ave. NE, Bellevue; 746-5824
- 3805 196th Ave. SW, Lynnwood; 744-1611
- *Tip-free*

The '90s mean that even Mexican fast food has gone health-conscious. In fact, Macheezmo Mouse is so serious about it that they print up pamphlets on weight management, diabetic exchanges, heart health—and how their food fits in. Every item on the menu is accompanied by nutritional information: The chicken burrito, for example, has 580 calories, 17% from fat—while the veggie power salad has 200 calories, 1% from fat. Make your informed decision.

Mr. C was a bit put off by a display of sample platters at the Queen Anne location. It's nice to see the choices before you order, but this food sits out all day, and looks a bit um, *faded* after a few hours. Is this the best way to tout healthy food? Well, most branches just show you photos, a better idea. After ordering and paying at the counter, give your name, and they'll call you once your order is ready.

Most burrito, enchilada, and taco plates are $4, including rice and beans on the side. There are also salads, quesadillas, and a children's menu as well; and nothing on the menu tops $5.25. To add a little kick to your meal, stop by the fixin's bar and try a unique but delicious concoction of spicy-sweet citrus barbecue sauce called Boss Sauce. Beer is available too—draft pints are $2-$3, while a bottle of Bud is $1.75.

Macheezmo Mouse restaurants are spacious, clean, and done up in a brightly colored Southwestern motif. Most have tables both inside and out. These features, plus a few children's items on the menu, make it a good bet for families, as well. Open for lunch and dinner, seven days a week.

Maharaja

- 500 Elliott Ave. W, Seattle; 286-1772
- 4542 California Ave. SW, Seattle; 935-9443
- 26108 Pacific Hwy. S, Kent; 946-0664

Folks who know of Maharaja swear by it for huge portions of spicy Indian food, especially the daily lunch specials, which will easily carry you all the way through the day for just $4.95. These specials include lamb curry and chicken tandoori, with a pile of side dishes that will make your plate runneth over. A daily buffet, also $4.95, rounds out the fantastic lunchtime deals.

Dinner entrees are also very reasonable; most are $5.95 to $8.95, while vegetarian dishes come in under $5. Try *keema aloo*, minced lamb cooked with herbs, spices, and potatoes ($6.50); "Dancing Chicken,"

cooked with lentil sauce ($6.95); or beef *sagg*, pieces of meat marinated in spices and cooked with spinach and ginger ($6.95). Light eaters can stick with mixed vegetables and rice for $4.95, or choose from the selection of appetizers, soups, and salads. Of course, if you came here to eat light you're probably in the wrong place! Maharaja is open every day from 11 A.M. to 2:30 P.M. for lunch, and from 4 to 10 P.M. for dinner.

Maybe Monday Caffé

- 10 Boston St., Seattle; 283-7118
- *Tip-free*

Maybe Monday has one of those "frequent flyer" coffee cards; after ten cups, you get the next one free. That'll *keep* you flying. Mr. C knows some folks who could get through the card in a day or two. Anyway, this place adds a nice extra touch by giving you a free cookie, too, with that free cup.

Serving a simple menu of breakfast and lunch treats along with the java, Maybe Monday dishes up home-cooked favorites like Belgian waffles ($2.75) and tarragon chicken sandwiches ($4.50). Eat inside the simply-decorated dining room, or outside as weather—and the warmth from your cup—will allow. Open from 7 A.M. to 6 P.M. Mondays through Fridays; Saturdays and Sundays from 8 A.M. to 5 P.M. only.

Mecca Cafe

- 526 Queen Anne Ave. N, Seattle; 285-9728

Opened in 1929, "The Oldest Family-Owned Cafe and Lounge in Seattle" does indeed reek of retro character, along with a few touches of modern, artsy hipness. Fortunately, these two styles have come together these days. The Mecca divides into two long rooms: a classic diner of counter and booths, and a classic lounge and bar.

On the diner side, you can get breakfast all day. Have a huge cheddar omelette for $5.25; it comes with crisp home fries and toast, or an "Australian muffin"—a variant of the English type. Good luck finishing it all. A plate of homemade biscuits and gravy, comfort food at its heaviest, is four bucks. Plenty of refills on the fresh coffee, too.

That same $4 will get you a juicy hamburger, a large patty of freshly rolled beef, with terrific hand-cut French fries ($4.75 at night). Full dinner plates like a hot open-face turkey sandwich with mashed potatoes ($5.50) and fried chicken ($6.75) are equally hearty. And, if you have room, they still make good ol' fashioned fountain treats too. Have a giant (enough for two people!) malted milkshake for only $2.75.

The Mecca's lounge is a true hangout in the best local dive tradition—that is, it's dark even by day, with a full bar and a ceiling high enough to handle the smoke. Dressing up the room considerably is an extensive collection of beer mats tacked up all over the walls, which have been doodled upon by various barroom Picassos over the years. Open until 1 A.M., with food 'til midnight.

Olympia Pizza & Spaghetti House
- 1500 Queen Anne Ave. N, Seattle; 285-5550

Pizza of the gods? You decide. It *is* good, though. It can also be pizza of modern-day paupers, considering the fact that you can get an individual pizza topped with hot pepperoni and cheese for around $7. For a dollar more, get a little ritzy and order a combination of sun-dried tomato, eggplant, and fresh garlic (make sure your date has some too!) piled onto a base pesto sauce.

Pastas, like ravioli and lasagna, range between $7 and $8; however, pizza is considered the specialty here—in fact, there are thirty-four kinds to choose from. Beer and wine is available, too. Olympia Pizza is open late seven days a week.

Pizzeria Pagliacci
- 550 Queen Anne Ave. N, Seattle; 285-1232
- 4003 Stone Way N, Seattle; 632-1058
- 4529 University Way NE, Seattle; 632-0421
- 426 Broadway E, Seattle; 324-0730

- 2400 Tenth Ave. E, Seattle; 632-1058
- *Tip-free*

Pizza is not the only supper you'll sing for on this menu. Calzone, soup, and pastas—both hot dishes and unique salads—are also served fresh daily. The atmosphere is casual, but nicer than your average pizzeria; fresh flowers in recycled juice bottles adorn every table, while artsy black and white photos and sketches decorate the walls. The most exciting thing you'll see is the occasional Frisbee of dough being flung up in the air by the chef behind the counter. All pizza dough is made fresh daily and tossed in this manner—"no rolling pins or sheeters to take the life out of the dough," as the menu boasts. This attention to quality definitely results in a superior pie.

Ordering takes place after you've viewed everything in the glass display cases. Mr. C particularly enjoyed a delicious $3.95 pesto and artichoke pasta salad; the basics, such as the "extra-pepperoni" pizza, are always on hand, either by the slice or the whole pie. Pizzeria Pagliacci is open from 11 A.M. to 11 P.M. Sundays through Thursdays, and 'til 1 A.M. Fridays and Saturdays.

Queen Anne Cafe
- 2121 Queen Anne Ave. N, Seattle; 285-2060

At the top of the hill, the Queen Anne Cafe is a diner-style restaurant that knows how to please its customers; breakfast is served all day, and dinners always include vegetables, bread, and rice, plus soup or a salad. This cafe even has a special senior citizens menu, with items like fish and chips or liver and onions—and each dish is just $4.

Burgers and omelettes are the specialties of the house—most are in the $4 to $5.50 range. All omelettes are served with homemade hash browns and toast, and come with a variety of fillings. The "Vegetable" is loaded with mushrooms, onions, tomatoes, broccoli, zucchini, and cheddar cheese ($4.50); the "Italian" overflows with a quarter-pound of Italian sausage, onions, green peppers, and cheese ($5.25).

Hamburgers come with potato chips or French fries. The "King" is topped with bacon, Swiss cheese, and grilled green peppers ($4.50); "Ben's Burger" is actually two quarter-pound patties, two slices of cheese, two slices of bacon, and thousand island dressing ($5.25). Hefty! The Queen Anne Cafe is open from 6 A.M. to 10 P.M. every day.

Taco Del Mar
- 615 Queen Anne Ave. N, Seattle; 281-7420
- 705 Madison Ave., Seattle; 467-0603
- 1301 Alaskan Way, Seattle; 233-9457
- 3526 Fremont Pl. N, Seattle; 545-8001
- *Tip-free*

These places are hardly bigger than a taco themselves, but if you're visiting the Queen Anne location, you'd never know it from looking at the large beach scene mural inside—complete with frolicking dinosaurs, an opera diva, mermaids, and a dude named Ray. The crew working here is enthusiastic, the music is loud, the deals are good, and the food is even better.

Batches of guacamole and salsa are made fresh throughout the day. The Jumbo Burrito is filled with beans, rice, salsa, onions, and either chicken, pork, or beef; at just $2.95, your wallet will yell "*Olé!*'" The vegetarian burrito may cost slightly more, but it's still a bargain at $3.50. Nachos, tacos, and all of the other standard Mexican fare are also available, at prices that make it easy to fill up. Taco del Mar is open every day.

Thailand on Queen Anne
- 1517 Queen Anne Ave. N., Seattle; 283-3663

Thailand on Queen Anne wants to be sure you don't leave hungry. Their entrees are good and filling; but, if you're absolutely famished, you may want to make your dish into a full meal by adding a cup of soup and Thai dessert for an extra $2.75.

Like all good Thai eateries, the degree of spiciness is indicated next to each dish on the menu; and, like the best, those spices can be altered according to your preference—ye of delicate taste buds need not worry. Among the specialties is a dish of green beans and onions sauteed with curry—your choice of beef, pork or chicken—for $6.25. Other scrumptious dishes include lemon grass-seasoned beef, and prawns sauteed with garlic, pepper, carrots and broccoli—each is priced at $7.25.

Take a trip to Thailand (on Queen Anne, that is) between 11:30 A.M. and 10 P.M. during the week, between 3 P.M. and 11 P.M. Saturdays, and 'til 10 P.M. Sundays.

UNIVERSITY DISTRICT

Araya Place
- 4732 University Way NE, Seattle; 524-4332

Araya Place is a rather elegant (for this area), yet relaxed cafe specializing in vegetarian Thai dishes only. The Bangkok Cafe (see below) is Araya's sister restaurant, so don't be surprised to see that name appear among the list of entrees here—such as the "Bangkok Cafe Green Curry."

Efficiency is virtue.

Entrees, noodle and rice dishes all range in price between $5.95 and $6.95. Try the tofu red curry for $6.50—tofu, sliced bamboo shoots, and zucchini, cooked in red curry paste and coconut milk. Enjoy the exotic food and atmosphere Mondays through Saturdays from 11:30 A.M. to 9 P.M.; Sundays, from noon to nine.

Atlantic Street Pizza

- 5253 University Way NE, Seattle; 524-4432
- 941 Holman Rd. NW, Seattle; 783-9698

Here's the take-out-only sibling of a popular Crown Hill restaurant. Their pizza is made with a gourmet flair; the special dough is all natural, made without sugar or yeast. Also, there are five homemade sauces to choose from, including five-cheese, and a mild, sweet crushed tomato sauce.

Toppings...there are so many, they've been broken down into categories like seafood, vegetables, and cheese. Peppers get their own heading. If you're feeling particularly indecisive, plenty of combinations are laid out for you—for example, the "Cinque Formaggi" ($10.75) with mozzarella, parmesan, Havarti, Swiss, and feta. The "Delaurenti's" ($12.75—named for movie mogul Dino?), smothered in green peppers, black olives, mushrooms, and tomatoes, is also just fabulous. The prices quoted here are for the 12" medium size; the 15" larges are a few dollars more. If it's just you eating, try the 7" small size, starting at only $3.40. Open daily until 1 A.M., an hour later on weekends.

Bangkok Cafe

- 4730 University Way NE, Seattle; 523-3220

The Bangkok Cafe, sibling of the vegetarian Araya Place (above), serves the full range of Thai dishes containing meat, although there is quite an extensive selection of vegetarian choices here as well. This distinction is good to know if your party is a mixed bag of carnivores and non-carns.

The menu includes beef, pork, poultry and seafood dishes, ranging in price between $5.95 to $9.95. Such tempting treats as chicken sauteed with baby corn, onion and mushrooms ($6.15) and prawns sauteed with basil, hot pepper, onion and curry paste, topped with peanuts ($8.50) will make your mouth water. Possibly your eyes, too. The Bangkok Cafe is open from noon to 10 P.M.

Mondays through Saturdays, and from 5 P.M. to 10 P.M. Sundays.

Big Time Brewery and Alehouse

- 4133 University Way NE; Seattle; 545-4509
- *Tip-free*

Before you sit down, you have to walk half-way through Big Time just to find the counter where you place your order. To enjoy some sunshine (*if* the sun happens to bless your visit), sit under the large skylight and enjoy the natural lighting. To enjoy good food at decent prices, order one of the sandwiches, which all come with tortilla chips, pepperoncini, and a fruit garnish—not bad for a college hangout.

Mr. C recommends the "Seattle Sub" ($4.10), made with ham, salami, Swiss and cheddar cheeses, tomato, and onion, all on a baguette roll. The "Swamp" ($4.25) is more appealing than it sounds, filled with turkey, provolone, and a zesty three-pepper relish. Most sandwiches are available in half portions too, and you can get a half with a cup of chili for just $4.95.

As this is a bar, no minors are allowed on the premises. Big Time is open from 11:30 A.M. through to 12:30 A.M. on weekdays, and 'til 1:30 A.M. Fridays and Saturdays. The kitchen closes at 11 P.M. during the week, and midnight on the weekends.

Black Cat Cafe

- 4110 Roosevelt Way NE, Seattle; 547-3887
- *Tip-free*

You won't have bad luck running into this Black Cat. Just about everything is under $5, and all of it is vegetarian. The atmosphere is colorful, busy, and laced with a touch of mischief. Christmas lights and a multi-colored fence greet you outside, while plastic floral tablecloths and potted plants make the interior festive. Operated by a health-conscious commune, the bustling kitchen maintains a folksy spirit.

The food here is homemade, filling, and dee-licious. There tends to be a Mexican slant to a lot of the menu offerings, like breakfast chilaquilas ($4.50), and garbonzo burritos ($3.50). Wonderfully hearty soups, too, good enough to warm up the bleakest winter's day. The desserts are tasty, and a meal in themselves; Mr. C had a "Monster Brownie" ($1.50) that certainly lived up to its name—it was huge! The Black Cat Cafe is open Tuesdays through Saturdays, from 10:30 A.M. to 8:30 P.M.; it's closed Sundays and Mondays.

Boat St. Cafe
• 909 NE Boat St., Seattle; 632-4602

What's that? Never heard of Boat Street? Well, it is a bit off the beaten path, but not so out of the way as all that. In fact, it's right under the University Bridge. Pull into a narrow parking lot, go all the way to the end of a cluster of marine shops, and there you'll find this charming little cafe. Its two-room interior is small, but light and airy; during the summer months, they add a table and a few Adirondack chairs outside the front door. Overall, the atmosphere is relaxed and in a way romantic, the serenity only occasionally broken by the horn from a passing vessel.

All of the food here is made on the premises by a young and engaging staff. As the menu points out, they make a point of using top-notch ingredients, with no frying whatsoever. It's a simple menu, just a handful of light foods and desserts. Things like chicken, apricot and ginger salad ($7.50), baked fresh oysters ($9.25), and smoked fish salad ($8.95). Their wonderful pasta salad, $6.50, is tossed with herbs, tomatoes, and roasted walnuts, in a garlic vinaigrette, served over spinach. *Tres chic.*

These folks must figure that such healthy platters allow a bit of cheating afterwards, since their fresh-baked desserts lean toward the rich and sinful. French apple shortbread, $3.25, is one of several choices served with heavy cream. There's always a good variety of creations on hand.

Weekends feature a special brunch menu, consisting of such unusual choices as "Barcelona Frittatas" ($4.75), with ingredients like smoked turkey sausage, potatoes, and onions baked up into a sort of quiche. French baked eggs in lemon herb cream is another winner, if not exactly a friend to the arteries. It's served with potatoes, fruit and a baguette for $5.75. Plus soups, salads, sandwiches, homemade granola, and more sweets—like banana nut bread with orange cream cheese ($1.95).

Given the location and the rarefied cooking, the Boat St. Cafe keeps limited hours, which vary through the year. Off-season hours are from 7:30 A.M. to 3 P.M. on weekdays ('til 5 on Fridays), and 8 A.M. to 5 P.M. on weekends. During the summer, they add dinner on Friday, Saturday, and Sunday evenings, serving until 9:30 P.M.

Chin Viet Thai Restaurant
• 4518 University Way NE, Seattle; 633-4800
• *Tip-free*

Chin Viet Thai is a sparse but busy cafeteria-style restaurant that serves inexpensive Asian dishes. As the name implies, these cuisines are all mix-and-match here. Egg rolls and barbecue pork sticks are 90¢ apiece, and *hombows*—a Vietnamese steamed pork-filled bun—are 80¢ each. For something more filling, try one of the combination plates, like almond chicken with vegetable chow mein and rice, all for $3.50. Even if you're not ordering a combo, most dishes, like beef satay and black bean ginger chicken, are served with rice. The wonton or beef noodle soup ($3.35 per bowl) are excellent choices for a lighter meal. Chin Viet Thai is open Mondays through Saturdays, from 10 A.M. to 9 P.M.

Costa's
• 4559 University Way NE, Seattle; 633-2751

This comfortable Greek and American restaurant offers classics from those two distinctly different, yet so often paired, cuisines. A basic hamburger and fries goes for four bucks. But c'mon, you can get a burger anyplace. For something a little different, try fettucine alla Greco—pasta with cream, butter, and feta cheese ($7). Most lunch and dinner prices come in around the same low numbers; but when the price does go up from afternoon to evening—as with the tasty *spanakotiropeta*, spinach and feta cheese in phyllo pastry, which rises from $4.50 at lunch to $8.50 at dinner—it's because you're truly getting twice as much. Good deal!

Costa's is open from 7:30 A.M. until 10:30 P.M. weekdays, and until 11:30 P.M. on weekends.

Flowers Cafe
- 4247 University Way NE, Seattle; 633-1903

Flowers Cafe is mainly geared toward the vegetarian or health-conscious palate, although you will find some red meat on the menu. The $5.50 all-you-can-eat lunch buffet certainly caught Mr. C's eye. Tabouli, pasta and vegetable salads were among the items to choose from. Or, order something from the grill. Burgers ($4.95) are available in both the falafel and beef variety, and come with salad and home fries. There's also a full bar. Flowers Cafe is open seven days for lunch only, from 11 A.M. to 4 P.M.

The Garden of Eat'n
- 5000 University Way NE, Seattle; 528-5357

At this lovely corner cafe in the U-District, complete with aquarium and lush plant life, omnivores and vegetarians alike may dine together in perfect harmony. The menu features home cooking that is strong in both areas, with lots of sandwiches, pastas, and full entrees to choose from.

A shrimp salad sandwich ($4.85) is great for those who want to indulge a craving for seafood, while a veggie pita pizza topped with feta cheese and olives ($4.75) is perfect for someone avoiding meat. Meanwhile, a good ol' hamburger goes for a *svelte* $3.95. A cup of soup or a trip to the salad bar accompanies each entree, while waffle fries, cole slaw, macaroni or potato salad accompanies each sandwich and burger—even the "designer sandwiches" you can customize yourself.

Breakfast is available too, with such favorites as buttermilk hotcakes ($2.95) and design-your-own omelettes ($5.65). Enjoy eat'n at this Garden from 9 A.M. to 9 P.M. on weekdays; on Saturdays and Sundays, they open an hour later.

Grand Illusion Cafe
- 1405 NE 50th St., Seattle; 525-9573
- *Tip-free*

Part of the art-house cinema of the same name (see the listing under "Entertainment—Movies"), this comfortable eatery offers good food in addition to coffees and pastries. Lounge on a sofa in front of a fireplace, read the day's papers, and nibble on a slab of olive asparagus quiche, $3.75. With fresh fruit, in season, it's only $4. Other choices may include things like vegetarian burritos ($3.50), lemon tahini salad ($2.75), or a bowl of gazpacho and fresh bread ($2). And if coffee is not your beverage (can that be?), you can order your own pot of tea instead.

The Grand Illusion Cafe is the perfect complement to the films shown here—for a quick bite beforehand, something to fuel the discussion afterward, or even if you're not going to a film at all. Open daily from 8:30 A.M. through 10:30 or 11 P.M.

Kidd Valley
- 135 15th Ave. NE, Seattle; 328-8133
- 5502 25th Ave. NE, Seattle; 522-0890
- 531 Queen Anne Ave. N, Seattle; 284-0184
- 4910 Green Lake Way N, Seattle; 547-0121
- 14303 Aurora Ave. N, Seattle; 364-8493
- *And other suburban locations*
- *Tip-free*

Kidd Valley is Seattle's own answer to McDonald's, though most locals would argue that Kidd Valley is better. And they're right. There's more of a selection, and your order is prepared while you wait. The classic hamburger is $2.29; the cheeseburger is $2.44. These burgers are juicy and delicious; 'nuff said.

For those who may be suffering from burger burn-out, there are also quite a few sandwiches to choose from, like a BLT ($2.49), broiled chicken ($3.54), and grilled ham and cheese ($2.99). The homemade onion rings ($1.19) and specialty shakes ($1.49) should not be missed, though only the strong of stomach will want to have both in the same sitting.

Kidd's atmosphere is strictly early-American fast-food joint—kinda sparse, a few prominent colors, and lots of booths. Open seven days a week.

Kyoto Teriyaki

- 1016 NE 65th St., Seattle; 525-9090

This northern U-District eatery isn't much to look at from the outside, but inside it's clean, well-kept and brightly decorated. Actually, it looks pretty much like any old diner or luncheonette, with a counter and a few small tables (a lot of their business is take-out); but you won't find them slinging any corned beef hash here.

Kyoto offers lots of food for little money. The specialty, of course, is—guess what—teriyaki. You can get a half-chicken, marinated in teriyaki sauce, then broiled and served with rice and vegetables for $3.50. What a bargain! That's not a typo, gang. Same price for chicken curry and pork teriyaki.

In fact, the most expensive item on the menu is a combination of pork, beef, and chicken teriyaki with rice and veggies for $6.50. Chow mein and noodles are also popular selections. Chow down at Kyoto Mondays through Saturdays from 10:30 A.M. to 9 P.M.

The Last Exit

- 5201 University Way NE, Seattle; no phone
- *Tip-free*

Recently moved up from its former digs on Brooklyn Avenue, the Last Exit is loads more fun than *No Exit* and *Final Exit* (remember that cheery ditty?) combined. In fact, not only will you not want to exit, this "oldest coffeehouse in Seattle" encourages you to

---

MR. CHEAP'S PICKS
University District

✔ **Black Cat Cafe**—Nothing but good luck here—as in cheap, tasty vegetarian dishes. Short on atmosphere.

✔ **The Garden of Eat'n**—Just as cute as its name, with tomatoes growing in the window and a colorful aquarium.

✔ **Grand Illusion Cafe**—Popular hangout for cappuccino and light foods, with classic art cinema attached.

✔ **Nasai Teriyaki**—Literally a hole-in-the-wall spot on The Ave., yet somehow the plates bulge with good Asian fare.

---

stay. Relax, hang out, and unwind.

They are even considerate enough to separate smokers and non-smokers into two wildly decorated rooms—play chess or read the paper in whichever one tickles your fancy (or lungs). Food runs to the standard pub fare, with a few twists: Try the tuna melt on a muffin ($4.10) or the vegetarian chili ($2.50). Needless to say, the Seattle beverage of choice is readily at hand, as are sodas, juices, and teas. The Last Exit is open daily.

La Vaca

- 4129 University Way NE, Seattle; 632-4909
- 613 Third Ave., Seattle; 622-0154
- 7910 Green Lake Dr. N, Seattle; 517-2949
- *Tip-free*

That's "The Cow," for those of us not fluent in Spanish. Don't take it personally—go ahead and um, pig out. This busy little take-out joint serves

Mexican food in *gigante* portions at low prices. Burritos are $3.25; choose from vegetarian, beef, chicken, or beans and cheese. Large enchiladas and tacos are $1.25, tostadas $2.50. Ordering by number speeds up the process—this is a good pit stop for a cheap, quick, and filling lunch. Stop by between 11 A.M. and 5 P.M., during the week; La Vaca on Third Avenue is closed on the weekends, and the University location is closed Saturdays. The Green Lake restaurant is open seven days.

Nasai Teriyaki
- 4305 University Way NE, Seattle; 632-3572

In their small storefront window, Nasai Teriyaki has posted a newspaper review which raves about the food and calls it the "best teriyaki in town," a large claim that's easily matched by the large, large plates of food everybody was eagerly wolfing down during Mr. C's visit.

This U-District restaurant is rather unusual looking; it actually appears to be nothing more than a hallway, a long and very narrow room leading from the door all the way to the back, where you turn sharply to the right into a (slightly) larger room. There aren't many tables; they do a brisk take-out business.

As the name implies, the entrees are pretty simple. Teriyaki. Whether you like chicken ($4.25), beef ($5.25), pork, or prawns (each $4.95), you'll get a heaping plateful, plus rice and salad. If you can't pick just one, there are various combinations for $5.45. Side orders are all way cheap, like a half-dozen gyoza dumplings for $2.45. Another bonus: everything is MSG-free. Nasai Teriyaki is open Mondays through Saturdays from 11 A.M. to 9:30 P.M., Sundays from noon to 9 P.M.

Pizzeria Pagliacci
- 4529 University Way NE, Seattle; 632-0421
- 550 Queen Anne Ave. N, Seattle; 285-1232
- 4003 Stone Way N, Seattle; 632-1058

- 426 Broadway E, Seattle; 324-0730
- 2400 Tenth Ave. E, Seattle; 632-1058
- *Tip-free*

Pizza is not the only supper you'll sing for on this menu. Calzone, soup, and pastas—both hot dishes and unique salads—are also served fresh daily. The atmosphere is casual, but nicer than your average pizzeria; fresh flowers in recycled juice bottles adorn every table, while artsy black and white photos and sketches decorate the walls. The most exciting thing you'll see is the occasional Frisbee of dough being flung up in the air by the chef behind the counter. All pizza dough is made fresh daily and tossed in this manner—"no rolling pins or sheeters to take the life out of the dough," as the menu boasts. This attention to quality definitely results in a superior pie.

Ordering takes place after you've viewed everything in the glass display cases. Mr. C particularly enjoyed a delicious $3.95 pesto and artichoke pasta salad; the basics, such as the "extra-pepperoni" pizza, are always on hand, either by the slice or the whole pie. Pizzeria Pagliacci is open from 11 A.M. to 11 P.M. Sundays through Thursdays, and 'til 1 A.M. Fridays and Saturdays.

Poco Loco
- 4518 University Way NE, Seattle; 548-9877
- *Tip-free*

Poco Loco has the same owners as Nueva Cocina and Burrito Express (see separate listings), so you can expect similar things from this location. However, the completely unbiased Poco Loco staff thinks they're the best of the trio, and that you'll get the best deals here. All burritos are $3.75, whether you want shredded beef, chicken, or vegetable fillings. Tostadas and crispy tacos are all $3, while soft tacos are $3.50.

In fact, these prices are the same as those of their brethren. Superior quality, or superiority complex? Put 'em to the test! If you want to sit down, there are a couple of counters with stools—otherwise, this is better as a take-out place. Open from 11 A.M. to 5 P.M. daily.

Ricardo's Juice Bar and Espresso Cafe

- 4217 University Way NE, Seattle; 633-1327
- *Tip-free*

In the front section of the Pilgrim's Nutrition store (see the listing under "Shopping—Food Shops"), you'll find a few tables and a little bit of counter space, better known as Ricardo's. Here, you can tend to your physical or emotional well-being, whichever is more in need of pampering. If your bod seeks a boost, try one of their veggie juices, and "smart drinks," like the "Quadruple C" with carrot, cucumber, cabbage, and celery for $2.50. If it's your spirit that needs a lift, how about "Death by Chocolate" ($2.75), made with blended espresso, milk, two types of chocolate, banana, and whipped cream. What a way to go. Juices and smoothies are priced from $2 to $3.75, depending on size and ingredients.

Don't worry, Ricardo's has solid food too—all very healthy and very cheap. Their "burgers" (none have red meat) go for $4.95, including a lemon-broiled tempeh burger and a grilled salmon and wild rice burger. Wow! These are served with fresh homemade potato or pasta salad. All other sandwiches are under $4; try the "Very Veggie" ($3.50), made with nine different vegetables, on your choice of honey wheat, sunflower wheat, onion dill rye, or wheat-free spelt bread. Naturally (no pun intended), they also have a selection of salads and soups.

Ricardo's also serves breakfast all day: breakfast burritos, scrambles with a variety of ingredients, and the like, all under $4.50. No doubt about it, this is a great place to hang out with a cup of herb tea, perhaps some vegan cookies, and recharge the old batteries. Even the "full spectrum" lighting does you good. Open Mondays through Fridays from 7:30 A.M. to 7 P.M., Saturdays from 9 A.M. to 7 P.M., and Sundays from 9 to 6.

Shultzy's Sausage

- 4142 University Way NE, Seattle; 548-9461
- *Tip-free*

Not many cafes would call themselves "the best of the wurst," but Shultzy's handily earns that title. As in knockwurst, bratwurst, and the rest, that is. That's what has made Shultzy's a UW landmark, and that's all this zany hole-in-the-wall serves up. No chemical preservatives are used, no MSG, and no fillers. As for fat content, they claim that a quarter-pound sausage has less fat than most McChain offerings. The turkey sausage has even less. So much for the nutrition lesson. Let's face it—you don't come here to be on a diet.

The items on the menu are rated from mild to HOT! (their emphasis). Tender tastebuds would probably enjoy the "Shultzy" ($3.25), a mild Italian pork sausage patty on a grilled roll with fresh garlic and olive oil. For a little kick, the "Ragin' Cajun" ($3) will wake up your mouth; it's a spicy Cajun smoked sausage, laced with garlic, on a fresh French roll. Kind of a po' boy that'll make you say "whoa boy."

The daily special allows you to pick any sausage, add a cup of chili or pork and beans, and a large soda, all for five bucks. That chili, with its own spicy sausage m ixed in, is just $2.50 a bowl, by the way. There are a few other (non-sausage) sandwiches, too.

There's not much seating at Shultzy's—you may be better off calling ahead for a take-out order. Or grab one to keep you company on a stroll down "the Ave." Shultzy's is open from 11 A.M. to 9 P.M. daily, 'til 7 P.M. on Sundays.

Silence-Heart-Nest Vegetarian Restaurant

- 5247 University Way NE, Seattle; 524-4008

Silence-Heart-Nest creates original, scrumptious, vegetarian and vegan dishes with an East Indian flavor. Try the "Calananda" ($7.25), a sort of Asian calzone; it's a crispy, deep-fried pastry loaded with spinach, mushrooms, tomato, mozzarella and ricotta, flavored with Indian spices, and served with garlic-cilantro tomato sauce. Mmmm. The "Masala Dosai" ($7.50) is also zingy and unique—an Indian sourdough crêpe, made from rice and lentils, filled with curried potatoes and served with coconut chutney.

There are actually seven different kinds of chutney to choose from at S-H-N; apricot, spicy tomato, and tamarind raisin are just a few. Most unusual. There are also sandwiches, mostly around $4.75; and a cup of homemade soup is $1.50. Mr. C especially enjoyed the *dal*, a traditional Indian soup, made with lentils, carrots, onions, tomatoes, and lots of spices.

One final note: Silence-Heart-Nest closes for two weeks, twice a year—in April, and August. During those months, call to check the schedule. Otherwise, stop by the nest any day but Sunday and eat to your heart's content—truly. Open for lunch and dinner daily.

Sunlight Cafe
- 6403 Roosevelt Way NE, Seattle; 522-9060

This cozy eatery does bring in a fair amount of sun, when it's available; but regulars probably rate its degree of *en*lightenment more noteworthy. That's because the place has an all-vegetarian menu, and goes beyond

that to include many vegan items. Mr. C had never even heard of vegan cinnamon rolls, but you can get 'em here—or non-vegan, your choice.

Lunch, served daily from 11 A.M. to 3 P.M., features morning-type dishes, like "Eggless Sesame Crunch Waffles" ($3), indistinguishable from the traditional kind. Throw some blueberries on top for 70¢ more. "Huevos Picantes" ($4.25) however, do give you an egg option. And you can skip the whole issue with something like a bowl of Thai garlic soup for $2.25. In fact, for just $4.95, you can get soup, salad, and bread, all freshly made on the premises. Good deal, no matter what your diet.

Dinner takes over from 4 to 9 P.M.; Mr. C was delighted with sauteed vegetables in a Thai peanut sauce, served over brown rice for $7.75. That includes, as do all dinner entrees, soup and a salad. Again, other choices will keep everyone happy: "Nutburgers" ($6.75), vegetarian lasagne ($7.75), spinach salad ($4.35) with sprouts, vegetables, and almonds.

Desserts offer lots of homemade pastries and the same all-encompassing choices. Have a slice of cappuccino cheesecake, or one made with tofu as a substitute. These, as well as a few lunch items if still available, are also served during the in-between hour before dinner.

WEST SEATTLE

Alki Cafe
- 2726 Alki Ave. SW, Seattle; 935-0616

Along the Alki beachfront, there tend to be two choices when it comes to food: cheap but unappetizing fast-food, or good-but-pricey sit-down meals. The Alki Cafe may not be the cheapest restaurant you'll find in this book, but given the aforementioned

choices, it's Mr. C's pick in this popular locale. The offerings here are more reasonable than similar places in the area, and certainly delicious. As an added bonus, the atmosphere here is elegant, yet relaxed—with folk music playing in the background, blond wood tables, and fresh carnations on each one.

For dollar value, the best bets are

found at breakfast and lunch; so if you're here for a day in the sun, that works out just fine anyhow. Two eggs with bacon, ham, or sausage, fried red potatoes, and a muffin or toast go for $4.25. Sourdough French toast is just $3.95 and there are plenty of other morning sweets, which of course come from the yummy Alki Bakery next door (more on that in a moment).

At lunch, Cheapsters can stick with sandwiches or burgers. Good choices here include fresh roasted turkey and Swiss ($5.75), and smoked salmon with avocado and caper mayonnaise ($6.95), along with a nice selection of soups and salads.

Dinner gets more expensive, but you'll still find entrees at or below $10. Try *yaki soba*, quick-fried beef with vegetables in ginger glaze over noodles ($8.95). Even oysters *muniere* (fried and topped with lemon, butter, and white wine sauce) is moderately priced at $9.95. All of these are served with a house salad and fresh-baked breads. Pastas are a good deal, too; try penne marinara ($8.50) or linguini primavera ($8.95), each served with salad. The menu includes a serious selection of beers and wines.

Now, about desserts. As mentioned above, all kinds of delectable pastries here come from the sibling across the street, appropriately named the Alki Bakery (2738 Alki Avenue SW, Seattle; 935-1352). If you're not in need of a full meal, this is a fine place to sit over a slice of caramel dome cake ($2.95) or chocolate peanut butter mousse torte ($3.25), sip an espresso, and read the P-I. Or, just stop in for breads, cakes, pies, cookies, muffins, pastry, and more. If you're lucky, they may even have some day-old bargains for you. Alki Bakery is also the sometimes home to "Lively, Local, and Free," a community arts series. See the listing for ArtsWest under "Entertainment—Arts and Cultural Centers" for more information.

Bangkok Shack
- 1333 Harbor Ave. SW, Seattle; 937-9771
- *Tip-free*

Okay, you're out for a day around Alki, and all you want is a quick bite to eat. Check out "The Shack," one of the only roadside take-out joints serving Thai food that Mr. C has ever found. A mere $3.95 gets you a plate of red curry chicken, and the prices range up to only $5.95 for things like Thai barbecued beef. There are plenty of concessions (pardon the pun) to American take-out as well, from half-pound burgers to fish and chips—and, of course, the ubiquitous espresso.

Enjoy your meal at a picnic table under a canopy; or, if it's a fine summer day, make your way across the street to Seacrest Park for some spectacular views of Puget Sound and the Seattle skyline. Who needs those expensive waterfront restaurants along the same stretch?

If you prefer this food inside, the same folks operate a full restaurant, Thai on Alki, next door at 1325 Harbor Avenue SW (telephone 938-2992); and they have another take-out location downtown, Bangkok Hut, at 2126 Third Avenue (441-4425).

Capers Espresso Cafe
- 4521 California Ave. SW, Seattle; 932-0371

This spacious, airy cafe doubles as a store displaying all manner of coffee and cooking paraphernalia. While precious few of these items are inexpensive, the food is surprisingly affordable for such a yupscale eatery.

It's all homemade, starting with the hot-from-the-oven scones, muffins, and assorted pastries. Espressos to sip with these start at a mere 75 cents. But why stop there? Capers is a find for lunch, brunch, or an early dinner. Mr. C loved a hearty bowl of carrot-tomato-rosemary soup for $3; they may have roasted garlic and potato soup or some other variety when you stop in. A smoked turkey sandwich, with pesto, sprouts, and cranberry sauce is $4.25, though you may be satisfied with a half-size handful for $2.35.

For a more substantial meal, try black pepper chicken and vegetables, served over a green salad, for $5.60; sweet-glazed meatloaf with red potato salad, $5.50; or angel-hair pasta marinara with fresh sourdough-rosemary bread and a green salad, $5.90. The limited but adventurous menu changes every week, and it's served with a smile in this attractive, refined atmosphere. When the weather allows, there are more tables on a patio out back (no view, but...).

Capers serves from 6:30 A.M. to 8:00 P.M. on weekdays; until 6 P.M. on Saturdays, and 5 P.M. on Sundays.

Guadalajara Hacienda
- 5923 California Ave. SW, Seattle; 932-2803
- 1531 Queen Anne Ave. N, Seattle; 283-0788

Guadalajara Hacienda strives to create the illusion that you're eating in a grand old Mexican plantation house; music, natural light, and murals all help to complete this effect. Of course, what good are the murals, if the cooking reminds you more of Air Mexico? Not to worry—the food is as splendid as the decor, and you won't have to spend too many pesos either.

Fajitas are the house specialty—each platter comes with rice, beans, sour cream, guacamole, and tortillas. Mr. C recommends the prawn fajitas ($9.75) with sauteed peppers, onions, zucchini, tomatoes, and mushrooms. A variety of deluxe enchiladas (you get two of them) are topped with cheese and served with rice and beans. All but one are $6.95; the chile verde enchilada, spicy and filled with pork, is $7.45.

Lunch specials, as always, are the best buys; all entrees are $4.75, with refried beans and rice. You can choose a pair of beef enchiladas, or the chile-colorado burrito (flank steak in a mild sauce, with rice, beans, and sour cream), or any of the other thirteen lunch selections. Also good to know, Guadalajara Hacienda will gladly make vegetarian versions of any dish upon request. The restaurant is open from 11:30 A.M. daily until 9:30 P.M. during the week; 'til 11 P.M. Fridays, 10 P.M. Saturdays, and 9 P.M. Sundays.

Iron Kettle Cafe
- 4533 California Ave. SW, Seattle; 938-2722

Stop into this place on California, in Seattle, and you'll feel like you've wound up in New England. It's cozy, country kitchen sort of a place. The kind of place where the waitresses wear period-style aprons and bonnets, the tables have checkered tablecloths, and the walls are decorated with hammered iron kitchen implements. It's the sort of place where they serve up large portions of good, simple food.

Dinners are modest, straightforward American meals like pot roast ($7.95) and "Mom's Meat Loaf" ($6.95). These include your choice of salad or a cup of soup, plus potatoes and biscuits. The Kettle also makes up big burgers—1/3-pound of hand-formed ground beef. Try a "Plain Jane" for $4.50, or the "Iron Works," topped with bacon, cheddar cheese, grilled onions, and mushrooms for $6.25. If chicken is more to your liking, try "The Hula": a breast of chicken covered with mozzarella cheese, pineapple, and teriyaki mayonnaise, also $6.25. And here's an unusual burger bonus: each is served with your choice of French fries, homemade soup, or a green salad.

On weekends, the Iron Kettle is a great place for that all-important meal, breakfast! You can get two eggs with bacon, sausage, or ham for $4.50, served with hash browns and toast, an English muffin, or a homemade biscuit. Three-egg omelettes and scrambles are filled with a variety of yummy ingredients. For a special treat, try a bacon waffle ($2.25) or "Three Pigs in a Blanket" ($3.50).

The Kettle serves lunch Tuesdays through Fridays from 11 A.M. to 2:30 P.M. and dinner from 4 to 9 P.M.; Saturdays add breakfast from 7 A.M. to noon; on Sundays, only breakfast is served, available from 7 A.M. to 2 P.M.

Jalisco Mexican Restaurant

- 8517 14th Ave. S, Seattle; 767-1943
- 1467 E Republican St., Seattle; 325-9005
- 122 and 129 First Ave. N, Seattle; 283-4242
- 12336 31st Ave. NE, Seattle; 364-3978
- 115 Park Lane, Kirkland; 822-3355

A shop owner of Mexican extraction told Mr. C to be sure to include Jalisco, for truly authentic regional food. Named for one of that country's more scenic states, this restaurant upholds that tradition of beauty—at least one branch sports a wall mural depicting a village center, complete with guitarist serenading a dancing couple by a fountain. Piñatas and plants are perched high above, and high-backed booths provide a secluded dining experience.

Try one of the huge "Especiáles de la Casa," like the chimichangas or enchiladas rancheras, for $7.55 each. All of these specialties are served with rice and beans, making for a gigantic plateful. For the lighter appetite, a single tamale ($2.65) or taco salad ($4.50) will do you right.

Be sure to try something with Jalisco's homemade *mole* sauce; usually made from unsweetened chocolate (yes, for dinner), these folks make it as a nifty peanut sauce instead. If you're not entirely familiar with such native culinary terms, there's a helpful glossary on the back of the menu.

The First Avenue location, just outside Seattle Center, has recently spawned a quicker-fare "taqueria" right across the street; the Lake City location adds a cocktail lounge. All branches are open daily from 11 A.M. to 10 P.M., and to 11 P.M. on Fridays and Saturdays.

Maharaja

- 4542 California Ave. SW, Seattle; 935-9443
- 26108 Pacific Hwy. S, Kent; 946-0664

MR. CHEAP'S PICKS
West Seattle

✔ **Alki Bakery and Cafe**—Cool coffeehouse and more formal restaurant, across the street from each other, for your day at the beach.

✔ **Capers Espresso Cafe**— Surprisingly affordable, wonderfully creative cuisine, considering its yuppified airs.

- 500 Elliott Ave. W, Seattle; 286-1772

Folks who know of Maharaja swear by it for huge portions of spicy Indian food, especially the daily lunch specials, which will easily carry you all the way through the day for just $4.95. These specials include lamb curry and chicken tandoori, with a pile of side dishes that will make your plate runneth over. A daily buffet, also $4.95, rounds out the fantastic lunchtime deals.

Dinner entrees are also very reasonable; most are $5.95 to $8.95, while vegetarian dishes come in under $5. Try *keema aloo*, minced lamb cooked with herbs, spices, and potatoes ($6.50); "Dancing Chicken," cooked with lentil sauce ($6.95); or beef *sagg*, pieces of meat marinated in spices and cooked with spinach and ginger ($6.95). Light eaters can stick with mixed vegetables and rice for $4.95, or choose from the selection of appetizers, soups, and salads. Of course, if you came here to eat light you're probably in the wrong place! Maharaja is open every day from 11 A.M. to 2:30 P.M. for lunch, and from 4 to 10 P.M. for dinner.

OUTER SUBURBS

Fresh Choice

- Sea Tac Mall, Federal Way; 941-3860
- 1733 Northup Way, Bellevue; 822-2548
- Northgate Mall, Seattle; 440-8136
- *Tip-free*

One of the cleanest, brightest and spiffiest of the shopping center buffet restaurants, these are (as of this writing) the only Northwest outposts of this California chain. But, before you give it the la-la-land snub, give it a try. You'll find food that is both fast and healthy—an overwhelming choice of salads, soups, pastas, and fixings. It's the G.C. (Gastronomically Correct) answer to the King's Table chain.

Everything here is "made from scratch" using all natural ingredients; many items are available in low-fat or non-fat versions, with color-coded name tags (everything here is clearly labeled, with ingredients listed out). And one price, $7.25, covers all the food you want—including seconds. Children pay half of that, and kids under five eat free.

Grab a tray! The first display is the lengthy salad bar, which includes prepared salads such as Caesar and Chinese almond. Or, make up your own creation from literally dozens of fresh vegetables, dressings, and toppings. This could be enough for some appetites, but oh, there's more! Move on to the baked potato bar for a spud heated up with your choice of stuffings; the pasta bar, where you can slather sun-dried tomato cream sauce on linguine or cheese tortellini; the soup bar, with different homemade selections daily, like Southwestern corn chowder and Cajun black bean; and the bread/muffin table, which even has crispy slices of cheese pizza (we need this too?). Oh yeah, and you can help yourself to desserts, from fruits to "Chocolate Decadence" brownies.

Needless to say, it's not hard to get your money's worth; it's just hard to finish it all. Empty tables with lots of food left behind show folks' tendency to order with dazzled eyes. How can the place stay in business with so much waste? Well, they do get you with the drinks, which cost extra—how 'bout $1.75 for a bottle of apple juice—but, if you're a hearty eater, things should still work out in your favor. Those drinks include bottled wines, wine coolers, and beers, by the way.

The atmosphere is as refined as you'll see at any shopping mall. The large dining room is carpeted. White walls are decorated with framed art prints. Classical music plays in the background. A busy staff keeps the place spotless, bussing tables promptly (if you get up for seconds, there's a "Be Right Back" card). In all, this could be the healthiest pigout you'll ever have. Open daily, with mall hours.

The Harbour Public House

- 231 Parfitt Way, Bainbridge Island; 842-0969

This quaint old house—built in 1881—is now the home of a fun and cozy pub. Inside, high ceilings expose wooden beams, lovingly restored for that country feel. Outside, as weather permits, a rear deck offers romantic views of Eagle Harbor with sailboat masts waving like reeds in the wind.

The simple menu features standard pub fare, nicely done up. Batter-dipped fish and chips come in hefty portions at $5.95; meaty cheeseburgers ($5.50) are also a handful, slathered with grilled onions and thick-cut fries. "Hearty Beef Chili" ($3.50) is just that, topped with cheese and onions. There are several sandwiches and salads; and the "Ploughperson's Lunch" tops out the menu, in politically correct fashion, at $7.95.

Needless to say, there is a full bar, and an impressive selection of wines and microbrewed beers. Here, Mr. C even sampled a Widmer beer made with strawberries for a unique flavor (yes, it works). Adding to the warm and convivial atmosphere is live folk music: Tuesday is open-mike night from 8 to midnight, while Sundays feature established performers from 8 to 10 P.M. There is no cover charge. The Harbour is open daily from 11 A.M. to 12 midnight.

Izzy's Pizza
- 10117 Evergreen Way, Everett; 355-3207
- 20500 108th Ave. SE, Kent; 859-0950
- 12301 120th Ave. NE, Kirkland; 820-9279

Buffet restaurants have become big business in the suburbs around Seattle. This chain, spreading throughout Washington and Oregon, offers a new twist: pizza meets salad bar. There is a brief menu, from which you can choose your pie (starting as low as $2.95 for an individual pan pizza); the menu also includes a couple of sandwiches, soups, and pastas. Then, there's a salad bar, brimming with greens, vegetables, fruits, dressings, prepared salads, soups, and even desserts. Finally, there is also a hot buffet of pizza slices, fried and barbecued chicken, side dishes like baked beans and roasted potatoes, and Izzy's very popular warm cinnamon buns.

Confusing? Mr. C thought so, too. But wait—here come the dining options and combinations! Now. . . . You can have a pizza. You can have the salad bar, once through or in unlimited trips. You can have one pass through the salad bar and all the pizza you can eat. You can have just the chicken and potatoes. Or, for the total pig-out, you can have the hot buffet, which includes pizza and chicken, plus unlimited trips to the salad bar. And this doesn't even get to the different *kinds* of pizza, like Five-Cheese, West-

ern BBQ Chicken, and Hawaiian Supreme, each in three sizes.

Talk about one-restaurant-fits-all. Well, it seems daunting, but apparently it works, especially with the family crowd. The prices sure help: The hot buffet/salad bar deal, which offers the most diversity, costs $5.95 per person at lunch and $6.95 at dinner. In fact, no buffet option here costs more than that—just add the drinks (sodas and beers are both available by the glass or pitcher). Made-to-order pizzas, of course, go higher; most range from about $6 to $16, depending on the toppings and size. For chain restaurant pizza, they're not bad.

Whichever way you go, you can feed an army—or anybody who eats like one—without increasing the defense budget. Open daily for lunch and dinner.

King's Table
- 4111 Wheaton Way, Bremerton; (360) 377-7044
- 137 SW 160th St., Burien; 244-1883
- 3802 Broadway, Everett; 252-6555
- 12120 NE 85th St., Kirkland; 828-3811
- 1545 NW Market St., Seattle; 784-8955
- *Tip-free*

Perhaps the lowest in overall quality of the Seattle area's many buffet restaurants, King's Table nevertheless offers a ton of food for the money. Dinners cost $6.99 per person (lunches about a dollar less), payable at the beginning of what is basically a cafeteria line. KT also offers a "Gold Card" for $1, allowing you to then save 50¢ on every visit; and Thursday is "Family Night," when kids under 12 pay just 39¢ for every year of their age.

The food is adequate, centering on such entrees as fried chicken, fish and chips, and hand-carved roast beef; along with these are a salad bar, side dishes, taco shells and fillings, and basic desserts, including a do-it-yourself soft ice cream machine. They also serve a breakfast buffet,

313

priced at $4.99. King's Table certainly fits the bill for families and for seniors, who can have a fixed-income night on the town. Open daily.

Macheezmo Mouse Mexican Cafe

- 3805 196th Ave. SW, Lynnwood; 744-1611
- 211 Broadway E, Seattle; 325-0072
- 701 Fifth Ave., Seattle; 382-1730
- 1815 N 45th St., Seattle; 545-0153
- 425 Queen Anne Ave. N, Seattle; 282-9904
- 2028 148th Ave. NE, Bellevue; 746-5824
- *And other suburban locations*
- *Tip-free*

The '90s mean that even Mexican fast food has gone health-conscious. In fact, Macheezmo Mouse is so serious about it that they print up pamphlets on weight management, diabetic exchanges, heart health—and how their food fits in. Every item on the menu is accompanied by nutritional information: The chicken burrito, for example, has 580 calories, 17% from fat—while the veggie power salad has 200 calories, 1% from fat. Make your informed decision.

Mr. C was a bit put off by a display of sample platters at the Queen Anne location. It's nice to see the choices before you order, but this food sits out all day, and looks a bit um, *faded* after a few hours. Is this the best way to tout healthy food? Well, most branches just show you photos, a better idea. After ordering and paying at the counter, give your name, and they'll call you once your order is ready.

Most burrito, enchilada, and taco plates are $4, including rice and beans on the side. There are also salads, quesadillas, and a children's menu as well; and nothing on the menu tops $5.25. To add a little kick to your meal, stop by the fixin's bar and try a unique but delicious concoction of spicy-sweet citrus barbecue sauce called Boss Sauce. Beer is available too—draft pints are $2-$3, while a bottle of Bud is $1.75.

Macheezmo Mouse restaurants are spacious, clean, and done up in a brightly colored Southwestern motif. Most have tables both inside and out. These features, plus a few children's items on the menu, make it a good bet for families, as well. Open for lunch and dinner, seven days a week.

Maharaja

- 26108 Pacific Hwy. S, Kent; 946-0664
- 4542 California Ave. SW, Seattle; 935-9443
- 500 Elliott Ave. W, Seattle; 286-1772

Folks who know of Maharaja swear by it for huge portions of spicy Indian food, especially the daily lunch specials, which will easily carry you all the way through the day for just $4.95. These specials include lamb curry and chicken tandoori, with a pile of side dishes that will make your plate runneth over. A daily buffet, also $4.95, rounds out the fantastic lunchtime deals.

Dinner entrees are also very reasonable; most are $5.95 to $8.95, while vegetarian dishes come in under $5. Try *keema aloo*, minced lamb cooked with herbs, spices, and potatoes ($6.50); "Dancing Chicken," cooked with lentil sauce ($6.95); or beef *sagg*, pieces of meat marinated in spices and cooked with spinach and ginger ($6.95). Light eaters can stick with mixed vegetables and rice for $4.95, or choose from the selection of appetizers, soups, and salads. Of course, if you came here to eat light you're probably in the wrong place! Maharaja is open every day from 11 A.M. to 2:30 P.M. for lunch, and from 4 to 10 P.M. for dinner.

O'Char

- Loehmann's Plaza, Bellevue; 641-1900
- Gilman Village, Issaquah; 392-2100

No, you won't find corned beef and cabbage here. Though it sounds Irish, O'Char serves up traditional Thai cuisine. The atmosphere is quite elegant, with its pink linen tablecloths and napkins; it's cozy and mellow with scrumptious food. Yet, the place is inexpensive. And, with locations in two popular shopping centers, O'Char is convenient, too.

Lunch specials offer the biggest bargains. $4.95 gets you a spring roll, salad, and your choice of an entree, like pad Thai, beef pepper steak, or green curry. Many of the entrees are available in vegetarian versions, bringing the price down to $4.50.

Dinners are very reasonable, as well. Start off with an order of those spring rolls ($3.95), deep-fried and dee-lish. Several wonderful entrees are priced in the $5.50 to $7 range, including a mix-and-match section of eight preparations (sweet and sour, ginger and vegetables, etc.), to which you add your choice of meat; Mr. C also recommends the char-broiled pork (or beef) marinated in garlic, pepper, and coriander; it's served with hot chili sauce. Quite a potent combination of flavors.

One unique dish which has brought O'Char a lot of attention is its "Red Wine Angel Wings" ($5.95), deep-fried chicken wings marinated in garlic and vegetables, and served in a red wine sauce. You won't find *these* wings in any sports bar. O'Char is open daily.

Red Robin

- 1305 SE Everett Mall Way, Everett; 355-7330
- Sea Tac Mall, Federal Way; 946-TOGO (8646)
- 1600 E Olive Way, Seattle; 323-1600
- 3272 Fuhrman Ave. E, Seattle; 323-0918
- Pier 55, 1101 Alaskan Way, Seattle; 623-1942
- 1100 Fourth Ave., Seattle; 447-1909
- Northgate Mall, Seattle; 365-0933
- 11021 NE Eighth St., Bellevue; 453-9522
- 2390 148th Ave. NE, Bellevue; 641-3810
- *And other suburban locations*

Red Robin is a popular chain where families, business types, mall creatures, and others all come together for standard American fare. The atmosphere is bright, lively, and convivial. Separate bar areas, fully outfitted

for beers and cocktails, include televisions showing various ball games.

The menu is dominated by the "Gourmet Burgers" (the world's greatest, in their humble opinion), in more than a dozen varieties. Try the "Banzai Burger," marinated in teriyaki sauce and topped with grilled pineapple and cheddar cheese ($5.95), or the "Lone Star Burger," with jalapeño jack cheese, salsa, and guacamole ($5.25). Non-carnivores may want to try the "Amazing Meatless Burger," made with veggies and grains ($5.25). In fact, you can have any style made with a meatless patty.

The one-size-fits-all menu also includes soups and sandwiches, entree-sized salads, pastas, and plenty of bar-food appetizers. Red Robin is a safe bet for bringing the gang to munch on wings and nachos. And save room for desserts like mud pie, cheesecake, brownie sundaes, shakes, and root beer floats. There's also a kiddie menu, with half a dozen meals all priced at $2.99 each. Most Red Robins serve food daily until midnight.

Streamliner Diner

- 397 Winslow Way E, Bainbridge Island; 842-8595

Just a little ways in from the ferry terminal, and not far from the Bainbridge Performing Arts Cultural Center (described in the "Entertainment" section of this book), the Streamliner Diner is a good place to stop if you're coming to Bainbridge Island for the day. It's even better if you live here! The place is a daily nostalgia fest—a classic luncheonette, with stainless steel kitchen walls (clean and shiny), soda fountains, a counter and stools, and lots of other old-time touches.

The Streamliner nevertheless turns something of a modern twist on classic diner food. After all, luncheonettes never turned out fresh grilled quesadillas in the old days—but you can get one here.

The place is only open for breakfast and lunch, and it fills up. Morning people will not be disappointed with selections like two eggs with country fried potatoes and a buttermilk biscuit, all for $3.75. Spend a few more dollars to add spicy Italian sausage or "Mrs. Murphy's Meatloaf" on the side. Omelettes come in an endless variety. Try the Italian omelette, filled with artichoke hearts, pesto, sun-dried tomatoes, and parmesan cheese ($6.50). Other breakfast faves include huevos rancheros, a veggie tofu scramble, and waffles.

Mrs. Murphy returns for lunch; a sandwich plate of her inimitable homemade meatloaf, piled up on sourdough bread and garnished with something called "Cajun Power Mayo" (it's a condiment *and* a cause) is $4.95. Same price for the daily quiche special, served with a green salad. And where else but a diner like this could you find a peanut butter, banana, and honey sandwich for $3.25? Yet, on the very same menu, you'll find a veggie pita pocket with hummus, cucumber, bell peppers, avocado, tomato, sprouts, and a lemon tahini dressing. Welcome to the '90s. The Streamliner is open 7 A.M. to 3 P.M. on weekdays, 8 A.M. to 2:30 P.M. on weekends.

The Yankee Diner

- 6812 Tacoma Mall Blvd., Tacoma; 475-3006
- 13856 Bellevue-Redmond Rd., Bellevue; 643-1558
- 5300 24th Ave. NW, Seattle; 783-1964
- *And other suburban locations*

This place is tailor-made for families of any size, as the usually packed waiting room will attest. You may hang out there as long as an hour before getting a table; yet, no one leaves. If you can manage to keep the kids quiet long enough, you won't be disappointed. This place is BIG: big on portions, and big on old-time, American-style foods. These go beyond the trademark Yankee pot roast, to include steaks, roast turkey, pot pies, and more. Best of all, you can get the whole brood in and out and still have enough money for the violin lessons.

The aforementioned pot roast, for instance, is just $8.75. Even cheaper is meat loaf ($7.95) or chicken fried steak ($7.45). Of course, it's the side dishes that make these entrees such a great value: Each one comes with a cup of soup or a green salad, vegetables, a choice of potato (including homemade mashed!), and biscuits baked from scratch. If you do have little ones to feed, a kids' menu includes turkey and pot roast dinners for under five bucks.

Folks with (slightly) lighter appetites can go for one of 35 different sandwiches, hot and cold, at lunch or dinner. Most of the dinner entrees are also available for lunch, at two or three dollars less. Come in midday and enjoy breaded veal cutlets or hickory smoked ham, with all those trimmings, for $5.95. At night, these go for $8.45.

Early risers aren't left in the cold, either. Mr. C *has* seen lower-priced breakfasts, but then, you won't need to eat again all day. The "Diner Special," for example, includes juice, fresh fruit, three eggs, bacon, ham or sausage, fried potatoes and toast or pancakes. Even at $6.25, it's a bargain—if you can finish! French toast made with the Yankee's home-baked cinnamon bread is another winner. Speaking of sweets, the diner is also popular for its desserts, malted milkshakes, and home-baked goodies. Open seven days a week.

Zoopa

- 393 Strander Blvd., Tukwila; 575-0500
- Bellevue Square Mall, Bellevue; 453-7887

• *Tip-free*

Along with Fresh Choice, described elsewhere in this book, Zoopa is swooping down upon the suburban Northwest, putting a new spin on shopping center dining. Of all the buffet restaurants encircling Seattle, these two chains are clearly ahead of the rest—in terms of quality and sheer quantity of offerings.

Zoopa also starts you off with a salad bar, consisting not only of a zillion fresh greens, vegetables, and fruits, but specially prepared salads like "Turkey Taco" and "Confetti Couscous" as well. There's also a "Kidstall" buffet which adds bins of Froot Loops and such among the veggies—clever strategy, eh, moms?

Meanwhile, it's off to the pasta counter next, for your choice of noodles and sauces—marinara, pesto, Alfredo. Soups, on Mr. C's visit, included minestrone, hearty onion, and chili. Add a few hunks of fresh bread, along with sodas, juices, beers, and wines, and it's a full meal.

Not to leave out the most important part—dessert. Help yourself to brownies, muffins, and/or soft-serve ice cream machines with a toppings bar of nuts and candies. Whew! Somewhere along the way, maybe they should add an Alka Seltzer counter, too. Eat as much as you can stand for $7.35, or $6.35 at lunch. Children (ages 5-11) are half-price at all times; and for kiddies up to age four, it's all-you-can-throw, absolutely free. Seniors over 60 get a 10% discount, too.

The atmosphere at Zoopa is a lively one; it rocks, while Fresh Choice rolls along to classical music. Potted trees reach up to the mauve-painted air ducts along the high ceilings. The place gets noisy, but one thing's for sure—no one walks away hungry. The Tukwila branch is in Southcenter Plaza, across Strander from the main Southcenter Mall. Open seven days a week.

LODGING

All area codes (206) unless otherwise noted

Always on the lookout for a bargain, Mr. C has tried to wade through the tricky waters of the hotel biz to find rooms where you can stay for well under $100 a night. In fact, some offer rooms for under $50 a night. These waters are tricky because hotel rates ebb and flow with the seasons. And don't forget that taxes are always going to be added on top of any quoted price. Here, then, are the results of this not-necessarily scientific survey.

Two important tips: First of all, you should always, *always* ask about discounts. No hotel room ever has only one price. Take advantage of any discounts you can—including corporate, AAA, military personnel, American Association of Retired Persons, and others. Furthermore, if you're going to be in town long enough, ask about weekly rates.

Finally, if you can at all, be sure to make reservations—and make them *early*.

HOTELS AND MOTELS

Aurora Seafair Inn

- 9100 Aurora Ave. N, Seattle, WA
  98103; 522-3754 or 800-445-9297

This commercially bustling highway at the northern end of the city is a haven for inexpensive motels. Recently renovated, the Seafair Inn is one of the better-quality establishments among the crowd. Not all are AAA approved, but this one is; all 32 rooms have color TV with cable, direct-dial phones, and air conditioning; some even have a Jacuzzi. Kitchenette efficiencies, with weekly rates as low as $180-$200, are also available. Otherwise, prices range from $40 to $55 for one person, and from $45 to $65 for two.

As roadside motels go, this one is quite comfortable. Its location is close to Green Lake, Northwest Memorial Hospital, and the Northgate Shopping Center. Also worth noting, they offer senior citizen discounts, and pets are allowed. There is plenty of parking space; access to the motel is only possible heading north on Aurora, which is a divided highway. Take exit 172 from Interstate 5.

Also worth checking in this same area is the **Emerald Inn** at 8512 Aurora Ave. N, Seattle, WA 98103 (telephone 522-5000). It too gets the nod from AAA; its 42 modern rooms are equipped with air conditioning, color TV (free HBO), and free local phone calls. Some kitchenettes are available. Rates range from $50 for one person up to $90 for a two-room suite.

Commodore Motor Hotel

- 2013 Second Ave., Seattle, WA
  98121; 448-8868

Located in the heart of downtown Seattle, the Commodore is an old-time, inexpensive hotel that provides the minimum creature comforts for the economical traveler. Decent beds, private bathrooms, and cable TV make for a pleasant enough stay, as do the maid service and laundry facilities.

It's hard to beat these prices, especially with this location. Nightly rates for a single range between $27 and $42; doubles, $31 to $49. There are also hostel-style accommodations for $12 a night (with a valid American Youth Hostels membership card); the rate is $15 if you don't have your own sleeping bag.

Eastgate Motel

- 14632 SE Eastgate Way, Bellevue,
  WA 98007; 746-4100 or
  800-628-8578

The Eastside has become quite ritzy over the years; Bellevue in particular is a mini-Seattle in itself, with its own busy downtown of glass skyscrapers and fancy restaurants. But 'twas not always thus, and if you want to do Bellevue on a super-tight budget, this older motel may be for you.

Located right off Interstate 90, on the north side (exits 11 A-B; careful, the access roads are tricky), the Eastgate is just a few miles south and east of central Bellevue. I-90 also takes you straight into downtown Seattle; if you aren't traveling by car, forget it. Rates start as low as $35 a night for one person, $40-$50 for two.

As for amenities, this is strictly your basic roadside stopover. The furnishings are spartan—what do you want for $35? It is AAA approved, with air conditioning, free parking, color TV (no cable), and free local phone calls. There are some kitchenette rooms, equipped with a small refrigerator and a microwave oven.

Much the same can be said for another old-timer in the area, the **Bellevue Motel** (1657 Bellevue Way NE, Bellevue, WA 98004; 454-3042). It's closer to central Bellevue, within walking distance. The small parking lot is ringed with a dozen rooms, all on one level; these are inexpensively furnished, and clean enough. There is no air conditioning. Color TVs are equipped with basic cable. The folks from AAA do not appear to have dropped by recently. Rates range from $40 to $50 a night; this place is even more "no-frills" than the Eastgate, but the location is convenient for drivers—midway between Route 520 and Bellevue's main business area. Bellevue Way leads directly to both.

Eastlake Inn
- 2215 Eastlake Ave. E, Seattle, WA 98102; 322-7726

Now, here's an interesting find. Slightly out of the way, in a neighborhood that is gentrifying nicely, the Eastlake Inn is like a hidden treasure.

It used to be a dive, in an area with a poor reputation. But then, such areas are often ripe for rebirth, which is just what's been happening in Eastlake. Trendy restaurants (too expensive for Mr. C!), students, and yuppies have all moved in. And, in the summer of '93, new owners took over this motel and renovated it completely. They appointed a hands-on manager, who lives on the premises. Now, each of the twelve rooms is comfortably furnished with "real" furniture and linens; each has a kitchen and a full-size bathroom, as well as cable TV. The parking lot is downright claustrophobic, but you do get one off-street space with each room.

Some of those restaurants are within walking distance, and a car puts you just a few minutes from downtown, Seattle Center, the Eastside, and UW. Perched as it is on a ridge, the motel even has one special room outfitted with "wraparound" windows for a spectacular view of Lake Union and downtown. Perfect for a romantic weekend.

The rates are simple. Rooms with one queen-size bed are $59 a night in summer, $49 after Labor Day; suites with two bedrooms are $79/$69. The room with the super-duper view is always $10 above the highest rate. Some rooms may be available by the

MR. CHEAP'S PICKS
Hotels/Motels

✔ **Eastlake Inn**—Surprisingly homey, in a neighborhood that's becoming very hip.

✔ **Inn at Queen Anne**—Kitchenettes fit for budget-conscious royalty, right next to Seattle Center.

✔ **Kings Inn**—For low-priced, basic lodgings in the heart of downtown.

✔ **Silver Cloud Inns**—Affordable elegance around the suburbs.

week (from $250) during the off-season. But, as word has gotten around about this place, it's become quite popular pretty much through the year; try to call well in advance. A 10% senior citizen discount is also offered to those over 55 at all times.

Georgetown Inn
- 6100 Corson Ave. S, Seattle, WA 98108; 762-2233

The Georgetown section at Seattle's south end is a heavily industrial district, bustling by day with tractor-trailers and lots of folks conducting wholesale business. If your business takes you to this part of the world, the Georgetown Inn is the class of the area—and yet, considering how nicely appointed it is, it's quite affordable.

This is a completely new building, built in '93, and fully equipped for the working traveler. It's located off exit 162 from Interstate 5, near Boeing Field; Route 5 will also take you directly north into downtown Seattle or south to the popular Southcenter shopping area and the Sea Tac airport. Parking, color TV with cable, laundry, continental breakfast, and a sauna/exercise room are all included free, and the rooms are truly attrac-

tive and comfortable. Rates start as
low as $59 a night for one person,
$69 for two; corporate rates start at
$52/$59. Kitchenettes and Jacuzzi
suites are also available, from $87 a
night. Weekly rates are not offered.

Again, the location is out of the
way (though not out of the question)
for tourists, and a car is a must. But,
for visitors who want a comfy budget
stay, this is well worth considering.

Inn at Queen Anne

• 505 First Ave. N, Seattle, WA
  98109; 282-7357 or 800-952-5043
Formerly a residential apartment
building, this "inn" makes no grand
claims to deluxe accommodations;
however, considering its economical
price range and location just outside
of Seattle Center, it delivers more
than its low rates would suggest.

The rooms—spruced up but not
modernized—are cheerful, cozy, and
tastefully decorated. A comfy bed,
spacious closet, full bath, and cable
TV also add to feeling of being
home. Each room has a tiny but fairly
complete kitchenette, making the inn
especially nice for long-term guests,
as does the laundry facility in the
basement. A continental breakfast is
offered to all guests; alas, don't count
on there being enough for everyone.

Bordering Seattle Center's west
side, IQA is conveniently located
near northward and southward bus
stops; getting anywhere in the city
from here is not a problem. The average one-night price for a single is
$55, and $65 for a double. During
the summer season, these rates go up
to $70 and $80, respectively, with a
10% discount by the week. If you're
staying over a week or a month, rates
can go as low as $37-$45 per night;
housekeeping is included.

Kings Inn

• 2106 Fifth Ave., Seattle, WA
  98121; 441-8833 or 800-546-4760
Here's a good budget choice for a motel right in downtown Seattle. The
cool cafes and restaurants of Belltown are around the corner; Pike
Place Market, and Westlake Center
(the south terminus of the Monorail)

are in walking distance. So are some
of Mr. C's favorite bargains, like Cinema 150, a four-screen theater where
all seats cost $1.50 (see the listing un-
der "Entertainment—Movies").

The KI itself feels kind of like a
motel where a hotel should be; its 70
rooms are comfortably basic. There's
free parking, color TV with HBO, and
a few kitchenettes are available. Rates
start at $55 for one person and $60 for
two; winter rates go as low as $40-$45.
There are also special discounts for
senior citizens. Weekly rates are also
available, from $250 and up.

Marvin Gardens Inn

• 2301 Third Ave., Seattle, WA
  98121; 443-1030 or 800-443-3031
The rooms at this Belltown hotel are
cozy garden studios, each with a bathroom and kitchenette. Laundry facilities and snack vending machines are
"just steps from the main lobby," and
many of the cafes and nightclubs described in this book are just steps
from the front door. For further assistance, the Marvin Gardens staff is
available 24 hours.

The inn caters particularly to
long-term residents. The weekly
rate for a single room is $210, and
$559 per month; it's also possible to
rent for six months with proof of
employment (if you earn less than
$20,000) at just $385-$420 per
month. Call for more details.

Pacific Plaza Hotel

• 400 Spring St., Seattle, WA 98104;
  623-3900 or 800-426-1165
Mr. C is often asked for at least one
lodging recommendation that's somewhat higher than the bottom of the
budget barrel, and here it is. The Pacific Plaza Hotel offers all the posh
elegance of its ritzy downtown neighbors, but for significantly less money.
Call this a cheaper alternative to the
Hilton, the Westin, and the like. The
lobby and rooms are stylish, classy,
and comfortable. A free continental
breakfast is offered daily, a laundry
service is available, and the front
desk is staffed 24 hours a day.

Considering that the Pacific Plaza
is located in the heart of downtown,

along busy Fourth Avenue, the rooms are fairly quiet. Of course, higher floors are obviously further away from the traffic, and probably even better for light sleepers.

Nightly rates start around $74 for a single, with a full-size bed; $84 for one to two people, with a queen-size bed; and $94 for a room with a king-size bed. Special rates are also available; weekend package deals may also be offered from time to time. Call the Plaza for more details.

Park Inn
- 225 Aurora Ave. N, Seattle, WA 98109; 728-7666

Another in-town choice is the Park Inn, located just three blocks east of the Space Needle. It's an older motel in a somewhat grimy corner of town, but what you get for the price can't be beat. The rooms are strictly basic, but PI also offers an indoor swimming pool and exercise facility, a separate children's play area, and a continental breakfast, plus a conference room and other business facilities.

There is a wide variety of rooms (including a non-smokers' floor) and prices, but rates range from about $50-$100 a night. Discounts are offered to AAA members, senior citizens, military personnel, and many others. Also, for a $6 fee, you can join Park Inn's "Performance Plus Club," which gives you extra privileges year-round: discounts of 30% on room rates, free local phone calls, later check-out times, and so on. Call for more info.

Silver Cloud Inns
- 5036 25th Ave. NE, Seattle, WA 98105; 526-5200
- 10621 NE 12th St., Bellevue, WA 98004; 637-7000
- 12202 NE 124th St., Kirkland, WA 98034; 821-8300
- 15304 NE 21st St., Redmond, WA 98052; 746-8200
- *And other suburban locations*
- Reservations for all branches: 800-551-7207

Silver Cloud is a Northwest chain which offers very comfortable rooms with lots of extra amenities. The look is bright and modern, rather luxurious; it feels more like a hotel than a motel. Yet, in-season rates start as low as $59 for one person, and around $70 for two.

These prices include features like swimming pools and/or fitness centers; conference rooms; plus continental breakfast, free local phone calls, free parking, laundry facilities, and more. Some rooms have their own Jacuzzis. Even suites, with two queen-size beds and a queen hide-a-bed (or a king-size bed with a queen hide-a-bed) and a small kitchen can cost as little as $80 to $95 a night; just the thing for families or small groups. There are no weekly rates, but Silver Cloud's "Frequent Guest" program gives you one free night for every nine. Most recently, the chain has added its first in-town branch, in the University District.

ALTERNATIVE LODGING

Green Gables Guest House
- 1503 Second Ave. W, Seattle, WA 98119; 282-6863 or 800-400-1503

For folks who want a quiet and supremely comfortable stay in Seattle—and who can afford a bit more than budget motel rates—Green Gables is a delightful private home on Queen Anne Hill. Seven guest rooms are available through the year (three of the rooms are in the recently acquired Mercer House, right next door). The main house itself dates from the turn of the century, with a front porch and a parlor inside for all guests to share.

Owners David and Lila Chapman are devoted collectors of vintage Americana, and the houses virtually overflow with period touches: furnishings, dolls and toys, and costumes (their side business!). Each room is unique, lovingly decorated with antiques, traditional American quilts, lace pillows, and stained glass windows. The neighborhood, and some rooms, offer scenic views of Elliott Bay.

Rates start as low as $65-$75 per night for rooms with one double bed and a shared bathroom; don't forget, you won't be sharing with many others. Rooms with private baths start at $95. The largest, a private suite with its own entrance, is $125; but this can be shared by up to four people, making an economical deal for families. All prices include full breakfasts, and there is a common room with a television, VCR, and games. Weekly rates are often available in the off-season; call as early as you can for any reservations, as the houses do fill up. For those who like to know these things, there's also a large (but friendly) dog who roams about the place.

Green Tortoise Backpacker's Guest House

- 715 Second Ave. N, Seattle, WA 98109; 322-1222

The northern base for the legendary "Green Tortoise" bus service, which offers cheap travel between Seattle and San Francisco, includes this hostel-style house for those explorers when they arrive. Actually, it's open to anyone, regardless of how you get there; anyone, that is, who seeks a laid-back, communal atmosphere in which college, the sixties, or both, live on eternally.

So, if you don't mind sleeping on a floor mattress or a bunk bed, with a few new friends for company and a bathroom down the hall, GT can be your home base too. It sure won't set you back much: How does $11 a night sound? That's the rock-bottom rate, but there are other options. Most cost no more than $20, including some rooms with their own baths. And a few private rooms, intended for couples, are available for $30-$35 a night.

In fact, this quaint three-story house somehow fits in 80 beds of all shapes and sizes; even so, on weekends (especially in summer), every one can be taken. Weekly and monthly rates are usually available, except during August and September; calling in advance is a good idea for *any* stay.

The house is located on Queen Anne Hill, just a few blocks up from the Seattle Center and convenient to several local bus lines. It's a residential neighborhood, so the atmosphere around the place is pretty mellow. There's no curfew; they do request quiet after 10 P.M. and no drinking after midnight. No smoking is allowed anywhere in the building. A back garden area offers ping-pong, picnic tables, and a group barbecue on Wednesday nights—you supply the food and drink, GT supplies "the coal and the potato salad."

Like traditional hostels, they also supply you with free locked storage, laundry and cooking facilities, some space in the fridge, and tons of maps and info on the area. Unlike most, they provide free coffee and tea all day; they don't charge extra for bed sheets; and they don't close up during the afternoon. Cool. Office hours are from 8 A.M. to 11 P.M. daily; call for directions from anywhere.

Hosteling International—Seattle

- 84 Union St., Seattle, WA 98101; 622-5443

Though it's Seattle's primary youth hostel, your stay here begins with an exciting round of "find-the-building." Here's a hint for when you're at the base of Union Street and see that the numbers don't go down to 84: Look for staircase rails. Waaaay down, at the bottom of a long stairway, is the hostel. Eureka.

Oh, and one other tip: Before you hike down, do make sure that you've got reservations. Otherwise, you'll only have to lug all your gear back up all those stairs.

That being said, AYH members pay a rate of $14 per night (*only* members are allowed from June through September). In the off-season, non-members can stay at a rate of $17. There are 138 beds in these dormitory-style rooms—and a shared lock box is available at the foot of each bunk. If trust is not one of your better attributes, or you just plain want your own quarters, private rooms are available for an additional charge. Bathrooms are down the hall; a laundry facility, vending machines, TV room, and kitchen area are available to all guests.

For those travelers looking to stay outside of town, other Hosteling International locations in the area include **Hosteling International—Port Townsend**, 272 Battery Way, in Fort Worden State Park, Port Townsend, 385-0655; **Hosteling International—Fort Flagler**, 7850 Flagler Road, #17, Nordland, 385-1288; and **Hosteling International—Vashon**, 12119 SW Cove Road, Vashon Island, 463-2592. Happy trails.

Vincent's Guest House
- 527 Malden Ave. E, Seattle, WA 98112; 323-7849

Like the Green Tortoise (above), this is another alternative to formal hostels, perfect for backpackers, students, and anyone who wants super-cheap accommodations without memberships and curfews. Unlike GT, Vincent's prices include a daily breakfast of bagels, coffee, and tea. It's also in a residential neighborhood, though a somewhat gritty one in the Capitol Hill area. That means livelier nightlife nearby, along with all the riffraff that goes with it. Some people don't mind this, some do.

Anyway, the prices are simple: $12 a night for a bed in a shared, dormitory-style room. Private rooms for couples are $25-$35 a night. Weekly rates are $70 in summer, $60 in the off-season. Sheets are included, and each room has its own attached bathroom and small kitchenette. You also get the standard communal kitchen, laundry, lockers (for rent), and TV room (with HBO). No smoking is allowed.

Vincent's also hosts a free barbecue and free beer night, each weekly; like the area itself, the folks here tend to be a loose, lively crowd. You can even borrow free passes to lots of

---

Capitol Hill nightclubs.

With about 40 beds, half as many as Green Tortoise, Vincent's requests that you call at least two days in advance for any booking. And, if you're staying for three nights or more, they'll pay for your cab ride from the railroad station or the Greyhound bus terminal. Otherwise, do call for directions; finding the place can be tricky if you're unfamiliar with the area.

YMCA
- 909 Fourth Ave., Seattle, WA 98104; 382-5000

The good ol' YMCA offers lodging for both male and female travelers at economical rates. In addition to being a hotel and a center for social services, the YMCA also has a health facility; hotel guests may use the pool, sauna, and other equipment at no additional cost. For further comfort, there are laundry facilities on every floor. And for your safety, the front doors are closed at 10 P.M. (this is not a curfew—there's always someone at the desk to let you in), and no overnight visitors are allowed.

Single rates start from $39 (no TV, shared bath), up to $53 (with TV, private bath). Weekly rates do not include a private bath option, only the television choice: without for $170 a week, with for $178.

Double rates range from $43 to $57, with the same respective choices as the single rates. Again, weekly rates for a double do not include private bath—without TV it's $196; with, $205. There is no limit to the length of your stay here, other than room availability.

YWCA
- 1118 Fifth Ave., Seattle, WA 98101; 461-4868

As far as lodging goes, the YWCA only accommodates women. No men, kids, or pet iguanas. Just women, that's it. In fact, as at most YWCA residences, men are not permitted inside beyond the lobby.

The rooms are small, dormitory-style, and their white tile floors give a feeling of cleanliness. Not deluxe, but very neat. A single goes for $31 per night; for just $5 more, you may add the convenience of a private bathroom. Weekly rates for the same rooms are $186 and $216 respectively. Unlike the YMCA (above), there is a two-week limit to your stay here, unless you get permission to remain longer.

As a hotel guest, you are allowed to use the facilities, like the pool and laundry room, for small fees. Plenty of nearby cafes, and a 24-hour front desk also make the YWCA convenient. There is no curfew, but for security reasons, the doors are locked at 7 P.M.

ALPHABETICAL INDEX